THE FUNCTION
IN THE
INTERNATIONAL
COMMUNITY

THE FUNCTION OF LAW

IN THE

INTERNATIONAL

COMMUNITY

BY

H. LAUTERPACHT

LL.D., Dr. Jur., Dr. Sc. Pol.

*Lecturer in Public International Law
in the
London School of Economics and
Political Science*

OXFORD
UNIVERSITY PRESS

OXFORD

UNIVERSITY PRESS

Great Clarendon Street, Oxford OX2 6DP

Oxford University Press is a department of the University of Oxford.
It furthers the University's objective of excellence in research, scholarship,
and education by publishing worldwide in

Oxford New York

Auckland Cape Town Dar es Salaam Hong Kong Karachi
Kuala Lumpur Madrid Melbourne Mexico City Nairobi
New Delhi Shanghai Taipei Toronto

With offices in

Argentina Austria Brazil Chile Czech Republic France Greece
Guatemala Hungary Italy Japan Poland Portugal Singapore
South Korea Switzerland Thailand Turkey Ukraine Vietnam

Oxford is a registered trade mark of Oxford University Press
in the UK and in certain other countries

Published in the United States
by Oxford University Press Inc., New York

© Sir Hersch Lauterpacht, 1933;
introduction: Martti Koskenniemi, 2011

First published 1933
This edition 2011

British Library Cataloguing in Publication Data
Data available

Library of Congress Cataloging in Publication Data
Library of Congress Control Number : 2011920653

Typeset by SPI Publisher Services, Pondicherry, India
Printed in Great Britain
on acid-free paper by
CPI Antony Rowe, Chippenham, Wiltshire

ISBN 978–0–19–960881–2

1 3 5 7 9 10 8 6 4 2

To

ARNOLD DUNCAN M^cNAIR

FOREWORD BY SIR ELIHU LAUTERPACHT

CBE, QC, LL.D

Amongst the many contributions of my father, the late Sir Hersch Lauterpacht, to the literature of international law, *The Function of Law in the International Community* may properly be regarded as the most important by reason of the rigour of its exposition of the judicial role in the settlement of international differences. To say this is not to detract from the originality and value of the other books that he published – *Private Law Sources and Analogies of International Law, International Law and Human Rights, Recognition in International Law*, and the *Development of International Law by the World Court*. However, there is about *Function of Law* an intensity of thought, comprehensiveness of vision and display of erudition which gives it a special quality that has been widely recognised.

The work was originally published in 1933 and the possibility of preparing a second edition certainly engaged my father's attention in the intervals of his work as a judge of the International Court of Justice between 1955 and 1960.[1] He left behind a partially edited text of the first sixty pages of the volume, for which no use could be found until the idea of this reprint emerged. It is, therefore, fortunate that it has been possible to incorporate in the present reprint the amendments that he contemplated.

The initiative of the Oxford University Press in producing this reprint, with the addition of a learned introduction by Professor Koskenniemi, which will be widely appreciated, is much to be valued.

---

[1] See *The Life of Hersch Lauterpacht*, by myself, published by the Cambridge University Press in 2010, pp. 399 and 414.

NOTE FROM THE PUBLISHER

This paperback edition of *The Function of Law in the International Community* features revisions and updates made by Sir Hersch Lauterpacht after the book first published in 1933, which have never before been implemented in the text. These revisions occur in the first three chapters of the book. As a result, eight pages have been added to the length of the work and the pagination may thus differ from that of the original edition of *The Function of Law*. A full overview of all the revisions made to this new paperback can be found on our website at http:// ukcatalogue.oup.com/product/9780199608812.do.

PREFACE

THE plan of this book has undergone in the course of its preparation a series of substantial changes. It has grown out of an article, published in 1928 in *Economica* under the title 'The Doctrine of Non-Justiciable Disputes in International Law' and a course of lectures with a similar title given at the Academy of International Law at The Hague in 1930. Its original purpose was to examine the current doctrine—a doctrine accepted by most international lawyers and embodied in leading international conventions for pacific settlement—of the inherent limitations of the place of law and of the judicial process in the society of States. According to this doctrine, international disputes are, by virtue of the peculiar structure of international law and relations, necessarily divided into two categories variously described as 'legal' and 'political', as 'justiciable' and 'non-justiciable', or as disputes as to 'rights' and conflicts of 'interests'. In the opinion of the adherents of this doctrine, this distinction not only affords a satisfactory basis for scientific exposition, but also can, and ought to, be used in international treaties having for their object the creation of a legal duty of pacific settlement in all possible contingencies. This doctrine the writer believes to be juridically unsound, and the original object of the book was to substantiate this view.

As the work progressed, however, it became clear that a merely critical approach might fail to bring into relief the true implications of the scope of the judicial function in international society. As in any other system of law, so also in that which governs the relations of States *inter se*, the question of the limits of the rule of law is the central problem of jurisprudence. It may not be difficult to prove that there is no merit in a classification which is based on the opinion that certain categories of disputes are not amenable to judicial settlement on account of the absence of relevant rules of law. But even when this particular aspect of the doctrine has been disposed of, there still remain special problems confronting international tribunals on account of the shortcomings of the international legal system; for it is a system in which general principles have not always found specific expression in concrete rules, in which law frequently lags behind morals to an extent unknown to the law obtaining within the State, and in which the process of adapting the law to changed conditions is still in a rudimentary stage. It may be easy to demonstrate that the absence from international society of law-making machinery which might effect a compromise between legal stability and social change is neither a sufficient basis for the classification of international disputes nor a reason for urging any limitation of the rule of law among States. But when this has been done there still remains the task of examining how the dangers arising from the absence of an international legislature may be overcome, and what is the solution, in the international sphere, of the perennial conflict between security and justice. To refute a doctrine and to avoid an issue of practical urgency and abiding legal interest would be too rigidly academic. Thus it happens that what was originally intended as a criticism of the orthodox doctrine of the inherent limitations of the international judicial function has been subordinated to an attempt to examine underlying legal problems of a more general nature. Subsequently, the extension of the original plan of the work made it necessary to consider the problem of the limitation of the place of law as a general problem of jurisprudence with special reference to the so-called 'specific' character of international law.

These are the reasons why what was originally intended as a monograph written *cum ira et studio* has developed into an examination, with reference to the relations of States, of some of the persistent problems of legal philosophy, such as the place of law in society, the nature of the judicial function, the problem of judicial discretion, and the antinomies of stability and change. This book is thus no longer a plea in support of a definite doctrine or an argument against a particular theory. It is an attempt at an exposition, by reference to the problem of the international judicial function, of what are believed to be the principal issues of the philosophy of international law.

I am deeply indebted to Professor Brierly for the care which he has bestowed upon the manuscript of this book. He has read it twice and made many suggestions, most of which I have adopted. My gratitude is the greater, because he is, as I know, not always in agreement with the views expressed in these pages. Mr. C. R. L. Fletcher, formerly one of the Delegates of the Clarendon Press, has also read the manuscript. The usefulness of his suggestions is only surpassed by the modesty and courtesy with which he made them. Dr. McNair has read large portions of the manuscript in its earlier stage and parts of the proof. An international lawyer is fortunate to receive his advice.

My thanks are also due to the Editors of the *British Year Book of International Law and of Economica* for permission to make use of material published in these periodicals, and to the Curatorium of The Hague Academy of International Law for a similar permission in regard to my lectures given at The Hague in 1930 and published in the *Recueil des Cours.*

Miss G. Bloch, of the London School of Economics, has borne the brunt of copying the manuscript and the successive stages of the typescript, and I wish to express to her my warm thanks.

Both the Laura Spelman Foundation through its London Committee and the University of London through its Publications Fund have generously contributed towards the cost of publication.

To the Delegates and Staff of the Clarendon Press I wish to express my thanks for their patient and careful co-operation.

The manuscript of this book was concluded in June 1932. It has not been practicable to consider or cite the literature or decisions published after that date.

H. L.

LONDON SCHOOL OF ECONOMICS
AND POLITICAL SCIENCE.
1 *February* 1933.

TABLE OF CONTENTS

PART I

INTRODUCTORY

CHAPTER I. THE SCIENCE OF INTERNATIONAL LAW AND THE LIMITATION OF THE PLACE OF LAW IN THE SETTLEMENT OF INTERNATIONAL DISPUTES

I. *The Doctrine of the Limitations of the Judicial Process in International Law*

II. *The History of the Doctrine*

CHAPTER II. CONVENTIONS OF PACIFIC SETTLEMENT AND THE LIMITATION OF THE JUDICIAL FUNCTION

PART II

THE INTERNATIONAL JUDICIAL FUNCTION AND THE COMPLETENESS OF INTERNATIONAL LAW

Chapter III. LIMITATION OF THE JUDICIAL FUNCTION ON ACCOUNT OF THE ABSENCE OF RULES OF INTERNATIONAL LAW

I. *The Meaning of the Doctrine*

II. *The Completeness of the Legal System as a General Principle of Law*

Chapter IV. 'LACUNAE' IN INTERNATIONAL LAW

Chapter V. THE PROBLEM OF THE JUDICIAL FUNCTION
IN INTERNATIONAL LAW

Chapter VI. NOVELTY OF ACTION AND NATURE OF
JUDICIAL ACTIVITY IN INTERNATIONAL LAW

PART III

POLITICAL DISPUTES AND THE JUDICIAL
FUNCTION IN INTERNATIONAL LAW

Chapter VII. IMPORTANCE OF DISPUTES AS A TEST
OF JUSTICIABILITY

I. *Political Disputes in General*

II. *The History of International Arbitration and the Justiciability of Important Issues*

III. *Relation between Legal and Political Disputes*

Chapter VIII. INTERNATIONAL LAW AND JUDICIAL DETERMINATION OF IMPORTANT ISSUES

Chapter IX. THE DOCTRINE 'DE MAXIMIS NON CURAT PRAETOR' AS PART OF LEGAL OBLIGATIONS

Chapter X. THE IMPARTIALITY OF INTERNATIONAL TRIBUNALS

PART IV

STABILITY AND CHANGE IN INTERNATIONAL LAW

Chapter XI. INTERNATIONAL CHANGE AND THE JUDICIAL SETTLEMENT OF INTERNATIONAL DISPUTES

Chapter XII. INTERNATIONAL CONCILIATION AS AN INSTRUMENT OF CHANGE

CHAPTER XIII. THE JUDICIAL APPLICATION OF THE
DOCTRINE 'REBUS SIC STANTIBUS'

CHAPTER XIV. THE DOCTRINE OF ABUSE OF RIGHTS AS
AN INSTRUMENT OF CHANGE

CHAPTER XV. EXTENSION OF JUDICIAL LEGISLATION BY
THE WILL OF THE PARTIES

Chapter XVI. JUDICIAL DECISION AS THE STARTING POINT FOR THE MODIFICATION OF THE LAW

I. *By the Will of the Parties*

II. *As Part of International Constitutional Machinery*

PART V

DISPUTES AS TO RIGHTS AND CONFLICTS OF INTERESTS

Chapter XVII. 'DISPUTES AS TO RIGHTS' AS A LEGAL CONCEPTION

C<small>HAPTER</small> XVIII. OBLIGATORY SETTLEMENT OF SO-CALLED CONFLICTS OF INTERESTS

PART VI

THE LIMITS OF THE RULE OF LAW

C<small>HAPTER</small> XIX. LIMITATIONS OF THE RULE OF LAW WITHIN THE STATE

C<small>HAPTER</small> XX. THE 'SPECIFIC' CHARACTER OF INTERNATIONAL LAW AND THE RULE OF LAW IN INTERNATIONAL SOCIETY

I. *The Nature of International Law as a Problem of General Jurisprudence*

II. *International Law as a Law of Co-ordinate Entities*

III. *The Judicial Function and the Legal Nature of International Law*

APPENDIX

LIMITATION OF THE JUDICIAL FUNCTION IN DISPUTES BETWEEN STATE-MEMBERS OF COMPOSITE STATES

TABLE OF CASES CITED

LIST OF ABBREVIATIONS OF
TITLES OF BOOKS AND PERIODICALS

Actes et Documents	Deuxième Conférence internationale de la Paix, Actes et Documents (1907).
A.J.	American Journal of International Law.
Lauterpacht, Analogies	Lauterpacht, Private Law Sources and Analogies of International Law (1927).
Annuaire	Annuaire de l'Institut de Droit international.
Annual Digest	Annual Digest of Public International Law Cases.
Arbitration and Security	Arbitration and Security: Systematic Survey of the Arbitration Conventions and Treaties of Mutual Security deposited with the League of Nations (2nd ed., 1927), C. 653. M. 216. 1927. V.
A.S., Proceedings	Proceedings of the American Society of International Law.
B.Y.	British Year Book of International Law.
Fauchille	Fauchille, Traité de Droit international public (8th ed. of Bonfils' Manuel de Droit international public), 2 vols. (1921–6).
Fischer Williams, Chapters	Chapters on Current International Law and the League of Nations (1929).
Hague Reports	Reports to The Hague Conferences of 1899 and 1907 (ed. by J. B. Scott, 1917).
Hall	Hall, A Treatise on International Law (8th ed. by Pearce Higgins, 1925).
Hyde	Hyde, International Law chiefly as Interpreted and Applied by the United States, 2 vols. (1922).
J.C.L. and I.L.	Journal of Comparative Legislation and International Law
L.N.T.S.	League of Nations Treaty Series.
Lafontaine	Lafontaine, Pasicrisie internationale (1902).
Lammasch, Rechtskraft	Lammasch, Die Rechtskraft internationaler Schiedssprüche (1913).
Lammasch, Schiedsgerichtsbarkeit	Lammasch, Die Lehre von der Schiedsgerichtsbarkeit in ihrem ganzen Umfange (1914).
Lapradelle and Politis	Lapradelle-Politis, Recueil des Arbitrages internationaux, vol. i (1905), vol. ii (1924).
Mérignhac, Conférence	Mérignhac, La Conférence internationale de la Paix (1900).
Moore	Moore, History and Digest of International Arbitrations to which the United States has been a Party, 6 vols. (1898).

Moore, Digest	Moore, A Digest of International Law, 8 vols. (1906).
Nielsen's Report	American and British Claims Arbitration (under the special agreement of 18 August 1910), Report by Nielsen (1926).
Nippold	Nippold, Die Fortbildung des Verfahrens in völkerrechtlichen Streitigkeiten (1907).
Official Journal	Official Journal of the League of Nations.
Oppenheim	Oppenheim, International Law (4th ed. by McNair), vol. ii (1926), vol. i (1928).
P.C.I.J.	Publications of the Permanent Court of International Justice.
	Series A—Judgements.
	B—Advisory Opinions.
	A/B—Cumulative Collection of Judgements and Advisory Opinions given since 1931.
	C—Acts and Documents relating to Judgements and Advisory Opinions given by the Court.
	D—Collection of Texts governing the Jurisdiction of the Court.
	E—Annual Reports.
Procès-Verbaux	Proceedings of the Committee of Jurists of 1920 appointed to draft the Statute of the Permanent Court of International Justice.
R.G.	Revue générale de Droit international public.
R.I.	Revue de Droit international et de la Législation comparée.
R.I. (Paris)	Revue de Droit international.
Recueil	Recueil des décisions des tribunaux arbitraux mixtes.
Recueil des Cours	Académie de Droit International, Recueil des Cours
Rivista	Rivista di diritto internazionale.
Schücking-Wehberg	Schücking und Wehberg, Die Satzung des Völkerbundes (2nd ed., 1924).
Verdross, Verfassung	Verdross, Die Verfassung der Völkerrechtsgemeinschaft (1926).
Westlake	Westlake, International Law, 2 vols. (2nd ed., 1910–13).
Z.f.a.ö.R. und V.	Zeitschrift für ausländisches öffentliches Recht und Völkerrecht.
Z.V.	Zeitschrift für Völkerrecht.

THE FUNCTION OF LAW IN THE INTERNATIONAL COMMUNITY: INTRODUCTION

Martti Koskenniemi[*]

I

In the recent advisory opinion by the International Court of Justice on the lawfulness of the unilateral declaration of independence of Kosovo, several States confronted the Court with the argument that in one way or another this was a 'political question' to which it was impossible or at least inappropriate to give a legal response. This claim has been made in most advisory proceedings at The Hague, and many States finding themselves in the position of respondent in contentious cases have used it to challenge the Court's jurisdiction. The Court answered in 2010 as it had done in all those prior cases. It stated that '[w]hatever its political aspects, the Court cannot refuse to respond to the legal elements of a question which invites it to discharge an essentially judicial task, namely, in the present case, an assessment of an act by reference to international law'. The Court continued by stressing that, 'in determining the jurisdictional issue of whether it is confronted with a legal question, it is not concerned with the political nature of the motives which may have inspired the request or the political implications which its opinion might have'. [1]

This is a response that Hersch Lauterpacht might have given, and it is likely to have been inspired by his insistence on the point. The claim that the 'political' nature of some issue—the way it touched the 'vital interests and honour' of a State—will automatically exempt it from legal settlement had been frequently heard in late nineteenth and early twentieth-century arbitral practice and *The Function of Law in the International Community* was conceived as an extended refutation of it. In

[*] Professor of International Law, University of Helsinki. This text is based on my 'The Function of International Law in the International Community: 75 Years After' (2008) 79 BYIL 353–66.

[1] ICJ, *Accordance with international law of the unilateral declaration of independence in respect of Kosovo* (Advisory Opinion of 22 July 2010), 13 (para 27).

particular, Lauterpacht wanted to reject the view that the reservation for 'essential interests' in an arbitration clause or a declaration of compulsory jurisdiction would operate in a self-judging way. Today, this question has arisen anew in the context of investment treaty arbitration. For example, the 2004 model treaty of the United States contains a clause according to which:

> Nothing in the Treaty shall:
> ... preclude a Party from applying measures that it considers necessary for the fulfillment of its obligations with respect to the maintenance or restoration of international peace or security, or the protection of its own essential security interests.[2]

The operative phrase here is: 'that it considers necessary'. Similar types of expression are now included in many investment treaties, inspiring or prompting to inspire what would be a fully 'Lauterpachtian' debate. Does such a formulation (or equivalent formulations) prevent an arbitral tribunal from examining whether the conditions in the State actually concerned its 'essential security interests' or at least whether the determination by the State that they did was made in good faith? Lauterpacht's response to such questions would have been a resounding 'of course not'.

The problem raises a series of perennial questions regarding the relationship between international law and that which at least prima facie appears outside it: political judgment. These questions have rarely been discussed in more detail or with more sense of urgency than here. This is no surprise. *The Function of Law in the International Community* was written at a time when persistent economic problems in the world had precipitated a constitutional crisis in many European countries as well as endangered international peace. A pressing need to clarify the relationship between law and politics had emerged. Many jurists, especially in the German realm, contributed to this debate, a fact that is visible on practically every page of this book. The work is thus much larger than a mere commentary on a technical aspect of the law concerning the jurisdiction of international tribunals. The author himself regarded it as his most important work. It is understandable why he would think so. The book is a restatement of practically all the important principles of law

---

[2] Article 18 of the Treaty Between the Government of the United States of America and the Government of [Country] Concerning the Encouragement and Reciprocal Protection of Investment (2004 Model BIT), <http://ita.law.uvic.ca/documents/USmodelbitnov04.pdf>.

in which Lauterpacht's generation of European international lawyers put their faith. It is an interwar book, no doubt, in many senses of that well-worn expression. But many of us still regard those principles as important, even as we no longer feel we can restate them with equal directness or sense of self-evidence. The book can in any case be read from two perspectives: as a masterful analysis of a problem of international jurisdiction, and a statement of a legalistic cosmopolitanism—'Rule of Law'—that continues to exert influence in the debates over the sense and direction of globalization today.

II

What was the world like into which *The Function of Law in the International Community* appeared?

Fifteen million Americans were out of work as President Roosevelt took office in 1933. A World Monetary and Economic Conference met in the summer to debate a programme of currency stabilization and adjustment of inter-governmental debts. Even contemporaries tended to describe this as a 'period of crisis'.[3] They were right. 1933 was the year of Hitler's accession as *Reichskanzler* and Europe's definite turn to the path of darkness. By now Hitler had been joined by Mussolini who insisted that Italy should be treated as a Great Power, especially in terms of its colonial designs in Eastern Africa. Japan's attack on China had led to the establishment of the puppet regime of Manchukuo. Diplomats kept on talking about non-recognition and economic sanctions but with little effect. The Soviet Union turned unexpectedly away from the policy of world revolution. In the following year it would join the League where it would become a staunch opponent of 'revision'.

The League of Nations was in a bad way. The Manchurian situation had demonstrated the fragility of the Covenant's collective security provisions. The Disarmament Conference had been undermined by Hitler's accession and Japan's withdrawal. No country had worked more to support the conference than Britain. Against a general atmosphere of hopelessness, Prime Minister Ramsay MacDonald suggested in the spring a new draft convention with definite levels of matériel and

---

[3] G.M. Gathorne-Hardy, *A Short History of International Affairs 1920–1939* (4th edn, Oxford University Press, 1950), p 258.

provision for conference in case of threatened violations of the peace.[4]

The League's Codification Conference had ended three years earlier in general disappointment. No significant progress had been made in the conclusion of multilateral treaties in order to solidify the basis of international law. Two years earlier the Permanent Court of International Justice had been faced with the trickiest problem it had so far encountered, namely the legality of the planned Austro-German customs union. Was the union or was it not contrary to the pledge of neutrality Austria had made in the Peace of Saint-Germain of 1919? The case immediately raised the problem that formed the main subject of *The Function of Law in the International Community*— namely the relationship between political developments and legal rules: was the growth of German hegemony in Europe a justiciable matter?[5]

III

In 1933 Hersch Lauterpacht was 36 years old. He had received his doctorate in Vienna in 1922 and had arrived in Britain with his wife Rachel in the following year. He enrolled in the London School of Economics (LSE) where he began to collaborate with Arnold McNair and to prepare his London dissertation, *Private Law Sources and Analogies of International Law*. The work was published in 1927, and in the same year Hersch received an assistant lectureship that was upgraded to full lectureship in 1930. In the following year, he received British citizenship.[6] At that time, he was busily giving lectures and publishing articles on international law matters, including the treatment of the Manchurian situation by the League organs. In Lauterpacht's view, the organs had not strictly speaking violated the Covenant in failing to take affective action. The Covenant did leave them discretion. But they had failed in their *political* obligation to use that discretion so as to give effect to the purposes of the League.[7]

---

[4] See eg F.S. Northedge, *The League of Nations. Its Life and Times 1919–1946* (Leicester University Press, 1986), pp 130–1.

[5] PCIJ, *Customs Regime between Germany and Austria*, Series A/B, No 41 (1931).

[6] On these biographical facts, see my 'Hersch Lauterpacht 1897–1960' in Jack Beatson and Reinhard Zimmermann, *Jurists Uprooted. German-Speaking Emigré Lawyers in Twentieth-Century Britain* (Oxford University Press, 2004), pp 604–16. See also now, Elihu Lauterpacht, *The Life of Sir Hersch Lauterpacht* (Cambridge University Press, 2010).

[7] Hersch Lauterpacht, 'Japan and the Covenant' (1932) 3 Political Quarterly pp 174–94; Eli Lauterpacht (ed), International Law; Collected Papers, Vol 5 (Cambridge University Press, 2004), 409–423.

No doubt owing to his readiness to speak on politically interesting topics, Lauterpacht's lectures were widely attended by students not working toward a law degree. He also collaborated actively with the professor of international relations at the LSE, C.A.W. Manning. Even if the British legal community did not hold international law in very high value, a persistent strand of interwar political idealism did. In the course of the 1930s, Lauterpacht worked to support the Disarmament Conference and participated in the drafting of the abortive Peace Act, proposed by Labour's Arthur Henderson and Lauterpacht's LSE colleague, Philip Noel-Baker. In a predominantly positivist legal environment, Lauterpacht was a natural lawyer—albeit one whose views were more evident in his critique of sovereignty than in any well-formulated normative theory. Unlike the Professor of International Law at the LSE, H.A. Smith, Lauterpacht was not a predominantly technical international lawyer but returned constantly to the foundational questions. In 1932, for example, he lectured to the LSE's famous Sociological Club on 'Is International Law Different in Nature from Other Law?'—a text that became the basis of Chapter XX of *The Function of Law in the International Community*.

IV

The Function of Law in the International Community (hereinafter *The Function of Law*) joins a wide European debate about the relationship between the 'political' and the 'legal' in the international world—a debate that had by that time received particular acuity in problems relating to the application of the League Covenant. After all, the Covenant's system of dispute settlement was based on the distinction between two types of disputes—those that were 'suitable for arbitration or judicial settlement' (Covenant 13.1 Article) and those that were not and were therefore to be directed to political organs such as the Council. The question of the 'nature' of particular disputes, and therefore of their justiciability, had been raised in practically every case in the Permanent Court that had not been submitted to it as a result of special agreement. It had been conventionally accepted that arbitration or judicial settlement were unsuitable for dealing with disputes over 'vital interests and honour', and many arbitration treaties contained a specific reservation to that effect. Although Lauterpacht dealt with the topic as it arose in the international realm, he was well aware that it was a general problem of jurisprudence, in particular the kind of jurisprudence that had been developed in German public law and that had peaked in the legal debates in Weimar Germany about the nature of sovereignty and the role of the republican constitution in times of economic and political crisis.

In a significant sense, much of the way we speak about international law has been received from German public law as it developed from constitutional commentaries about the nature of the Holy Roman Empire in the seventeenth century to the natural law of the eighteenth and the public law formalism of the nineteenth centuries. No legal tradition in this period compares with the German in the depth, complexity, or sense of urgency of its questions. Lauterpacht had been brought up in that tradition. One of his teachers in Vienna had been Hans Kelsen who at the time of the first publication of *The Function of Law* was intensively engaged in a debate about the relationship between law and political sovereignty under the Weimar Constitution—the application of the infamous Article 48 on emergency powers so as to strengthen the position of the Reich, and in particular the *Reichskanzler*, against deviating factions in the realm. The debate concerned the foundations of the legal-constitutional order. For the legalists, with Kelsen as their spokesman, law itself regulated the limits of its validity. When and how emergency powers, for example, could be used was a question of legal interpretation, properly within the jurisdiction of the Constitutional Court. For Kelsen's opponents—led by the *Kronjurist* of the regime, Carl Schmitt—the foundation of the constitutional order must necessarily lie outside that order itself. In particular, it must lie in a political sovereignty that can guarantee the efficiency of the constitution, if necessary by sending in the police.[8] For Kelsen, in other words, the political decisions needed to uphold the law must be received from the law (constitution). For Schmitt, the constitution is powerless in itself—its force and effect must lie in a prior political *decision* about whether to follow the constitution or to make an exception to it.

The question of the respective relations of law and politics in the international world had also been frequently dealt with in the German academia. For instance, Karl Strupp in Frankfurt had devoted a good quarter of his 1922 *Habilitation* on State responsibility to the question of *Notrecht* and gave his trial lecture

---

[8] For one brief but useful description of this debate, see David Dyzenhaus, *Legality and Legitimacy. Carl Schmitt, Hans Kelsen and Hermann Heller in Weimar* (Clarendon Press, 1997).

on precisely Article 48 of the Weimar Constitution.[9] More significantly, the question of the respective roles of law and politics in international dispute settlement was taken as the object of his 1929 doctoral dissertation by Strupp's most famous student, Hans Morgenthau, the future father of the discipline of international relations in the United States.[10] Morgenthau had argued that there were two kinds of international conflict: 'disputes' that focused on well-defined single issues that could be made the object of legal settlement, and what he chose to call 'tensions' that implicated a wider—political—antagonism and that could not usefully be submitted to legal mechanisms. There was no general rule by which the two could be identified. The 'political' nature of a problem depended simply on how intensely a State felt about it. When the intensity was high enough, a legal procedure would not only be useless but quite harmful.[11]

The Function of Law could only have been written from within the German tradition, from a vivid sense of the urgency of the question of the legal system's ultimate foundation. Things seemed completely different in Britain. The validity of the British constitution, or of the legal system, was an unreflective second nature of British politics and in no need of elaborate doctrinal defence. In the troubled waters of the German and the international world of the 1930s, no such self-evidence was present. *The Function of Law* is thus German; not only in its sentence structure, but in the sensibility it transmits to its readers. In an early essay on Spinoza, Lauterpacht had written that '[i]t is the ultimate results of the theory of the state which are resorted to by international lawyers as the foundation of their systems'.[12] Few assumptions can be more un-English, in fact more German, than

---

[9] For Strupp's treatment of the legal disputes/political disputes distinction in his various later works, see Sandra Link, *Ein Realist mit Idealen—Der Völkerrechtler Karl Strupp (1886–1940)* (Nomos, 2003), pp 241–7.

[10] Hans Morgenthau, *Die internationale Rechtspflege. Ihr Wesen und ihre Grenzen* (Noske, 1929).

[11] For Lauterpacht's positive review, see (1931) XII *BYIL* 229. For the grounding of Morgenthau's sceptical attitudes towards law and legal institutions in his professional experience in the Weimar Republic, see William E. Scheuerman, *Morgenthau. Realism and Beyond* (Polity Press, 2009), pp 12–24. See now also Oliver Jütersonke, *Morgenthau, Law and Realism* (Cambridge University Press, 2010) (highlighting the importance for Morgenthau of his 'debate' with Lauterpacht), pp 37–74.

[12] Hersch Lauterpacht, 'Spinoza and International Law', (1927) VIII BYIL 368; Eli Lauterpacht (ed), *International Law: Collected Papers*, vol. 2 (Cambridge University Press, 1975), p. 366–383.

the view that the law emerges as deductive inferences from the political philosophy of statehood.

This, however, is the perspective adopted in *The Function of Law*. It asks the question about the proper role of law in the international world, especially vis-à-vis that which is 'politics', often appearing under the vocabulary of 'sovereignty'. For, as Lauterpacht states at the outset of the book, the 'limitation of the place of law [is] an expression of the theory of sovereignty'.[13] The question is not approached in an openly philosophical or a political theory vocabulary, however, but through a technique of legal argument that almost presupposes the answer that Lauterpacht will produce by it. The perspective taken here is legal-institutional. What, *The Function of Law* asks, is the (legal) force of the claim, often raised in the practice of judicial and arbitral tribunals, that some disputes cannot be dealt with by law—that they are 'non-justiciable'—owing to their nature as 'political' disputes?

V

The Function of Law is an attack on the commonly held view that there were two types of international conflict—legal and political disputes—and that, consequently, only some of them are justiciable whereas others are not. Lauterpacht has no sympathy for these distinctions. For him, they are unfounded in logical, jurisprudential, as well as practical terms. In fact, as he puts it, the distinctions are simply ideological, being '… first and foremost, the work of international lawyers anxious to give legal expression to the State's claim to be independent of law'.[14] Lauterpacht agrees—perhaps surprisingly, but in fact quite coherently—with Morgenthau and Schmitt that it is impossible to draw a clear distinction between the political and the legal by a determinate rule. Anything can, from some perspective, be labelled 'political'. In particular, as he puts it with special reference to Morgenthau's dissertation, '[t]he State is a political institution, and all questions which affect it as a whole, in particular in its relations with other States, are therefore political'.[15] But surely the mere fact that all disputes are 'political' in this way does not provide a reason for regarding them as non-justiciable. In fact, Lauterpacht writes, 'it is the refusal of the State to submit the dispute to judicial settlement, and not the

---

[13] *The Function of Law*, p 3.   [14] Ibid, p 6.   [15] Ibid, p 161.

intrinsic nature of the controversy, which makes it political'.[16]
This is what it means to say that the theory of non-justiciability is
a consequence of the doctrine of sovereignty—it defers to the
sovereign will of the State itself. But if the will of the State were a
conditio sine qua non for a dispute being justiciable, then it would
always remain open for a State to opt out from the law's
constraint. Like Morgenthau and Schmitt, Lauterpacht believes
that the distinction between legal and political disputes, combined with the principle that its application is dependent on the
State's own view ('self-judgement'), would lead international law
beyond the vanishing point of jurisprudence. But where Morgenthau would conclude that this was indeed the case, and that
the absence of a delimiting rule meant that everything was
politics, Lauterpacht draws the contrary conclusion. For him:

> all international disputes are, irrespective of their gravity, disputes of
> a legal character in the sense that, so long as the rule of law is
> recognized, they are capable of an answer by the application of legal
> rules.[17]

In other words, the fact that a State may feel strongly about
some matter—for example, that it relates to its 'vital interests'—
does not exempt the matter from the law but, on the contrary,
calls for the application of legal rules concerning precisely those
types of (important) matters. The State will not have a veto. The
last word remains, and must remain, with the judge. *The Function
of Law* then goes methodologically through each of the four non-
justiciability doctrines that Lauterpacht is able to identify in the
international debates, showing how each attempt to delimit a
realm of the 'political' outside the 'legal' in international affairs
will eventually become an apology for unlimited freedom of
action of States and thus impossible to accept within a system
of law.

The first item dealt with is the claim that when there is 'no
law' at all a matter must be dealt with in a political way. To treat
this issue Lauterpacht chooses the jurisprudential vocabulary of
'lacunae'. What force is there to the argument that in cases of
'gaps', judicial and arbitral bodies must decline jurisdiction and
declare '*non liquet*'? As he had already done in his London
doctoral dissertation of 1927, Lauterpacht shows that, as far as
legal practice is concerned, courts and tribunals appear constantly to decide cases by analogy, by general principles of law,

---

[16] Ibid, p 172.   [17] Ibid, p 166.

balancing conflicting claims or having recourse to abstract points about the needs of the international community.[18] The alleged novelty of a dispute has never prevented a tribunal from giving a legal answer to it.[19] Of course, situations must arise every now and then for which the legislator has provided no prima facie applicable solution. No legislator will have prepared for every contingency. But the fact of there not existing positive (in the sense of 'posited') law on every conceivable aspect of human behaviour has not, at least not in practice, led to a wide acknowledgement of the correctness of the theory of 'gaps'.

But Lauterpacht does not merely wish to demonstrate the absence of cases of *non liquet* in international practice. He derives this state of affairs from a wider principle—namely the jurisdictional axiom 'that the judge is bound to give a decision on the dispute before him'.[20] There are no gaps for Lauterpacht. This does not follow from the (naive) assumption that the legislator would have foreseen everything. The completeness of the law is, instead, 'an *a priori* assumption of every system of law, not a prescription of positive law'. Though particular laws or particular parts of the law may be insufficiently covered, '[t]here are no gaps in the legal system as a whole'.[21] This is not a result of arguing from formal completeness of the Kelsenian type—that is to say, from the perspective of the assumption that in the absence of law, the plaintiff has no valid right and that *ergo*, his claim must be rejected.[22] For Lauterpacht, the very notion of 'law's absence' is untenable. For it presumes that law consists of isolated acts of State will that may or may not have extended to the matter under consideration. But this is not at all how Lauterpacht understands the law. He is, after all, a natural lawyer; although for good prudential reasons he refrained from trumpeting this in his British legal environment. But it led him to suggest that 'gaps' were in fact only *primae impressionis* difficulties to decide cases. If law is thought of in terms of general principles, judicial balancing, and social purposes—as Lauterpacht held it to be—then there is no principled difficulty to respond to novel situations in the end.[23] Even 'spurious gaps' may be filled: an unsatisfactory single rule may be bypassed to give effect to a major principle of law, the intention of the

---

[18] Ibid, pp 118–43.   [19] Ibid, pp 113–43.   [20] Ibid, p 143.
[21] Ibid, p 72.   [22] Ibid, pp 85–6, 93–112.
[23] Hence McNair's apt characterization of Lauterpacht's writing as 'constructive idealism': A. McNair, 'Hersch Lauterpacht 1897–1960' (1961) Proceedings of the British Academy 378.

parties, or the purposes of the legal system as a whole. In this way, even legal change is regulated by the law.[24]

A second, widely held view presupposed that only technical or otherwise minor disputes were amenable to legal settlement, while 'important' issues needed to be dealt with in a political vein. *De maximis non curat praetor*. This was the view on which Morgenthau had written his doctoral dissertation, and had proposed the distinction between political 'tensions' and legal 'disputes'.[25] Sometimes, Morgenthau wrote, even a minor issue must be understood as a 'tension' rather than a dispute because it has become a *symbol* of the antagonism between the relevant States: the real issue is the political conflict, not the legal form it takes. Again, Lauterpacht begins by noting that since the *Alabama* case (1872), tribunals have dealt with a wide number of important questions.[26] Having surveyed the practice of the Permanent Court of International Justice, he concludes that adhering to this principle 'would mean the speedy and radical liquidation of the activities of the Court'.[27] Again, however, the main argument is not about what tribunals may have done in practice. An issue of principle is involved. Lauterpacht agrees— perhaps surprisingly—with Morgenthau and even with Carl Schmitt that whether a matter touches on the State's 'vital interests' or 'honour' cannot be decided in abstraction from the State's own view of it.[28] These are purely subjective notions. If important issues were excluded from judicial settlement, and if the determination of the 'importance' of an issue were left to the party itself, then there would in fact exist an unlimited right to opt out from third party settlement. And this would be absurd.

On the other hand, Lauterpacht does not want to overlook the importance of arguments about 'vital interests' or 'honour'. It is true that they had been widely used in arbitration treaties and that they do reflect important State concerns. To discard or ignore them would be unrealistic and counterproductive. To avoid the absurdity of self-judgement, however, the decision on whether a matter might in fact touch on the 'honour' or 'vital

---

[24] *The Function of Law*, pp 87–95, 262–5 and *passim*. Cf also 'The Absence of an International Legislature and the Compulsory Jurisdiction of International Tribunals' (1930) XI BYIL 134, 144–54.

[25] Morgenthau, *Die internationale Rechtspflege*, above n 10.

[26] *The Function of Law*, pp 153–61.

[27] Ibid, p 163.

[28] Ibid, p 167.

interests' of a State must be allocated to the tribunal itself in which the claim has been made. That is to say, it should be dealt with no differently from any other claim made by a party regarding a treaty provision or customary law principle. As such, it is tantamount to calling for a decision on the merits of the claim. But this means, of course, that the matter is fully justiciable.[29] For instance, it is often held that issues of immigration are non-justiciable. 'In fact', responds Lauterpacht, 'they are a typically appropriate subject for judicial settlement. An international court will in most cases invariably presume that the claim will be dismissed.'[30]

The third group of arguments that presumed a distinction between legal and political disputes concerned the need for accommodating the needs of change in law. Sometimes—and Lauterpacht must have had the debate about the revision of the Versailles peace settlement in mind—law might represent an obsolete political situation, a status quo that no longer exists. An arrangement made long ago may have come to seem too burdensome or otherwise unjust for a party. Owing to the absence of an international legislature, it may often be impossible to correct the matter by formal means. In such cases—so the argument goes—it would be unjust, counterproductive, or even dangerous to insist on the application of the law.[31] For Lauterpacht, however, arguments about the clash between law, on the one hand, and justice or peace, on the other hand, are completely vacuous. Political realists mistake complexity for conflict. Problems of the obsolete or unjust rule may always be tempered by reference to the larger purposes of the law, *rebus sic stantibus*, abuse of rights, or principles of equity or reasonableness.[32] The view that law lags behind and must therefore sometimes be offset by new 'political' objectives that provide a better response to the requirements of the moment is again based on the old (positivist) idea that law is a matter of a definite number of legislated rules—typically rules laid out by the sovereign legislator—that are carved in stone and become inevitably outdated as the reasons for their enactment have disappeared.

Yet it is a primitive legal theory that views the law in such a way, Lauterpacht argues. For as legal practice shows, judges and arbitrators have not lacked means to apply the law in innovative ways, and to set aside rules that appear to be obsolete or unjust:

[29] Ibid, pp 361–9.   [30] Ibid, p 182.
[31] Ibid, pp 253–355.   [32] Ibid, pp 278 et seq.

'much of this amending process is actually and necessarily performed by international judges in the ordinary course of their judicial function'.[33] It is a matter of the normal interpretation of the rules, often by reference to their object and purpose. Rules operate in normative environments in which there are many kinds of interpretative techniques, principles of proportionality, and reasonableness, as well as other argumentative resources that enable the adjustment of the law according to important needs. The concerns of realism are incorporated in the law, for example, by the State's undoubted right to determine the conditions of self-defence for itself and in the exception to the vitiating effect of duress in the law of treaties. The realists' main concern is that law might sometimes fail to give due regard to the liberty and the fundamental rights of the State. As Lauterpacht responds, however:

> It is not sufficiently realized that fundamental rights of States are safe under international judicial settlement, for the reason that they are fundamental legal rights.[34]

The fourth and last group of arguments seeking to uphold the law/politics distinction referred to here points to a difference between 'disputes as to rights' and 'conflicts of interest'. This, too, is an empty distinction for Lauterpacht. Every right worth having makes reference to some interest, and merely having an interest in something is not a legitimate ground for imposing the burden of a legal duty on someone. Legitimate and illegitimate interests, and the connected duty on someone to contribute to the fulfilment of legitimate interest, can only be identified by making the distinction between 'raw' interests and interests upgraded into (legal) rights. If a State demands a piece of territory from another because this is vital for its development, it is easy to understand why it may want to deal with this as a conflict of interests rather than as a conflict of rights (because it has no right). But if it were entitled to do this unilaterally—that is to say, if it had the opportunity to change the terms of the debate from 'rights' to 'interests' by an *ipse dixit*—then, of course, this would violate the interests of its opponent in a way that would be absurd. In fact, Lauterpacht says, to presume such a distinction 'very nearly amounts to a rejection of the institution of obliga-

---

[33] Ibid, p 352.
[34] Ibid, p 181, and generally pp 185–90, 279.

tory judicial settlement'.[35] For the same reason, proposals to set up specialized institutions to deal with 'conflicts of interest' cannot be accepted. As 'interest' is not amenable to objective determination, this would only create a unilateral veto from juridical settlement and an authorization to discard the rights of others.[36]

VI

The refutations of the distinction between legal and political disputes in *The Function of Law* turn on Lauterpacht's hermeneutic view of the law—the assumption that no event is 'essentially' or in itself a legal or a political event. Its character as such is the result of projection, interpretation from the particular standpoint of the speaking subject. If the distinction were upheld, it would always allow a State to present its unwillingness to submit itself to the legal process as a result of its 'application' of the distinction. And:

> An obligation whose scope is left to the free appreciation of the obligee, so that his will constitutes a legally recognized condition of the existence of the duty, does not constitute a legal bond.[37]

That the problem of self-judgement (or auto-interpretation) becomes the central problem of Lauterpacht's doctrinal work follows from his view that the law is always relative to interpretation. This was a basic tenet of German legal theory; both Kelsen and Schmitt shared it, as did such new streams of continental jurisprudence as Hermann Kantorowicz's 'free law'.[38] If rules do not have essential meanings but those meanings result from interpretation, then the project to chain States

---

[35] Ibid, p 363.

[36] Ibid, pp 380–5.

[37] Ibid, p 197. This is, paradoxically, the very point E.H. Carr makes against Lauterpacht. Precisely because there can be no distinction between law and politics, the latter will always prevail: E.H. Carr, *The Twenty-Years' Crisis 1919–1939* (2nd edn, Macmillan, 1981 [1946]), p 195.

[38] In *The Function of Law* there is only one reference to the free law school or to Kantorowicz himself. Nevertheless, Lauterpacht's discussion of 'spurious gaps'—that is, gaps that result from the unsatisfactory character of clear rules—is practically indistinguishable from 'free law' arguments. For Lauterpacht, too, the distinction between 'real' and 'spurious' gaps is 'relative' (just like, he says, the difference between the legislator and the judge), and cases 'may occur in which a decision, which at first sight is *contra legem*, can be brought within the pale of law conceived as a whole'. Like Kantorowicz, Lauterpacht refrains from associating judicial freedom with arbitrariness. 'It is freedom within the law conceived as something more comprehensive than the sum total of its positive rules': *The Function of Law*, p 88.

into the rule of law by legislation is insufficient. Instead, 'Who judges?' (*Quis judicabit?*) becomes the key question. In *The Function of Law*, the lawyer—as judge and arbitrator—becomes the foundation of the rule of law. This is why Lauterpacht is led to focus on their impartiality and to examine their ability to interpret the law so that everyone's vital interests are secured.[39] To us, an inquiry into judicial honesty and competence seems a somewhat facile solution for world peace. But Lauterpacht's rule-scepticism is ours, too. Our own pragmatism stands on the revelation that it is the legal profession (and not the rules) that is important. As Lauterpacht puts it:

> There is substance in the view that the existence of a sufficient body of clear rules is not at all essential to the existence of law, and that the decisive test is whether there exists a judge competent to decide upon disputed rights and to command peace.[40]

The Function of Law puts forward the image of judges as 'Herculean' gap-fillers by recourse to general principles and the law's moral purposes that is very similar to today's Anglo-American jurisprudential orthodoxy.[41] Moreover, it heralds the end of jurisprudence and grand theory in the same way legal hermeneutics does, by focusing on the interpretative practices of the legal profession.[42] Simultaneously, however, it remains hostage to and is limited by the conventions and ambitions of that profession. In this sense, *The Function of Law* is the last book on international theory—the theory of non-theory, the sophisticated face of legal pragmatism.

VII

And what has *The Function of Law* to say to us today? As pointed out at the beginning, the distinction between 'legal' and 'political' disputes remains an important consideration—or at least it is often invoked to decide (that is, to exclude) the jurisdiction of international bodies or agencies. Moreover, many, though by no means all, constitutional systems subscribe to the distinction and

---

[39] Ibid, pp 210–49.
[40] Ibid, p 432.
[41] I have argued about the essential similarity of Lauterpacht's constructivism and Ronald Dworkin's jurisprudence in my *From Apology to Utopia. The Structure of International Legal Argument. Reissue with a New Epilogue* (Cambridge University Press, 2005), pp 52–6.
[42] This point is emphasized in Anthony Carty, 'Why Theory? The Implications for International Law Teaching' in P Allott et al, *Theory and International Law: An Introduction* (BIICL, 1991), pp 77, 78–99.

exempt issues of foreign policy from the jurisdiction of domestic supreme courts.[43] The 'political questions doctrine' followed by the US Supreme Court is one well-known, though controversial, example of the view of foreign policy being essentially non-justiciable.[44] A counter-example is provided by Germany in which important foreign and even defence policy issues are regularly submitted to the scrutiny of the Constitutional Court (*Verfassungsgericht*).[45] In Britain, the matter came up in the *Pinochet* case where it was pointed out by Lord Nicholls that any suggestion that the matter might be non-justiciable was mooted by the Parliament's having specifically legislated for it.[46] This presumes (*contra* Lauterpacht) that when there is no such (positive) legislation, there is also no jurisdiction. But, in fact, non-justiciability reaches further. In a 2006 case the Court of Appeal highlighted 'a general principle of the separation of powers between the executive and the courts, including the principle that there remain some areas which are essentially matters for the executive and not the courts'.[47]

International lawyers may have thought that the settled practice by the International Court of Justice of dismissing claims by parties according to which the Court would not enjoy jurisdiction owing to the 'political' nature of the case, should have finished with the matter internationally. The Court, it appears, also from the *Kosovo* case cited above, has endorsed Lauterpacht's position, and routinely asserts that the fact that a case has political implications does not mean that the Court could not pronounce on its legal aspects.[48] A small dent in that practice is constituted by the partial *non liquet* given by the Court in the 1996 Advisory Opinion on the *Legality of the Threat and Use of*

---

[43] See eg Thomas M. Franck, *Political Questions / Judicial Answers. Does the Rule of Law Apply to Foreign Affairs?* (Princeton University Press, 1992).

[44] For a recent case, see *Schneider v Kissinger* 412 F3d 190 (DC Cir 2005).

[45] For a recent case concerning the violation of parliamentary procedure in a contribution by Germany of troops for a NATO operation in Turkey in 1983, see BVerfG, 2 BvE 1/03 (7 May 2008).

[46] *Ex parte Pinochet (No 1)*, Lord Nicholls (2002) 119 ILR 96.

[47] *R (on the application of Gentle and Clarke) v Prime Minister, Secretary of State for Defence and Attorney General* (12 December 2006) (2008) 133 ILR 752 (para 75).

[48] The 'Lauterpachtian' language is particularly clear in the *Tehran Hostages* case where the Court pointed out that 'disputes between sovereign States by their very nature are likely to occur in political contexts' and that if the Court 'contrary to its settled jurisprudence' were to see this as a reason for refusing to deal with the case, 'it would impose a far-reaching and unwarranted restriction upon the role of the Court in the peaceful solution of international disputes': ICJ, *Tehran Hostages*, Reports 1980, 20 (para 37). The most exhaustive discussion of the matter is now in ICJ, *Construction of a Wall* (Advisory Opinion), Reports 2004, 155–6 (para 41).

Nuclear Weapons.[49] Moreover, the debate in the 1990s over judicial review of Security Council decisions highlighted many of the aspects of the old debate and although it remained inconclusive, there has been marked hesitation (to put it no higher) among international lawyers to affirm the Court's jurisdiction over Council activities.[50] In the European Union, the exclusion of the jurisdiction of the European Court of Justice (ECJ) from matters of common foreign and security policy and, a fortiori, common security and defence policy, reflects precisely the types of arguments against which Lauterpacht wrote *The Function of Law.* Nevertheless, when the jurisdiction of the ECJ has been triggered in matters that are related to foreign policy—such as in the application of economic sanctions—a remarkable development has taken place, from an outright refusal to deal with such matters to a close scrutiny of sanctions from the perspective of their conformity with human rights and due process standards under the novel *Kadi* jurisprudence.[51] The European Court of Human Rights (ECtHR), too, has frequently dealt with cases in which respondent governments have claimed that the matter pertained to the exclusive jurisdiction of the domestic authorities. The Court has never adopted a formal non-justiciability doctrine—indeed, it would be hard to see how such would work in a human rights context. But it has often been sensitive to the concerns of member governments endowing them with a wide margin of appreciation when they were conducting policies intended to safeguard national security.[52]

---

[49] Here the Court concluded that 'in view of the current state of international law, and of the elements of fact at its disposal, the Court cannot conclude definitively whether the threat or use of nuclear weapons would be lawful or unlawful in an extreme circumstance of self-defence, in which the very survival of a State would be at stake': ICJ, *Threat or Use of Nuclear Weapons* (Advisory Opinion), Reports 1996, *Dispositif*, 266 (E).

[50] Out of the huge literature, see eg Kamrul Hossain, *Limits to Power? Legal and Institutional Control over the Competence of the United Nations Security Council under Chapter VII of the Charter* (Acta Universitatis Lapponiensis, 2007).

[51] For an overview of the attitude of the ECJ until 2002, see my 'Judicial Review of Foreign Policy Discretion in Europe' in Petri Helander, Juha Lavapuro, and Tuomas Mylly (eds), *Yritys eurooppalaisessa oikeusyhteisössä* (Turun Yliopisto, Oikeustieteellinen tiedekunta, 2002), pp 155–73. For the *Kadi* cases, see Case T-306/01 and Case T-315/01 *Ahmed Ali Yusuf and Al Barakaat International Foundation and Yassin Abdullah Kadi v Council of the European Union and Commission of the European Communities* (21 September 2005) and the overturning of the judgment of the CFI by the Grand Chamber of the ECJ in its Judgment of 3 September 2008 in Joined Cases C-402/05 P and C-415/05 P *Kadi & Al Barakaat v Council of the European Union* (2008) 3 CMLR 41.

[52] In an early case, the Court held that 'having regard to the high responsibility that a government bears to its people to protect them against any threat to the life of the nation, it is evident that a certain discretion—a certain margin of appreciation—must be left to the government': ECtHR, *Lawless* case, Series B, 1960–61, 82 (para 90). In a 1993 case

If the terms of the interwar debate are applied to the question about the jurisdiction of the ECJ or the ECtHR, it is possible to see that behind the apparently conceptual problem of the limits of the 'political' vis-à-vis the 'legal' there is a more pragmatic concern about who should have the final say about foreign policy—and thus occupy the place political theory has been accustomed to calling 'sovereignty'. Kelsen, Schmitt, and Lauterpacht all had much to say about this, and very little that would have been both new and intelligent has been added to the topic thereafter. But to phrase this debate as being about 'sovereignty'—the 'Weimar' perspective—does not really lead far towards resolving it. In a pluralist world, there is simply no such 'ultimate' place from which authoritative direction could be received for any and all disputes. Perhaps the whole question should be rather brought down from conceptual abstraction and the inconsequential debates about the 'nature' of particular grievances. Perhaps it could be examined in terms of the subtle institutional politics that we witness in national administrations as well as international institutions—the jurisdictional tug of war between technical experts, lawyers, and policy-makers. A question of economic sanctions, for example, can be described and dealt with from the perspective of politics, economics, security, human rights, development, and international legality. Accordingly, it may trigger the expertise and jurisdiction of political and economic experts, security institutions, human rights bodies, and development organizations—as well as, of course, international judicial or arbitral tribunals. Who should be entitled to decide? Framed in these terms, drawing a line between 'legal' and 'political' (or indeed, other fields such as 'economics', 'security', 'human rights', etc) by an abstract rule begins to seem increasingly less important than to accept that, however it is done, the matter will remain controversial and will require attention to such institutional safeguards as representation, transparency, and accountability. Each of these various institutions and forms of expertise appears to itself as the 'ultimate' point from which matters ought to be decided. For those outside the relevant institution—the expert committee, the council of diplomats, the court, or tribunal—however, it may be anything

concerning terrorism and the derogation from rights under Article 15 of the Convention under public emergency, the Court affirmed that 'a wide margin of appreciation should be left to the national authorities'. Nevertheless, this margin was not unlimited and its use was examined by the Court: ECtHR, *Brannigan and McBride*, Series A, No 258 B, 49 (para 43).

but self-evident which of them should have jurisdiction and the privilege to decide. This highlights the importance of what could be called a 'politics of re-description': the constant effort exercised by legal and other experts to describe important matters in the language of their particular expertise so as to achieve the allocation of decision-making power on that matter to their preferred institution—the one in which they, or their values, are well represented.[53]

Hersch Lauterpacht was committed to the belief that international lawyers, in particular international judges, should rule the world. This was a part of what I have elsewhere called the project of gentle civilizing. It was a legal but also a political project. Putting trust in the good sense and responsibility of lawyers for resolving international disputes has its advantages, of course. But judicalization also has its well-known disadvantages. It prefers some interests against others; some voices are easily heard in courts and tribunals whereas other voices only with difficulty, if at all. There is still much work to be done on how interests and preferences come to be filtered in different institutions and thus contribute to form the structural bias of such institutions. I have said this before and I will say it again: *The Function of Law* is the most important English-language book on international law in the twentieth century. It is not so because of the invulnerability of its arguments but because of the acute sensitivity it shows to institutional choices for the distribution of spiritual and material values in the world. We know now that neither lawyers nor diplomats should have the final say in the absolute terms of the old debate. There is surely room for both. Instead, we should choose the available vocabulary, and the institutional alternative that it supports, with a keen eye on the foreseeable effects that this will have in the global games of power in the twenty-first century. It is hard to think of a better way to prepare for them than by reading this book.

---

[53] See further my 'The Fate of International Law: Between Technique and Politics' (2007) 70 Modern Law Review 7–9 and *passim*.

PART I

INTRODUCTORY

THE SCIENCE OF INTERNATIONAL LAW AND THE LIMITATION OF THE PLACE OF LAW IN THE SETTLEMENT OF INTERNATIONAL DISPUTES

I

The Doctrine of the Limitations of the Judicial Process in International Law

§ 1. The Limitation of the Place of Law as an Expression of the Theory of Sovereignty. The function of law is to regulate the conduct of persons, natural or juridical, by reference to rules whose formal—as distinguished from their historical—source of validity lies, in the last resort, in a command imposed from outside. Within the community of nations this essential feature of the rule of law is constantly put in jeopardy by the conception of the sovereignty of States which deduces the binding force of international law exclusively from the will of each individual member of the international community. This is the reason why any inquiry of a general character in the field of international law finds itself at the very start confronted with the doctrine of sovereignty. The same applies to the question of the limitations of the function of law in the settlement of international disputes—a problem which, to a large extent, is the creation of the doctrine of sovereignty. For the impact of the theory of the sovereignty of States reveals itself in the international sphere mainly in two ways: first, as the right of the State to determine what shall be for the future the content of international law by which it will be bound; secondly, as the right to determine what is the content of existing international law in a given case. The first aspect, according to which the State is not bound by any rule of law unless it has accepted it expressly or tacitly, has found its theoretical expression in the positivist doctrine. Its effects have been particularly conspicuous in the field of international legislation as the result of the requirement of unanimity, frequently appearing in the form, or as a corollary, of the doctrine of equality of States. The second aspect connotes that, in case of dispute, the State is in principle the sole judge of the existence of any individual rules of law, applicable to itself. It is a canon of international law that the jurisdiction of international tribunals is one voluntarily accepted by States.[1] The arbitrament of disputes by law is not regarded as a fundamental duty owed by one member of the community of nations to another, but as a self-imposed and essentially reversible concession, conditioned by the nature of the present and future relations with the State or States concerned.[2]

The legal shortcomings of the doctrine of sovereignty in the international sphere would have been revealed much earlier but for the fact that it has surrounded itself with doctrines derived from it, which, suitably elaborated by Governments and writers, have subsequently acquired a standing of their own and contributed powerfully towards perpetuating the influence of the original doctrine. Thus in regard to the State's claim, now fully admitted by existing law, to remain, as between itself and other States, the judge over a disputed right, international lawyers have called into being the doctrine of the inherent limitations of the international judicial process, commonly called the doctrine of non-justiciable disputes. That doctrine is based on an alleged fundamental difference between two categories of disputes: legal and non-legal, legal and political, justiciable and non-justiciable, disputes as to rights and disputes arising out of conflicts of interests. It connotes that by the very nature of international relations there are certain types of international disputes which are not an appropriate object for judicial settlement, in

---

[1] 'It is well established in international law that no State can, without its consent, be compelled to submit its disputes with other States either to mediation or to arbitration, or to any other kind of pacific settlement'—Permanent Court of International Justice in the *Eastern Carelia* case, Series B, No. 5, p. 27. See also Series A, No. 2 (*Palestine Concessions* case), p. 16 ('The Court, bearing in mind the fact that its jurisdiction is limited, that it is invariably based on the consent of the respondent and only exists in so far as this consent has been given . . .'); Series A, No. 9 (*Factory at Chorzów: Jurisdiction*), p. 32; Series A, No. 15 (*Minorities in Upper Silesia* case), p. 22; *Ambatielos case (Merits)*, *ICJ Reports* 1953, p. 19; and, in particular, the case of *Monetary Gold Removed from Rome* where the court declined jurisdiction, at the instance of Italy who originally invoked it, on the ground that in deciding the issue before it the Court would have to pronounce on the international responsibility of Albania who was not a party to the proceedings. The Court said: 'To adjudicate upon the international responsibility of Albania without her consent would run counter to a well-established principle of international law embodied in the Court's Statue, namely, that the court can only exercise jurisdiction over a "State with its consent"': *ICJ Reports* 1954, p. 32. That principle does not fully apply to advisory jurisdiction. See the Advisory Opinion on the *Interpretation of the Peace Treaties with Bulgaria, Hungary and Roumania*: *ICJ Reports* 1950, p. 65, which, to that extent, constitutes a modification of the principle laid down in the case of *Eastern Carelia*. For comment on this aspect of the requirement of consent, see Lauterpacht, *Development*, pp. 353–8.

[2] See below, pp. 167, 168.

particular for judicial settlement following upon an obligation undertaken in advance within the frame of so-called 'compulsory' or 'obligatory' arbitration. The examination of that doctrine is one of the main objects of this book.

§ 2. The Doctrine of the Limitation of the Judicial Process as an Argument in Favour of Obligatory Arbitration.

The doctrine of the inherent limitation of the judicial process has not only been an instrument for reconciling the uncompromising claims of sovereignty with the necessity, dictated by the needs of international intercourse and by the pressure of public opinion, of concluding treaties of judicial settlement creating—by providing an argument in favour of realistic caution—the appearance of effective legal obligations. For some lawyers and statesmen, that doctrine has been an instrument in support of the cause of obligatory arbitration. In the Memorandum submitted by the Russian delegation to the First Hague Conference, we find the following significant passage: 'In introducing international arbitration into the international life of States, we must proceed with extreme care in order not to extend unreasonably its sphere of application so as to shake the confidence which may be inspired therein, or discredit arbitration in the eyes of Governments and peoples.'[1] This passage expresses one of the principal reasons which underlay the doctrine of the limitations of the international judicial function at a time when the idea of compulsory arbitration first began to occupy the minds of lawyers and statesmen. At that time lawyers began to think of introducing the distinction between 'legal' and 'political' disputes; such a distinction might, they said, help to overcome the general unwillingness of Governments to submit their disputes to international adjudication. This function the doctrine of the limitation of the judicial process has preserved up to the present day. In 1930 the author of a thorough exposition of the history and of the principles of the General Act of 1928 for the Pacific Settlement of International Disputes, in discussing the distinction between disputes as to respective 'rights' and other controversies—a modern formulation of the traditional distinction between legal and political disputes—adopted the same attitude. He admitted the classification to be antiquated, and realized that it could easily become an element of confusion, but he justified

---

[1] Explanatory Note concerning Article 10 of the Russian draft, printed in *The Reports to the Hague Conferences of 1899 and 1907*, ed. by J. B. Scott (1917), p. 99.

its retention on the ground that it might serve the useful purpose of overcoming the distrust of Governments.[1]

With other writers the doctrine in question has been resorted to as a well-meant attempt to lend the authority of a legal principle to an attitude of Governments inimical to any real recognition of the sovereignty of law. The law of nations is in many respects a deficient system of law, and international lawyers, anxious to stress the legal character of their discipline, are apt to invest the deficiencies of international law *qua* law with the authority of legal principles derived from the very nature of international society. The idea underlying these attempts has been that, so long as the obligatory jurisdiction of international tribunals does not form part of positive law, it is better, through an appropriate legal doctrine, to represent that situation as compatible with the rule of law in international society. These attempts at embellishment, dictated by a specifically conceived legal positivism, and frequently resulting in the provision of a legal justification for backward aspects of international relations, are of frequent occurrence in the field of international law. Whatever may have been the reasons which prompted writers to accept the doctrine of non-justiciable disputes, in turn, there is little doubt that it, i.e. the doctrine of the inherent limitations of justiciability of international disputes, has powerfully influenced the subsequent practice of Governments. In point of time, it was formulated before the Hague Peace Conferences of 1899 and 1907, and long before the first general arbitration treaties were concluded. This fact goes far to answer the question whether what international lawyers have done has been merely to formulate the existing practice and tendencies of Governments, or whether the object and effect of their teaching has not been to provide Governments with a ready formula for expressing their unwillingness to undertake the commitments of obligatory judicial settlement.

From that point of view, the doctrine of the inherent limitations of the judicial process among States is, first and foremost, the work of international lawyers intent upon giving legal expression to the State's claim to be independent of law. They have sought to do this in reliance upon a general theory on the place of law and courts in international society. The practical problem of obligatory arbitration has thus been linked up with the central problems of the philosophy of international law and of legal philosophy in general.

[1] Gallus in *R.I.*, 3rd ser., xi (1930), pp. 224–9.

II

The History of the Doctrine

§ 3. The Original Scope of the Doctrine. Vattel. The principal function which the doctrine of the 'inherent limitations' has been called upon to fulfil since its inception, has been to supply a legal cloak for, or explanation of, the traditional claim of the sovereign State to remain the ultimate judge of disputed legal rights in its controversies with other States. A plausible solution of the conflict between the factors pressing for the assumption of some measure of obligatory judicial settlement and the determination to retain freedom of action, lay in confining obligatory arbitration to matters of small import. Consequently international lawyers applied themselves with zeal towards demonstrating the necessity for such a limitation. Yet, it was soon felt that to accept the *importance* of disputes as a basis both for the obligation to arbitrate and for a scientific classification of disputes would amount to the adoption of a test so subjective and so indeterminate as to render it valueless in theory and in practice. The remedy was found in linking up this highly subjective test with one capable of objective determination. The test thus found was the suitability of a dispute to be settled by the application of legal rules. What remained was to show that, owing either to the specific structure of international law or to the actual incompleteness of its rules, the law of nations can be applied only to matters less important than the independence and the vital interests of States. This task was begun as early as 1758 by Vattel.

Vattel, whose elegant manner of evasion has remained typical of the attempts to reconcile the insistence on the rights of sovereignty with the appearance of a recognition of a legal order among nations,[1] may be regarded as the writer who, without using the *terminus technicus* in question, first introduced the doctrine of non-justiciable disputes into international law.[2]

---

[1] See Van Vollenhoven, *The Three Stages of International Law* (1919), for a somewhat outspoken estimate, from this point of view, of Vattel's place in the history of international law.

[2] The absence of direct reference, among early writers on international law, to any distinction between different classes of disputes explains itself by the fact that arbitration, as such, occupies only a little space in the treatises on international law in the two hundred years following upon the appearance of the *De jure belli ac pacis*. Grotius himself discusses arbitration in some detail in the twenty-third chapter of Book II in a section entitled 'How War may be obviated by Arbitration'. He shows no inclination to limit the duty to resort to peaceful solution. He says: 'It would be advantageous, indeed in a degree necessary, to hold certain conferences of Christian powers, where those who have no interest at stake may settle the dispute of others, and where, in fact, steps may be taken to compel parties to accept peace on fair terms': ii. xxiii. viii. 4. (*Classics of International Law*, Kelsey's translation, 1925).

His chapter on 'The Manner of Settling Disputes between Nations'[1] presents an appearance of a clear logical distinction between different kinds of settlement. He distinguishes between, and deals in separate paragraphs with, Amicable Adjustment, Compromise, Mediation, Arbitration, and Conferences and Congresses. He is full of approval for arbitration. It is even possible that he has in mind not only isolated arbitration agreements, but arbitration treaties of a more general character, since he speaks with commendation of the Swiss Cantons which 'have taken the precaution, in all their alliances with one another, and even in those which they have contracted with neighbouring powers, to arrange in advance the manner in which they are to submit their differences to arbitrators in case they cannot adjust them by a friendly settlement'.[2] But side by side with this recognition of the beneficent influence of arbitration there runs persistently a call to caution in terms which explain clearly one of the bases of the modern doctrine of non-justiciable disputes. 'Arbitration', he says, 'is a very reasonable means, and one that is entirely in accord with the natural law, of terminating every dispute which does not directly affect the safety of the State.'[3] 'In the disputes', he continues, 'which arise between sovereigns, a careful distinction must be made

Neither will such a limitation be found in Pufendorf's chapter on 'The Way of Deciding Controversies in the Liberty of Nature': *Jus Naturae et Gentium* (1672), Book V, chapter xiii. See also *De officio hominis et civis juxta legem naturalem libri duo* (1682 edition), p. 102. And see Zouche, *Juris et Judicii Fecialis* (1650), Part II, section 1; Wolff, *Jus Gentium* (1749): the sixth chapter of the sixth book entitled 'De modo componendi controversias gentium'; Moser, *Versuch des neuesten Europäischen Völkerrechts in Friedens-und Kriegszeiten* (1777–80), Book XVI, part viii, sections 16, 17, and 18. It is typical of the part played by arbitration in Moser's day that there is in this voluminous work only one instance of an arbitration treaty—that between Turkey and Russia in 1741. He attempts a purely technical classification of controversies into claims, complaints, and disputes. Burlamaqui, *Principes du droit de la nature et des gens* (Dupin's ed., 1820), vol. iii, chapter xvii, pp. 490ff., discusses in some detail the procedure of arbitration and the question of rules to be applied. There is no attempt at a classification of disputes except for the passage in which, like Pufendorf (op. cit.), he urges that the plaintiff State is, more than the defendant, under a duty to seek arbitration. See Bynkershoek in *Questionum Juris Publici Libri duo* (1737), Book II, chapter xxiv, entitled 'De modis conciliandi dissentientes Provincias'. See also Wagner, *Zur Lehre von den Streiterledigungsmitteln des Völkerrechts* (1900), for a number of references to early writers.

   [1] *Le Droit des Gens, ou Principes de la Loi Naturelle, appliqués à la Conduite et aux Affaires des Nations et des Souverains* (1758), Book II, chapter xviii. The quotations which follow are from Fenwick's translation of 1916 (*Classics of International Law*).

   [2] Ibid., § 329.

   [3] Ibid. It is not surprising, having regard to the manner in which Vattel used to cloak his views, that some authors regard him as one of the first champions of

between essential rights and less important rights, and a different line of conduct is to be pursued accordingly.'[1] There is a
duty to negotiate and to seek arbitral decisions 'where interests
that are not essential, or are of small consequence, are
involved'.[2] He obviously attached importance to that distinction
for he repeats it, for the third time, in the paragraph which
follows. He is very eloquent on the duty of a nation 'when one
should seek to rob it of an essential right, of a right without
which it cannot hope to maintain its existence' not even to
attempt pacific settlement, but to 'exhaust its resources, and
nobly shed the last drop of its blood'.[3] It is for our purpose less
important, though it is characteristic of Vattel, that even within
this orbit he limits the duty of reference to arbitration to 'doubtful cases'. Where the right is 'clear, certain and indisputable . . . a
sovereign may, if he has the power, boldly prosecute it and
defend it without submitting it to arbitration'.[4]

§ 4. **The Modern Origins of the Doctrine.** The modern
origin of the distinction between legal and political disputes can
be traced to three events of outstanding importance in the
history of international arbitration. The first was the Alabama
arbitration in 1872, and the discussion preceding and following
that most important arbitration.[5] Of the many attempts, private
and official, to arrive at an amicable settlement of the underlying dispute, a letter written by Thomas Balch, and published, on
31 March 1865, in the *New York Tribune*, was not the least significant. Although not referring *eo nomine* to legal or political disputes, it drew attention to the fact that the reciprocal claims
rested upon questions of law, and, being claims of individuals,
were not 'strictly national'.[6] This latter argument was intended
to convey that the question was not one of 'high policy'.

The second event of importance was the foundation of the
Institute of International Law, which took up, as one of its first
tasks, the formulation of a plan of arbitral procedure. In 1873
Professor Goldschmidt was entrusted with the preparation of
Draft Regulations for International Arbitral Procedure. In the

---

arbitration. See, for instance, Ralston, *International Arbitration from Athens to Locarno* (1929), p. 121.

[1] § 332.
[2] Ibid.   [3] Ibid.   [4] § 331.   [5] See below, p. 147.
[6] The letter is reprinted in Balch, *International Courts of Arbitration* (1874), p. 12.

Preliminary Remarks to the draft[1] dealing with the question of the *compromis*, he pointed out that, an arbitral decision being essentially a judicial decision, arbitration was not applicable to 'non-legal disputes whose nature does not admit of a judgment according to the rules of law'. He gave a definition of legal differences (*Rechtstreit, contestation juridique*) which he described as disputes 'which ought to be decided by the application of principles of law'. In this class he included territorial claims and questions of interpretation of treaties. He then proceeded to elaborate the distinction between legal and political disputes. He found that the latter are disputes of a complex nature concerned with questions of nationality, of equality, or of supremacy, which, being by their very nature questions of power, and not of law, are unsuitable for arbitral settlement. This change of position was typical. For the secure basis of the applicability of a legal rule as a test whether the dispute is legal or not, he substituted a fundamentally different criterion in the second part of the definition.

The third stage in the development of the new doctrine began with the Hague Conventions, the official memoranda there presented,[2] and the discussions which preceded and followed the Conferences. It is apparent, when the First Hague Conference, by refusing to embody the principle of obligatory arbitration in a rule of positive law, and by introducing the conception of legal disputes, inaugurated a new period in the history of international arbitration, it merely gave formal expression to an opinion persistently voiced by international lawyers of the time.

§ 5. Views of Writers Prior to the Hague Conferences.

Thus already in 1870, Trendelenburg, in a much quoted monograph,[2] insisted that arbitration is an unsuitable method of settlement of disputes in cases where historical events work to create new legal relations between States; that only the legal element in the conflicts of nations is amenable to arbitration; and that judicial settlement must accordingly be excluded in questions of national development and aspirations. For the settlement of such disputes he recommended the process of conciliation on the initiative of third States. Bluntschli, in a paper entitled 'The Organization of the European Federation of

---

[1] Printed in *R.I.* vi (1874), pp. 421–52, and in *Resolutions of the Institute of International Law*, ed. by J. B. Scott (1916), pp. 205–43. See also the same in *Zeitschrift für das Privat- und öffentliche Recht der Gegenwart*, ii (1875), p. 716.

[2] *Lücken im Völkerrecht* (1870), p. 21.

States'[1] drew a distinction, which he regarded as being of great importance for the proposed Federation, between 'higher politics in international law' and matters of 'mere international administration and justice'. The former, he said, include 'all questions which concern the existence, the independence, the freedom of States, and on which the conditions of life of the nations, their safety and development are dependent'. In regard to such interests he asserted, in a passage vividly reminiscent of Vattel, that nations prefer to sacrifice life and property for the maintenance of their rights rather than to submit to a foreign administrative authority, or even to an arbitral or judicial award of international courts. Such questions, he said, must be left to the Supreme Council of the Federation. But in regard to matters of small importance in the domain of international administration and justice, which 'can be looked after without danger to individual sovereign States, arbitration, including even permanent international tribunals for certain disputes, is the proper procedure'. Thus, he thought, the reform of prize law was a suitable subject for an international court of justice.[2]

Prominent writers who championed the cause of arbitration, shared that attitude of caution. Rouard de Card, while recognizing the suitability of arbitration for many questions of importance, for instance, delimitations of frontiers, conflicts of jurisdiction and, generally, violations of international law, was emphatic in excluding from its purview questions affecting national independence.[3] Lacointa, in his Introduction to Kamarovsky's leading treatise on arbitration, excluded from the domain of judicial settlement all questions of a 'nontangible' character, i.e. questions 'which solely excite international hatreds and antagonisms and which do not offer any precise object for a decision'.[4] Mougin de Roquefort adopted a similar attitude.[5] Kamarovsky himself emphasized the fact that only the legal side of the external relations between States is capable of judicial determination, namely, such disputes as by virtue of positive international law and of conventions concluded between States are capable of objective and juridical determination.[6]

---

[1] Printed in *Gesammelte kleine Schriften* (1881), ii. 281 ff. Parts of this paper were published and somewhat freely translated in Darby, *International Tribunals*, 4th ed. (1904), pp. 195–213.

[2] His enumeration of 'matters of small importance' included, *inter alia*, interpretation of treaties relating to trades and tariffs, extradition of criminals, nationality, international private and criminal law, controversies regarding damages, &c.

[3] *Les Destinées de l'arbitrage international* (1892).   [4] p. xix.

[5] *De la solution juridique des conflits internationaux* (1889), p. 85.

[6] *Le Tribunal international* (1887), p. 504. However, he was of the opinion that an international tribunal once established will attract also questions of a political character which it will solve by the application of general principles of law.

Textbook writers of that period were no less ready to take over the distinction between legal and political disputes. Bulmerincq, writing in Holtzendorff's *Handbuch des Völkerrechts*,[1] limited himself to stating that disputes between States are due to political or legal causes and that only the latter can be settled by arbitration. Rivier,[2] who defined as legal disputes such differences as can be decided by recourse to legal principles, gave a very liberal interpretation of that definition, and included in it questions affecting the property of the State, its territory and frontiers, claims for idemnity on the ground of alleged breaches of neutrality or of violation of rights of aliens, interpretation and execution of treaties, diplomatic privileges, rights of navigation, and so on. Geffcken, in his edition of Heffter,[3] confined arbitration to claims capable of juridical formulation—claims which he regarded as the least frequent and least important type of conflicts. Calvo expressed the opinion that international arbitration must stop short of disputes which involve directly the national honour and independence, which 'affect the deeply-lying, almost personal, national sentiment, of which no third state can be a judge, each nation being the sole judge of its own dignity and of the rights which guarantee that dignity'.[4] The doctrine was at that time also clearly recognized by Fiore,[5] Ullmann,[6] F. de Martens,[7] and other writers.[8]

§ **6. Kaltenborn.** Before proceeding with the account of the further development of the doctrine special reference may fittingly be made to three writers whose contributions to the subject are of particular importance. They are Kaltenborn, Lorimer, and Westlake. Kaltenborn's contribution entitled 'The Revision of the Doctrine of International Legal Procedure' appeared in 1861.[9] There is little in it which is devoted to arbitration proper. In particular he makes no attempt at a classification of international disputes. But his contribution is of interest as an attempt to vindicate the principle that States are not only parties but also judges and policemen in their own

---

[1] (1889), iv. 1, 31.   [2] *Principes du droit des gens* (1896), ii. 179.
[3] 8th ed. (1888), p. 231.
[4] *Le droit international théorique et pratique* (6th ed., 1888), vol. iii, p. 472.
[5] *Nouveau droit international* (translation from the Italian), ii (1885), No. 1205.
[6] *Völkerrecht* (1898), p. 131.
[7] *Traité de droit international* (translation, 1887), iii. 154.
[8] See, for instance, Féraud-Giraud in *R.I.* xxix (1897), pp. 333–66, and authors there cited.
[9] *Zeitschrift für die gesammte Staatswissenschaft*, xvii (1861), pp. 69–124.

cause. He rejects the view that obligatory judicial settlement is necessarily an instrument for securing peace. For, he says, if the State against which judgement is given refuses to comply with the decision, what remains is to give effect to it by the application of force—which again means war. On the other hand, he finds no insurmountable difficulty in the fact that, in international law, the parties are at the same time judges of the dispute. He doubts whether that peculiarity of international organization must necessarily result in injustice. For, he argues, States are moral beings of whom it may be assumed that they are less under the influence of passion and partiality than individuals,[1] and that they are therefore unlikely to abuse their position in this unusual cumulation of functions. There are in it, he added, some advantages not to be found in the ordinary judicial procedure among individuals. One of these is that sovereign States, acting as judges in their cause, will not permit their just claims to be defeated as the result of formal procedural rules which, within the State, often obstruct the path of justice. Neither, according to Kaltenborn, are the interests of justice necessarily compromised because in international disputes the State acts not only as party and judge, but also as legislator. He pointed to the results of some successful wars—war being regarded as a lawful means of settling disputes—waged by Prussia as showing that the ultimate effects of what he called the specific judicial organization of international society may be consistent with reason and justice.

§ 7. **Lorimer.** Lorimer's views, expressed with characteristic vigour and independence of judgement, are of interest as an early attempt 'to eliminate impossible cases' from the purview of obligatory judicial settlement.[2] Without using the term 'political', he expressed the opinion that arbitration is inapplicable where the question at issue has reference to the relative value of States—where it is asked, for example, 'whether their historical position in relation to each other is or is not now their true position'. He referred to the Franco-German war of 1870, which was a struggle for the hegemony over continental Europe, as an example of this type of question. But he was of the opinion that the questions whether Germany was entitled to claim Alsace and Lorraine on historical and ethnological

---

[1] Ibid., p. 89.
[2] They are expressed in a letter written to Thomas Balch in 1874 and reprinted in Balch's *International Courts of Arbitration* (1874), pp. 28–38.

grounds, or whether France was entitled to the Rhine as a frontier for geographical reasons, were proper subjects for arbitration. 'Arbitration', he said, 'like judicial action in any other form, can only declare a relation which already exists, whereas war brings about new relations, or at least converts those which existed *in posse* into relations *in esse*.'[1] However, when referring to the Eastern Question as a dispute in which the conflict ranged over the question whether Russia was or was not the preponderating Power in the east of Europe and the west of Asia, he expressed the opinion that even in this case there existed an arbitrable element owing to Turkey's willingness to place herself in the hands of third Powers.[2]

§ **8. Westlake.** Westlake's contribution to the problem was, and has remained, by far the most searching and original exposition of the question of the limitations of the international judicial process. His treatment of the subject is admirable and weighty, although there is no escape from the conclusion that the distinction which he set up between political and legal disputes is essentially of a verbal character. He oscillates, without making a final choice, between an objective criterion for legal disputes and a construction which, being based on a very orthodox view of State sovereignty, leaves to the States an unlimited freedom of action.

On the one hand, he lays down an objective test for legal disputes, easily ascertainable by the fact that 'they can be settled by reference to known rules, having at their back that force which is derived from the general consent of the international society';[3] or, as he puts it in another place, political action determining the non-legal character of the dispute is allowed when the rule of international law needs to be supplemented or precisely defined.[4] This objective test Westlake still formally maintains, although he stretches it to breaking-point, when he

---

[1] Ibid., p. 38. See also below, p. 167.

[2] Lorimer's rather pessimistic attitude as to the ultimate efficacy of arbitration for the purpose of insuring lasting international peace was due to his opinion that this end cannot be achieved by anything short of an efficient international legislature, an international judicature, and an international executive. He had no patience with a movement which, through the usual reservations, restricted so much the scope of matters for arbitration that one had to ask 'whether the class of cases which remain to it be not precisely those which have hitherto been disposed of just as surely and economically and far more quietly by diplomacy'. See *The Institutes of the Law of Nations* (1884), ii. 212.

[3] *International Law* (2nd ed., 1910), i. 338.

[4] Ibid., p. 302.

limits the scope of legal disputes by excluding from it differences
in which the legal point is clear and established, but is overridden by considerations of higher distributive justice, namely,
when 'opinion is felt to be outgrowing a rule, so that a change in
the law may be asserted in good conscience to be necessary and
yet from the want of an international legislature it is difficult to
effect such change otherwise than by setting an example of it'.[1]

On the other hand, he puts forward a different test of justiciability, whose only connexion with the first appears to be that it
renders it irrelevant. According to that test, disputes are political
(as distinguished from legal) and not suitable for arbitration if
they touch upon important matters, i.e. matters included in the
very elastic conception of independence.[2] Moreover, for the
independence of a State to be affected it is not necessary, he
says, that the existence of the State should be at stake; it is
sufficient if 'it is hindered in doing or not doing anything that
an independent State may justly do or abstain from doing'; the
mere possibility of an adverse judgement being given in such
matters is sufficient to render the dispute non-justiciable.[3]
Accordingly, he is of the opinion that, as every general arbitration treaty should contain a general reservation of independence, and as that reservation must leave it substantially to the
parties to decline arbitration whenever they think fit, it would be
on the whole better, except between parties in which good faith
can be assumed in advance, not to conclude general arbitration
treaties in order not to aggravate the original difference by
adding to it a charge of bad faith.[4] This result of the argument
shows the practical sense and logical consistency worthy of the
great lawyer. It is less easy to see what useful function the
distinction, so elaborately developed, of different kinds of disputes could fulfil in the light of the negative comprehensiveness
of the final result.

[1] Ibid., p. 301.
[2] See his article on 'International Arbitration', published in 1896, and reprinted
in *International Law* (2nd ed., 1910), i. 350–68.   [3] Ibid., p. 357.
[4] This limitation, or rather exclusion, of justiciability does not, according to
Westlake, stop short of pure questions of law. Even if the law applicable is clear, the
dispute is not justiciable if one party puts forward a claim which its opponent
regards as put openly in defiance of the law. Thus when Venezuela, in 1896, put
forward claims which he regarded as frivolous, he wrote to *The Times* that 'it did not
lie in the mouth of any nation that its claim was reasonable enough for it to be
entitled to an arbitration,' ... and that arbitration was possible only subject to
certain rules laid down for the guidance of the arbitrators or to the exclusion of
claims based 'on the inadmissible doctrines' (10 February, 1896).

§ 9. The Method of Enumeration. While one group of writers were thus basing the justiciability of disputes on the existence of legal rules applicable to the dispute,[1] another was confining it to small issues,[2] and a third attempting to combine the two heterogeneous elements, others attempted to solve the difficulty by proposing a more pragmatic test of the distinction between the two classes of disputes, namely, the method of enumeration. Thus Morizault-Thibault, in a careful discussion of the subject, confined international arbitration to the examination of questions of fact and to the settlement of juridical disputes, i.e. (a) claims for compensation; (b) territorial disputes; (c) interpretation and execution of treaties.[3] Sir Frederick Pollock distinguished between the following classes of disputes: (a) disputes relating to boundaries and territorial rights; (b) claims arising out of breaches of conventional or customary international law; (c) disputes analogous to civil actions for wrongs, for instance, claims arising out of denial of justice.[4] That method of enumeration underlay the wording of the Optional Clause of Article 36 of the Statute of the Permanent Court of International Justice and, subsequently, of the International Court of Justice. Thus in Woolf's *International Government* (1916)[5] there appeared a classification of 'justiciable' disputes in the following terms: (1) questions of fact; (2) questions of title to territory and of boundaries; (3) questions as to the interpretation and application of treaties or international law, of claims founded on treaties or on international law, or alleged breach of treaties or of international law; (4) questions as to the responsibility or blame attached to national agents or representatives for the results of acts of such agents or representatives; (5) questions as to certain kinds of pecuniary claims. It will be noted that with the exception of class (2) the other categories have found a place in the list of disputes contained in Article 36.[6]

---

[1] For more detailed references to this group see below, pp. 52–4.

[2] See below, pp. 139 et seqq.

[3] *Essai sur l'arbitrage international* (1877), pp. 49–56.

[4] *The Cambridge Modern History*, vol. xii (1910), p. 716. See also the definition, partly incomplete and partly tautological, of Oppenheim: 'Legal differences arise from acts for which States have to bear responsibility, be it acts of their own or of their parliaments, their judicial and administrative officials, their armed forces, or individuals living on their territory. Political differences are the result of a conflict of political interest.' *International Law*, vol. ii, 4th ed. by McNair (1926), p. 3. And see De Louter, *Le Droit international public positif* (1920; French translation), ii. 150.

[5] pp. 52–4.

[6] See also Woolf, *The Framework of a Lasting Peace* (1917), Appendix IV, 'Proposals for the Prevention of Future Wars,' by Viscount Bryce and others, in which the present enumeration of Article 36 appears, it seems, for the first time.

§ 10. Other Tests of Applicability of the Judicial Process: Justice and Adequacy of the Existing Law. The Attitude of the Parties.

The years following upon the First World War witnessed the wide adoption of new tests of the justiciability of international disputes. While the insufficiency of the existing law was originally accepted as a reason for the limitations of the judicial function, on the ground that the law was not complete, the new reason assigned for the exclusion of the judicial process, as the result of obligations undertaken in advance, in regard to certain categories of disputes, owes its origin to the belief that, owing mainly to the difficulty of adapting existing international law to new and changing conditions, there will always remain a class of disputes which, if decided by the application of strict law, may be productive of injustice and prejudicial to the peace of the world. As it is impossible to determine in advance, by a classification embodied in an arbitration treaty, to what disputes this test may prove to be applicable, some went so far as to oppose obligatory arbitration altogether on the ground that any such general commitments, while on the face of it progressive, would in fact be dangerous seeing that they would divert attention from the equally essential and urgent task of changing the law in accordance with justice.[1]

Simultaneously with that test there was put forward another criterion of justiciability of disputes, namely, that which determines the character of the dispute by reference to the attitude of the parties. If the parties ask merely for the application or interpretation of existing international law the dispute is a legal one; it is a controversy in which the parties are in dispute as to existing legal rights. If, on the other hand, the parties profess to disregard an existing rule and claim a change in the law, the dispute is a political one; it is a conflict of interests.[2] The terminology of some leading instruments of compulsory arbitral and judicial settlement after the First and the Second World Wars, is expressive of the wide acceptance secured by the test thus formulated.[3]

§ 11. Determination by International Tribunals.

For reasons discussed elsewhere[4] some of these tests of the distinction between legal and political disputes are being gradually

---

[1] See below, pp. 245 et seqq.
[2] See below, pp. 351–3.
[3] See below, pp. 37 et seqq.   [4] See below, pp. 353–7.

abandoned. However, even then writers are reluctant to jettison altogether the distinction between legal and political (or justiciable and non-justiciable) disputes. While agreeing that a clear definition of the two classes of disputes cannot well be embodied in treaties of obligatory arbitration and judicial settlement, they have suggested the delegation, to the arbitral or judicial tribunal, of the task of determining in each particular case whether a dispute is justiciable or not.[1]

This is well illustrated by the discussions in the Institute of International Law at its meeting at Grenoble in 1922. The *rapporteurs* proposed in their draft resolution that the following three tests be adopted for the exclusion of the normal judicial process: (*a*) the absence of a generally recognized rule of law applicable to the case; (*b*) the impossibility of deciding the question without taking into account general principles of justice and equity; (*c*) the necessity of proceeding to a regulation of interests. The Institute rejected this part of the draft and adopted the following resolution:

1. 'All disputes, whatever their origin and character, are, as a general rule, and subject to the following reservations, susceptible of judicial settlement or arbitral decision.'

2. 'At the same time, when, in the opinion of the Defendant State, the dispute is not susceptible of being settled judicially, the preliminary question, whether it is or is not justiciable, is to be submitted to the Permanent Court of International Justice, which will decide in accordance with its ordinary procedure.

    'If the Court by a majority of three-fourths declares that the objection is not sustainable, it will retain the case for a decision on its merits.'[2]

Thus the Institute, although still willing to recognize that at least some disputes may not be justiciable, thought it desirable to leave to the Permanent Court of International Justice the solution of a question which neither the Institute itself nor two generations of jurists have been able to solve. That disappointing result of the attempt of a highly qualified body of jurists to find a scientific basis for the traditional classification of disputes did not have the effect of eliminating it from legal discussion as

[1] See below, pp. 357–9.
[2] See *Annuaire*, xxix (1922), pp. 23–58, 258–9. See for a commentary on the three tests of non-justiciability proposed by the *rapporteurs* Hostie in *R.I.*, 3rd ser., ix (1928), pp. 265–81, 568–80.

illusory and possibly misleading. It continued to be the object of patient and elaborate investigation. The question was again before the Institute in 1927, when Professors Borel and Politis prepared a report on 'Extension of Obligatory Arbitration and the Obligatory Jurisdiction of the Permanent Court of International Justice',[1] and in 1929 when the report, supplemented by additional observations by Professor Borel,[2] came up for discussion.[3]

§ 12. The Conception of Justiciable Disputes.

As seen from the survey of authorities in the preceding sections, the confidence with which writers speak of the distinction between legal and political—or justiciable and non-justiciable—disputes is not reassuring when contrasted with the absence of any measure of agreement as to its meaning. For it appears that out of the multitude of definitions there emerge at least four clear—although not mutually exclusive—conceptions of legal or justiciable disputes:

(*a*) Legal disputes are such differences between States as are capable of judicial settlement by the application of existing and ascertainable rules of international law.

(*b*) Legal disputes are those in which the subject-matter of the claim relates to questions of minor and secondary importance not affecting the vital interests of States, or their external independence, or internal sovereignty, or territorial integrity, or honour, or any other of the important interests covered by the 'restrictive clauses'—the reservations—contained in treation of obligatory arbitral or judicial settlement.

(*c*) Legal disputes are those in regard to which the application of existing rules of international law is sufficient to ensure a result which is not incompatible with the demands of justice and with a progressive development of international relations.

(*d*) Legal disputes are those in which the controversy concerns a claim of legal right as distinguished from a claim admittedly aiming at a change of the existing law.

---

[1] *Annuaire*, xxxiii (2) (1927), pp. 669–761. See also ibid., pp. 762–833, for illuminating comments by Huber, Hammarskjöld, Le Fur, Dupuis and Hobza. And see ibid., pp. 565–85, for the report of De la Barra and Mercier on arbitral procedure.
[2] *Annuaire*, xxxv (1) (1929), pp. 467–98.
[3] Ibid. xxxv (2) (1929), pp. 170–83.

When, in a treaty of pacific settlement, the obligation to have recourse to, and abide by the decision of, a judicial or arbitral body is limited by a qualifying reference to 'legal' or 'political' disputes, this limitation of the arbitral or judicial process may refer to one or more—possibly to all—of the above meanings of the doctrine.

The conception of justiciability, viewed as a formal concept, may be used with a double meaning. It may refer to the suitability of a dispute, or of a category of disputes, to form the subject-matter of a judicial procedure; or—and this is the meaning of the term generally adopted in municipal jurisprudence—it may refer to the existence of the jurisdiction of a competent tribunal to pronounce on the dispute.[1] Thus when a dispute arises between State A and State B in respect of a portion of territory, that dispute may be described as non-justiciable on the ground of its allegedly inherent unsuitability for judicial settlement, for instanced, because there are no rules of international law to decide the matter, or because the dispute involves a major interest of the State, or because other methods of settlement are deemed to be more likely to remove the cause of friction. Or it may be described as non-justiciable on the ground that, whatever its nature may be, the contesting States are not bound by any treaty-provision conferring upon an international court jurisdiction in regard to that particular dispute and that, therefore, no tribunal has jurisdiction in respect of it.

In municipal law the lawyer is inclined to regard a 'justiciable' dispute as one over which a competent court has jurisdiction,[2] and he would argue that in a civilized country all disputes are justiciable, at the instance of any of the interested parties.

---

[1] The *Oxford Dictionary* defines 'justiciable' as 'liable to be tried in a court of justice, subject to jurisdiction'. See Strong, arbitrator, in the *Pelletier* case (Moore, p. 1773): 'It is the general rule of the law of nations that offences committed by a vessel at sea or on board while in a port of a foreign country are justiciable, or triable, only in the courts of the country to which the vessel belongs.'

[2] 'The acts of a belligerent Power in right of war are not justiciable in its own Courts ...' (Lord Parker of Waddington in *The Zamora* [1916], 2 A.C. 77). Objection is sometimes raised to the use of the term 'justiciable' on the ground that it tends to confuse the printer. See Madariaga, *Disarmament* (1929), p. 223, for a reference to 'compulsory jurisdiction for justifiable disputes'. It is in this connection that that term has often been used in the constitutional law of the United States by reference to so-called political questions with regard to which it is established that it is not within the province of courts to pass judgment upon certain aspects of legislative or executive action. See Willoughby, *The Constitutional Law of the United States*, vol. iii (1929), pp. 1326–36, and Jaffe, *Judicial Aspects of Foreign Relations* (1933), pp. 12–78. See also below, p. 381 as to Act of State.

Within the State all conflicts between citizens are cognizable by courts which either pronounce on the merits or definitely dismiss the claim on the ground that, whatever its moral or other justification may be, it is not entitled to protection and enforcement by the law.[1] In this latter case, the court, although not necessarily removing the cause of friction which underlies the dispute, disposes of it definitely, insofar as it purports to be based on an appeal to law, by the implied prohibition of enforcement of the claim through recourse to violence, or by the refusal to lend the aid of the State in enforcing it. It is in that sense that the courts settle the dispute with finality. The decision thus given may still leave one of the parties—or, possibly, both of them—unsatisfied and suffering from a sense of grievance on account of the inadequacy of the law as applied by the Court. But that factor is relevant only to the question whether it is the business of courts to remove causes of friction within society. It is not relevant to the question of the capacity of all disputes to be the subject of a judicial decision definitely adjudicating upon the legal merits of the issue. This applies also to cases in which, because of the absence of jurisdiction to grant a remedy, a court declines to give a remedy and, in effect, dismisses the action. In that sense all disputes—all claims of a legal right—are justiciable.

While within the State the question of terminology causes little difficulty, the situation is different in international law. There the general justiciability of disputes is not part of the existing law; it is in the nature of a specifically undertaken, and restrictively interpreted, obligation. Accordingly, in international law, when the question arises whether any actual dispute is justiciable or not, the proper procedure is necessarily to inquire whether the contesting States have in regard to that particular dispute undertaken to accept the jurisdiction of an international tribunal. It is here that the difficulty begins. For, as will be shown in the second chapter, when States undertake the obligations of compulsory arbitral or judicial settlement, they circumscribe their obligation by adopting the conception of justiciability as connoting suitability—expressed by one or more of the four tests of a legal dispute indicated above—for judicial settlement. That is to say, they recognize as justiciable (from the point of view of the competence of an international tribunal) such disputes as are justiciable (from the point of view of their inherent suitability for judicial settlement). This is the

---

[1] See below, pp. 60 et seq.

reason why in this book the conception of justiciability, in its formal aspect, is necessarily used in two meanings. The context will leave the reader in no doubt to which meaning reference is being made. But it is a disquieting gloss on the present position of international law in regard to obligatory arbitral or judicial settlement that a double and uncertain formal connotation is added to the four substantive meanings of the conception of justiciability of international disputes.

§ 13. The Scheme of the Work. After having surveyed in the present chapter the history of the doctrine of the inherent limitations of the judicial function in international law, and the part played thereby, it is proposed to consider, in the second introductory chapter, the extent of the adoption of that doctrine in treaties of pacific settlement, as well as the question of the authority attaching to it by reason of such adoption. It is then intended to consider the four current aspects of the doctrine. Thus in Part II there will be discussed that aspect of the distinction between legal and political disputes which bases the justiciability of disputes on the existence of applicable rules of law. It will be necessary to examine, as general problems of positive law, the questions of the completeness of the legal system and of the difficulties raised by novelty of action and by cases *primae impressionis* (Chapter III). The problem of the lacunae—and of their peculiarities—in international law will then be examined by reference to the distinction between genuine and spurious interpretation of the existing law (Chapter IV). With reference to these aspects of the question, there must be discussed the nature and the special tasks of the judicial function in international law when confronted with the theoretical completeness and the actual shortcomings of an undeveloped system of law (Chapter V). It is then proposed to verify the affirmation of the compteness of international law for the purpose of settling disputes by reference to the history of international arbitration—in particular by an inquiry how far international tribunals have been impeded in their work by the absence of rules of international law applicable to the cases submitted to them, and by what methods they have met novel situations confronting them in the course of their activity (Chapter VI).

In Part III it is proposed to examine that asserted limitation of the international judicial function which adopts the importance of the issues involved as a basis for the determination of the suitability of disputes for obligatory judicial settlement. We shall inquire, first, whether that doctrine is substantiated by the history of international arbitration, and whether the distinction, so conceived, between legal and political disputes can be established by a criterion other than the will of the State to submit any particular dispute to adjudication (Chapter VII). We shall examine whether a doctrine which bases the future obligation to have recourse to judicial settlement on a necessarily subjective test of the importance of a particular issue can suitably form the basis of a *vinculum juris* inherent in every legal obligation, and how far it can properly find a place in international conventions of obligatory judicial settlement (Chapter IX). Further, it is proposed to examine how far the restriction of justiciability of disputes to matters of minor importance is compatible with some governing principles of international law, with the protection afforded by international law to the fundamental rights of States, with the function of the law in general, and with recent conventional international law which curtails the right of recourse to force for the purpose of giving effect to claims (Chapter VIII). It is, in particular, in connexion with the limitation of the judicial function in respect of important issues that the question of the impartiality of international tribunals may be regarded as one of the vital problems in the matter of obligatory judicial settlement, and it is therefore intended to consider that question separately (Chapter X).

The problem of reconciling, in the field of international law, the conflicting demands of stability and change has found expression in that conception of non-justiciability according to which obligatory judicial settlement of certain categories of disputes may, in view of the absence of an international legislature modifying or abolishing obsolete law, result in judicial pronouncements dangerous to the cause of justice and of international peace. Part IV will be devoted to an examination of this aspect of the doctrine. It will be necessary to investigate the special aspect in international law of the general problem of the relation between security and justice, in particular with reference to the possibilities of international legislation (Chapter XI) and the respective merits of the judicial procedure and so-called 'alternative means of settlement', in particular of conciliation (Chapter XII). As the absence of an international legislature able to modify and develop the law admittedly imposes a heavy strain upon a system of compulsory international judicial settlement, it will be necessary to consider what are the existing and possible substitutes for an international legislature. In particular we shall have to examine what are the possibilities of obsolete law being brought up to date by judicial legislation in international law either in general, or by the judicial application of the doctrine *rebus sic stantibus* (Chapter XIII) and of the doctrine of the prohibition of abuse of rights (Chapter XIV). As elsewhere, so also in the international sphere, judicial legislation is necessarily limited, and the avenues will have to be explored through which the basis of judicial legislation may be extended by the will of States through the conferment upon international courts of the power to lay down regulations, or propose recommendations, or to decide *ex aequo et bono*. In particular it will be necessary to examine how the exercise of such powers is consistent with the judicial function of international tribunals (Chapter XV). Finally, it will be submitted that the extension of the legislative function of tribunals by the will of the parties is limited to individual cases and cannot fittingly form part of a scheme of obligatory settlement. Proposals will therefore have to be examined for making judicial decisions the starting-point for the modification of the law, in particular by way of subsequent political action of the organs of the international community (Chapter XVI).

In Part V an analysis will be attempted of the fourth, and last, conception of justiciability of disputes, i.e. that based on the distinction between 'disputes concerning rights' and 'conflicts of interests'. The question will be examined, *inter alia*, whether that distinction can accurately be used as the basis of a classification of international disputes for the purposes of obligatory judicial or arbitral settlement (Chapter XVII). The possibility will then be considered of rendering obligatory the settlement of disputes in which a party asks for a change in the existing law. In particular, the provisions of the General Act of 1928 will be examined from this point of view (Chapter XVIII).

The doctrine of the limitation of the judicial function appears, in the field of international law, not only in one of the four formulations referred to above. It appears, regardless of any of the current classifications of disputes, in the form of the rule according to which the submission of disputes to international tribunals is essentially voluntary in its nature. Some aspects of that general rule will be considered in Part VI, in which the question of the place of law in the international society is considered as a problem of general jurisprudence. In particular, as the obtaining rule is frequently supported by reference to the limitation of the place of law in every political society, it will be inquired how far the existing limits of the judicial process within the State justify the wider assertions of the limitation of the place of law in general (Chapter XIX). Concurrently with the opinion that the limitation of the function of law and of courts is a general legal phenomenon, the view is frequently expressed that it is the consequence of what has been called the 'specific character' of international law. Accordingly it will be necessary to inquire what is meant by the 'specific character of international law', and how far the shortcomings of existing international law can legitimately be regarded as necessarily inherent in it and, as such, as contributing to a more general conception of law of which international and municipal law are the constituent elements (Chapter XX).

CHAPTER II

CONVENTIONS OF PACIFIC SETTLEMENT AND THE LIMITATION OF THE JUDICIAL FUNCTION

§ 14. In General. The vast number of treaties of obligatory judicial or arbitral settlement concluded since the beginning of the twentieth century offers at first sight a chaotic picture of various types of treaties, differing from one another in respect of the comprehensiveness of their reservations and of the machinery devised for securing their professed object. Yet, notwithstanding the great variety of form and method, the more important of these treaties can be conveniently reduced to a limited number of clearly defined and representative types. In all of them the doctrine of the limitation of the international judicial function (as expressed in the distinction between justiciable and non-justiciable disputes) constitutes the backbone of the treaty or, at least, the framework of its structure. The effect of the adoption of the classification varies in the different types of convention. In some it results, notwithstanding their description, in an actual elimination of any obligation to have recourse to a procedure involving a binding settlement; in others, the adoption of the doctrine renders, in effect, the jurisdiction of an international court dependent upon the discretion of the parties interested in the dispute; finally, in others, notwithstanding the adoption of the *termini technici* of the doctrine, there is express provision for a binding settlement of all disputes.

There are five principal types of these conventions: (1) The arbitration treaties concluded under the aegis of the Hague Convention of 1899 for the Pacific Settlement of International Disputes. (2) What may be called the American type of arbitration treaties which follow the model of the unratified treaties of 1911 between the United States and Great Britain, and the United States and France. (3) The most general arbitration treaty constituted as the result of the signature of the Optional Clause of Article 36 of the Statute of the Permanent Court of International Justice and, its successor, namely, the International Court of Justice. (4) The group of treaties framed in accordance of what may be conveniently referred to as the Locarno type of conventions. (5) A growing number of all-inclusive instruments for pacific settlement on the lines of the General Act for the Pacific Settlement of International Disputes approved in 1928 by the Assembly

of the League of Nations and revised in 1949 by the General
Assembly of the United Nations. These include the European
Convention for the Peaceful Settlement of Disputes adopted in
1957.

§ 15. The Hague Conventions for Pacific Settlement. The
distinction between justiciable and non-justiciable disputes was
taken over for the first time as part of positive international law
in the Hague Conventions for the Pacific Settlement of International Disputes in 1899 and 1907. Article 16 of the Convention of
1899, and Article 38 of the Convention of 1907, laid down:

> 'In questions of a legal nature, and especially in the inter-
> pretation or application of international conventions, arbitra-
> tion is recognized by the signatory Powers as the most effective,
> and at the same time the most equitable, means of settling dis-
> putes which diplomacy has failed to settle.'

In thus introducing into the field of international law the
distinction between two categories of disputes, the Governments
represented at the First Hague Conference accepted almost
literally the wording proposed in the draft convention submitted
to the Conference by the Russian delegation.[1] The reasons for
introducing the distinction were ably stated in the elaborate
Russian Memorandum, in which the distinction between legal
and other disputes served the purpose of supporting a cautious
proposal for a limited scheme of obligatory arbitration—a proposal which failed to secure acceptance.[2] However, the passages
of the Memorandum relating to legal and political disputes
subsequently proved a source of inspiration for many a lawyer
and statesman; they constitute an important contribution to
the history of the doctrine of the inherent limitations of the
international judicial process.

The Explanatory Note concerning Article 5 of the draft
relating to mediation insisted that, although arbitration was
in general more effective than mediation, the application of
the former 'is essentially and even exclusively restricted to
cases where there is a conflict of international rights, while
mediation, although of a political character, is equally
applicable to the conflicts of interests which most often
threaten peace among nations'.[3] In the Note concerning

---

[1] See Article 7 of the draft: *Reports to the Hague Conferences of 1899 and 1907*
(hereafter referred to as *Hague Reports*), ed. by J. B. Scott (1917), p. 92.
[2] See Article 10 of the Russian draft, ibid., p. 93.   [3] Ibid., p. 95.

obligatory arbitration, it was pointed out (in a passage reproduced in substance in Article 10 of the draft) that, subject to the saving clause of honour and vital interests, the disputes suitable for arbitration were those arising out of demands for an indemnity for damages. Such disputes, it was said, relate to questions of law, and do not as a rule concern the vital interests or the honour of the States, 'it being understood that a State whose national honour or vital interests had been attacked would not, of course, limit itself, and could not limit itself, to demanding material indemnity for damages and losses suffered by it'.[1] Disputes arising out of demands that another State 'shall or shall not exercise certain given attributes of the sovereign Power' were described as not suitable for arbitration. However, non-justiciability of disputes concerning the exercise of the rights of sovereignty did not prevent the authors of the Note from describing as suitable for arbitration such disputes as concern the exercise of sovereign rights in times of peace and war so long as they assume the form of a claim for damages. As distinctly unsuitable for obligatory arbitration were described political treaties 'which are nothing but the temporary expression of chance and transitory relationships between the various national forces'.[2] The authors of the Memorandum then proceeded to show that such treaties restrict the freedom of action of the contracting parties only so long as conditions remain unchanged; that disputes concerning them turn, not so much on the interpretation of their provisions, as on their change or complete abrogation; and that it would therefore be inappropriate to submit such disputes to arbitral tribunals, 'in whose eyes the principle established by the treaty would be just as obligatory, just as inviolable, as the principle established by the positive law in the eyes of any national tribunal whatever'.[3]

In the general report of the Committee presented to the Conference the limitation of the scope of disputes recommended as suitable for arbitral settlement was explained on the ground that, as the arbitrator is a judge and as such is

---

[1] *Hague Reports*, p. 98.

[2] Ibid., p. 97. In view of the historical events connected with the repudiation by Russia in the years 1871 and 1886 of her obligations in respect of the Black Sea and the Port of Batoum the Russian delegation might have felt that they were particularly entitled to urge that latter argument.

[3] Ibid., p. 97. See, for an illuminating discussion of the Russian Memorandum, Baker in *B.Y.*, 1925, pp. 81–6.

bound to act according to law, arbitration is not applicable to disputes about 'conflicting interests' and 'differences of a political nature'. These differences, it was pointed out, in which the claims of the parties cannot be stated in the form of legal propositions, are by their very nature outside the jurisdiction of tribunals called upon to adjudicate on the basis of law.[1] Nothing can illustrate better the slow rate of progress in the matter of justiciability of disputes than the fact that all the four elements of the doctrine, as outlined in the preceding chapter and as still in vogue to-day, underlay the proposals submitted at the First Hague Conference in terms almost identical with those at present in use.

The formula put forward by Russia at the First Hague Conference seems to have secured general acceptance without much discussion, largely owing to the fact that the proposed article was in the nature of a mere recommendation clearly distinguished from an undertaking of obligatory arbitration. In fact, commentators did not fail subsequently to point out that the qualifying reference to legal disputes was unnecessary seeing that the article did not imply any obligation.[2] When at the Second Hague Conference attempts were made to introduce some measure of obligatory arbitration by reference to the formula of legal disputes,[3] this basis of classification was vigorously criticized by the German delegate, Baron Marschall von Bieberstein, in two frequently quoted speeches.[4]

§ 16. The Hague Arbitration Conventions. Although the Hague Convention of 1899 marked the first recognition in conventional international law of the doctrine of 'inherent

[1] Ibid., p. 56.
[2] See Mérignhac in *R.G.* x (1903), p. 803, and Nippold, p. 207. Apart from this, the formula does not seem to have incurred the criticism of the commentators at the time. See Mérignhac, *Conférence*, pp. 269, 291, 292; Nippold, pp. 177, 178, 207-9; Meurer, *Das Friedensrecht der Haager Konferenz* (1905), vol. i, pp. 190-5. Objection was, however, raised to the obviously superfluous reference to interpretation of treaties—in itself a legal matter.
[3] It was then proposed, mainly by the United States and Great Britain (see *Hague Reports*, pp. 436, 482, 486), that what constituted in the Convention of 1899 a mere recommendation should be incorporated as the basal provision of a general arbitration treaty, subject to the usual reservations, and to the right of the parties to be the sole judges whether the differences which arise affect the interests safeguarded in the reservation clauses. See on this point Lémonon, pp. 121-87, and, as to the discussions in the Committee, *Hague Reports*, pp. 366-488.
[4] See below, p. 185. And see Huber, 'Die Fortbildung des Völkerrechts auf dem Gebiete des Prozess- und Landkriegsrechts durch die II. internationale Friedenskonferenz', in *Das öffentliche Recht der Gegenwart*, vol. ii (1908), pp. 519, 520.

limitations', that doctrine did not properly become part of the law until the several States had acted upon the opinion expressed in Article 16 of the Convention.[1] This was done in a series of arbitration conventions concluded after 1903, which followed upon the initiative given by the treaty between Great Britain and France. Apart from a number of treaties concluded among, and by, South and Central American States, these treaties constitute the bulk of pre-war arbitration conventions. With a slight modification,[2] they incorporated the formula adopted by the Hague Conventions, which they then proceeded to qualify by the typical general reservation. Thus the first of these treaties, namely, the arbitration treaty between Great Britain and France of 14 October 1903, provided in Article 1 as follows:

> 'Differences which may arise of a legal nature, or relating to the interpretation of treaties existing between the two contracting parties, and which it may not have been possible to settle by diplomacy, shall be referred to the Permanent Court of Arbitration established at The Hague by the Convention of 29 July 1899, provided, nevertheless, that they do not affect the vital interests, the independence, or the honour of the two contracting States, and do not concern the interests of third Parties.'[3]

The so-called Root arbitration treaties concluded by the United States in and after 1908 contained an identical provision, modified by an additional clause reserving for the Senate of the United States the right of advice and consent in regard to any special arbitration agreements to be made by the United States in pursuance of the general arbitration treaties.[4]

---

[1] See *Procès-verbaux* of the First Conference, part i, pp. 138 et seq. (and *Hague Reports*, pp. 111–25) for a detailed statement, prepared by Baron Descamps, of arbitration and mediation provisions prior to the Hague Conferences.

[2] These treaties referred to disputes of a legal nature *or* those relating to the interpretation of treaties, whereas the Hague Convention spoke of 'questions of a legal nature, *and especially* in the interpretation or application of international conventions'. Much criticism was levelled against this change on the ground that the interpretation and application of treaties were legal questions, and that the use of the word 'or' was therefore misleading. Perhaps the reproach was not quite justified, seeing that the word 'legal' does not necessarily mean the possibility of applying legal rules, and that it may equally connote the absence of the political element; in which case 'or' seems to have been correctly used.

[3] Hertslet, *Treaties*, vol. xxiii, p. 492. Great Britain alone concluded, before the First World War, sixteen of these treaties.

[4] See, for instance, the treaty of 4 April 1908 between the United States and Great Britain; Hertslet, *Treaties*, vol. xxv, p. 1203. Twenty-five of these treaties were negotiated by Secretary Root. See, on these treaties and, generally, on the

Before the First World War the number of treaties of the former type amounted to over one hundred.[1] A number of them were renewed in the period following the war,[2] some substituting the Permanent Court of International Justice for the Permanent Court of Arbitration. Several treaties of this type were also concluded after the First World War, for instance, between the United States and Sweden on 24 June 1924,[3] between Venezuela and Norway on 13 May 1935,[4] and between the Netherlands and Japan on 19 April 1933.[5] However, most of these treaties have been replaced by instruments of a different type referred to below.[6] The American Root treaties have given way either to the General Inter-American Arbitration Convention of 1929[7] or to the uniform treaties concluded by the United States since 1928 after the model of the treaty with France of 6 February 1928.[8] However, for a period of nearly twenty years these treaties constituted the basis of obligatory arbitration of

arbitration treaties of the United States, Jessup, *The United States and Treaties for the Avoidance of War*, International Conciliation Pamphlet, 1928, No. 239; Wilson in A.J., 25 (1931), pp. 474–9; and *The International Law Standard in Treaties of the United States* (1953), pp. 34–43.

[1] Most of these treaties concluded between 1903 and 1914 are printed in *Traités généraux d'arbitrage, communiqués au Bureau International de la Cour Permanente d'Arbitrage*, First Series (1911); Second Series (1914). See also for another list of these treaties *N.Z.* xxxix (1928–9), pp. 413–15; and Clad, *Wesen und Grenzen der internationalen Schiedsgerichtsbarkeit* (1928), pp. 15 et seq. However, such individual arbitration as occurred between the contracting parties as a rule took place by reference not to these arbitration treaties, but to the Hague Conventions for Pacific Settlement, with the exception of the arbitration agreement between Norway and the United States concerning the shipping claims of 30 June 1921 (*A.J.*, vol. xvi (1922) Suppl., p. 17), and the arbitration agreement between the United States and the Netherlands concerning the Palmas Island of 23 January 1925 (ibid. xix (1925), p. 108).

[2] See, for instance, the arbitration treaties between Great Britain and Italy (1 February 1904; renewed 14 August 1923); Great Britain and the United States (4 April 1908; renewed 23 June 1923); Great Britain and Spain (27 February 1914; renewed 9 February 1924); Great Britain and Holland (15 February 1905; renewed 12 July 1925); United States and Netherlands (2 May 1908; renewed 13 February 1924); United States and Japan (5 May 1908; renewed 23 August 1923). These treaties will be found in *Arbitration and Security*, pp. 92, 93, 98, 115, 99, and 106 respectively.

[3] Ibid., p. 108.

[4] *Systematic Survey*, p. 1078. See also ibid., pp. 1010 and 1063 for treaties concluded in 1933 between the Netherlands and Venezuela, and Denmark and Venezuela, respectively.

[5] Ibid. p. 1024.

[6] Almost all the treaties here referred will also be found in Habicht, *Post-War Treaties for the Pacific Settlement of International Disputes* (1931), and in *P.C.I.J.*, Series D, No. 6.

[7] See below, p. 38.   [8] See below, p. 37.

Governments, and had the effect of firmly entrenching the doctrine of its inherent limitations in the practice in that period and the science of international law.

§ 17. The Covenant of the League of Nations and the Charter of the United Nations. Before considering the extent of the adoption of the doctrine of non-justiciable disputes in the Optional Clause of the International Court it may be convenient to examine how far it was incorporated in the Covenant of the League of Nations. The first two paragraphs of Article 13 of the Covenant ran originally[1] as follows:

'1. The Members of the League agree that whenever any dispute shall arise between them which they recognize to be suitable for submission to arbitration, and which cannot be satisfactorily settled by diplomacy, they will submit the whole subject-matter to arbitration.

'2. Disputes as to the interpretation of a treaty, as to any question of international law, as to the existence of any fact which, if established, would constitute a breach of any international obligation, or as to the extent and nature of the reparation to be made for any such breach, are declared to be among those which are generally suitable for submission to arbitration.'

This enumeration of subjects suitable for judicial settlement was subsequently included in Article 36 of the Statute of the Court, in which, however, as the result of the interpolation of the term 'legal', there took place, according to some, the formal incorporation of the doctrine. No such formal incorporation was attempted in the Covenant. But did the latter adopt the doctrine in substance? That it had been so adopted to a considerable extent was the view of a large number of writers.[2] This was also the view of several Governments during and after the Peace Conference of 1919. In particular in the British Official Commentary to the Covenant, a document particularly entitled to respect having regard to the part played by British draftsmen in the framing of the Covenant, it was stated that Article 13, while not providing for compulsory arbitration in any class of disputes, 'to some extent recognizes the distinction between justiciable and non-justiciable causes, by declaring that in certain large classes of disputes recourse to arbitration is *prima facie* desirable'.[3] That view, however, cannot be accepted without

---

[1] As to the amendments to this article see below, p. 357, n. 1.

[2] It seems, however, that some of these use the term merely for the sake of description. See, for instance, Schücking-Wehberg, pp. 517–19; Pollock, *League of Nations* (2nd ed., 1922), pp. 143, 145.   [3] Parl. Pap. (1919) (Cmd. 151).

serious qualification. In the first instance, as the main purpose of the doctrine of non-justiciable disputes is to limit the general obligation undertaken in a treaty of compulsory arbitration, and as Article 13 contained no such obligation, it is difficult to accept the view that the doctrine of the necessary limitations of the international judicial function is impliedly contained in the Covenant. Not only did no express reference to the doctrine appear in the Covenant, but a study of the origin of Article 13 shows that such reference was deliberately excluded.

Article 3 of the Phillimore Plan for a League of Nations of 20 March 1918 provided:

> 'If a dispute should hereafter arise between any of the Allied States as to the interpretation of a treaty, as to any question of international law, as to the existence of any fact which if established would constitute a breach of any international obligation, or as to the nature and extent of the reparation to be made for any such breach, if such dispute cannot be settled by negotiation, arbitration is recognized by the Allied States as the most effective and at the same time the most equitable means of settling the dispute.'[1]

In the interim report accompanying the draft it was stated that Article 3 was adapted from Article 38 of the Hague Convention of 1907 for the Pacific Settlement of International Disputes.[2] The only—and significant—change was the omission of the word 'legal' and the substitution for it of the detailed enumeration of the four categories of disputes. The formula of the Phillimore Plan was subsequently adopted in General Smuts's draft[3] from which it apparently found its way to the second[4] and third[5] draft of President Wilson and eventually to the draft of the Covenant as finally adopted.[6] Notwithstanding the various changes which

---

[1] R. S. Baker, *Woodrow Wilson and World Settlement* (1922), vol. i, p. 75.

[2] Ibid., p. 70.   [3] Ibid., p. 98.

[4] See R. S. Baker, op. cit., p. 103; the first draft, ibid., p. 90, did not contain the enumeration.   [5] Ibid., p. 120.

[6] The enumeration of four categories of disputes did not appear either in the official British Plan, in which reference to arbitration was of a very rudimentary nature, nor in the subsequent so-called Hurst-Miller compromise draft (there was only, in Article 11, a provision to the effect that the High Contracting Parties agree that whenever any dispute or difficulty shall arise between them, which they recognize to be suitable for submission to arbitration, and which cannot satisfactorily be settled by diplomacy, they will submit the whole subject-matter to arbitration: R. S. Baker, op. cit., p. 147). It was absent, therefore, from the draft which was laid before the League of Nations Commission of the Peace Conference as a basis of discussion. Later, however, on the proposal of Lord Robert Cecil (Miller, *The Drafting of the Covenant* (1928), i, p. 327 (Twelfth Meeting of the Committee on the League of Nations)) it was again inserted in the Covenant as finally adopted. It was thought that some slight measure of progress would be achieved by at least defining

the original Phillimore Plan had undergone, there was significance in the determination not to adopt the *termini technici* of the doctrine of non-justiciable disputes.

Although the Covenant is no longer a binding instrument it has been thought useful to retain this lengthy footnote in view of its bearing on the interpretation of Article 36 of the Statute of the Court.

§ 18. The Optional Clause of Article 36 of the Statute of the Permanent Court of International Justice and the International Court of Justice.

Article 36 of the Statute of the Permanent Court of International Justice provided that any State signatory to the Protocol establishing the Court may recognize in advance the jurisdiction of the Court, in relation to any Member of the League or State accepting the same obligation 'in all or any of the classes of *legal*[1] disputes concerning: (*a*) the interpretation of a treaty; (*b*) any question

---

in concrete terms the disputes which were regarded as generally suitable for arbitration. See note by the British delegation of 7 April 1919 on the redraft submitted by the Drafting Committee, where it was stated that the insertion of the enumeration took place in deference to the argument that the draft, as originally submitted to the Committee, was in this respect 'actually retrogressive as not sufficiently recognizing the distinction evolved in recent years between justiciable and non-justiciable disputes' (Miller, op. cit., vol. i, p. 416). It must be noted that the term 'generally' was intended to refer not to the comprehensiveness of the enumeration, but to the duty to submit to arbitration disputes thus enumerated. There is little doubt, if the various drafts of the Covenant may serve as a guide, that there was no intention to make arbitration compulsory. See on this point Schücking-Wehberg, pp. 524–6; Baker in *B.Y.*, 1925, pp. 70–4. See also Loder, ibid., 1921–2, pp. 18–24.

At the fifteenth meeting of the Drafting Committee objection was taken by the Portuguese delegate to the word 'generally' which originally did not appear in the British amendment (see Miller, op. cit., vol. ii, p. 352). It was, however, retained following upon Lord Robert Cecil's insistence that it would be dangerous for the principle of arbitration to impose it too strictly in a great number of cases. Thus he pointed out that it would not always be desirable that the question of the interpretation of a treaty should be submitted to arbitration in matters involving the honour and the vital interests of a country. See Miller, op. cit., vol. ii, p. 378. See also the views of a number of the members of the Committee of Jurists in 1920, who drafted the Covenant, *Procès-verbaux*, pp. 228, 235, 240, 278. See also *Records of the Second Assembly*, pp. 697, 826, on the rejection by a sub-committee of that Assembly of the proposal of the Norwegian, Swedish, and Danish delegations to omit the word 'generally'. The sub-committee was of the opinion that such an amendment would be contrary to the intention of the Covenant not to adopt obligatory arbitration. For a complete list, see Hudson, pp. 703–5.

[1] The italics are the writer's.

of international law; (c) the existence of any fact which if established would constitute a breach of any international obligation; (d) the extent and nature of the reparation to be made for any such breach'. By the end of 1939 that so-called Optional Clause had been accepted by over fifty Governments. It constituted the most important and most widely accepted instrument of compulsory political settlement. In so far as the doctrine of non-justiciable disputes forms part of the Optional Clause it does so as the result of the term 'legal' preceding the enumeration of the four classes of disputes in respect of which the obligation is undertaken. It is unlikely that Article 36 has that effect. For reasons of which the detailed presentation lies outside the scope of this book the writer believes that the term ought to be interpreted in a descriptive sense only.[1] This is so although,

---

[1] By admitting the possibility of the term 'legal' being descriptive, we obviate the necessity of regarding it either as qualifying or as meaningless (see Fischer Williams, *Chapters*, pp. 38, 39, who expresses hesitation in regarding the word as meaningless).

The history of this article in the Committee of Jurists is strongly in favour of the view that the term is merely descriptive. The original draft of the Statute which Lord Phillimore laid before the Committee of Jurists in 1920, reproduced the four classes of disputes (the enumeration included a fifth item referring to the Court's interpretation of its own judgements (*Procès-verbaux of the Proceedings of the Committee*, p. 253): this item, which was adopted in the final draft, was struck out by the Assembly), mentioned in Article 13 of the Covenent, but contained no reference to 'legal' disputes. It seems that it was the learned President of the Committee who was specially intent on having the phrase included. Baron Descamps had taken a leading part in the deliberations of the Hague Conferences of 1899 and 1907, and he found it difficult to discard a notion which was both time-honoured and generally believed to safeguard an important aspect of State sovereignty. As may be seen from his Note on the Question of Compulsory Jurisdiction laid before the Committee, Baron Descamps's insistence on adding the qualifying term 'legal' was originally due to his opinion that there are disputes which can neither be stated nor decided legally, such as conflicts of interests and political disputes, and also that there exist disputes of a legal character 'in which the adoption of legal methods would imply, according to the views of certain States, the abandonment of rights considered rightly or wrongly inalienable' (*Procès-verbaux*, p. 254). However, judging from the subsequent discussion before the Committee, there is reason to believe that the purpose of the proposed qualifying term was more in the nature of an expression of respect for a phrase which has become dear to the hearts of lawyers and statesmen, than of a wish to formulate actual reservations. When M. Ricci Busatti proposed the omission of the expression 'questions of a legal nature', the sole reason of the President's opposition to this amendment was that the term played an important part in the Conferences of 1899 and 1907, and that 'legal conscience and world opinion would be astonished not to find this term in the Committee's plan' (ibid., p. 283). That the term 'legal' was not regarded as qualifying in any way the subsequent enumeration may be seen from the fact that in the Root-Phillimore Plan, in which following upon the insistence of the President the term 'legal' was included, the relevant passage ran as follows: 'The Permanent Court of International Justice shall be competent to hear and determine cases between States concerning questions of a legal nature, *that is to say*'

as a matter of terminology, it may be argued that the Optional
Clause recognizes the doctrine of non-justiciable disputes, and a

(italics ours), which affect: the interpretation of a treaty, &c. (ibid., p. 547). Little
importance was subsequently attached to the proposed addition, and in the scheme
prepared by the drafting sub-committee the term 'legal' did not appear at all (ibid.,
p. 566; Article 29 of the draft). When the draft was considered by the Committee, at
the final stages of its work, the President again reverted to this subject. That his
insistence upon the retention of the term was largely intended to ensure continuity
in terminology may again be seen from the fact that the wording proposed by him
at that final meeting was: 'Between States which are members of the League of
Nations, the Court shall have jurisdiction (and this without any special convention
giving it jurisdiction) to hear and determine cases of a legal nature, *that is to say*
(italics ours) cases concerning . . . .' (ibid., p. 582). This shows that even with the
President, who was most insistent on the subject, that term did not serve the
purpose of qualifying or limiting the enumeration. 'This wording was adopted', it
is then stated in the *Procès-verbaux*, 'except that the words "that is to say, cases", were
deleted' (ibid.). Nothing is said of the reasons for this fateful omission. Was it due to
a misguided passion for economy in speech?

In the final, and authoritative, report submitted by the Committee to the
Council of the League, the relevant passage, which forms part of the introduction
to Article 34 of the draft stated expressly that disputes of a legal nature to which that
article refers are *defined* 'in the terms of Article 13 of the Covenant'.

The fact that the enumeration of disputes in the Optional Clause of Article 36
was originally a textual reproduction of the list of disputes enumerated in Article 13
of the Covenant—in which, as again its history shows (see above, p. 33), the word
'legal' was deliberately omitted—supports the view that the adjective is merely
descriptive. The present writer has suggested elsewhere (*Economica*, 1928, p. 291) an
explanation why the term 'legal', which did not appear in Article 13 of the
Covenant, appeared subsequently in Article 36 of the Statute. Article 13 did not
imply any undertaking for obligatory arbitration, and there was therefore no
necessity to qualify its terms. The original draft of the Statute of the Court, as
proposed by the Committee of Jurists, provided for compulsory arbitration, and
the qualification appeared necessary in order to make the proposal less radical and
more acceptable. The First Assembly subsequently rejected the Jurists' interpretation of Article 13 of the Covenant, as implying obligatory arbitration, but it left
intact the word 'legal' whose *raison d'être* had in the meantime disappeared.—See
also Hammarskjöld in *Annuaire*, xxxiii (2) (1927), p. 819, and Hudson, pp. 456 and
459 (following largely the analysis undertaken in the present footnote), to the effect
that the term is solely descriptive and declaratory. And see below, p. 201, on the
interpretation of Article 36.

Although the term 'legal' may properly be regarded as descriptive, the view has
been expressed that it need not necessarily be taken as a definition of which the four
categories constitute an exhaustive elaboration (see Hammarskjöld, op. cit.). This
caveat is due to the opinion that there may arise disputes obviously capable of legal
determination, but not comprised in any of the four categories. It may be doubted
whether such a contingency is likely to arise. The clause 'any question of international law' is wide enough to cover the three remaining classes, and, indeed, any
conceivable dispute in which the parties ask for their legal rights. See also below,
p. 281. It does not appear that in the Phillimore Plan (see above, p. 33) the
enumeration was regarded as a definition of justiciable disputes. See Miller,
op. cit., i, p. 327, ii, p. 352. However, President Wilson regarded the four classes
only as instances. See his speech at the Plenary Session of the Peace Conference,
28 April 1919, in Miller, op. cit., ii, p. 700. See also ibid., pp. 348 and 378, for a
similar statement by President Wilson.

Government wishing to lean on the letter of that Article may be tempted to argue that, although a dispute may fall within one of the categories there enumerated, it does not come within the purview of the jurisdiction of the Court on the ground that it is not a 'legal' dispute—the word 'legal' being interpreted in all, or some of, the possible meanings outlined above. This was actually the case in one dispute in which an attempt was made to invoke the Optional Clause before the Permanent Court of International Justice.[1]

Except for minor changes, which are not relevant in the present context, the Optional Clause of Article 36(2) of the Statute of the International Court of Justice adopted in 1945 is the same as that of its predecessor. Accordingly, there apply to it the comments made above as to the effect of the term 'legal disputes' as employed therein. It has not given rise to difficulties—possibly for the reason that the contentious jurisdiction of the Court has but rarely been invoked by reference to the Optional Clause. Only in one case, brought before the Court under Article 36(2), did the defendant State raise a Preliminary Objection on the ground that there did not exist before the Court a legal dispute in the sense of that provision. In the *Case concerning right of passage over Indian Territory (Preliminary Objection)* the Indian Government challenged the jurisdiction of the Court for various reasons, of which two had reference to the term 'legal disputes'. In the first instance it was maintained by India that as the Portuguese Government brought the dispute before the Court before exhausting the possibilities of negotiation and of a requisite definition and determination of the subject matter of the dispute 'there was not yet any legal and justiciable dispute between the Parties which could be referred to the Court under the Optional Clause'.[2] The Court did not accept that contention. It found that protracted negotiations had taken place; that they had reached a deadlock; and that Portugal had throughout the negotiations described the denial of the right of passage as being inconsistent with established custom and international law in general.[3] Secondly, it was maintained by India that as the subject matter of the Portuguese claim pertained to a matter which according to international law was exclusively within the domestic jurisdiction of India and

---

[1] See below, p. 200.
[2] See the Submission of the Government of India *ICJ Reports* 1957, p. 133.
[3] Ibid., p. 149.

as the two States had accepted the jurisdiction of the Court 'only for legal disputes which may be decided by the Court under the provisions of Article 38(1), of Statue [relating to the sources of law to be applied by the Court], the dispute submitted to the Court by Portugal was not such a dispute'.[1] It did not prove necessary for the Court to decide upon that particular objection. However, the manner in which these terms of the Statute were used as grounds for a preliminary objection, which in this respect proved to be of a somewhat unsubstantial character, throws light upon the comprehensive possibilities of challenge to the jurisdiction latent in the expression 'legal disputes'.

It may be added that the formula of the Optional Clause has been taken over, expressly or by reference, in a number of multilateral and bilateral treaties of pacific settlement. Thus in Article 8 of the Brussels Pact of 17 March 1948 between the United Kingdom, Belgium, France, Luxembourg and the Netherlands the Parties undertook to 'settle all disputes falling within the scope of Article 36, paragraph 2, of the Statute of the International Court of Justice, by referring them to the Court' (subject to the reservations made by the Party concerned when accepting the compulsory jurisdiction of the Court).[2] In Article 31 of the American Treaty of Pacific Settlement (Pact of Bogota) of 30 April 1948 the Parties 'in conformity with Article 36, paragraph 2, of the Statute' of the Court undertook, *verbatim*, the obligations of that Article—the expression 'disputes of a juridical nature' instead of 'legal disputes' being probably no more than a nuance of translation.[3]

§ 19. Treaties with the American Formulation of Justiciability of Disputes.

Another group of treaties in which the distinction between justiciable and non-justiciable disputes has found clear expression is that inaugurated by the unratified arbitration treaty concluded by the United States on 3 August 1911 with Great Britain and, on the same date, with France.[4] Article 1 of these treaties provided for arbitration of 'all differences hereafter arising between the High Contracting Parties, which it has not been possible to adjust by diplomacy, relating to international matters in which the High Contracting Parties are concerned by virtue of a claim of right made by one against the other under a treaty or

---

[1] Ibid., p. 134.   [2] *Systematic Survey*, p. 1160; Misc. No. 2 (1948) Cmd 7367.
[3] *Systematic Survey*, p. 1161; *UNTS* 1, p. 449.
[4] See *A.J.* v. (1911), Suppl., pp. 253 and 249 respectively.

otherwise, and which are justiciable in their nature by reason of being susceptible of decision by the application of the principles of law or equity'.[1] These treaties, which did not contain the usual sweeping reservations, were subsequently amended by the Senate of the United States in a manner which caused the Executive to refrain from proceeding with their ratification.[2] However, they did not remain altogether without effect. The discussion in the legal literature which grew up round these treaties contributed largely towards investing the formula with a certain amount of authority, and, when in 1928 the Government of the United States took the initiative in concluding a number of arbitration treaties, the draft of 1911 supplied a ready model. Article II of the arbitration treaty with France, of 6 February 1928, repeated verbatim the formula of 1911. As this treaty contains a number of extensive reservations,[3] and, as it expressly safeguards the powers of the Senate in regard to the conclusion of a special agreement in each case, it has proved acceptable to that body.[4] It was followed by a large number of identical treaties replacing the Root treaties of 1908.[5]

---

[1] Article 2 of the treaty provided for a Mixed Commission composed of an equal number of nationals of the two States to decide any preliminary controversy on the question whether the dispute is justiciable or not.

[2] For these amendments see *A.J.* vi (1912), p. 460; on the treaties themselves see ibid., pp. 167–77. See also in support of the view opposing ratification Snow, 'Legal Limitation of Arbitral Tribunals', reprinted from *University of Pennsylvania Law Review*, vol. lx, in *The American Philosophy of Government* (1921), pp. 233–66.

[3] The reservations exclude from the operation of the treaty disputes the subject-matter of which: (*a*) is within the domestic jurisdiction of either of the contracting parties; (*b*) involves the interests of third parties; (*c*) depends upon or involves the maintenance of the Monroe Doctrine; (*d*) depends upon or involves the observance of the obligations of France in accordance with the Covenant of the League of Nations. The reader will note the wide scope of the first reservation. It refers not to matters which according to international law are within the domestic jurisdiction of the State, but to matters of domestic jurisdiction pure and simple.

[4] See *A.J.* xxii (1928), Suppl., p. 37. For a discussion of this treaty and of its reservations see Jessup, op. cit., pp. 200–6; Hudson in *A.J.* xxii (1928), pp. 368 et seqq.; Anderson in *A.S. Proceedings*, 1929, pp. 113–19; Wilson in *AJ*, 25 (1931), pp. 479–85.

[5] See, for instance, the treaties concluded in 1928, 1929, and 1930 with Austria, Bulgaria, Czechoslovakia, Denmark, Germany; Hungary, Norway, Roumania, Yugoslavia, Sweden, Egypt, Holland, Greece, and China. See *A.J.* xxiii (1929), Suppl., pp. 197–234; *Systematic Survey*, pp. 58 and 59. And see *ibid.*, pp. 803, 825, and 872 for the treaties, respectively, with China (1930), Iceland (1930), and Switzerland (1933). Most of these treaties have survived the Second World War. See, for instance, the Note of the United States of America to Bulgaria of 8 March 1948 notifying the latter of the pre-war treaties between the two countries which the United States desired to keep alive: *UNTS* 29 (1949), p. 104. And see *UNTS* 48 (1950), p. 9, as to the similar treaty with Roumania.

The same formulation of justiciable disputes is, with a slight modification, adopted in the General Treaty of Inter-American Arbitration signed on 5 January 1929 by almost all States of the American Continent, including the United States.[1] Article 1 of that treaty provides as follows:

'The High Contracting Parties bind themselves to submit to arbitration all differences of an international character which have arisen or may arise between them by virtue of a claim of right made by one against the other under treaty or otherwise, which it has not been possible to adjust by diplomacy and which are juridical in their nature by reason of being susceptible of decision by the application of the principles of law.

'There shall be considered as included among the questions of juridical character: . . . '

There follows the list of the four categories of disputes enumerated in Article 13 of the Covenant.

§ 20. Arbitration Conventions of the Locarno Type. The prominent feature—from the point of view of the question discussed here—of this comprehensive group of arbitration treaties is that the doctrine of non-justiciable disputes, which is here incorporated either by reference to disputes 'as to respective rights' or to 'legal' disputes or by enumeration of the four classes of disputes of Article 13 of the Covenant, far from resulting in a mere difference of procedure, has the effect of withdrawing 'non-justiciable' disputes from the purview of binding settlement, for which it substitutes the procedure of conciliation.

Foremost in this group are the four arbitration treaties of Locarno of 16 October 1925 between Germany and Belgium, France, Poland, and Czechoslovakia.[2] According to these treaties, controversies of every kind with regard to which the parties are in dispute as to their respective rights shall be submitted either to an arbitral tribunal or to the Permanent Court of International Justice. Identical provisions were contained in several other treaties of the Locarno type, for instance, in the treaties of France with the Kingdom of the Serbs, Croats, and Slovenes of 11 November 1927,[3] of France with Roumania of 10 June 1926,[4] of Sweden with Czechoslovakia of 2 January 1926,[5] Luxemburg and the Netherlands of 17 September 1929,[6] and of the Netherlands and Czechoslovakia of 14 September 1929.[7]

---

[1] Printed in *A.J.* xxiii (1929), Suppl., p. 82, and in *B.Y.*, 1929, pp. 22–5; *Systematic Survey*, p. 499. See on this treaty Murdoch in *A.J.* xxiii (1929), pp. 282–91; Fischer Williams in *B.Y.*, 1929, pp. 14–22; Anderson in *A.S. Proceedings*, 1929, pp. 112–19; Whitton and Brewer in *A.J.* xxv (1931), pp. 447–68.

[2] *Arbitration and Security*, pp. 408, 412, 416, 421, respectively.

[3] Ibid., p. 325.   [4] Ibid., p. 253.   [5] Ibid., p. 232.

[6] *L.N.T.S.*, vol. cvii, p. 37.   [7] Ibid., p. 203.

A number of treaties of this group refer to 'legal' disputes instead of to disputes 'as to respective rights'.[1] The absence of any provision whatsoever for the case of the failure of the conciliation procedure in regard to non-justiciable disputes, is found in a series of treaties of arbitration and conciliation concluded separately by Denmark, Sweden, Norway, and Finland in 1925 and 1926. The treaties of arbitration provide for the final settlement of legal disputes; the treaties of conciliation provide, *inter alia*, for a report by a conciliation commission in regard to all other disputes.[2] While with regard to these disputes a preliminary conciliation procedure is optional, it is obligatory with regard to other disputes. These, if not settled by conciliation, were to be submitted to the Council of the League of Nations to be dealt with under Article 15 of the Covenant—a procedure which, even if resulting in a unanimous recommendation to the Council of the League of Nations, did not bind the parties to accept its recommendation (except to the extent of not going to war with the State accepting it). There was thus absent in these treaties an effectively binding procedure of settlement with regard to the—elastic and indefinite—category of 'political' disputes.

In this category there ought also to be mentioned the group of arbitration and conciliation treaties concluded by Germany prior to the Locarno agreements, such as the treaty with Switzerland of 3 December 1921,[3] with Sweden of 29 August 1924,[4] with Finland of 14 March 1925,[5] and with Estonia of 10 August 1925.[6] In these treaties the doctrine of non-justiciable disputes found expression both by an enumeration of subjects suitable for

---

[1] See the following treaties: Hungary and Italy, of 5 April 1927, *Arbitration and Security*, p. 317; Hungary and Switzerland, of 18 June 1924, ibid., p. 210; Hungary and Poland, of 30 November 1928, *L.N.T.S.*, vol. c, p. 69; Hungary and Turkey, of 5 January 1929, ibid., p. 139; Bulgaria and Hungary, of 22 July 1929, ibid., vol. ci, p. 42; France and the Netherlands, of 10 March 1928, ibid., vol. cii, p. 111; and, in effect, The Netherlands and Siam, of 27 October 1928, ibid., vol. xciii, p. 131.

[2] See treaty of arbitration between Finland and Sweden of 29 January 1926, *Arbitration and Security*, p. 120, and treaty of conciliation of 27 June 1924, ibid., p. 152; treaty of arbitration between Denmark and Sweden of 14 January 1926, ibid., p. 124, and treaty of conciliation of 27 June 1924, ibid., p. 62; treaty of arbitration between Norway and Sweden of 25 November 1925, ibid., p. 130, and treaty of conciliation of 27 June 1924, ibid., p. 149; treaty of arbitration between Denmark and Norway of 15 January 1926, ibid., p. 133, and treaty of conciliation of 27 June 1924, ibid., p. 168; treaty of arbitration between Finland and Norway of 3 February 1926, ibid., p. 135, and treaty of conciliation of 27 June 1924, ibid., p. 155.

[3] *Arbitration and Security*, p. 200.   [4] Ibid., p. 219.

[5] Ibid., p. 226.   [6] Ibid., p. 284.

arbitration, an enumeration covering in substance the classes of disputes of Article 13 of the Covenant, and by the exclusion of arbitration in cases in which one party pleaded (and wherein the plea, if contested, is recognized by the tribunal) that 'the dispute is mainly political and, for this reason, does not allow a decision based exclusively on legal principles'.[1] In these treaties again no procedure was provided in case the parties do not accept the recommendation of the Conciliation Commission.

Under this head there must be included a series of treaties which use a variant of the Locarno formula in referring to 'all disputes of any kind relating to a right asserted by one of the High Contracting Parties and contested by the other'.[2] These are to be submitted to the Court or an arbitral tribunal. The Treaty provides for no effective procedure of settlement for the residuum of disputes with regard to which conciliation is obligatory. Similar provisions are found in the treaties between France and the Netherlands of 10 March 1928,[3] France and Spain of 10 July 1929, Spain and Netherlands of 30 March 1931,[4] Netherlands and Turkey of 16 April 1932[5] and Turkey and Yugoslavia of 27 November 1935.[6]

Under the provisions of this Treaty the two countries submitted in 1956 to an Arbitral Tribunal a dispute concerning the arbitration of the Lake Lanoux in the Pyrenees. For the award of 16 November 1957, see ILR, 1957.

§ 21. The 'General Act' Conventions of Pacific Settlement.

In this group of treaties the adoption of the distinction between justiciable and non-justiciable disputes, although productive of uncertainty, does not result in sanctioning the possibility of a refusal of final and binding settlement. Foremost in this group is the General Act recommended in 1928 by the Ninth Assembly of the League of Nations and a number of treaties framed on the same lines. The General Act distinguishes between disputes with regard to which parties are in conflict as to their respective rights and other disputes. In regard to the first, the

---

[1] See e.g., article 4 of the Swiss-German treaty.

[2] In these treaties 'it is expressly agreed that the disputes referred to above shall include, in particular, those mentioned in Article 13 of the Covenant of the League of Nations'.

[3] *Systematic Survey*, p. 348.

[4] Ibid., p. 884. In Article 19 of the Treaty there is provision for settlement by arbitration *ex aequo et bono* if the parties so agree.

[5] Ibid., p. 696.   [6] Ibid., p. 1056.

parties agree to submit the dispute to the decision of the Permanent Court of International Justice or, if they so agree, of an arbitration tribunal, either directly upon the failure of diplomatic negotiations or, after abortive conciliation, which is optional. In regard to other disputes conciliation is obligatory. If within the month following the termination of the work of the conciliation commission the parties are unable to reach an agreement, the dispute may be brought before an arbitral tribunal by either party (Article 27). Unless the parties agree otherwise, the tribunal is bound to apply the rules of law enumerated in Article 38 of the Statute of the Permanent Court of International Justice. If there exists no such rule applicable to the dispute the tribunal shall decide *ex aequo et bono* (Article 28). These provisions are analysed elsewhere.[1] In 1949 the General Assembly of the United Nations brought the General Act up to date by way of minor changes which consisted mainly in the substitution of the International Court of Justice for the Permanent Court of International Justice.[2] It is in force between a considerable number of States.

The General Act gave a stimulus to a large number of bilateral treaties which are, necessarily, of three types. In the first instance, some of the treaties follow the substantive procedural pattern as described above. The same machinery of settlement of disputes is adopted, with slight modifications, in the treaties between Poland and Norway of 9 December 1929;[3] Norway and Czechoslovakia of 9 September 1929;[4] Poland and Spain of 3 December 1929;[5] Switzerland and Czechoslovakia of 20 September 1929;[6] Spain and Czechoslovakia of 16 November 1928;[7] Spain and Norway of 27 December 1928;[8] Portugal and Switzerland of 17 October 1928;[9] Rumania and Czechoslovakia of 21 May 1929;[10] and in a number of other treaties.[11] Belgium

---

[1] See below, p. 374.
[2] For a detailed account of the proceedings, see *AJ* 43 (1949) p. 706. For the revised text, see *UNTS* 71, p. 161; Sohn, *Basic Documents of the United Nations* (1956), Appendix, p. 76. The Revised General Act entered into force in 1950. By 1956 only four States had acceded to it: Belgium, Denmark, Norway, and Sweden (the latter without accepting the Chapter on Arbitration). For those parties to the General Act which have not adopted the version revised in 1949, the Act of 1928 continues in force unless otherwise validly terminated. For the view that the Court had jurisdiction by virtue of the General Act, which was not invoked by either Party to the case, see the Dissenting Opinion of Judge Basdevant in the *Case of Certain Norwegian Loans: ICJ Reports* 1957, p. 74.
[3] *L.N.T.S.*, vol. ci, p. 337. [4] Ibid., p. 357. [5] Ibid., p. 503.
[6] Ibid., vol. cii, p. 125. [7] Ibid., vol. c, p. 315.
[8] Ibid., vol. xcvii, p. 341. [9] Ibid., vol. xcvi, p. 289. [10] Ibid., p. 313.
[11] See also the treaties of Belgium with Switzerland on 5 February 1927 (*Arbitration and Security*, p. 320); and with Portugal on 9 July 1927 (ibid., p. 337).

and Turkey of 1931;[1] Bulgaria and Belgium of 23 June 1931;[2] Bulgaria and Norway of 26 November 1931;[3] Sweden and Turkey of 19 February 1932;[4] Denmark and Greece of 13 April 1933;[5] Denmark and Yugoslavia of 14 December 1935;[6] and Denmark and Bulgaria of 7 December 1945.[7] Another group of treaties lay down that all disputes are subject, in the first instance, to the procedure of conciliation; to be followed, if the recommendations of the conciliation commission are not accepted, by a final judgement of the International Court of Justice. If in the opinion of the Court the dispute is not of a juridical nature—it is here that the distinction enters—the parties bind themselves to agree to its being settled, by the Court or an arbitral tribunal, *ex aequo et bono*. Treaties of this type have been concluded between Italy and Switzerland on 20 September 1924,[8] Italy and Spain on 7 August 1926,[9] Italy and Chile on 24 February 1927,[10] Spain and Portugal on 18 January 1928,[11] Spain and Switzerland on 20 April 1926,[12] Roumania and Switzerland on 3 February 1926,[13] Switzerland and Greece on 21 September 1925,[14] and Luxemburg and Switzerland on 16 September 1929;[15] Greece and Turkey on 30 October 1930;[16] Bulgaria and Spain on 26 June 1931;[17] between Italy and: Colombia (18 March 1932),[18] Luxembourg (15 March 1932),[19] Panama (14 December 1952),[20] and Costa Rica (31 October 1933);[21] Persia and Turkey on 23 January 1932;[22] and Luxembourg and Norway on 14 December 1932.[23]

---

[1] *Systematic Survey*, p. 892. [2] Ibid., p. 903. [3] Ibid., p. 920.
[4] Ibid., p. 949. [5] Ibid., p. 1016. [6] Ibid., p. 1093.
[7] Ibid., p. 1085. See also the Treaty of 27 June 1930 between Iceland and Sweden which lays down that 'any legal dispute arising between Sweden and Iceland which falls within any of the categories specified in Article 36, paragraph 2, of the Statute of the Permanent Court of International Justice, and which it has not been possible to settle by diplomacy, shall be referred for settlement to the said Court in accordance with the provisions of the said Statute'. All other disputes are, subsequent to a failure of agreement after a procedure of conciliation, to be submitted to an arbitral tribunal for a binding decision 'in accordance with law and equity'—a somewhat unexpected provision in relation to disputes which are not of a binding character: *Systematic Survey*, p. 822. And ibid., pp. 814, 817, and 820, for identical treaties with Denmark, Finland, and Norway.
[8] *Arbitration and Security*, p. 206. [9] Ibid., p. 314.
[10] *L.N.T.S.*, vol. lxix, p. 278. [11] Ibid., vol. lxxvii, p. 115.
[12] *Arbitration and Security*, p. 257. [13] Ibid., p. 249.
[14] *L.N.T.S.*, vol. lxxvii, p. 188. [15] *L.N.T.S.*, vol. cvii, p. 31.
[16] *Systematic Survey*, p. 858. [17] Ibid., p. 912. [18] Ibid., p. 961.
[19] Ibid., p. 965. [20] Ibid., p. 992. [21] Ibid., p. 1052.
[22] Ibid., p. 939.
[23] Ibid., p. 992. Similarly, the Treaty of Friendship, Conciliation and Judicial Settlement between Turkey and Italy of 24 March 1950 (*UNTS* 96 (1951), p. 209) provides for the procedure of conciliation of all disputes of whatsoever nature and, in case either Party fails to comply with the proposals of the Commission, for the

Finally, in the third group of these treaties, legal disputes or disputes 'as to respective rights' are to be submitted to the International Court of Justice, either before conciliation, which is optional, or after the failure of the conciliation proceedings. 'Political' disputes are, in the first instance, to be submitted to conciliation, failing which the dispute must be submitted to an arbitral tribunal, which shall decide *ex aequo et bono*. To this group belong, among others, the treaty between Austria and Sweden of 28 May 1926;[1] France and Switzerland of 3 March 1928;[2] of Belgium with Sweden of 30 April 1926;[3] Denmark of 3 March 1927;[4] Finland of 4 March 1927;[5] and Spain of 19 July 1927;[6] the treaty of Sweden with Spain of 26 April 1928;[7] of Finland with Spain of 31 May 1928;[8] France and Finland of 28 April 1930;[9] and Sweden and Portugal of 6 December 1932[10]

Some treaties of this type, such as the Treaty for the Pacific Settlement of Disputes between Brazil and Venezuela of 30 March 1940, although on the face of it they do not resort to the traditional distinction between justiciable and non-justiciable disputes, do so in fact. Thus Article 3 of that Treaty provides that 'all disputes shall be submitted to the Permanent Court of International Justice or to an Arbitral Tribunal' if they have not been previously settled by conciliation procedure established by the Treaty and if they arise from one of the four named categories (these being identical with those enumerated in Article 36 (2) of the Statute of the Court).[11] The Treaty provides for conciliation in respect of disputes not submitted to arbitration or judicial settlement. If, within six months of the Opinion rendered by the Conciliation Commission, the Parties have failed to

---

compulsory jurisdiction of the International Court of Justice (Article 18). It is provided that should the latter 'find that the dispute does not involve a question of law, the Parties agree that it should be decided *ex aequo et bono*'.

[1] *Arbitration and Security*, p. 260.   [2] *L.N.T.S.*, vol. xcv, p. 91.

[3] *Arbitration and Security*, p. 297.   [4] Ibid., p. 305.   [5] Ibid., p. 333.

[6] *L.N.T.S.*, vol. lxxx, p. 28. In some of the treaties of this group the expression *amiable compositeur* or *amigable componedor* is translated in the *League of Nations Treaty Series* as 'special referee'. See also the treaty between Spain and Luxemburg of 21 June 1928, ibid., vol. cix, p. 139.

[7] Ibid., vol. lxxvii, p. 79.   [8] Ibid., vol. lxxxii, p. 231.

[9] *Systematic Survey*, p. 785. See also ibid., p. 343 for the Treaty of 3 March 1928 between France and Sweden.

[10] Ibid., p. 987. The Treaty between Greece and Poland of 4 January 1932 bypasses the difficulty by not referring to the rules of law to be applied by the Tribunal (ibid., p. 932).

[11] *Systematic Survey*, p. 1127.

reach an agreement, the dispute shall be submitted to an arbitral tribunal constituted in accordance with the Treaty. The latter contains no express provision as to the basis of the decision, which they agree to respect, of the arbitral tribunal—though it appears that the intention was that the Tribunal shall decide *ex aequo et bono*.[1] There are other treaties in that category to the same or similar effect.[2]

The European Convention for the Peaceful Settlement of Disputes of 29 April 1957 follows, in a manner which is not without interest, the lines of the General Act. The Parties agree, in Article 1, to submit to the International Court of Justice 'all international legal disputes which may arise between them including, in particular, those concerning' the four categories of disputes as enumerated in Article 36 of the Statute. They may, with regard to these disputes, agree to a prior procedure of conciliation. With regard to other—non-legal—disputes the procedure of conciliation is obligatory (unless the parties agree to resort to arbitration forthwith). So is the procedure of arbitration with regard to non-legal disputes with respect to which conciliation has failed.The sources of the award to be rendered by the Arbitral Tribunal are formulated differently—though only with a controversial approximation to precision—then in the General Act: 'If nothing is laid down in the special agreement or no special agreement has been made, the Tribunal shall decide *ex aequo et bono*, having regard to the general principles of international law, while respecting the contractual obligations and the final decisions of international tribunals which are binding on the parties.' (Article 26). Some aspects of the Convention are commented upon elsewhere in this book. In the present context it is sufficient to note that the expression 'international legal disputes' in Article 1 was adopted after considerable discussion in substitution for the draft previously approved by the European Assembly on the unanimous recommendation

---

[1] This may be gauged from the provision of Article 21 in which, as an alternative to settlement by the arbitral tribunal, the 'Parties reserve the right to agree to submit the dispute to the Permanent Court of International Justice which shall then decide *ex aequo et bono*.'

[2] The Treaty of Non-Aggression, Conciliation, Arbitration, and Judicial Settlement of 17 December 1939 between Colombia and Venezuela provides, subject to important reservations: (a) for conciliation for all disputes; (b) for a judicial decision, based on law, of the Permanent Court of International Justice or of an arbitral tribunal of the four classes with regard to disputes enumerated in Article 36 of the Statutes: *Systematic Survey*, p. 1121. See also Treaty of Conciliation and Obligatory Arbitration of 22 August 1934 between Brazil and Uruguay: ibid., p. 1073.

of its committee on Legal and Administrative Questions. That Committee expressed preference for the formula used in the Locarno Agreements and the General Act—'all disputes with regard to which the parties are in conflict as to their respective rights'—on the ground that there was 'every advantage in retaining a terminology which has been in force twenty-five years and whose meaning has been made clear by international opinion and practice'.[1] That explanation probably erred on the side of overstatement—although there may have been substance in the view of the Committee that the words 'all international legal disputes' may lead to uncertainty as to their interpretation. There is an element of uncertainty in both formulas.

§ 21(a). **Treaties without the Traditional Classification of Disputes.** It is only in exceptional cases that treaties providing for obligatory judicial or arbitral settlement contain no reference, either express or implied, to the traditional classification of disputes. Thus the Treaty of 22 September 1930 between Panama and Spain provides that the Parties 'undertake to submit to arbitration all disputes of every kind which may for any reason arise between them and which it may not be possible to settle by direct negotiation' (Article 1).[2] Article 2 of the Treaty of Friendship between Greece and the Philippines of 28 April 1950 provides that 'should any dispute arise between the two High Contracting Parties which cannot satisfactorily be adjusted by diplomacy, or through mediation or arbitration, the Parties shall not use force for settlement, but shall refer the dispute to the International Court of Justice for final adjudication'.[3] In some cases, the absence of the current terminology is accompanied, or explained, by the fact that in fact no substantive obligation is being undertaken.[4] The Treaty of 28 May 1931

---

[1] *Council of Europe. Consultative Assembly.* 7th Ordinary Session (First Part), 1955, Recommendation 79 (Article 1).

[2] *Systematic Survey*, p. 840.

[3] *Yearbook of the Court, 1955–1956*, p. 214. See also ibid., 1947–1948, p. 157 for an identical provision in the Treaty of 18 April 1947 between China and the Philippines.

[4] See, e.g. the Treaty of 18 February 1950 between Iran and Pakistan in which the Parties agreed that 'all disputes, of whatever nature they may be, arising between them shall be settled by friendly means through the usual diplomatic channels in a peaceful manner and within a reasonable space of time': ibid., *1952–1953*, p. 199.

between Siam and Switzerland is to the same effect;[1] so is the Treaty, most comprehensive in its determination to secure the effectiveness of its provisions, between Colombia and Peru of 24 May 1934.[2]

§ 22. The Effect of the Doctrine of 'Inherent Limitations' Incorporated in Treaties.

The survey of the arbitration conventions undertaken in this chapter shows that the notion of inherently non-justiciable disputes has found a place in all leading conventions of obligatory judicial and arbitral settlement. In these instruments the doctrine of non-justiciable disputes finds its official and authoritative formulation under the general designation of legal or justiciable disputes, or disputes as to respective rights. It gives there expression to the idea that international disputes are, by the very nature of their content, divided into two categories which not only exist, but exist so clearly that they may be taken as the basis of international obligations. As shown, the doctrine is embodied in these conventions with varying effect. In some it merely results in interposing an alternative method of procedure prior to the recourse to judicial or arbitral settlement which is adopted as obligatory in regard to all disputes. In others, including some of the principal conventions now in force, it affects the fundamental obligation of the treaty. In numerous treaties concluded by the United States and other American countries, it clearly removes from the field of obligatory judicial settlement a large, though indefinite, body of possible disputes. In others, in which the incorporation of the doctrine of non-justiciable disputes proves upon detailed analysis to be a matter of terminology rather than of substance, it introduces an element of uncertainty and confusion which distinctly diminishes the value of the obligation. Thus, as has been pointed out, in case of a dispute of grave importance between two States signatories to the Optional Clause under Article 36 of the Statute of the Permanent Court, it might be open to one party to refuse to submit the case to the Court on the ground that, although the dispute is covered by one of the four categories enumerated in Article 36 of the Statute, it is nevertheless a political, and not a 'legal', dispute—'political' not

---

[1] *Systematic Survey*, p. 903; *LNTS.*, 125, p. 357.
[2] *Systematic Survey*, p. 1073; *LNTS*, 164, p. 21. The Treaty lays down expressly that it is not limited by any reservations which the parties may attach to their acceptance of the Optional Clause.

only as being a dispute of a grave political character in the current meaning of the word, but also as being political in any, or all, of the three other meanings in which the term is being used. The party thus questioning the jurisdiction of the Court would be able to adduce a formidable array of authorities in support of its contention in regard to every one of these interpretations.

The problem has been simplified to a very small extent only by the fact that, in certain treaties, the question whether a dispute is a 'legal' one or not is left to the decision not of the interested party but of the tribunal. For that practice amounts to imposing upon international courts a task which has so far baffled individual and collective efforts of lawyers, and which by its very nature may be insoluble.

A survey of the history of treaties of obligatory arbitral and judicial settlement since the First World War shows some general, though not uniform, movement[1] in the direction of eliminating restrictive clauses of a sweeping character which in fact deprived the principal undertaking of its binding force. Treaties in which there appear the reservations of honour, vital interests, and independence are few and provoke comment by virtue of their exceptional character. Some elastic types of reservation, such as matters of domestic jurisdiction, interests of third parties, territorial integrity, and disputes belonging to the past, are still to be found in a number of treaties, but the dangers of their elasticity are reduced as the result of the power conferred upon or inherent in tribunals to decide on their applicability in each particular case.[2] The nature of that development may be gauged by a comparison of two treaties concluded between Turkey and Italy. In the first, concluded on 30 May 1928,[3] the contracting parties not only inserted the reservation of questions which according to international law concern national sovereignty, but also reserved for themselves the right to 'determine unilaterally, in a written declaration, whether a question should come within its sovereign rights' are in the nature of an exception.[4] Finally, the current distinctions—either separately or in their cumulative effect—between disputes which are and those which

---

[1] See above, p. 37, n. 5.   [2] See below, p. 187.

[3] Printed in *Documents on International Affairs*, Systematic Survey, p____. 1928, edited by Wheeler-Bennett (1929). See also Article 2 of the treaty of 16 May 1929 between Germany and Turkey, according to which the treaty does not apply to disputes 'which, in the opinion of either Party, relate to its sovereign rights,' *L.N.T.S.*, vol. cix, p. 465.

[4] Which, however, again includes the United States treaties referred to above.

are not suitable for decision on the basis of law tend to perpetuate the view that, in the international sphere, the function of law
conceived as a regulative force governing the external conduct
of persons is inherently limited in the sense that in a comprehensive and indefinite sphere of action and omission, they are
the only and the ultimate judges of their rights and duties. Any
such notion is incompatible with the idea of a society under the
rule of law. The rule of law does not mean that it is substantially
ubiquitous and uniformly effective. To use a much abused and
self-evident phrase—the law is not a panacea, it does mean that
it is the law which determines the border line between its
compulsive authority and that of moral and political obligation
left to the autonomy of human will and the interplay of social
forces. The distinction, in various forms, between justiciable and
non-justiciable disputes is being maintained. As the notion of
non-justiciable or political disputes is wide enough to include
any of the restrictive clauses, even those of a most sweeping
character, there is a danger of the progress achieved being in
many instances altogether illusory. At best, the confusion and
doubts which it is bound to create tend to defeat to a large extent
the essential object of those treaties, whose practical reason of
existence lies not so much in the frequency of their application
as in their effect in fostering a sense of security and recognition
of the ultimate arbitrament of law.

The second, concluded on 24 March 1950, provides for conciliation and, eventually, for the compulsory jurisdiction of the
International Court of Justice of all disputes of whatsoever
nature and lays down (in Article 3) that its provisions shall not
apply to questions which 'under treaties in force between the
High Contracting Parties, are within the competence of either
Party,[1] nor to questions relating to sovereign rights'. However,
while the Treaty lays down that either Party shall be entitled to

---

[1] The unorthodox formulation of this Treaty probably explains why it excludes
only such matters within the competence of either Party as are provided for in
Treaty and not those following from general international law. The answer is
probably that, in the view of the present writer, any reservation of matters domestic
jurisdiction is probably otiose inasmuch as it makes no material difference to the
question of the competence of the tribunal. If a matter is in law within the exclusive
domestic jurisdiction of a State, the tribunal will find that it is so regardless of
whether a reservation to that effect has been appended. The more substantial
difficulty is that of the legal standard by reference to which the Court or the arbitral
tribunal will decide whether the subject matter of the dispute refers to sovereign
rights.

determine, by a written statement, whether a question involves
sovereignty, it qualifies that right by providing that the other
Party, if in disagreement, may resort to arbitration or may
apply to the International Court of Justice for a ruling on this
preliminary question. The important exception to that tendency
to impart an element of reality and of absence of artificiality, to
the major undertaking of obligatory judicial or arbitral settlement, however limited it may others be, consists: (a) in the express
reservation of the right to determine unilaterally the extent of the
obligation undertaken by a State and (b) the effective assertion of
the right of a State, after it has undertaken a general commitment
in this sphere, to insist on a special agreement, dependent upon its
will, submitting a particular dispute to a tribunal. These two
exceptions are discussed elsewhere in this book. They do not
detract from the general trend as here indicated.

On the other hand, there has been no abatement in this
doctrine, variously expressed, of the inherent non-justiciability
of certain categories of disputes. However, as the doctrine
of non-justiciable disputes forms part—through its various
designations—of the conventional law on the subject, the question must necessarily by answered.

§ 23. **The Authority of the Doctrine of the Limitations
of the International Judicial Function as adopted in
Treaties.** What is the authority of these treaties in so far as
they incorporate the doctrine in question? How far is the lawyer,
bound as he is to consider the actual practice of States, under the
duty of accepting the notion of non-justiciable disputes both as
part of positive international law and as expressing a correct
legal proposition? Undoubtedly, the lawyer ought to recognize
fully that the doctrine, as accepted in its various current designations, has been adopted by the practice of States. Having
regard to the treaties in question, he may have to use, in his
presentation of the subject, the terminology adopted in these
treaties. But further than that his duty does not go. On the
contrary, his task is to examine whether the doctrine and its
current formulations are otherwise in conformity with other
rules of conventional and customary international law; whether
they are consistent with the whole body of international law
conceived as a scientific system; whether the several meanings of
the doctrine are mutually compatible or mutually contradictory;
and, above all, whether they are capable of application while
leaving intact the principal object of these treaties conceived as
instruments embodying legal rights and obligations. By giving

currency to the doctrine of non-justiciable disputes, Government not only give expression to their desire not to accept without limitations the jurisdiction of international tribunals in disputes which may arise between them. They adopt at the same time a classification of disputes; they set up a legal category. They may legitimately do so. Treaties of pacific settlement, in particular those of a general character, are law-creating expressions of the will of States. As the legislator is at liberty to take over, from the armoury of legal science, terms, classifications, and categories for the purpose of expressing his will—and he does so frequently—so may Goverments do when laying down rules which shall bind them in the future. But the intrinsic, legal, and logical value of any such term or classification is a matter for legitimate examination and criticism on the part of the lawyer.

It has been rightly said, with reference to the legislator's attempts at scientific construction, that he who could make a threefold classification adequate when there are four elements to be classified, or who could make a fiction a reality, could more easily change a man into a woman.[1] The same applies to States in general and to the doctrine of non-justiciable disputes in particular. It is legitimate for Governments to reserve for themselves, in regard to the judicial settlement of their disputes, freedom of action in certain spheres and in a manner compatible with the assumption of some legal obligation, however limited. But if, with this object in view, they avail themselves of juridical terms expressive of a distinction which does not in fact exist, to which are attached a variety of contradictory meanings, and whose constitutive elements are incompatible with one another and with existing international law, then, as authors of this attempt at legal construction, they cannot claim the immunities otherwise enjoyed by sovereign States. Their desire, effectively embodied in treaties, not to be bound irrevocably and unequivocally by any obligations apparently undertaken forms part of international law and must be respected like most emanations of their will. No such authority attaches to the theoretical garb with which they choose to cloak their determination to retain the ultimate freedom of action.

§ 24. Limitations of the Judicial Function through Reservation. The recourse to the terminology of the doctrine of non-justiciable disputes is not the only means of limiting the

---

[1] Tourtoulon, *Philosophy in the Development of Law* (English translation, 1922), p. 380.

compulsory jurisdiction of international tribunals. The substance of the doctrine, namely, the restriction of the scope of judicial and arbitral settlement, and its method, namely, the use of indefinite terms depriving the obligation of an objective criterion of its applicability, will be found in the treaties—current before the First World War—which contain the comprehensive and elastic reservations of vital interests, national honour, and independence.[1] It was generally accepted that these reservations implied the right, on the part of the State making the reservation, to determine whether it applied in a particular case. Reasons are given elsewhere in this book for the view that reservations thus conceived divest such treaties of an element of legal obligation.[2] The same applies to all reservations with regard to which such right of unilateral determination is granted in a treaty or effectively asserted in a unilateral declaration purporting to assume obligations of compulsory arbitral or judicial settlement. This, as will be shown, is particularly the case with regard to the reservation of matters essentially, or exclusively, within the domestic jurisdiction of a State as determined by that State.[3] That category includes also treaties which, while laying down the general obligation of arbitral or judicial settlement, make that obligation dependent upon the conclusion of a special agreement, dependent upon the will of both parties. These treaties are in fact entered upon subject to the reservation that when a particular dispute arises the Parties will determine whether and to what extent there applies to them the major undertaking embodied in the treaty.[4] The position is different with regard to those numerous treaties in which a tribunal, such as the International Court, is entrusted with the task of laying down the terms of the special agreement.

---

[1] For a discussion of these reservations before the First World War see Wehberg in *A.J.* vii (1913), pp. 301–14, and Calvalcanti, ibid., viii (1914), pp. 723–37. For a recent examination of this category of reservations see Morgenthau, *Die internationale Rechtspflege, ihr Wesen und ihre Grenzen* (1929), pp. 98–104, 112–30, with extensive bibliographical references. For a careful discussion of reservations in general see Wilson in *A.J.* xxiii (1929), pp. 68–93, See also Clad, *Wesen und Grenzen der internationalen Schiedsgerichtsbarkeit* (1928), pp. 59–72, 111–14. and Schindler, *Die Schudsgerichtsbarkeit seit 1914* (1938), pp. 81–94. A useful synopsis of reservations in post-war treaties will be found in *Arbitration and Security*, pp. 23–6 and *Systematic Survey*, pp. 23–8.

[2] See below, p. _____.

[3] See below, p. _____.

[4] That particular form of reservation is a conspicuous feature of numerous arbitration treaties concluded by the United States of America. See above, p. _____. And see, in particular, Wilson in *AJ*, 25 (1931), pp. 469–89.

On the other hand, reservations, however elastic and comprehensive, do not deprive the treaty or the declaration of its character as a legal instrument so long as their applicability is one for the decision of the tribunal. These include those relating to disputes involving the interests of third parties,[1] or territorial integrity, or the Monroe Doctrine, or—a reservation of frequent occurrence—that exempting from the purview of the undertaking disputes occurring prior to it or arising out of facts and situations anterior to it.[2] There are, further, in this category specific reservations such as those relating to disputes arising out of hostilities in which the parties were engaged, or to disputes with a State which has refused recognition to the State which it attempts to bring before the Court, and the like.[3]

Finally, there are reservations of a suspensive and procedural character such as those making the obligation of judicial or arbitral settlement dependent upon previous attempts at settlement by negotiation and diplomatic means generally; those excepting from the operation of the undertaking disputes for the settlement of which a different procedure is provided for in another instrument; or those concerning disputes falling within the jurisdiction of the administrative or judicial authorities of the defendant State pending the final decision of the authorities—a reservation which does no more than affirm the established rule

---

[1] On this reservation see Morgenthau, *op. cit.*, pp. 110–12 and Lammasch, *Rechtskraft*, pp. 95–104. And see below, p. 198, for an instance of actual recourse to that reservation.

[2] See below, p. ____. And see Fischer Williams in *BY* XI (1930), pp. 74–5; Lauterpacht in *Economica*, 1930, pp. 139–44; Politis, in his argument before the Court in the *Chorzów* case, Series C, No. 1391, pp. 35 *et seq.*

[3] Unlike in the case of ordinary treaties, where as a rule—and, possibly, subject to the broad qualifications formulated by the Court in the Opinion on *the Reservations to the Genocide Convention (ICJ Reports)* 1951, p. 15—the assent of the other signatories is required to reservations not included in the treaty as originally signed, a different practice obtains with regard to instruments of obligatory judicial and arbitral settlement. Attempts, of a somewhat nominal character, have been made to circumscribe that freedom of appending reservations. Thus the General Act for the Pacific Settlement of International Disputes of 1928 provides, in Article 39, that these reservations may refer only: (a) to so-called past disputes; (b) matters which according to international law are solely within domestic jurisdiction; (c) 'disputes concerning particular cases or clearly specified subject-matters, such as territorial status, or disputes falling within clearly defined categories'. It is difficult to visualise the kind of reservation which is not covered by the latter provision. The same applies to the provision of Article 35 of the European Convention for the Peaceful Settlement of Disputes of 1957 which is identical with Article 39(2)(c) of the General Act of 1928 cited above.

of international law relating to exhaustion of legal remedies.[1] An examination of these reservations does not fall within the scope of this book. They have been referred to in order to draw attention to the fact that the incorporation in treaties, through the orthodox classification, of the doctrine of the limitation of the international judicial function does not constitute the only limitation upon the normal function of international tribunals. But it probably constitutes the most widely adopted and, in view of the authority lent to it by the doctrine of international law, perhaps the most fundamental limitation of the duty and the function of obligatory judicial settlement of disputes involving the members of the non-territorial community. Above all it has provided the main support for the principle, which is still a valid part of existing international law, that—unlike in other civilised political communities—a member of what is called the society of States may lawfully withhold from another member the other-wise elementary right to a judicial decision based on law.

---

[1] It lies in the nature of things that reservations are as a rule inserted only in general arbitration treaties. But see the *Portendic* case, decided on 30 November 1843, for an example of reservations attached to an *ad hoc* arbitration agreement: Lapradelle and Politis, vol. i, pp. 522, 523, and *British and Foreign State Papers*, xxxiv, pp. 1064 and 1068. These are not, in effect, reservations but agreed formulations of the law to be applied by the tribunal. See, for instance, Rule A of Article 4 of the terms of submission of Treaty of 1897 between Great Britain and Venezuela concerning the arbitration in the matter of British Guiana. That Rule laid down that in 'adverse or prescription during a period of fifty years should make good title' and that 'the arbitrators may deem exclusive political control of a district, as well as actual settlement thereof, sufficient to constitute adverse holding or to make title by prescription'.

PART II

THE INTERNATIONAL JUDICIAL
FUNCTION AND THE COMPLETENESS
OF INTERNATIONAL LAW

CHAPTER III

LIMITATION OF THE JUDICIAL FUNCTION ON ACCOUNT OF THE ABSENCE OF RULES OF INTERNATIONAL LAW

I

The Meaning of the Doctrine

§ 1. In General. International judicial settlement—a term which in its essential meaning includes international arbitration—is a method of settling disputes between States by a binding decision based upon rules of law. This exclusive authority of rules of law as a source of decision has from the very inception lent to the notion of international judicial settlement and arbitration most of its moral and political strength. Accordingly, it was natural to propound and to act upon the view that in all cases where there are no rules of international law applicable to the case, there is, by virtue of the very conception of international judicial settlement and arbitration, no room for settlement by that method as a matter of binding obligation accepted in advance, and that controversies the solution of which may be affected by such absence of legal rules are non-legal and, in consequence, non-justiciable. This is the origin of the time-honoured and, in point of time, probably the first definition of legal disputes: legal disputes are those which are capable of decision by the application of rules of international law. This reference to the non-existence of a rule of international law applicable to the case is most frequently made in the sense that, owing to its recent origin, to the indefinite character and the scarcity of its rules, and to the constitutional difficulty of creating new and amending obsolete law, international law exhibits, more than any other system of law, considerable gaps and deficiencies, with the result that a decision in accordance with the law is frequently impossible. It is in that sense that Westlake spoke of legal disputes as controversies which 'can be settled by reference to known rules, having at their back that force which is derived from the general consent of the international society',[1] or that he stressed the political character of disputes in cases when international law needs to be supplemented or precisely defined. In the works of writers, at

---

[1] *International Law* (2nd ed., 1910), i. 358.

international conferences, in the pronouncements of statesmen, and in the provisions of treaties of compulsory settlement there runs a persistent current of opinion to the effect that the international judicial function is necessarily limited as the result of the material insufficiency of international law. That view, which has behind it the appearance of a purely juridical method of approach to the problem, is to-day only slightly less emphatic than it was at the time when international lawyers first began to discuss the limitations of international judicial settlement.

§ 2. The History of the Doctrine. The first attempt to deal on this basis with the question of the limitation of the judicial function was made in 1873. Professor Goldschmidt, in his capacity of *rapporteur* to the Institute of International Law, when dealing with the question of the possible range of international arbitration, referred to the monograph of Trendelenburg on gaps in international law,[1] in which the view was expressed that an arbitral award in an international dispute may not be rendered except on points which are of a legal nature. He fully agreed with that opinion, and submitted that 'there are no grounds for a judicial decision, nor consequently for an arbitral decision, in differences which are not of a legal character (*Rechtsstreitigkeiten*), and whose nature does not admit of a judgement according to rules of law'.[2] Several years later, Kamarovsky, in his comprehensive treatise on international arbitration, pointed out that the jurisdiction of international tribunals must be confined to disputes which, by virtue of positive international law and of conventions concluded by the parties, admit of an objective and juridical determination.[3] This view was subsequently adopted and amplified by a large number of writers.[4] When in 1922 the Institute of International Law again discussed the question of the classification of international disputes, the *rapporteurs* in their draft resolution proposed that the Institute should include 'the absence of a generally recognized rule of law' as one of the reasons of non-justiciability of disputes.[5] Professor Politis, one of the authors of the report, writing some time later, gave detailed reasons in support of

[1] *Lücken im Völkerrecht* (1870), p. 21.
[2] 'Draft Regulations for International Tribunals. Preliminary Remarks.' Printed in *Resolutions of the Institute of International Law*, ed. by J. B. Scott (1916), p. 207.
[3] Ibid., pp. 504–5.
[4] See above, p. 11.
[5] *Annuaire*, xxix (1922), p. 36. See above, p. 18.

the view that an international tribunal in general and the International Court in particular might find themselves in the position of not being able to give judgement because of the absence of positive rules or principles of law recognized by civilized States.[1]

When in 1920 the Committee of Jurists charged with the drafting of the Statute of the Permanent Court of International Justice considered the matter of the sources of law to be applied by the Court, there were members of the Committee who believed that, in view of the insufficient development of international law, there was a possibility of the Court's being confronted with the necessity of pronouncing a *non liquet* on the ground that there was no law applicable to the dispute. For some members that necessity of avoiding the possibility of a *non liquet* was the main reason for urging the insertion, in paragraph 3 of the present Article 38 of the Statute, the provision empowering the Court to render decisions in accordance with principles of law generally recognized by civilized States.[2] It seems that, in the minds of some, even that provision was not sufficient to exclude the possibility of gaps in the law.[3] This appears to be one of the reasons why the Committee thought it necessary to append to its draft a Resolution urging in the interest of 'the extension of the sway of justice and the development of international jurisdiction', the convening of an international conference charged with reconciling divergent views on

---

[1] *La Justice internationale* (1924), pp. 84, 85, 170. See also Lammasch, *Rechtskraft*, pp. 43–9; Brown in *R.I.*, 3rd ser., v (1924), p. 317; Verzijl, ibid., vi (1925), pp. 742, 743; Mulder, ibid., vii (1926), pp. 555–76; Hostie, ibid., ix (1928), pp. 267–72; Spiropoulos, *Die allgemeinen Rechtsgrundsätze im Völkerrecht* (1928), pp. 16ff.; Le Fur in *Annuaire*, xxxiii (2) (1927), pp. 788–802; Fischer Williams, *Chapters*, pp. 52–5; Morgenthau, pp. 37–42. See also Ch. de Visscher in *Recueil des Cours*, 1925 (i), pp. 403–5, and Reeves in *A.J.* xv (1921), pp. 373, 374, who regards as non-justiciable those controversies in regard to which 'there is no legal rule of action'.

[2] Thus M. Hagerup said: 'There might be cases in which no rule of conventional or general law was applicable. A rule must be established to meet this eventuality, to avoid the possibility of the Court's declaring itself incompetent (*non liquet*) through lack of applicable rules.' *Procès-Verbaux*, p. 296. See also the opinion of Mr. Root (ibid., pp. 309, 310) who envisaged the possibility of the Court declaring itself incompetent or limiting itself to a recommendation; of M. de Lapradelle (ibid., p. 312) who urged that it was impossible to admit a declaration of *non liquet*, and that such a declaration would amount to a denial of justice which it was necessary to exclude from an international court; of M. Fernandes (ibid., p. 345); and of Lord Phillimore (ibid., p. 332) who indicated that the insertion of 'general principles of law' as one of the sources of law avoided the difficulty of 'the blind alley of *non liquet*'. See also Cheng, *General Principles of Law as Applied by International Courts and Tribunals* (1953), pp. 6–20 for an account, from a different point of view, of this aspect of the discussion before the Commission.

[3] See Politis, op. cit., p. 170.

particular topics of international law and 'giving special consideration to those points which are not at the present time adequately provided for'.[1]

§ 3. **Opinions of Statesmen. The Practice of States.** This persistent view that there are gaps in international law which act as a limitation of the justiciability of disputes, found clear expression in the resolution adopted in 1928 by the Ninth Assembly of the League of Nations urging the members of the League to sign the Optional Clause of Article 36 of the Statute of the Court, and expressing the hope that 'the efforts now being made through progressive codification to diminish the uncertainties, and supply the deficiencies, of international law will greatly facilitate the acceptance of the Optional Clause'.[2]

Of the numerous utterances of statesmen bearing upon the subject the views of two British statesmen may fittingly be recalled. When in 1896 Lord Salisbury explained to the United States Secretary of State the reasons prompting Great Britain to resist the inclusion of territorial claims within the orbit of the proposed general arbitration treaty, he pointed to the rudimentary condition and the uncertainty of international law on the subject.[3] 'There is', he said, 'no enactment or usage or accepted doctrine which lays down the length of time required for international prescription; and no full definition of the degree of control which will confer territorial property on a nation has been attempted.'[4] A similar view, in relation not to any particular branch of international law, but to the law of nations as a whole, was expressed over thirty years later by another British statesman

---

[1] *Procès-Verbaux*, p. 747.

[2] It is in particular in the United States that there was for a time an insistence on the necessity of codifying international law as one of the means of extending the scope of 'justiciable' disputes and of obligatory arbitration in general. It was the American representative who was mainly responsible for the resolution, referred to above, of the Committee of Jurists in 1920. See also Scott, 'Advancement of International Law Essential to an International Court of Justice', in *A.S. Proceedings*, 1921, pp. 21–8. However, while this attitude of these and other lawyers was in no way inimical to the extension of the limits of obligatory arbitration, there was in the United States, and in other countries, a large body of opinion which regarded codification of international law as a condition precedent to the assumption of effective obligations in the field of judicial settlement. In view of the limited scope and possibilities of codification at the present stage, that attitude amounts to a negation of obligatory settlement on the basis of law.

[3] Dispatch to Sir Julian Pauncefote, of 18 May 1896, Moore, p. 973.

[4] Ibid., p. 974.

who for a long period was responsible for the conduct of the foreign policy of Great Britain.[1]

Finally, the idea of the limitation of the function of international tribunals on account of the lack of rules of international law has found direct or indirect expression in a long series of arbitration conventions. It constitutes at least one of the possible meanings of the crucial qualification in treaties and declarations which limit the duty of judicial settlement to 'legal' disputes,[2] or 'disputes as to respective rights'.[3] It is expressed, more clearly, in those instruments which refer to disputes which are justiciable by being capable of a decision by the application of rules of law or of law and equity.[4] It has been incorporated in the numerous treaties in which the Tribunal is instructed to decide *ex aequo et bono* in case there are no rules of law applicable to the dispute.[5] The much-debated Article 28 of the General Act for the Pacific Settlement of International Disputes[6] contains a provision to the same effect. Other treaties are even more explicit. Thus Article 5 of the Treaty of Arbitration and Conciliation between Switzerland and Germany of 3 December 1921, after referring to the rules of law applicable by the Tribunal, and including the sources of law enumerated in the first three paragraphs of Article 38 of the Statute of the Permanent Court of International Justice, laid down that 'if, in a particular case, the legal bases mentioned above are inadequate, the Tribunal shall give an award in accordance with the principles of law which, in its opinion, should govern international law. For this purpose it shall be guided by decisions sanctioned by legal authorities and jurisprudence.'[7] There are instances of international tribunals which, although equipped with the rich depository of law embodied in the first four paragraphs of Article 38 of the Statute of the International Court, have nevertheless thought it necessary to provide for the emergency in which they might be placed

[1] Sir Austen Chamberlain, on 5 July 1929, in the House of Commons: 229 *House of Commons Deb.*, col. 404.

[2] See above, pp.29 et seq. It will be noted that almost all arbitration treaties concluded before the World War, and limiting the duty of judicial settlement to 'legal' disputes, contained sweeping reservations excluding important, i.e. political, disputes from the purview of the obligation. This may serve as an indication that the term 'legal' referred in that connexion to the existence of legal rules applicable to the dispute.

[3] See pp. 38 et seq. *infra*.

[4] See p. 37 *supra*.

[5] See p. 41 *supra*, and p. 372 *infra*. See also *Annuaire*, xxxiii (2) (1927), p. 708, for another enumeration of some of these conventions.

[6] See below, p. 377.   [7] *Arbitration and Security*, p. 202.

by the absence of rules of law applicable to the case before them.[1]

The above survey of authorities shows that the conviction of the substantive insufficiency of international law has not wholly lost its hold over writers and statesmen, and that the orthodox conception of legal (or justiciable) disputes as disputes capable of decision through the application of existing, ascertained, and generally recognized rules of international law is still one of the bases of the doctrine of the limitation of the judicial function in the international society. The examination of this aspect of the doctrine falls under several headings. First, we must inquire into the meaning of the phrase 'rules of law applicable to the settlement of the dispute'. Secondly, that aspect of the doctrine of non-justiciable disputed must be examined by reference to general principles of law and the rules of positive international law as well as to the history of international arbitration. Thirdly, it must be considered from the point of view of the practical and theoretical problems of the judicial function in international law.

§ 4. Analysis of the Phrase 'Rules of International Law Applicable to the Settlement of the Dispute'. It has been noted above that the first practical consequence of the doctrine of the limitation of obligatory settlement on the basis of law on account of the possible absence of rules of law applicable to the dispute is that it has been adopted in instruments of pacific settlement. It is necessary, before examining the substantive aspects of the doctrine, to inquire into its usefulness and applicability in treaties imposing obligations upon the parties. Assuming that the term 'legal' or 'justiciable' refers to the existence of 'rules of international law applicable to the settlement of the dispute', the question arises what is meant by that latter phrase. In particular it must be asked: (*a*) What is meant by 'rules of international law' upon which the decision

---

[1] Thus the arbitration tribunal which, in July 1928, gave an award in the matter of certain Portuguese claims against Germany, when confronted with the absence, in the relevant treaty provisions, of any reference to the law to be applied by the Tribunals, decided in the first instance to have recourse to the sources of law enumerated in Article 38 of the Statute. But apparently it did not regard these sources of law as a sufficient protection from the possibility of a *non liquet*, for the relevant part of the decision runs as follows: 'A défaut de régles du droit des gens applicables aux faits litigieux, les arbitres estiment devoir combler la lacune, en statuant suivant les principes d'équité tout en restant dans le sens du droit des gens appliqué par analogie, et en tenant compte de son évolution.' *Recueil*, viii. 413. See also *Annual Digest*, 1927–8, Case No. 317. And see below, p.

must be based? (*b*) What is implied in the term 'applicable'? (*c*) What is meant by the 'settlement of the dispute' on the basis of applicable rules of international law?

(*a*) A formula which refers to decisions based on existing international law inevitably raises the question of the nature of the sources of international law. The question whether a dispute is 'legal', in the meaning here discussed, will be answered in one an way by an adherent of the law of nature and the principles of natural justice as forming part of international law; in another by the rigid positivist, for whom nothing short of a rule of conduct expressly accepted by States possesses the authority of a rule of international law; and in still another by the follower of a middle course who, now powerfully supported by Article 38 of the Statute of the Permanent Court, recognizes the practice of States as the principal source of law, but is prepared to extend the sphere of applicable international law by the approved scientific methods of analogy with, and deduction from, general principles of law. Thus a claim, like that put forward in 1912 by Russia against Turkey, for moratory interest on account of the delay in the payment of a war indemnity,[1] would be regarded by the rigid positivist as outside the scope of judicial settlement, on the ground that it is based on a rule not expressly recognized by States and relating to a situation without precedent in the practice of States. The same claim will be regarded by others as forming the subject-matter of a distinctly legal dispute, to be settled by the application not only of general principles of law, drawn by analogy from the relevant branches of private law, but also by the application of a more comprehensive rule of international law enjoining reparation for any non-fulfilment of an international obligation for which the State bears responsibility.[2] The same applies to all disputes for the decision of which there exist no specific rules of international law, but which can be decided by the application of a more general principle of the law of nations.[3] It will be seen, therefore, that the term 'legal', adopted in this connexion by lawyers or in a treaty, does not in

---

[1] See below, p. 115.

[2] See below, p. 117.

[3] See below, p. 111. And see Thayer in *Harvard Law Review*, xxvi (1912–13), p. 416, for the suggestion that treaties restricting the jurisdiction of international tribunals to disputes capable of solution by the application of rules of law and equity are not 'as far behind treaties for the arbitration of all controversies of any nature as is generally supposed'.

fact convey any clear indication of the intention of those using this term, or the extent of the obligation of undertaken in any particular treaty. It might be said that nothing short of complete codification of the entire body of international law would remove the uncertainty created by this particular conception of justiciable disputes.[1] Yet it may be doubted whether even total codification would meet the difficulties involved in this particular limitation of justiciability. For codification does not necessarily eliminate the possibility of gaps. It frequently accentuates it by limiting the freedom of the judicial development of the law.

(*b*) The second difficulty arising out of this conception of the limitation of the judicial function is that the reference to the existence of rules of law *applicable* to the case reveals, upon analysis, a confusing variety of possible meanings. For once the emphasis is placed upon the *applicability* of the existing rule of law, the question of the existence of the relevant rule recedes into the background. Such emphasis means that, although there exist rules of law bearing prima facie upon the case in question, they are in fact not 'applicable', either because the subject-matter of the dispute is too important for judicial cognizance in a society where the precarious reign of law is a matter of voluntary acceptance, presumptively restricted to subjects of minor importance; or because the application of an existing rule of law might yield a result which, owing to the rudimentary character of the law-amending process in international society, would be unjust and dangerous to the peace of the world; or because the claim of the plaintiff, or the defence of the defendant, State is admittedly placed outside the sphere of law. Thus when Article 28 of the General Act for the Pacific Settlement of International Disputes[2] lays down that in so far as there exists no rule of law—as provided in Article 38 of the Statute of the Court—applicable to the dispute, the Tribunal shall decide *ex aequo et bono*, it is by no means certain that the article refers solely to the actual existence of rules which are prima facie applicable. Any criticism, therefore, of this and similar provisions on the ground that the idea of the substantive insufficiency of international law is unscientific, touches only one of the possible meanings of this conception of justiciable disputes. In fact, any effective criticism of this

---

[1] See here Verzijl in *R.I.*, 3rd ser., vi (1925), pp. 733–6; and Politis in *Annuaire*, xxix (1922), p. 226.

[2] See above, p. 41, and below, p. 377.

particular meaning of the term[1] may have the indirect result of emphasizing these alternative meanings.

(*c*) It is not clear what is meant by the phrase 'settlement of the dispute' on the basis of rules of international law. Is the word 'settlement' used here in the merely formal sense, or does it refer to the settlement of the dispute in the sense that a final and satisfactory solution can be achieved as the result of the application of the existing rule of law? Thus, for instance, when Professor Hyde defines those issues as justiciable which 'are capable of *reasonable*[2] adjustment by reference to accepted principles of international law',[3] it is apparent that it is the substantive appropriateness of the decision (as distinguished from the formal applicability of rules of law) on which stress is being laid.

The difficulties indicated above are not merely of a terminological nature. They tend to emphasize the uncertainty and ambiguity which attach to this particular conception of legal disputes and thus diminish its usefulness as an instrument for circumscribing a treaty obligation in which certainty and clarity are of the essence of the undertaking.[4] It may be admitted that a tribunal endowed with the power of interpreting the instrument in question will ultimately decide upon a proper interpretation of the phrase here discussed, but this does not alter the fact that, prior to such judicial interpretation (which is in itself a formidable task), the extent of the obligation of settlement on the basis of law will remain a subject of conjecture.

Finally, there arises the question of the nature of the judicial procedure in the matter of ascertaining whether there exists a rule of law applicable to the dispute. When one State meets the claim of the other with the assertion, put forward before the Tribunal, that the dispute is not a legal one (in the sense here discussed), what will the Tribunal do? Assuming—in order to simplify a subject bristling with difficulties—that the Tribunal will disregard the possible interpretation of the

---

[1] See, for instance, the weighty remarks by Brierly in *B.Y.* xi (1930), pp. 127–9.

[2] Italics ours.

[3] Vol. ii, p. 112. However, Professor Hyde apparently adopted a somewhat different test when he states, on p. 113, that a justiciable controversy exists whenever 'the principles of international law are sufficiently broad and flexible in their scope and application, and sufficiently well understood, to mark clearly the lawfulness or unlawfulness of the conduct or contentions giving rise to complaint'.

[4] See pp. 435, 436 *infra*.

phrase as discussed under (*b*) and (*c*), and will limit itself to ascertaining whether, contrary to the contention of the plaintiff, there is a rule of international law applicable to the case, must not a decision on this question be essentially one on the merits? A judgement stating that there is no applicable rule of international law will be in effect tantamount to the rejection of the claim on the ground that there is no rule of law to support it. A decision that the claim is covered by a rule of international law may, in many cases amount to an admission of the claim.[1] It will thus be seen that this conception of the limitation of the judicial function, when embodied in treaties, not only gives rise to ambiguities frustrating their essential purpose, but may not even be capable of achieving the purpose of the parties who desire to limit the jurisdiction of the tribunal.

II

The Completeness of the Legal System as a General Principle of Law

§ 5. The Completeness of the Legal System as a Problem of Municipal Law. Serious as they are, the difficulties described above do not constitute the principal drawback of the doctrine of the limitation of the judicial function as based on the applicability of legal rules. Its fundamental shortcoming consists in the underlying assumption that there are, in the international community, which is *ex hypothesi* a community under the rule of law, disputes between its members which, owing to the absence of rules of law, cannot be legally disposed of by a judicial decision. This conception illustrates more eloquently than anything else the slow progress of the science of international law, in which solutions, long accepted in national jurisprudence as being dictated by the very existence of the legal order, have failed to secure acceptance by international lawyers for almost two generations. For the problem of the completeness of the legal order, and of so-called gaps in positive law, is not one confined to international law. It is an ever-present problem in jurisprudence and legal philosophy. It has produced, mainly in the last fifty years, a considerable literature, centring round the question of the nature and the

---

[1] The point is elaborated in more detail below, at pp. 357–63.

limits of the judicial function,[1] in Germany,[2] France,[3] Switzerland,[4] the United States,[5] and, to a smaller extent, in England.[6]

However, although the question whether law provides an answer for every conceivable situation that may arise has been widely discussed, the question whether the judge is at liberty to refuse to give a decision on the ground of the

---

[1] The student will find a representative selection of authors dealing with this subject in the Modern Legal Philosophy Series in the volume entitled *Science of Legal Method* (1921).

[2] Some of the more representative works bearing on the subject may be mentioned here: Bergbohm, *Jurisprudenz und Rechtsphilosophie* (1892); Stammler, *Die Lehre vom richtigen Recht* (1902); Ehrlich, *Freie Rechtsfindung und freie Rechtswissenschaft* (1903); Zitelmann, *Lücken im Recht* (1903); Gnaeus Flavius (Kantorowicz), *Der Kampf um die Rechtswissenschaft* (1906), and the same, *Rechtswissenschaft und Soziologie* (1911); *Aus der Vorgeschichte der Freirechtslehre* (1926), and in the *Columbia Law Review*, xxviii (1928), pp. 698–707 (jointly with Patterson); Jung, *Positives Recht* (1907), *Problem des natürlichen Rechts* (1912) and 'Von der logischen Geschlossenheit des Rechts', in *Festgabe für Dernburg* (1900); C. Schmitt, *Gesetz und Urteil* (1912); Reichel, *Gesetz und Richterspruch* (1915); Binder, *Die Philosophie des Rechts* (1925), pp. 970–94; Sauer, *Lehrbuch der Rechts- und Sozialphilosophie* (1929), pp. 231–43

[3] See in particular Gény, *Méthode d'interprétation et sources en droit privé positif* (1919 ed.), ii, sec. 176; *Science et technique en droit privé positif* (1924), iv, in particular pp. 213–65; Malberg, *Contribution à la théorie générale de l'État* (1920–2), i, Nos. 236–8. Saleilles's contribution is well presented by Gény in *L'Œuvre juridique de Raymond Saleilles* (1914), pp. 3–63. See also Charmont, *La Renaissance du droit naturel* (1910); Ripert, *Droit naturel et positivisme juridique* (1918). And see the works of Page, a Belgian jurist, *De l'interprétation des lois*, 2 vols. (1915); *A propos du gouvernement des juges* (1931).

[4] See Williams, *Zu den Einleitungsartikeln des schweizerischen Zivilgesetzbuches* (1926) and the literature compiled therein, and the same in *Kommentar zum schweizerischen Zivilgesetzbuch*, introductory volume (1911), pp. 4–9; E. Huber, *Recht und Rechtsverwirklichung* (1921); Burckhardt, *Die Lücken des Gesetzes und die Gesetzesauslegung* (1925), and the same, *Die Organisation der Rechtsgemeinschaft* (1927), pp. 105–18.

[5] See Pound, *An Introduction to the Philosophy of Law* (1922), pp. 100–43; 'Courts and Legislation', in *The Science of Legal Method* in Legal Philosophy Series (1921), pp. 202–28; 'Justice according to Law', in *Columbia Law Review*, xiii (1913), pp. 696–713, and xiv (1914), pp. 103–21; *Law and Morals* (1924); *Harvard Law Review*, xxv (1911–12), pp. 140–68 and 489–516; xxvii (1913–14), pp. 195–234 and 605–28; xxx (1916–17), pp. 201–25; xliv (1930–1), pp. 697–711; Cardozo, *The Nature of the Judicial Process* (1925); Frank, *Law and the Modern Mind* (1929); Hutcheson in *Cornell Law Quarterly*, xiv (1929), pp. 274 et seqq.; Dickinson in *University of Pennsylvania Law Review*, lxxix (1931), pp. 833 et seqq.; F. Cohen in *Yale Law Journal*, xii (1931), pp. 201–20; Llewellyn in *Harvard Law Review*, xliv (1930–1), pp. 1222–56. See also Gray, *The Nature and Sources of the Law* (1909), sections 602 et seqq.

[6] Allen, *Law in the Making* (2nd ed., 1930), pp. 177–88. See also, as bearing indirectly upon the problem, Pollock, 'Judicial Valour and Caution', in *Law Quarterly Review*, xlv (1929), pp. 293–306, and *Expansion of the Common Law* (1904), pp. 107–38; *The Genius of the Common Law* (1912), pp. 75–125. And see Salmond, *Introduction to the Science of Legal Method*, in Legal Philosophy Series (1921), pp. lxxv–lxxxvi, and Jethro Brown, *The Austinian Theory of Law* (1906), pp. 288–302, and in *Yale Law Journal*, xxix (1919–20), pp. 394–400.

supposed absence of a rule of law applicable to the individual case has seldom been the object of controversy or discussion. It has been answered, with decisive determination, in the negative—not by elaborate jurisprudential considerations, but by the very fact of the establishment of a community under the reign of law. This is a legal phenomenon of so cogent a nature that it is only in exceptional cases that the law finds it necessary to enjoin *expressis verbis* upon the judge the duty to give a decision in any case whatsoever in regard to which he has jurisdiction. The French *Code Civil* and several codes framed in accordance with it[1] constitute this much-quoted exception. The Civil Code lays down in its Article 4 that the judge who refuses to decide a case on the ground that the law is silent, obscure, or insufficient in regard to the matter before the Court is guilty of a denial of justice. Other systems of law do not regard it as necessary to insert an express prohibition to this effect. Their codes undertake the more positive task of supplying the judge with a source of decision in cases of this nature.[2] Thus the Civil Code of Switzerland lays down in Article 1 that if in a particular case the positive law does not in the opinion of the judge provide a sufficient basis for decision, he shall decide in accordance with custom, or, in the absence of the latter, in accordance with a rule which he would follow if he were legislator, and that, in so doing, he ought to be guided by tradition and by recognized legal authorities. The Austrian Civil Code refers the judge in similar cases to natural law,[3] and the Italian Code to general principles of law.[4] In Germany the legislator, after having deliberately[5] refused to lay down any specific rule on the matter, so framed some of the crucial provisions of the law as to leave to the judiciary the widest possible measure of discretion, excluding any possibility of the judge having to consider

---

[1] See, for instance, Article 15 of the Argentine Code.

[2] Some, like the Argentine Code, combine the two methods: see Article 15 and 16 of the Code.

[3] Article 7. Article 1 of Chinese Civil Code of 1929 provides that 'in the absence of applicable legal provisions, custom is to be followed, and, in the absence of custom, general principles of law'.

[4] Article 3 (2).

[5] Thus the first paragraph of the first draft of the new German Code contained a provision relating to situations for which the law does not provide a rule. The paragraph laid down that in such cases the judge shall have recourse to analogy, or, should that prove impossible, that he should draw his decision from principles resulting from the law as a whole. However, in subsequent deliberations in committee this paragraph was dropped on the ground, *inter alia*, that its substance was a matter of course. See Planck's *Kommentar zum bürgerlichen Gesetzbuch* (4th ed., 1913), vol. i, p. lix.

himself under a disability due to the apparent absence of a rule of law.[1] In England a long series of cases *primae impressionis* has shown clearly that novelty of action and absence of precedent are not in themselves a bar to recognition of a claim—a rule which Sir Frederick Pollock has called 'the first and greatest rule of our customary law'.[2] It may well happen that the novelty is of such a nature as to raise a matter of new principle to which, in the opinion of the judge, effect cannot be given without the interposition of the legislature. The only practical result of such a view is, obviously, not a refusal to give a decision, but the rejection of the claim. But, as mentioned above, the absence of a major principle governing the case is not easily assumed, however great may be the embarrassment[3] caused by the absence of direct precedent and authority.

§ 6. The Prohibition of 'non liquet' as an 'a priori' Legal Principle.

As a matter of fundamental legal principle, no express provision of the positive law is necessary in order to

[1] See, for instance, §§ 157, 162, 320, 815 of the Civil Code referring to 'good faith' (*Treu und Glauben*); §§ 138, 817, 819 referring to 'good morals' (*gute Sitten*); or §§ 315, 317, 319, 660, 745, 1430, 1619, 1668 referring to the free and equitable discretion of the judge. For numerous other examples see Stammler, *Die Lehre vom richtigen Recht* (1902), Book III; and Sauer, *Lehrbuch der Rechts- und Sozialphilosophie* (1929), pp. 236, 237.

[2] See this Note *in fine*. And see *Ashby* v. *White* (1704), 2 Ld. Raym. 938, where the majority of the Court clearly rejected the view, purporting to be based on Littleton, that the case was *primae impressionis*. This rejection was emphasized in a case which occurred about sixty years later, i.e. in *Chapman* v. *Pickersgill* (1762), 2 Wilson 146, where Pratt C.J. said: 'I wish never to hear this objection again. This action is for a tort; torts are infinitely various, not limited or confined, for there is nothing in nature but may be an instrument for mischief.' See also *Vaughan* v. *Menlove*, 3 Bing, N.S. 468; 4 Scott 244; *Le Caux* v. *Eden*, 2 Doug. 594 (1781); *Pasley* v. *Freeman*, 3 T.L.R. 51. Professor Winfield has clearly demonstrated in a recent study that mere novelty of action has never been in English law a conclusive objection to judicial recognition of any new remedy in general, and of an action in tort in particular: 'The Foundation of Liability in Tort', in *Columbia Law Review*, xxvii (1927), pp. 1–11. See also Smith, *Leading Cases*, 12th ed., vol. i, pp. 293–5; Allen, *Law in the Making* (2nd ed., 1930), pp. 178ff., who points out that the judge is not embarrassed by the absence of authority, 'for no authority is needed for the affirmation of the very essence of the law'; and see in particular Sir Frederick Pollock's note in Maine's *Ancient Law* (1920 ed.), p. 46: 'They [judges] are bound to find a decision for every case, however novel it may be . . . . Perhaps this is really the first and greatest rule of our customary law: that, failing a specific rule already ascertained and fitting the case in hand, the King's judges must find and apply the most reasonable rule they can, so that it be not inconsistent with any established principle . . . .' It is, therefore, somewhat difficult to see what are the authorities for the view of Le Fur in *Annuaire*, xxxiii (1927), p. 789, to the effect that the admissibility of *non liquet* is an Anglo-American, as distinguished from the continental, doctrine.

[3] See Allen, loc. cit., for interesting examples of such cases.

impose upon the judge the duty to give a decision, for or against the plaintiff, in every case brought before him. The completeness of the rule of law—as distinguished from the completeness of individual branches of statutory or customary law—is an *a priori* assumption of every system of law, not a prescription of positive law.[1] It is impossible, as a matter of *a priori* assumption, to conceive that it is the will of the law that its rule should break down as the result of the refusal to pronounce upon claims. There may be gaps in a statute or in the statutory law as a whole; there may be gaps in the various manifestations of customary law. There are no gaps in the legal system taken as a whole.[2] The first function of the legal organization of the community is the preservation of peace. Its fundamental precept is, 'there shall be no violence'. But this primordial duty of the law is abandoned and the reign of force is sanctioned as soon as it is admitted that the law may decline to function by refusing to adjudicate upon a particular claim, at least to the extent of pronouncing that violence must not be used for the purpose of enforcing it. Thus viewed, the function of the judge to pronounce in each case *quid est juris* is pre-eminently a practical one.[3] He is neither compelled nor permitted to resign himself to the *ignorabimus* which besets the perennial quest of the philosopher and the investigator in the domain of natural science. As a matter of legal history, courts and other law-administering agencies preceded formal codes and elaborate rules of law.[4] A most rudimentary system of law, with only a few abstract rules to guide the judge, may not inaccurately be said to be complete so long as there is a clear duty incumbent upon the members of the community to submit their disputes to a final decision of the judge. Under the normal rule of law it is inconceivable that a court should pronounce a *non liquet* because of the absence of law. This is certainly not so, because the positive law has provided a solution for all possible

---

[1] See here Radbruch, *Grundzüge der Rechtsphilosophie*, p. 188, and Bruns, 'Völkerrecht als Rechtsordnung', in *Z.f.a.ö.R. und V.* i (1), 25–31.

[2] Bergbohm, *Jurisprudenz und Rechtsphilosophie* (1892), pp. 372 ff., gave a lead to continental jurists in stressing this aspect of the completeness of the rule of law. He seems, however, to have made himself liable to misunderstanding (see Bruns, op. cit.) by propounding the view that the entire field of events and human actions is divided into the domain regulated by law and into a legal vacuum of mere facts (*rechtsleerer Tatsachenraum*).

[3] This is well put by Jethro Brown. The function of the judge, he says, is 'to decide disputes in accordance with law so far as that may be possible, but in any case somehow—in short, to administer justice': *The Austinian Theory of Law* (1906), p. 296.

[4] See below, p. 424.

emergencies. The reason for it is that law conceived as a means of ordering human life—unlike theoretical sciences including the science of law itself—cannot without abdicating its function concede that there are situations admitting of no answer.[1] This is so obvious that even in the centuries-old struggle between the formalistic and free interpretation of law—a struggle representing in the last two centuries the opposition between the historical and the so-called 'free' law schools—it was agreed on both sides that in no case may the judge refuse to give judgement on account of a supposed gap in the law. The only difference between the two schools was that, whereas the latter professed consciously to transform the law by way of creative interpretation, the former, regarding the law as a perfect and closed system, gave to their judicial activity the form of a strict application of existing rules.[2]

§ 7. The Positivist Doctrine and 'Lacunae' in International Law.

The insistence on the possibility of international tribunals having to refuse to adjudicate because of the absence of applicable provisions of the law draws its main strength from the so-called positivist doctrine in international law. It is principally in the domain of judicial settlement that the full implications of that doctrine reveal themselves. And it is in the very fact that the logical consummation of the positivist doctrine, as taught in international law, is the insistence on the admissibility of judicial *non liquet* that we can find its condemnation as a legal doctrine. Even if it had not been proven that the theoretical implications of the positivist teaching are a postulate not realized in the writings of the positivists themselves,[3] and even if the positivist doctrine in international law had not been shown to be inconsistent with the practice of States which it professes to follow, its ultimate conclusions in the field of the actual application of international law through the instrumentality of judicial settlement would in themselves signify its futility as a legal theory.

[1] See here the illuminating article by Del Vecchio, 'Essai sur les principes généraux du droit', in *Revue critique de législation et de jurisprudence*, xlv (1925), pp. 153–92, 231–52.

[2] Lauterpacht in *Economica*, 1928, pp. 293, 294. This point of view has since been given expression by writers like Fischer Williams, *Chapters*, pp. 50, 51; Brierly in *B.Y.*, 1930, pp. 127–32; and Bruns, op. cit. See also Redslob, *Das Problem des Völkerrechts* (1917), pp. 315–19, on the tendency of legal systems to exclude the possibility of a legal vacuum.

[3] See Lauterpacht, *Analogies*, pp. 51–71.

However, as the positivist doctrine is frequently adduced in support of this aspect of the doctrine of the limitation of the judicial function, it ought to be pointed out, by way of summary of a view fully developed elsewhere, that uncompromising positivist tendencies have, to say the least, recently relaxed their hold upon international lawyers. This weakening of their influence has been the unavoidable consequence of the process of developing international law from a mere registration and generalization, frequently arbitrary and exaggerated, of the practices of States to a system of rules drawing its reinforcements from *all* legitimately available sources of law.[1] The practice of States recognizes that international law both may and must avail itself of subsidiary sources for the purpose of settling disputes between States. It is especially in numerous arbitration conventions in which the contracting States define the law which ought to guide the arbitrator that this fact comes clearly to light. The writer has attempted in another place to examine this aspect of the practice of States, and has there arrived at the conclusion that there is a customary rule of international law to the effect that rules of law otherwise independent of customary and conventional international law are to be regarded as binding upon international tribunals in individual cases.[2] Article 38, paragraph 3, of the Statute of the Permanent Court of International Justice, which authorizes the judges to apply, in the absence of conventional or customary rules of international law, 'general principles of law recognised by civilised nations', was therefore of a revolutionary character only by reason of its almost universal acceptance both by the signatories to the Statute and in other international instruments.[3] That article is in essential har-

---

[1] It has been said by a competent authority that international law is theoretically able to solve every question, owing to the historical influence which the law of nature exercised over it since the beginning. (See Huber in *Annuaire*, xxxiii (1927), vol. ii, p. 764, and Redslob, *Das Problem des Völkerrechts* (1917), p. 316.) It is submitted, with deference, that there is no necessity for such explanation. The reason lies in the *horror vacui* common to all law, both municipal and international, although it may be true that international law is, more than any other legal system, in a position to fill its gaps as the result of its being able to draw upon the legal experience of all nations.

[2] Lauterpacht, op. cit., p. 63.

[3] The first three paragraphs of Article 38 have been incorporated in most of the general arbitration treaties concluded since the War. See, for instance, the Pan-American Arbitration Treaty, above, p. 38; as to Article 28 of the General Act, see p. 377. For examples of arbitral tribunals following the same sources of law, see p. 56, n. 1. And see *A.J.* xviii (1924), p. 179, for a statement of the law applied by the Mixed Claims Commission between the United States and Germany. It will be noted that Article 19 (1) of the

mony with the attitude which the law of every legal community (in so far as it refuses to sanction the use of force as a means of settling disputes between its members) must expect from its judiciary. It has definitely removed the last vestige of the possibility of gaps conceived as a deadlock in the way of the settlement of a dispute. The disinclination to repeat themselves ought not to prevent international lawyers from drawing repeated attention to the fact that the terms of Article 38 of the Statute, and in particular of its third paragraph, are broad enough to allow a legal answer to every dispute. The prohibition of *non liquet* is one of the 'general principles of law recognised by civilised nations'.

The student of international law must be warned that, particularly in respect of the matter under discussion, the positivist doctrine in international law resembles only in name the corresponding tendencies in other branches of law. One of the objects of positivism, both in international law and in municipal law, is to ensure that the judge shall have recourse only to sources of law clearly laid down in the express provisions of the law. According to both, the judge should be merely, as Montesquieu said, 'la bouche qui prononce les paroles de la loi'.[1] At the time of the French Revolution (which was responsible for much of the juristic formalism embodied in that maxim) the citizen regarded it as derogatory to his liberties to be subjected, not to the law of the State, but to the magistrate's personal judgement of what was right. Similarly international positivism thought it derogatory to the sovereignty of the State to subject it to rules other than those which it has expressly recognized. However, here the similarity ends, and the substantial difference begins.

In other branches of law it is of the essence of positivism that it denies the existence of gaps in the law. For only so is it in a position to insist that there is neither necessity nor justification for judicial activity other than that of the strict application of existing law. In the international sphere

---

Règlement adopted in 1875 by the Institute of International Law laid down as follows:

'An arbitral tribunal must not refuse a pronouncement on the ground that there is not sufficient law or facts to base the opinion upon.

'22. If it finds the pretensions of the parties unfounded, it ought to declare so and, if not limited by the *compromis*, to say what the law between the parties is.'

[1] *De l'Esprit des Lois*, Book I, 6.

positivism expresses itself principally in the assertion that there do exist *lacunae* in international law, and it postulates on this ground the exclusion of the judicial function in the sphere said to be affected by the absence of law. In municipal law positivism does not transgress the limits of a theory of the judicial function; in international law it is tantamount to the negation of the rule of law in a large and indeterminate sphere of relations.

There is, secondly, another difference which reveals even more clearly the exceptional character of the positivist idea in international law. In the field of general jurisprudence positivism denies the existence of gaps, and asserts its belief in the completeness of the existing law, because it is of the essence of its teaching to pay attention to what the law is, not to what the law ought to be. Now the idea of gaps in the law is largely a teleological idea; it is an expression of a view *de lege ferenda*.[1] Once the fundamental principle is accepted that the rule of law is complete, then an affirmation of a *lacuna* in the law amounts in fact to a statement that a result reached by the application of the law as it stands is unsatisfactory, and that a different solution is dictated by considerations of the purpose and unity of the law as a whole. In this sense it may be said that to assume that there is a gap is tantamount to suggesting how the *lacuna* should be filled. This is the reason why the absence of gaps and the completeness of the rule of law are, in the municipal sphere, a positivist postulate *par excellence*. In international law the position is reversed.

Caught in a dilemma in which he finds himself compelled to depart from the principal tenets of the original doctrine in municipal law, the adherent of the positivist doctrine in international law may retort that the teleological conception of gaps, as relating exclusively to an existing but unsatisfactory legal rule, does not obtain in the international community where the jurisdiction of adjudicating agencies is optional. It is not believed that this argument is legally sound. The duty to have recourse to judicial settlement may be imperfect in an imperfect system of law. But once it is accepted, either in general or in a particular arbitration treaty, there is accepted with it the fundamental principle of law which

---

[1] See on this point the very clear observations of Brierly in *B.Y.*, 1930, p. 128, and of Binder, *Philosophie des Rechts* (1925), pp. 976–85. And see below, pp. 86 et seq., 134.

imposes upon the judge the duty to give a decision in all circumstances.[1] This consequence cannot be avoided by the plea of the special character of international law and the lack of development of its rules—unless by the 'special character' of international law is meant that, in certain cases, the rule of law breaks down and the unilateral enforcement of claims takes its place.[2] In so far as positivism in international law denies these basic assumptions of the rule of law, it cannot be recognized as a sound legal doctrine. It is a misnomer to identify it with positivism as taught in other branches of law. In its ultimate conclusions it constitutes the very negation of its prototype in the sphere of municipal jurisprudence.

[1] We are therefore unable to accept the view put forward by Professor Politis that there is in this respect a difference between the judge within the State and an international tribunal. (*La Justice internationale*, 1924, p. 84.) Professor Politis does not produce any evidence in support of what he believes to be the practice of international tribunals and of arbitration-conventions. See also the Report of Mercier and de la Barra in *Annuaire*, xxxiii (2) (1927), p. 583. See pp. 127 et seqq. below.

[2] See below, Chapter XX.

CHAPTER IV
'LACUNAE' IN INTERNATIONAL LAW

§ 8. The Peculiarities of the Problem of Gaps in International Law. It has been submitted in the preceding chapter that the problem of gaps is fundamentally the same in international and municipal law. This does not mean, however, that the question does not present in international law certain peculiar features, a proper realization of which is necessary for an adequate understanding of the intricacies of the international judicial function. In what, then, does the peculiarity of the question of gaps in international law lie? It lies in the fact that in addition to the reasons which create that problem in municipal law there are a number of factors which aggravate it in the domain of international law.[1] They are the scarcity and indefiniteness of substantive rules of international law as the result of the comparative immaturity of the system, of the scarcity of precedent, both judicial and in the practice of States, and of the imperfections of the law-creating and law-amending process;[2] the difficulties in the ascertainment of the existing law and the consequent uncertainty as to the exact legal position in many of its branches; the revealed lack of agreement between States on a number of subjects; the emphasis laid on the principle of independence and presumptive freedom of action with the resulting check upon a creative interpretation of the existing law; and, finally, the existence of substantive rules like the validity of treaties concluded under duress which, although forming part of positive international law, nevertheless constitute such a departure from general principles of law that they tend to create the feeling that there exists a gap which may well be remedied. The peculiar nature of the question of gaps in international law may be admitted without denying

---

[1] On the question of gaps in international law see, in addition to the authorities cited above, p. 35, n. 1, Trendelenburg, *Lücken im Völkerrecht* (1870); Zitelmann, *Die Unvollkommenheit des Völkerrechts* (1919); Burckhardt, *Die Unvollkommenheit des Völkerrechts* (1923), and in *Organisation der Rechtsgemeinschaft* (1927), pp. 377–82; Verdross, *Die Verfassung der Völkerrechtsgemeinschaft* (1926), pp. 69–75.

[2] The actual content of international law is even more meagre than may appear from its presentation in text-books, when we consider that most rules of international law are concerned with a definition of subjective rights established by particular or general treaty. Rights of this nature would hardly appear in a presentation of a system of municipal law which is composed of abstract rules of an objective nature.

its essential identity with the analogous problem in municipal law, or asserting that international law consists of gaps, or denying on this account its legal nature.[1]

The peculiarities of the problem of gaps in international law will now be considered.

§ 9. Genuine Interpretation in International Law.

There arise, in the first instance, situations which, although covered by a general rule and principle of international law, are not, owing to the defects of international law-making, in fact specifically regulated by a concrete law. They correspond largely to a category of gaps in municipal law which are attributed to the oversight, lack of foresight, or, generally, to the imperfections of the law-making agency. In such cases the process of filling the gap is regarded as a legitimate realization of the will of the legislator. Austin refers to them as gaps which may be filled by genuine as distinguished from spurious interpretation.[2] In German jurisprudence they are

---

[1] There are a number of writers who deny the legal character of international law, not on the ground of the absence of a legislature, of a judiciary, and of an executive, but on the ground that its rules are scarce, indefinite, and only superficially regulating the life of States. This is, for instance, the view of Hold-Ferneck, who expresses the opinion that international law does not in fact constitute a legal order, for, he says, whereas in the State legal regulation affects important matters and leaves outside its province minor matters, the situation is reversed in international law ('Anerkennung und Selbstbindung', in *Zeitschrift für Rechtsphilosophie*, iv (1929), pp. 179 ff.). The same reason has induced Felix Somló, a distinguished positivist jurist, to deny the legal nature of international law (*Juristische Grundlehre* (2nd ed., 1927), pp. 160 ff.). In his opinion international society could only then be regarded as a true legal community if, by dint of numerous rules, it could succeed in regulating a relatively wide field of relations between States. If, he says, the rules by which the State regulates individual conduct did not go further than those by which international law regulates the conduct of States, no one would venture to assert the existence of the rule of law within the State. See also Baumgarten, *Die Wissenschaft vom Recht und ihre Methode*, 2 vols. (1920–2). But see for a criticism of this point of view Walz, *Wesen des Völkerrechts und Kritik der Völkerrechtsleugner* (1930), p. 197.

Possibly the scarcity of rules of international law could be partly explained by reference to the sociological rule, according to which the larger the community subject to law the smaller is the compass of detailed regulation (Simmel, *Soziologie*, pp. 473, 474). This means that, as international law regulates the relations of a more comprehensive community than that regulated by municipal law, both the intensity and the amount of its rules are smaller. This explanation seems also to be in accordance with that feature of law which lies in the possibility of its universal application. It follows that the larger the community the smaller is the possible number of such rules. With this view as to the necessarily general character of the rules of international law should be contrasted the opinion of Anzilotti, *Corso* (3rd ed., French translation), p. 46, according to which, in view of the absence of a regular legislative process, rules of international law are mostly and necessarily particular in their application.

[2] *Jurisprudence* (4th ed., 1873), i. 1023, 1028.

given by some writers the designation of real gaps (*echte Lücken*), as distinguished from spurious gaps which are the product of the critical attitude of the lawyer dissatisfied with a clearly expressed provision of the law.[1] Gaps of this description arise within the State when the existing law is confronted with new economic or social developments which it is found necessary to bring within the orbit of legal principles of more general nature than the rules of law directly applicable. Another variation of gaps within this category arises out of sheer inadvertence or lack of foresight in legislative enactments when the legislator is guilty of obvious inconsistencies, or of a failure to provide for contingencies directly arising out of the provisions of the law which ought to have been foreseen at the time when the rules in question were enacted. All these varieties of gaps occur in the sphere of international law. For reasons peculiar to the society of States they occur here more frequently than elsewhere.

(*a*) *Imperfections of Conventional International Law.* Gaps due to deficiencies and inconsistencies in drafting are more frequent in international law where the necessity of arriving at a solution by way of compromise results in law-making conventions whose meaning is deliberately obscure. There are treaties which, under cover of a mutual consensus, in fact register an agreement to disagree. In other cases the circumstances attending the concluding stages of international conferences produce treaties whose draftmanship compares unfavourably with that of national laws; for these go through a series of readings in the legislative chambers and in committees.[2] Even carefully and competently prepared international documents show gaps of this nature. Thus the Statute of the Permanent Court of International Justice, a document carefully prepared by an authoritative committee of jurists, contains such gaps as the absence of any direct reference to Advisory Opinions, or to resignation of judges,

---

[1] See Zitelmann, *Die Lücken im Rechte* (1903), pp. 24 ff.; Burckhardt, *Die Organisation der Rechtsgemeinschaft* (1927), pp. 105, 106.

[2] For an example of such a mistake see Annex IV of Article 190, paragraph 2, of the Treaty of St. Germain referred to and discussed by Ehrlich, 'L'interprétation des traités', in *Recueil des Cours* (1929), pp. 52, 53. See the case *Polyxene Plessa* v. *Turkish Government*, decided on 9 February 1928, by the Graeco-Turkish Mixed Arbitral Tribunal, in which the Tribunal acted on the view that the wording of the treaty did not reproduce with necessary precision the intention of the parties (*Recueil*, viii. 224, and *Annual Digest*, 1927–8, Case No. 299).

or to the amendment of the Statute.[1] There must also be mentioned gaps occasioned by obvious discrepancies in bilingual treaties. Even the Covenant of the League of Nations[2] and the Statute[3] of the Permanent Court of International Justice are not free from such blemishes.

(b) *Static Character of Customary International Law.* Of particular importance is that aspect of the problem of gaps which arises out of the defective adaptation of existing law to new developments. The different branches of the law of war, especially those relating to contraband and blockade and to submarine and air-warfare, are typical illustrations of this feature of international law. Prior to the World War, the entire body of laws of war, as partly codified by the First and Second Hague Conferences, was under the sway of the continental distinction between the State, as the formal subject of the relation of war, and its subject. It is sufficient to refer to the maintenance, although in an emaciated form, of the distinction between different kinds of contraband, the rules as to requisitions in occupied territory defined by the needs of the occupant's armed forces as distinguished from those of its entire population, the treatment of enemy merchantmen

---

[1] The last-mentioned example suggests that there may be gaps which are deliberate. Thus the mandates under Article 22 of the Covenant of the League of Nations do not contain provisions as to the remuneration of a mandatory or the methods of the termination of a mandate after fulfilment of its object. The 'gap' in the Statute of the Court consisting in the absence of an age-limit for judges may be an intentional one. And see, as to the so-called 'gaps' in the Covenant, below, p. 84.

[2] Thus, for instance, in paragraph 4 of Article 4 the English text contains the words 'at its meetings' which do not occur in the French text; in paragraph 2 of Article 11 the words '*par suite*' in the French text do not occur in the English text. The French text of Article 14 refers to the advisory function of the Court in the mandatory terms 'la Cour donnera un avis', whereas the English text lays down that 'the Court may give an advisory opinion'. See *Annuaire*, xxxiv (1928), p. 437, and Steiger, *Die Unparteilichkeit bei Schlichtung von Staatskonflikten* (1929), pp. 91–3. In the wording of Article 18 the English text imposes the duty of registration on the contracting party, whereas the French text is so worded as to impose that duty upon the Secretariat; in Article 23, paragraph 2, the English text refers to 'all such international bureaux and all commissions', whereas the French text speaks of 'tous autres bureaux internationaux et toutes commissions'. For minor discrepancies see Schücking-Wehberg, pp. 160, 188, 388, 672, 766.

[3] Thus, for instance, the French text of Article 16 of the Statute speaks of 'les membres de la Cour', whereas the English text refers to 'the ordinary members of the Court'. See also, as to the differences in regard to Articles 38 (4) and 45, the minutes of the Committee of Jurists in 1929 entrusted with the revision of the Statute (Doc. C. 166, M. 66. 1929. V. pp. 62, 65). On the question of interpretation of bilingual treaties see Ehrlich, op. cit., pp. 98 ff.; *P.C.I.J.*, Series A, No. 2, p. 19; and *Annual Digest*, 1925–6, Cases Nos. 281 and 282.

at the outbreak of war, the treatment of enemy private property on land. The effective persistence of this view, which was in itself evidence of a disregard of the tendencies and realities of modern warfare, resulted in a number of 'gaps' which could be filled only by the crude process of setting aside the existing law.

However, the existence of gaps as the result of the deficient process of adaptation is not confined to the laws of war. It is equally acute in the international law of peace. It is sufficient to mention the rigidity with which it adheres to the three miles' limit of territorial waters regardless of the large variety of interests to be protected by the littoral State, or to the rule of jurisdictional immunities of States regardless of the nature of the particular State activity.[1] There is an obvious relation of cause and effect between this lack of adaptation and the fact that international law is pre-eminently under the domination of abstract principles of great generality. Many of these general principles may have been adequate in the formative period of international law. Their static character in the subsequent period of growing complexity of international relations has tended to emphasize their irrelevance to the concrete situations created by new developments. Thus international law has fully accepted the principle of responsibility of States, but the number of clear and agreed rules in which that principle is applied to possible causes of action proves, upon analysis, to be small. It lays down the general principle of respect for private rights in the matter of state succession, but it does not say what these private rights are.

(c) *Absence of Co-ordinating Agencies.* Finally, in this category are included gaps in which apparently contradictory rules, or actually conflicting competencies, equally recognized by international law, result in situations calling for their solution for reference to major juridical principles. Thus international law, by conferring upon States in the matter of nationality a large degree of freedom of action, sanctions indirectly the institution of double nationality, but at the same time fails to provide rules for the solution of conflicts, possibly of a grave character, arising out of the fact that two States may claim diplomatic protection over the same individual or impose upon him conflicting duties. It will be

---

[1] See here the article by Dickinson in *Michigan Law Review*, xxv (1926–7), pp. 622–44. As to air law, see below, p. 301.

shown later how international tribunals solve some of the difficulties thus created.[1] Similarly, international law indirectly sanctions statelessness, but it fails to provide rules for conflicts like those arising out of the claim of one State that another should consent to receive a deported person whom it has denationalized.[2] It subjects the alien to the unrestricted territorial supremacy of the receiving State, upon which it imposes at the same time the duty to respect his property, but it provides no answer to the question of the responsibility of the State for measures of confiscation of property affecting the alien and the subject alike.[3] Or, to mention a more specific instance, it grants to consular authorities, in countries with extraterritorial jurisdiction, exclusive jurisdiction over the subjects of their State, and it confers on the army of occupation the exclusive jurisdiction over persons belonging to it. But it does not solve the conflict arising out of the fact that a person belonging to the army of occupation may be a subject of the State enjoying the rights of extraterritoriality. Thus when the Permanent Court of Arbitration, in the *Casablanca* case, was confronted with a dispute between Germany and France arising out of a conflict of jurisdiction of this nature, the Tribunal, in its award of 22 May 1909,[4] while deciding in favour of France, refused to lay down a general rule in the matter. 'The conflict of jurisdictions', it said, 'cannot be decided by an absolute rule which would in a general manner accord the preference to either of the two concurrent jurisdictions.'[5]

In all these three groups of case the gaps are the result of the imperfections of the law-making process. They are not a deliberate creation of the law. The filling of these gaps may be regarded as being legitimately within the scope of judicial activity. Reasons peculiar to international law have rendered the possibilities of this aspect of the function of international tribunals wider than in any other branch of law. There is therefore in international law a particularly wide scope for bona fide genuine interpretation. So long as there is no departure

---

[1] See below, p. 126.

[2] See Fischer Williams, *Chapters*, pp. 123–46. And see below, p. 300.

[3] See Fischer Williams, ibid., pp. 147–87, and Fachiri in *B.Y.*, 1925, pp. 159–71, and the bibliography noted in Oppenheim, i. 294, n. 2. And see below, p. 121.

[4] Scott, *Hague Court Reports*, p. 111.

[5] Ibid., p. 114. See also Rousseau in *R.G.* xxxvii (1930), p. 438, and von Bar in *Das Werk von Haag*, ed. by Schücking, 2nd series, ii (1927), pp. 45, 46.

from an express rule of international law the interpretation is 'genuine', even if recourse is had to a most abstract and general rule, and even if, as the result, the function of interpretation seems to assume the character of judicial legislation proper. It will be shown in one of the chapters which follow in what manner international tribunals exercise this function.

§ 10. Gaps due to Revealed Discrepancies in the Practice of States. There are in international law a number of subjects which, although obviously falling within the domain of matters subject to regulation by international law, cannot be said to be actually so regulated, because the practice of States shows, in respect of them, conflicting legal views based in part on conflicting interests. This category of gaps is well illustrated by the difference of views revealed at the First Codification Conference at The Hague in 1930 in regard to such subjects as the breadth of territorial waters, or certain aspects of the responsibility of States for injuries done on their territory to the persons and property of aliens, or certain questions of nationality. The differences, already referred to, of legal views which obtained before the World War in regard to certain matters of prize law offer another example. In some of these matters the divergencies are clearly manifested and accentuated by an actual or supposed clash of interests. In others the lack of agreement is due less to any divergence of interests than to mere discrepancies of practice resulting from historical peculiarities and purely accidental reasons. There is no underlying conflict of interests behind the fact that American and English Courts claim the jurisdiction, as a matter of legal right, in regard to criminal acts committed on board a foreign vessel stationed in American and English ports, and refrain from the exercise of such jurisdiction, as a matter of international comity, except in cases of grave crimes where the public order in the port may be disturbed, whereas the Courts of many other countries, adhering to the so-called French rule, refuse to exercise such general jurisdiction—again except in regard to grave offences—as a matter of legal obligation. There is no actual clash of interests in the differing practice of various States in regard to the treatment of foreign public ships engaged in commerce; or in regard to the immunities to be granted to diplomatic envoys in respect of acts done in their private capacity; or in the matter of the discrepancies, so clearly revealed in the *Lotus* case,[1] in the practice of States in regard to the question of jurisdiction over foreigners for crimes committed abroad.

§ 11. Judicial Activity and Gaps due to Discrepancies of Practice.

What is the legal position in respect of these unequivocal discrepancies? If consent is the essential condition for the existence of a rule of international law, then a revealed and deliberate absence of agreement should clearly point to the existence of a gap on the subject. In fact, this category of gaps is regarded by some as the main instance of *lacunae* in international law.[2] It is submitted that this view can be adopted only subject to the qualification that the gap is virtually filled when the States recognize the authority of obligatory judicial settlement. The absence of agreement does not mean that the States in question desire the controversial subject to remain altogether outside the sphere of law, so as to render it impossible for the judge to decide the case. Such a desire could not in any case produce legal effects. The utmost that can be said is that its consequence would be to leave the controversial subject out of the sphere of express legal regulation; with the result that, in the absence of an agreed rule, the judge would have to reject the demand of the plaintiff State on the ground that no evidence of a rule of international law limiting the freedom of action of the defendant State has been produced. The fundamental principle of the formal completeness of the international legal system cannot be affected by the mere fact of a number of States disagreeing on a particular subject.

However, it is not believed that the fact of discrepancy must necessarily have the result of reducing the judicial activity to passive reliance on the principle of the formal completeness of international law, a principle which, as will be shown, is not always calculated to yield results satisfactory from the point of view of justice and of the wider purpose of the law.[3] There is no reason why an international tribunal, confronted with a dispute involving a controversial subject of this nature, should not disregard altogether the conflicting views and proceed to give judgement by reference to a more general principle of international law, on which there exists a substantial measure of agreement. Thus, to give an example

---

[1] *P.C.I.J.*, Series A, No. 10.
[2] See Fischer Williams, *Chapters*, pp. 52 ff.   [3] See below, pp. 85 et seqq.

from the field of State responsibility, an international tribunal confronted with the question of the international responsibility of a State for the acts of an official committed outside his authority, but under cover of his official character (i.e. within the general scope of his employment), would hardly refuse to give a decision, or to admit a claim, for the mere reason that there is a divergence of views on the matter as clearly revealed during The Hague Codification Conference in 1930.[1] It would have recourse to such international decisions as exist on the matter.[2] In their absence it would base its judgement on those general principles of State responsibility in regard to which there exists already a certain measure of agreement. In the atmosphere of an international conference labouring under the assertiveness of the triple doctrine of sovereignty, equality, and unanimity, unessential differences, dictated by considerations of passing political interests, are elevated to the authority of a conflict of legal principles. It is in that atmosphere that differences of this nature are able to produce a deadlock. No such deadlock is likely or admissible before an international tribunal governed by the paramount duty of arriving at a decision governed by rules of law of general application. Thus the divergence of views on the legal position in regard to the so-called plea of non-discrimination in the treatment of aliens has not prevented, and is not likely to prevent, arbitral tribunals from deciding disputes involving this issue.[3] It is one of the chief advantages, as it is the unavoidable result, of submission to judicial settlement that disputes are no longer decided by the attitude of the disputants—even if that attitude amounts to a disagreement, revealed before the occurrence of the dispute, as to the position of international law on the matter—in regard to the merits of the dispute, but by reference to explicit or latent principles of law.[4] It cannot be said that by assuming in such

---

[1] See Borchard in *A.J.* xxiv (1930), pp. 529–31.

[2] See Borchard, op. cit., p. 530, n. 17, for reference to some of them.

[3] See below, p. 121.

[4] It may therefore be necessary to scrutinize closely the view which sees in the recent attempts at codification undertaken under the auspices of the League of Nations a source of danger for judicial settlement on the ground that codification conferences, such as the First Hague Codification Conference in 1930, tend to give official and deliberate expression to divergent views of States. It is pointed out that, whereas these divergences were before the Conference so inarticulate that an international tribunal could afford to disregard them, this is no longer possible after the only result of the Conference has been to lend to these disagreements the authority of formal declarations of sovereign States. This view is rebutted in the text. Thus in the matter of State responsibility the

cases jurisdiction on the merits, an international tribunal assumes the function of a legislator. For its decision is given on legal grounds possessing a degree of generality transcending the individual issue before the tribunal and agreed upon by members of the international community, including the States in dispute.

§ **12. Spurious Interpretation in International Law.** While the filling of 'real' gaps by the process of 'genuine' interpretation of the existing law, with a view to giving effect to the intention of the law-making agencies, falls within the normal scope of judicial activity and has occasioned only mild controversy, the question of 'unreal' gaps which, it is said, can be filled only by recourse to 'spurious' interpretation is a more difficult one. An unreal gap exists when the solution dictated by a clear rule of positive law is found by the judge to be unsatisfactory from the point of view of the major purpose of the law conceived as a whole. To fill it, in the opinion of many, is in fact to override the existing law and to embark upon judicial law-making pure and simple. It is this aspect of gaps which has become the object of controversy between the various schools on the nature of judicial activity. The cleavage of opinion is well illustrated by the fact that, in the terminology of continental legal philosophy, the 'real' gaps of the positivists are referred to by the Free Law School as mere textual gaps, while the 'unreal' gaps of the former appear to the latter as material gaps.[1] Probably the difference between these two views is in most cases a relative one, as is in the last resort the difference between the

abortive Hague Conference of 1930 showed unanimous agreement in regard to the *bases* of State responsibility, and an international tribunal may safely be permitted to deduce the specific rule from the generally agreed principle.

It is typical of the exaggeration which characterizes some of the discussion on matters of international law that, while codification is regarded by some as an essential condition of obligatory judicial settlement (see above, p. 54), others have, for reasons indicated above, begun to regard it as dangerous to that very cause. In the present state of international organization the possibilities of codification are undoubtedly limited, and the major part of the task of developing and clarifying existing law devolves therefore upon international tribunals. There are in *gremio juris gentium* as it exists to-day the elements for such development and clarification, although the somewhat excessive zeal of the advocates of codification has had the result of obscuring these possibilities. See Brierly in *B.Y.*, 1931, pp. 1–12, on the possibilities of codification in the light of the experience of the Conference in 1930. On the vanishing prospects of codification, in the light of the Resolution of the Twelfth Assembly in 1931, see Hudson in *A.J.*, xxvi (1932), pp. 137–43.

[1] See Kantorowicz and Patterson in *Columbia Law Review*, xxviii (1928), pp. 699–706.

activity of the legislator and the judge, or the answer to the question whether a case is covered by existing principle or not.[1] Cases may occur in which a decision which at first sight is *contra legem* can be brought within the pale of law conceived as a whole. Such a decision need not necessarily be the result of a purely subjective discretion and individual idiosyncrasy; it may, when regard is had to the entirety of legal and social relationships within the community, be described as fulfilling what the legislator would have intended if he could have foreseen the changes occurring in the life of the community. Judicial freedom need not, as has been said before, be identified with the reign of arbitrariness. It is freedom within the law conceived as something more comprehensive than the sum total of its positive rules.

However serious may be the controversy regarding the limits of judicial freedom within the State, and however pregnant with consequences this controversy may be from the point of view of its effects on legal philosophy in general, it is clear that the opportunities within the State for the exercise of judicial discretion in the direction of filling gaps *de lege ferenda* are not frequent. There is not only the bulk of the existing law to be reckoned with[2]—that would not in itself be an obstacle in the way of the exercise of judicial freedom. The real check lies in two facts. The first is that judicial freedom is in municipal society not the main or normal instrument for filling the gaps *de lege ferenda*; it is the legislature which is normally charged with this function, and which may do it openly and avowedly in cases in which judicial law-making would amount to a clear usurpation of powers. The other fact is that, in the modern State, municipal law taken as a whole represents a mature system of law, in which the contractual and voluntary basis of the binding force of law has given way to the generally accepted idea of the subjection of the individual to the law; in which the law embraces all relations which seem to be conveniently capable of legal regulation; in which the recourse to violence for the

---

[1] See below, pp. 100 et seqq. 'It would be no easy task even in theory to set a boundary between a new principle and the extension of an old one, and practice shews that in many cases it is impossible': Winfield in *Columbia Law Review*, xxvii (1927), p. 9, with special reference to the dictum of Ashurst, J., in *Le Caux* v. *Eden* (1781), 2 Doug. 594.

[2] 'Insignificant is the power of innovation of any judge, when compared with the bulk and pressure of the rules that hedge him on every side'—says Judge Cardozo, op. cit., p. 136, himself no grudging interpreter of 'the field of discretion that remains' (p. 141).

purpose of giving effect to claims is reduced to a minimum; and in which a substantial approximation of law to morals and to general principles of law is not only an ever-present postulate, but also a matter of actual occurrence.[1]

Neither of these factors obtains with equal intensity in the international society. The absence, and its implications, of an appropriate legislative agency are discussed in another part of this book.[2] In this place we are concerned with the low degree of maturity of international law as compared with that of the law within the State. The lower that degree of maturity—in regard to the emphasis on the external character of the law, its comprehensiveness, its abhorrence of *vis privata*, and its approximation to the canons of morality and general principles of law—the more are cases likely to occur in which the solution given by positive international law is regarded as unsatisfactory. Thus we find writers who regard the existence of the wide field of so-called matters of domestic jurisdiction as indicating a serious gap in international law.[3] Others regard as a gap the legal admissibility of war, as for instance did Trendelenburg, who first dealt in a comprehensive manner with the problem of gaps. 'It is a radical gap in international law,' he said, 'that war can break out at all.'[4] The disregard of the vitiating influence of duress upon the validity of treaties may be mentioned as a further example. In general, every shortcoming of international law *qua* law can be regarded as coming within this category of gaps. It is clear that in an imperfectly organized political community like the society of States the field of this class of gap is particularly large. It is larger than in municipal law not only in bulk, but also in intensity. Within the State it relates to possible improvements in occasional shortcomings in the existing law; in international law it affects some of its fundamental aspects.

§ 13. Judicial Activity and Spurious Interpretation. How much of these gaps *de lege ferenda* is the international judge in a position to fill, while remaining at the same time loyal to

---

[1] 'In general, law cannot depart far from ethical custom nor lag far behind it . . . . One need but look at a mass of legal precepts that make up the bulk of legal systems to-day in order to see that they are anything but authoritative promulgations of ethical custom': Pound, *Law and Morals* (2nd ed., 1926), p. 115.

[2] See below, pp. 245–58.

[3] See, for instance, Mulder in *R.I.*, 3rd ser., vii (1926), p. 560.

[4] *Lücken im Völkerrecht* (1870), p. 32.

his judicial function of applying the existing law? As these gaps touch some of the typical—and generally regarded as funda-mental—aspects of present-day international law, his discretion in filling them is more limited than in municipal law. Thus, to give one instance, it may appear to some as a serious gap that an international tribunal should be compelled to give a decision which in effect confers a premium upon the aggressive disposi-tion of a State to the disadvantage of other States who refrained from resorting to warlike action in order to enforce a demand. However, so long as war or reprisals are a recognized means of enforcing claims, it is difficult to see how recourse to them can adversely affect the legal rights of a State. The Permanent Court of Arbitration was actually confronted with that problem in the *Venezuelan Preferential Claims* case in 1904.[1] It was contended before the Tribunal, on behalf of the States which had refrained from participating in the coercive measures applied against Venezuela, that to recognize the claim for priority would in fact amount to encouraging recourse to force in a manner contrary to the necessities of peace and to the obligations of the parties to the dispute bound by the first article of the Convention of 1899 for the Pacific Settle-ment of International Disputes. It was pointed out that an award in favour of the States claiming priority would in fact confer a premium upon the State which forestalls another in the application of force. 'Il ne suffira pas,' it was said in the French 'Mémoire', 'd'être violent, il faudra l'avoir été le premier; ce sera une prime à la vitesse.'[2] The Tribunal refused to let itself be guided by these considerations,[3] and based its decision on the interpretation of the several protocols signed in 1903 between Venezuela and the blockading

---

[1] For a summary of this case and the award see Scott, *Hague Court Reports*, pp. 54 ff. For an analysis of the award see von Bar in *Das Werk von Haag*, ed. by Schücking, 2nd ser., i (1917), pp. 253–307, and Mallarmé in *R.G.* xiii (1906), pp. 423–500.

[2] *Mémoire français*, pp. 42, 43. See the *Preliminary Brief on behalf of Venezuela*, p. 109. And see the French 'Mémoire' as printed in *Proceedings of the Venezuelan Arbitration*, U.S.A., 58th Congress, 3rd Session, Doc. No. 119, pp. 886, 887, and the argument of Mr. Wayne M. Veagh on behalf of the United States, ibid., pp. 1120, 1121.

[3] 'Whereas the Tribunal considers itself absolutely incompetent to give a decision as to the character or the nature of the military operations undertaken by Germany, Great Britain and Italy against Venezuela. Whereas also the tribunal of arbitration was not called upon to decide whether the three blockading Powers had exhausted all pacific methods in their dispute with Venezuela in order to prevent the employment of force': Award, op. cit., pp. 58, 59.

Powers in which the customs' revenues of two Venezuelan ports were allocated for the purpose of satisfying the claims of the Powers, as well as on the interpretation of the agreement between Venezuela and the so-called neutral Powers. Only by dint of disregarding the effects of a process, fully recognized by law as obtaining at that time, could the Tribunal have arrived at a decision unfavourable to the claims of the blockading Powers. Sir Robert Finlay, who appeared on behalf of Great Britain, said in his opening argument that 'nothing more fatal to arbitration could be conceived than any attempt to ignore the legitimate consequences of war'.[1]

International tribunals are, for reasons already stated, more frequently than municipal courts confronted with problems of this nature. They are in a position of great responsibility in all cases in which a rule of positive international law deviates from the path of just law, and thus creates the appearance of a 'gap'. Such cases stimulate the tendency to interpretation in which a decision apparently going beyond the existing law reveals itself upon analysis as derived from a major principle of law or from the intention of the parties. Two cases decided by the Permanent Court of International Justice will illustrate this point. The Covenant of the League of Nations provides, in its Article 5, that apart from matters of procedure, appointment of commissions, and cases expressly laid down in the Covenant—for instance, in Article 15, paragraph 6, and in Article 16, paragraph 4— unanimity is required for the decisions[2] of the Council and the Assembly. It would thus seem that, having regard both to the interpretative rule *inclusio unius est exclusio alterius*, and to general rules of equality of States resulting in the requirement of unanimity, Article 5 of the Covenant leaves no room for ambiguity. However, this explicit provision apparently creates a gap when gauged by the major legal principle that, by the very nature of the thing, unanimity including the parties to the dispute cannot be required when a body acts in a judicial capacity. In its Twelfth Advisory Opinion concerning the interpretation of the Treaty of Lausanne in the matter of the boundary between Iraq and Turkey, the Court adopted the view, which is of

---

[1] Award, op. cit., p. 1239.
[2] Probably as distinguished from mere recommendations. See on this question Oppenheim, i. 327, 328, and Fischer Williams, *Chapters*, p. 432.

far-reaching importance for the interpretation of the Covenant in general,[1] that the clear provisions of the Covenant must, in the case before it, be read subject to the general principle that no one is judge in his own suit.[2] In the Advisory Opinion concerning the Danzig Railway Officials, the Court gave its *imprimatur* to the view, which twenty years before would have appeared as revolutionary, that individuals can under certain conditions directly acquire rights under international law.[3] In this case the Court, while professing to adhere to the orthodox doctrine,[4] based its opinion on the intention of the parties. But in doing this it modified a rule hitherto regarded as one grounded on a basic principle of international law.[5] The alternative attitude would have consisted in interpreting the intention of the parties by reference to an accepted doctrine of international law. Both Advisory Opinions show that, if only the decision can be brought within the frame of a major legal principle or the will of the parties, it is rendered in conformity with existing international law. This leaves to the international judge a considerable scope of discretion, so long as he does not admittedly go beyond the limits of the existing law. His position is in this respect the same as that of the judge within the State, although, owing to the shortcomings of international law *qua* law, particular juridical restraint and particular judicial valour are required in the dangerous course of steering between the Scylla of the complacent assumption of the completeness of the law and the Charybdis of the attempt at fulfilling the function of an international legislature.

[1] See, for instance, Articles 10, 11, 13 (paragraph 4), 15 (paragraph 8), 16 (paragraph 2), and 17 of the Covenant. Under all these articles there is a possibility of the Council acting in a judicial capacity, in particular in regard to the interpretation of the Covenant.

[2] *P.C.I.J.*, Series B, No. 12, p. 32.

[3] Ibid., No. 15, p. 18.

[4] There are writers who interpret this Opinion as expressly confirming the traditional doctrine on the position of individuals in international law. See Beckett in *B.Y.*, 1930, p. 4.

[5] It will be noticed that the orthodox position of international law in regard to rights of individuals and their direct enforcement through the agency of international tribunals is regarded by many as a 'gap' in international law. See *Annuaire*, xxxiii (2) (1927), p. 629, in which the *rapporteurs* speak of 'une lacune grave dans l'organisation judiciaire internationale au point de vue de la protection des intérêts privés, considérés dans le plan international'.

CHAPTER V

THE PROBLEM OF THE JUDICIAL FUNCTION IN INTERNATIONAL LAW

§ 14. The Formal and Material Completeness of International Law. It has been shown in the preceding chapters that, so long as we are content to apply to international law the fundamental principles of jurisprudence and the general principles of law, there are no 'gaps' in international law, if that term is meant to imply that in certain cases an international tribunal is obliged or entitled to refuse to give a decision on the ground that there is no recognized rule of international law applicable to the case. There is always open to the Tribunal the possibility of rejecting the claim on the ground of the absence of an agreed rule of law supporting the demand. In doing so the Tribunal may proceed on a number of rules of varying degrees of elasticity. It may act on the view that the freedom and the independence of States are the basis of international law, and that no claim aiming at a restriction of a State's freedom of action can be recognized unless it is based on an expressly agreed rule of international law. It may adopt as a guiding principle the rule that whatever is not expressly prohibited is permitted. It may, by a rigid adherence to the maxim *qui utitur jure suo alterum non laedit*, reject any claim challenging the exercise of rights recognized by the law. With the help of these formal rules and principles it may be possible to deal—by rejecting it—with every claim for which there is no express and explicit warrant in the law. Very frequently this method of dealing with claims will be in accordance with the judicial function of international judges as distinguished from that of legislators or mediators. As often as not it will also be in accordance with the purpose of the law, whose silence may be as emphatic as any of its explicit pronouncements, and in which the absence of restriction may as a rule be legitimately interpreted as a conceded permission of freedom of action.

However, there exists a danger, ever present in the administration of justice in general and in international law in particular, that a rigid application of tests based on these formal principles may, by reducing the activity of the judge to a merely automatic function, defeat the very end of law.

Undoubtedly it secures what may be called the formal justiciability of disputes, inasmuch as it produces a judicial pronouncement on the legal merits of any claim whatsoever submitted to a Court. But at the same time it may make us forget that the necessary aim of any legal system is also material completeness. In order to achieve that material completeness the judge must consider not only the letter of the law, but also its spirit and purpose. While, therefore, rejecting the view that there is a practical or theoretical possibility of an international Court being compelled, in the exercise of its judicial duty, to decline jurisdiction on account of the absence of a legal rule applicable to the case, and while rejecting also the distinction between legal and non-legal disputes as based on that possibility, it is important to bear in mind the problem which in this respect confronts international judicial settlement, and the dangers which beset it in the fulfilment of its task.

The view that there are gaps in law is theoretically false, and practically dangerous only if it is understood as meaning that the legal order as a whole may break down in cases of supposed insufficiency of law for the reason that the judge is in such cases entitled or obliged to abdicate his judicial function by refusing to give a legal decision. But if it is false to assume that there exists a gap in the sense that the legal order contains no solution at all, it is equally false to assume that there exist no gaps in any sense whatsoever, and that the necessary consequence of the presumed silence of the law is a rigidly negative attitude towards interests claiming legal protection. The conception of the completeness of the legal order is a beneficent notion inasmuch as it excludes the anarchical possibilities of a *non liquet*. But there is little doubt that this very notion may obstruct the path of the law by being used as a justification for the renunciation on the part of the judge of his power to apply the existing law in a just, creative, and scientific manner. It is easy to say that as there is no gap in the law, its silence in a particular case must be regarded as having a decisive and negative effect on the claim before the Court. Such reasoning may frequently be correct. But, at times, it may be an expression of intellectual inertia or of short-sightedness. It is the idea that there *do* exist gaps in law—material gaps in the teleological sense as judged from the point of view of the general purpose of the law, and as distinguished from formal gaps identical with a break in the continuity of the legal order—it is this idea which has throughout the ages been a powerful and indispensable factor in the development of law, in enacting remedial legislation, in the daring application of general principles to altogether new facts of social development, in ingenious but indispensable 'distinguishing' of cases, in creating fruitful fictions. How could law have developed if the assumed absence of gaps expressive of its formal completeness were to be identified with the absence of gaps pointing to material perfection? How could law develop if the fact that there is always a formal 'yes' or a 'no' to a claim were always to be used as a stimulus or justification for the complacent exercise of judicial logic? These dangers of exaggerated importance being attached to the formal completeness of law are particularly great in international law, where the field of detailed regulation is limited, where the postulate of presumptive freedom of action is more authoritative, and where the resulting checks upon an extensive interpretation of the existing law are more pronounced.

Moreover, it must be borne in mind that the formal rules of great elasticity enumerated at the beginning of this chapter are in themselves only an imperfect guide. To a large extent they beg the question which they purport to answer. Thus when we mean to rely on the rule that what is not prohibited is permitted, we may be pursuing only the shadow of a rule. For the actual decision in each case will depend on the question whether we have in mind an express prohibition, specifically and unequivocally laid down—and such prohibitions may be very few in an undeveloped system of law labouring under a traditionally exaggerated conception of freedom—or a prohibition deduced from the general body of the law.[1] If, starting from the proposition that the law is complete and that there is therefore no room for looking behind the few specific rules and prohibitions, we accept the first alternative, then we come dangerously near to lending ourselves to the use of a narrow and unscientific method which will defeat the very end of law. Or, when we accept the principle that every claim must be rejected unless there are agreed rules of law in support of it, all depends on what we understand agreed rules of law to mean. If we understand thereby agreement, express and formal, on every individual aspect of a major principle, then, finding as we do in

---

[1] See below, pp. 286 et seq., on the application of the doctrine of abuse of rights.

international law few manifestations of agreement of this nature, we shall be compelled to refuse legal satisfaction to claims which, if related to a more comprehensive rule bearing on the matter and agreed upon by States, would justify themselves before the bar of the law.

There are many cases decided by international tribunals which show clearly how an attitude which takes the silence of the law on a particular point as an expression of its substantive completeness may produce results highly questionable when weighed in the balance of international law as a whole.

§ 15. Absence of an Express Rule. The 'Savarkar' Case.

Cases may occur in which the peculiarity of the facts underlying the action is such that, by the nature of things, it can hardly be expected that there should exist an express rule embracing the particular situation.[1] In such cases it is easy to identify the unavoidable absence of a specific rule with the denial of a legal remedy. The *Savarkar* case is an instructive example of a decision determined by a purely formal approach to a question submitted to an international tribunal. In this case, decided in February 1911, by the Permanent Court of Arbitration,[2] France demanded the restitution of an Indian political prisoner who, while on board an English merchant vessel at Marseilles, escaped to the shore where, with the help of Indian police officers, he was captured by a French police officer and handed over to the British authorities on board the vessel. France contended that the capture—which was due to a mistake of the French officer acting under the belief that the fugitive was a member of the crew—of the prisoner on French territory, and his delivery to British authorities, were acts contrary to international law. The Tribunal rejected the French demand on the ground that there was no rule of international law imposing upon Great Britain an obligation to restore to France a prisoner apprehended in these circumstances. In giving judgement the Tribunal pointed out, in support of its decision, that the case was not one of recourse to fraud or force in order to obtain possession of the prisoner, that there was no violation of French sovereignty,

---

[1] For some examples of such situations see below, pp. 105 et seq.

[2] The award is printed in *The Hague Court Reports*, ed. by J. B. Scott (1916), p. 275. The case is analysed in detail by Kohler in *Das Werk von Haag*, ed. by Schücking, 2nd ser., part iii (1914), pp. 69–166. For a decision of the German *Reichsgericht* in a somewhat similar case on 24 March 1922, see *Juristische Wochenschrift*, 1922, p. 1558.

and that the British officials in question acted in good faith and had no intention of committing any unlawful act.

This judgement was subjected to much criticism. Thus, Anzilotti pointed out, *inter alia*, that the responsibility of Great Britain was engaged, as 'there existed a relation of cause and effect between a fact contrary to international law . . . and the conduct of British police officers' for which Great Britain was responsible.[1] Van Hamel maintained that the question which the Tribunal ought to have answered in its judgement was: Could the prisoner have been extradited if the demand for his extradition had been dealt with in accordance with law?[2] Whatever may be the justification of these and similar criticisms,[3] they all point to the principle that the existence of a rule directly and specifically applying to the case before the Court is not an essential requisite for the recognition of a claim. It is true that there was no rule of international law 'imposing, in circumstances such as those which have been set out above, any obligation on the Power which has in its custody a prisoner, to restore him because of a mistake committed by the foreign agent who delivered him up to that Power',[4] but the circumstances were so exceptional that it would be surprising if there had been one. This was clearly a case where the absence of a specific rule need not necessarily have been regarded as decisive, and where recourse might have been had to a more general legal rule calculated to remedy the effects of what was admittedly a mistake culminating in an injury to a State. It was irrelevant that the interest involved was of a moral, not of a material, nature, namely, the interest which a State may attach to the respect for its territorial sovereignty or to the giving effect to the principle of asylum to political offenders.[5]

---

[1] *Rivista*, 2nd ser., i (1912), pp. 258–68.

[2] *R.I.*, 2nd ser., xiii (1911), pp. 370–403.

[3] See Strupp in *Z.V.* v (1911), Supplement, pp. 12–18; Robin in *R.G.* xviii (1911), pp. 303–52; and Kohler, op. cit. But see Oppenheim, i, § 332, who, however, does not give reasons in support of his view.

[4] Award, op. cit., p. 279.

[5] Both these interests are combined in Anzilotti's statement to the effect that: 'Una violazione internazionalmente rilevante del diritto d'asilo è . . . una violazione del diritto subiettivo dello Stato di rifugio', op. cit., p. 266. And see *P.C.I.J.*, Series A, No. 2, p. 22, and Series C, part i, p. 445, as bearing on the question whether, in regard to the mandates system under Article 22 of the Covenant of the League, a direct material interest must be involved in order to confer upon a Member of the League the right to challenge the legality of the acts of the mandatory in a mandated territory. See on this question Wright, *Mandates under the League of Nations* (1930), pp. 474–6.

Such an interest was violated, and the absence of fraud or force was material only to the extent of relieving Great Britain from any further responsibility—financial or otherwise—in addition to that of restoring the prisoner. It was also obvious that, as the result of the prisoner being handed over by mistake, effects were produced which were contrary to the spirit and the general conceptions of the law obtaining between the two countries in regard to the extradition of political offenders. This general consideration could have been taken as the basis of the decision even without the Tribunal adopting the view—and it might have found it difficult to adopt it—that non-extradition of political offenders formed part of international law, or that individuals in the position of the fugitive in question acquired direct rights under international law. It was suggested by Lammasch, who was one of the arbitrators in this case, that the decision of the Tribunal would probably have been different if the question put to the Tribunal had been whether France was bound to grant the extradition of the prisoner, or whether the French police officer had not acted under the influence of a mistake in helping to apprehend the fugitive,[1] but that the formulation of the *compromis* being what it was, it was impossible for the Tribunal to give a different decision. This explanation seems to be singularly unconvincing, in particular when we consider the pronouncements of the Permanent Court of International Justice to the effect that the form which the parties give to the arbitration agreement is not invariably decisive for the determination of the jurisdiction of the Court.[2]

§ 16. The Same. Questions of State Succession. The dangers of a purely technical conception of the completeness of international law are well illustrated by the attitude of national and international Courts in regard to certain aspects of State succession. This branch of international law offers a particularly good example of a general consensus of opinion in regard to the abstract principle, and a conspicuous lack of agreement in regard to its application. It is dominated by the principle that the successor State must respect the private rights acquired under its predecessor. In the words of Chief Justice Marshall, in the frequently quoted case of *United States* v. *Percheman*:[3]

---

[1] *Rechtskraft*, p. 25.   [2] See below, p. 327.   [3] 7 Peters' Reports, 51, 86.

'The modern usage of nations, which has become law, would be violated; that sense of justice and of right which is acknowledged and felt by the whole civilized world would be outraged, if private property should be generally confiscated, and private rights annulled. The people change their allegiance; their relation to their ancient sovereign is dissolved: but their relations to each other, and their rights of property, remain undisturbed.'

How far has this generally accepted abstract principle been equally accepted in relation to the different aspects of State succession? How far, for instance, is the successor State under a duty to respect the private rights of individuals in their capacity as the creditors of the former State? It would appear that the respect of rights thus acquired follows as a necessary consequence from the principle of respect of private rights. The same relates to other contractual and concessionary rights. A considerable number of treaties, of opinions of international lawyers, and of judicial opinions can be cited in support of that view.[1] But there are judicial decisions and opinions of writers which point in a different direction, and seem to lend authority to the view that the treaties in question, far from giving effect to a recognized rule of international law, contain provisions rendered necessary by the absence of relevant rules of international law. Unless therefore the international judge is prepared to disregard the absence of a specific rule bearing upon the respect for a particular category of private rights, and unless he is willing to assume that there is a provisional gap in positive law necessitating the recourse to the general legal principle which enjoins respect for private rights, he will be adopting a formalistic attitude little in keeping with positive law itself. Thus, for instance, when the arbitrator in the Ottoman Debt Arbitration, in his award of 18 April 1925, expressed the view that, notwithstanding the existing precedents, it was impossible to assume the existence of a rule of international law obliging the State which acquires territory by cession to take over a corresponding part of the public debt of the ceding State, he was assuming a pseudo-positivistic attitude which can hardly be regarded as being in accordance with the general principle governing State succession.[2]

---

[1] For a survey of authorities and treaties to this effect, see Lauterpacht, *Analogies*, §§ 54, 56, 57. See also Oppenheim, i, §§ 82–4, and, in particular, Feilchenfeld, *Public Debts and State Succession* (1931). And see generally on the conception of acquired rights Cavaglieri in *R.G.* xxxviii (1931), pp. 257–96.

[2] *Annual Digest*, 1925–6, Case No. 57.

Another aspect of State succession illustrates with equal clearness the unsatisfactory results of this method. There is certainly no clear-cut rule of international law relating to the duties of the successor State in regard to the officials in the service of its predecessor. Treaties of international law contain no reference to this subject at all. The temptation is therefore great to solve the difficulties surrounding this matter by the simple device of pointing to the absence of any rule of international law imposing upon the successor State the duty to take over the officials of its predecessor. There are decisions not only of municipal courts,[1] but also of international tribunals in which recourse has been had to this summary method in regard to this particular aspect of State succession.[2] Any result must be unsatisfactory which is based on the view that what is not expressed in law—and how relatively few rules are expressly prescribed by international law—is not law at all. The respect of private rights *is* an express rule of international law, and this general rule ought to be taken as a basis for decision in each relevant case. The question is, Are the acquired private rights, if any, affected by the decision of the successor State to dispense with the services of the official without pension or compensation? In some countries, like Great Britain, members of the Civil Service hold office at the pleasure of the Crown; they do not acquire any contractual or quasi-contractual rights. In other States, like France and Germany, they have rights of this nature to continued employment. Obvious reasons of public policy may make it impracticable to continue the employment of officials appointed by the former power, but even then there still remains the question of adequate compensation, in particular in regard to such employment as that in the inferior ranks of the railway, postal, and other purely administrative offices in which there is hardly room for apprehension that their continuance in employment might endanger the security or administrative unity of the successor State. It is from the point of view of the generally recognized principle of respect for private rights, and not from that of the merely negative consideration that there is no relevant rule of international law, that cases of this description must

---

[1] See *Annual Digest*, 1925–6, Case No. 68 (*Saar Territory* (*Prussian Officials*) case).

[2] See, for instance, the decision of the Polish-German Arbitral Tribunal for Upper Silesia of 27 January 1928 in the case *Frystatzki* v. *Polish State*, *Annual Digest*, 1927–8, Case No. 62.

be treated if effect is to be given to broad and generally recognized principles of international law.

§ 17. Restrictive Interpretation of Available Sources. Extinctive Prescription.

The history of international arbitration in regard to the question of extinctive prescription offers similar instances of a purely formal and restrictive interpretation of the applicable sources of international law. Thus we find a recent arbitral award in which the view is expressed that 'there is, of course, no rule of international law putting a limitation of time on diplomatic action or upon the presentation of an international claim to an international tribunal'. The award referred to was given by the Mexican-American General Claims Commission on 3 June 1927 in the *George W. Cook* case.[1] This decision was rendered only two years after the Institute of International Law had recognized that extinctive prescription ought to be regarded as having a place in international law;[2] after the arbitrators in a number of well-known cases, like the *Williams*[3] and *Gentini*[4] cases, had acted upon that rule; and after the only arbitration case—the *Pious Fund of California* case—which was interpreted by some as denying extinctive prescription in international law, was clearly shown to have referred not to any international rule of law of extinctive prescription, but to municipal statutes of limitation.[5] Technically the commissioners in the *George W. Cook* case were entitled to assert categorically that there was nothing in the nature of an international statute of limitations. There is no express rule of conventional international law of a legislative nature enacting the rule of extinctive prescription, or the period necessary for its completion; and it may be argued that, notwithstanding the ample support of the doctrine by writers and by some arbitral tribunals, there is no sufficient amount of international practice to constitute extinctive prescription part of positive international law. But it is the restrictive interpretation of the available sources of law which seriously diminishes the value of the award in the *George W. Cook* case. It disregards important subsidiary sources of international law as expressed in the practice of tribunals and in the opinions of writers. It fails to pay

---

[1] See *Annual Digest*, 1927–8, Case No. 174.

[2] *Annuaire*, xxxii (1925), p. 477.

[3] Moore, pp. 1449–68.

[4] Ralston, *Venezuelan Arbitrations*, pp. 724–30.

[5] See on this point Lauterpacht, *Analogies*, § 113, and the observations of the arbitrator in the *Gentini* case, *supra*.

attention to considerations of convenience, of the reason of the thing, and of the general principles of law which lie at the basis of international law. The inappropriateness of such a rigidly positivistic conception of existing international law will appear even more clearly when we compare this award with another decision, and its reasons, given on the subject of extinctive prescription on 14 February 1927 by the Graeco-Bulgarian Mixed Arbitral Tribunal in the case of *Sarropoulos* v. *Bulgarian State*.[1] Confronted with a demand put forward in 1921, and arising out of an event which had taken place in 1906, the Tribunal held that the exception of prescription could validly be raised. The reasoning of the Tribunal bears so closely upon the subject under discussion that the following extract appears to be justified:

'Positive international law has not so far established any precise and generally adopted rule either as to the principle of prescription as such, or as to its duration. Neither do arbitral decisions or opinions of writers yield any agreed solution.

'However, prescription appears to constitute a positive legal rule in almost all systems of law. It is an expression of a great principle of peace which is at the basis of the common law and of all civilized systems of jurisprudence. Stability and security in human affairs require that a delay should be fixed outside which it should be impossible to invoke rights or obligations....

'Prescription being an integral and necessary part of every system of law must be admitted in international law.'

§ 18. Freedom of Action as a Regulative Principle. The 'Lotus' Case.
The misguided insistence upon the explicitness of rules of international law—an attitude which is expressive of a purely formal conception of the completeness of the law—finds expression also in the treatment of the principle of freedom and the independence of States as a direct source of law and as a vehicle of judicial reasoning. In sound legal theory it should not be allowed to fulfil either of these functions. The Permanent Court of International Justice seems to have adopted this course in the *Lotus* case, where it accepted as one of the bases of its decision the principle that 'international law governs relations between independent states', and that 'restrictions upon the independence of states cannot, therefore, be presumed'.[2] It held that its function was not to find the principle which would permit Turkey to exercise jurisdic-

---

[1] *Recueil*, vii. 51, and *Annual Digest*, 1927–8, Case No. 173.
[2] Series A, No. 10, p. 18.

tion over a foreigner for an offence committed on the high seas, but to inquire into the existence, if any, of principles prohibiting Turkey from exercising such jurisdiction. Any criticism of this view of the Court ought to be mitigated by the fact that it was not the only consideration on which the Court based its judgement. Neither can exaggerated regard for claims of State sovereignty be regarded as typical of the work of the Permanent Court in general.[1] The Court adduced in support of its ruling in the *Lotus* case reasons of a far more substantial character based on a careful consideration of the merits and demerits of the proposed solutions.[2] But there is a danger that in the hand of a less authoritative body than the Permanent Court of International Justice the conception of the independence of States may be used with results foreign to the purpose of the law.[3] From the point of view of legal philosophy freedom may, as the Hegelians would have it, be regarded as the ultimate object of the rule of law in the wider sense.[4] But it is not the basis or the essence of law. As law consists in the regulation of human conduct, it results in practice in the limitation of freedom of action. The

[1] See below, p. 208.

[2] The Court said in the concluding part of the judgement: 'Neither the exclusive jurisdiction of either state, nor the limitations of the jurisdiction of each to the occurrences which took place on the respective ships would appear calculated to satisfy the requirements of justice and effectively to protect the interests of the two States. It is only natural that each should be able to exercise jurisdiction and to do so in respect of the incident as a whole. It is therefore a case of concurrent jurisdiction.' Series A, No. 10, pp. 30, 31.

For an interesting if somewhat hesitating juxtaposition of the two principles, see the award of Judge Huber in the Moroccan claims, in which the arbitrator said in 1924 (*Rapports* [quoted below, p. 120] at p. 53): 'The territorial sovereignty constitutes such a fundamental feature of modern public law that foreign intervention in the relations between the State and the individuals under its territorial sovereignty can only be admitted by way of exception.' However, he proceeded to admit that this respect for freedom of action was only one of the material considerations; that the right of intervention (not in its technical sense) in order to protect subjects abroad has been claimed by all States; and that the only question was to determine the limits of this right of intervention. He pointed out that a different view would mean depriving international law of a remedy against injustices amounting to a negation of human personality.

[3] This aspect of the judgement is criticized by Bruns in *Z. f. a. ö. R. und V.*, i (1929), pp. 31–40, and Brierly in *Law Quarterly Review*, xliv (1928), pp. 156, 157, who points out that 'we are not entitled to deduce the law applicable to a specific state of facts from the mere fact of sovereignty or independence' and who quotes Westlake, i. 237, to the effect that 'so far from sovereignty being the key to the solution of the questions indicated, it is only by putting together the solutions which they shall have severally received that it will become possible to form the complete picture or definition of international sovereignty'.

[4] See, for instance, Hegel, *Grundlinien der Philosophie des Rechts* (1820), p. 61; Lorimer, *Institutes of Law* (2nd ed., 1880), p. 354. And see Pound, *Interpretations of Legal History* (1923), pp. 46–8.

sovereignty of the State in international law is a quality conferred by international law. It cannot, therefore, be either the basis or the source of the law of nations. In international law this reliance upon freedom and independence as a substantive source of law is the more dangerous as, because of reasons peculiar to international law, the number of explicit rules restricting freedom of action is limited and their ascertainment is difficult. A combination therefore of a rigid theory of the formal completeness of international law (which renders it difficult to define restrictions of freedom of action through the normal exercise of judicial activity) with an emphasis upon the sovereignty of States as a law-creating principle may easily produce results inimical to the purposes of law.

§ 19. The Principle 'neminem laedit qui jure suo utitur' Closure of Buenos Ayres. The principle of sovereignty and independence are not the only possible source of the assumption of freedom of action. A source of this nature can be found in a one-sided use of certain general legal maxims like *neminem laedit qui jure suo utitur*, or of particular permissive rules of international law, like that relating to the freedom of the sea. The former rule was adopted as the basis of the decision by the arbitrator in the dispute between Argentina and Great Britain concerning the closure, in February 1845, of the port of Buenos Ayres. The port was closed, without sufficient notice, to vessels communicating with Montevideo, the Uruguayan port blockaded at that time by Argentina. Great Britain demanded compensation on account of the damage caused by the closure of the port without due notice. The arbitrator rejected the claim on the ground that the State closing its ports to foreign commerce is the sole judge of the conditions under which it will admit foreign vessels. The fact, he said, that such closure may cause damage to foreign vessels was not relevant. *Neminem laedit qui jure suo utitur.*[1] It is not necessary to discuss here the merits of this decision, which does not seem to be inconsistent with justice, seeing that it may be difficult to expect from a State that it should offer the hospitality of its ports to foreign vessels about to break a blockade proclaimed by it. Possibly it could have been asserted that in cases of this nature the analogy of

---

[1] For an account and analysis of this award see Lapradelle and Politis, ii. 637 ff.

blockade for which previous notification is required[1] could hardly apply, seeing that the closure was regarded by Argentina as an imperative measure of warfare. But to appeal to the formal absence of restrictions upon freedom of action is a procedure of doubtful value. The maxim *neminem laedit qui jure suo utitur* frequently begs the question as to what is that *suum jus*. It is the extent of that *suum jus* which is the subject of judicial inquiry.[2] Freedom of action must be the result, not the starting-point, of the investigation. A right which prima facie falls within the exclusive competence of a State may be restricted by a number of rules of international law. Such possible rules must be fully explored and discarded as inapplicable before the principle of freedom of action is elevated to the authority of a source of decision. But their absence must not be assumed from the lack of an express restrictive provision. Here, as elsewhere, it may be the duty of the judge to go behind the formal completeness of the law. Freedom of action cannot be regarded as a regulative principle.[3]

§ 20. Limits of Permissive Rules. The Behring Sea Arbitration.

The award of the Tribunal in the *Behring Sea* arbitration is a further illustration of the inadequacy of the use of the principle of freedom of action as an automatic source of decision, even when such principle is seemingly based on a specific rule of international law. In this arbitration, which was a typical case *primae impressionis*, the United States contended that they had the right to restrain British subjects from engaging in capturing and killing seals in the Behring Sea in a manner regarded by the United States as uneconomic, wasteful, and destructive of the sealing industry,[4] in which the United States claimed a proprietary interest.

---

[1] The use of this analogy for the present case has been suggested by Politis (in *Recueil des Cours*, 1925 (i), p. 100), who criticizes the award adversely.

[2] See below, Chapter XIV, on the application of the doctrine of abuse of rights.

[3] That the principle of sovereignty and independence thus conceived is a double-edged sword may be seen from the *Lotus* case, where the opposing parties had recourse to it in support of opposing contentions. Its small practical value is clearly shown by the fact that it reduces a major issue to a question of the burden of proof.

[4] The indiscriminate exercise of the right of fishery in the Behring Sea was described in the United States *Argument*, p. 175 (as quoted below) as 'conduct inhuman and barbarous beyond the power of description, criminal by the laws of the United States and of every civilised country so far as its municipal jurisdiction extends'.

They also based their claim to exclusive jurisdiction in the Behring Sea on certain alleged prescriptive rights of a jurisdictional nature originally belonging to Russia. Both these claims were opposed by Great Britain and rejected by the Tribunal on legal grounds into which it is not necessary here to inquire.[1] However, one of the main arguments adduced by Great Britain in the course of the proceedings was that based on the principle of the freedom of the sea, described in the British Argument as 'the right to come and go upon the high seas without let or hindrance, and to take therefrom at will and pleasure the produce of the sea'.[2] It was contended that the claim of the United States to the protection of the seal industry was in violation of the principle of the freedom of the sea. 'It is with no mere idle use of high-sounding phrase', it was said in the British Argument, 'that Great Britain once more appears to vindicate the freedom of the sea.'[3]

The Tribunal answered in the negative the question whether the United States had any right of protection in the fur-seals frequenting the islands of the United States in the Behring Sea when such seals are found outside the ordinary three miles' limit. This answer was partly determined by the weakness of the American legal position in regard to the proprietary and prescriptive rights, but it is submitted that the absence of prescriptive and proprietary rights *stricto sensu* need not necessarily have led to the denial of the right of protection, or at least of the right to demand an agreed measure of common or international protection. It is true that the decision was largely due to the manner of presentation of the claim by the United States. Entangled in the assertion of a prescriptive right of jurisdiction, which proved to be non-existent, and of a proprietary right, whose legal foundation was problematic, it failed to make full use of the notion of 'abuse of rights' as well as of the more general arguments that the freedom of the sea could not mean absence of any legal regulation whatsoever, and that it was inherent in the very idea of the common user of the produce of the sea that it implied reasonable limitations of its exercise. It was only as an occasional side-issue that the United States had attempted this approach to the controversy. When they did so they rendered such approach largely ineffective by an

---

[1] Some of them are summarized in Lauterpacht, *Analogies*, §§ 98, 99.
[2] (1893) [C. 6921] United States, No. 4, pp. 7, 8.
[3] Ibid.

exaggerated recourse to the idea of self-defence.[1] It may never-theless be doubted whether, even given the line of argument adopted by the United States and the formulation of the crucial question put to it, the Tribunal was under the necessity to adopt in the decision a clearly negative attitude towards the general contention of the United States. In substance, the Tribunal was confronted with a new and unprecedented situation; there was so far a gap in the law. One course open to the Tribunal was to assume, as it did, that international law on the subject, embodied in the principle of the freedom of the sea, was com-plete. The other course was to go beyond this formal complete-ness, to recognize the provisional existence of a gap, and to have recourse to broader principles of law. This was the view which the United States urged the Tribunal to adopt. The way in which, throughout the arbitration, it impressed upon the Tribu-nal the necessity of having recourse to general principles of law and justice forming the very foundation of international law, constitutes the most spirited defence ever officially undertaken by a Government of the law of nature as the foundation of international law.[2] It was urged that the particular circum-stances of the case justified the application of a universal and necessary principle 'to an exigency that has not arisen in this precise form before'.[3]

It is permissible to maintain that the demand for a restriction of freedom of action could in this case legitimately have been brought within an overruling principle more comprehensive than that of the freedom of the sea itself. The award of the Tribunal on this particular question is an illustration of the consequences of a rigid conception of the completeness of inter-national law.[4] The judge's vision must not be blurred

---

[1] See the *Argument* of the United States (cited below), pp. 170ff. And see below, p. 179, n. 1.

[2] See in particular *Written Argument* of the United States (British edition: United States, No. 8 (1893) [C. 6951], pp. 1–26) (Mr. Carter's argument on 'What law is to govern the decision').

[3] Ibid., p. 172.

[4] A probable explanation of this aspect of the decision of the Tribunal lies in the fact that, by the terms of submission, it was enabled, if not indirectly invited, to grant by way of a recommendation what it refused to grant in its formal award. Article VII of the arbitration agreement of February 1892 provided that if the answer of the Tribunal to the question of jurisdiction shall be such as to make the concurrence of Great Britain necessary to the framing of regulations for the proper protection or preservation of the fur-seals, the arbitrators shall determine what concurrent regulations are necessary. The recommendations made by the Tribunal contained drastic limitations, including the prohibition to kill or capture seals within sixty miles around the islands

by permissive rules which although elastic are anti-social in their nature. An all too easy assumption of the formal completeness of international law must not be allowed to weaken the very essence of judicial activity.

§ 21. Cases 'primae impressionis' and the Judicial Function in International Law.

As will appear more clearly from the next chapter, in which it is proposed to inquire into the character of the judicial activity of international tribunals when confronted with new situations, the cases discussed above are not typical of judicial activity in the field of international arbitration. Their consideration has been thought necessary in order to show that the rejection of the idea of formal gaps in international law, although theoretically correct, does not, when taken by itself, necessarily supply a satisfactory solution of the difficulties with which tribunals are confronted. The rejection of the admissibility of *non liquet* implies the necessity for creative activity on the part of international judges. Legal philosophy in the domain of municipal jurisprudence has shown the possibilities and, indeed, the inevitability of the law-creating function, within defined limits, of the judge within the State.[1] Undoubtedly, for reasons stated elsewhere, the problem of gaps in international law shows certain features peculiar to the present state of international society. But the peculiarity of the

---

frequented by them, the prohibition to capture or kill them in May, June, and July, the prohibition to use nets, fire-arms, and explosives in the fur-seal fishery, &c. (See Moore, pp. 948 ff.)

[1] Austin, in the Note to Lecture V, says: 'I cannot understand how any person who has considered the subject can suppose that society could possibly have gone on if the judges had not legislated, or that there is any danger whatever in allowing them that power which they have in fact exercised, to make up for the negligence or the incapacity of the avowed legislator. That part of the law of every country which was made by judges has been far better made than that part which consists of statutes enacted by the legislature.' And see on judicial legislation, Holmes, *The Common Law*, pp. 35, 36. See also McIlwain, *The High Court of Parliament and its Supremacy* (1910). *An Historical Essay on the Boundaries between Legislation and Adjudication in England.* An excellent exposition of the problem will be found in Dickinson, *Administrative Justice and the Supremacy of Law* (1927), pp. 122 et seqq. ('For law ends by being what it is made to be by the body which applies it to concrete situations; it takes shape only at the moment when it is fitted to the facts of an actual case.') And see Pound, *Law and Morals* (2nd ed., 1926), p. 62: 'There are many situations where the course of judicial action is left to be determined wholly by the judge's individual sense of what is right and just.' In England the conception of public policy has played a not unimportant part in promoting judicial legislation. See Winfield, 'Public Policy in the English Common Law', in *Harvard Law Review*, xlii (1928–9), pp. 76–102; and Knight, 'Public Policy in English Law', in *Law Quarterly Review*, xxxviii (1922), pp. 207–19. And see p. 255, *infra*.

problem of gaps in international law must not be allowed to obscure the fact that as a matter of broad principle the question is the same in both spheres of law, inasmuch as it is in both a question of the interpretation of the existing law taken in its entirety. As in other systems of law, so also in international law, there are no gaps from the point of view of the duty of tribunals to pronounce upon the legal merits of any claim that may be submitted to them. But, as elsewhere, so also in international law, however formally complete, there exist gaps from the point of view of the logical unity and consistency of the law, of its actual effectiveness in meeting emergencies, and of the moral and social ends of the international legal system. Whenever there is a gap of this nature there is, provisionally at least, a case *primae impressionis*. The *lacuna* does not lie in the fact that there is no legal answer to the case in question—there are no such gaps. The gap lies in the fact that the legal answer obtained by recourse to a rule directly applicable seems to be legally unsatisfactory. As in such cases the law cannot be presumed to aim at an unsatisfactory result, the seemingly applicable rule is regarded as not applicable, and the case itself appears to be, in relation to that rule, novel. In such cases the judge, unless limited by a clear and unmistakable rule of positive law, feels constrained to have recourse to a more general, although undoubtedly recognized, legal rule in order to obtain a legally more satisfactory result. The gap thus proves to be provisional. As a matter of juridical logic it appears therefore that, even from the point of view of the material appropriateness of the law, there are no gaps at all. However, this relates to the final result of judicial activity. The fact that the gap is provisional shows that it exists as an actual problem in the course of the process of the judicial application of the law.

When it is said that there are no gaps in law, because, in view of the judge's duty to give a decision in any event, the actual rule of law, although uncertain and unrevealed in certain stages of the dispute, is nevertheless *in gremio judicis*, we thereby admit that that rule, prior to its final enunciation, existed only potentially. *Quod est in posse, non est in esse.* The very necessity of having recourse to analogy or to deduction from a more general principle of law, points in a sense to the provisional existence of a blank space in the positive law. It could, of course, be said with almost equal cogency that every judicial pronouncement involves, to a lesser or larger extent, a deduction from a more general rule, inasmuch as judicial activity is essentially the last link in the chain of the crystallization of the rule of law, that is to say, it is the bridge between the necessarily abstract legal rule and the necessarily individual nature of the particular case. Every case is in a sense *primae impressionis*, inasmuch as every case is individual and every rule abstract. On the other hand, even a most obviously novel case is typical when we consider that law is originally and ultimately not so much a body of legal rules as a body of legal principles.[1] The gap between the abstract legal rule and the individual case may be infinitesimal when the rule is perfectly specific and the case perfectly normal. It becomes substantial when the absence of a detailed or socially appropriate individual rule makes the individual case appear less typical and the need for a more general rule more urgent. The question of existence of gaps in this sense is a question of determining the degree of the intensity and of the creativeness of judicial activity.

Thus viewed, the controversy as to whether judges 'make' or 'discover' law becomes somewhat unreal.[2] It is futile to maintain that in 'making' law the judge is as free of the existing legal materials as is the legislator;[3] he is bound by the existing principles of law; he is bound by them even, to take the extreme case of his giving a decision apparently *contra legem*, when he finds that the major purpose of the law compels him to have regard to its spirit rather than to the letter and to disregard its express words.[4] On the other hand,

---

[1] Thus the question whether a man is responsible for the predatory habits of his cat engaged in killing the birds of his neighbour may, to the surprise of the Court, prove to be a case *primae impressionis*, inasmuch as there may be no precedent or authority for dealing with the predatory habits of cats (*Buckle* v. *Holmes*, [1926] 2 K.B. 125). At the same time, however, it is clear that the case is covered by abundant authority in the form of legal principle, either in the law of trespass, or in the principle imposing upon the owner of a dangerous animal or thing the obligation to take measures to restrain it from doing damage.

[2] The classical English theory, propounded by Hale and Blackstone and rejected by Austin, to the effect that the applicable rule of law is safely hidden *in gremio legis* and that the judge has only to uncover and to apply the pre-existing rule, is pungently criticized by Sir Henry Maine in *Ancient Law* (1920 ed.), pp. 35, 36. The conflicting theories are lucidly stated by Cardozo, op. cit., pp. 124–7.

[3] See Cardozo, op. cit., pp. 135–8, where the student will find a detailed exposition of these limitations upon the law-making possibilities of the judicial function.

[4] 'Scire leges non est verba earum tenere sed vim ac potestatem.' See the pronounced views of Salmond on the danger of the unqualified acceptance of

it is futile to assume that the process of 'discovery' of the pre-existing law is a mechanical function of human automata. The process of 'discovering' a thing is, as the very word implies, a not less creative function than the 'making' of it. In recognizing this, one need not go to the extreme point of urging a view which makes of the judge a legislator, instead of seeing in him the servant of the existing law. There is no need to accept either the view that the function of the judge is merely one of automatic, formal, and logical deduction from the rule of law, or the view that it is a highly subjective operation in which the judge's outlook and predilections as a thinking and feeling human being are of decisive importance. The essence of the freedom of judicial decision is not freedom from the existing law, but, so far as is humanly possible, freedom from the purely subjective inclination of the judge. This purely subjective element may be limited by the judicial duty of respect for the supremacy of the law, or by express legal provisions, as in the Swiss Code, which, while empowering the judge to act as legislator, limits his discretion by commanding him to remain within the orbits of customary law and legal tradition embodied in the writings of publicists. But limited it must be so long as the judge remains loyal to his judicial function. Undoubtedly the postulate of government by laws, not by men, is an ideal which can never be fully realized, seeing that it is through the instrumentality of feeling and willing men that the law is to be declared, but the part of the purely subjective factor in judicial activity must not be exaggerated. This applies both to municipal and to international law.[1] However extensive the scope of law-creating judicial interpretation may be, it is always limited, although not totally determined, by existing legal materials. The undeniable freedom of judicial decision is one within the law.

The actual result of judicial activity is a conscious or

---

the maxim, *Ita scriptum est*, as leading to absurdities and to a defeat of the true purpose of the law: Introduction to the volume of the *Science of Legal Method*, in Modern Legal Philosophy Series (1921), pp. lxxxiv and lxxxv.

[1] In regard to the latter, these limits of judicial discretion have been well defined by Lammasch, one of the greatest authorities in the field of international arbitration. When dealing with the problem of gaps, and while denying the right of an international tribunal to refuse to give a decision on the ground of the absence of an applicable legal rule, he argued that the award must be given, 'having regard, so far as this is possible, to the existing rules of international law and to the spirit of the principles governing the law of nations' (*Schiedsgerichts-barkeit*, p. 179).

subconscious compromise between these two factors. But, although it is not the business of jurisprudence to investigate the details of the psychological process by which the judge arrives at his decision,[1] it may be noted that this aspect of judicial activity is of special interest in the international sphere. It is so because, while the inducements to the exercise of creative judicial discretion are here stronger than within the State,[2] the judicial activity of international tribunals is surrounded by the important check inherent in the voluntary nature of the jurisdiction conferred upon them by States. The very existence of an international judiciary might be imperilled if, in the present state of international organization, the conviction gained ground among Governments that circumspection and restraint are absent in the conflict between what has been called judicial idealism[3] and the claims of State sovereignty.

---

[1] This point is well put by Somló, *Juristische Grundlehre* (1917), p. 421.
[2] See above, pp. 81 et seqq.   [3] See below, p. 205.

CHAPTER VI

NOVELTY OF ACTION AND NATURE OF JUDICIAL ACTIVITY IN INTERNATIONAL LAW

§ 22. Novelty of Action in International Judicial Settlement. The history of international arbitration is a continuous proof of the view that the alleged absence of legal rules does not in actual practice constitute an obstacle in the way of judicial settlement of international disputes. For three lessons emerge with convincing clearness from the practice of international arbitration in the last hundred and thirty years: the first is that in the majority of cases international tribunals have been confronted with novel situations for which international law has had no ready-made solutions at hand. The second is that there is, so far as the writer is aware, no dispute on record in which an international tribunal has refused to adjudicate on the ground that there was no law applicable to the case. The third is that this consistent fulfilment of the judicial duty to pronounce the law in each case has not been achieved at the cost of sacrificing the strictly legal character of international arbitration.[1]

International tribunals are, for a number of reasons, even more frequently than municipal courts, confronted with the phenomenon called 'novelty of action'. The first of these reasons is the relative scarcity of judicial precedent, due not so much to the lack of occasion for judicial determination of disputed questions as to the absence of the obligation to have recourse to this method of pacific settlement. This is the explanation why only in regard to a small segment of the rules, as distinguished from principles of international law, it is possible to refer to an international judicial decision corroborating or throwing light upon the rule in question. Thus, to mention one instance, reprisals and retorsion, to which resort is not infrequent, constitute, for obvious reasons, an appropriate subject-matter for judicial determination both of their justification in a given case and of the limits of their application, but until very recently[2] there has been no judicial pronouncement on either of them.

---

[1] As to some aspects of the problem of the judicial character of international arbitration see below, pp. 380 et seqq.

[2] See, on the question of reprisals, in particular on the justification of reprisals, the necessity of previous request to redress the injury and the question of proportionality of reprisals, the *Naulilaa Incident* case between Portugal and

The second reason, closely connected with the first, is that the predominance of general principle and the scarcity of detailed rules give to many a case the impress of novelty, not as the result of any exceptional peculiarity of the facts involved in the dispute, but merely owing to the absence of a clear and ascertained rule relating thereto. Some cases are indeed novel by reason of the circumstances which underlie them. Thus the cases of the *Comet*, the *Encomium*, and the *Creole*[1] in which the British-American Mixed Commission, sitting in London under the Convention of 8 February 1853, was confronted with claims arising out of the liberation by British authorities of slaves owned by American subjects and brought on American ships into British ports, were cases *primae impressionis*, not merely on account of the unsettled state of the law as to the jurisdiction of the State in regard to foreign ships within its ports. They were novel primarily by reason of the exceptional nature of the facts which gave rise to the controversy, and which in turn brought forth a number of questions, such as the implications of the freedom of navigation of the high seas, the territorial character of ships, the rules of international law in regard to slavery, and the question of respect of the property of aliens, especially in relation to considerations of public policy.[2] The *Savarkar* case, discussed above, is another example of a case novel on account of the peciliar nature of the facts underlying the action.[3] On the other hand, in cases like the *Lotus* case, the facts were typical and simple, and only the scarcity of relevant judicial precedent and the unsettled state of the law made the case one *primae impressionis*.

Finally, novelty of action before international tribunals is frequently due to the combination of the limited number of what may be called international causes of action, as embodied principally in the rules relating to State responsibility, with the large variety of occurrences giving rise to inter-

---

Germany, of 31 July 1928, decided by a Special Arbitral Tribunal: *Recueil*, viii. 409, 422–5, and *Annual Digest*, 1927–8, Case No. 360. And see, on the question of retorsion, the case of *Jules Baranyai* v. *Yugoslavia*, decided on 15 September 1927 by the Hungarian-Yugoslav Mixed Arbitral Tribunal: *Recueil*, vii. 858, and *Annual Digest*, 1927–8, Case No. 359.

[1] See Moore, pp. 408, 410, 4369, 4375.

[2] For an admirable analysis of these questions see Strisower in Lapradelle and Politis, i. 705 ff. The question was no longer a novel one in 1875, when an award was given on a similar matter in the dispute between Peru and Japan in the case of the *Maria Luz*, a Peruvian vessel, which carried Chinese coolies to Peru via Japan. For the award see Lafontaine, p. 199, and Moore, p. 5034.

[3] See above, p. 88.

national disputes. International law does not recognize individuals as subjects of international law, and its causes of action are framed correspondingly. But, as is pointed out in another part of this book,[1] the great majority of cases which come before international tribunals have their origin in injuries to private interests as distinguished from general State interests. A survey of the judgements given by the Permanent Court of International Justice illustrates this point very clearly.[2] With the exception of the judgement concerning the territorial jurisdiction of the International Commission of the Oder, and the Orders relating to the Swiss Free Zones, as well as of the two judgements (Nos. 3 and 4) given in summary procedure, all judgements of the Court have had their origin in a direct injury to a private interest. It is the State which takes up the private claim in the last resort, but this does not alter either the original nature or the large variety of the claims. This is one of the main reasons for the continuous novelty of action confronting international tribunals.

§ 23. Interpretation of Treaties and Novelty of Action.

The circumstance that the bulk of international disputes relates to the interpretation of treaties does not result in reducing the number of cases *primae impressionis*.[3] A dispute may technically refer to the interpretation of a treaty, but that does not necessarily mean that the tribunal is not confronted with new or substantial questions of law. The *Venezuelan Preferential Claims* case, referred to above,[4] was a case with a strikingly novel accumulation of circumstances,[5]

---

[1] See below, p. 154.

[2] See the *Wimbledon* case (Judgement No. 1): in substance a claim on behalf of the Company which sustained the loss caused by the refusal of passage through the Kiel Canal; Judgements Nos. 2, 5, and 10: in substance a claim on behalf of Mr. Mavrommatis in regard to his concessionary rights in Palestine; Judgements Nos. 6, 7, 8, 11, and 13 and three Orders (Series A, Nos. 8, 12, and 19)—all concerning the violation of private German rights in Upper Silesia; the *Lotus* case (Judgement No. 9) arose out of the alleged unlawful exercise of jurisdiction over a French subject; Judgement No. 12 was concerned with the alleged violation of minority rights; Judgements Nos. 14 and 15 were concerned with the payment of loans owned by private individuals.

[3] See, however, on this point and on that discussed in the preceding section, Fischer Williams, *Chapters*, pp. 56 and 51 respectively.

[4] See p. 82.

[5] See *Final Report* of the agent of the United States: 'It was conceded by counsel on both sides that the law of nations afforded no clear rule for the decision of the controversy. No such case had ever before arisen, and in the course of the trial neither the counsel nor the arbitrators were able to cite any

but technically it was, and was dealt with by the Tribunal as a matter of interpretation of a specific set of agreements. The *North Atlantic Fisheries* arbitration[1] was formally concerned with the interpretation of the treaty of 1818 conferring certain rights upon American fishermen, but one of the principal issues of the dispute was, for the first time in the history of international arbitration, the controversial question of so-called 'State servitudes'. The question, raised in the *Wimbledon*[2] case before the Permanent Court of International Justice, whether the opening of an international waterway to the ships of all nations at peace with the riparian State exempted that State from some of the normal duties of neutrality in respect of that waterway, was a novel one in the practice of international tribunals, but technically it was a question of the interpretation of Article 380 of the Treaty of Versailles. The *Lotus* case, in which an international tribunal was for the first time required to pronounce on the question of jurisdiction in respect of offences committed outside the territory of the State claiming jurisdiction, was technically a case of interpreting Article 15 of the Convention of Lausanne of 24 July 1923, respecting the conditions of residence and business and jurisdiction, which provided that 'all questions of jurisdiction shall, as between Turkey and the other contracting Powers, be decided in accordance with the principles of international law'. The question before the Court was whether Turkey acted in accordance with the above treaty stipulation, i.e. whether the assumption of jurisdiction over a French subject was, in the circumstances, contrary to international law. The same applies to Advisory Opinions which, with no exception, were all given on a disputed interpretation of treaties, awards, or other international documents. Thus, to give one example, the typically novel question involved in the Twelfth Advisory Opinion on the matter of voting and unanimity before the Council of the League of Nations in cases when that body is asked to act in an arbitral capacity, was one of the interpretations of the relevant provisions of the Treaty of Lausanne and of the Covenant of the League.[3] The statement may be ventured that almost the entire history of the work of the Permanent

---

authority, either from decisions of arbitral tribunals or from the writings of publicists which was plainly applicable to the case': *Proceedings of the Venezuelan Arbitration*, U.S.A., 58th Congress, 3rd Session, Doc. No. 119, p. 15.

[1] See below, p. 149.   [2] See below, p. 112.   [3] See above, p. 83.

Court of International Justice could be given in terms of cases arising out of the interpretation of treaties.[1]

It is not difficult to explain this phenomenon. It lies in the fact that the work of interpretation is one of discovering the intention of the parties not only by reference to rules of interpretation, but to rules of international law bearing upon the subject-matter of the disputed contractual stipulation. These rules may be ready at hand, or they may have to be developed by the legitimate methods of judicial activity. The parties may, so far as it lies within their power, expressly exclude the operation of certain otherwise applicable rules of international law—*modus et conventio vincunt legem*—but if they have not done so the substantive rules of international law must be resorted to as a vehicle of interpretation. The treaty must be taken to have been made within the frame of international law, in relation to which the facts of the case may present an entirely novel situation. In concluding treaties the parties must frequently avail themselves of current legal forms and institutions, and thus the interpretation of their intentions assumes necessarily the character of a construction, by reference to the specific facts of the case, of these legal terms and institutions. The parties conclude a treaty not in a legal vacuum, but against a background of existing rules of international law.[2] It may be true that the treaty has to be interpreted by reference to the intention of the parties. But the intention of the parties must be interpreted by reference to rules of international law, in so far as their application has not been expressly excluded by the parties.[3] This is the

[1] A recent case—*Steiner and Gross* v. *Polish State*—decided by the Upper Silesian Arbitral Tribunal on 30 March 1928, may be quoted as another example illustrating this point. In this case the Tribunal was called upon to interpret Article 4 of the German-Polish Convention of 15 May 1922, concerning Upper Silesia, which conferred direct access to the international tribunals on any person *ayant droit* injuriously affected in his property rights. It was contended by Poland that the expression *ayant droit* did not comprise Polish subjects, as it was a principle of international law that an individual could not invoke an international authority against his own State. The interpretation of the treaty was thus made dependent upon the view of the Tribunal as to the existence of the principle of international law invoked by Poland and qualifying the clear wording of the treaty. The Tribunal refused to admit that there was such a principle. See for this case *Annual Digest*, 1927–8, Case No. 287.

[2] See *P.C.I.J.*, Judgement No. 8, pp. 21–3, in which a clause conferring jurisdiction upon the Court was interpreted by reference to the history of international arbitration since the end of the eighteenth century.

[3] The above considerations will perhaps suggest to the reader a certain criterion for gauging the relative importance of the first two paragraphs of the enumeration of the sources of law to be applied by the Permanent Court of International Justice according to Article 38 of its Statute. In particular, he

reason why the possibilities of novelty of action are not decreased on account of the fact that the great majority of cases coming before international tribunals have been, and are likely to continue to be, disputes as to the interpretation of treaties.

§ 24. International Tribunals and the Function of Filling Gaps.

The realization of the extensive scope of cases *primae impressionis* confronting international tribunals helps to throw into relief some of the most important aspects of their activity. In meeting the exigencies of novel cases, international tribunals seem to be fully conscious of the strictly juridical nature of this aspect of their activity, and of its compatibility with international law and with the powers conferred upon them by States. This attitude was given clear expression in the case *Eastern Extension, Australasia and China Telegraph Company, Ltd.*, decided on 9 November 1923 by the British-American Arbitral Tribunal under the Convention of 18 August 1910.[1] Discussing the contention that there was no rule of international law on the question of the right of the belligerent to cut neutral submarine cables, the Tribunal said that, even assuming that there was no specific rule of international law governing the case of the cutting of cables by belligerents, it could not be said that there was no principle of international law applicable.

> 'International law, as well as domestic law, may not contain, and generally does not contain, express rules decisive of particular cases; but the function of jurisprudence is to resolve the conflict of opposing rights and interests by applying, in default of any specific provision of law, the corollaries of general principles, and so to find—exactly as in the mathematical sciences—the solution of the problem. This is the method of jurisprudence; it is the method by which law has been gradually evolved in every country resulting in the definition and settlement of legal relations as well between States as between private individuals.'[2]

In what manner do international tribunals proceed when confronted with novel situations in the course of their judicial

---

may be inclined to think, not without good reason, that the order in which the first two sources of law have been placed, although technically correct, is not necessarily indicative of the function which they fulfil in the process of bringing about the decision.

[1] Nielsen's *Report*, pp. 73–81.

[2] Ibid., pp. 75, 76. In the *Argument* of Mr. Cecil J. B. Hurst (as he then was), the British agent, the student will find a lucid exposition of the function of international tribunals when confronted with novel situations (pp. 70, 71).

activity? There is a variety of ways in which they accomplish their task when confronted with an emergency of this nature:

(*a*) They may proceed either by analogy with specific rules of international law or by recourse to general principles of international law.

(*b*) They may apply general principles of law, notably of private law.

(*c*) They may bridge the gap by an even more conspicuous recourse to creative judicial activity, aiming at solving the controversy by shaping a legal rule through the process of judicial reconciliation of conflicting legal claims entitled to protection by law.

(*d*) They may accomplish the same task by a consideration of the larger needs of the international community and, in particular, by the necessity of rendering the contractual relations between States effective rather than ineffective. Instances of these four methods will now be considered.

§ 25. Filling of Gaps by Recourse to Analogy with Rules of International Law.

It happens frequently that when an international tribunal is confronted with a seemingly novel situation, although there is no rule of international law directly applicable to the case before the Court, international law regulates expressly some similar situation. It is to these rules that the Tribunal has recourse in dealing with a case *primae impressionis*. This is well illustrated by the case, referred to above, of the *Eastern Extension, Australasia and China Telegraph Company, Ltd.*, in which Great Britain, on behalf of the said company, claimed compensation for losses sustained by the company whose submarine telegraph cables were cut by the United States naval authorities during the Spanish-American war in 1898. Great Britain admitted that there existed in 1898 no conventional or customary rule of international law imposing upon the United States the duty to pay compensation for the cutting of the cables, but she contended that, in the absence of any rule of international law on the point, the Tribunal was both bound and entitled to lay down such a rule. The Tribunal declined to act on the somewhat technical view that, as there was no rule of international law limiting the freedom of action of the defendant State, the proper solution would be to reject the claim. After having defined in general terms, quoted above,[1] its duty in

---

[1] See p. 110.

cases *primae impressionis*, it proceeded to show that the point was indirectly covered by existing international law. It recalled the principle of international law which admitted that the legitimate object of sea warfare is to deprive the enemy of the means of communication which the high seas afford to States, and which even entitle the belligerent to prevent the use of the sea by neutrals who afford assistance to the enemy by carrying contraband or by transporting hostile dispatches or troops. 'It is difficult to maintain in the same breath that a belligerent is justified by international law in depriving the enemy of the benefit of the freedom of the high seas, but is not justified in depriving him of the use of the seas by means of telegraphic cables.'[1]

The case of *Coenca Brothers* v. *Germany*, decided on 1 December 1927 by the Graeco-German Mixed Arbitral Tribunal, offers a similar example of the application of the process of analogy to other existing rules of international law. This was a claim for compensation for damage suffered by the claimants in the course of the bombardment of Salonica by German air forces in January 1916. The bombardment was carried out during the night without warning. It was held that the bombardment was contrary to international law and that Germany was liable in damages. The Tribunal admitted that there were no specific rules of international law relating to aerial bombardment, but it held that the rules of international law referring to land bombardment, in particular those laid down in Article 26 of the Fourth Hague Convention respecting the laws and customs of war on land, were applicable to bombardment from the air.[2]

Another example of recourse to the analogy of express rules of international law obtaining on a subject germane to that before the Tribunal is the *Wimbledon* case, decided in the first judgement given by the Permanent Court of International Justice. Analogy did not constitute here the only source of the decision of the Tribunal, but it played a prominent part in the process of formulating judgement. After having discarded the argument of Germany as to the necessity for restrictive interpretation, the Court proceeded to point to other international agreements placing restrictions upon the exercise of rights of sovereignty; in particular it referred to the rules established with regard to the Suez and Panama

[1] Nielsen's *Report*, p. 76.
[2] *Recueil*, vii. 683, and *Annual Digest*, 1927–8, Case No. 389.

Canals. While admitting that the rules are not the same in both cases, the Court pointed out that 'they are of equal importance in that they demonstrate that the use of the great international waterways, whether by belligerent men-of-war, or by belligerent or neutral merchant ships carrying contraband, is not regarded as incompatible with the neutrality of the riparian sovereign'.[1] After discussing in detail the provisions relating to these two international waterways the Court said: 'The precedents therefore afforded by the Suez and Panama Canals invalidate in advance the argument that Germany's neutrality would have necessarily been imperilled if her authorities had allowed the passage of the "Wimbledon" through the Kiel Canal, because that vessel was carrying contraband of war consigned to a state then engaged in armed conflict.'[2]

With the method of meeting new cases by recourse to analogy with germane rules of international law, there is closely connected the method of filling of gaps by making a general principle of international law apply to the specific facts confronting the Court.[3] The manner in which the Permanent Court of International Justice applied, in its Sixth Advisory Opinion, the general principles of State succession to an altogether novel situation illustrates this method quite clearly. The situation with which the Court was presented was a typically novel one. It was confronted with a category of private rights which had baffled the doctrine of State succession before, but which had never before come for judicial determination. The combination of political and private law elements of the leasehold rights of the German colonists, in some of the territories ceded to Poland, was of such a nature as to emphasize with special force that aspect of the doctrine of State succession which subjects the State's duty to respect private rights to its political necessities and to requirements of public policy. The Court met the

---

[1] Series A, No. 1, p. 25.
[2] It will also be noted that some of the reasons which led arbitrators to adopt the doctrine of extinctive prescription were based on the analogy of acquisitive prescription of territorial title which was held to form part of international law. This was the line of reasoning adopted by Commissioner Little in the *Williams* case, decided under the Convention of 1885 between the United States and Venezuela (Moore, p. 4195)—a case which marked the entrance of the doctrine of an international statute of limitations into international law.
[3] The slight difference between this method and that discussed in the first part of this section is mainly a formal one. In the latter the process is one of deduction, in the former one of analogy.

novel situation by disregarding the political peculiarities of the case before it and by applying the general principles of international law on the matter of State succession.[1] At the same time it proceeded by way of analogy with treaty-provisions bearing upon a similar matter. It referred to Article 75 of the Treaty of Versailles, relative to contracts between the inhabitants of Alsace-Lorraine and the former German authorities, which lays down that these contracts should be maintained, and if terminated in the general interest that equitable compensation should be accorded. 'If this rule', the Court said, 'prevails in Alsace-Lorraine, which under Article 51 was restored to French sovereignty as from the date of November 11th, 1918, it is hardly conceivable that it was intended by the Treaty to give discretionary powers as regards similar rights in territories the sovereignty of which was acquired only by cession.'[2] The judgement of the Court relating to the territorial jurisdiction of the International Commission of the river Oder also combines recourse to general principles of international law and analogy with certain specific rules of international law. In this case the Court was confronted with the somewhat novel question whether the internationalization of a waterway, traversing or separating different States, stops short at the last political frontier, or whether it extends to the whole navigable river. After having rejected a series of arguments submitted by the Polish Government in support of the former alternative, the Court, in order to decide the case before it, decided to 'go back to the principles governing international fluvial law in general'.[3] These principles the Court found in the practice of States relating to international rivers and in 'the possibility of fulfilling the requirements of justice and the considerations of utility' which that practice throws into relief. That practice showed that 'a solution of the problem has been sought not in the idea of a right of passage in favour of upstream States, but in that of a community of interest of riparian States'.[4] The Court then proceeded to examine the analogous provisions of the Act of the Congress of Vienna of 1815 and

[1] See Series B, No. 6, p. 36.

[2] Ibid., p. 38. And see ibid., pp. 38, 39, for a similar reference to paragraph 2 of the Annex to Section V of Part X of the Treaty, and the Court's statement that 'if as between enemies such contracts are maintained, it seems impossible that the Treaty should have countenanced the annulment of contracts between a State and its newly acquired nationals'.

[3] Judgement No. 16, Series A, No. 23, p. 26.   [4] Ibid., p. 27.

of the corresponding articles of the Treaty of Versailles—all of which it regarded as corroborating the view that the disputed Article 331 of the latter treaty 'must be interpreted in the light of' the above general principle.[1]

§ 26. Filling of Gaps by the Application of General Principles of Law and of Principles of Private Law.

The second method of meeting new cases is to fill the gap by applying general principles of law and jurisprudence. The application of this method is open to international tribunals either by virtue of express reference in arbitration agreements empowering them to apply general principles of law,[2] or, in default of such express reference, as the consequence of the legitimate view that general principles of law are in any case necessarily included within the sources of the arbitrator's decision. These general principles of law are, in the great majority of cases, in substance coextensive with the general principles of private law. The writer has attempted in another place to show how constant is the practice of international tribunals in relying upon this particular source of law.[3] However, as will be seen from the analysis of the *Fabiani* case,[4] general principles of public law are equally applicable for this purpose. The same may be said of general maxims and principles of jurisprudence.[5] It is intended to refer here only to some of the more typical cases.

One of the most instructive instances of this aspect of international judicial activity is the *Russian Indemnity* case, decided by the Permanent Court of Arbitration in 1912. Novelty of action was its outstanding feature; so also was the way in which the tribunal had recourse to general principles of private law in order to answer the question whether and how far Turkey was bound to pay moratory interest for delays in the payment of the war indemnity to Russia by virtue of Article 5 of the Treaty of Constantinople of 1879. It affirmed, in the first instance, the obligation of Turkey to pay

---

[1] Ibid., p. 29.

[2] Paragraph 3 of Article 38 of the Statute of the Permanent Court of International Justice furnishes the most important example of a reference of this nature. It will be noted that a large number of recent arbitration treaties incorporate Article 38 bodily. See, for instance, Article 5 of the arbitration treaty of 3 December 1921 between Germany and Switzerland (*Arbitration and Security*, p. 201). For an analysis of Article 38 and for further references to treaties containing clauses of this nature see Lauterpacht, *Analogies*, § 29.

[3] See Lauterpacht, *Analogies*, § 28.

[4] See below, p. 116.   [5] See below, p. 117.

moratory interest by way of deduction from the general principle of State responsibility which, in the opinion of the Tribunal,
implied a special responsibility in the matter of delay in the
payment of a money debt. Having once determined the general
principle of responsibility, the Tribunal proceeded to apply
principles of private law in order to define both the extent of
the obligations arising therefrom and the exception to it. The
basis for determining the extent of the obligation was found in
the fact that 'all the private legislation of the States forming the
European concert admits, as did formerly the Roman law, the
obligation to pay at least interest for delayed payments as legal
indemnity when it is a question of the non-fulfilment of an
obligation consisting in the payment of a sum of money fixed
by convention, clear and exigible, such interest to be paid at
least from the date of the demand made upon the debtor in due
form of law'.[1] It was also in private law that the Tribunal, at the
very last stage of its reasoning, and after having devoted practically the whole judgement to the vindication of the Russian
claim, found the reason for acquitting Turkey from liability.[2]

The *Fabiani* case between France and Venezuela, decided in
1896 by the President of the Swiss Confederation[3] in a careful
and closely reasoned judgement, offers another example of
recourse to general principles of law, in particular of public
law. This was a claim based on denial of justice on the part of
Venezuelan Courts, and, by reason of the novelty of the circumstances accompanying the case, it afforded a good opportunity
for a bold application of general legal principles. Thus, in giving
an affirmative answer to the question whether undue delay
inpronouncing judgement constitutes denial of justice, the Tribunal said that it relied upon 'general principles of international
law concerning denial of justice, that is to say on rules common
to the majority of legal systems or as taught by writers'.[4] It was
almost exclusively by reference to numerous authorities
on municipal public law that he dealt with, and decided, the
question of the responsibility of the State for acts of its agents,

---

[1] See the award, Scott, *Hague Court Reports*, p. 316.

[2] 'In private law, the effects of demand for payment are eliminated when the
creditor, after having made legal demand upon the debtor, grants one or more
extensions for the payment of the principal obligation, without reserving the rights
acquired by the legal demand.' (Ibid., p. 322.)

[3] For the award see Lafontaine, pp. 344–69.

[4] Lafontaine, pp. 356, 362.

and in particular of its judicial officers, committed in the exercise of their functions.[1] The same authorities were his guide on the question whether any distinction ought to be made in respect of State responsibility between administrative and judicial officers, or between different degrees of fault.[2] Having thus disposed of the claim itself, he proceeded, on the basis of general principles of law, to assess the damages.

> 'In modern law,' he said, 'the person responsible for an Aquilian fault is in principle liable to repair the damage which may reasonably be anticipated as the direct or indirect consequence (*damnum emergens* and *lucrum cessans*), but while certain legal systems, like those of France and Germany, do not make the amount of damages and of interest dependent upon the gravity of the fault, other legal systems, like the Austrian Civil code and the Federal (Swiss) Code of Obligations, do not accord total reparation except in cases of fraud or grave fault.'[2]

There followed an enumeration of a representative array of private law authorities on the subject.[3] As the arbitrator found that grave fault attached to the acts and omissions of Venezuelan authorities, he awarded damages both for *damnum emergens* and *lucrum cessans*. Finally, he relied on the Swiss Code of Obligations and on Laurent's treatise for answering the question how far compound interest should be included in the computation of the sum due under the award.[4]

The question of award of damages in general, and of measure of damages in particular, furnishes, as shown already in the *Fabiani* case and in the *Russian Indemnity* case, another clear example of filling a gap in the law by recourse to general principles of law. When the Permanent Court of International Justice in the *Factory at Chorzów* case[5] stated that the duty of making reparation in case of a breach of an engagement is not only a principle of international law, but also 'a general conception of law', it gave its sanction to a long series of arbitral decisions. The same applies to the question of measure of damages. Thus in the case of the *Cape Horn Pigeon* and other vessels, decided in 1902, between the United States and Russia, the arbitrator based his decision on the view that 'the general principle of private law

---

[1] Ibid., p. 363.   [2] Ibid., p. 364.

[3] Ibid., p. 365. The judgement, which constitutes an important contribution to the general question of State responsibility, seems to be somewhat neglected by writers urging the elimination of the conception of culpability from the doctrine of State responsibility.

[4] Ibid., p. 368.

[5] Judgement No. 13 (*Claim for Indemnity, Merits*), Series A, No. 17, p. 29.

according to which damages ought to comprise an indemnity, not only for the damage suffered, but also for the loss of profits, is equally applicable to international disputes'.[1]

The way in which the doctrine of prescription has become part of international arbitral law offers yet another instructive example of the filling of an apparent gap by recourse to rules generally adopted in the systems of private law. Reference was made in one of the preceding chapters to the recent case of *Sarropoulos* v. *The Bulgarian State*, in which the Tribunal recognized extinctive prescription on the ground, *inter alia*, that it formed part of all systems of jurisprudence.[2] This was also one of the reasons for the adoption of the doctrine in the *Williams* case,[3] and for its reaffirmation in the *Gentini* case between Italy and Venezuela in 1903.[4,5]

The recourse to general maxims and principles of jurisprudence is well illustrated by the practice of the Permanent Court of International Justice, in particular in its Twelfth Advisory Opinion concerning the method of voting in the Council of the League when acting in an arbitral capacity.[6] This case, already referred to,[7] shows in an illuminating fashion how a judicial tribunal, after refusing to assume too rigidly the completeness of a legal instrument, prefers to bridge the provisional gap by recourse to a general principle of law. The general principle adopted in this case, namely, that no one is judge in his own cause, is of paramount importance for the interpretation of the Covenant of the League. There are other cases in the practice of the Court in which the same method has been adopted.[8]

---

[1] For the award see Descamps and Renault, *Recueil international des traités du XXème siècle* (1902), p. 299. See also the award in the Delagoa Bay Railway Arbitration of 1900 between Portugal and Great Britain, in which damages for *damnum emergens* and *lucrum cessans* were awarded on the basis of the 'general principles of common law of modern nations' (*Sentence Finale*, pp. 155 ff.).

[2] See above, p. 94.

[3] Moore, p. 4195.

[4] Venezuelan Arbitrations, Ralston's *Report*, pp. 726–8. The arbitrator referred, among others, to Savigny, Laurent, and Bouvier.

[5] For another instance of the application of a general principle of law see the case of *H. J. R. Hemming*, decided on 18 December 1920 by the British-American Mixed Claims Commission (Nielsen's *Report*, p. 622), in which the Tribunal held that the United States were responsible for the acts of an official acting outside the scope of his competence, on the ground that their subsequent conduct must be regarded as an implicit ratification of the contract entered into by the official in question.

[6] Series B, No. 12, p. 32.

[7] See above, p. 83.

[8] See, e.g., Judgement No. 8 (*Factory at Chorzów. Claim for Indemnity. Jurisdiction*), p. 31, for a reference to 'a principle generally accepted in the jurisprudence of international arbitration, as well as by municipal courts' to the effect 'that one Party cannot avail himself of the fact that the other has not

§ 27. Finding of Rules by Judicial Reconciliation of Conflicting Legal Claims.

This aspect of creative judicial activity has already been referred to in connexion with the question of gaps due to discrepancies in the legal views and the practice of States. Cases frequently occur in which the pretension of neither party is entirely consistent with justice or with sound juridical principle. The absence of political and legal organization in the international community makes it possible for both sides to maintain legal claims which, while not wholly unjust or unsound, are extreme and lacking in sufficient consideration for the claims of others. In such cases the judicial function asserts itself by performing the essential task of the law-creating process, namely, by effecting either a judicial compromise between two conflicting claims or, if that is not possible, by giving effect to the claim which is stronger in law. This aspect of the judicial function stops short of legislation, in that it is grounded on the existing law in so far as the latter is applicable. It is pre-eminently a judicial function, inasmuch as it is based on rules capable of general application in future similar cases. Some examples taken from the history of international arbitration will perhaps illustrate with more precision this aspect of judicial activity.

In the *Palmas Island* arbitration, decided in 1928 and referred to below,[1] the arbitrator, after affirming his duty to give a decision, even if neither party had entirely substantiated its claim to the disputed island, laid down the general rules which ought to guide the judge in giving a decision by weighing the relative merits of the titles invoked. He said:

> 'International law, like law in general, has the object of assuring the coexistence of different interests which are worthy of legal protection. If, as in the present instance, only one of two conflicting interests is to prevail, because sovereignty can be attributed to but one of the Parties, the interest which involves the maintenance of a state of things having offered at the critical time to the inhabitants of the disputed territory, and to other States, a certain guarantee for the respect of their

---

fulfilled some obligation, or has not had recourse to some means of redress, if the former Party has, by some illegal act, prevented the latter from fulfilling the obligation in question, or from having recourse to the tribunal which would have been open to him'. See also Advisory Opinion No. 16 (*Interpretation of the Graeco-Turkish Agreement of 1 December 1926*), p. 25, for another example of recourse to an 'accepted principle of law'.

[1] See below, p. 133.

rights ought, in doubt, to prevail over an interest which—supposing it to be recognized in international law—has not yet received any concrete form of development.'[1]

Accordingly, he held that the Island of Palmas ought to be attributed to the Netherlands, on the ground, *inter alia*, that 'the establishment of Netherlands authority, attested also by external signs of sovereignty, had already reached such a degree of development that the importance of maintaining this state of things ought to be considered as prevailing over a claim possibly based either on discovery in very distant times and unsupported by occupation, or on mere geographical position'.[2]

An instance of similar method is provided by the award of Judge Huber of October 1924 concerning the British claims in the Spanish Zone of Morocco, arising out of injuries done to the life and property of British subjects as the result of acts or omissions of Spanish authorities.[3] The arbitrator was confronted with two conflicting propositions advanced by the parties. According to the Spanish contention, the ascertainment of the responsibility of the authorities for damages suffered by aliens is always an internal matter, not subject to international jurisdiction. Great Britain contended that international responsibility arose whenever a State was guilty of negligence in the prevention or repression of acts injurious to nationals of other States. The arbitrator admitted that he was confronted with a situation of some difficulty. He pointed out that the abundant diplomatic correspondence concerning claims for indemnity afforded no guidance, as Governments have abstained from laying down abstract and rigid rules for situations of this description; that although the great majority of writers showed an inclination to limit the responsibility of the State, their views were often inspired by political considerations and represented a natural reaction against unjustified intervention in the affairs of certain nations; and that, although there was a considerable output of arbitral practice on the matter of the responsibility of States for damages suffered by aliens, caution was required in accepting the findings of the various commissions as authoritative, seeing that the manner of setting up the commission may determine in advance the principle of

---

[1] *A.J.* xxii (1928), p. 911.   [2] Ibid. p. 912.
[3] *Réclamations britanniques dans la zone espagnole du Maroc* (Accord anglo-espagnol du 29 Mai 1923), *Rapports*, La Haye, Mai 1925.

responsibility. In view of this the arbitrator regarded himself as justified in having recourse to general legal considerations. He said:

> 'It is accepted that every law aims at assuring the coexistence of interests deserving of legal protection. That is undoubtedly true also of international law. The conflicting interests in this case, in connection with the question of indemnification of aliens, are, on the one hand, the interest of the State in the exercise of authority in its own territory without interference or supervision by foreign States, and, on the other hand, the interest of the State in seeing the rights of its nationals in a foreign country respected and effectively protected.'[1]

While expressing the view that, by weighing the relative importance of the conflicting interests, a just and equitable solution of the difficulty could be achieved, the arbitrator remarked that 'nevertheless there will always remain, as in the majority of practical juridical questions, a fairly considerable margin or a subjective element of appreciation which cannot be removed'.[2] He then proceeded to lay down the various rules of State responsibility in regard to aliens.

The above instances show[3] that a decision yielding a result which lies half-way between the claims advanced by the parties is not necessarily the consequence of a non-judicial compromise. As between individuals so also among States it is not unusual that legal claims and defences are on both sides stated in extreme terms. It is the function of the judicial process to find the exact balance.[4] On the other hand, in the field of international disputes there are a number of questions which have remained unsolved because there has been an inclination on the part not only of States but also of tribunals to adopt a rigid and uncompromising attitude. The question of the so-called plea of non-discrimination in the treatment

---

[1] Ibid., p. 52.   [2] Ibid.

[3] This point is developed in more detail below, pp. 130 et seqq.

[4] This persistent problem in international arbitration revealed itself clearly in the proceedings and the decision of the Commission acting under Article V of the Jay Treaty of 1794—the first modern arbitral proceedings. Discussing the allegation that the award of the Commissioners laying down the St. Croix boundary was effected by diplomatic negotiation rather than by judicial determination, Moore justly observed that the result reached was 'after all an example of the necessary process of adjustment, of the weighing of one consideration against another, by which, in the presence of proofs concerning the effect of which opinions may inevitably differ, concurrent and just human judgements, judicial and otherwise, are daily reached' (*International Adjudications* [1930] ii. 368).

of aliens,[1] in particular in regard to the respect due to their property, affords an instructive example. Whereas some tribunals have adopted the view that equality of treatment provides a full answer to claims under this head,[2] others have held that absolute respect for property rights or compliance with a minimum international standard is essential if the State is to escape responsibility.[3] The same may be said of the attitude of Governments[4] and writers,[5] although there are examples on record of the same Government adopting an opposite attitude in substantially similar circumstances.[6] But the course which is believed to be the proper one, and which is suggested by the position adopted by international tribunals in other cases, would be to evolve a legal rule constituting a judicial compromise between the legally recognized claims of territorial sovereignty, on the one hand, and the internationally recognized rights of aliens, on the other hand. Thus in regard to interference with rights of property, neither full compensation nor total denial of redress might in sound law meet the requirements of justice.[7] Partial compensation adjusted to the particular circumstances of each case, while giving the impression of a compromise, might nevertheless represent a juridically sound and equitable solution.[8]

---

[1] For the literature on the plea of non-discrimination see Oppenheim, i. 294, n. 1, and 558, n. 1.

[2] See, for instance, *Standard Oil Company* case, *Annual Digest*, 1925–6, Case No. 169; *Canadian Claims for Refund of Duties* case, ibid., Case No. 168; the *Cadenhead* case, Nielsen's *Report*, p. 508.

[3] See *George W. Hopkins* case, *Annual Digest*, 1925–6, Case No. 167; *H. Roberts* case, ibid., Case No. 166.

[4] As revealed, for instance, at The Hague Codification Conference in 1930.

[5] See, e.g., the resolution of the International Law Association in 1930: 36th *Report*, p. 361; but see Cavaglieri, in *R.G.* xxxviii (1931), pp. 293–6, and, in particular, Fischer Williams, *Chapters*, pp. 147–87.

[6] Compare, for instance, the attitude of the United States in the controversy with Mexico concerning the provisions of her constitution affecting the property of aliens (see Bullington in *A.J.* xxi (1927), pp. 685–705) with their communication to the Norwegian Government following upon the award in the Norwegian shipowners' claim in 1922: '...due process of law applied uniformly, and without discrimination to nationals and aliens alike, and offering to all just terms of reparation or reimbursement, suffices to meet the requirements of international law' (*A.J.* xvii [1923], p. 288).

[7] Probably the failure to realize fully the possibilities of this aspect of judicial activity was responsible for the protracted and juridically unsatisfactory course of the well-known Hungarian-Roumanian Optants dispute. The parties apparently thought that a judicial decision on the merits must result either in an award of full compensation or the total rejection of the claims.

[8] A certain approximation to this method will be found in Judgement No. 7 of the Permanent Court (*German Interests in Polish Upper Silesia. Merits*) in which, while laying down that a measure prohibited by a treaty cannot become lawful 'by reason of the fact that the State applies it to its own nationals' (p. 33), the

§ 28. Filling of Gaps by reference to the Needs of the International Community and the Effectiveness of Treaty Obligations.

When, in meeting a novel situation, there is no room for exclusive application of any of the methods described above, there still remains that source of judicial activity which consists in the realization of the purpose of the law, namely, in finding, in case of doubt, solutions most conducive to the benefit of the community as a whole and to the necessity of stable and effective legal relations between its members. The operation of this method is illustrated by the principal reasons which caused international tribunals to recognize extinctive and acquisitive prescription, that is to say, the consideration of stability, of the necessity for maintaining, so far as possible and equitable, the established order of things, and of discouraging endless litigation. Thus, in regard to acquisitive prescription, the arbitrator in the above-mentioned *Island of Palmas* case, when stressing the importance of peaceful, continuous, and effective display of State activity as a title of acquisition of sovereignty, expressed the view that the recognition of the law-creating effect of prescription in international law is particularly necessary in view of the particular needs of the international society. He pointed out that although municipal law, owing to its complete judicial system, is able to recognize, subject to rules of prescription and protection of property, abstract rights of property as existing apart from any material manifestation of them, 'international law, the structure of which is not based on any super-state organization, cannot be presumed to reduce a right such as territorial sovereignty, with which almost all international relations are bound up, to the category of an abstract right, without concrete manifestation'.[1] The same reason underlay the decision of The Hague Tribunal in the *Grisbadarna* case between Sweden and Norway, when it stated that 'a state of things which actually exists and has existed for a long time should be changed as little as possible';[2] and it was given expression, in regard to extinctive prescription, in the *Gentini* case, by reference, *inter alia*, to the maxim 'interest rei publicae ut sit finis litium'.[3]

Court nevertheless admitted that 'expropriation for reasons of public utility' may not necessarily be prohibited by international law (p. 22).

[1] *A.J.* xxii (1928), p. 876.
[2] Award of 23 October 1909, Scott, *Hague Court Reports*, p. 130.
[3] Ralston's *Report*, p. 726.

The award of the Swiss Federal Council of 24 March 1922, in the boundary dispute between Colombia and Venezuela, affords another example of meeting a novel situation by the application of the principle of effectiveness of treaties and of awards given in pursuance thereof. In this case the arbitrator was called upon to decide whether either of the disputant parties was entitled to take possession, without formal rendition, of the territories given to it by a previous arbitral award,[1] and clearly defined either by natural frontiers or as the result of the work of delimitation commissions set up in pursuance of that award. The arbitrator answered this question in the affirmative for the reason, *inter alia*, that the disputed and novel question as to the necessity of formal delivery must be answered by reference to the necessity of rendering effective the relations between the parties: 'Thirty years have elapsed since the Spanish award was given; that award cannot indefinitely remain in the nature of a judicial abstraction.'[2]

The work of the Permanent Court of International Justice shows how novel situations are met by an application and interpretation of the law which, although based on the existing conventional and customary rules of law, is guided by a constructive consideration of the needs of the international community. When in the *Lotus* case the Court refrained from limiting itself to a mere affirmation of freedom of action as derived from the principle of State sovereignty, and formulated the rule of concurrent jurisdiction—as best calculated to protect the interests of States and to meet the requirements of justice—in regard to crimes committed by foreigners outside the national territory;[3] when in the Advisory Opinion relating to the powers of the Council of the League of Nations in fixing the boundary between Iraq and Turkey, the Court explained the necessity for a unanimous decision[4] on the ground that, only if the decisions of the Council are backed by the unanimous consent of its members, will they possess the necessary degree of authority, and in particular on the ground that it is necessary that decisions affecting the peace of the world should have the support of those Members of the Council who by reason of their political position might have to bear the major share of responsibility for putting these

---

[1] Given on 16 March 1891, on behalf of the King of Spain.

[2] *Sentence Arbitrale*, p. 106. See also *Annual Digest*, 1919–22.

[3] Judgement No. 9, Series A, No. 10, p. 30.

[4] Not requiring, however, the votes of the parties to the dispute. See above, p. 83.

decisions into effect;[1] when in the Second and Thirteenth Advisory Opinions the Court expressed the view that the exclusion of agriculture from the purview of the activities of the International Labour Organization, or the failure to regulate conditions of work in agriculture by way of international agreement, might act as a check on the adoption of more humane conditions of labour by constituting 'a handicap against the nations which had adopted them, and in favour of those which had not, in the competition of the markets of the world',[2] and that 'it is not conceivable' that the parties to the Treaty of Versailles intended, by excluding the right of regulating the work of employers when such regulation is essential for, and incidental to, the regulation of the work of employees, to prevent the Organization from accomplishing its essential object of assuring humane conditions of work and the protection of workers;[3] when in the Sixth and Seventh Advisory Opinions the Court refused to interpret the Minorities Treaties in a manner which would deprive them of a great part of their value;[4] when in the *Chorzów Factory* case, in the plea to the jurisdiction in respect of the claim for indemnity, the Court affirmed its competence to give a decision on the question of reparation for a breach of an international engagement,[5] on the ground that otherwise its judgements, 'instead of settling a dispute once and for all, would leave open the possibility of further disputes',[6] and that an interpretation which would limit the Court 'simply to recording that the Convention had been incorrectly applied or that it had not been applied, without being able to lay down the conditions for the re-establishment of the treaty rights affected, would be contrary to what would, prima facie, be the natural object of the clause'[7]—all these

[1] Series B, No. 12, p. 29.
[2] Series B, No. 2, p. 25.
[3] Series B, No. 13, p. 18.
[4] See Series B, No. 6, pp. 23, 24, and No. 7, p. 17.
[5] Although the treaty in question conferred upon it jurisdiction only in regard to differences concerning the interpretation and the application of its provisions.
[6] Judgement No. 8, Series A, No. 9, p. 25.
[7] Ibid. For an interesting cumulation of various sources of decision in a novel case, see the Judgement of the Permanent Court of International Justice of 30 August 1924 (Judgement No. 2, *The Mavrommatis Palestine Concessions, P.C.I.J.*, Series A, No. 2, p. 16), in which the Court was confronted with the fact that neither the Statute nor the Rules of the Court contained any rule regarding the procedure to be followed in the event of an objection being taken *in limine litis* to the Court's jurisdiction: 'The Court therefore is at liberty to adopt the principle which it considers best calculated to ensure the administration of justice, most suited to procedure before an international tribunal and most in conformity with the fundamental principles of international law.'

cases show how creative judicial activity, while remaining within the orbits of the existing law, fills the gaps by a consideration of the practical needs of international co-operation and of the effectiveness of the treaties concluded by States.[1]

Finally, as to the last instance of this aspect of judicial activity, reference ought to be made to the manner in which international tribunals solve the difficulties arising out of the fact of double or triple nationality. Under international law the nationality of individuals is in principle a matter of municipal law.[2] There are no rules of customary or conventional law in existence which could serve as a guide for an international tribunal in a case in which it is incumbent upon it to decide to which of the two or three nationalities preference ought to be given. Such a decision may be necessary not only for the protection of the interests of individuals, but also of the interests of States in all cases in which, for the sake of more or less transient advantages, an individual deems it proper to acquire and to claim the status of a given nationality. In all cases of double nationality, the international tribunal is confronted with two nationalities, both of which are equally valid under international law. The absence of a regulative principle rendering possible a choice between the two constitutes, in a sense, a gap in the law. But the history of international arbitration does not provide instances of tribunals refusing on this ground to give a decision. Their task is to solve the conflict with which they are confronted. They do it, without calling into question the validity of either nationality, 'in accordance with rules of international law'— to use the words of the arbitrator in the *Arata* case between

[1] See here also for another example of meeting a novel case by recourse to the principle of effectiveness of treaties, the award of the Upper Silesian Mixed Commission of 15 November 1925, on the question as to the language in which testimonials of minority schools in Upper Silesia should be issued to pupils. There was no provision in the Geneva Convention of 15 May 1922 between Poland and Germany regulating this matter. It was held that the fact that the treaty did not regulate this matter was not decisive; that the type of minority schools created by the Convention in question was a new one, and admitted of no such detailed regulation; that in the absence of special regulations the general purpose of the treaty must serve as the basis for the solution of questions arising in practical life; and that 'if claims of minorities, justifiable in themselves, were to be rejected on the ground that there was in the treaty no express provision to uphold them, then the minority schools would become a parody of the intentions of the makers of the treaty': *Annual Digest*, 1925–6, Case No. 237, and *Zeitschrift für ost-europäisches Recht*, ii (1926), p. 73.

[2] See for an affirmation of this principle—subject to the existing treaty obligations—Advisory Opinion No. 4, p. 24.

Italy and Peru in 1903.[1] In these decisions, international tribunals, while leaving aside the supposed differences between the Anglo-American and continental schools of thought on the subject of nationality, have evolved a working rule based on the conception of 'active nationality'.[2] A series of judgements given by the Mixed Arbitral Tribunals established by the Peace Treaties of 1919 brings clearly to light this aspect of the activity of international courts.[3]

§ 29. The Problem of 'non liquet' in the History of International Arbitration.

Both the fundamental prohibition of *non liquet*, conceived as the prohibition to refuse the adjudication of a claim on the ground of absence of law, and the great variety of methods by means of which international tribunals are in a position to meet novel situations,[4] explain why, contrary to some loose statements on the matter, the history of international arbitration shows no single instance of an arbitral tribunal refusing to give a decision because of the supposed absence of a rule of law. A case frequently referred to as supporting the view of the admissibility of *non liquet* is the award given on 10 January 1831 by the King of Holland, acting as arbitrator between Great Britain and the United

---

[1] See for the award of 30 September 1903 Descamp and Renault, op. cit., i. 709. See also the award in the *Medina* case between Costa Rica and the United States of 31 December 1862 in Lapradelle and Politis, i. 167–70, and a learned note on the general aspects of the problem, ibid., pp. 170–7.

[2] It is immaterial that in doing this they frequently avail themselves of the term 'domicile', thus lending colour to the view that a certain particular conception is being adopted. See, for instance, the *Brignone* case before the Italian-Venezuelan Claims Commission, and the opinion of Ralston, Umpire, *Venezuelan Arbitrations*, p. 716. See also the *Maninat* case, before the French-Venezuelan Commission in 1902, Ralston's *Report*, supplementary volume (1906), p. 74, and further cases cited therein.

[3] See, for instance, *Baron Frédéric de Born* v. *Yugoslav State* (*Annual Digest*, 1925–6, Case No. 205) and *Barthez de Montfort* v. *Treuhänder Hauptverwaltung* (ibid., Case No. 206).

[4] With regard to the varieties of judicial method referred to in the three preceding paragraphs, it must be kept in mind that in all of them the activity of international tribunals remains within the orbit of the application of the existing law to cases *primae impressionis*. It was not necessary to refer here to cases in which the legal basis of the decision is broadened by an express provision of a general or particular arbitration treaty which empowers the tribunals to make recommendations, or to decide *ex aequo et bono*, or in accordance with principles of justice or of equity. Treaties of this description are discussed in another part of this book. (See below, pp. 317 et seqq., 372 et seqq.) The extension of the legal basis of the decision by a special agreement of the parties is not necessary in order to relieve an international tribunal of the necessity of having to pronounce a *non liquet*. As has been shown before, an international tribunal is in any case prevented from adopting such a course.

States in the matter of the north-eastern boundary. Under the Treaty of Ghent of 24 December 1814 a mixed commission was entrusted with the task of rendering a decision on the disputed frontier. Article IV of the same treaty provided that, in case of failure of the commissioners to arrive at a decision, the two Governments shall submit the reports of the commissioners to 'some friendly sovereign or State to be then named for the purpose'. In pursuance of that treaty, and following upon the disagreement of the commissioners, a further convention was concluded on 29 September 1827, in which the contracting parties undertook to choose a friendly sovereign or State as arbiter to act and give a 'just and sound decision' in case the commissioners should be unable to agree within two years after the arbitrator thus chosen had signified his consent to act in that capacity. The contracting parties agreed to ask the King of the Netherlands to act as the arbitrator.

The arbitrator found that 'the arguments adduced on either side, and the documents exhibited in support of them, cannot be considered as sufficiently preponderating to determine a preference in favour of either one of the two lines respectively claimed' by the parties; that 'the nature of the difference and the vague and not sufficiently determinate stipulations of the Treaty of 1783' did not permit 'the award of either of those lines to one of the said Parties, without violating the principles of law and equity with regard to the other'; and that the circumstances upon which the decision depended 'could not be further elucidated by means of fresh topographical investigations, nor by the production of additional documents'.[1] However, he did not on these grounds decline to give a decision. 'Nous sommes d'avis', he said, 'qu'il conviendra d'adopter pour limites de deux États une ligne...', and he proceeded to indicate a line which he regarded as most suitable and as most in accordance with the treaty of 1783. The representative of the United States protested against the award, on the ground that the arbitrator exceeded his powers by making a recommendation instead of pronouncing an award. The question, he said, on what lines the boundary should run if the treaty of 1783 could not be

---

[1] The award is printed in Moore, pp. 119–36; Lapradelle and Politis, i. 371–7; and Lafontaine, p. 11. For a full account of the case see Moore, pp. 85–161; Asser in Lapradelle and Politis, i. 355–400; and White, *Boundary Disputes and Treaties* (1914): Extract from *Canada and its Provinces*, pp. 751–825.

executed was not one which the United States were prepared to submit to the arbitration of another sovereign power. Subsequently the Senate of the United States resolved that the award was not obligatory; and Great Britain did not insist on its acceptance.[1] The award met with some strong criticism on the part of several writers.[2] It has, in the absence of better examples, become the *casus classicus* of excess of jurisdiction. It may be doubted whether this case constitutes in fact an example either of excess of jurisdiction or of a judicial *non liquet*. It certainly cannot be both. What apparently is contended by the critics of this award is that there ought to have been pronounced a *non liquet*, and that the failure to pronounce it resulted in a clear excess of jurisdiction. This latter assertion is a controversial one, and will be discussed presently. In any case, notwithstanding the considerable difficulties involved in giving a decision, the award is a clear example of assumption of jurisdiction, and not of a refusal to adjudicate.

It has been maintained that the boundary line chosen by the arbitrator disregarded the treaty of 1783; that, although he was at liberty to lay down a line other than that claimed by either party, the line ought nevertheless to have been one grounded in the treaty; that as the terms of the treaty had proved impossible of effective interpretation, the arbitrator ought to have declared a *non liquet*; that although it is true that municipal courts are not at liberty to refuse a decision, seeing that they are bound to give effect not only to the will of the parties, but also to administer the law as a whole, this is not so in the case of international tribunals which are expected and entitled to give effect to the arbitration agreement only and exclusively.[3] It is difficult to follow these arguments. The passage of the award, quoted above, shows that the arbitrator was conscious of his duty to give a legal award in conformity with 'law and equity'. There is no warrant to assume that he disregarded the treaty of 1783. On the contrary, the reasoning of the award indicates that the decision was inspired by the wish to render that treaty effective rather than ineffective. Admittedly, the wording of the decision is open to reproach on the ground that it was apt to create the impression of being a mere recommendation and

[1] However, it may not be strictly accurate to maintain that there was 'a mutual waiver of the award' (Moore, p. 137).

[2] See, for instance, Asser in Lapradelle and Politis, i. 392–400.

[3] These points are clearly put by Asser, op. cit., pp. 398 ff.

that it failed to make express reference to the treaty of 1783, to
which the decision given was the nearest approximation. But the
formal defects cannot invalidate the substance of the award. In
particular, the undoubted fact that the arbitrator is bound by
the terms of the *compromis* ought not to lead to the conclusion
that he is not bound by anything else. When two parties constitute a judicial tribunal to *decide* a controversy they must first be
presumed to mean what they say, namely, that they wish the
arbitrator to dispose finally, so far as a legal decision can do it, of
the object of the dispute; secondly, they must be presumed to
wish that the international tribunal should regard itself as bound
by the entire body of substantive and adjective rules of international law, including those rules of interpretation of treaties
which postulate the effectiveness of treaty provisions.

An arbitrator who arrives at the final conclusion, that a
provision of a treaty means nothing, has failed in his duty as a
jurist and a judge. When necessary, even the most rudimentary
evidence of the intention of the parties, coupled with the rich
armoury of rules of logical and historical interpretation, ought to
be sufficient to produce a substantive result preventing the treaty
from becoming ineffective. It is submitted that it is irrelevant
to say that when the judge is unable to elucidate the intention
of the parties he ought to pronounce a *non liquet*.[1] It is his duty to
find what, having regard to the available data, was the intention
of the parties or what the intention of the parties must be
presumed to have been.[2] When certainty is unattainable, the
nearest approximation to the proper construction of the treaty
must be the object aimed at. When Great Britain and the
United States concluded on 8 May 1871 an arbitration convention to settle the Vancouver Island boundary dispute,[3] they in-

---

[1] Lammasch, *Schiedsgerichtsbarkeit*, p. 184.

[2] It was only excess of caution, prompted by the experience of the award of 1831,
which induced the Emperor of Russia, when invited in 1888 to act as arbitrator
between France and Holland concerning the frontier dispute in Guiana and
Surinam, to insist that he be given the right to fix a boundary line other than
that demanded by the parties. These powers were conferred upon him in the
supplementary convention of 28 April 1889 (printed in Lafontaine, pp. 328ff.).
However, in his award of 13 May 1891 he found no occasion to avail himself of
these additional powers (for the award see Moore, p. 4869). See on this matter
Rolin-Jaequemyns in *R.I.* xxiii (1891), p. 84, who disapproves of the new departure,
and Renault in *R.G.* i (1894), who approves of it. See also Mérignhac, p. 108, and
Lammasch, *Schiedsgerichtsbarkeit*, p. 182.

[3] The convention and the award, given on 21 October 1872 by the German
Emperor, are printed in Lafontaine, pp. 149–51.

structed the arbitrator to decide which of the claims put forward
by the parties 'is most in accordance with the true interpretation' of the relevant treaty provisions. When France and Brazil
concluded on 10 April 1897 an arbitration agreement for the
settlement of the dispute concerning the boundary between
Brazil and French Guiana, they equally conferred a substantial
measure of discretion upon the arbitrator.[1] And the arbitration
conventions between Colombia and Venezuela of 14 September
1881 and of 15 February 1886 expressly empowered the arbitrator to 'fijar la línea del modo que crea más aproximado á los
documentos existentes'.[2] However, it is only *ex abundanti cautela*
that these express provisions are inserted. Their existence in no
way derogates from the right and the duty of arbitration tribunals to pronounce judgements on the basis of the closest possible
approximation to the existing rule in all cases of doubt. Uncertainty can never be regarded as a reason for the abdication of
the judicial function. Thus, in the *North Atlantic Fisheries* arbitration of 1910 between Great Britain and the United States, the
Tribunal, in answering the question whence must be measured
the three marine miles of the 'coasts, bays, creeks, or harbours'
referred to in the treaty of 1818, recognized that the law on the
matter was far from being clear. But that circumstance did not
prevent it from answering the question as put to it in the
arbitration agreement. The answer was necessarily a general
one, and the Tribunal availed itself of the right, conferred upon
it in the *compromis*, to propose by way of recommendation more
concrete rules calculated to enhance the usefulness of its
answer.[3]

§ 30. The Question of 'non liquet' in Boundary and Territorial Disputes. The Island of Palmas Arbitration.

It
is in particular in respect of boundary disputes that
writers are inclined to propound the view that the arbitrator
may frequently find himself under the necessity of refusing
to give a decision, namely, in cases where the parties put
forward contrary pretensions which neither of them proves
able to substantiate before the Court by sufficient evidence.
It is pointed out by these writers that, unless specifically

---

[1] See Lafontaine, pp. 563ff., for the convention and the award.
[2] Ibid., p. 513. The award of 16 March 1891 is printed ibid. See also Lammasch,
Schiedsgerichtsbarkeit, pp. 181–4, for more detailed references.
[3] See below, p. 311.

entrusted, the Court is not at liberty to choose a third intermediate line; that its function is to ascertain the frontier as given by the existing law; and that the effect of its decision is not to create new rights, but to declare the existing ones. While these last two submissions may be readily assented to, it is difficult to admit that they are relevant to the first—the accuracy of which is open to question. This view is put forward by writers of authority,[1] but it is not supported by the practice of international tribunals. If the business of the judge is to declare the existing frontier in regard to the disputed territory, then it is difficult to see why, in ascertaining the existing law, he should be bound by the assertions of the parties which may go beyond what they are legitimately entitled to claim.[2] In fact, it may be assumed that they will tend to exaggerate their legal rights. It is the frontier as given by law, and not as arbitrarily defined by the litigants, that the arbitrator has to lay down. If he chooses an intermediate line, there is no reason for maintaining with any degree of cogency that the boundary chosen is a common denominator arrived at through a process of compromise and mediation, as distinguished from a strictly judicial procedure.[3] Unless he is expressly precluded by the terms of the arbitration agreement from adopting such a course, he may—in fact, he must—by balancing the relative value of the arguments and proofs adduced by the parties, fix a line which he deems to be correct in law. He may choose a line suggested by one party. But he need not necessarily do so.[4]

---

[1] See Lammasch, *Rechtskraft*, p. 31; Renault, Lapradelle, and Politis in *R.G.* xiii (1906), p. 319; Paul de Lapradelle, *La Frontière* (1928), pp. 142, 143.

[2] Since these lines were written, the view expressed in the text has found authoritative confirmation in the final Judgement of the Permanent Court of International Justice of 7 June 1932, in the case of the Free Zones of Upper Savoy and the District of Gex (Series A/B, No. 46): 'From a general point of view, it cannot lightly be admitted that the Court, whose function is to declare the law, can be called upon to choose between two or more constructions determined beforehand by the Parties, none of which may correspond to the opinion at which it may arrive' (at p. 138). See also Series A, No. 2, p. 24, for a similar instance.

[3] See above, p. 121.

[4] The logical arguments adduced in support of the contrary view are more plausible than convincing. Thus it is said by Renault, Lapradelle, and Politis: 'La mission de l'arbitre est de vérifier une ligne. L'arbitre ne statue pas sur le partage d'une masse territoriale considérée comme superficie, mais sur l'identité d'une *frontière* considérée comme ligne. La sentence ne porte pas directement sur une quantité, mais directement sur une identité. La quantité est susceptible de plus ou de moins. L'identité n'est susceptible que d'être ou

Even if the arbitrator is expressly instructed to adopt one of the contrary claims, that circumstance does not prevent him from arriving at a decision by gauging the relative merits of the claims put forward by the parties, or compel him to pronounce a *non liquet* when he finds that neither of the parties has succeeded in proving its contentions up to the hilt. This is very clearly illustrated by the concluding remarks of Professor Huber, the sole arbitrator in the *Palmas Island* arbitration.[1] Article I of the arbitration agreement of 23 January 1925 provided expressly that the sole duty of the arbitrator shall be to determine whether the Island of Palmas belongs *in its entirety* to either of the parties.[2] The arbitrator, having considered the respective claims based on discovery, cession, and effective occupation, found that the disputed island formed in its entirety a part of Netherlands territory. But he admitted in the concluding section of the award that the same conclusion would be reached even if it were admitted that the evidence laid before the Tribunal did not suffice to substantiate the Dutch title as based on continuous and peaceful display of sovereignty. 'In this case', he said, 'no party would have established its claims to sovereignty over the island and the decision of the arbitrator would have to be founded on the relative strength of the titles invoked by each party.' And he added: 'The possibility for the Arbitrator to found his decision on the relative strength of the titles invoked on either side must have been envisaged by the Parties to the Special Agreement, because it was to be foreseen that the evidence produced as regards sovereignty over a territory in the circumstances of the island in dispute might prove not to be sufficient to lead to a clear conclusion as to the existence of sovereignty.'[3]

---

de ne pas être. Une ligne peut être autre, elle ne peut pas être moindre. Une masse est divisible, une frontière ne l'est pas.' (Op. cit., p. 319.)

The argument, it is submitted, misses the point. The question is certainly not one of *dividing* the frontier. The question is to *fix* the indivisible frontier as it exists in law.

[1] The award is printed in *A.J.* xxii (1928), pp. 867–912.

[2] Ibid., p. 868.

[3] The arbitrator, in pointing to his duty to give a final decision, seems to have attached importance to the fact that in the Preamble to the arbitration convention the parties expressed the desire to have the dispute 'terminated'. This expression showed, said the arbitrator, that 'it is the evident will of the Parties that the arbitral award shall not conclude by a *non liquet*'. It is suggested, with deference, that such a final decision must always be regarded as being intended by the parties. In submitting a case for judicial settlement, States contemplate primarily the termination of the dispute.

§ 31. Conclusions. It may be useful to summarize the conclusions reached in this Part.

In so far as the doctrine of the limitation of the international judicial function rests upon the supposed non-existence of legal rules applicable to disputes, the doctrine is contrary to generally accepted principles of positive municipal law and of general jurisprudence with which the completeness of the legal system and the prohibition of judicial *non liquet* are fundamental principles admitting of no exceptions. It disregards the fact that the so-called gaps of international law, while admittedly presenting a more serious problem than in municipal jurisprudence, are capable of being filled in the course of the normal exercise of international judicial activity. The history of international judicial settlement supplies a continuous proof of this process. It has produced no instance of a refusal on the part of an international judicial tribunal to give a decision on the ground of the absence of applicable rules of law.

Notwithstanding the admitted peculiarities and comprehensiveness of its gaps, international law, like any other system of law, is complete from the point of view of its adequacy to deal with any dispute brought before an international judicial tribunal. At the same time it has been shown that, like any other system of law, international law contains gaps from the point of view of the approximation of its rules to the essential purposes of international law and to the requirements of international justice. To disregard this fact, in deference to a purely mechanical conception of the completeness of international law, is to thwart the judicial activity of international tribunals in a manner contrary to the spirit of international law. The juxtaposition of these apparently contradictory submissions, namely, that in one sense there exist gaps and that in another sense there cannot be a question of gaps, is apt to prove confusing. But the confusion must disappear when the significance of the double meaning of the term 'gap' is fully realized. According to one meaning, which has gained currency in international law, it connotes the inability of the law to give any decision at all in a given case; according to the other it connotes the inability to give a decision consistent with the social purpose of the law and with the requirement of unity within the law. The analysis here undertaken has revealed that *ultimately* there are no gaps in the law either from the jurisdictional (i.e.

formal) or the material point of view. From the jurisdictional point of view there are no gaps, inasmuch as it is axiomatic that the judge is bound to give a decision on the dispute before him. From the point of view of the material adequacy of the existing law, such gaps as undoubtedly occur to the judicial mind are merely provisional. They are ultimately either filled by the legitimate process of developing the existing legal materials or eliminated, however reluctantly, from the purview of judicial, as distinguished from legislative, cognizance.

At the same time we have shown that the problem of what may be called the material completeness of the law is a general legal problem whose urgency and importance are in international law greater than elsewhere. The international lawyer who is satisfied with having attempted to prove the unsoundness of the doctrine of the limitation of the judicial function in international law, in so far as it is based on the existence of rules of law applicable to the case, is therefore accomplishing only one half of his task. The juridical shortcomings of this doctrine ought not to be regarded as a reason for disregarding one of the most important problems of judicial settlement of international disputes, namely, the magnitude of the task with which international judges are confronted in solving, in the course of their judicial task of creatively applying and developing international law, the eternal antinomy between rule and discretion.[1]

[1] The gaps of international law reveal themselves not only in the absence of adequate legal rules in respect of definite situations. As consent is generally regarded as the condition of the existence of a rule of international law, a clear divergence of views or practice constitutes prima facie evidence of a gap in international law. This is the reason why the widespread belief in the existence of two substantially different schools of thought in international law, namely, the Anglo-American and the Continental schools, is of paramount importance for the problem of the international judicial function. For if we admit that the differences between them are as substantial and as fundamental as is generally assumed, then we question to a large extent the existence of that community of law between nations which is the essential condition of the proper functioning of an international judiciary. This is the explanation why the question of the existence of these two schools of thought has been given prominence, especially in connexion with the problem of obligatory arbitration and the justiciability of international disputes. The writer has attempted to show elsewhere that the alleged fundamental differences between the Continental and Anglo-American schools of thought in international law are grossly exaggerated and, so far as the international law of peace is concerned, practically non-existent. See *B.Y.*, 1931, pp. 31–62.

PART III
POLITICAL DISPUTES AND THE JUDICIAL FUNCTION IN INTERNATIONAL LAW

CHAPTER VII
IMPORTANCE OF DISPUTES AS A TEST OF JUSTICIABILITY

I

Political Disputes in General

§ 1. Political Disputes as involving Important Issues. Writers and statesmen desiring to endow the doctrine of the limitations of the international judicial function with the authority of a legal theory feel attracted by the view that, owing to the material insufficiency and inadequate development of the law of nations, there are disputes which are incapable of settlement by the application of generally recognized rules of international law, and which are therefore political. However, the test of the limitation of the judicial function based on the applicability of legal rules is not the most important one in practice. This attribute must be reserved for the distinction between legal and political disputes based on the relative importance of the subject-matter of the controversy. According to this test those disputes are political, and therefore non-justiciable, which affect the important, or—to use the current expression—the vital interests of States.

As shown in the introductory part of this book, it was Vattel who, without referring to the doctrine *eo nomine*, first gave clear, although discreet, expression[1] to the view that arbitration in international disputes must stop short of grave matters affecting the safety of the State. This limitation of the function of arbitration was the central theme with most of the writers in the second half of the nineteenth century during the discussions concerning obligatory arbitration and the future of arbitration in general.[2] Some of these writers confined themselves to stating this limitation in terms of an obvious proposition not requiring any detailed elaboration. Thus Westlake, as we have seen, regarded as political, and therefore not suitable for arbitration, disputes affecting the independence of nations, independence being here synonymous not merely with the existence of the State, but with its

---

[1] See above, p. 7.   [2] See above, pp. 10 et seqq.

right not to be hindered 'in doing or not doing anything that an independent state may justly do or abstain from doing'.[1] Von Bar expressed the view that 'courts of arbitration are the proper agency for securing the peace in respect of international disputes of minor importance which are not likely to become questions of honour', and that 'they are not the appropriate instrument for deciding very important national issues, seeing that such questions cannot, either wholly or in part, be described as legal questions'.[2] Revon, the author of a leading monograph on international arbitration, regarded questions referring to the 'autonomie souveraine d'un peuple' as affected by an 'incompétence absolue de l'arbitrage'.[3] Similar were the views of writers like Rivier, Trendelenburg, Mougin de Roquefort, Fiore, Calvo, Lacointe, Dreyfus, Ullmann, and others referred to in another part of this volume.[4]

Other writers, while adopting substantially the same view, explained it by asserting that as arbitration is a process of applying legal rules, and as questions of political power and honour are not capable of legal formulation, they were not a suitable object of arbitration. Thus, says Geffcken: 'A state will not lightly submit to arbitration questions relating to its position of power and honour. Arbitration is possible only when the opposing claims can be formulated juridically. Such cases, however, are the least frequent and the least important.'[5] F. von Martens, who played a leading part in the First and Second Hague Conferences, was emphatic that matters suitable for arbitration must be capable of juridical analysis. But, he said, it could hardly be assumed that in matters of world historical importance, parties would submit to an arbitral tribunal, and that the latter would be in a position to base its judgement on legal grounds. Accordingly, in all international disputes in which the political element predominates, settlement by arbitration is impossible. The latter, he submitted, was applicable only to disputes of minor importance relating to interests capable of legal determination.[6] The same attitude found clear expression in what may be regarded as the first scientific attempt by a jurist to deal with the distinction between legal

---

[1] *International Law* (2nd ed., 1910), i, No. 357.

[2] Quoted after Nippold, p. 174.

[3] Quoted after Nippold, p. 496.

[4] See above, p. 12.

[5] In Heffter, *Das europäische Völkerrecht der Gegenwart* (8th ed., 1888), p. 231. See also Klüber, *Völkerrecht* (2nd ed., 1851), p. 377, n. *a*.

[6] *Völkerrecht* (German ed. by Bergbohm, 1883) vol. ii, p. 466.

and political disputes, namely, in a Memorandum prepared by Professor Goldschmidt in 1872 for the Institute of International Law.[1]

This method of approach remained predominant in the twentieth century. It was countenanced in substance, if not in form, by writers like Nippold[2] and Wehberg,[3] scholars who were admittedly warm adherents of obligatory arbitration, but who regarded the inclusion of broad reservations identical with the 'honour clause' as politically or theoretically indispensable. The only points of difference were such questions as whether these reservations were so essential as to render their express inclusion unnecessary,[4] or whether in lieu of a number of elastic reservations it might not be advisable to agree on a single one of adequate comprehensiveness. Thus Fauchille[5] defined as 'political' any dispute, even one calling for an examination of questions of law, which affects the independence, the vital interests, or the national honour of the State. Balch, who made the distinction between political and legal disputes the subject of special study, was emphatic that the distinction between legal and political disputes does not depend on the question whether there is a generally recognized rule of international law applicable to the case. The proper test, he says, is whether the award of the arbitrator may have the effect of seriously lessening the power of either of the parties to the dispute. Legal disputes are, according to him, such disputes as do not involve 'the life and future of nations... whereas political questions are differences that do involve in their solution the future relative power, and so

---

[1] See above, p. 52.

[2] pp. 201–30; and the same, 'Das Problem der obligatorischen Schiedsgerichtsbarkeit', in *Jahrbuch des öffentlichen Rechts*, viii (1914), pp. 43–5.

[3] In *A.J.* vii (1913), pp. 308–12, and *Z.V.* vii (1913), Supplement, pp. 11–13.

[4] According to that view, the 'honour clause', i.e. the reservation of freedom of action, whether clearly expressed or not, forms an essential element of any commitment in the field of international arbitration; and, similarly as in the case of the 'clausula rebus sic standibus' there is no obligation to arbitrate strong enough to exclude that tacit reservation. This view was clearly expressed by Zorn (op. cit., pp. 22, 23), a leading German lawyer.

[5] *Traité de droit international public*, 8th ed. of Bonfils, i (1926), No. 947 (i). See also, to the same effect, Kohler, *Völkerrecht* (1918), p. 14. When, therefore, Hyde, 'Legal Problems Capable of Settlement by Arbitration', in *Judicial Settlement of International Disputes*, No. 11, p. 9, says that 'It must be obvious that the legal character of an international dispute is not dependent upon the magnitude of the issue involved, or upon the degree of interest with which one state may cherish a principle decisive of its own conduct,' this statement, which we believe to be a correct formulation of the legal position, is not expressive of an opinion generally held.

the fate of nations'.[1] Senator Elihu Root, a statesman with a deservedly great reputation as a lawyer, when discussing in 1911 the proposed arbitration treaty of the United States with Great Britain regarded it as axiomatic that questions of any nature which might affect the fundamental rights of States could never be justiciable.[2] When in 1922 the Institute of International Law discussed the question of classification of international disputes, many of its members were content with describing as political all disputes affecting the independence, honour, and the vital interests of nations.[3]

Governments have frequently given expression to the view that obligatory judicial settlement of disputes must be confined to small issues. This, as we have seen, was the basis of the well-known Memorandum prepared by the Russian delegation for the use of the First Hague Conference.[4] The conception of legal disputes as identical with unimportant matters formed the key-note of both Hague Conferences. Baron Descamps, a jurist and statesman prominent in the arbitration movement, referred repeatedly to the fact that 'apart from important disputes, which require a machinery of mediation, there are legal disputes'.[5] When in 1928 the then British Government explained, in a weighty State paper, the reasons for its refusal to subscribe to the obligations of obligatory judicial settlement, it referred to the existence of political questions which, although justiciable when viewed from the point of view of application of legal rules, were not so on account of the importance of the issues involved, in respect of which no Government could assume with any degree of assurance that public opinion would be in favour of giving effect to an unfavourable award.[6]

[1] *Legal and Political Questions between Nations* (1914), p. 131. But see op. cit., p. 19, for an entirely different test of political disputes as occasioned by the wish of one State to appropriate the rights of another.

[2] Quoted after Wilson in *A.J.* xxii (1928), p. 72.

[3] See, for instance, Strisower in *Annuaire*, xxix (1922), pp. 52, 53. See also Nyholm in *Origine et l'œuvre de la Société des Nations*, ed. by Munch, i (1923), p. 241. See also Verzijl in *R.I.*, 3rd ser., vi (1925), pp. 733–54; Morgenthau, *Die internationale Rechtspflege, ihr Wesen und ihre Grenzen* (1929), pp. 69 and 70; Mulder in *R.I.* (Geneva), 1925, p. 83.

[4] See above, p. 27.

[5] See also Lammasch in *Zeitschrift für internationales Privat- und Staatsrecht*, xii. 31, for a similar classification of disputes current at The Hague Conference. He pointed out that the Conference envisaged three types of machinery: (*a*) mediation for political, i.e. grave disputes; (*b*) commissions of inquiry for disputed questions of fact not affecting the honour and vital interests of nations; (*c*) arbitration for other disputes.

[6] 'Observations of His Majesty's Government in Great Britain on the Programme of Work of the Committee on Arbitration and Security of the

However, it is by their conduct, rather than by expression of general legal formulas, that States have endorsed the view that obligatory judicial settlement must be limited to matters of minor importance. This conduct has manifested itself in the general arbitration treaties in which, through the institution of reservations, the view has found expression that disputes affecting important interests of the State are unfit for compulsory arbitration. The limitation, thus expressed, of the function of arbitration to unimportant matters is almost as old as treaties of general arbitration. The wording of the arbitration engagements concluded in the period after the World War, and in particular the gradual abandonment of general reservations of independence, vital interests, and honour, have tended to create the impression that the elimination of important issues from the purview of judicial settlement has now receded into the background. Such an impression is misleading. Not only must it be borne in mind that other reservations of an indeterminate and comprehensive nature—like those of domestic jurisdiction, national legislation, interests of third States, the Monroe Doctrine[1]— still continue to form part of arbitration treaties. The principal fact is that, as has been shown in Chapter II, the theory of the necessary limitation of the judicial function forms part of practically all recent arbitration agreements, including the Optional Clause of Article 36 of the Statute of the Permanent Court. Whenever a treaty confines the obligation of judicial settlement to legal, or juridical, or justiciable disputes, or disputes concerning rights, the door is open for invoking the doctrine of the non-justiciability of important issues. Thus, for instance, the limitation, real or apparent, in the Optional Clause of the jurisdiction of the Court to *legal* controversies may be pleaded as excluding political, i.e. important, issues from the range of the obligation. A formidable array of authority may be adduced in support of this conception of political disputes which, as will be shown, is confirmed by a significant amount of State practice.[2] Finally, there must be added to this group the new—and not the least important—category of disputes declared non-justiciable by declarations and reservations accompanying the General

Preparatory Commission for the Disarmament Conference', *League of Nations, Official Journal*, May 1928, pp. 694–704.

[1] See for references to the literature on these reservations above, pp. 46–8.
[2] See below, pp. 194–201.

Treaty for the Renunciation of War, i.e. disputes relating to the exercise of the reserved right of recourse to war in self-defence.[1]

§ 2. The Legal Construction of Political Disputes.

The juridical problem created by the support given by States to the doctrine of the elimination of important issues from obligatory arbitration has been a difficult one since the inception of the discussion on the subject. Undoubtedly, part of the difficulty was due to the fact that the term 'political', by referring to disputes of a grave character, assumed in the international sphere a meaning altogether different from that associated with that conception in other branches of law or social science. The most serious difficulty, however, consisted in the fact that as it became increasingly clear that if legal disputes were generally described as those which can be decided by the application of rules of law, it was impossible, without discarding an authoritative theory, to adopt an altogether different test based on the importance of the issues involved. And yet it was in a successful overcoming of this contradiction that lay the only possibility of placing on a legal basis this aspect of the doctrine of the limitation of the international judicial function.

There are two ways in which the doctrine thus conceived can be given the form of a juridical doctrine: (a) If we assume that rules of international law neither do nor can embrace matters of grave importance, then the non-justiciability of grave issues falls with perfect ease within the major definition, according to which legal disputes are those which can be settled by the application of rules of international law.[2] (b) The other possible juridical explanation of the limitation of justiciability of international disputes to matters of small importance can be based on the argument derived from the sovereignty of the State, namely, that as submission to the jurisdiction of an independent international tribunal is in the nature of a voluntary concession, any conferment of jurisdiction in advance, which thus develops into a compulsory submission, must be limited to minor matters; that it would be incompatible with the dignity and sanctity of national interests to submit them without any limitation to decisions of a foreign tribunal; that such a limitation is particularly dictated by reason of the absence of certainty either as to the

---

[1] See below, p. 177.   [2] See here Giraud in *R.G.* xxix (1922), p. 496.

impartiality of international tribunals or their strictly judicial character; that any obligation of a general character must therefore be framed so as to leave to the State the ultimate freedom of action; and that such freedom of action can be best secured by limiting the scope of the obligation to matters of small importance the determination of which is, either by their nature or by express reservation, as a rule exclusively within the province of the State undertaking the obligation of judicial settlement.

These are the two possible legal bases of the international doctrine 'de maximis non curat praetor'. It is proposed, in this and the following chapters, to examine as a legal proposition this aspect of the doctrine of the limitation of the function of law in international relations. As in other parts of this volume, so also in the present chapter, the method of investigation is an analytical one. It is intended to inquire whether the doctrine is in accordance with the relevant practice of States and international tribunals; whether it is in itself capable of forming the subject-matter of a legal obligation; whether it is in conformity with the current conceptions of the function of law in general; and, finally, whether it is consistent with the character and the rules of present-day international law.

II

The History of International Arbitration and the Justiciability of Important Issues

§ 3. The British-American Arbitrations. Arbitrations under the Jay Treaty and other Mixed Commissions. The history of international arbitration in the last hundred and thirty years does not substantiate the view that important issues are unsuitable for judicial settlement. The scope of this book does not permit of an examination from this point of view of the entire field of international arbitration, but it is believed that the history of British-American arbitrations sufficiently illustrates the point at issue. Between few countries has history created more frequent or important occasions for dispute than between these two States, and the part played by judicial settlement in solving these differences is therefore particularly instructive.

Some of the questions which the Jay Treaty of 1794 submitted for decision by mixed commissions are typical examples of the issues on which the two countries, in the subsequent course of their mutual relations, were content to submit to arbitral determination. The position which the Jay Treaty, as the first modern arbitration agreement, occupies in the history of international arbitration, has tended to obscure another feature of that treaty, which is no less important, namely, the gravity of the issues which the commissioners were empowered to decide. In addition to its Fifth Article, which provided for the determination by a mixed commission of the fate of a vast stretch of disputed territory in connexion with the St. Croix river boundary, the treaty contained the formidable Article VII which dealt with the British claims arising out of the alleged violation of duties of neutrality by the United States and with the American claims arising out of British measures of blockade in the course of the war with France. In that Article the two States submitted for adjudication by a mixed commission contested claims arising out of matters which subsequently disturbed the relations between the two countries during the nineteenth century, which nearly culminated in a rupture during the World War prior to the United States joining the ranks of the belligerents, and which still constitute one of the unsolved problems between the two countries. It was under this Article that the question of contraband in regard to foodstuffs and the legality of requisitions of goods of this description came up for able argument and the decision of a majority.[1] Under the same Article a mixed commission was entrusted with the task of deciding claims, not unlike some of those put forward in the *Alabama* arbitration, arising out of alleged violations of duties of neutrality by the United States in the war of Great Britain against France.[2] The history of the protracted proceedings of some of the commissions under the Treaty of Ghent of 24 December 1814, adjudicating boundary disputes relative to large territories, in particular those relating to the north-eastern boundary from the source of the St. Croix to the St. Lawrence river and to the boundary line to the Lake of Woods, bear testimony to the importance

[1] See *The Neptune*, Moore, p. 3843, and the Opinions of the Commissioners Gore, Pinkney, and Trumbull, pp. 3844–85. See also Lapradelle and Politis, i. 137–78. And see Moore, *International Law and Some Current Illusions* (1924), pp. 26–35, on the close analogy between the belligerent measures taken in the World War and in the Napoleonic War.

[2] See for a detailed examination of the work of this Commission Lapradelle and Politis, i. 178–215.

of these controversies.[1] The cases of the *Comet*, the *Encomium* and, in particular, of the *Creole*, adjudicated by a mixed commission under the Convention of 8 February 1853, which arose out of the liberation of rebellious slaves on American ships in British ports, were cases regarded by many as involving national honour, and said to have nearly embroiled the United States and Great Britain in war.[2] However, it is the *Alabama* and the *British Guiana* arbitrations which best illustrate the thesis here put forward.

§ 4. The Alabama Arbitration. The *Alabama* controversy[3] not only involved questions of maritime law of considerable importance. It was a dispute in which both countries claimed that their national honour was involved. For the American people the question became one not only of material reparation for an alleged wrong, but of vindication of the dignity of their country. One of the reasons why a previous convention, concluded in 1869, and providing for a settlement of the American claims, was rejected by the American Senate was the circumstance that it did not contain an expression of regret on the part of Great Britain. This act of expiation was performed by the British Commissioners negotiating the Treaty of Washington of 8 May 1871, who in a friendly spirit expressed the regret felt by Her Majesty's Government for the escape, under whatever circumstances, of the *Alabama* and other vessels from British ports and for the damage caused by these vessels. It is doubtful whether the intensity of feeling on both sides is sufficiently expressed by the information that 'the American commissioners accepted this expression of regret as very satisfactory to them and as a token of kindness'.[4] However, it was in particular the attitude originally assumed by Great Britain which made that dispute appear as one not suitable for arbitral settlement. When, in 1865, the United States asked for an impartial determination of the controversy, Earl Russell, the British Secretary of State, was emphatic that neither the question whether Great Britain observed her duties of neutrality in good faith, nor the question whether

[1] See Lapradelle and Politis, i. 375, and Moore, pp. 127 et seqq.
[2] See Moore in *International Conciliation*, No. 48, p. 28. And see Lapradelle and Politis, i. 704–32.
[3] For an exhaustive treatment of this dispute see Moore, pp. 494–682, and Lapradelle and Politis, ii. 712–983.
[4] See Moore, p. 544.

the Law Officers of the Crown properly interpreted the neutrality laws of the country, 'could be put to a foreign government with any regard to the dignity and character of the British Crown and the British nation'. Lord Russell was insistent that 'Her Majesty's Government are the sole guardians of their own honour'.[1] The subsequent course of events proved that the non-justiciability of this serious controversy, which imperilled the peaceful relations between the two countries, far from being inherent in the dispute itself, was an external factor resulting from the unwillingness of a Government to have the controversy settled judicially.

§ 5. **The British Guiana and Alaska Arbitrations.** The *British Guiana* controversy in and before 1897 offers an even more instructive instance. In the whole history of international arbitration there hardly occurred a dispute of a more 'political' character. It is sufficient to refer to the invocation of the Monroe Doctrine by the United States as a matter of fundamental political principle; to the lengthy and highly polemical diplomatic correspondence; to the unusually drastic action of the President of the United States in proposing to the Senate the appointment of an American Commission entrusted with the task of an independent investigation of the dispute, and the submission of a report to be acted upon by the United States; to the widespread indignation created in Great Britain both by this proposal and by the very fact of an authoritative intervention of the third party;[2] to the equally general feeling of resentment in the United States against Great Britain; and, finally, to the vast size of the territory in dispute.[3] As in the *Alabama* controversy, so also in this case the British Government originally regarded arbitration as an unsuitable method of settlement. In his dispatch to Sir Julian Pauncefote of 27 February 1896, Lord Salisbury pointed out that the American proposal for arbitration went too far; that he was not prepared in matters of high political importance to admit unrestricted arbitration; and that it was doubtful whether an impartial arbitrator could be

---

[1] See Moore, p. 496.

[2] In his letter to *The Times* on 6 June 1896 Westlake wrote: 'The President's message had first to be met in this country by an assertion of our own dignity and independence'.

[3] See Hyde, i. 143–7, for the details of this controversy. See also Cleveland, *The Venezuelan Boundary Controversy* (1913), and Hall, 8th ed., by Higgins (1924), pp. 136–7.

obtained, and whether there were clear rules of law to guide the arbitrators on the points on which they were called upon to give a decision.'[1] This matter of 'high political importance' eventually resolved itself into a lengthy legal contest[2] on such questions as acquisition of title by occupation, discovery, and prescription, and on such procedural technicalities as the function of estoppel in relations between States—just as the *Alabama* controversy was eventually reduced to a protracted legal debate on certain aspects of the law of neutrality, on the meaning of 'due diligence' in modern and Roman law, on the admissibility of indirect damages and of award of interest in international law.[3]

The Alaskan boundary dispute submitted to arbitration in 1903 was of a less serious nature than the two preceding disputes, but it was undoubtedly a 'political' dispute from the point of view of the important economic and strategic interests at issue. In this case it was Great Britain who had to overcome the original unwillingness of the United States to submit the matter to arbitration. There was a disposition in the latter country to regard the Canadian claims as of such a frivolous nature as to constitute an abuse of arbitral procedure.[4]

§ 6. The North Atlantic Fisheries Arbitration.

Finally, the *North Atlantic Fisheries* arbitration of 1910 ought to be mentioned as an example of a dispute which prima facie does not create the impression of affecting the vital interests or the dignity of the parties, but which in fact, owing to the importance of the economic interests involved, to the protracted course of the controversy, and, generally, to the circumstance

---

[1] *British and Foreign State Papers*, lxxxviii. 1245 et seqq. See also ibid. lxxxvii. 1093 and 1107.

[2] See *British Guiana Boundary Arbitration with the United States of Venezuela: Case, Counter Case, and Argument*, 9 vols., printed at the Foreign Office, London, 1898; the parallel volumes representing the American case; and Minutes of Proceedings, *British Guiana-Venezuelan Boundary Arbitration*, 11 vols., Paris, 1899.

[3] See on some of the legal aspects of these arbitrations Lauterpacht, *Analogies*, pp. 216–23, 227–33.

[4] In his *The Alaskan Frontier* (1903), T. W. Balch wrote: 'There is no more reason for the United States to allow their right to the possession of this unbroken Alaskan lisière to be referred to the decision of foreign judges, than would be the case if the British Empire advanced a claim to sovereignty over the coast of the Carolinas or the port of New York and proposed that this demand should be referred to the judgment of subjects of third Powers' (p. 178).

of the issue, was so regarded by the two States. A passage from the opening remarks of the Oral Argument of Senator Root before the Tribunal in this case may fittingly be quoted as illustrating this aspect of the matter:

> 'It is not alone a controversy that, through lapse of time, has acquired historic interest, that, through the participation of many of the ablest and most honored statesmen of two great nations through nearly a century, has acquired that sanctity which the sentiment of a nation gives to the assertion of its rights, but it is a controversy which involves substantial and, in some respects, vital interests to portions of the people of each nation. . . .
>
> 'When two great nations, bound to protect the interests of their citizens, however humble, find themselves differing in their views of rights which are substantial, find themselves differing so radically that each conceives itself to have a right which it cannot abandon without humiliation, and cannot maintain without force, a situation arises of the gravest importance and the first dignity.'[1]

These opening remarks in no way exaggerated the political importance of the controversy. The same applies to the *Behring Sea* controversy which arose out of the action of the United States, undertaken with the view to preventing the destruction of an important industry which it regarded as rightfully belonging to it.[2] These are border-line cases occupying a position midway between those disputes whose political importance is patent and those in which it is hidden behind the purely economic or technical aspect of the controversy. As such they are typical illustrations of the fact that the vast majority of international disputes settled by a legal award were cases of a political character from the point of view of the importance of the interests involved or the sentiments raised. For it is only following upon protracted negotiations, and after other means of settlement have failed, that a question is deemed of sufficient importance to warrant submission to arbitration. It has been deemed sufficient to illustrate the general proposition here put forward by reference to British-American arbitration only. To do it with regard to cases of judicial settlement between other countries

---

[1] 'Argument of the Honorable Elihu Root on behalf of the United States', edited by J. B. Scott, *The World Peace Foundation* (1912), pp. 1, 2.

[2] See above, p. 97.

would amount to covering almost the entire field of international arbitration.

§ 7. Relevance of the Historical Instances of Judicial Settlement of Important Issues. It is necessary at this stage to consider the view which questions the relevancy of the actual judicial settlement of grave issues such as the *Alabama* or *British Guiana* arbitrations to the question of justiciability of important disputes. Thus it is pointed out that the arbitration conventions in question, far from entrusting the Tribunal with the task of deciding the substance of the controversy, merely amounted to a formal registration, in a manner calculated to spare the susceptibilities of the parties, of a previous agreement disposing of the subject-matter of the dispute on its merits. It is contended that in the *Alabama* controversy the arbitration agreement and the arbitration proceedings were merely a convenient instrument for disguising a diplomatic defeat of Great Britain compelled to yield to the persistent American demands for compensation; that the task of the Tribunal merely consisted in putting in the form of a legal award an agreement previously arrived at and laying down a new rule of law specially designed for the occasion; and that in this, as in other similar cases, arbitration, far from being an instrument essential for the preservation of peace, was only a diplomatic device.[1]

Only an imperfect acquaintance with the history of this particular dispute can justify that view as to the part played by the *Alabama* arbitration. The unusual solemnity of the proceedings before the Tribunal; the bulk and quality of the legal argument put before it; the protracted deliberations of the arbitrators; and the unabated interest and feeling of suspense which accompanied the work of the Tribunal, do not substantiate the view that its work was merely of a formal character. Rules of substantive law were undoubtedly laid down for the guidance of the Tribunal, but neither in municipal law nor in international law does the existence of clear rules applicable to the case tend to diminish the decisive importance of the judicial function. Such questions as the meaning of the vital clause of 'due diligence', whether and to what extent there had taken place a breach of the duties of

---

[1] See, for instance, Morgenthau, op. cit., pp. 97 and 94, n. 17, and the authorities there cited (who, however, do not in fact substantiate the view in support of which they are cited).

neutrality as laid down in the 'three rules', whether the Tribunal had the power to decide on the scope of its jurisdiction, whether indirect damages constituted a good ground for an award under international law—a decision on these questions rested with the Tribunal so as to make it impossible in advance to determine the outcome of the dispute. In regard to the sum actually awarded, the judgement, which was for over fifteen million dollars, might as well have been for one-tenth of that sum. Equally, in regard to the *British Guiana* arbitration, it cannot be correctly maintained that the task of the Tribunal was a nominal one, inasmuch as, in consequence of the adoption, in the arbitration agreement, of the rule of prescription by adverse holding for a period of thirty years, the major issue had been decided in advance. No one who has studied the voluminous award of the proceedings before that Tribunal can agree with that contention. In addition to the intricate questions of occupation and discovery as modes of acquisition of title, the problem as to the meaning of prescription and adverse holding constituted an important issue before the Tribunal.[1]

The argument, that arbitration in cases of this description is rather the consequence of the will to adopt a peaceful solution than the cause of the preservation of peace, is irrelevant to the question of suitability of grave issues for judicial settlement. Undoubtedly the recourse to arbitration is dependent upon the will of States to respect the law—a disposition which cannot be secured by any formal machinery, not even by that of arbitration. The relevant question is whether, given the will to peace and the determination to recognize the reign of law, not only in regard to a particular dispute, but in general, judicial settlement is a suitable instrument for securing the peace also in such disputes as affect important interests of the disputants. The essential elements of the situation are not affected by the fact[2] that in all these cases recourse to judicial settlement was had by way of an *ad hoc* agreement, in which the parties were in a position to estimate the gravity of the risk involved in that procedure. The view has been expressed that the situation is altogether different when such disputes must be submitted for determination by foreign judges as the result of an obligation undertaken in advance in entirely different circumstances

---

[1] See *Proceedings*, ix. 2690–707.
[2] See for a contrary view Lapradelle and Politis, ii. 902.

and many years before the actual dispute occurs. The objection is hardly convincing. If a dispute is suitable for judicial settlement by way of an *ad hoc* agreement, such suitability is not affected by the duty of submitting a dispute to arbitration as the result of a general treaty.

III

Relation between Legal and Political Disputes

§ 8. Political Character of All International Disputes, including Legal Controversies. The consequences of the exclusion of 'political', i.e. important, issues from the domain of normal judicial settlement appear clearly from the consideration that, as a rule, every international dispute is of a political character, if by that is meant that it is of importance to the State in question. Thus viewed, the proposition that some legal questions are political[1] is an understatement of what is believed to be the true position. The State is a political institution, and all questions which affect it as a whole, in particular in its relations with other States, are therefore political. As such they are deemed to be important. A matter which in relations between citizens belongs to the ordinary incidents of business intercourse acquires special importance when it is related to a State. When in 1912 Russia brought before the Permanent Court of Arbitration a claim against Turkey for interest on delayed payments of a war indemnity, Turkey contended that to compel a State to pay moratory interest might have the result of compromising its finances and its political existence.[2] Disputes between States, even if of a trifling origin, are important because the atmosphere of international relations, with the menacing shadow of force lurking behind a precarious recognition of the reign of law, makes them so. The shortcomings of the international legal organization tend to increase the importance and political character of every controversy. Controversies between States are objectively important because they affect large numbers of individuals. They are subjectively important because frequently the fact of the dispute having proved incapable of settlement in

---

[1] See, for instance, Morgenthau, op. cit., p. 60.
[2] See Contre-memoire of Turkey, p. 33 (cited in Meurer, *Der russischtürkische Streitfall*; in Schücking, *Das Werk von Haag*, vol. i, part iii, p. 271).

the normal course of abortive diplomatic negotiations has necessarily enlarged the scope of the controversy.[1]

Neither is their importance, and, therefore, their political character, excluded because they affect an individual and not the State as a whole. A wrong done to the individual is a wrong done to his State. The overwhelming majority of cases which come before international tribunals are grounded in the alleged unlawful treatment of individuals and of claims arising therefrom, in particular in alleged denial or miscarriage of justice. Recent awards of arbitration commissions have described some cases of denial of justice as an indignity inflicted upon the individuals concerned, and it is not unnatural in such cases to identify the injured honour of the alien with that of his State. Modest awards of pecuniary indemnity are here as a rule regarded as sufficient to placate the injured honour of a nation.[2] When in 1896 Lord Salisbury negotiated with the United States Secretary of State a permanent arbitration treaty, he was prepared to conclude a treaty without any reservations in regard to disputes 'of a private origin', i.e. disputes involving private claims, but he was not inclined to undertake an obligation of this scope in respect of disputes affecting the State as a whole.[3] In stipulating for this exception, Lord Salisbury apparently had in mind territorial claims, which, by the method of a generalization usual in such cases, he promoted to the authority of a special class of disputes. But a survey of arbitration cases suggests that, apart from territorial disputes, there are hardly any disputes coming within the description of disputes affecting the State as a whole.

By the same token it may be difficult to admit that a dispute is deprived of its political character by virtue of having assumed the form of a claim for damages. It was pointed out in the Russian Memorandum submitted to the First Hague Conference that such claims do not affect the exercise of important sovereign rights, or involve the national honour

---

[1] For an interesting example of the use of the term political see the decision of the umpire in the case of *McLeod*, arising out of the well-known Caroline incident. He pointed out that as the British Government assumed responsibility for the acts, and pleaded justification on the ground of urgent necessity, 'from this time the case of the claimant became a political question between the two governments' (Moore, p. 2425).

[2] See the numerous cases on denial of justice decided by the American-Mexican Mixed Claims Commission and reported in the *Annual Digest*, 1925–6 and 1927–8.

[3] See dispatch to Sir Julian Pauncefote of 5 March 1896, Moore, i. 963.

or vital interests of the claimant State, which otherwise would not limit itself to a claim for material indemnity, but would resort to war.[1] However, claims for damages may, and as a rule do, directly involve the exercise of rights of jurisdiction and other rights of sovereignty. It is sufficient to refer to a number of cases which occurred before the Russian Memorandum was written and which were concerned with the exercise of belligerent rights, like that between Great Britain and France in 1843 arising out of the blockade of the Portendic coast;[2] or the case of the *Macedonian*, in 1863, between the United States and Chile concerning the seizure of private property in land warfare;[3] or between Great Britain and Argentina, in 1870, arising out of the closure of the port of Buenos Ayres in the course of military operations.[4] The fact that a claim for damages does not involve the honour or important interests of the plaintiff State is not decisive, seeing that it may affect the honour and important interests of the defendant country. The *Alabama* controversy ought to have been remembered in this connexion, as ought to have been some minor conflicts like the *General Armstrong*,[5] or the *Virginius*,[6] which took place before the Russian Memorandum was composed, and which, although concerned with a demand for damages, were described by competent authorities as having brought the disputants to the very verge of war. There is no escape from the fact that all international disputes are 'political' to a larger or smaller degree.

A learned writer, anxious to preserve the strictly judicial character of the Permanent Court of International Justice, suggested that the Court should refrain from dealing with political questions.[7] A survey of the work of the Court up to date would show that strict adherence to this counsel of caution would mean a speedy and radical liquidation of the activities of the Court. The long series of judgements, both as to jurisdiction and on the merits, concerning certain German interests in Polish Upper Silesia, can hardly be

---

[1] The Memorandum is printed in Scott, *Reports to The Hague Conferences*, pp. 94 ff.

[2] See Lapradelle and Politis, i. 512–44.

[3] Ibid. ii. 188–229.

[4] Ibid. ii. 637–67. See above, p. 96.

[5] Between the United States and Portugal (1852). See Lapradelle and Politis, i. 635–50. In this case the United States originally refused the offer of arbitration and recalled their minister to Portugal.

[6] Between the United States and Spain. See Moore, *International Law and Some Current Illusions* (1924), p. 87.

[7] See Brown, *International Society* (1923), p. 85.

separated from the political background of the relationships between Poland and Germany in the period after the World War and the problem of protection of minorities. The importance of the judgements relating to the Palestine concessions, although only indirectly concerned with the principles of mandatory government, cannot be said to be limited to the private rights of Mr. Mavrommatis. The highly political aspect, both of the accompanying circumstances and of the question at issue, raised in the *Wimbledon* case in connexion with the neutralization of the Kiel Canal, needs no elaboration. All these cases were brought before the Court by way of a unilateral application. Neither was the political element absent from cases brought before the Court by common agreement, like the question of the jurisdiction of the International Oder Commission in the Polish parts of the river and its tributaries, or certain questions connected with the language of instruction in minorities schools in Polish Upper Silesia, or the interpretation of Article 435 of the Treaty of Versailles relating to the régime of Free Zones round Geneva. The highly political character of nearly every Advisory Opinion rendered by the Court is apparent not only from the fact of their constituting one phase in the course of a political dispute dealt with by the Council of the League of Nations, but, even more so, from their subject-matter. They decided, in effect, important territorial disputes; they laid down guiding principles in regard to the procedure and substance of the protection of minorities; they dealt with matters of delicacy peculiar to the relations between Poland and Danzig, and Poland and Lithuania; they defined the competence of the International Labour Organization in matters vitally affecting its existence and its functions; and—last but not least—they made a pronouncement on the question of the proposed customs union between Germany and Austria.[1]

---

[1] The Advisory Opinion of the Permanent Court of International Justice in the matter of the *Austro-German Customs Union* controversy, given on 5 September 1931 (*P.C.I.J.*, Series A/B, No. 41), is an example of a judicial pronouncement on a matter of grave importance intimately connected with international politics in one of their most controversial aspects. The very importance of this pronouncement has given rise to doubts whether the Court ought to have given an Opinion on a question of this nature. (For a criticism of the Opinion of the Court from this point of view see Borchard in *A.J.* xxv (1931), pp. 711–16; Brierly in *Z.f.a.ö.R. und V.* iii (1932), pp. 68–75. For an answer to these criticisms see Jessup in *A.J.* xxvi (1932), pp. 105–10, and Manning in *New York University Law Quarterly Review*, ix (1932), pp. 339–43.) Much of the criticism

§ 9. Legal Character of All International Disputes, including Political Controversies.

While it is not difficult to establish the proposition that all disputes between States are of a political nature, inasmuch as they involve more or less

levied against the Opinion is in general terms, and it may therefore be difficult to refute it. Thus when it is said that the matter submitted to the Court was 'highly political', the answer is that—apart from the indefiniteness of the term 'political'—nearly all the other judgements or advisory opinions of the Court were more or less 'political' in the sense that they raised issues affecting international politics or important interests of States. A more tangible objection is expressed in the view that the Court was in a position to answer the question put to it only by going outside its judicial province and by taking into account future political contingencies. It is doubtful whether these objections are well founded.

The Court had to answer the question whether the proposed Customs Union was contrary to the obligation undertaken by Austria in Article 88 of the Treaty of St. Germain 'to abstain from any act which might directly or indirectly or by any means whatever compromise her independence', and in the Geneva Protocol of 1922 to the effect that she will 'abstain from any negotiations or from any economic or financial engagement calculated directly or indirectly to compromise' her independence. The Court was thus called upon to exercise a typically judicial function consisting in the interpretation of a contractual obligation. The question submitted to the Court was what is described in Article 36 of the Statute as a 'legal' question. It did not lose this character, because in order to answer it it was necessary to consider questions of fact. A question of fact may not be a question of law, but—in so far as the fact is relevant to the interpretation of a legal rule or obligation—its ascertainment is a legal matter. Undoubtedly, the Court's task was rendered more difficult by the fact that in interpreting the relevant instruments it had to consider also the probable future results of the contemplated union. But this added difficulty could not impair the judicial character of the task conferred upon the Court. Municipal courts are frequently called upon to consider the probable effects of acts or omissions. Many a question relating to the law of negligence may be mentioned as an example. The question in the *Customs Union* case was one of the probable effects of a step covered prima facie by a treaty provision. The question was admittedly a complicated one, but this is an additional reason why it should have been answered by an impartial and authoritative body approaching the matter in a judicial temper. In point of actual accuracy the opinion of a body of judges on the probable political consequences of a measure is not necessarily superior to that of a body composed of the political representatives of States. But once it has been found necessary to have an opinion which in the nature of things cannot partake of scientific certainty, it is prudent to endeavour to obtain an opinion which approximates to moral certainty and relative finality. A court of law is more likely to attempt successfully such an approximation than a political body. It may be regarded as regrettable that conventional international law should contain provisions of an indefinite character, but it is a matter for statesmen to avoid treaties of this description. Once such provisions have become part of the law, their interpretation forms legitimately part of the judicial function.

The Court, it is submitted, would not have acted in accordance with its judicial duty if it had refused to comply with the request of the Council to give an opinion. It is conceivable that the Court could have arrived at an opinion to the effect that the treaty provisions were so vague as to be meaningless, and that therefore no question of their violation arose. This would be an opinion of a most serious character, but one which the Court would in law be entitled to take. But, for reasons stated above, it is doubtful whether the Court could properly have refused to give a decision on the ground that it would have to be

important interests of States, it is equally easy to show that all international disputes are, irrespective of their gravity, disputes of a legal character in the sense that, so long as the rule of law is recognized, they are capable of an answer by the application of legal rules. The principle that there is always *in gremio legis* an answer to the question whether a given claim is grounded in the existing law or not,[1] applies with no less force to controversies in which the connexion of the dispute with the major aspects of the external policy of the State seems to render judicial determination particularly inappropriate. In fact, unless the doctrine be accepted that international law is capable of regulating matters of secondary importance only, it is difficult to see how the political importance of the matter can be related to the question of its being amenable to a legal decision. This applies, to mention some instances of recent history, to questions of such a preeminently 'political' nature as the responsibility of Serbia in 1914 for the irredentist preparations against Austria-Hungary;[2] whether the intervention of the Allied Powers in Greece in 1917 was legally justified, not only on account of the alleged unneutral conduct of the Greek Government, but also by virtue of the treaties of 1830 and, particularly, of 1863, guaranteeing to Greece a constitutional régime; whether the interpretation by Italy during the World War of her treaty of alliance with the Central Powers was legally well founded;[3] whether the French occupation of the Ruhr in 1923 was warranted by the terms of Annex II of Part VIII of the Treaty of Versailles;[4] or whether Article 431 of that treaty in fact supported the claim of Germany for the evacuation of the

---

based on 'a personal estimate of future political probabilities' (Brierly, op. cit., p. 75).

The fact that the Opinion was given by a majority of six against a minority of five, and the composition of the majority and the minority, gave rise to some exaggerated criticism. For a much needed correction of these criticisms see Jessup, op. cit., p. 107; Manning, op. cit., p. 343; and J. W. Davies in *Atlantic Monthly*, January 1932.

[1] See above, pp. 63 et seqq.

[2] See *A.J.* viii (1914), Supplement, p. 278, for the Serbian attitude, to the effect that she was 'perfectly ready to meet any reasonable demands of Austria-Hungary, so long as such demands were kept on the "terrain juridique"', namely, as to satisfaction to be given by Serbia for any neglect of her international duty.

[3] See, for instance, *A.J.* ix (1915), Supplement, p. 26, for the Italian interpretation of the treaty, to the effect that its character was purely defensive and that, therefore, the war undertaken by Austria, and believed to be aggressive, did not fall within its terms.

[4] See McNair in *B.Y.*, 1924, pp. 17–37, and Schuster in *A.J.* xviii (1924), pp. 407–18.

Rhineland subsequent to the adoption of the Dawes Plan and the conclusion of the treaties of Locarno.[1] No one of these issues was submitted to judicial determination, not because judicial settlement was inapplicable or because the disputes were not about contested legal claims, but because there was a determination, obviously liable to be backed by force, to refuse such settlement. Undoubtedly, the very idea of a legal pronouncement on such questions as the Italian treaty of alliance may appear to some as strikingly dogmatic, if not pedantic. But, in fact, the non-justiciability of a dispute of this nature is nothing else than the expression of the wish of a State to substitute its own will for its legal obligation—an attitude which it may otherwise be difficult to condemn, seeing that in treaties of this description the other contracting party is fully aware of the aleatory and highly contingent character of the advantage gained by the treaty. The interpretation of a controversial treaty of alliance is a political dispute which affects the vital interests of a nation. But the dispute is at the same time a legal dispute *par excellence* involving a judicial interpretation of the terms of the treaty. It may be argued, with some impatience, that a State can hardly be expected to risk a decision of foreign judges on questions of this kind. The answer to this is that the way of avoiding such risks is to refrain from concluding treaties of this nature. Failing that, it is difficult to escape the logic of the alternative: either a State is determined to abide by obligations as laid down in the treaty, in which case a judicial interpretation of a disputed point is the logical consequence of the treaty. Or else it is determined to cloak its refusal to fulfil the treaty in the garb of a legal interpretation of its own, supported by the doctrine of non-justiciability of political issues. It is this doctrine which has enabled States to defy important legal obligations while professing to remain within the pale of the law.

The same considerations apply to the interpretation of one of the most important general treaties concluded after the World War, i.e. the Pact for the Renunciation of War. The question of the fulfilment of that treaty has been treated as non-justiciable matter as the result of the determination of its principal signatories to remain the sole judges whether a case for self-defence (that is for disregarding the object of the treaty) has arisen. The question is undoubtedly of the highest

---

[1] See *Parl. Debates, House of Lords*, lxxi, No. 14, cols. 453–74.

importance for the State concerned, but it is at the same time *par excellence* a question capable of judicial cognizance. The claim that it should be removed from the purview of judicial determination is not an illustration of non-justiciability of important matters, but a controversial interpretation calculated to reduce the value of the Pact of Paris as a legal instrument.[1]

§ 10. Historical Instances. The problem under discussion can best be illustrated by instances in which judicial settlement was refused and recourse had to armed force in disputes obviously capable of judicial determination, on the ground that the controversy was political and therefore unsuitable for arbitration.

When in 1837 France put forward a series of demands arising out of the alleged unjust treatment of her subjects in Mexico, the latter offered to submit the claims to arbitration—an offer which was described by France as ridiculous, and rejected. It was pointed out in the French ultimatum that claims of this nature were not a proper subject of arbitration in relations either of States or of individuals. The French Government insisted that the dignity and duty of France did not permit her to allow a third person to decide (even if in form only, as there 'could be no possible difference of opinion on the substance of such matters between civilized States') the question whether the spoliations, violence, and murder to which French citizens had been subjected should or should not be adequately compensated.[2] As Mexico refused to comply with this ultimatum, France proceeded to reprisals and, subsequently, to warlike action.

The study of the diplomatic correspondence and of the negotiations preceding the war between Great Britain and the South African Republic shows that the subject-matter of the controversy, which gave rise to the war, was in itself one capable of solution by the application of rules of international law.[3] The question of the legality of the treatment

---

[1] See on this matter pp. 177–82, *infra*.

[2] See Lapradelle and Politis, i. 546, and, generally, on the whole dispute, pp. 544–79. See also ibid., p. 584, on the refusal of the British Government to accept the Greek offer of arbitration in the well-known *Don Pacifico* case. And see *British and Foreign State Papers*, lxxxvii (1894–5), pp. 220, 221, 255, 316, on the rejected Siamese offers of arbitration in the dispute with France in 1893. See Ralston, *International Arbitration from Athens to Locarno* (1929), pp. 222, 223, and 227, for examples of exaggerated demands put forward by claimant States refusing arbitration.

[3] The demand for arbitration was one of the conditions of the ultimatum which the Republic addressed to Great Britain and whose rejection formally

of aliens affected by the immigration law of the South African Republic was a legal question and was treated as such by the Republic, which repeatedly proposed arbitration; so was the question of the interpretation of the treaties concluded between the two countries in 1881 and 1884. But these proposals for arbitration were rejected[1] by Great Britain, partly on the ground that the relation of suzerainty said to have been established by the treaties of 1881 and 1884 was incompatible with arbitration, and partly on other grounds.[2]

The history of the events which in 1902 led to the declaration of war by a number of European Powers against Venezuela offers another example of a legal issue being converted into a highly political and therefore non-justiciable controversy, solely by the refusal of one party to submit a dispute to arbitration. The controversy concerned certain claims of a number of European States, including Great Britain, arising out of alleged injuries suffered by the nationals of those States as the result of the action of Venezuelan ships during the civil war. Venezuela offered to submit the claims for judicial determination, but the offer was rejected by the Powers. In a Memorandum communicated on 23 December 1902 by the Marquess of Lansdowne, it was stated:

> 'Some of the claims are of a kind which no government could agree to refer to arbitration. The claims for injuries to the person and property of British subjects owing to the confiscation of British vessels, the plundering of their contents, and the maltreatment of their crews, as well as some claims for the ill-usage and false imprisonments of British subjects, are of this description. The amount of these claims is comparatively insignificant, but the principle at stake is of the first

led to war. See ibid., p. 947, and also p. 880. See also pp. 570ff. for an exposition by the South African Republic of the legal aspects of the controversies with copious references to Field's *Code of International Law* and to the treatises of Hall, Phillimore, and others.

[1] It seems that at one stage Great Britain was willing to submit some aspects of the controversy to arbitration 'without introduction of a foreign element' (*British and Foreign State Papers*, xci (1898–9), p. 798).

[2] It may be useful to quote a passage from the dispatch of Sir Alfred Milner to Mr. Chamberlain referring to the South African proposal for arbitration: 'I expressly guarded myself against the idea that arbitration was applicable to all differences. I was thinking ... more especially of the question whether the laws and administration of the South African Republic were fair towards its foreign residents. It is, of course, absurd to suggest that the question whether the South African Republic does or does not treat British subjects resident in that country with justice, and the British Government with the consideration and respect due to any friendly, not to say "suzerain" Power, is a question capable of being referred to arbitration. You cannot arbitrate on broad questions of policy any more than on questions of national honour' (ibid., p. 705).

importance, and His Majesty's Government could not admit that there was any doubt as to liability of the Venezuelan Government in respect of them.'[1]

The dispute between Colombia and the United States in 1903 and 1904 arising out of the setting up, by way of revolution, of the new State of Panama, and its recognition by the United States, offers another instructive example. The establishment of Panama as a State was made possible by an act of intervention on the part of the United States, who prevented the Colombian Government from quelling the rebellion by force of arms. Throughout the controversy the United States insisted upon the strict legality of its action. In particular it supported its attitude by reference to the treaty concluded by it in 1846[2] with New Granada, the predecessor of Colombia. In Article 35 of that treaty New Granada guaranteed to the United States the right of way and transit across the Isthmus of Panama in regard to any modes of communication then existing, or to be constructed in the future. It was contended by the United States that the attitude of the Colombian Government amounted to a frustration of the purpose of that provision, and that, therefore, another provision of that article, guaranteeing the territorial integrity of Colombia, had lost its binding force.[3] The Colombian Government denied this allegation, and proposed that the Colombian claims arising out of the events in Panama be submitted to the Permanent Court of Arbitration at The Hague.[4] To this request the United States refused to accede, on the ground that the claim put forward by Colombia was 'of a political nature, such as nations of even the most advanced ideas as to international arbitration have not proposed to deal with by that process'. 'Questions', it was said, 'of foreign policy and of the recognition or non-recognition of foreign States are of a purely political nature, and do not fall within the domain of judicial decision.'[5] It will be noted that the demands of Colombia were based not on the fact of recognition of the new Panama Republic by the United States, but on its alleged disregard of the obligation of the

---

[1] *British and Foreign State Papers*, xcv (1901, 1902), p. 1131. See also ibid., pp. 1118, 1124, 1129.

[2] Printed in *A.S., Proceedings* (1913), p. 283; Malloy, *Treaties*, i. 312.

[3] See the note of Hay, Secretary of State, of 5 January 1904, *Foreign Relations*, 1903, pp. 294–306.

[4] Colombian Note of 23 December 1903, ibid., pp. 284–94.

[5] Ibid., p. 306.

treaty of 1846 relating to the guarantee of the territorial integrity of New Granada.[1] The binding force of that treaty, or the applicability of the relevant provision, were not contested by the United States. It was its interpretation that was disputed. But the question was described as one pertaining to a matter of foreign policy, and therefore not capable of solution by way of a judicial decision. This case is an example of a solemn assertion that the foreign policy of a State, i.e. the way in which its relations with other States are shaped, is a matter not capable of legal determination. It is an example of an attitude clearly illustrating the real meaning of the assertion that a dispute is political.[2]

§ 11. The Will of States as Determining the Justiciability of Political Disputes.

In attempting to establish the borderline between legal and political questions—political questions meaning disputes involving important issues—international lawyers have, it appears, been confronted with two sets of apparently contradictory facts. One was that disputes of high political importance were submitted to, and settled by, a purely judicial process. The other was that disputes obviously capable of decision on strictly legal lines were withheld from that procedure, on the ground that they were essentially political in their nature. One tended to show that international disputes, while capable of legal decision, are of a political nature; the other that important political disputes are amenable to a legal process. This experience was in the long run bound to impress upon the mind of the international lawyer the fact that, when referred to as connoting important conflicts, the term 'political' is in no way connected with the legal nature of the dispute in the sense of being capable of decision on the basis of a rule of law, or of being concerned with claims put forward by virtue of a rule of international law.[3]

---

[1] See Colombian Note of 11 January 1904, ibid., p. 313. The whole correspondence is printed in Moore, *Digest*, § 344. And see, in support of the view that the dispute was capable of a legal answer, Fenwick in *A.S.*, *Proceedings* (1917), p. 73; and *R.G.* ii (1904), pp. 590–4.

[2] In the cases here discussed, the disputants were not bound by any existing arbitration treaty. In the next chapter there will be discussed instances of refusal of arbitration in cases obviously capable of judicial determination, but described by the refusing party as highly political, and not coming therefore within the purview of an existing arbitration treaty.

[3] See on this point Morgenthau, op. cit., pp. 62 ff.; Giraud in Lapradelle and Niboyet's *Répertoire de Droit International*, i. 675; Salvioli in *Rivista di Studi di diritto publico e corporativo*, i, No. 6. See also Lammasch, *Über isolierte und institutionelle Schiedsgerichte*, vi (1912), p. 103; Nippold, pp. 180 ff.

The same dispute may be purely legal, and purely political, i.e. it may be capable of legal decision so as to admit of a judicial settlement, and it may be regarded as 'important' so as to make arbitration appear dangerous. There have been attempts, renewed from time to time, to solve the difficulty by improvements in terminology. Thus Professor Verzijl suggested that, instead of using the term 'political' as applied to disputes incapable of solution by the application of a rule of law, the term 'non-legal' should be used for that purpose.[1] But gradually the lesson of facts is being assimilated, namely, that it is the refusal of the State to submit the dispute to judicial settlement, and not the intrinsic nature of the controversy, which makes it political. Lawyers are beginning to abandon the vicious circle presented by the situation in which a dispute is deemed to be important and therefore not compatible with the judicial process, whereas it is its alleged non-justiciability that renders it 'political'.

This is the reason why, alongside the orthodox view adopting the relative importance of the subject-matter of the dispute as decisive for the determination of the scope of judicial activity in international relations, there has been a persistent undercurrent of opinion expressive of the view that there is no fixed limit to the possibilities of judicial settlement; that all conflicts in the sphere of international politics can be reduced to contests of a legal nature; and that the only decisive test of the justiciability of the dispute is the willingness of the disputants to submit the conflict to the arbitrament of law. This tendency can be traced to the early leading treatises on the subject of international arbitration—those of Revon,[2] Mérignhac,[3] and Nippold.[4] It seems that a growing number of jurists are now prepared to accept this view,[5] although the traditional terminology still continues to exer-

---

[1] See in *R.I.*, 3rd ser., vi (1925), p. 733. See also Ch. de Visscher, ibid., 3rd ser., ix (1928), p. 36, where he attaches great hopes to the setting up of 'a more rational classification of international disputes' as a substitute for indefinite and destructive reservations.   [2] p. 496.

[3] pp. 184 et seqq., and in *R.G.* x (1903), p. 803.

[4] pp. 168–230. See also to the like effect Arnaud, *Un traité d'arbitrage permanent entre la France et l'Angleterre* (1903), p. 7; Redslob, *Das Problem des Völkerrechts* (1917), pp. 315–30; Reinsch in *A.J.* v (1911), pp. 604–14.

[5] See Scott in *A.S.*, *Proceedings* (1924), pp. 79, 80; Borchard, ibid., pp. 50–7; Dupuis in *Annuaire*, xxxiii (1927), vol. ii, pp. 808, 810; Politis and Brown, ibid., p. 669; Ch. de Visscher in *R.I.*, 3rd ser., ix (1928), p. 36; Gallus, ibid., xi (1930), p. 226. See also Pollock, *The League of Nations* (2nd ed., 1922), p. 145, while referring to Article 13 of the Covenant, and Strisower, *Der Krieg und die Völkerrechtsordnung* (1919), p. 63, and in *Annuaire*, xxix (1922), pp. 50–6.

cise a confusing fascination, revealing itself in attempts to maintain a form whose content has become discredited. The determination is still lacking to give full scientific recognition to the resounding words uttered by Mr. Justice Baldwin in the case of *Rhode Island* v. *Massachusetts*, and revealing clearly the true source of the 'political' character of disputes.[1] The science of international law has not altogether discarded the questionable function of an *ancilla regnorum*, supplying States with a convenient terminology calculated to cloak the negation of the reign of law with the garb of a law-abiding disposition. Instead of being compelled to admit openly that they intend to remain judges in their own cause, Governments are still in the position to avail themselves of the time-honoured phrase, endowed by jurists with the authority of a juridical conception, and to proclaim that an actual dispute is, or that future disputes may be, 'political' and therefore not amenable to judicial process.

[1] See below, p. 442.

CHAPTER VIII

INTERNATIONAL LAW AND JUDICIAL DETERMINATION OF IMPORTANT ISSUES

§ 12. The Function of the Doctrine 'de maximis non curat praetor'. The elimination of important issues from the purview of obligatory judicial settlement is the principal manifestation of the generally recognized rule of present-day international law, according to which, in the absence of an express agreement to the contrary, a State is under no duty to submit its disputes with other States for judicial determination. This rule is, in turn, one of the three principal modes of expression of the doctrine of sovereignty in the international sphere: The sovereign State does not acknowledge a central executive authority above itself; it does not recognize a legislator above itself; it owes no obedience to a judge above itself. Although the cumulative effect of these three expressions of sovereignty is to bring international law to the vanishing point of law—notwithstanding well-meant attempts to show that these shortcomings are common to primitive societies[1]—they are frequently regarded as inherent in international law, and as conditioning its very existence. It is in particular in regard to the possibility of a compulsory international judiciary[2] that writers frequently paint the picture of an international law destined, under the penalty of extinction, to remain at the stage of a primitive law. Whatever may be the justification for this generalization of the present legal position, there is no doubt as to the voluntary nature of judicial settlement under the present-day international law. The expression 'obligatory', when applied to arbitration treaties in which States agree to submit future disputes for judicial determination, is to this extent a misnomer.[3] At present both optional and obligatory arbitration are grounded in the will of States, and are, as a rule,[4] subject

---

[1] See below, p. 424.

[2] 'International law does not know of any automatic and universal unity of judicial determination, and cannot know of any so long as it remains international law and so long as States remain sovereign'—Heller (*Die Souveränität* (1927), p. 157). See also to the same effect Zorn, *Das deutsche Reich und die internationale Schiedsgerichtsbarkeit* (1911), p. 19.

[3] See on the relative value of the distinction between voluntary and obligatory arbitration *Annuaire*, xxxiii (2) (1927), p. 67. See also Renault, *Actes et Documents*, ii. 66–70; and Sir Edward Fry, ibid., p. 80.

[4] The Locarno arbitration treaties of 16 October 1925 do not contain a provision for denunciation.

to termination at the end of the period for the duration of which the obligation has been undertaken. It is not without significance that the most general existing instrument of 'obligatory' arbitration bears the name of an 'Optional Clause'. Only a treaty of a legislative character not subject to denunciation would make arbitration truly obligatory.

It is this absence of any general legal duty of judicial settlement which explains the prevalence among Governments, statesmen, and lawyers of an attitude which conceives of judicial settlement as of a concession granted to another State. The view is still widespread that only friendly and undisturbed relations between two States justify such an act of accommodation. The sense of values, to which life within a civilized community has in this respect accustomed private individuals, does not obtain in relations between States. When writing, about sixty years ago, on the limits of arbitration, Lorimer urged that the duty to arbitrate does not apply to the relations of Western States with savage and uncivilized communities, on the ground that they are devoid of a rational contracting will, that the decisions of the arbitrators appointed by them cannot be trusted, and that they themselves cannot be relied upon to give effect to the decisions of the arbitrator.[1] The relations between States belonging to the community of nations are, so far as judicial settlement is concerned, still to a large extent under the sway of limitations which Lorimer assigned to the field of relations with uncivilized peoples. A State does not regard the refusal of its offer of judicial settlement as an affront to its dignity or as a denial of its membership in a legal community. A Government rejecting an offer of arbitration, either generally or in regard to a particular dispute, does not feel that it offends against the legal sense of other members of the international society.[2]

At the same time, however, Governments have found it impossible to ignore entirely either the requirements of international security or the pressure of public opinion, and means had to be sought for reconciling their determination not to give up their freedom of action with the necessity of assuming some obligations in the field of judicial settlement.

---

[1] See his letter to Thomas Balch, reprinted in Balch's *International Courts of Arbitration* (1874), p. 28.
[2] See above, pp. 160 et seqq., and below, pp. 194 et seqq., for examples of refusals of offers of arbitration.

Such a reconciliation of freedom of action with a binding obligation is impossible of achievement in the domain of juridical logic, but it has been achieved as a matter of terminology in the domain of obligatory arbitration. The apparent solution of the difficulty was to adopt the duty of obligatory judicial settlement in respect of matters of minor importance, to reject it in regard to important issues defined as political, and, in some cases, to reserve to the State the right to decide which issues are, and which are not, important. This object has been achieved either by a general term limiting the obligation of judicial settlement to 'legal' as distinguished from 'political', i.e. important, matters, or by attaching reservations, referring to a more or less comprehensive class of important disputes.

The essential object of this aspect of the doctrine of the limitation of the judicial function embodying in the form of a legal principle the rule 'de maximis non curat praetor'—a rule expressive of the view that international law is too weak to take cognizance of questions involving important issues—is to reserve to States freedom of action in disputes of importance. This reservation of freedom of action is frequently, as in almost all arbitration treaties concluded before the World War, amplified by the additional safeguard consisting in preserving the right of the State to determine whether the controversy is of sufficient importance. The same safeguard will be found in one of the most weighty instruments of pacific settlement, namely, in the General Treaty for the Renunciation of War. In a number of recent arbitration conventions, including the Optional Clause, the determination of the applicability of the reservations is left to the competent tribunal. This undoubted progress has tended to obscure the significance of the fact that in either case, the elimination of disputes of importance most likely to disturb the friendly relations between the States in question forms an integral part of the instrument. It will now be considered whether the elimination of interests of vital importance from the domain of compulsory judicial settlement is in accordance with the function of law in general, and of international law in particular.

§ 13. The Principle 'de maximis non curat praetor' as a Legal Proposition. The widely accepted idea of the special character of international law has so accustomed the international lawyer to notions which depart from generally accepted legal principles that he is not perturbed by the idea of the reign of law being relegated to matters of little importance.[1] Thus, for instance, says Anzilotti:

> 'The interests protected by international law are not those which are of major weight in the life of states. It is sufficient to think of the great political and economic rivalries to which no juridical formula applies, in order to realize the truth of this statement. International law develops its true function in a sphere considerably circumscribed and modest, not in that in which there move the great conflicts of interests which induce states to stake their very existence in order to make them prevail.'[2]

The same view has been expressed in a different form by Cavaglieri, who has pointed out that, while according to the 'natural-law-school' all possible relations between States were covered by generally recognized principles of international justice, modern positivism insists that there exist limitations of the international legal system.[3] There ought to be little doubt as to the legal repugnancy of the doctrine in question. To restrict law to small matters is to reduce to a minimum its proper function, namely, that of preservation of peace and of prevention of recourse to force.[4] There is a tendency among writers on international law to support obvious shortcomings in the legal organization of the international community by reference to analogous shortcomings in primitive societies.[5] It would be difficult to find even within primitive communities a phenomenon corresponding to that of the limitation of law to trivial matters.

The idea of the limitation of the function of judicial settlement to matters of little importance, obnoxious as it is as a general legal proposition, is also misleading from the point of view of the actual content and scope of international law. Can it, with any degree of accuracy, be said that international

---

[1] In the sphere of municipal law there have been, in the United States, attempts to refer to 'political' questions in regard to the activity of the Supreme Court when passing upon the constitutionality of social and industrial legislation. It has been suggested that questions of this description are too important for judicial cognizance, and that 'the legislative industrial policy of a state or nation can hardly even be stated in classical legal terminology': Finkelstein in *Harvard Law Review*, xxxvii (1923–4), pp. 338–64, at p. 363. And see for a refutation of this view Weston, ibid., xxxviii (1824–5), pp. 296–333.

[2] *Corso*, i. 311. See also on this question Cereti, *La tutela giuridica degli interessi internazionali* (1929).

[3] *Lo stato di necessità nel diritto internazionale* (1917), p. 119.

[4] See on this matter below, pp. 171 et seq.　　　[5] See below, pp. 424, 432.

law is concerned only with minor issues between States? Such an assertion is on the face of it contrary to the actual content of international law as at present constituted. International law may not possess clear-cut rules governing certain specific situations; it may fail to reconcile conflicting views of States on a number of questions; and some of its rules may not have gone beyond the stage of a statement of general principles. But the major questions of the existence of States, and their rights as members of the international legal community, do form the subject-matter of clear, although general, rules. When, therefore, it is being stated that international law still persists in regarding some questions as too great for legal regulation,[1] the intention is obviously to convey that States in their mutual dealings, in particular in their arbitration treaties, refuse to accept as actually binding, rules of international law so far as they affect vital questions of their international policy. It has been suggested that although the major aspects of international relations may have belonged for a long time to the domain of politics, as distinguished from law, they have ceased to be so now, when the domain of law increasingly pervades the domain of international relations.[2] This suggestion is believed to understate the position. The legal regulation of the major aspects of international relations is as old as international law, and the fact that major questions of international relations have long been regarded as pertaining to the domain of politics and not of law, is merely the expression of the deficient vitality in practice of these fundamental rules of international law. The doctrine 'de maximis non curat praetor' is as abhorrent to the ordinary notions of the function of law as it is unwarranted by the actual content of substantive international law.

From the point of view of the question how far the rule 'de maximis non curat praetor' satisfies the wants of the international community, there should be little doubt as to its inadequacy. At the Second Hague Conference, Renault, a jurist of high standing, while describing this limitation of the function of the law to matters of small importance as a *malum necessarium* in the present state of international society, expressed the opinion that judicial settlement in minor matters is not without importance, as it is bound to inculcate in States the habits of legality, and gradually to accustom

---

[1] See, for instance, Hershey, in *Proceedings, Judicial Settlement of International Disputes*, 1911, p. 107.   [2] See Nippold, pp. 144, 145.

them to submit to arbitration disputes of major import.[1] It must be a matter for serious consideration whether any possible advantages of such development are not necessarily counterbalanced by the disadvantages, psychological and political, of a system in which a solemn machinery of peaceful settlement is put in motion and maintained in regard to matters of little consequence, whereas in major issues defiance of the law, expressed either in aggressive force or in the perpetuation of a wrong by passive force, is allowed to have full play.

Nothing will illustrate better the paradoxical results of a doctrine which limits the full duty of judicial settlement to minor matters than the distinction, frequently referred to in this connexion, between individual and general arbitration treaties. Thus it is widely believed that permanent treaties of arbitration are possible only among nations between whom there exists a sufficiently high degree of mutual confidence, and between whom that relation of confidence is likely to continue.[2] At the Second Hague Conference the chief German delegate urged that whereas a treaty of obligatory arbitration might be possible between two States where the scope of possible controversies is more or less clearly defined (because determined by a series of concrete and known factors, like their geographical position, their financial and economic relations, and the entire history of their relations), such concrete factors are absent in a general treaty of obligatory arbitration which necessitates vague and elastic reservations destructive of the value of the treaty.[3] The same line of reasoning was advanced over twenty years later, with a striking similarity of expression, in the British Official Memorandum submitted in 1928 to the Committee on Arbitration and Security, in which the British Government gave as one of the reasons of its reluctance to undertake the obligations of compulsory arbitration, the fact that

---

[1] *Actes et Documents*, ii. 67.

[2] See, for instance, Dupuis in *Annuaire*, xxxiii (2) (1927), p. 810; Huber, ibid., p. 766.

[3] See Speech of Baron Marschall von Bieberstein, *Actes et Documents*, ii. 286. It was Westlake (see above, p. 5) who first drew attention to the necessity for carefully choosing the partners to an arbitration treaty. He regarded it as fundamental to include the reservation of independence and vital interests in every treaty of obligatory arbitration. These reservations, he admitted, leave ample scope for abuse and evasion, aggravating the original controversy. Accordingly, such treaties should be concluded between States between whom the community of legal outlook and the absence of deeply lying political differences are such as to render improbable any such abusive interpretation of the reservations.

'obligations which it may be willing to accept towards one State it may not be willing to accept towards another'.[1] This is tantamount to saying that arbitration treaties should be concluded between States among whom no serious grounds of disagreement are likely to occur, and that they ought not to be concluded between States whose reciprocal relations are unsettled, and therefore particularly in need of an effective machinery of peaceful settlement agreed upon in advance. Some writers go even further, and express quite openly the opinion that treaties of obligatory arbitration containing no reservations of matters of importance ought not to be concluded between States among whom relations are strained as the result of a permanent tension, so that grave disagreements are likely to occur between them.[2]

The very institution of reservations, which has now acquired a permanent status in treaties of pacific settlement, is an expression of the view that important controversies which are likely to occur must be excluded from the scope of obligatory arbitration. For reservations are, as a rule, ingeniously framed generalizations of anticipated possible disputes, in regard to which either of the contracting parties is anxious to preserve freedom of action by recourse to force if necessary. The close connexion between this differentiation among the parties to the mutual obligation of judicial settlement, and the reservation of the right to have recourse to force, was shown at the Second Hague Conference by the chief American delegate with unusual force and frankness.[3]

---

[1] See above, p. 142, n. 1. That considerations of this nature were not entirely alien to the official discussions centring round the 'General Act' recommended by the Ninth Assembly of the League of Nations, may be seen from the admirable article by Gallus in *R.I.*, 3rd ser., xi (1930), pp. 205–19.

[2] Morgenthau, op. cit., pp. 130, 131. A reasoning of this nature necessarily recalls to mind the view expressed at the Second Hague Conference, to the effect that the arbitration treaties with the proposed reservations provided for arbitration, so long as there existed no dispute, but that their legal force was reduced to a minimum as soon as a controversy arose incapable of settlement by diplomatic means. Statesmen frequently wish to 'have it both ways', and, while opposing obligatory arbitration in matters of importance, they deprecate the recourse to it in trivial matters. Thus at the Second Hague Peace Conference the German delegate insisted that 'nowadays all these small disputes are being settled in an amicable way by a conciliation', and that 'it does not appear desirable that this state of affairs should be replaced by a régime which would permit every state to invoke against another a formal engagement calculated to drag it before an arbitration court, with its long and costly procedure that would rather aggravate than settle the difference'. (*Actes et Documents*, ii. 287.)

[3] Mr. Choate said: 'But suppose you do agree with twenty nations, and conclude such treaties with that limited number, either separately or jointly, what do you mean with regard to the twenty-five other nations whom you will have

§ 14. The Protection of Vital Interests of States by International Law and by International Tribunals.

One of the reasons underlying the hesitation of Governments to recognize that important issues are a proper subject for judicial settlement, is the belief that the activity of international tribunals, far from constituting a judicial process which attributes to every one what is legally his due, is a method of adjusting conflicting issues by way of compromise, and that, accordingly, the vital interests of the State ought not to be submitted to that procedure, at least by way of an obligation undertaken in advance. This view was clearly expressed by many of the earlier writers on international arbitration, like Rouard de Card,[1] Dreyfus,[2] and Carnazza Amari.[3] It has not ceased to exercise its fascination over lawyers and statesmen of to-day, who, with a dogmatism expressive of the lack of appreciation of the true legal position, repeat that arbitration is impossible on such matters as questions of domestic jurisdiction or immigration or similar fundamental and inalienable rights. It is not sufficiently realized that fundamental rights of States are safe under international judicial settlement, for the reason that they are fundamental legal rights; that inalienable rights are safe under international judicial settlement, because nothing—except force—can alienate them; that matters which according to international

refused to admit into your charmed circle of arbitral accord? You must reserve, must you not, you must mean to reserve, the right to resort to war against the twenty-five non-signatory States when differences with them cannot be settled by diplomatic means. Those are the two alternatives always, arbitration or force. And if you will not agree to arbitration, it must be because you reserve the right, if not the intent, to resort to force with them.' Ibid., p. 74 (as translated in the *Proceedings of The Hague Conferences*, ed. by J. B. Scott (1921), ii. 75).

In a Memorandum addressed in July 1907 to the German Emperor, and relating to the question of obligatory arbitration to be dealt with at The Hague Conference, the German Chancellor explained that the conclusion of a general treaty of obligatory arbitration was wholly unacceptable, 'as it would deprive us of the possibility to bring into play the factor of power, both generally and also in regard to obnoxious smaller States'. (*Grosse Politik der europäischen Kabinette*, xxxiii (2), p. 330.) The same point of view underlies the opinions of Admiral Mahan, an able opponent of obligatory arbitration before the World War (*Armaments and Arbitration*, p. 4). See also André, *De l'arbitrage obligatoire dans les rapports internationaux* (1903), p. 196, for a similar explanation of the refusal of Governments to limit their freedom of action.

[1] *Études de droit international* (1890), p. 230.

[2] *L'arbitrage international* (1892), p. 278.

[3] *Traité de droit international* (translations from the Italian; 1882), ii. 560: 'Les différends dans lesquels s'agite un droit primitif, l'indépendance et l'intégrité d'une nation, par exemple, ne sont pas susceptible d'être la matière d'un arbitrage... dont la décision dernière a la valeur d'une transaction.'

law are within exclusive domestic jurisdiction are safe under the aegis of obligatory arbitration, because a tribunal acting judicially will necessarily adjudge them to be so.

Undoubtedly, international law, like other law, does not act with automatic rigidity, and there is full scope for a liberal and creative administration of the law by international tribunals.[1] But where the claim runs counter to a clearly ascertainable right or an uncontroverted principle of international law—for instance, when a State claims a portion of the territory of its neighbour or denies its right to regulate the admission of aliens—then the judge has no option but to give a decision in accordance with the law as it stands. This, however, does not mean that the dispute is a non-justiciable one, that is to say, that it cannot be decided by an international tribunal pronouncing according to law. The Court will here be in the position to state clearly that the position of one party is wholly untenable in law, and to dismiss the claim. Eminent statesmen and jurists insist that questions like immigration are not 'arbitrable'. In fact, they are a typically appropriate subject for judicial settlement. An international court will in such cases invariably pronounce that the claim must be dismissed. To submit questions of immigration to arbitration does not mean to expose it to the risks of bargaining and compromise by political mediators; it means having the right to exclusive regulation of immigration upheld by an impartial decision more authoritative than the fiat of the State concerned.[2] Governments are probably aware of that fact, and their unwillingness to submit such questions to judicial settlement is not the result of the conviction that their rights cannot be upheld by a clear pronouncement of the law, but of their reluctance to entrust the decision on matters of vital national importance to outside bodies over

[1] See above, Chapters V and VI.
[2] Apprehension on this ground was expressed, as frequently as unnecessarily, during the prolonged discussion centring round the abortive general arbitration treaty between this country and the United States in 1911. See, for instance, the speeches of Knox and Taft in *Proceedings of the American Society for Judicial Settlement of International Disputes*, ii (1911), pp. 19 and 178, respectively. See also Politis in *Recueil des Cours* (1925), i. 43: 'Les affaires domestiques ne sont pas justiciables. Elles ne peuvent pas, en principe, être soumises à l'arbitrage.' However, the real intention, unfortunately concealed behind this vague generalization, is to say that an international tribunal 'ne s'occupe pas des affaires domestiques au point de vue matériel pour indiquer comment elles doivent être réglées. Il s'en occupe seulement au point de vue formel pour dire à qui en revient le règlement.' And see ibid., p. 52. See also, for a criticism of Politis, Bruns in *Z.f.a.ö.R. und V.* i (1929), pp. 36–9.

which they have no control. It is the absence of confidence in the judicial character[1] and impartiality of international tribunals,[2] and the traditional assertion of national sovereignty as the ultimate judge in matters of importance, that lie at the bottom of the supposed non-justiciability of such disputes. Only so is it possible to explain the otherwise incomprehensible fact that powerful States, with large territorial possessions, whose title-deeds of their position in the world have full and uncontroverted validity in international law, and which have, therefore, nothing to fear from an international judicial tribunal, refuse to commit themselves to compulsory arbitration—whereas small States, whose 'place in the sun' is limited as the result of historical development, and whose aspirations must necessarily be defeated when weighed in the impersonal scales of law, are, as a rule, more willing to undertake the commitments of obligatory arbitration. The same applies to most of the reservations in the arbitration treaties, for instance, reservations of disputes involving interests of third parties or of domestic jurisdiction. They are unnecessary, inasmuch as they are implied in the judicial character of the activity of international tribunals. The irrelevance of the reservation of domestic jurisdiction appears clearly from what has been said above. As to the interests of third parties, it is generally recognized that decisions and awards of international tribunals cannot legally affect States which are not parties to the dispute.[3]

The history of international controversies shows, it is believed, that there is among States a clear appreciation of the legal position in regard to disputes affecting certain rights generally regarded as fundamental. This may be seen from the position taken up by Japan in regard to the restriction of immigration of Japanese subjects into the United States. The attitude of Japan was prompted not by a refusal to admit the right of a State to regulate in principle questions of immigration, and generally the treatment of aliens, but by their objection to discriminating between different nations. Thus while not questioning 'the sovereign right of any country to regulate immigration to its own territories', the Japanese Government protested against the discriminatory

---

[1] See below, p. 379.   [2] See below, Chapter X.
[3] See above, p. 47, n. 1. As to this reservation see the literature referred to in Morgenthau, op. cit., pp. 110–12.

clause of the United States Immigration Act of 1924, on the ground that 'international discriminations in any form and on any subject, even if based on purely economic reasons, are opposed to the principles of justice and fairness upon which the friendly intercourse between nations must, in its final analysis, depend', and that discriminations based on race are still more to be deprecated. The actual number of Japanese nationals admitted into the United States was regarded as immaterial, but the principle was insisted upon that discrimination is not compatible with the respect and consideration which one nation is entitled to expect from the other.[1] The protest of the Italian Government in the same matter was based on similar grounds.[2]

As the belief in the impartiality and the truly judicial character of international arbitration gains ground, there must necessarily be less disinclination to entrust to international tribunals the competence to decide disputes involving rights of States firmly embedded in international law.

---

[1] See the Note of the Japanese Ambassador to the Secretary of State, *World Peace Foundation Pamphlets*, vi (1924), pp. 361, 372, and Matsushita, *Japan in the League of Nations* (1929), pp. 162–5. See also as to the Japanese amendment, on matters of domestic jurisdiction, to the abortive Geneva Protocol, ibid., pp. 64–75, and Fifth Assembly, *Minutes of the First Committee*, pp. 29, 45, 55, 80, 85, 102.

[2] The exclusion of matters of this description from the purview of *judicial settlement* must not be confused with their exclusion from the scope of *conciliation* so far as its findings may be endowed, totally or in part, with a binding effect. Thus it was not inappropriate for the United States to insist, when the Covenant of the League was framed in 1919, on the exclusion of matters which, according to international law, fall exclusively within the domestic jurisdiction of the State, from the sphere of the Council's report under Article 15 of the Covenant. For the function of the Council is one of mediation and conciliation—a procedure which is not bound up with a strict regard for rules of existing international law. This is the reason why paragraph 8 of Article 15 of the Covenant, laying down that the Council shall refrain from making a recommendation in a dispute arising out of a matter which by international law is solely within the domestic jurisdiction of a State, does not constitute a class of disputes non-justiciable in themselves. If the Council decides that the dispute is according to international law within the domestic jurisdiction of the State, does such a decision amount to a pronouncement that the dispute is non-justiciable? The very reverse is true. If the same dispute were submitted to a decision of an international court, then its decision that the matter is one of exclusive domestic jurisdiction could not be interpreted as laying down that the dispute is non-justiciable. It would rather amount to a clear statement that, justiciable as the dispute is, the plaintiff's claim cannot be entertained or have effect given to it, as no grounds of international law have been disclosed limiting the autonomy of the State affected. While the recommendations of the Council, acting under Article 15, need not necessarily be grounded in existing international law, its function under paragraph 8 of Article 15 is judicial. It has to decide whether by *international law* a matter is or is not within the exclusive domestic jurisdiction of the State. By definition such a function is a strictly judicial one. This is the reason why the Council, when confronted with a plea of domestic jurisdiction, takes the advice of the Permanent Court of International Justice (see Advisory Opinion No. 4).

This change of attitude must also strengthen the conviction of States that, in so far as the vital interests of States require protection, they are better protected by the recognition of the reign of law administered through the agency of international tribunals than by formally safeguarding, through the usual reservations, the ultimate right to have recourse to force.[1] Nothing will illustrate this tendency better than the following extract from a message of the Swiss Federal Council concerning the arbitration and conciliation treaty between Switzerland and Italy of 20 September 1924:

> 'This treaty is entirely lacking in the cautious and frequently quite unjustifiable reservations which States, in accordance with the almost unanimous opinion of jurists, used to incorporate in arbitration treaties; thus the present treaty implicitly gives expression to the view that the full application to international relations of principles of law and equity, far from affecting injuriously the sovereignty of the State, is, on the contrary, its best safeguard.'[2]

In a message, published on the same day and referring to a similar treaty with Brazil, the view is described as incomprehensible that an arbitral award might endanger the principles of international law which it is expected to respect.[3] This expression of opinion, recognizing the authority of the law as the proper agency for the protection of fundamental legal rights, is particularly significant when contrasted with the attitude of Switzerland at the Second Hague Conference at which that country was prominent against the abandonment of the reservations now declared to be unjustifiable.[4]

§ 15. Judicial Determination of the Right of Self-defence.

It is of importance to consider, as one aspect of the problem discussed above, how far it is possible to accept the view

---

[1] See here the Report of Borel and Politis in *Annuaire*, xxxiii (2) (1927), pp. 737, 738.

[2] *Bundesblatt* (1924), iii. 667 et seqq.

[3] Ibid., pp. 653 et seqq. Heller, *Souveränität* (1927), pp. 157 ff., suggests that these passages amount to an indirect recognition of the supremacy of national sovereignty. He then uses this inference as an argument against obligatory arbitration.

[4] *Actes et Documents*, ii. 65. However, it will be noted that in 1883 Switzerland proposed to the United States a general arbitration treaty without any reservations. See *Bundesblatt* (1884), ii. 577. The draft was accepted by the Government of the United States, but rejected by the Senate. In the message of 19 December 1904 (printed in Nippold, p. 656) the Federal Council intimated that the draft of 1883 went 'too far'. See Burckhardt, *Schweizerisches Bundesrecht* (1930), pp. 341–82, for a thorough presentation of the arbitration treaties concluded by Switzerland. See also Schindler in *R.I.*, 3rd ser., vi (1925), pp. 816–75.

according to which there is no room for judicial determination of the question of the legality of recourse to force in self-defence. In particular it is proposed to consider this question in relation to one of the principal international instruments of pacific settlement, i.e. the General Treaty for the Renunciation of War. In declarations preceding, accompanying, and following upon the signature and ratification of this treaty, its leading signatories not only excepted the right of self-defence from the operation of the terms of the treaty, but interpreted that right as implying that each nation 'alone is competent to decide whether circumstances require recourse to war in self-defence'.[1] (It is assumed, for the purpose of the observations which follow, that these declarations cannot be disregarded in the interpretation of the treaty.)

The conception of self-defence as used in connexion with the General Treaty for the Renunciation of War, and by the great majority of writers, is a classical example of a purely legal question being endowed with the qualities of a political and, therefore, non-justiciable controversy, by dint of the assertion that the interested States are the sole judges in the matter. Probably the view as to the impossibility of judicial determination of the recourse to force in self-defence is due to the confusion, which is almost general, of two different aspects of this question. There is, first, the actual use of force when there is *periculum in mora*, when a State believes its very life and vital interests to be endangered beyond possibility of redress if immediate action is not taken, when in the words of the classical definition there is a necessity for action which

---

[1] See, for instance, American Note of 23 June 1928 to some of the original signatories, printed in Miller, op. cit., p. 213, and in *International Conciliation*, Pamphlet No. 243, October 1928, p. 496. It may be useful to quote the relevant passage quoted in the Note: 'There is nothing in the American draft of an anti-war treaty which restricts or impairs in any way the right of self-defence. That right is inherent in every sovereign State and is implicit in every treaty. Every nation is free at all times and regardless of treaty provisions to defend its territory from attack or invasion and it alone is competent to decide whether circumstances require recourse to war in self-defence.... Inasmuch as no treaty provision can add to the natural right of self-defence, it is not in the interest of peace that a treaty should stipulate a juristic conception of self-defence since it is far too easy for the unscrupulous to mould events to accord with an agreed definition.' (Ibid., p. 497.) See also the Note of the French Minister of Foreign Affairs to the American Ambassador of 14 July 1928: 'Nothing in the new treaty restrains or compromises in any manner whatsoever the right of self-defence. Each nation in this respect will always remain free to defend its territory against attack or invasion; it alone is competent to decide whether circumstances require recourse to war in self-defence.' (Ibid., p. 504.) See also Cmd. 3153.

is 'instant, overwhelming, and leaving no choice of means and no moment for deliberation'.[1] It is of the essence of the legal conception of self-defence that recourse to it must, in the first instance, be a matter for the judgement of the State concerned. For if recourse to it were conditioned by a previous authorization of a law-administering agency, then it would no longer be self-defence; it would be execution of a legal decision. When therefore Governments and writers insist that recourse to self-defence is not subject to judicial determination, they give expression to a self-evident truism—so long as it is clear that what is permitted is the provisional right to act. This is one meaning of the contention that the conception of aggression (and of its complement—self-defence) is incapable of being defined in advance, and that it must therefore be left to the State concerned to decide in each individual case whether the circumstances justify recourse to war in self-defence.[2]

The other meaning usually attaching to the assertion of the non-justiciability of disputes arising out of recourse to force in self-defence is that the legitimacy—as distinguished from the act itself—of the exercise of the right of self-defence is incapable of judicial determination. This doctrine cannot be admitted as juridically sound. If the conception of self-defence is a legal conception—and it becomes so, *inter alia*, by forming part of a treaty or of declarations organically connected with it—then any action undertaken under it must be capable of legal appreciation. If the precedents usually enumerated in connexion with the exercise of the right of self-preservation (which is identical with, or closely akin to, that of self-defence) are taken into consideration, it will be seen that in each case the parties attach importance to proving the legality of the action undertaken under this head. Writers justify or condemn it on the ground of its conformity or otherwise to the legal principle which it professes to follow; so do statesmen; so do international tribunals whenever they have had occasion to pass judgement on the matter.[3] The right of

---

[1] This is the definition by Mr. Webster, an American Secretary of State, Moore, *Digest*, ii, § 217, p. 412.

[2] See in particular Spaight in *J.C.L. and I.L.*, 3rd ser., xiv (1932), pp. 20–9. See also Shotwell, *War as an Instrument of National Policy* (1929), pp. 207–11, and Cohn, *Kriegsverhütung und Schuldfrage* (1931), pp. 115–41. See in particular Wright in *International Conciliation*, Pamphlet No. 243, October 1928.

[3] For a fairly exhaustive enumeration of the relevant instances and of the literature on the subject see Strupp, *Das völkerrechtliche Delikt* (1920), pp. 139–42, 162–4. See also Rodick, *The Doctrine of Necessity in International Law* (1928). For

self-defence is a general principle of law, and as such it is necessarily recognized to its full extent in international law. But it is not a right fundamentally different from the corresponding right possessed by individuals under municipal law. In both cases it is an absolute right, inasmuch as no law can disregard it; in both cases it is a relative right, inasmuch as it is recognized and regulated by law. It is recognized to the extent—but no more—that recourse to it is not in itself illegal. It is regulated to the extent that it is the business of the Courts to determine whether, how far, and for how long, there was a necessity to have recourse to it.[1] There is not the slightest relation between the content of the right to self-defence and the claim that it is above the law and not amenable to evaluation by law. Such a claim is self-contradictory, inasmuch as it purports to be based on legal right, and as, at the same time, it dissociates itself from regulation and evaluation by the law. Like any other dispute involving important issues, so also the question of the right of recourse to war in self-defence is in itself capable of judicial decision, and it is only the determination of States not to have questions of this nature decided by a foreign tribunal which may make it non-justiciable.

It is, therefore, not the right of self-defence which threatens to introduce the principal element of disintegration into the General Treaty for the Renunciation of War.[2] The possible element of disintegration lies in the assertion that recourse to self-defence is not amenable to judicial determination. If this were the correct interpretation of the treaty, then the result would be to deprive it of its legal value as a means of preventing war, and to reduce its legal effect to a mere theoretical change, to be registered by text-books of international law, in the conception of war as a legally recognized

an interesting reminder of the possibilities of the plea of self-defence see Moore, pp. 839, 840, 919, 920, on the argument of the United States in the *Behring Sea* arbitration. See also the opinions of the American Commissioners in the *Betsey*, on the admissibility of the plea of self-defence, Moore, pp. 3853, 3873, 3884. Oppenheim, who expresses the view that the reason of the thing 'makes it necessary for every State to judge for itself whether a case of necessity in self-defence has arisen' (i, § 130), discusses at length the lawfulness of some of the historical instances of self-defence. See Verdross in *Recueil des Cours* (1929), v. 481–90, for a clear exposition of the whole question.

[1] See below, p. 393.

[2] It may also be said that such right would, given an unstrained interpretation of the conception of self-defence, be logically included in that provision of the preamble to the treaty which provides that 'any signatory Power which shall hereafter seek to promote its national interests by resort to war should be denied the benefits furnished by this Treaty'.

form of international procedure.[1] If that were so, the treaty would stamp as unlawful such wars only as the belligerents might openly declare to be undertaken with the intention of aggression. It could not be described as rendering unlawful wars which States, fully conscious of the moral and political implications and risks of their action, honestly declared to be undertaken in repelling a danger, actual or threatened, to their vital interests. It would be immaterial that, under this interpretation, the exercise of discretion in the exercise of the right of self-defence would be subject to the general legal requirement of good faith in the performance of treaty obligations. Various systems of law contain provisions which expressly refer to the requirement of good faith. It is the elimination of any objective legal authority endowed with the competence to ascertain whether the duty of good faith has been complied with, which would largely be destructive of the legal object of the treaty so interpreted.[2] Only the befogging generality of phrases, which envelops some of the fundamental aspects of relations between States, could then explain why many lawyers have failed to point to the element of pure discretion, entirely removed from grounds possessing any legal relevance, introduced into the General Treaty for the Renunciation of War by such an interpretation of the right of self-defence. For such an interpretation would create a new and formidable category of non-justiciable matters, including the very purpose of the treaty within the rule 'de maximis non curat praetor'. As in other matters, the exclusion of the judicial process would lie not in the nature of the issue, but in the determination of the States to make it non-justiciable.[3]

[1] See, for an estimate of this aspect of the treaty, Morris in *A.S.*, *Proceedings* (1929), pp. 88–91, and the following discussion. See also Borchard in *A.J.* xxiii (1929), pp. 116–20, and in *Z.f.a.ö.R. und V.* i (1929), pp. 126–31, in an article entitled 'The Kellogg Treaties Sanction War'. See also Cohn in *Z.V.* xv (1930), p. 181.

[2] Even if that were so, cogent reasons might be adduced in support of the contention that, notwithstanding its legal imperfections, the Treaty for the Renunciation of War is, on account of its rejection of the conception of war as a legitimate means of legal procedure, of supreme moral and political value for the preservation of peace. Equally convincing arguments could be put forward in support of the view that, by lulling the conscience of the world into a false sense of security, and by perpetuating the actual elimination of the idea of law from a most important manifestation of the will of sovereign States, the treaty is morally and politically dangerous. However, such considerations are beyond the province of a legal investigation.

[3] If the view expressed above is accepted, then the question of the definition of 'aggression' becomes less important than is usually assumed. Aggression

However, there is nothing in the declarations or reservations referring to the Pact for Renunciation of War, and concerning the right of self-defence, which necessitates the assumption that the signatories of the treaty intended to adopt this second interpretation which, as has been shown, would deprive the treaty of most of its legal value. It is possible, perhaps probable,[1] that the intention was merely to reaffirm a principle necessarily valid without any express declaration, namely, that implied in the first-mentioned interpretation of the non-justiciability of the right of self-defence.[2]

would simply mean such recourse to war—or to acts of force deemed to be tantamount to war—as a judicial tribunal would, having regard to the circumstances of the case, hold to be unwarranted by self-defence, and therefore unlawful. There may still exist a necessity for defining aggression for purposes of provisional police action. For such purposes a technical and automatic definition might be necessary. Such definition, it is believed, would not be contrary to justice or impracticable.

[1] This view is different from that formerly expressed by the writer in *Recueil des Cours* (1930), iv. 611, 612. It appears to him, on reconsideration of the question, that there is no warrant for the interpretation adopted therein.

[2] The principal difficulty is that there is no machinery provided in the Pact for Renunciation of War for a legal regulation of the recourse to self-defence. Such a machinery exists in the Covenant of the League of Nations. A power of this nature is, for instance, exercised by the Council or Assembly of the League of Nations in determining whether there has been a violation of Article 12 of the Covenant obliging States not to go to war before having recourse to the machinery provided in the Covenant. According to the Report of the Committee of Jurists of 1923, following upon the dispute between Italy and Greece, the Council of the League is entitled to determine whether recourse to force not intended as war is contrary to the provisions of Articles 12, 13, or 15 of the Covenant. Such determination would necessarily include a judicial expression of opinion on the admissibility, in a given case, of the principle of self-defence. In general, the Council and the Assembly of the League provide a possibility for evolving not only a moral but also a legal judgement on the observance of the provisions of the Covenant as to recourse to war. See, for instance, the Resolution of the Institute of International Law of 1923 (*Annuaire*, xxx [1923], p. 384, and Schücking-Wehberg [2nd ed., 1924], p. 464), on the duty of the Council to form an opinion on the question whether there has taken place 'aggression' within the meaning of Article 10 of the Covenant. See also the unratified amendment to Article 16 of the Covenant, according to which 'it is for the Council to give an opinion whether or not a breach of the Covenant has taken place' (Second Assembly, *Plenary Meetings*, p. 806).

CHAPTER IX

THE DOCTRINE 'DE MAXIMIS NON CURAT PRAETOR' AS PART OF LEGAL OBLIGATIONS

§ 16. The Subjective Element in the Conception of Political Disputes. It has been shown in the preceding chapter that the conception of political disputes, inasmuch as it excludes judicial determination of important issues among States, is not in accordance with existing international law, and that it is contrary to the accepted notions of the purpose of law in general. This principal defect of the conception of political disputes has been obscured by the view, which has recently been gaining ground, that it is not so much the exclusion of the judicial process in respect of important issues that is to be deprecated as the freedom of States to determine which issues are important. This view, it is believed, underestimates the difficulties of the problem. Whenever in an arbitration treaty issues of importance are excluded from legal determination—either by the use of the term 'legal' as distinguished from 'political' ('political' meaning a grave issue), or by reference to the general reservation of independence, vital interests, or honour—the limitation of the competence of the Tribunal to decide upon the applicability of these limitations lies not so much in the will of the States as in the nature of the restrictions adopted. No juridical test has so far been devised by which the degree of the exclusion of the judicial process in disputes involving important issues could be determined. It may be doubted whether such a test is possible at all. A juridical criterion, like any other test, can be formed only on the basis of data capable of objective ascertainment. But the history of international controversies shows that a dispute may be 'important' for a variety of reasons: it may be so because of the supposed magnitude of the material interests involved; it may be important because of the amount of feeling and sentiment raised by it;[1] it may be regarded as comparatively important

---

[1] See *Actes et Documents*, ii. 299, for the suggestion that disputes concerning the fulfilment of financial obligations are particularly likely to affect the national honour of the State. There are writers who see the only difference between justiciable and political disputes in the fact that in the former the issue is of a direct and concrete nature, whereas in the latter the attitude of the disputants has rendered the issue emotional and complex. See Shotwell in *Foreign Affairs* (American review), April 1928, pp. 465–7.

so as to justify exclusion from judicial process because of the supposed lack of an impartial arbitrator,[1] or the weakness of the opponent from whom better terms may be exacted in a different manner; it may be regarded as important because of the possible difficulty in giving effect to an adverse award; it may be looked upon as involving vital interests because of the special position of the State concerned.[2] An altogether insignificant dispute may become important because of the refusal of the opponent to have it determined by an impartial investigation; a dispute which is of a trifling nature among two States between whom there exist friendly relations will become of unusual significance in the mutual relations of countries between whom there is a state of permanent political tension; or it may be important because of the nature of the satisfaction demanded.

There is in fact no dispute, however trifling in origin, which cannot in certain circumstances be regarded as affecting some important interest of the State as expressed in the usual restrictive clauses. At the Second Hague Conference an attempt was made by the British and American delegations to set up a list of conventions, the interpretation of which could never be regarded as a political matter involving the vital interests, the independence, and the honour of a State. These conventions were:

I. Disputes concerning the interpretation and application of conventional stipulations relative to the following subjects:
   1. Reciprocal free aid to the indigent sick.
   2. International protection of workmen.
   3. Means of preventing collisions at sea.
   4. Weights and measures.
   5. Measurement of ships.

---

[1] It is significant that Hyde, ii. 114, when referring to the lack of popular confidence in the competence of available tribunals, states that a refusal of a State to arbitrate does not necessarily signify its intention to ignore the law of nations, but is the result, *inter alia*, 'of the seriousness of its doubt as to the likelihood of obtaining judicial recognition of the justice of its claim'.

[2] Thus at the First Hague Conference it was pointed out, on behalf of the United States, that the question of international canals, such as the Panama Canal, may be of secondary importance to many States, while it is a question of vital interest for the United States, and that it could not therefore be included within the list of treaties whose interpretation it was proposed to make subject to unconditional arbitration treaties. Conversely, territorial questions, which European States regard as political *par excellence*, are not always so regarded by South American States. See, for instance, a Memorandum submitted by Peru to the Second Pan-American Conference in 1902, cited by Morgenthau, op. cit. p. 64; and see *Actes et Documents*, ii. 269, and *Committee on Arbitration and Security*, 2nd Session, p. 37

6. Wages and estates of deceased seamen.

7. Protection of literary and artistic works.

II. Pecuniary claims for damages, when the principle of indemnity is recognized by the parties.[1]

This enumeration shows how limited is the scope of matters in regard to which it was deemed possible to exclude in advance the likelihood that important political interests will be involved. But even this modest list failed to secure unanimity.[2] As the German delegate to that Conference said, even the interpretation of a technical convention concerning the use and exchange of railway cars may become a non-justiciable matter, for instance, in time of mobilization. 'A question may be juridical for one country, and political for the other. There are purely juridical matters which become political as the dispute begins.'[3] When in 1899, at the First Hague Conference, Russia proposed obligatory arbitration in regard to a similar list of conventions of a technical character, including conventions relating to sanitation and veterinary surgery and for the prevention of phylloxera, she

---

[1] See Scott, *Reports to The Hague Conferences, 1899 and 1907* (1917), p. 437.

[2] The list was adopted by 31 votes against 8, with 5 abstentions. Germany, Austria-Hungary, Belgium, Bulgaria, Greece, Roumania, Switzerland, and Turkey voted against; Italy, Japan, Luxemburg, Montenegro, and Siam abstained. In addition, the British and American delegations put forward another proposal for attaching to the Convention, for future adhesion, a protocol enumerating a large number of technical conventions subject to obligatory arbitration without reservations. See Scott, ibid., pp. 445, 448.

A large number of arbitration treaties have been concluded in which the comprehensiveness of the general reservations is limited by an enumeration of matters not considered to fall within the purview of the reservations. Thus the Final Protocol to the treaty between Germany and Switzerland, of 3 December 1921 (*Arbitration and Security*, p. 201), which exempts from arbitration matters affecting the territorial integrity of the contracting parties, lays down that ordinary frontier disputes shall not be considered as disputes affecting territorial integrity. The treaty between Argentina and Italy, of 18 September 1907 (Martens, 3rd ser., iv. 84), which excepts matters affecting the constitution from the purview of the treaty, provides that, apart from questions of nationality, controversies relating to the interpretation of treaties, and to disputes on questions of international law, shall not be regarded as affecting the constitution. The treaty between France and Denmark, of 9 August 1911 (Martens, 3rd ser., v. 682), which contained the usual wide reservations, laid down that these reservations cannot be invoked in disputes concerning claims for damages (if there is agreement on the question of principle governing the claim), claims for contract debts claimed by nationals and taken up by their State, and the interpretation of treaties of commerce and navigation and of a number of technical conventions. See for an enumeration of a considerable number of similar treaties Clad, *Wesen und Grenzen der internationalen Schiedsgerichtsbarkeit* (1928), pp. 64–8, and A. Niemeyer in *N.Z.* xxxix (1928–9), pp. 415 et seqq.

[3] Baron Marschall von Bieberstein at the Second Hague Conference, *Actes et Documents*, ii. 51. See also Lammasch, *Die Lehre von der Schiedsgerichtsbarkeit* (1914), p. 105.

did not omit to qualify her proposal by the usual reservation clauses of vital interests and national honour.[1]

There are in existence a number of recent technical conventions, the clauses of which bring out with equal clearness the fact that the character of a convention is not in itself a sufficient indication of the nature of disputes likely to arise under it. Thus in the conventions, concluded on 9 December 1923, and relating to the transmission in transit of electric power or to the development of hydraulic power, it has been found necessary to exempt from the provisions concerning the application or interpretation of the conventions any State which represents that the transit or the development of hydraulic power will be seriously detrimental to its national economy or security.[2] Similar provisions as to the non-applicability of the obligatory judicial process in cases in which, in the opinion of the State concerned, its vital interests are affected, will be found in the Statute on the Régime of Navigable Waterways of International Concern.[3] (In other cases, the question whether the vital interests are involved seems, in the last-mentioned convention, to be left for ascertainment by an international tribunal.[4]) The Convention for the Abolition of Import and Export Prohibitions and Restric-

---

[1] For the full list see Scott, op. cit., p. 93. See also treaties like those between Belgium and Roumania of 27 April 1905, Martens, *N.R.G.*, 3rd ser., ii. 236, which include the typical reservations of independence, &c., in regard to the interpretation of treaties on international private law, customs, treatment of ships, navigation, trade-marks, artistic and literary property, and civil and criminal procedure.

[2] See *P.C.I.J.*, Series D, No. 5, pp. 209 and 211 (Article 12 of both Conventions). See also *L.N.T.S.* xxxvi. 76.

[3] Article 10, paragraph 3, *L.N.T.S.* vii. 57: 'It is understood, however, that such works [relating to the maintenance of the waterway] cannot be undertaken so long as the State of the territory on which they are to be carried out objects on the ground of vital interests.' See Hostie in *R.I.*, 3rd ser., ii (1921), p. 562, who says that this provision constitutes 'un retour partiel à la néfaste conception suivant laquelle un État prétend se mettre au-dessus de la justice en se réservant de juger lui-même'. And see Rousseau, *La compétence de la Société des Nations dans le règlement des conflits internationaux* (1927), pp. 193, 194. A similar provision will be found in paragraph 3 of Article 43 of the Elbe Navigation Act of 22 February 1922 (*A.J.*, Supplement, vii (1923), p. 227).

[4] See Article 19: 'The measure of a general or particular character which a contracting State is obliged to take in case of emergency affecting the safety of the State or the vital interests of the country may, in exceptional cases, and for as short a period as possible, involve a deviation from the principles of the above Articles.' The exceptions laid down in this Article are subject to Article 22 of the Convention which provides for the judicial settlement of the disputes as to the interpretation or the application of the Convention. The difference between Articles 19 and 10 (3) is substantial. But see Smith in *Grotius Society*, xvi (1931), p. 99. The Convention on the Freedom of Transit of 20 April 1921 contains provisions similar to those of Article 19 referred to above (*L.N.T.S.* vii. 29).

tions of 8 November 1927 contains an unusual combination of restrictions of judicial process. It not only lays down, in Article 8, that there shall be excluded from judicial determination, *inter alia*, prohibitions of a non-economic character (Article 4) and temporary and exceptional prohibitions dictated by vital interests (Article 5). It also provides that in other controversies the dispute as to the interpretation or application of the treaty must be of a legal character, it being, in case of dispute, for the Permanent Court or an arbitral tribunal to determine whether the dispute is of a legal nature or not.[1]

§ 17. Ascertainment of the Political Character of the Dispute.

The international conventions referred to above show how wide is the possible scope of grave issues and how necessarily subjective must be any attempt to determine the gravity of the issue as an element of the justiciability of the dispute. There is in existence a number of arbitration treaties in which, in case of a disagreement between the parties, the determination whether the question is a political one or not is left for the decision of the Tribunal. In the arbitration treaties concluded in 1905 between Italy and Peru,[2] and in 1908 between Norway and Portugal,[3] and several other States, it was laid down that the Tribunal shall be competent to decide the preliminary question whether the dispute involves the vital interests, the independence, or the national honour of the disputants. Similarly, Article 4 of the treaty of arbitration and conciliation between Switzerland and Germany of December 1921,[4] provided that, if one of the parties pleads that the question at issue is one which affects its independence, the integrity of its territory, or other vital interests of the highest importance, and if the plea is not recognized by the other party, this point shall be settled by means of arbitration. The same provision is made in regard to the plea that the dispute, although not falling within these exceptions, is 'mainly political and, for this reason, does not allow of a decision based exclusively on legal principles'.[5]

---

[1] For an analysis of these provisions, see Lacour-Gayet in *R.I.* (Paris), ii (1928), pp. 216–23.

[2] Martens, *N.R.G.*, 2nd ser., xxxiv. 320.   [3] Ibid., 3rd ser. iii. 208.

[4] *Arbitration and Security*, p. 201.

[5] These provisions must be distinguished from those encountered in a considerable number of recent arbitration treaties (enumerated in *Arbitration and Security*, p. 26) which confer upon the Tribunal the power to determine whether a dispute is or is not covered by a specific reservation. Such an authorization

It might also be said, although this is not the view held by the writer, that the same power has been conferred upon the Permanent Court of International Justice in Article 36 of its Statute, in so far as the power, granted to it in the last paragraph of that Article, may possibly extend to determining whether a dispute is 'legal', i.e. not involving issues of importance—this being one of the possible meanings of the qualifying term preceding the enumeration of the four categories of disputes in that Article.

Attempts calculated to restore an element essential to any legal obligation, namely, its independence of the discretion of the party under an obligation, are certainly praiseworthy, but it is by no means certain that this object is possible of achievement. It may be within the province of a judicial tribunal to decide on the applicability of a specific reservation, however comprehensive, for instance, the Monroe Doctrine or interests of third parties, or of national legislation, or of self-defence. But it means stretching judicial activity to the breaking-point to entrust it with the determination of the question whether a dispute is political in the meaning that it involves the independence, or the vital interests, or the honour of the State. It is therefore doubtful whether any tribunal acting judicially can override the assertion of a State that a dispute affects its security or vital interests. As we have seen, the interests involved are of a nature so subjective as to exclude the possibility of applying an objective standard not only in regard to general arbitration treaties, but also in regard to each individual dispute.[1] We are therefore unable to follow the view expressed by Professor Huber and other members of the Institute of International Law, according to which it is not the insertion of comprehensive reservations (such as those used in the Franco-British treaty of 1903), which ought to be deprecated, but the right of the parties to decide as to their applicability.[2] The line of progress does not lie in devising an appropriate agency

may be given by a provision conferring upon the Tribunal jurisdiction in regard to the interpretation or application of the arbitration treaty. The treaties referred to in the text confer upon the Tribunal this power in regard to the general reservations of political issues.

[1] See, however, Lammasch, *Über isolierte und institutionelle Schiedsgerichte*, p. 83.

[2] See *Annuaire*, xxxiii (2) (1927), p. 765. According to Professor Huber this right of the parties deprives the treaty of its political value. It is suggested in this and in the following sections that such right, which is inherent in the reservations of this nature, affects substantially the legal value of the treaty. See also the Report of Borel and Politis, ibid., pp. 672, 673, 709–14, 739–43.

to decide whether an international court has no jurisdiction for the reason that a particular case affects the vital interests, independence, or honour of a nation, or because it is a political dispute involving grave matters, in contradistinction to a legal or juridical dispute. It lies in abandoning conceptions which are incapable of forming part of a legal obligation.

§ 18. Conception of Political Disputes as part of Legal Obligations.

Whatever may be the value of entrusting to judicial tribunals the decision whether a dispute is political (i.e. involving important issues), the fact remains that in many recent instruments of pacific settlement they have been denied this power. Apart from the doubtful case of the elimination of judicial decision, in the Pact for the Renunciation of War, from the determination of the legitimacy of recourse to self-defence, it is sufficient to mention the 'vital interests clause' in the technical conventions quoted above;[1] or the General Treaty of Inter-American Arbitration of 1928;[2] or the large group of treaties concluded by the United States in and subsequent to 1928.[3] The legal value of instruments of this nature may now properly be considered. These international conventions constitute, it is believed, obligations without the *vinculum juris*. An obligation whose scope is left to the free appreciation of the obligee, so that his will constitutes a legally recognized condition of the existence of the duty, does not constitute a legal bond. It is even impossible to say that its effect is to create what is called in Roman law 'a natural obligation', or in English law an 'agreement of imperfect obligation'. The position is in this respect different from that arising, e.g., under Articles 10 or 16 of the Covenant whose obligations are not deprived of their legal character as the result of the right of the Members of the League to determine whether a case for the application of these provisions has arisen. There is here no right *ab initio*, as there is, for instance, in regard to the imperfect obligation arising out of the operation of a statute of limitations. There is, in the vital aspect of the stipulation, no legal right vested in one party to determine the action of the other, because that other party has reserved for itself freedom of action. 'Nulla

---

[1] See above, pp. 186, 187.
[2] See above, p. 38. And see Whitton and Brewer in *A.J.* xxv (1931), pp. 458–63, who express the view that 'the individual parties to the treaty are the sole judges of such general reservations as bind all, and of such particular reservations as involve them individually'.
[3] See above, p. 37.

promissio potest consistere, quae ex voluntate permittentis statum capit.[1] The opposition between *obligatio* and *mera facultas* is a fundamental one, and cannot be removed by technical formulas aiming at reconciling the State's freedom of action with an obligation to submit disputes to judicial settlement. An international lawyer, who had occasion to devote special study to this question, remarked that the problem how to combine freedom of action with a definite obligation admitting of no ambiguity had been baffling the student for a long time, and that it may take another fifty years before the problem will be solved.[2] It is submitted that the estimate is an optimistic one. A reconciliation of this kind is in law a matter impossible of achievement.

The juridical form in which this ultimate right of free action expresses itself most frequently has been—in almost all pre-war arbitration treaties, and in many post-war treaties embodying the elimination of important issues[3]—the requirement of a special *compromis* to be concluded as occasion should arise, in addition to the general arbitration treaty.[4] The much debated question whether a State bound by a general arbitration treaty of this nature is bound to conclude the special *compromis* has been answered, with a consensus approaching unanimity, that there is no such duty if one party is of the opinion that its vital interests or honour, or some matter exclusively within its domestic jurisdiction, are at stake. Lammasch, an authority by no means averse to the

---

[1] *D.* 45. 1 *de verb. obl.* 108, § 1. See also Article 1162 of the Italian Code: 'È nulla l'obbligazione contratta sotto una condizione, che la fa dipendere dalla mera volontà di colui che si è obbligato.'

[2] Brown in *A.S., Proceedings* (1924), p. 77. See on attempts to define 'honour' and 'vital interests'. *Annuaire*, xx (1904), p. 181.

[3] This question does not, naturally, arise when the arbitration treaty contains no reservations whatsoever, although, if the treaty does not confer jurisdiction upon a permanent tribunal with a fixed procedure and organization, the framing of the *compromis* is of considerable importance and may be decisive for the outcome of the issue. The whole matter of the conclusion of the *compromis* is treated by Lammasch, *Über isolierte und institutionelle Schiedsgerichte*, pp. 92–110. See also Wehberg, *Kommentar*, pp. 90ff., and Nippold, pp. 180ff. For a recent admirable study see Wilson in *A.J.* xxv (1931), pp. 469–89. As to the particular necessity of a special agreement in the case of the United States, in the form of a treaty as distinguished from an executive agreement, see Fleming, *The Treaty Veto of the American Senate* (1930), pp. 104 et seqq. See also Moore, *International Law and Some Current Illusions* (1924) pp. 87, 90, and Renault, at the Second Hague Conference, *Actes et Documents*, ii. 69, and the literature concerning the unratified treaties of 1911, p. 37, *supra*.

[4] The recent treaties concluded by the United States combine freedom of appreciation of the applicability of reservations with the necessity of a special *compromis*.

cause of obligatory arbitration, says 'The vital interests and the honour of a State are matters so individual, and so dependent on subjective valuation, that it is hardly possible to entrust a foreign agency with the decision whether they are involved in a dispute or not.'[1] He had no doubt that, failing an express provision to the contrary, an international tribunal is not competent to decide on the matter.[2] He could perhaps have added that even if it were competent, it might have found it difficult to fulfil that function when acting in a judicial capacity.[3]

§ 19. The Element of Good Faith.

The legal inadequacy of instruments of pacific settlement embodying the conception of political disputes as determined by the importance of their subject-matter, is so obvious that an explanation may

[1] Ibid., p. 102.

[2] Apart from the few treaties referred to above, p. 185, the pre-war arbitration treaties contained no provisions in this matter, as it was generally understood that the decision on the question of the applicability of the reservation lies within the discretion of the State concerned. Article 53 of Convention No 1 of 1907 for the Pacific Settlement of International Disputes provided, *inter alia*, that the Permanent Court of Arbitration shall be competent to settle the *compromis* following upon a unilateral request. But the same Article laid down that recourse cannot 'be had to the Court if the other party declares that in its opinion the dispute does not belong to the category of disputes which can be submitted to obligatory arbitration'. It also conferred, unconditionally, that right upon the Tribunal in case of a dispute arising from contract debts claimed to be due to private persons, and for the settlement of which the offer has been accepted. For a discussion of this Article see *Actes et Documents*, ii. 638 ff., 675 ff., 747 ff., 750 ff., and Lammasch, op. cit. Most of the signatures of the Convention were accompanied by reservations as to Article 53. This also was the case in regard to the treaties concluded after the World War and based on the Franco-British treaty of 1903. For an enumeration of the treaties see *Arbitration and Security*, p. 34. Other post-war treaties provide for a special procedure in the event of the parties being unable to agree upon the *compromis*. Some entrust with that task the Conciliation Commission, others an arbitral tribunal. See ibid., pp. 35, 36. It is difficult to draw a rigid line between the question of applicability of reservations, i.e. the duty of agreeing to conclude a *compromis*, and the details of the *compromis*. Article 53 of The Hague Convention probably refers to both. See on the whole question Wilson, op. cit. The question of applicability of reservations falls, as a rule, under the general heading of disputes arising out of the interpretation or application of the arbitration convention. See *Arbitration and Security*, p. 26. See also Jessup in *A.J., Proceedings* (1929), pp. 128, 129.

[3] See on this point Morgenthau, op. cit., p. 90, n. 10, with copious references; Wehberg in *A.J.* vii (1913), p. 310, and in *Kommentar*, pp. 98 ff.; Ch. de Visscher in *R.I.*, 3rd ser., ix (1928), p. 40.

Article 41 of the General Act of 1928 provides that disputes relating to the interpretation or application of its provisions, including those concerning the classification of disputes and the scope of reservations, shall be submitted to the Permanent Court of International Justice. However, it will be noted that, apart from matters of domestic jurisdiction, Article 39 of the Act indirectly excludes the comprehensive reservations of a general character.

be necessary of the persistence of this type of international engagement. The confusing artificiality of language is here typical of the intercourse of Governments in matters in which the insistence on the rights of sovereignty makes concessions to public opinion, and to the necessities of orderly international relations, by the use of general terms of an all-embracing elasticity.[1] Writers anxious to further the cause of international arbitration have been in the habit of minimizing the possible effect of the lack of legal obligation in treaties of this description, and of magnifying the possibilities, said to be inherent in the formal residuum, that is, in matters of small importance. They insist that, however insignificant the actual legal obligation may be, there is no doubt that States intended to enter into some legal obligation of a binding character which, like any other treaty, has to be executed in good faith; that no State which attaches importance to its prestige and reputation, not only as a law-abiding State, but as a powerful State, will be apt to plead that its independence or honour is affected by some trifling occurrence or claim; that, granted that the obligation extends to matters of small importance only, their submission to arbitration will foster respect for the law in general, and will pave the way for the submission of more important disputes; and that the submission to judicial settlement of trivial issues will at least prevent such issues from becoming magnified and from embittering international relations as the result of the refusal to submit them for impartial adjudication.[2]

In so far as these and similar views point to the possible political and moral value of such obligations, they may be a matter of discussion. In particular, it may be asked whether the policy of confining the judicial function in international relations to small issues, and of extolling the value of the advantage thus achieved, may not have the effect of perpetuating the idea of the reign of law being confined to trivial matters. But these are matters which are outside the scope of legal analysis. The question is, what is the legal

[1] When necessary, Governments do not hestitate to stress the actual legal position. See, for instance, Argument of Mr. Arthur Cohen in the *Venezuelan Preferential Claims* case, p. 1258 (as quoted above on p. 82), when replying to the reproach that the declaration of war was contrary to the new obligations of The Hague Convention: 'His Majesty's Government... insists most strongly that neither the peace conference nor The Hague Convention impliedly altered any rule of international law that existed previously.'

[2] See the remarks of Renault at the Second Hague Conference, *Actes et Documents*, ii. 67; Lammasch, *Schiedsgerichtsbarkeit*, p. 69.

value of such obligations. It may be true, as Sir Edward Fry said at the Second Hague Conference, that *vincula juris* are not the only bonds which bind States, and that treaties of this nature are at least an expression of the conscience of the civilized world;[1] but this very submission, noble as it is, negatives the value of such treaties as legal obligations. The account, which follows, of some of the relevant cases seems to confirm the view of the somewhat cynical opponent of obligatory arbitration that the vital stipulation of these treaties says 'thou shalt', qualified by 'if it pleaseth thee'.[2] In treaties of this description a State may exercise its discretion without acting illegally. Whether it will lower its prestige by pleading vital interests at the slightest provocation is its own concern, as is the question whether its honour is involved. But there is no question of a breach of a legal obligation. There is no such obligation *ab initio*. There may or may not be justification for the unreality of language attempting to elevate the generalizations and technicalities of mere evasion to the dignity of a legal obligation,[3] but the lawyer can be no party to any such attempt.[4]

---

[1] *Actes et Documents*, ii. 298.

[2] Baron Marschall von Bieberstein, ibid., pp. 49 ff., 285 ff.

[3] The Second Hague Conference, at which the very modest attempts at introducing obligatory arbitration met with no success, adopted the following resolution, whose meaninglessness justifies, in this connexion, quotation in full:

'The Commission is unanimous:

'1. In admitting the principle of obligatory arbitration.

'2. In declaring that certain disputes, in particular those relating to the interpretation and application of the provisions of international agreements, may be submitted to obligatory arbitration without any restriction.

'Finally, it is unanimous in proclaiming that, although it has not yet been found feasible to conclude a Convention in this sense, nevertheless, the divergences of opinion which have come to light have not exceeded the bounds of judicial controversy, and that, by working together here during the past four months, the collected States of the world not only have learned to understand one another and to draw closer together, but have succeeded, in the course of this long collaboration, in evolving a very lofty conception of the common welfare of humanity.' Scott, *Reports*, p. 454. Baron Marschall von Bieberstein's comment on this resolution was short but pungent. He said, in his report to the German Government: 'It is difficult to say less in more words.' *Die grosse Politik der europäischen Kabinette*, vol. xxiii, part ii, p. 346.

Baron Guillaume, Chairman of the first Committee, ended his Report on the abortive discussions in the Committee in the following confident manner: 'All the positions won were maintained, the rights of all were safeguarded, a spirit of concord and wise conciliation permitted the Commission to appear before the Conference united and conscious of the usefulness of its efforts.' Scott, *Reports*, p. 454.

[4] It may be a matter of interest for the student of social psychology to inquire how far the principle 'virtutem credant habere et habebunt' applies to the problem under discussion. But such considerations are beyond the province of the lawyer, whose sole duty is to discover how far a provision embodies a legal

In particular he must refuse to attach exaggerated importance to the argument that the legal obligation still subsists in matters of obviously minor importance which no amount of discretion can, without a breach of faith, interpret as falling under the designation of important disputes. Whenever a State attaches so much importance to the refusal to submit a dispute to judicial settlement as to expose itself to the charge of breaking its obligations, the dispute is apparently of such importance, at least from the subjective point of view of the State concerned, as to bring the refusal with perfect justification within the conception of non-justiciability. In matters whose insignificance is so obvious as to preclude them from being brought within the right of freedom of action, a State will be under no necessity of refusing to comply with an inconvenient treaty obligation. For such cases will, as a rule, be disposed of through the machinery of negotiation. The fact that diplomatic negotiations have proved abortive and that a demand has been put forward to have recourse to the costly and cumbrous machinery of arbitration will have the effect of rendering a dispute sufficiently important to remove it from the purview of the obligation.

§ 20. Historical Instances. German State Succession Claims against Great Britain.

A survey of some historical instances of refusal of arbitration in situations apparently covered by general arbitration treaties will, it is submitted, show that the view developed above as to the weakness of the legal bond, if any, of treaties of pacific settlement embodying the principle of non-justiciability of important disputes, is largely substantiated by the practice of States.

After the annexation of South Africa by Great Britain, Germany put forward certain claims on behalf of some German subjects for deliveries said to have been made to the South African Government. The German Government contended that Great Britain was bound to compensate the claimants by virtue of the rules of international law governing State succession. Great Britain denied that international law

---

obligation, and how far it is merely a pretence at a legal obligation. However, even lawyers of authority do not easily resign themselves to a simple acceptance of the results of a juridical analysis. Compare, for instance, Lammasch's praise of the results of the Second Hague Conference in *Schiedsgerichtsbarkeit*, p. 69, with his more confidential expressions of opinion on the 'inner falsehood' of the final resolution of that Conference: see Marga Lammasch and Hans Sperl, *Heinrich Lammasch*, p. 58.

imposed upon her any such obligation. It would seem that a claim of this nature does not involve either vital interests or honour, and is therefore a proper subject for arbitral adjudication, particularly when the two States in question are bound by a general arbitration convention. Yet, when in 1907 and in the following years Germany repeatedly proposed to Great Britain that the matter should be submitted to the Permanent Court of Arbitration, Great Britain refused to accede to that request. Both States were at that time bound by a general arbitration treaty concluded on 12 July 1904, incorporating the reservations of vital interests, the independence, and the honour of the contracting parties. The British Note refusing the German request was sent on 16 September 1907, at the time when the Second Hague Conference was sitting. In the instructions, which in June[1] and September[2] 1907 the German Government sent to its delegation at The Hague, reference was made to the British refusal and to the German Government's feeling of 'most painful surprise' evoked by it, and the delegation was instructed to draw the attention of the British delegates to the incompatibility of the British attitude at the Conference (favouring obligatory arbitration) with that country's unwillingness to abide by the provisions of a treaty already in existence. In February 1911 the German Government proposed that at least the preliminary question, namely, whether the dispute created by the German claims was one of a legal nature in accordance with Article 1 of the arbitration treaty, should be submitted to the Permanent Court of Arbitration.[3] No definite answer to that request had been given at the time of the outbreak of

---

[1] Draft of 14 June 1907, *Die grosse Politik der europäischen Kabinette, 1871–1914*, vol. xxiii, part i, p. 260. The claims were those on behalf of a certain C. F. Sunkel, a German subject, but they were representative of a larger number of claims of this description. See also on this case Simons, *The Evolution of International Public Law in Europe since Grotius* (1931), p. 135.

[2] Draft of 27 September 1907, ibid., vol. xxv, part ii, p. 342. This case is also referred to in Schücking, *The International Union of The Hague Conferences* (English translation, 1918), p. 125.

[3] Ibid., p. 343. The above instance of refusal of arbitration is taken from the German official documents quoted above. The writer has been unable to verify this account by reference to an official British source. In the case of the *Bundesrath* (see Oppenheim, ii, § 402) Germany also proposed, in 1900, arbitration on all disputed points. It was reported by Count Bülow in his speech in the Reichstag on 19 January 1900, that the British Government expressed the hope that there will be no necessity for arbitration, but have declared their concurrence in the institution of a tribunal, if necessary, to arbitrate upon the claims for compensation. See *British and Foreign State Papers*, xciv (1900, 1901), p. 1007.

war in 1914. This was the reason why, when in 1909 the arbitration treaty concluded in 1904 had lapsed and a new treaty had to be negotiated, the German ambassador was directed not to assume the initiative in the matter.[1]

§ 21. The Panama Canal Tolls Controversy.

In 1912 the American Congress passed a Bill fixing the tolls to be paid for passing through the Panama Canal, and added to it a clause which exempted American vessels engaged in coasting trade from paying tolls, thus giving them a privileged position as compared with the vessels of other nations. Great Britain protested against this measure as being in violation of the Hay-Pauncefote Treaty of 18 November 1901. That treaty had laid down that the canal shall be free and open to the vessels of commerce and of war of all nations on terms of entire equality, so that there shall be 'no discrimination against any such nation, or its citizens, or subjects, in respect of the conditions or charges of traffic or otherwise'. The United States denied that they were guilty of such violation, on the ground, *inter alia*, that the expression 'all nations' did not include the United States. As the United States and Great Britain were bound by an arbitration treaty, concluded in 1908, analogous to that between Great Britain and France in 1903,[2] Great Britain proposed that, should the United States be disinclined to withdraw the measure, the question should be submitted to arbitration.[3] This course the United States seemed, on somewhat technical grounds, to be unwilling to accept. It was contended that the mere passing of the Act did not in itself constitute an injury, and that, although the United States now possessed the power to act in a manner said to be contrary to the interests of British shipping, it was the improper exercise of a power, and not merely its possession, which alone gave rise to an international cause of action.[4]

---

[1] *Die grosse Politik der europäischen Kabinette*, xxiii (2), p. 344.

[2] See above, p. 30.

[3] See Dispatch to His Majesty's Ambassador at Washington respecting the Panama Canal Act, 14 November 1912, Cd. 6451, *Parl. Papers*, 1912–13, cxii. 646.

[4] See Dispatch from Secretary of State at Washington to the United States Chargé d'Affaires, 20 January 1913, Cd. 6585, *Parl. Papers*, 1912–13, cxii. 663. And see *A.S.*, *Proceedings* (1913), pp. 212–22, on the question whether 'it is necessary in international law that injury actually be suffered before a justiciable action arises'. See also a letter by Westlake, ibid. A similar question was considered and answered by the Permanent Court of International Justice in *Mavrommatis Palestine Concessions* case, *P.C.I.J.*, Series A, No. 5, pp. 39, 40.

It was suggested that a further examination of the relevant facts should be undertaken by both Governments, and that, should there still be a difference of opinion between them, the controversy should be submitted to a commission of inquiry for examination and report on the lines of the unratified arbitration treaty of 3 August 1911, between the United States and Great Britain. The Act was subsequently repealed by both Houses of Congress,[1] but the general feeling at the time was that, if it had not been repealed, there could not have been obtained the consent of two-thirds of the American Senate required for the submission of the question to arbitration.[2] The controversy gave ample opportunity for a discussion of the question of the applicability of the arbitration treaty of 1908, and there was general agreement among publicists that the question fell within the obligations of the treaty.[3] This, however, was not the opinion of the Government of the United States.

§ 22. The Tunis and Morocco Nationality Decrees Case.

The British-French controversy in the years 1922 and 1923 concerning the French nationality decrees in Tunis and Morocco may be referred to as a third example. On 8 November 1921 the French Government published in Tunis and Morocco (French Zone), under the sovereignty of the Bey of Tunis and the Sultan of Morocco respectively, certain Nationality Decrees, the effect of which was to confer French nationality on persons, including British subjects, born in those countries of persons also born there. In pursuance of these decrees the British subjects were made liable to French military service. Great Britain protested against this measure as being in violation of treaty rights entitling her to claim for her subjects in Tunis the same rights as were accorded to the subjects of all other Powers, and also on the ground that France was not entitled to impose French nationality and its obligations on British subjects on account of their birth in a country which, although under French protection, did not form part of French territory. As the French Government did not agree with these contentions, Great Britain proposed

---

[1] See *A.J.* viii (1914), p. 592.   [2] Ibid., p. 597.

[3] See, for instance, Hershey in *A.S.*, *Proceedings* (1913), pp. 232–8; Latané in *A.J.* vii (1913), pp. 17–26; Oppenheim, *The Panama Canal Conflict between Great Britain and the United States of America* (1913), pp. 44–57. See also Note addressed by His Majesty's Ambassador at Washington to the United States Secretary of State, 28 February 1913, Cd. 6645, *Parl. Papers*, 1912–13, cxii. 672.

that the dispute, being of a legal nature, should be submitted to arbitration under the Franco-British Arbitration Agreement of 1903 and under Article 13 of the Covenant of the League of Nations.[1] The French Government, however, refused to admit that the dispute was one of a legal nature. It pointed out that the treaty of 1903 excepted from the purview of arbitration matters involving the vital interests, the independence, and the honour of the contracting parties and affecting the interests of a third Power; that the dispute affected the interests of Tunis; that questions of nationality were too intimately connected with the constitution of the State to permit of their designation as legal questions; and that the French Government was not therefore in a position to submit to arbitration questions 'qui touchent intimement à l'exercice du droit souverain de légiférer'.[2] In a subsequent memorandum the British Government reiterated its opinion that the question was entirely juridical, and expressed the view that 'a refusal to submit to arbitration such a question, if persisted in by the French Government, would seem to reduce to mere empty words the arbitration conventions on which hope had been placed as the best means of ensuring the pacific settlement of international disputes'.[3] However, the risk of laying itself open to the reproach of reducing to 'mere empty words' a solemn obligation did not induce the French Government to recede from its original attitude.

This last case is of particular interest, as the subsequent course of the controversy made it possible to ascertain by way of a judicial pronouncement the accuracy of a substantial part of the French contention that the dispute was not a legal one. Great Britain brought the dispute before the Council of the League of Nations under Article 15 of the Covenant, and, as France contended that the Council was precluded, in virtue of Article 15, paragraph 8, from dealing with the dispute, the Permanent Court of International Justice was asked to give an Advisory Opinion whether the dispute was,

[1] See the Notes of Lord Hardinge to M. Poincaré of 6 and 28 February 1922, printed in *P.C.I.J.*, Series C, No. 2, additional volume, pp. 173, 178.

[2] Note of M. Poincaré to Lord Hardinge, of 22 March 1922, ibid., p. 184. And see the oral argument of Professor de Lapradelle before the Permanent Court of International Justice on 11 January 1923, Series C, No. 2, p. 55: 'But although the question which is in dispute between us at this moment has a considerable number of juridical aspects, it is none the less fundamentally and in its nature a political question of the first importance.'

[3] Memorandum communicated to the French Government on 14 July 1922, ibid., p. 192.

on the principles of international law, solely a matter of domestic jurisdiction.[1] The answer of the Court was in the negative. Formally, the question whether the dispute was one solely of domestic jurisdiction was different from that whether as a non-legal dispute it came within the reservations of the arbitration treaty of 1903. In substance, however, the two questions were identical, and the Opinion of the Court may legitimately be regarded as a test, both of the value of the arbitration treaties embodying the doctrine of non-justiciability of political disputes, and of the spirit in which the contracting parties give effect to these treaties. In each of the three instances here mentioned the dispute was obviously capable of judicial determination; in none of them was involved any really important State interest justifying, as a matter of good faith, the refusal to concede to the other disputant the benefit of judicial settlement; in each case the party offending against the spirit of the treaty was a Great Power professing to lead the van in the cause of international arbitration.[2]

§ 23. Political Character of Legal Disputes under the Optional Clause. The Belgian-Chinese Controversy in 1926. The controversy between Belgium and China con-

---

[1] See *P.C.I.J.*, Series B, No. 4. For some of the literature on the subject see Oppenheim, ii. 61, n. 2.

[2] It is not proposed to discuss here other cases of refusal of arbitration claimed under an arbitration treaty. Mention should, however, be made of the dispute between the Union of Sweden and Norway and Spain in 1888, and of that between Italy and Switzerland in 1893. The first dispute arose out of the Spanish law of 1883 regulating the levying of the tax on alcohol products. It was maintained by Sweden and Norway that the law amounted to conferring a bounty on Spanish alcohol products, which privilege was said to be excluded by the commercial treaty in force between the two countries and providing for arbitration in regard to the interpretation of its provisions. Spain contended that the law in question was not governed by the provisions of the treaty as being 'une question du régime interieur'. This preliminary question was submitted to an arbitrator who upheld the Spanish contention. See Lammasch, *Isolierte und institutionelle Schiedsgerichte*, pp. 99, 100; *R.G.* i (1894), p. 286. The dispute between Italy and Switzerland was of a similar nature. The controversy arose out of an Italian decree of 1893 prescribing that custom dues should be paid in gold. Switzerland maintained that the decree was contrary to the commercial treaty of 1892 and invoked the arbitration clause of the treaty. Italy refused to accede to the request, on the ground that the decree was one relating to the internal monetary policy of Italy. For a discussion of this case and further literature see Lammasch, ibid., pp. 100–2; Langlade, *De la clause compromissoire*, pp. 202 ff.; Stoykovitch, *De l'autorité de la sentence arbitrale en droit international public* (1924), p. 52; *R.G.* i (1894), pp. 81 ff., 279 ff. As to the dispute and war, notwithstanding a previous arbitration treaty, between Guatemala and Salvador in 1894, see Fauchille, § 969.

cerning the interpretation of the treaty of 2 November 1865, unilaterally denounced by China in April 1926, shows that the existing wording of the Optional Clause of Article 36 of the Statute may give rise to the contention that the term 'legal' preceding the classification of the four categories of disputes enumerated therein is meant to exclude 'political' disputes, i.e. disputes of importance. Both parties to this dispute were bound by the Optional Clause. But the Chinese Government refused to agree to the proposal of Belgium to submit to the Permanent Court of International Justice the question of the interpretation of Article 46 of the treaty of 1865 relating to the renewal of the treaty. It maintained that the dispute, which was said to be one on the application of the principle of equality of treatment in relations between Belgium and China, was political in character and that 'no nation can consent to the basic principle of equality between States being made the subject of a judicial inquiry'.[1] It was prepared to agree to the submission of the dispute to the Court only if the Belgian Government agreed to its being settled *ex aequo et bono*.[2] Belgium subsequently brought the matter before the Court by way of unilateral citation, and the Court issued a number of formal orders, including one indicating measures of interim protection.[3] Subsequently Belgium withdrew the case,[4] and the question of the competence of the Court under the terms of the Optional Clause never came up for argument and decision. It is, however, instructive that, in the only case in which the Optional Clause was invoked, there was revealed the cloven hoof of the doctrine of the elimination of important issues from the obligatory jurisdiction of international tribunals.[5]

[1] Memorandum of the Chinese Government of 16 November 1926. Series C, No. 16 (1), p. 78.

[2] See below, p. 326.

[3] See Series A, Nos. 8, 14, 16.

[4] Series A, No. 18.

[5] That this readiness to use to the full the measure of discretion left open by the treaty is not confined to Great Powers may be seen also from the British-Spanish Moroccan Claims controversy. It appears from the award rendered in August 1924 by Huber, arbitrator, in the case of British claims against Spain in connexion with damage alleged to have been suffered by British subjects and protected persons in the Spanish Zone in Morocco between 1913 and 1921, that Great Britain had considerable difficulty in inducing Spain to submit the matter to arbitration. (See p. 42 of the *Rapports* of the arbitrator, printed at The Hague, 1925.) There existed between the two countries an arbitration treaty originally concluded on 27 February 1904, and framed after the pattern of the treaty between Great Britain and France of 1903. (See above, p. 80.) But Spain seems to have invoked the reservations of the treaty, and eventually it proved possible to obtain her consent to the submission of the dispute to impartial adjudication only by dint of an agreement providing, in regard to the

This does not, of course, mean that, had the case not been withdrawn, the Court would have recognized the validity of the objection. We believe that it would have held that the term 'legal' preceding the enumeration of the four categories of disputes referred to in the Optional Clause is merely descriptive of these disputes and does not contain any additional or restrictive qualification; that, in any case, it could not be interpreted as excluding judicial determination of important interests of States; that such a limitation of the jurisdiction of international tribunals would be contrary to general notions of law and to the purpose and actual content of existing international law; that a restriction of this nature, when inserted in a treaty of obligatory judicial settlement, would tend to deprive the treaty of the element of legal obligation and cannot therefore be assumed to have been intended by the parties; and that, therefore, the doctrine of the non-justiciability of political, i.e. important, issues cannot be recognized. This hypothetical reasoning of the Court constitutes, it will be noted, a summary of the conclusions reached in the last three chapters of this book.

---

most important aspect of the dispute, not for arbitration proper, but for an examination and report, and restricting the report in advance to claims which the arbitrator may find 'arbitrable'. (See below, p. 201.) In the initial stages of the dispute between Switzerland and France concerning the Free Zones (see below, p. 315), France refused to submit the matter to arbitration. On 26 March 1921 the French Ambassador addressed a Note to Switzerland, stating that 'le Gouvernement français, bien entendu, ne saurait envisager la possibilité de soumettre à un arbitrage . . . une question touchant ainsi directement la souveraineté de la France': *P.C.I.J.*, Series C, No. 17, iii. 1650. See also ibid., iv. 2233.

CHAPTER X

THE IMPARTIALITY OF INTERNATIONAL TRIBUNALS

§ 24. The Impartiality of International Tribunals and the Problem of Obligatory Judicial Settlement. Of the various historical reasons which, in the international society, have led to the perpetuation of the legal position expressed in the maxim 'omnis civitas judex in re sua', one of the most important is the lack of confidence in the impartiality of international tribunals. Comprehensive commitments, like the obligations of the so-called Optional Clause of Article 36 of the Statute of the Permanent Court, and, to some extent, of the General Act for the Pacific Settlement of International Disputes, have become part of positive law. But these very documents, as the result of their elastic reservations and of the adoption of the distinction between so-called legal and political disputes, qualify substantially the duty of judicial settlement by eliminating from it disputes of importance in regard to which Governments deem it safer to preserve freedom of action. The exclusion of grave issues from the purview of the international judicial function has for a long time been countenanced by the practice of States and by opinions of lawyers. As has been shown in the preceding chapters, the real difficulty lies not in the inability of international law to protect important interests of States, but in the apprehension that it would be dangerous to expose such interests to the risks of a decision by judges whose impartiality is regarded as problematical.

It is only in terms of that apprehension that it is possible to understand the persistent emphasis on the inherent limitations of the judicial function in matters of independence of States, of questions of domestic jurisdiction, of recourse to force in self-defence, of immigration[1]—all of which are interests which are recognized and protected by international law. The same applies to the other aspects of the supposed limitations of the judicial function. If States refuse to treat disputes as justiciable on account of alleged lack of legal rules, it is because they distrust the impartiality of international judges in the unavoidable exercise of their creative function of filling the gaps in an undeveloped legal system.[2]

---

[1] See above, pp. 173 et seq.   [2] See above, pp. 105–35.

This is also true with regard to the third principal issue of the asserted limitation of the international judicial function, namely, the difficulty, aggravated by the absence of an international legislature, of the adaptation of legal stability to social change in the sphere of international relations.[1] A considerable proportion of this task of adaptation lies legitimately and necessarily within the domain of the judicial function. Here again judicial discretion plays an important part, and the question of impartiality of the international judge becomes once more decisive for the purpose of determining the range of disputes suitable for obligatory adjudication. The problem of the impartiality of the international judge is the Cape Horn of international judicial settlement. It has proved to be an important factor in the efforts to establish a permanent international tribunal and, generally, in the history of obligatory arbitration. Its urgency was clearly recognized in the course of The Hague Conferences.[2] It has been a persistent theme of lawyers[3] and political writers.[4] It is undoubtedly one of the most urgent problems of the political organization of the international community, a problem the consideration of which requires a combination of conscientious abstention from imputation of motives with the determination not to avoid the issue because of the necessity of taking into account factors of a psychological and personal nature.

§ 25. Impartiality as between the Parties to the Dispute.
The aversion, so frequently voiced, against national issues

---

[1] See below, pp. 245 et seqq.

[2] See Don José Battle y Ordoñez, *Actes et Documents*, ii. 156. At the Second Hague Conference Mr. Root said: '... The great obstacle to universal adoption of arbitration is not the unwillingness of civilised nations to submit their disputes to the decision of an impartial tribunal; it is rather an apprehension that the tribunal selected will not be impartial' (Second Hague Conference, *Proceedings of The Hague Peace Conferences*, ii, 'Meetings of the First Committee', ed. by Scott (1921), p. 316).

[3] See, for instance, Westlake (2nd ed., 1910), p. 363; Hyde, ii. 114, who points, as a factor explaining a refusal to arbitrate, to the seriousness of the State's 'doubt as to the likelihood of obtaining judicial recognition of the justice of its cause' and to the 'added difficulty of securing an impartial umpire': Kohler, *Grundlagen des Völkerrechts* (1918), p. 14; Zitelmann, *Die Unvollkommenheit des Völkerrechts* (1919), pp. 53, 54; Morgenthau, op. cit., pp. 84–93. See also the writers quoted below, p. 204.

[4] See, for example, Sidgwick, *Elements of Politics* (4th ed., 1919), p. 265: 'Even when there is no definite conflict of principles, the ties of interest and alliance that bind nations together may render it difficult to find an arbiter whose absence of bias can be trusted when the question to be decided is of great importance.'

being determined by 'foreigners' is not always the outcome of a falsely conceived sense of national dignity. The conviction that international judges in their capacity as members of their national communities may not always be capable of the required detachment, refers not only—not even principally— to the attitude of judges in disputes in which their own State is directly interested as a party. For it is not with these judges that the decision will rest as a rule—although cases do occur in which the vote of the national judge is in effect decisive, for instance, when the decision is given by the casting vote of the President, as in the *Lotus* case[1] or in the French-Swiss Free Zones Order,[2] or by a majority of one, as in the Advisory Opinion concerning the Austro-German Customs Union.[3] The doubts refer to the attitude of judges nationals of States which are not direct parties to the dispute, i.e. of what might be described as neutral judges. For, in fact, the view is widespread that in international disputes there are in practice no neutrals. It is pointed out that in the international sphere the possible number of litigants is incomparably smaller than within the State; that, while, as a rule, the outcome of the dispute is a matter of indifference to the municipal judge, who does not know the parties, the situation is different in the domain of international relations where any appreciable change in the political relations of two States has ultimately repercussions on the position of other States; and that, in addition to the fact of the interdependence of nations in general, formal alliances and specific common interests make third States and their nationals directly interested in the outcome of a dispute.[4] Lord Salisbury gave clear expression to this objection in 1896 in the course of the negotiations for a treaty of obligatory arbitration between the United States and Great Britain. In insisting on the limitation of the scope of the proposed treaty to matters in which the State is representing its own subjects as individuals, and on the exclusion of questions concerning the State considered as a whole, Lord Salisbury pointed out that in regard to the latter it would be impossible to find impartial arbitrators. In such disputes, he said, 'in the existing conditions of international sentiment, each great power could point to nations

---

[1] *P.C.I.J.*, Series A, No. 10.   [2] Ibid., No. 24.
[3] Series A/B, No. 41.
[4] See Lasson, *Das Prinzip und Wesen des Völkerrechts* (1870), p. 25. For a recent exposition of the question see Morgenthau, pp. 84–9. See also Gonsiorowski, *Société des Nations et problème de la paix* (1927), i. 501, 502.

whose admission to any jury by whom its interests were to be tried, it would be bound to challenge; and in a litigation between two great powers the rival challenges would pretty well exhaust the catalogue of the nations from whom competent and suitable arbiters could be drawn'.[1] This was a somewhat surprising statement by a minister of a country which in 1870 and in 1893 co-operated—in the *Alabama* and *Behring Sea* arbitrations—in setting up authoritative tribunals composed largely of neutral judges, but it must nevertheless be regarded as an authoritative expression of a frequently voiced argument.[2]

§ 26. **Impartiality between Judicial Idealism and Claims of Sovereignty. The Right to determine Jurisdiction.** The possible bias in favour of one of the parties does not exhaust the problem of impartiality of international judges. The question has another aspect which is peculiar to the international judicial function. It arises out of the frequent necessity for a decision between the claim, grounded in many a rule of international law, of sovereign States to freedom of action and what may be called judicial idealism intent upon extending the domain of law. This problem confronts international judges in the first instance in regard to the question of the scope of their own jurisdiction. In the fulfilment of their judicial duty they are frequently called upon to decide between two conflicting tendencies which, although they may in practice be covered by the conflicting claims of the two parties, do in fact represent a conflict between, on the one side, the natural tendency of a judge to act on the rule 'boni judicis est ampliare jurisdictionem' and, on the other side, the application of the rule of international law according to which the jurisdiction of international tribunals is strictly limited by the will of the States.

There ought to be little doubt as to the importance of this aspect of the problem. The powers which States confer upon international tribunals by the mere fact of endowing them

---

[1] Dispatch of 5 March 1896: Moore, p. 964.

[2] It is of interest to note the American reply to this part of the British argument: Mr. Secretary Olney said in a note to Sir Julian Pauncefote (11 April 1896: Moore, p. 970): 'It may be pointed out, too, that if bias on the part of foreign jurists is feared, the United States, being without alliances with any of the countries of Europe, is certainly not the party to expect any advantage from that source. Great Britain could at least not fail to know in what quarters friendliness or unfriendliness might be looked for.'

with jurisdiction are in a sense unlimited. They are so owing to the well-recognized rule according to which international tribunals possess the legal right to pass judgement on the scope of powers conferred upon them by the general or special arbitration agreement. The right of arbitral tribunals to decide on the scope of their jurisdiction means that with the signature of an arbitration agreement—be it a general arbitration agreement, or a *compromis ad hoc*, or an arbitration clause in a commercial or any other treaty—the State has handed over to a foreign body the interpretation of the cherished right of remaining judge in its own cause. The most modest arbitration agreement may, if the tribunal invoked is not impartial and is not adhering strictly to the terms of the *compromis*, be construed so as to enable the tribunal to explain away any of the reservations and to enlarge the scope of the undertaking.[1] A tribunal acting in this way would doubtless bring its decision within the operation of the rule according to which judgements rendered in excess of jurisdiction are null and void, but the very necessity of putting forward this charge imposes upon the State in question a heavy burden and responsibility. And while there is a possibility of a higher international court reviewing from this point of view the judgement of a less authoritative tribunal,[2] such possibility does not exist at all when the Court in question is the highest international tribunal.

---

[1] It would appear that a State which becomes a member of the Permanent Court of International Justice by adhering to the Protocol of Signature of the Statute of the Court does not in fact assume any substantial obligations, and, in particular, that membership of the Court does not, in itself, imply any new commitments in the sphere of obligatory arbitration. This is so to a large extent. However, a State adhering to the Protocol of Signature becomes bound by the last paragraph of Article 36 of the Statute according to which the Court is competent to decide whether a given dispute falls within the scope of its jurisdiction. By virtue of that provision the Court is bound and entitled to consider the question of jurisdiction in regard to any claim, however remote from the scope of the State's obligation to arbitrate, which a State may care to put forward. Undoubtedly it must be assumed that the Court in the impartial exercise of its judicial duty would declare that the claim is not covered by the arbitration agreement, but the fact remains that it has the legal power to decide on these matters in the first instance.

[2] In 1929 the Assembly, at the proposal of Finland, adopted a Resolution inviting the Council to submit to examination the question: What would be the most appropriate procedure to be followed by States which desired to enable the Permanent Court of International Justice to assume in a general manner, as between them, the functions of a tribunal of appeal from international arbitral tribunals in all cases where it is contended that the arbitral tribunal was without jurisdiction or exceeded its jurisdiction? For the Report of the Committee entrusted by the Council with the study of this matter see League of

The possible implications of the problem of jurisdiction appear clearly from the well-known Hungarian Optants dispute between Roumania and Hungary in 1927 concerning the jurisdiction of the Mixed Arbitral Tribunals by virtue of Articles 239 and 250 of the Treaty of Trianon. Roumania, in refusing to recognize the decision of the Mixed Arbitral Tribunal,[1] contended that while the Tribunal was given jurisdiction only in regard to a definite and rigidly circumscribed category of disputes (affecting measures of liquidation and confiscation of property of persons in their capacity as former enemies), it assumed jurisdiction over matters of a very wide compass in the domain of internal legislation and affecting vital interests of Roumania as an independent State. The assertion may or may not have been justified, but this aspect of the dispute shows the possible extent of the obligation assumed by States in conferring jurisdiction upon international tribunals. That the question is not of an academic character may be seen from the fact that in the bulk of the contentious cases which came before it for judgement, the Permanent Court of International Justice was concerned with pleas to its jurisdiction.[2] In some of these cases the Court did not shrink from giving an extensive interpretation to the scope of the powers conferred upon it by the parties. Thus in the Judgement of 26 July 1927, concerning its competence in the claim for indemnity in the case of the *Factory at Chorzów*, the Court declared that a convention conferring upon it jurisdiction in the matter of the interpretation and application of a treaty, also gave to it jurisdiction in the matter of claims for reparation of the damage caused in disregard of the treaty provisions.[3]

Finally, it will be noted that the conferment of jurisdiction upon international tribunals is frequently accompanied by provisions empowering these tribunals either to lay down with a binding effect, or to 'indicate', provisional measures calculated to prevent conduct or measures which a subsequent judgement on the merits may declare to be unlawful. It lies in the nature of things that such provisional measures

Nations, Document C. 338. M. 138, 1930, V. For the literature on the subject of excess of jurisdiction see the bibliography compiled by Lauterpacht in *B.Y.*, 1928, p. 120, and the Notes by Brierly, ibid., pp. 114–17, and Lauterpacht, ibid., pp. 117–20.

[1]   *Emeric Kulin* v. *Roumanian State*, 10 January 1927, *Recueil*, vii. 138.
[2]   See below, p. 427.   [3]   Series A, No. 9, pp. 20–5.

may be 'indicated' even in regard to matters on which the Court may subsequently arrive at a decision that it has no jurisdiction.[1]

§ 27. International Tribunals and State Sovereignty. The
right to determine the scope of jurisdiction is not the only occasion on which the question of impartiality between judicial idealism and rights of sovereign States becomes relevant. In the course of their judicial activity international tribunals are frequently called upon to adopt an attitude in regard to other cherished claims of State sovereignty. This may be best illustrated by reference to the work of the Permanent Court of International Justice. It is not an exaggeration to say that a large part of the work of that Court may be followed and described in terms of a restrictive interpretation of the rights of State sovereignty. Whether it be the consistent refusal to regard treaty obligations as limitations of State sovereignty warranting restrictive interpretation; or its interpretation, disregarding procedural niceties, of the obligations of States in the matter of minorities;[2] or its refusal to mitigate the rigour of the principle of respect of private rights in regard to State succession, notwithstanding the political origin and implications of the private rights in question;[3] or its reluctance to yield to the disinclination of States to acquiesce in a supposed extensive interpretation of

---

[1] Article 41 of the Statute of the Permanent Court provides as follows: 'The Court shall have the power to indicate, if it considers that circumstances so require, any provisional measures which ought to be taken to reserve the respective rights of either party. Pending the final decision, notice of the measures suggested shall forthwith be given to the parties and the Council.' See on this Article Salvioli in *Rivista*, xvi (1924), p. 119, and Hammarskjöld in *R.I.*, ser. III, vol. iii (1922), p. 142. And see the Court's Orders indicating provisional measures in the Chinese-Belgian dispute on the interpretation of the treaty of 2 November 1865 (Series A, Nos. 8, 14, and 16, and *Annual Digest*, 1927–8, Cases Nos. 350–2). And see *Arbitration and Security*, pp. 47 et seqq., for an enumeration of twenty-two arbitration treaties repeating the provisions of Article 41. It will be noted that the Orders of the Court under Article 41 have no binding effect; they merely *indicate* the provisional measures. See the Report of the Committee of Jurists of 1920, *Procès-Verbaux*, p. 735. See also Article 13 of the Barcelona Statute on the Freedom of Transit of 20 April 1921, providing for provisional recommendations in cases of urgency. In the Rules of Procedure of the Mixed Arbitral Tribunals provisional measures are endowed with binding effect. See Guggenheim, *Les Mesures provisoires de procédure internationale et leur influence sur le développement du droit des gens* (1931), pp. 18–32. This work constitutes an admirable study of the question of provisional measures.

[2] See Advisory Opinion No. 6, Series B, No. 6, pp. 19–26. And see above, p. 125.

[3] See above, p. 113.

the competencies of international bodies like the International Labour Organization,[1] or the European Danube Commission,[2] and of provisions relating to the free use of international waterways;[3] or the recognition on its part of the principle of the prohibition of abuse of rights;[4] or, finally, the gradual but consistent building up of a body of judicial precedent in apparent—but not actual—disregard of Article 59 of the Statute and of the natural aversion of sovereign States to admit sources of international law other than the express will of Governments.

It is not as if in acting thus the Permanent Court has not been proceeding in a strictly judicial manner. Judicial idealism is not tantamount to a dereliction of judicial duty. It merely signifies a definite choice between two possible legal tendencies, one of which is based on traditional assertions of State sovereignty, and the other on broad legal principle. Very frequently these assertions of State sovereignty prove, upon analysis, to be mere pretensions whose main claim to authority lies in the fact that some writers confuse unilateral claims of Governments with the law-creating practice of States. In such cases it is within the province of judges to put some exaggerated claims (raised to the authority of law by the fact that there has previously been no occasion for their judicial refutation) in their proper place by confronting them with the appropriate legal principle. This vindication of the authority of law, although referred to here as judicial idealism, is a legitimate function of judges. It ceases to be legitimate when, in the pursuit of a progressive and ethical solution, judges are driven to disregard a clear rule grounded in the practice of States and in the imperative requirements of the stability of the law. A high degree of impartiality as between the legitimate claims of States and the inclination to a 'natural law' solution is thus required. It is a problem which, for reasons which have already been indicated, is more serious in international relations than within the State.[5]

These aspects of the impartiality of judges have been noted here, not as the typical manifestation of the problem, but as

---

[1] See Advisory Opinions, Nos. 2 and 13.
[2] Advisory Opinion, No. 14.
[3] See, for instance, Judgements No. 1 (the *Wimbledon* case) and No. 16 (Jurisdiction of the International Commission of the Oder).
[4] See below, p. 288.   [5] See above, p. 104.

a phenomenon bearing closely upon the question of confidence of Governments in international tribunals. They are problems which judges in the fulfilment of their judicial function must keep constantly in mind. The possible lines of approach in regard to what has been called the conflict between judicial idealism and sovereignty of States have already been indicated. The problem of jurisdiction is no less intricate, but it is capable of treatment on the lines of broad principle. Undoubtedly, the powers conferred in this respect upon international tribunals are very extensive. A nation signing the Optional Clause, which includes the right of the Court to determine its own competence, has, theoretically, granted to it the right to decide, in the first instance at least, on most vital questions bearing upon its political existence, even if the signature is accompanied by wide reservations. But this omnipotence of a tribunal endowed with an unlimited jurisdiction is theoretically on the same plane as the possibility of the sovereign parliament enacting laws which are contrary to reason and impossible of execution. It exists in theory, but in practice it exists only as a reminder that an abuse of it would speedily bring to light the inherent limitations of sovereignty. The right of States to refuse to submit disputes with other States to judicial settlement is, subject to obligations expressly undertaken, undoubted. They are entitled to regard any deliberate extension of jurisdiction on the part of courts, in excess of the power expressly conferred upon them, as a breach of trust and abuse of powers, justifying a refusal to recognize the validity of the decision. So long as the jurisdiction of international courts is optional, the confidence of States, not only in the impartiality of these tribunals as between the disputants, but also in regard to the use of the powers conferred upon them, is one of the essential conditions of effective judicial settlement. This does not mean that the interpretation of arbitration agreements in the matter of jurisdiction ought to be artificially limited. In particular, the view cannot be countenanced that arbitration agreements, being in the nature of restrictions of sovereignty, ought to be interpreted restrictively. The intention of the parties, and the necessity of giving full effect to the will of the parties, must here as elsewhere be adopted as the guiding principle.[1] A not unimportant element of this will of the parties is the necessarily implied wish to have the dispute

---

[1] See above, pp. 123 et seq.

decided rather than to have it left unsettled. The practice of international tribunals must be a judicious compromise between these conflicting considerations.

§ 28. Political Impartiality and Personal Integrity. Before discussing the most important aspect of the problem of impartiality of international judges, i.e. their attitude in their capacity as nationals of a State, and the possibility of their being influenced in the exercise of their judicial function by the fact that they belong to a given national community, it is convenient to refer to the question of personal integrity and probity of judges. This question has now ceased to occupy the minds of writers to the extent which it did before. In the second half of the nineteenth century, when arbitration became the subject of scientific legal discussion, the question of the personal integrity of the arbitrators was given prominence in connexion with the validity of arbitral awards and the problem of appeal from the awards of arbitrators. Possibly the lack of reality which characterized international arbitration at that time was responsible for this detailed treatment of a problem whose gravity and practical application has proved to be altogether imaginary. At a time when both obligatory arbitration and permanent arbitral tribunals were practically non-existent, authors discussed, *faut de mieux*, with vigour the right of the parties to reject a *judex inhabilis* or *suspectus*, as well as the question of corruption.[1] But modern arbitration shows only one clear instance of proved corruption of an arbitral body, namely, in the case of the Mixed Commission between the United States and Venezuela sitting under the treaty of 25 April 1866. Charges of bribery were brought forward against some members of this Commission, and it was subsequently found by a Committee of the House of Representatives that the charges were 'not without foundation'. Thereupon a new convention was concluded,

---

[1] See Goldschmidt's Report to the Institute of International Law in 1874, printed in *Resolutions of the Institute*, edited by J. B. Scott (1916), pp. 219 et seqq. And see the elaborate discussion by Lammasch, *Rechtskraft*, p. 168, whether the award is null and void when the corrupt arbitrator has remained in a minority. The Statute of the Permanent Court does not mention the question of corruption, except, perhaps, to the extent of providing in Article 18 that 'a member of the Court cannot be dismissed unless, in the unanimous opinion of the other members, he has ceased to fulfil the required conditions'. It is very doubtful whether there is room for the application in this connexion of Article 61, which refers to the revision of a judgement in case of discovery of new facts of a decisive nature.

on 5 December 1885, for 'Re-opening of the Claims of the Citizens of the United States against Venezuela'.[1]

However, judicial integrity may be impaired not only by the somewhat crude process of accepting bribes, but also by other acts and situations imperilling the independence of the judge and his capacity for a detached appreciation of the case at issue, such as an official connexion with his Government, active participation in politics, appearing as counsel in international cases, or previous expression of opinion on disputed questions of law or fact. In fact, from Vattel to modern writers, publicists speak in one breath of corruption, bad faith, or obvious bias.[2] In this connexion there has been developed the doctrine[3] and, in a sense, the practice of *recusation*, i.e. challenging individual judges on the bench on account of their possible bias. This procedure is adopted in a number of municipal systems.[4] It has also, to some extent, been sanctioned in the Statute of the Permanent Court of International Justice. Article 17 of the Statute of the Court provides, *inter alia*: 'No member may participate in the decision of any case in which he has previously taken an active part, as agent, counsel or advocate for one of the contesting parties, or as a member of a national or international Court, or of a commission of enquiry, or in any other capacity. Any doubt on this point is settled by the decision of the Court.' It may be assumed that this article permits the parties themselves to raise the question of the impartiality

---

[1] Moore, p. 4808; Lammasch, *Rechtskraft*, p. 202. Barbeyrac, as quoted by Mérignhac (p. 314), refers to the attempts of the Emperor Maximilian and the Doge of Venice who both tried to bribe Pope Leo X when he had been chosen as arbiter. See also Pufendorf, *De jure naturali et gentium*, Book V, chap. 13, § 4. The standard in ancient Greece may have been a lower one. It seems that arbitrators did not receive a regular remuneration. But they received thanks and gifts from the victorious party. There are instances of the arbitrators receiving from the victorious party a crown of gold and the freedom of the city with all the privileges; also their city-state received tangible expressions of appreciation. Frequently the only source of information on an individual arbitration are the inscriptions in honour of the arbitrators. However, in the arbitration between Cos and Calymnia the oath to which the arbitrators subscribed contained the undertaking that they would not receive presents in any form from either party. See Raeder, *L'Arbitrage international chez les Hellènes* (1912), pp. 317 et seqq.

[2] See Vattel, Book II, chap. 38, § 329, who speaks of 'corruption ou partialité ouverte'; Fauchille, vol. i, part iii, p. 552, speaks of 'fraude ou déloyauté de l'arbitre'; Nys in *R.I.*, 2nd ser., xii (1910), pp. 597–614. And see on the whole question Schätzel, *Rechtskraft und Anfechtung von Entscheidungen internationaler Gerichte* (1928), pp. 17 et seqq.

[3] See in particular Schätzel, op. cit., pp. 45–55; Mérignhac, pp. 51 et seqq.; Lammasch, *Rechtskraft*, pp. 70 et seqq.

[4] See, for instance, § 41 of the German Code of Civil Procedure.

of individual judges, and that it is not limited to an *ex officio* action of the Court.[1] In conjunction with Article 17 there must be read Article 24 of the Statute which provides as follows:

> 'If, for some special reason, a member of the Court considers that he should not take part in the decision of a particular case, he shall so inform the President.
>
> 'If the President considers that for some special reasons one of the members of the Court should not sit on a particular case, he shall give him notice accordingly.
>
> 'If in any such case the member of the Court and the President disagree, the matter shall be settled by a decision of the Court.'

During the ten years of its existence the Court has had frequent occasion to apply and to put a practical interpretation on these articles.[2] While the provisions of Article 24 refer to

---

[1] However, see in regard to Article 24, Series E, No. 3, p. 186, for a decision of the Court in February 1922, to the effect that no provision should be inserted in the Rules enabling the parties to suggest that a judge should not sit on a case.

[2] Thus in regard to Article 17 the following internal decisions of the Court will prove of interest: In September 1926 the Court decided that there is no incompatibility between the functions of a member of the Court and those of a member of a conciliation commission. But it expressed the opinion that 'there is a certain effective incompatibility between the functions of judge and member of a conciliation commission when the same agreement provides for judicial settlement by the Court, failing a settlement by the conciliation commission' (*P.C.I.J.*, Series E, No. 3, pp. 177, 178). The Court had no doubt that a judge who sat on a conciliation commission would be debarred from sitting on the Court in the same case. See also Series E, No. 7, pp. 276, 277. In March 1928 the Court decided that Judge Huber, who acted as legal adviser to the Swiss Government from 1918 to 1921, could sit in the *Free Zones* case between France and Switzerland. The question was raised by Judge Huber himself. The reason for the Court's decision was that the functions referred to in Judge Huber's communication had been exercised before the dispute in question had arisen (*P.C.I.J.*, Series E, No. 4, p. 270). In February 1931 a question arose whether judges, who had sat as members of the Council of the League of Nations when a report was made on a matter connected with a question subsequently brought before the Court, were prevented from taking part in the examination of the question by the Court. The Court answered the question in the negative (Series E, No. 7, p. 277). However, the Court decided that there existed such incompatibility when the member of the Court acted as *rapporteur* to the Council on a kindred question, or acted as a member of a Committee of Jurists to inquire into a matter subsequently submitted to the Court (ibid., p. 287). In May 1931 the Court decided that it would not be proper for a judge to represent his country as delegate to the International Labour Conference, or to make official pronouncements regarding the international policy of his Government (ibid., pp. 277, 278). And see ibid. on the relation between Articles 17 and 24. On 30 July 1926 the Court adopted the following resolution: 'The Court holds that neither its members, nor the Registrar, nor the officials of the Registry, should accept decorations without the consent of the Court.' The following instances will illustrate the change of views which has taken place in this matter: vol.

incompatibility raised *proprio motu* by the judge concerned, Article 17 has reference to objective incompatibilities enumerated therein.

In addition, the Statute of the Court includes positive provisions calculated to safeguard the impartiality and the independence of its judges in the sense here discussed. Article 16 of the Statute lays down that members of the Court may not exercise any political or administrative function, and Article 17 provides that no member of the Court can act as agent, counsel, or advocate in any case of an international nature. In the Protocol for the revision of the Statute adopted on 14, September 1929 by the Assembly of the League,[1] these safeguards were made even more explicit. According to Article 16, as revised, judges must refrain not only from exercising any political or administrative function, but also from engaging in any other occupation of a professional nature. It was natural that this extension of incompatibilities should have been accompanied by a corresponding improvement in the emoluments of the judges and in the material conditions of their personal status.[2] As within the State so also in the international society this latter factor cannot be disregarded. Nothing in the nature of the absence of the necessary standard of material well-being and security

---

lxxxix (1896, 1897) of the *British and Foreign State Papers* contains a dispatch of the Marquess of Salisbury announcing the appointment of Signor Vigliani as a G.C.M. G. in recognition of the services rendered by him to Her Majesty's Government as arbitrator in the Manica frontier dispute with Portugal (p. 751). But see vol. iii, p. 178, of *P.C.I.J.*, Series E, on the refusal of the Court to allow the Registrar to accept a decoration conferred upon him by a Government which had recently been a party to suits before the Court. In 1927 the Court authorized the Registrar to accept a decoration conferred upon him by his own Government (*P.C.I.J.*, Series E., No. 4, p. 270). There has been no disposition on the part of the Court to discourage the acceptance of decorations for services unconnected with the work of the Court. See also the Report of the American Agent, *Venezuelan Arbitrations*, 1903 and 1904, pp. 18, 19, on a member of the panel of the Permanent Court of Arbitration acting as counsel for Venezuela.

[1] For an excellent account of the revision of the Statute see *P.C.I.J.*, Series E, No. 6, pp. 55–98, and No. 7, pp. 89–109. See also Cassin in *R.G.* xxxvi (1929), pp. 377–96; Raestad in *R.I.* (Paris), iii (1929), pp. 340–79; ibid. (1929), pp. 5–66; Michel de Grotte in *R.I.*; Jessup in *A.J.* xxiv (1930), pp. 353–6; and an anonymous article in *B.Y.*, 1931, pp. 122–31. And see also the Minutes of the Meetings of the Committee of Jurists on the Statute of the Permanent Court, 11–19 March 1929, Doc. C. 166, M. 66, 1929, v.

[2] In spite of the fact that the revision of the Statute as envisaged by the Protocol of 14 September 1929 had not taken place by the end of 1931, the provisions as to raising the salaries of judges, as to their pensions, and as to their judicial vacation within the frame of an organization of the Court based on its being permanently in session were adopted by way of a resolution of the Assembly or of an amendment of the rules of the Court. See *P.C.I.J.*, Series E, No. 7, pp. 90–109.

should stand in the way of a proper fulfilment of the judicial function on the part of international judges.

§ 29. The Problem of Political Impartiality.

While, as a rule, personal integrity may ordinarily be taken for granted, and while the dangers besetting it may successfully be lessened by external regulation, for instance, by provisions as to incompatibility and to the improvement of the status of judges, it is the task of securing what may be called political impartiality, i.e. impartiality *qua* members of a given national community, which constitutes the principal aspect of the problem under discussion. As a matter of fundamental principle the problem of impartiality of judges is in the international sphere the same as within the State. It is a problem of loyalty to the judicial oath of impartiality. Political integrity is only one aspect of personal integrity. The difference between a *judex corruptus* and a judge breaking his judicial oath on account of conscious bias in favour of his country is only one of degree. Only the false conception of the State as a higher and sacrosanct association makes the breach of the judicial oath appear less discreditable when the duty of impartiality is forsaken in the interest of a State and not for individual gain. As in other branches of international law, so also in this matter, the principle holds good that it is not permissible to apply to relations of States standards different from those obtaining within the State. An oath of judicial impartiality is an oath the deliberate disregard of which is morally as reprehensible as within the State. Conscious bias in favour of his own State on the part of an international judge constitutes a dereliction of duties and an abuse of powers. Undoubtedly, the fact that a judge is a national of a State may influence him subconsciously and independently of his will. The subconscious element of sentiment and national solidarity may prove stronger than a legal declaration. However, although the subconscious factor cannot be entirely eliminated, it is to a large extent a function of the human will, of the individual sense of moral duty, and of the enlightened consideration of the paramount interest of peace and justice entrusted to the care of judges. The Statutes both of the Permanent Court of Arbitration and of the Permanent Court of International Justice specify as one of the qualifications of the judges that they should be of the 'highest moral character'. This ideal of moral excellence has reference not so much to inaccessibility to corruption, as to the capacity to combat that form of judicial bias which the current exaggerations of State sovereignty and the dualism of ethical standards have deprived of the moral opprobrium justly attaching to it.[1,2]

There is no reason why a breach of the judicial duty of impartiality in the international sphere should be regarded differently from similar conduct on the part of the judge within the State. The exaggeration which usually attends the discussion of international matters makes us forget that the danger of judicial bias is not a problem confined to international tribunals. The constitutional history of many a country shows judgements which the unprejudiced verdict of history has declared to be due not to the application of existing law, but to its disregard by biased judges.[3] In matters of economic policy and in disputes involving the opposing interests either of capital and labour, or generally of the wealthy and the poor, the impartiality of courts

---

[1] On the day on which M. Mourawieff, a Russian national, had to deliver judgement in the *Venezuelan Preferential Claims* case in his capacity as President of the arbitral tribunal, there came the news of the outbreak of war between Russia and Japan. M. Mourawieff used the opportunity of his Presidential allocution in order to describe the Japanese declaration of war as a wanton act of aggression and the war on the part of Russia as a war of legitimate self-defence in the name of the honour and dignity of his country. The Japanese Minister at The Hague protested, in a letter addressed to the Secretary of the Permanent Court of Arbitration in February 1904, against the 'wrongful and unseemly use' of the Court. But there is no record of a more general condemnation of this deliberate and gratuitous refusal on the part of an individual entrusted with an international function to rise above the immediate interests of his country. (*The Venezuelan Arbitration before The Hague Tribunal*, 1903, *U.S. Senate Documents*, 58th Congress, 3rd Session, vol. vii, Doc. No. 119, pp. 99, 139.)

[2] Among the factors independent of the will of the international judge and likely to affect his impartiality, reference is frequently made to the absence of a common legal outlook. The writer has dealt with this aspect of the problem in an article on 'The So-Called Continental and Anglo-American Schools of Thought in International Law' in *B.Y.*, 1931, pp. 31–62. The supposed fundamental differences between these two alleged conceptions of international law may be taken as a fair test for judging the accuracy of the argument on the divergence of the legal outlook as a reason for questioning the impartiality of the international judge. What is conspicuous in the practice of international tribunals is not that international judges differ at times from one another, but the fact that, as frequently as not, they arrive at judgements which are unanimous or rendered by substantial majorities. Their deliberations do not result in a series of contradictory dissenting opinions.

[3] To the English lawyer there will occur here such cases as *Hampden's* case (1637), 3 St. Tr. 825, or *Godden* v. *Hales* (1686), 11 St. Tr. 1166, or, possibly, *Thomas* v. *Sorrell* (1676), K.L. 56. These cases ought to be distinguished from cases of real or alleged judicial misconduct or perversion of justice in some cases decided by Chief Justice Jeffreys, or the trial of Nuncomar before Sir Elijah Impey, or of Lord Cochrane before Lord Ellenborough.

composed, as a rule, of judges belonging by birth, training, and community of sentiment and interests to one section of the population, has never been universally admitted. It constitutes a problem requiring eternal vigilance even in countries with a judiciary of the highest degree of integrity.[1] For the argument that, unlike a judge in the international sphere, a judge in a municipal court has never a personal interest in the case, is only partly accurate. It is not accurate to say that while, within the State, the judgement affects the parties only and has no effect upon third parties, the position is different before an international tribunal where, in view of the very limited number of the members of the international community, each individual litigant is known to the judge. A decision of a municipal court frequently affects interests of a much wider circle of persons than the parties directly concerned. There are test cases in which a decision between the parties to the action creates or declares law directly affecting the widest circles of population, frequently including the judge himself. A case involving the interpretation of rent-restriction legislation may be mentioned as an instance. In such cases, although the judge may not know the parties *qua* individuals, they represent to him types of interests in regard to which his judgement may be influenced by his predilections, prejudices, and interests.

At the same time, however, the possibility of judicial bias is not regarded within the State as a reason for limiting the competence of courts. The occasions on which judges fail conspicuously to overcome the bias of political prejudice or economic interests are in the nature of an exception. Complaints that judgements constitute 'class judgments' are on the whole remarkably rare. For if judges, in common with other human beings, are susceptible to the claims of their private interests or those of their group, they are no less susceptible to the categorical imperative of duty and to the powerful voice of justice. This applies both to the municipal and the international judge. There is no warrant, in either

---

[1] See on this point McIver, *The Modern State* (1926 ed.), p. 266; Laski, 'Judicial Review of Social Policy in England' in *Harvard Law Review*, xxxix (1926), pp. 83–848. And see Pound in *Columbia Law Review*, xix (1914), p. 104, n. 175, for some references to the literature in regard to the United States. For comment on Mr. Justice Astbury's much discussed judgement in the course of the English general strike in 1926, in the case of *National Sailors and Firemen's Union* v. *Reed*, [1926] 1 Ch. 536, see the authoritative Note in *Law Quarterly Review*, xlii (1926), p. 289.

sphere, to doubt the faculty of man to lift himself above his own interests or those of his group, and to serve the cause of justice—a cause whose identity with the ideal of peace is in the society of States certainly not less than among individuals within the State. To deny the very possibility of international judges being impartial when their national interests are concerned is to exhibit a shallow scepticism which ignores both human nature and, as will be shown presently, historical experience. There is in international judges a deep and ever-growing consciousness that they are the trustees of the best and most urgent hopes of humanity and holders of a supreme position in the international hierarchy. President Huber, when opening in 1925 the Second Presidential Session of the Court, referred to the great responsibility of the members of the Court, a responsibility which, he said, it would be too difficult to bear but for the consciousness that 'so long as our (the judges') labours are devoted to the Cause...we are sustained by a force which is not merely our own'.[1] When, at one of the subsequent sessions of the Court, President Anzilotti paid homage to the work of Lord Finlay, the most eloquent tribute he was able to pay to the memory of a distinguished judge was to refer to numerous instances of his impartiality.[2]

The history of international judicial settlement certainly cannot be adduced as showing the inability of international judges to discharge their duties impartially when the interests of their State are concerned. It is sufficient to refer to the more recent history of arbitration between Great Britain and the United States in order to see how baseless is such an assertion. With the exception of the *Alabama* arbitration, when the British arbitrator, Sir Alexander Cockburn, did not conceal the fact that he regarded himself as an advocate rather than a judge,[3] the subsequent arbitration cases showed the American and British members of the successive tribunals as fully conscious of their duty of judicial impartiality. The

[1] Series C, No. 7 (1), p. 18. And see Series E, No. 5, p. 19, for President Anzilotti's references, in connexion with the problem of impartiality, to 'the greatness of our mission and the crushing responsibility which is ours'.
[2] He said: 'I think I am paying the greatest tribute to our lamented colleague...by saying here publicly that Lord Finlay did not hesitate to vote against the views put forward by his Government's representatives when he was convinced that right lay on the other side' (16th Session, 15 May 1929, *P.C.I.J.*, Series E, No. 5, p. 22). And see for similar reference to Judge Weiss's impartiality ibid., p. 19 (16th Session, 13 September 1928).
[3] See Moore, pp. 659–61, for somewhat depressing details as to Sir Alexander's attitude. See also Cushing, *The Treaty of Washington* (1873), pp. 128–49.

Alaska Boundary dispute was submitted for a majority decision by a tribunal composed equally of American and British members. The majority in favour of the American contention was secured by the vote of Lord Alverstone—a fact whose significance appears in its proper light when we consider that this tribunal was largely composed of persons acting rather as a commission of negotiators, firmly committed to a definite view,[1] than as a judicial tribunal. While, for this reason, the significance of the *Alaska* arbitration as evidence of judicial impartiality may be a matter of dispute, in the *Behring Sea*,[2] *British Guiana*,[3] and *North Atlantic Fisheries*[4] arbitrations, the concurrence of the American and British judges in the principal parts of each decision constitutes a persuasive example of judicial detachment. It would be an idle undertaking to enumerate instances of judges voting against their own country, just as it is unnecessary to expatiate in detail on the numerous unanimous decisions of mixed arbitral and claims commissions; on the frequent fact of the national of a disputant party being chosen as umpire with a decisive vote and of his discharging his task with admitted impartiality;[5] or on

---

[1] It appears that President Roosevelt, who rejected the proposal for arbitration, finally agreed to submit the matter for a decision by 'six impartial jurists of repute', three appointed by each party. In fact, the impartial jurists chosen by the United States were, in the President's words, 'men who had already committed themselves on the general proposition'. See *Selections from the Correspondence of Theodore Roosevelt and Henry Cabot Lodge*, ii. 67, and for further references, on this and other aspects of this arbitration, Garner, *American Foreign Policies* (1928), pp. 152 and 153.

[2] This arbitration illustrates the question of impartiality from a different angle. While Mr. Justice Harlan, the judge appointed by the United States, voted on some of the principal issues of the dispute together with other arbitrators, Senator Morgan, another nominee of the United States, consistently upheld the attitude of his country in the successive votings. The incident shows that the judicial mind may be capable of a degree of impartiality which is not easily obtainable by a politician. See for the record of the voting during the deliberations concerning the award, Moore, pp. 914–22.

[3] The award was unanimous. (See for a refutation of the view that this award constituted a compromise, Lauterpacht, *Analogies*, p. 65 n.)

[4] The award was unanimous, but for the dissent of Judge Drago. See below, p. 226.

[5] The choice, in 1923, of Judge Parker (in succession to Mr. Justice Day) as Umpire in the Mixed Claims Commission between the United States and Germany affords a recent example. It has been stated that Judge Parker made it clear at an early stage of his work as umpire that 'as a judge he regarded himself as denationalized, and he lived up to the fullest measure of this self-denying ordinance' (Borchard in *A.J.* xxiv (1930), p. 140). As to the choice of Mr. Bates, an American citizen resident in London, as umpire in the Mixed Commission between Great Britain and the United States of 1853, see Moore, pp. 398–400. Previously, the British commissioner agreed to the selection as umpire of Mr. Martin van Buren, formerly President of the United States, who, however, declined the nomination. See also Moore, pp. 1299–303, as to the

the instances in which national judges specially appointed by Governments to represent the interests of their country voted against the contention advanced by their Government.[1] But it is necessary to keep these instances in mind whenever the inaccurate view is expressed that impartiality is *impossible* when the interests of the judge's own State are involved. Far from being an impossibility, impartiality is a function of personality and of an elevated attitude of mind which can, within obvious limits, be secured by appropriate methods of election and provisions as to the status of the judges, and which can be fostered and maintained by a vigilant public opinion and by a general consensus as to the decisive importance of the judicial function for the preservation of law and peace among nations. For the fact that impartiality is possible does not mean that it does not constitute a very real problem in international judicial settlement. The source of danger lies not only in the obvious ties of sentiment and interest. It lies, in no less degree, in the historical circumstances in which international judicial settlement has developed. Only a clear realization of the nature of these circumstances can supply the necessary foundation for the provision of necessary safeguards and remedies.

§ 30. International Judicial Function and Representation of Interests. An important aspect of these peculiar circumstances consists in the fact that the history of judicial settlement in the past hundred and forty years is a history of an attempted—but not always achieved—compromise between the concession to the opponent of the benefit of the judicial process and the determination of the sovereign State not to bow to judicial authority entirely external to itself. This compromise was effected through mixed commissions, i.e. bodies composed exclusively or predominantly of the nationals of the disputant States, and combining, through the instrumentality of an appropriate procedure, the functions of negotiators, advocates, and judges. The history of international arbitration since the Jay Treaty can, with few exceptions, be written in terms of mixed commissions. And the few instances of judicial or quasi-judicial settlement in

choice in 1870 of Dr. Lieber, an American citizen, as umpire in the American-Mexican Claims Commission.

[1] See, for instance, Advisory Opinions Nos. 15 (*Jurisdiction of the Courts of Danzig*) and 17 (*The Graeco-Bulgarian Communities*), in which the national judges joined in the unanimous opinion of the Court. And see note 3 on p. 237.

the sixteenth and seventeenth centuries exhibit the same characteristics. The mixed commissions between Great Britain and the United States, which have constituted the bulk of arbitral settlement between the two countries in the nineteenth century, were frequently little short of bodies of negotiators putting forward their claims in the form of legal arguments. This feature of the mixed commissions manifested itself not only in the method of selecting the umpire, but also in the provision rendering impossible a decision against the determined wish of one of the parties. The Jay Treaty provided that the quorum necessary for the transaction of business was 'one of the commissioners on each side, and the fifth commissioner'. By withdrawing, the commissioners of either party were legally in a position to frustrate a decision. Of this opportunity the American commissioners availed themselves freely, to the point of rendering abortive the work of the arbitrators in the commission dealing under Article VI of the Jay Treaty with the impediments to the recovery of debts owed to British loyalists.[1] The British commissioners submitted a resolution reminding their American colleagues of their duty to decide all questions with perfect impartiality and without any regard to the source of their appointment, but the resolution shared the fate of the major business. As a measure of retaliation, British members announced their withdrawal from another commission, sitting at the same time under Article VII of the Treaty and concerned mainly with the encroachments by Great Britain on American neutral rights.[2] Subsequently this limitation upon the activities of commissions disappeared, but the other characteristic remained. Thus arbitration conventions usually contained a provision to the effect that in the absence of an agreement between the commissioners, the umpire was to be chosen by lot from among their nominees. These nominees were, as a rule, nationals of the disputant parties, and it was generally accepted that the outcome of judicial proceedings was largely dependent on obviously aleatory proceedings.[3] The opinions of the commissioners and the umpires thus chosen, in particular in the

---

[1] For an interesting account of the disagreements and 'temperamental differences', see Moore, pp. 288–97.

[2] Moore, p. 338.

[3] Thus the Convention of 8 February 1853 between the United States and Great Britain provided that in case the commissioners should not agree on the name of the umpire, they should each name a person and 'in each and every case in which the commissioners may differ in opinion as to the decision they ought to give, it shall be determined by lot which of the two persons so named

early stages of the history of British-American arbitration, although couched in legal language, read very much like the argument of a party to the dispute. They are of undoubted interest for the history of international law, but their authority as a source of international law is insignificant.[1]

Subsequent developments in the machinery of arbitral settlement brought a definite improvement as the result of the elimination of the necessity of a quorum, and of the addition of neutral members with whom, in the event of the failure of national commissioners to arrive at an agreement, rested the final decision. But the mixed commission remained. In fact the mixed claims commission composed of three members, i.e. of the nationals of the parties and of a neutral umpire, constitutes the most frequent type of arbitral machinery, in particular in cases of a large number of private claims to be dealt with individually by the commission. This element of representation of national interests is not confined to bodies expressly designated as mixed commissions. With the exception of cases submitted to a decision by a foreign sovereign, the arbitral tribunals constituted *ad hoc* between the disputants included nationals of the parties, and, notwithstanding their formal designation, preserved the essential characteristics of mixed commissions. The body constituted on 18 August 1910 between Great Britain and the United States for the settlement of a number of claims was designated as a tribunal. But as stated in the arbitration agreement, the tribunal was constituted in pursuance of The Hague Convention of 1907 for the Pacific Settlement of International Disputes, and in particular of its Article 87, which provided as follows:

> 'Each of the parties in dispute appoints an arbitrator. The two arbitrators thus selected choose an umpire. If they do not agree on this point, each of them proposes two candidates taken from the general list of the members of the Permanent Court

shall be the arbitrator or umpire in that particular case'. The same provision was inserted in the Convention of 1822. When, in regard to the latter convention, a computation was made of the lump sum to be accepted in lieu of the awards to be made under the convention, it was assumed, in respect of the award of interest, that assuming that the lot would fall equally on each of the persons appointed, one half of the claimants would obtain interest, whereas the other would not (Moore, p. 392).

[1] The student must therefore read with a certain reserve the, undoubtedly sincere, declaration of Commissioner Gore in the *Betsey*: 'Although I am a citizen of but one [nation], I am constituted a Judge for both. Each nation has the same, and no greater, right to demand of me fidelity and diligence in the examination, exactness and justice of the Decision' (Moore, p. 2288).

exclusive of the members appointed by either of the parties and not being nationals of either of them; which of the candidates thus proposed shall be the umpire is determined by lot.'

In fact, most of the tribunals established within the frame of the Permanent Court of Arbitration included representatives of the parties to the dispute, and some of them approached closely the type of mixed commissions.[1] The history of the Permanent Court of Arbitration shows occurrences which vividly bring to mind the element of representation of interests revealed in the attitude of some of the national judges thus appointed. It is sufficient to refer to the manner in which the Japanese judge in the *Japanese House Tax* case registered his 'absolute disagreement with the majority of the Tribunal with regard to both the grounds and the decision of the award';[2] or in which in the *Casablanca* case the parties appointed as arbitrators legal advisers of their respective Foreign Offices who had conducted the diplomatic correspondence in this case prior to its submission to arbitration; or in which the arbitrator appointed by the United States in the *Norwegian Shipowners Claims* case refused to be present when the award was announced, on the ground that the other arbitrators disregarded the terms of submission and exceeded the authority conferred upon them.[3] The element of representation of interests in some of the arbitral bodies of this type is shown by the fact that according to a preponderant body of opinion the national judges remain under the authority of their State, that they are bound to follow its instructions, and can be recalled at any time.[4] The history of the Mixed Arbitral Tribunals established by the Peace Treaties of 1919 shows that the withdrawal of the national arbitrator is not a mere theoretical possibility.[5] Neither is the element of representation entirely excluded when the

[1] See, for instance, the *Japanese House Tax* case, the *Grisbadarna* case, the *Orinoco Steamship Company* case, the *Canevaro* case, the *French Claims against Peru* case, and the *Norwegian Shipowners' Claims* case.

[2] Scott, *Hague Court Reports*, p. 84.

[3] See for the award *A.J.* xvii (1923), p. 399.

[4] See Schätzel, op. cit., p. 34; Oppenheim, ii, § 16, expresses the opinion that the award has no binding force if the arbitrators have failed to follow their instructions.

[5] See the decision of the Yugoslav-German Mixed Arbitral Tribunal of 19 December 1923 in the case of *Ventense* v. *Yugoslav State*, in which the Tribunal refused to interfere with the withdrawal of the German arbitrator by the German Government. And see *D.* v. *German Reich*, *Annual Digest*, 1925–6, Case No. 301, for an instance of withdrawal of an arbitrator. In this case the Tribunal referred to the French decree of 17 January 1920 (*Journal Officiel*, 1920, p. 946), according

parties nominate neutral arbitrators, for practice has shown that
the neutral members thus appointed frequently deem it to be
their duty to defend the interests of the State responsible for
their appointment.[1] It would be easy to multiply evidence in
support of the view that prior to the establishment of the Permanent Court of International Justice, impartiality in international arbitration was endangered as the result of the adherence
to the idea of representation of interests. Undoubtedly, experience shows that even in mixed commissions or similar bodies the
duty of impartiality asserts itself in the overwhelming majority of
cases, but the dangers resulting from the composition of these
bodies are obvious and must not be neglected. It is possible that
this combination of judicial function and of representation of
interests was necessary and justified as a transition stage from
the refusal of sovereign States to recognize a judge over themselves to a more advanced stage of legal organization. It is also
probable that for certain types of case a mixed commission
combining judicial and negotiating functions is the most appropriate instrument.[2] But the unavoidable effect of this infusion of
the element of representation of interests was to impart to the
judicial function in international society a feature which is, as a
rule, unknown to municipal tribunals. Even when, with the
establishment of the Permanent Court of International Justice,
the idea of representation of national interests on the part of the
judges was formally abandoned, it still received countenance
through the institution of so-called national judges.[3]

§ 31. The Impartiality of Neutral Judges. The other
factor complicating the problem of impartiality of international
tribunals is that arising from some specific aspects of im-

---

to which French members of the Mixed Arbitral Tribunals may be suspended or
withdrawn by the President of the Republic acting on the advice of the Minister for
Foreign Affairs.

[1] See Lammasch, *Schiedsgerichtsbarkeit*, p. 126, for an account of the withdrawal in
1884, by the Emperor of Brazil, of the Brazilian umpire appointed by him in a
dispute between Chile and some European States on the ground of his alleged bias
against Chile.

[2] It has been stated by a writer having practical experience of the work of the
Mixed Arbitral Tribunals that they have been most successful when acting by way
of compromise and accommodation rather than in a judicial capacity. The output
of the German-French Mixed Arbitral Tribunal increased from several hundred in
the first four years to seven thousand in the following three years, after both sides
had agreed to attempt in the first instance an agreed solution by way of compromise. See Schätzel, op. cit., p. 37. See also the same, *Das deutsch-französische gemischte
Schiedsgericht* (1930), pp. 16–48.

[3] See below, p. 228.

partiality of neutral judges. It is frequently pointed out that while in municipal courts the disputants are, as a rule, unknown to the judges, whose attitude is accordingly one of detachment, the position is different before international tribunals where the number of disputants is small and limited; that the political interdependence of States has the result of making neutral judges directly interested in the outcome of the disputes which come before them; and that it is accordingly impossible to speak with reliance of the impartiality of neutral judges.[1] The exaggerations of this argument have already been discussed in the preceding section, where it was shown that the apparent disinterestedness of municipal judges is not always expressive of the true position. But there is nevertheless some substance in the contention that the idea of representation of interests of the States directly concerned is not the only danger which besets the impartiality of international tribunals. Frequently, more frequently than in corresponding situations before municipal courts, a neutral State is vitally interested in the outcome of the dispute. The permanent identity of interests of small States as opposed to Great Powers; the abiding community of interests of States bound by ties of common race, culture, and language; the less immutable but equally strong solidarity of interests of States bound by political alliances, by transient agreements for *ad hoc* purposes, or by jealousies against neighbours richer and more powerful than themselves; and even the accidental identity of interests in particular claims and policies—all this renders the impartiality of neutral judges a problem which is not to be lightly dismissed. Some instances taken from the history of international arbitration will clearly illustrate this latter point.

In the *North Atlantic Fisheries* arbitration decided by the Permanent Court of Arbitration in 1910, Judge Drago

---

[1] See above, p. 204. See also Lapradelle and Politis, i. 379, on the Report of the Joint Select Committee of the Legislature of the State of Maine concerning the refusal to recognize the award given in 1831 by the King of Holland. One of the reasons for the refusal (see also above, p. 129) was that while at the time of the signature of the arbitration agreement the arbitrator was king of a State comprising Belgium and Holland, a substantial change of circumstances had taken place owing to the revolution and the declaration of Belgian independence. It was maintained that these events brought the King of Holland into a substantial measure of dependence upon England, and also that it might have inspired in him a lack of sympathy with the cause of the United States as a country with free institutions.

insisted on delivering a dissenting opinion against the unanimous view of the Tribunal on the question of the meaning of the term 'bay' in the British-American Treaty of 1818. But it was subsequently suggested by Lammasch,[1] the President of the Tribunal, and it appears from an article published by Judge Drago himself, that in acting in this manner the Argentine judge had in mind not only the interpretation of the treaty, but also the possibility of safeguarding the interests of his country in the issue of the River La Plata. The distinguished judge wrote with disarming simplicity: 'It is a particularly fortunate coincidence that in a case submitted for my examination and decision my convictions as arbiter and judge were in accord with the interests of my country in regard to Rio la Plata, which is in the same position as the Concepcion, Delaware and Chesapeake Bays, which are territorial notwithstanding their width.'[2]

A series of recent cases illustrate another aspect of the same problem. Neutral judges of the Mixed Arbitral Tribunals established after the World War were frequently called upon to pass judgement on the legitimacy of German belligerent action in connexion with the plea of necessity and effectiveness of military operations. It is not surprising that, in the fulfilment of their function, they should have thought of some of the arguments on the effectiveness of belligerent measures used in connexion with the encroachments upon the rights of neutrals. In the case of *Coenca Brothers* v. *Germany*,[3] decided in 1927 by the Graeco-German Mixed Arbitral Tribunal, the President, a Dutch subject, dealt with the German plea that bombardment from the air must necessarily be a surprise attack. He agreed that the plea was a correct one from the military point of view, but, he said, this did not imply that bombardment without warning ought to be permitted; on the contrary, the implication would be that such bombardment is generally inadmissible. There may, it is respectfully submitted, be much sound law in these words of the learned judge, but the emphasis on certain passages of this and similar decisions may, without any imputation of unseemly motives, be regarded as giving expression to the feelings of the much harassed neutral States. In addition, cases occur in which circumstances bring to light with particular emphasis the difficulties, real or asserted, of securing unimpeachable

---

[1] *Rechtskraft*, p. 33, n. 1.   [2] *R.G.* xix (1912), p. 37.
[3] *Annual Digest*, 1927–8, Case No. 389; *Recueil*, vii. 683.

neutrality. This happens notably in cases in which a number of States are directly interested, as parties or otherwise, in the outcome of the dispute, so that the bench includes a substantial proportion of judges who are nationals of the disputant parties.[1]

While the questions raised by the necessity of securing impartial detachment from neutral judges certainly aggravate the problem under discussion, they are of no more decisive importance than the problem of impartiality of judges who are nationals of the States appearing as parties to the dispute. What has been said above in regard to the latter applies also to neutral judges. At the same time, however, the securing of impartiality on their part constitutes a problem, and it is not permissible to neglect it or to regard it as solved.[2] The element of confidence has been and must remain the paramount factor in determining the extent to which States are prepared to confer jurisdiction upon international courts. It will therefore for a long time be the duty of statesmen, of lawyers, and of public opinion at large to contribute so far

---

[1] Thus in the *Wimbledon* case (Judgement No. 1), the first case to come before the Permanent Court of International Justice, the four plaintiff States (Great Britain, France, Italy, and Japan) were all represented on the bench by their nationals. But see the dissenting opinion of the Italian judge in opposition to the contention of the Italian Government. See also the case relating to the territorial jurisdiction of the International Commission of the River Oder (Judgement No. 16). The Advisory Opinion of the Permanent Court on the proposed Customs Union between Germany and Austria afforded another example of the multiplicity of interested parties and the consequent reduction of the neutral element on the highest international judicial tribunal.

[2] Care must be taken not to exaggerate this aspect of the matter. Thus it has been said that a judgement of an international court which would have the effect of altering the balance of power in the world or on a continent might directly interest third States and thus imperil the impartiality of neutral judges. Such a contingency is obviously of a hypothetical nature. International tribunals which administer existing law obviously are not in a position to give judgements altering the political constellation of the world. Similarly, it may be doubted whether the political interdependence of States is of such a nature as to make neutral States (and judges who are their nationals) directly interested in the outcome of every dispute between other States. Even if one were prepared to admit that the main preoccupation of neutral judges is to weigh scrupulously the effect of their judgement on their own State, it is clear that in actual practice there is in most cases no such interdependence of interests. A Central American State is not interested in the outcome of a dispute concerning the Customs Union between Austria and Germany. Japan or China are not interested in the outcome of a frontier dispute between Albania and Yugoslavia (Advisory Opinion No. 9), or between Poland and Czechoslovakia (Advisory Opinion No. 8). This actual disinterestedness on the part of a large number of judges—*qua* nationals of their States—occurs in every case submitted to the Permanent Court. It is perhaps in the attitude of detachment due to reasons of geography rather than in the much exaggerated necessity of having the various legal systems represented on the Court that lies the chief advantage of the composition of a Court whose judges are drawn from distant continents.

as in them lies to the strengthening of that confidence. Conscious endeavour by way of constitutional safeguards and critical watch-fulness should be directed towards removing from permanent international tribunals the last traces of representation of interests and towards emphasizing their character as agencies of impartial justice. We say '*permanent* tribunals', for it lies in the nature of things that the problem arises principally in connexion with permanent international agencies with a fixed body of judges. (In tribunals established *ad hoc* the parties are to a large extent in a position to select a body of judges in whom they have confidence.) Of the permanent tribunals the Permanent Court of International Justice is the principal, if not the only one.[1] Accordingly, the discussion, which follows, of some practical problems in connexion with judicial impartiality is confined to that Court. Of these problems the question of national judges and of the methods of electing the judges of the Court are believed to be the most important. The first relates to the elimination of the factor of representation of interests as represented in the institution of national judges; the other has reference to the methods of electing the judges of the highest international tribunal.

§ 32. Elimination of the Element of Representation of Interests. The Problem of National Judges. An impor-tant step towards strengthening confidence in the impartiality of international adjudication is to banish from it the factor of representation of interests. The first measure in the direc-tion of this objective is the removal of this aspect of the organization of the highest international tribunals which in itself is both a consequence and a perpetuation of the idea of advocacy of interests. This aspect is embodied in the institu-tion of so-called national judges. The fact that judges of the Permanent Court sit on that tribunal not as representatives of State interests, but as dispensers of impartial justice is fundamental, and solemn expression has frequently been given to it. At the same time, however, by having adopted the institution of national judges,[2] i.e. judges of the nationality of the disputant parties appointed for the purpose of a

---

[1] See below, p. 362, n. 1, on the element of permanency of other international tribunals.

[2] Article 31 of the Statute of the Court provides, *inter alia*, as follows:

'If the Court includes upon the Bench a judge of the nationality of one of the parties only, the other party may select from among the deputy-judges a

specific dispute, in addition to the Court as ordinarily constituted, the authors of the Statute of the Permanent Court have enshrined in it the idea of representation of interests. They have done so not without a previous consideration of the history of the problem[1] and of the possible alternatives. When, in 1929, at the time when the revision of the Statute was under consideration, the question of national judges came up for review, there was no disposition to consider the question of a change.[2] The principal reasons adduced both for the introduction and retention of the system of national judges have been that it is useful to have the assistance of judges acquainted with the legal system and the views of each of the parties to the dispute, and that the confidence of the disputants in the judgement of the Court and their willingness to accept an adverse decision would be strengthened by the knowledge that the judgement was given after due consideration of the views expressed by the national judge.[3] These reasons will be examined in the discussion which follows.[4] What is common to all of them—as indeed to most of the discussions on the subject—is the failure to appreciate

judge of its nationality, if there be one. If there should not be one, the party may choose a judge, preferably from among those persons who have been nominated as candidates as provided in Articles 4 and 5.

'If the Court includes upon the Bench no judge of the nationality of the contesting parties, each of these may proceed to select or choose a judge as provided in the preceding paragraph.

'Should there be several parties in the same interest, they shall, for the purpose of the preceding provisions, be reckoned as one party only. Any doubt upon this point is settled by the decision of the Court.'

By an amendment, adopted in 1926, to Article 71 of the Rules of the Court, the same principle has been made to apply to Advisory Opinions. For an interpretation of these articles see the Order of the Court of 20 July 1931 in connexion with the Advisory Opinion on the Customs Régime between Austria and Germany, Series A/B, No. 41, pp. 88–90. See also Series D, No. 2 (1931), p. 111.

[1] *Procès-Verbaux* of the Committee of Jurists of 1920, pp. 168–74, 529–39, 575–7. See also for a lucid account of the question Fachiri, *The Permanent Court of International Justice* (1925), pp. 47–50. For a more general survey see Hill in *A.J.* xxv (1931), pp. 670–83. See also Wehberg, *The Problem of an International Court of Justice* (English translation, 1918), pp. 55–9; Lammasch, *Schiedsgerichtsbarkeit*, pp. 123–6; Nippold, pp. 314ff.; *Actes et Documents*, ii. 741 and 880.

[2] But see the remark of Sir Cecil Hurst (*Minutes of the Committee of Jurists*, Doc. C. 166, M. 66, 1929. V. p. 51) that the arguments adduced by M. Fromageot in favour of abolishing dissenting opinions 'were strong arguments for excluding national judges from the Court on the ground that they would have insufficient courage to take a decision against their own countries'.

[3] For a restatement of these reasons see Fachiri, loc. cit., and the well-informed article of an anonymous writer in *R.I.* (Paris), iv (1929), pp. 29–31. See also the Report of a Committee of the Permanent Court to consider the question of national judges in connexion with Advisory Opinions, *P.C.I.J.*, Series E, No. 4, pp. 75–7.

[4] See below, p. 234.

the indirect but formidable influence of this system on the judicial character of the Court when viewed in terms of general confidence in its impartiality.

§ 33. The Attitude of the National Judges on the Permanent Court of International Justice.

An analysis of the work of the Court in regard to the attitude displayed by national judges shows that the problem is not purely a theoretical one. A survey of the judgements given by the Court shows that, in sixteen cases, the parties have availed themselves of the right to appoint a national judge. In three of these cases[1] the national judge voted with the majority in favour of the contention advanced by his State. In one case the record does not disclose the names of all the dissenting judges. In the remaining twelve cases[2] the national judges regarded it as their duty to disagree with the decision of the majority and to uphold in dissenting opinions the defeated views of their Governments.[3,4]

The above analysis has been undertaken with the greatest respect for the judges of the Permanent Court and after a consideration of the expediency and appropriateness of this line of investigation. The question of enhancing the impartiality of the Court can be discussed without impugning the sincerity and integrity of individual judges. It is a question which ought not to be avoided because of the fear of lowering the authority of the Court. But it must be stated, without impugning the motives of the national judges in the fulfilment of their judicial duty, that the result of the analysis here undertaken cannot be regarded as a mere coincidence.[5]

---

[1] Judgements Nos. 2, 9, and 5. In the latter judgement the decision favoured in a sense both parties. The Court, while stating that a breach of an international duty has been committed and that the concession in question ought to be readopted, refused to grant compensation on the ground that no damage has been proved. (The above survey is based on the activity of the Court up to June, 1932.)

[2] Judgement No. 11.

[3] Judgements Nos. 1, 6, 7, 8, 10, 12, 13, 14, 16, Series A/B, 46, and the two important Orders concerning the Swiss Free Zones (Series A, Nos. 20 and 22).

[4] No comprehensive picture of this aspect of the activities of the Court in the matter of advisory opinions is possible, as the appointment of national judges in such cases had not begun before March 1928. In two Advisory Opinions (No. 15 and in the *Railway Traffic between Lithuania and Poland* case) the national judge joined in a unanimous decision of the Court. The Advisory Opinion No. 17 seems to have favoured both parties equally. In Advisory Opinions Nos. 16 and 18 no national judges were appointed. In the others the national judges delivered dissenting opinions against the decision of the majority.

[5] It is somewhat difficult to see why, in view of the above result, writers are inclined to express the opinion that the institution of national judges has proved to be a success. See Hill, op. cit., p. 683, and *R.I.* (Paris), iv (1929), p. 30.

It shows that, whatever may be the postulated function of and the services rendered by the national judges in the course of the deliberations of the Court,[1] it has proved impossible to avoid the grave danger of the national judges of the Court acting and, with few exceptions, being looked upon as representing the interests of their States. Any usefulness of the national judges in that direction is overshadowed by the manner of the actual exercise of their judicial vote as disclosed in the statistics compiled here. It is not suggested that there have been no grounds of legal substance behind their vote, but the fact is profoundly disturbing that (barring the doubtful case of the eighth Judgement) in no case have national judges voted against their State where it was successful, and that in no case have they refrained from expressing their dissent when the Court rejected the view of their Governments. In several cases the situation was aggravated by the circumstance that the dissenting opinion was delivered against the unanimous (Judgements Nos. 6, 7, and 8) or practically[2] unanimous (Judgement No. 14) view of the Court.[3]

It would be not only unjust but also misleading to attribute the exclusive responsibility for the present state of affairs to individual national judges.[4] The responsibility rests with the dualism of a system which excludes, as a matter of fundamental principle, any idea of representation of interests, except those of the law, on the part of the permanent body of the judges, and which, notwithstanding the requirement of declaration of impartiality, admits in fact the idea of representation of national interests on the part of the non-permanent judges. It would be both idle and inaccurate to deny that the latter are by the very nature of their function under a definite obligation to their State to explain its views to the Court. When, therefore, they preface their dissenting opinions by a reference, whose sincerity cannot be doubted, to the dictates of conscience bidding them to record their

---

[1] See below, p. 235.

[2] The explanation of the other two dissenting opinions in this case will, if we may say so without disrespect, be found in Judgement No. 15 and the dissenting opinions there delivered.

[3] In the latter cases the national judge based his dissenting opinion largely on the ground that the Court had no jurisdiction, notwithstanding the fact that the case came before it by virtue of a special agreement.

[4] Some of the passages which follow are taken from the author's Note in the B.Y., 1930, pp. 182–6, entitled 'Dissenting Opinions of National Judges and the Revision of the Statute of the Court'.

dissent, it may be difficult to decide whether the reference is made to the duty of judicial impartiality, rendered problematical by the dualism of the system, or to the obligation to represent the interests and to put forward the view of their Governments. The border-line between explaining the legal views and defending the interests of the State concerned is in such cases so shadowy as to become utterly unreal. It has been said by a committee of the Permanent Court in connexion with the problem of representation of the interests of litigants that 'of all influences to which men are subject, none is more powerful, more persuasive or more subtle, than the tie of allegiance that binds them [judges] to the land of their homes and kindred and to the great sources of the honors and preferments for which they are so ready to spend their fortunes and to risk their lives'.[1] If this is true of judges in general, it must be particularly true of judges appointed *ad hoc* by their Governments.

§ 34. Representation of Interests and the Impartiality of the Court.
The creation in the Permanent Court of a body of judges regarded by the opinion of the world as conscious of their position in the hierarchy of international organization, and developing, and enabled by their status and organization to develop, a sense of priesthood in the service of an idea transcending any particular interest, continues to be at the present time of supreme importance for the international community. This last sentence has all the disadvantages of a high-sounding phrase, but it is believed nevertheless to give expression to the fact that the problem of putting beyond any possible doubt the impartiality and disinterestedness of the highest international tribunal constitutes, as we have seen, perhaps the most vital question in the field of international judicial settlement. The revision of the Statute by the Assembly in 1929 was to a large extent intended to improve the personal status of the judges and to add to the safeguards of their judicial independence, dignity, and integrity.[2] However, the securing of the personal

---

[1] *P.C.I.J.*, Series E, No. 4, p. 75.

[2] Thus, for instance, Article 16 of the revised Statute provides that the members of the Court may not exercise any political or administrative function, nor engage in any other occupation of a professional nature. This latter provision does not appear in the unrevised Article 16. The revised Article 17 provides that no member of the Court may act as agent, counsel, or advocate in any case. The unrevised Article 17 limited this prohibition to cases of an international nature.

integrity and independence of the judges of the Court solves only one part of the problem. The perfecting of their political impartiality and the securing of their independence of purely national considerations and sympathies is of even greater importance because of the impossibility of achieving this end through formal safeguards. This is a problem of the creation in the minds of judges of a sense of international solidarity resulting in a clear individual consciousness of citizenship of the *civitas maxima*, a development on which it would be inappropriate to offer advice or suggestions. But at least it can be said without impropriety that that process ought not to be impeded by the continuance of formal institutions perpetuating the idea of representation of national interests.[1] National judges are such an institution. The very presence of a national judge changes the character of the deliberations of the Court. They cease to be a contest between the various aspects of the impersonal claims of justice; they tend to degenerate into a contention between the conflicting claims of the parties. The fine scales of justice are loaded with the crude and incongruous element of partisan interest.

It is not denied that the abolition of the system of national judges presents a problem of extreme difficulty. Formally, considerations of nationality do not enter into the question of election of judges. But so long as by tacit convention and for political reasons, whose cogency and expediency are obvious,

---

[1] No one who studies the record of the proceedings of the Committee of Jurists who in 1920 drafted the Statute, or of the Committee which in March 1929 considered the question of its revision, can fail to realize that the idea of representation of interests underlay in a decisive manner the entire conception of national judges. This point of view seems now to have definitely prevailed. In the unrevised Statute there was still doubt whether national judges were expected to conform to the requirement of Article 16 of the Statute—at least in the French text—which laid down that the members of the Court must not exercise any political or administrative function in their respective States. (There was a curious discrepancy between the French text which spoke of 'les membres de la Cour' and the English text which spoke of 'the ordinary members of the Court'. However, even the English text was not quite clear whether the word 'ordinary' meant permanent members of the Court, or whether it was intended to cover all judges except deputy-judges.) This doubt was removed when in 1929, in the case concerning the Brazilian Federal Loans contracted in France, the French Government nominated as judge *ad hoc* the then Legal Adviser to the French Ministry of Foreign Affairs. Formally the French Government was represented in this case by the then Assistant Legal Adviser to the Ministry of Foreign Affairs, who was thus called upon to plead before his official chief acting in the capacity of a judge. The revised Article 31 quite clearly imposes no limitations in this respect, and there is now nothing to prevent a State from nominating as its national judge its official legal adviser, its minister for foreign affairs, or any of its civil servants.

Great Powers are certain of being actually represented on the Court, it is not easy to urge smaller nations to give up a right to which they attach importance. Neither can a proper remedy be found in a modification of the rights or functions of the national judges, for instance, in limiting the exercise of their vote or disregarding it altogether in certain contingencies.[1] Such a solution would have the result of sanctioning formally the position of national judges as advocates of their national interests, and would tend to aggravate the evil. The same objection attaches to any proposal to abolish the right of national judges to deliver dissenting opinions.[2] In addition, the dissenting opinions may have the advantage of checking manifestly partisan dissent by at least compelling the national judge to produce the reasons for dissent and by exposing the dissenter to the criticism consequent upon the weakness or frivolity of any such dissent—although experience teaches that that contingency has not prevented dissenting opinions, and that any criticism of the legal merits of dissent must be confined to a small number of experts. However, for the time being and in the absence of a more radical remedy there devolves upon international lawyers a distinct duty to examine the dissenting opinions, with due respect and without any implication of motives, but with a determination to call attention, if and when occasion arises, to any improper use of this right. Proposals may also be usefully considered for a working compromise between the claims of national representation and the necessary preservation of the character of judges as representatives of international justice. Thus it would be possible for the Council and the Assembly to elect, at the recommendation of the States, a standing list composed of two national judges for each State for a prolonged period to serve, if necessary, on the Court. The judges thus elected would be formally independent of their Governments.[3]

The major duty, upon which it is not necessary here to expatiate, rests with the national judges themselves. The fulfilment of that duty ought to be made easier by the realization both of the insignificance of the advantage which the dissent confers upon the national judge's own State and of

---

[1] See, for instance, the suggestion of Sir John Fischer Williams in connexion with the casting vote of the President in the case of the *Lotus*, in *Chapters*, p. 229.

[2] See on this question the *Minutes* of the Committee of 1929 entrusted with the revision of the Statute, pp. 50–5.

[3] See on this point *R.I.* (Paris), iv (1929), p. 31.

the immeasurable value of the benefit which could be conferred upon the institution of international justice as a whole by an attitude of studied restraint and painstaking disinterestedness. There is a fatal lack of rationality in a system which, while, in view of the size of the Court, conferring little actual benefit on the State appointing a national judge—in no case, not even in the *Lotus* case, did the vote of the national judge exercise a decisive influence[1]—by necessity threatens to imperil the quality of absolute disinterestedness which is essential to the effective functioning of the Court as a tribunal endowed with and exercising jurisdiction in matters of importance for the peace of the world.

§ **35. The Current Arguments in Favour of the Institution of National Judges.** Are the grave objections to which the institution of national judges is open counterbalanced by offsetting advantages? It is submitted that none of the reasons usually adduced in favour of the retention of the system will stand a critical examination. This applies in particular to the view that the presence of a national judge at the deliberations of the Court must tend to increase a State's confidence in the justice of the decision of the Court and make it less disinclined to accept an adverse verdict. An argument of this nature touches the very heart of the problem. Only in a Court in which in the public estimation there still lingers the factor of advocacy of interests does it matter whether a State is represented by its national or not. Only the total eradication of the idea of representation of interests can remove the main reason for the insistence on the retention of national judges and do away with the vicious circle in which the existence of national judges perpetuates the conception of a court whose judges represent interests of their States, and in which that conception in turn tends to entrench such 'judges *ad hoc*' as a permanent institution. There are other reasons why it is difficult to accept the opinion that the presence of the national judge will ensure a nation's confidence in the regularity and impartiality of the Court's proceedings.[2] Is such

---

[1] It will be noted, however, that although in this case the vote of the Turkish judge had no decisive effect in regard to the actual decision of the Court, it had the effect of giving to the world, with the authority of a formal majority of the Permanent Court, approval of a doctrine of great importance which some believe to be mistaken.

[2] It has also been said (see Fachiri, op. cit., p. 50) that the national judge may assist the Court in shaping the judgement so that it may avoid wounding

supervision necessary? And if necessary, can it be effective? The view has been expressed in this connexion that international justice must not only be done, but that it must appear to have been done. It is doubtful whether such appearance can be created by the mere fact of the presence of the national judge. Can it not be said that the presence of the national judge, symbolizing the idea of representation of interests, will rather tend to weaken that appearance? It is impossible not to gain the impression that the retention of the institution of national judges constitutes a concession to the uninformed respect for State sovereignty in what is essentially a minor detail—considering the negligible effect of the national judge on the outcome of the dispute—in comparison with the concessions which States have already made to the cause of impartial international justice by undertaking the commitments of obligatory arbitration.[1] The same element of unreality attaches to the argument, somewhat uncritically repeated with melancholy frequency, that the presence of national judges is essential in order that the bench may be properly informed of the legal and other views of the party to the dispute. In the course of the written proceedings frequently comprising bulky volumes of Cases, Counter-cases, Arguments, and Counter-arguments, there is ample opportunity for the Court to become acquainted with the views and the legal outlook of the parties. These opportunities are supplemented by the wealth of argument displayed with great industry during the oral proceedings. In case the judges are still in need of further instruction, there are available to them the usual channels of research in a library specializing in comparative law. And it has been repeatedly suggested that, should these safeguards be regarded as unsatisfactory, there remains the possibility of the bench being assisted by national assessors acting in an advisory capacity without the right to vote.[2]

national susceptibilities. It is safe to assume that a bench composed of distinguished lawyers, most of whom have had practical experience of governmental international intercourse, is not in need of such assistance.

[1] States themselves may not always attach decisive importance to being represented on the Court. See Advisory Opinion No. 16, pp. 7, 8, for an instance of a waiver by the parties to the dispute of their right to appoint a national judge.

[2] See the suggestion of Lapradelle in the course of the deliberations of the Committee of Jurists in 1920 (*Procès-Verbaux*, p. 535). And see Articles 26 and 27 of the Statute of the Court providing for technical assessors without the right to vote in Labour cases (compulsorily) and in Communication and Transit cases (optionally).

§ 36. Safeguards of Impartiality of Judges. Improvements in the Method of Election.

A change in the existing law in the matter of national judges is not the only, or even the principal, measure whose realization may assist the cause of securing the highest possible degree of impartiality in the work of the Court. For in the last resort the attitude of national judges is not in itself typical of the normal working of the Court, and the record of their voting on the Permanent Court is not in itself an accurate illustration of the question of impartiality of its judges. For national judges are in fact, if not in law, representatives of the States who appoint them. It is the attitude of the ordinary judges which must form the starting-point for a critical consideration of the work of the Court, namely, their attitude in cases in which their own State is involved. An analysis of the judgements shows that with the exception of one case[1] there has been no disposition on the part of judges to vote against the view adopted by their own Governments.[2] The tendency in regard to advisory opinions appears to be the same.[3] In addition, some cases decided by the Court have given rise to the apprehension that the impartiality of the Court may be threatened by the inclination of judges to support the cause of the State politically allied with their own country. It would betray an obvious lack of sense of proportion if any deductions from these necessarily speculative indications were allowed to blur the general estimation of the work of the Court since its inception. Seldom in the history of political institutions has there been such a general consensus of opinion on the steady increase of

---

[1] Judgement No. 1 (the *Wimbledon* case), when Judge Anzilotti joined in a dissenting opinion against the majority judgement.

[2] In Judgement No. 1 the judges in question, with the exception of Judge Anzilotti, favoured the contention of their Governments. This was also the case in Judgements Nos. 5 (in part), 10, 16, and in the two Orders relating to the Swiss Free Zones. In Judgements Nos. 2, 9, and 15 dissenting opinions were delivered by the nationals of the defeated party. In Judgements Nos. 6, 7, 8, 11, 12, and 13 judges *ad hoc* were appointed on both sides.

[3] The majority of the advisory opinions were given in cases in which the actual parties to the dispute had no nationals sitting as ordinary members of the Court. In addition, it is not clear whether the manner of recording the votes of judges at the earlier stage of the work of the Court permits of definite conclusions. The later advisory opinions exhibit the same tendency as that observed in regard to judgements. But see p. 220, n. 1. See also, to the same effect, Advisory Opinion, Series A/B, No. 42; possibly the same applies to the Fourth Advisory Opinion (*Tunis and Morocco Nationality Decrees*), where Judge Weiss seems to have voted against the contention of the French Government. In Advisory Opinion No. 14, and Series A/B, No. 40, judges delivered dissenting opinions against the otherwise unanimous view of the Court.

authority as in the case of the Permanent Court of International Justice. Much of this happy result is undoubtedly due to the inherent and inescapable usefulness of the Court as the highest organ of international justice. At the same time this result would have been impossible if the general body of judges had not been composed of persons who have approached their task with an almost religious sense of duty and determination on judicial impartiality. Thus viewed, the importance of the tendency noted above need not be exaggerated. Even if it be admitted that national judges or, perhaps, even some of the ordinary judges, when their own (or, possibly, an allied) State is concerned, have not succeeded in overcoming the powerful influence of national allegiance, their influence in shaping the results of the work of the Court would not be, and has not been, decisive.

These considerations, however, do not absolve those in a position of responsibility—and lawyers called upon to advise them—from the duty of enhancing by every possible means the element of impartiality in the Permanent Court. Any show of partisanship on the part of a judge, even if immaterial for the outcome of an actual dispute, necessarily imperils the estimation and the atmosphere of impartiality in the Court as a whole. Accordingly, apart from the removal of those features in the organization of the Court which amount to a formal recognition through the institution of national judges of the idea of representation of interests, the constant vigilance of statesmen and lawyers must be directed towards securing, so far as this is possible by external regulation, a composition of the Court in which the ideal—admittedly difficult of achievement—of impartiality transcending the ties of nationality is brought nearer realization. If this may be said with sincere humility and respect, the fullest possible effect must—as a matter of deliberate and conscientious policy—be given to those words of Article 2 of the Statute, according to which the Court 'shall be composed of a body of independent judges elected regardless of their nationality from amongst persons of high moral character'. For impartiality, when the interests of the judge's own State are concerned, is in the last resort a personal quality of intellect and conscience. It presupposes the determination on the part of judges to regard the international community, which is still to a large extent a postulate, as an entity as real as any sovereign State, and with an equal claim to allegiance. It presupposes on their

part the consciousness of being citizens of the world.[1] It presupposes on their part the realization of the moral consequences of
the fact that they are the trustees of one of the highest and
perhaps the most important function which can be put in the
hands of man. The securing of these qualities can never be
exclusively a question of machinery. But it can be so to a very
large extent. This is the reason why the task of securing a
morally and intellectually high type of judge constitutes one of
the most important tasks of the community of States organized
in the League of Nations.

The consideration of the adequacy of the existing methods of
electing the judges of the Court must form the subject of constant preoccupation on the part of responsible statesmen. The
elaborate procedure by which the Permanent Court gives its
judgements is generally known and appreciated.[2] The procedure by which judges are elected ought to be the object of
equally anxious care. It is therefore a duty of true statesmanship
to review periodically the existing machinery with a view to
eliminating any subsisting element of hap-hazardness or other
inadmissible influences in the election of judges. It is by no
means certain that these elements are entirely eliminated
under the present method of electing the judges of the Court.

When the Statute of the Court was drafted in 1920, the
main preoccupation of the authors of the Statute was to find
a method for reconciling the claims of the small and large
powers for representation on the Court—a problem which
had frustrated the attempt made in 1907 at The Hague to
establish a permanent international court. Accordingly,
when in 1920 that difficulty was satisfactorily solved by the
adoption of the so-called Root-Phillimore plan,[3] there was
a general feeling that the most important problem in the
election of judges was satisfactorily solved. It may be doubted
whether—quite apart from the fact that the main object of

---

[1] The British Commissioner in the London Commission of 1853, in submitting
his suggestions as to the choice of the umpire, referred to the persons concerned as
entitled 'to take rank among that class of citizens of the world in whom every nation
takes a pride, whose fame is the common property of all, and whose feelings,
sympathies, and interests may be fairly considered as not confined to one place or
people, but equally and indifferently spread over the whole world' (Moore, p. 395).

[2] See Hammarskjöld in *Michigan Law Review*, xxv (1927), pp. 327–53, and the
account by Judge Hughes reprinted in *B.Y.*, 1930, pp. 180, 181. See also the detailed
discussion of the question in 1931 by the Court itself in connexion with some
proposed changes, *P.C.I.J.*, Series D, No. 2, pp, 218–52.

[3] See Articles 8–12 of the Statute.

the Root-Phillimore plan has been rendered obsolete by the changes in the composition of the Council and the resulting preponderance of small Powers—there is sufficient justification for the continuance of this feeling. The Statute of 1920 failed to achieve, or even to consider, what ought perhaps to have been its principal object, namely, the securing of the election of judges through a most careful, deliberate, and responsible method. Apart from the submission of lists of candidates by the national groups,[1] the election of the judges by the simultaneous proceedings of the Council and the Assembly is the haphazard result of an electoral process pure and simple with all the disadvantages of haste, chance, physical fatigue, and political bargaining. These methods and the concomitant disadvantages have been subjected to well-informed criticism.[2] However, there seems to have been so far no general recognition of the fact that a change of the existing methods is necessary if the League of Nations is to fulfil properly one of its most important functions, i.e. the selection of an authoritative court inspiring the absolute confidence of the world.

The choosing of international judges must be a process not only of election, but of careful, conscientious, and mature selection by a body of some degree of permanence capable of developing an articulate common will and responsibility. It should not be the result of a chance vote of an unwieldy body whose responsibility is necessarily limited, but the outcome of a long process of weighing the personal qualifications of the candidates. A method could be devised by which the judges could, subject to the confirmation by a qualified majority of the Assembly, be appointed by the Council advised by a committee composed of its own permanent and non-permanent members and working for an extended period. Such a system would combine the uttermost care in the selection of the judges of the Court with the preservation of the rights of the Assembly of the League.[3] However, even a reform of

---

[1] It entrusted national groups appointed by their Governments, under the conditions laid down for members of the Permanent Court of Arbitration, with the task of nominating the candidates for election. These national groups are, according to the Statute, recommended to consult their highest Courts of Justice, Legal Faculties and Schools of Law, and National Academies and national sections of International Academies devoted to the study of law. It does not appear that this provision has been complied with in practice.

[2] See *B.Y.*, 1931, pp. 123–31.

[3] The process would resemble to a certain extent the procedure by which the judges of the Supreme Court of the United States are nominated.

this nature would not entirely remove the inconveniences resulting from a simultaneous election of fifteen judges. Ways must be
sought for doing away with the danger resulting from the necessity of electing all the judges at once, from the consequent
perfunctory character of the selection, and from the ensuing
impossibility of remedying mistakes until a further nine years
have elapsed. These risks would be eliminated by a system
under which only five judges would be elected at a time—a
procedure which could be effected by a rule under which, while
the nine years' period of office would be maintained, one-third
of the judges would retire every three years.

These suggestions are here put forward with diffidence and
with an apology appropriate to every attempt at propounding
new schemes. Their justification is the conviction of the writer
that the method by which the organized community of nations
elects its most important organ may legitimately be regarded as
the object of continuous investigation and improvement. The
Permanent Court is the solid rock upon which statesmen will set
their feet in time of trouble when all other means have failed.
'Interest civitatis maximae ut haec petra sit firma'. Impartiality
is a quality of mind and character which can only partly be
secured by dint of external regulation and machinery. But this
is the very reason why nothing ought to be left undone which
renders the part played by these external factors as effective as
is humanly possible.

PART IV

STABILITY AND CHANGE IN
INTERNATIONAL LAW

CHAPTER XI

INTERNATIONAL CHANGE AND THE JUDICIAL SETTLEMENT OF INTERNATIONAL DISPUTES

§ 1. The Absence of an International Legislature as a Reason for the Limitation of the Jurisdiction of Courts. While legal analysis, and the study of the working of international arbitration, have been proving that neither the supposed non-existence of legal rules applicable to the dispute, nor the importance of the subject-matter of the controversy, affords an adequate basis for a doctrine of the limitation of the international judicial function, another basis for such doctrine has been attracting the attention of international lawyers. According to this view, the judicial function, conceived as a compulsory procedure, is applicable to such disputes only as, having regard to the present state of international organization and law-making, can be solved by the application of rules of law in a manner consistent with the requirements of justice and of international peace and progress. As Professor Hyde says, a dispute is justiciable if it is 'capable of *reasonable*[1] adjustment by reference to accepted principles of international law'.[2] The basis of this conception of justiciability is the fact that there does not exist an international legislature capable of modifying or supplementing existing law. The adherents of this doctrine point to the consequently static character of international law, and to the possibility of controversies arising in which the decisions of an international organ acting judicially and giving, as it is bound to do, effect to an undoubted international right, would be manifestly unjust. These decisions, it is said, might be so little in accord with the changes continually taking place in international society that they would have the unavoidable effect of perpetuating injustice and friction. It is pointed out that the existence of the obligation of judicial settlement, in issues of this description, must cause the interested States to adopt a rigid attitude of reliance on formal rights, an attitude which they might possibly be induced to abandon or to modify in the course of a less rigid procedure. The upholders of this view look with impatience on those who regard judicial settlement as a panacea for securing peace, and for solving

---

[1] Italics are mine.   [2] Vol. ii, p. 112.

international conflicts; they insist that real progress in this direction can be achieved only by admitting the essential non-justiciability of such disputes, and by developing so-called alternative methods of settling them through international conferences, conciliation, and international legislation.

The origin of this aspect of the doctrine of the limitation of the judicial function goes back to Westlake's well-known discussion of the limitations of international arbitration. He was inclined to recognize the right of political action, to the exclusion of the duty to arbitrate, not only when there is no legal rule in existence, or when the existing rule is in need of being supplemented or more precisely defined, but also in cases where the legal aspect is clear, but is overridden by considerations of higher distributive justice, namely, when 'opinion is felt to be outgrowing a rule, so that a change in the law may be asserted in good conscience to be necessary, and yet, from the want of an international legislature, it is difficult to effect such change otherwise than by setting an example to it'.[1]

However, it was after the World War that clear expression was given to this view by a number of writers and statesmen of authority. Thus Professor Huber, when discussing in 1919 the bases of the Covenant of the League of Nations, and its provisions in regard to judicial settlement, drew attention to the essential difference, in this respect, between international and municipal law, inasmuch as 'the latter possesses in its legislature a regulative organ which normally ensures the adaptation of the law to the changing conditions of power within a society, whereas the essentially contractual nature of the relations of independent States enables States interested in the maintenance of the *status quo* to prevent or to obstruct the evolution of the law.'[2] At the first Assembly of the League of Nations, during the discussion on the inclusion of the principle of obligatory arbitration in the Statute of the Permanent Court of International Justice, Lord Balfour gave eloquent utterance to similar doubts.[3]

---

[1] *International Law* (2nd ed.), i. 301.

[2] *Zeitschrift für Völkerrecht*, xii (1922–3), p. 14; and *Annuaire*, xxxiii (2), pp. 763, 764.

[3] He said: 'Remember that this Court is set up to administer a system of international law. International law itself is a changing and growing subject. There is no provision—fortunately perhaps—within the limits of the Covenant for changing and reforming international law, and this Court is brought into existence not to change it or reform it, but simply to administer it. Therefore you may find yourselves, or some nation in the course of time may find itself, in the position that a rigid interpretation of what may be an antiquated system of international law (which would never be embodied in any authoritative code or authoritative work if all the circumstances were understood), nevertheless

When in 1922 the Institute of International Law discussed the problem of the obligatory jurisdiction of international tribunals, Professors Politis and Brown submitted a report in which they envisaged the possibility of disputes not being suitable for judicial settlement on the ground that they could not be decided without taking into account general principles of justice and equity. It was clear from the report and from discussion that such a possibility was regarded as the direct outcome of the absence of an international legislature able to develop the existing law in the spirit of justice and progress.[1] In general it can be said that this manner of approach is prevalent in the most notable of recent contributions to the subject of compulsory arbitration, like those by Brierly,[2] Hostie,[3] Schindler,[4] Morgenthau,[5] and, in particular, by Sir John Fischer Williams.[6]

has to be administered by a Court which, in administering it with strict regard to law with which it has to deal, but without any power of showing that larger vision which is sometimes given to statesmen and politicians, may affect interests so profoundly concerning the very existence of that state, that your whole machine would be destroyed before that state would submit itself voluntarily to legal destruction.

  'I do not think such cases are likely, but who among you will venture to say that they are impossible? . . .

  'The very thought that it might occur will throw discredit on your system, unless you allow some possible safety valve.' *Doc. concerning the Action by the Council of the League under Article 14 of the Covenant*, p. 247; *First Assembly, Plenary Meetings*, p. 488. The 'safety valve' was found in the rejection of obligatory arbitration.

  [1] *Annuaire*, xxix (1922), p. 36.

  [2] *The Law of Nations* (1928), p. 189.

  [3] In *R.I.*, 3rd ser., ix (1928), pp. 263–81, 568–87. Hostie, while rejecting other tests of justiciability of disputes, suggests that a dispute is non-justiciable if there is a clear divergence between the law applicable to the dispute and the requirements of equity. The existence of such a divergence must, he says, be left to the determination of the Court in each particular case. He thus envisages a situation in which a Court after having dealt with a dispute on its merits and having found on the question of law, ought to refuse to give judgement and pronounce the dispute non-justiciable. As he says, 'La guerre juste . . . est un mal affreux. Mais la paix injuste est un mal plus grand.' (Op. cit., p. 576.) See also Cimbali, *Le cause dei perpetui insuccessi dell'arbitrato internazionale* (1926), and other writings by the same author cited op. cit., at p. 7.

  [4] *Recueil des Cours*, 1928 (v), pp. 264–79.

  [5] *Die internationale Rechtspflege, ihr Wesen und ihre Grenzen* (1929), in particular pp. 72–84, 131–52. See also the interesting article of Decencière-Ferrandière in *R.G.* xxxvi (1929), pp. 416–51. He proposes a solution of the difficulty by way of establishing two organs competent to deal with international disputes. He suggests that every dispute should in the first instance be submitted to a judicial organ deciding in accordance with strict law; that if either party is unwilling to accept the judgement the dispute should be submitted to a non-judicial organ, which will be competent to decide the matter merely from the point of view of equity to the exclusion of any legal consideration whatsoever; and that the pronouncement of the 'organ of equity', if contrary to the judgement, should have the effect of suspending its operation.

  [6] *Chapters*, pp. 34, 35; *International Change and International Peace* (1932); *A.J.* xxvi (1932), pp. 31–6.

§ 2. The Problem of Change in International Relations. The problem of adjusting the functioning of the law to the perpetual antinomy of change and stability, and of justice and security, is not one peculiar to international law. It is a general legal phenomenon common to every political society. It is one of the central problems of legal philosophy.[1] Experience teaches that in this struggle the element of change is not always victorious, for the simple reason that stability and security are in themselves a powerful constituent element of justice. There is, as Montesquieu already pointed out, a limit to the possible sacrifice of security to progress.[2] The same experience teaches that there is ultimately no more effective challenge to the maintenance of the law than an immutability impervious to the needs of life and progress. As Ihering said: 'A concrete law, which, because it has once existed, claims absolute and accordingly perpetual existence, is like a child who strikes his own mother; it derides the idea of law even in invoking it, for the idea of law is perpetual becoming. . . .'[3]

The tendency of international lawyers to treat fundamental questions of international law apart from the corresponding phenomena in other fields of law has had the result of exaggerating the importance both of the element of change and of the absence of an international legislature as an instrument of change. There are undoubtedly reasons peculiar to international relations which have had the effect of distorting the true proportions of the problem. The principal of these reasons is the fact that, in international relations, the main source of conditions calling for change is obsolete or unjust rights of individual States grounded in contractual agreements of indefinite duration based on force. (Treaties, even of a legislative character, concluded in time of peace are as a rule of limited duration or subject to denunciation, and thus provide a possibility for giving effect to a change in conditions.) Thus when in the last ten years the problem of

---

[1] The problem has formed one of the main themes of Dean Pound's writings on legal philosophy. See in particular *The Spirit of the Common Law* (1921); *Interpretations of Legal History* (1923). See also Demogue, *Les Notions fondamentales du droit privé* (1910), chapter on Evolution and Security in Modern French Legal Philosophy, *Modern Legal Philosophy Series* (1921), pp. 446–70; Sauer, *Lehrbuch der Rechts- und Sozialphilosophie* (1929), pp. 228–31. Sir Henry Maine's Chapter II on Legal Fictions in his *Ancient Law* bears on the same subject.

[2] *Esprit des lois*, Book VI, ch. iii.

[3] *Der Kampf ums Recht* (1906 ed.), p. 9 (translated as in Demogue, op. cit., p. 447).

peaceful change is put in the foreground of international discussion, and when reference is made to the constant change in
conditions of relative power, the true objects aimed at are
changes in the territorial and other provisions imposed by
force in the recent peace treaties. It is the questionable political
and moral value of the source of many international obligations of indefinite duration which is responsible for some of the
exaggerations of the necessity for change. Law means inconvenience to those subjected to its obligations, and in the relations
of individuals its hardships are accepted as a necessary inci-
dence of social life. But when, as in relations between States,
this inconvenience has its origin in agreements imposed by
force, and when it is accompanied by the realization of the
difficulty of change by the intervention of the law, it produces a
psychological attitude in which the sense of grievance and the
original injustice are unduly magnified.

However, once the causes aggravating the problem of
change within international society have been realized, care
must be taken not to exaggerate its importance by regarding
it as *the* problem of international law.[1] In international
relations the securing of the observance of the law in regard
to its essential, as distinguished from its minor, aspects is still
the chief task which confronts the society of States. It must
also be borne in mind that, while in the international sphere
the problem of change is for some reasons more urgent than
within the State, there are other reasons which limit its importance. One of these factors is that the scope of matters
governed by international law is on the whole confined to the
regulation of the external relations of States. It does not and
cannot aim at regulating the lives of the members of the
international community in the same intensive and pervading
manner as municipal law does. It is mainly adjective law. It is,
more than any other kind of law, a regulation of competencies.
Only when the political organization of the international community has undergone a fundamental change, so as to regulate
in detail the life of its individual members in its internal
aspects—only then will it be possible to speak of a constant
flux of changes necessitating legislative remedies. At present
international law is more static than any other law not only
because of the absence of an international legislature,
but principally because it regulates relations which are not

---

[1] See Fischer Williams, *International Change and International Peace* (1932), p. 76.

in themselves liable to be affected in a decisive manner by economic and other changes.[1]

Closely connected with this aspect of the matter is the view that, as within the State legislation gives formal recognition to changed conditions of power and influence, it is unfortunate that in the international sphere there does not exist a machinery translating growing power into legal right. This view ignores the fact that one of the not least important functions of the law is to protect the weaker members of the community against the physical preponderance of others, and not invariably to give effect to it. However, the main fallacy of this attitude is the belief that the internal growth of the State, and the increase in its internal power, constitute a condition which must find an expression in external relations of power. The two are not necessarily related. It will be shown in the next Part how most so-called conflicts of interests are due, not to economic necessities, but to the imperfections of international legal organization, in particular to the legal admissibility of force and the absence of the duty of judicial settlement.

§ 3. International Legislation[2] as an Instrument of Change.

A legislature is the principal—although not the only—instrument for changing the existing law. In many cases it is, in the absence of a voluntary renunciation of a legal right, the only instrument of change. There ought to be no doubt that in some cases an international legislature—and

---

[1] It is of importance that the lawyer studying the problem of the conflict between stability and change in international relations should not allow himself to be misled by general phrases. Thus he frequently comes across a view that, while within the State the functions of decaying individuals are taken over by their successors, the constitution of the international society of sovereign States makes it possible for decaying States, which have become unable to discharge their responsibilities towards their peoples, to perpetuate the territorial *status quo* which, as a result, tends to become unjust and intolerable. For a recent statement of this point of view see Hawtrey, *Economic Aspects of Sovereignty* (1930), pp. 137 ff. But might it not be said that nations, far from decaying, are in a state of perpetual renovation for the very reason that they are composed of individual human beings of limited physical duration? In the course of history nations have frequently succumbed to physical force and lost independent statehood, but only a crude interpretation would invariably ascribe such occurrences to internal decay and regard them as just decrees of world history.

[2] The term 'legislation' is here used in its original meaning as referring to a law-creating activity of a sovereign authority. The term 'international legislation', when used with reference to international conventions of a general character, is convenient so long as it does not have the effect of concealing the actual absence of a true international legislature. See Hudson, *International Legislation* (1931), vol. i, Introduction.

only an international legislature—would be in the position
to remove dangerous causes of friction by a deliberate change of
the legal *status quo*. For this reason the absence of an international
legislature must be regarded as putting a heavy strain on the
obligatory rule of law in the international society. However, once
the importance of an international legislature in this respect has
been recognized, care must be taken not to exaggerate either its
possibilities or the results of its absence.

The existing legal *status quo* may be a source of friction, but
there is no certainty that legislation devised to alter it may not
prove even more dangerous to the cause of peace. It may lead
to actual recourse to force where formerly only dissatisfaction
and friction existed. In so far as it may deprive a State of rights
previously enjoyed, it may be regarded as an act of injustice
and usurpation of powers in the same way as legislation within
the State, dictated by class or other factional interests, may
prove productive of widespread indignation or disobedience
culminating in revolution.[1] A change in the law may be possible of achievement only at the expense of the growth of others,
in particular when the object of the claim is such that there is
not enough of the object desired to go round. An enactment by
an international legislature changing existing rights may leave
the out-voted State dissatisfied, resentful, and clamouring in
turn for a change.

In addition, the scope and the possibilities of legislation are
strictly limited on more general grounds. In the first place,
legislation is subject to the same limitation as legal regulation
in general. It cannot regulate matters which, having regard
to the nature and the function of the law, are beyond the
sphere of legal regulation. And it must stop short of relations
which, although in principle amenable to regulation by law,
cannot become so having regard to the state of the political and social development within the particular society.[2]
Secondly, its operation is necessarily limited by the fact
that some legal relations, although distasteful to those who
expect to benefit by a change of the law, ought nevertheless
to be maintained because of their conformity with material
or formal justice. It is not the function of the law to prevent

---

[1] It has been said that acts of injustice committed against individuals are less
dangerous in practice than acts of injustice committed against States; for 'To clash
even lightly with the interests of a group is to strike a beehive or an anthill...':
Tourtoulon, *Philosophy in the Development of Law* (1922; English trans.), p. 503.

[2] See below, p. 391.

individual hardship following upon the operation of rules of law. On the contrary, its task is to give effect to legal rights, notwithstanding the inconvenience of those subjected to a legal duty. Law is more just than loose conceptions of justice and equity. Nothing is more instructive in this respect than to note how often international tribunals, instructed to decide in accordance with equity, have insisted on deciding on the grounds of law because that solution seemed to them more just as tending to realize legitimate expectations.[1] It is only when such hardship and injury become socially detrimental that the legislator steps in. A change of the law, even if its continuance is detrimental to the interests of the person or the group asking for its removal, may violate reasonable expectations of others protected by law and just in themselves. A State 'sitting on its rights' is not necessarily in the wrong. Thirdly, the fact that, in the international sphere, demands for a change relate frequently to a change of territorial rights acquired in contractual agreements based on force, constitutes another source of difficulty. For legislation restoring rights of this nature would be necessarily retroactive. Within the State legislation is only in exceptional cases concerned with the invasion, with a retroactive effect, of private

---

[1] See, in particular, the decision in the *Maninat* case before the French-Venezuelan Mixed Commission, where the Umpire refused to identify equity with generosity and insisted on a decision based on law, on the ground that 'equity exists when exactly the right thing is done between the parties'. *Report of the French-Venezuelan Mixed Commission* (1906), pp. 44–80, United States Sen. Doc. No. 533, 59th Congress, 1st Session. See also the *Gentini* case, Ralston's *Report*, p. 727, where the claimant Government asked for the rejection of the plea of prescription on the ground of equity: 'We are told with truth that this is a Commission whose acts are to be controlled by absolute equity, and that equity will not permit the interposition of a purely legal defence as prescription is said to be. But is this position correct? . . . The principle of equity finds its foundation in the highest equity—the evidence of possible injustice to the defendant, the claimant having had ample time to bring his action, and therefore, if he has lost, having only his negligence to accuse.' See, in particular, the numerous decisions of the British-American Mixed Arbitral Tribunal under the Convention of 18 August 1910, which instructed the Tribunal to decide in accordance 'with treaty rights and with the principles of international law and of equity'. In these decisions—see below, p. 312—the Tribunal, while refusing to give effect to claims based on equitable considerations, but not supported by the existing law, recommended to the States concerned certain lines of action as an act of grace. And see the *Sambiaggio* case, Ralston's *Report*, p. 692, to the effect that it is the duty of the Tribunal instructed to disregard the technicalities of the local law, 'to apply equitably to the various cases submitted the well-established principles of justice, not permitting sympathy for suffering to bring about a disregard of law'. See also Nielsen's *Report*, pp. 51–67, for a learned argument by Counsel in the *Eastern Extension, Australasia and China Telegraph Company, Ltd.*, case, and p. 79 for the decision of the Tribunal. But see the award in the *Cayuga Indians* claim, ibid., pp. 314–20.

rights. The paramount legal postulate of security and stability is one which affects not only the administration of justice, but also the legislative function as well. This is the reason why legislation is not as a rule retroactive;[1] why it does not as a rule interfere with individual contractual engagements; and why the invasion of private rights is so far as possible subject to the duty of compensation.

These general observations may well be illustrated by a consideration of the possibilities of Article 19 of the Covenant, in which the postulate of international legislation modifying obsolete rights and legal conditions is expressed in a hesitating but unmistakable manner. There are very few who deny the imperative necessity of giving concrete shape and effectiveness to that article. Yet its present imperfection must not be allowed to cause us to exaggerate the possibilities of its application. What would be the scope of the operation of an international legislature, as foreshadowed in Article 19, in removing what are now regarded as the main obstacles to peace and the main causes of international friction? Would it, for instance, be able to effect any territorial changes of importance without provoking most determined and embittered opposition on the part of those threatened by the proposed change, an opposition which would shatter the very foundations of the international organization embodied in the League of Nations? Would an international legislature be in a position, without exposing the League to the danger of dissolution, to limit the freedom of States in the matter of tariffs and migration? It is not only the opposition of sovereign States, but the inherent difficulties of the problems involved which would act here as a powerful check upon the legislative activity. Thus, to mention one instance, who would make bold to maintain with assurance, justifying international enactments of a radical nature, that the opening, by virtue of such an enactment, of the thinly populated territories of some States to foreign immigration would be just, desirable, and expedient? Perhaps the historian, when viewing in the distant future the growth of the League of Nations in the first century of its existence, will comment on the rudimentary character of its legislative organs at that stage as having been a blessing in disguise, namely, as having

---

[1] On the principle of non-retroactivity of laws as a 'condition indispensable pour la sécurité et la stabilité des relations juridiques' see Duguit, *Traité de Droit constitutionnel* (2nd ed.), v. 310.

prevented its disruption as the possible result of attempts to settle matters of this nature with the help of the dangerous instrument of a majority-vote, and as having made possible their discussion in an atmosphere of persuasion and relative detachment.

An exaggerated estimate of the need of change and of the possibilities of an international legislature may also have the undesirable effect of inducing States, parties to a dispute, to seek shelter behind the immobility of the law, and to renounce the exploration of methods more likely to lead to a satisfactory solution than a formal change through legislative or quasi-legislative action. Nothing in the present state of international organization can be more detrimental to the prospect of effective change than to rely exclusively upon legislative action for its realization. This method of approach has the result of diverting the attention of nations and statesmen from constructive measures based on an attitude of reasonableness and responsibility for international peace; for these alone can in many cases produce a satisfactory solution. No legislative action can, for instance, remove such sources of friction as are due to the desire for territorial changes in respect of certain territories with racially mixed populations. Only neighbourly arrangements, conceived in a spirit of accommodation, can in such cases provide a satisfactory and lasting solution. Exaggerated emphasis on the necessity for legislative change may have the result of diverting the State which is clamouring for change from constructive efforts to contribute its share towards remedying a situation complained of. One may mention here, for instance, the claim for international legislative regulation of migration as a solution of the friction occasioned by the problem of over-population in some countries. Deliberate measures calculated to check unrestricted growth of population are no less vital for the solution of the difficulties involved than legislative international action.

§ 4. **Judicial Adaptation of the Law to Changed Conditions.** The discussion among international lawyers of the problem of peaceful change in connexion with the absence of an international legislature has been marked not only by overemphasis, ignoring the analogous phenomena within the State, of the element of change, but also by an under-estimate of the function of courts as an instrument for adapting the existing law to changed conditions. The fact that, normally, the function of changing the law is within the province of the legislature, and that the business of courts is to apply existing law, has at times led writers to deny that courts have any place at all in the scheme of change.[1] It is of importance not to accept this general statement without closest investigation. Undoubtedly legislation is the normal and the most effective means of changing the law, but it is not the only means. It is the instrument of a community in an advanced phase of its legal organization. It is the last stage in the evolution of law-making. The analogy of the creation and the application of the law within the State is highly instructive in this connexion.[2] Law is created not only by legislative bodies, or by custom, or by individual agreements of the parties. It is also created by judges by way of interpreting the existing law and applying its general principles. There are obvious limits to this law-making activity of judges,[3] but these limitations do not materially alter the fact that courts do not slavishly administer abstract rules without being able to exercise creative discretion. It is irrelevant whether this exercise of discretion is shown in recourse to conceptions of justice, or general principles of law, or the law of nature, or of public policy.

Judicial law-making is a general legal phenomenon in societies where justice is administered by judicial tribunals. Accordingly, like courts within the State, so also international tribunals, by the very nature of the judicial function, are not confined to a purely mechanical application of the law. When applying the necessary abstract rule of law to the concrete case, they create the legal rule for the individual case before them. The actual operation of law in society is a process of gradual crystallization of the abstract legal rule, beginning with the constitution of the State, as the most fundamental and abstract body of rules, and ending with the concrete

---

[1] See, e.g., Fischer Williams, *International Peace and International Change* (1932), p. 11.

[2] In Sir Henry Maine's *Ancient Law* (1920 ed.), pp. 29–33, the student will find an illuminating passage on the operation of the agencies by which law is brought into harmony with society. He points out that social necessities and social opinion are as a rule in advance of law; that, although the gap may be almost closed for a time, it has a perpetual tendency to reopen; and that there are three principal agencies which constantly adjust the law to the requirements of progress. They are legal fictions, equity, and legislation. The first two operate principally through the instrumentality of courts.

[3] See above, p. 80.

shaping of the individual legal relation by a judgement of a court, or by an adjudication or decision of an administrative authority, or by an agreement of the interested parties. The separation of powers as between the judiciary and the legislature is as legendary as it is between these two agencies and the administrative power. This creative exercise of judicial activity is no less real in common-law countries than in systems of law where the principle *stare decisis* has no formal validity.[1] In international law the scope of this aspect of judicial activity is much wider; for, in international society, conscious law-making by legislation is in a rudimentary stage, the creation of customary law is slow and difficult of ascertainment, judicial precedent is relatively rare and of controversial authority, and, in consequence, the field of detailed concrete regulation is small, and that of general principles of law wide and elastic. Accordingly, in international law judicial law-making is of special importance for the purpose of disposing of disputes by developing and adapting the law of nations, within the orbit of existing law, to the new conditions of international life through a process of equitable judicial interpretation and reasoning. The conception of international tribunals administering in a mechanical fashion obsolete rules of law is as far from the truth, although as easily assumed, as the conception that they may disregard clear provisions of the law in order to arrive at a compromise satisfying both parties. International tribunals are judicial tribunals administering rules of law. But, like the law applied by municipal courts, the law administered by them is tempered by a spirit of legal equity, common sense, and natural justice which, while paying full consideration to acquired rights, finds ways and means to prevent the law from becoming an instrument of oppression, or from giving its sanction to manifest absurdities. International tribunals are in this respect in a more favourable position, inasmuch as they are hampered by a comparatively small number of hard-and-fast rules, and are, therefore, more in a position to exercise their law-creating function in a spirit of progress. Thus viewed, the present imperfect state of international legislation, far from being a reason for questioning the applicability of obligatory judicial settlement, is a powerful argument in its favour.

The law-creating activity of international tribunals

---

[1] See Lauterpacht in *B.Y.*, 1931, pp. 53, 54.

formed the subject-matter of one of the preceding chapters in which their methods of meeting cases *primae impressionis* were examined.[1] They have been shown to be manifold and effective. But have cases *primae impressionis* discussed in these chapters any direct relation to the question of judicial adaptation of the law to changed conditions? It is submitted that they have. A case of first impression is simply one for which the existing law, statutory or other, provides, on the face of it, no solution, so that recourse to a more general legal rule or principle is necessary. This gap in the law may be due to an oversight of the legislator; it may be due to the fact that by mere accident a certain type of case has not previously come before courts; but it may also be the result of objective changes in society necessitating recourse to judicial law-making. Even this aspect of judicial activity is, it is true, limited by the existing law, and great are the difficulties and heavy the responsibility of international judges in reconciling the antinomies of genuine and spurious interpretation of the existing law; but this has not, as we have seen, prevented them from fulfilling their judicial function in the spirit of progress and with due regard to the phenomenon of change. In addition, while international tribunals are thus frequently, by the very nature of the judicial function, in a position to adapt the law to objective changes in the international community, there exist, in addition, certain specific legal rules and doctrines which emphasize in varying degrees the possibilities of this aspect of judicial activity in the international sphere. Some of these doctrines will be considered in this Part. They are the judicial application of the doctrine *rebus sic stantibus*; the doctrine of abuse of rights; and some aspects of so-called international inter-temporal law.

§ 5. The Absence of Provisions for Change and the Justiciability of International Disputes.

Nothing that has been said here about the limited possibilities of international legislation as an instrument of peace is intended to deny that the question of adapting existing law to new conditions is no less essential in international law than under any other system of law. But it has been thought necessary here to draw attention to these limitations of international legislation because the demand for it, put forward in connexion with the problem of change, has become an argument against the rule of law in international

---

[1] See above, pp. 105 et seqq.

relations as embodied in the principle of obligatory judicial settlement. The practical consequences of linking up the obligatory judicial settlement of international disputes with the establishment of an international legislature are obvious. There is in practice little difference between rejecting obligatory arbitration for the reason of its incompatibility with the State's freedom of action in the international sphere and rejecting it on the ground that the international society does not as yet possess a legislature in the accepted meaning of the word. The setting up of an international legislature would constitute the most fundamental change in the present organization of international society, and a derogation from the traditional attributes of national sovereignty immeasurably greater than a most comprehensive acceptance of the obligations of compulsory judicial settlement. To regard the establishment of an international legislature as a condition precedent to the setting up of a system of obligatory arbitration is in effect to reject an institution of vital importance to the existence of any legal community on the ground that that community has not as yet developed certain modes of creating law; it is to make the rule of law dependent upon the fulfilment of a condition which, if realized, would constitute the greatest inroad upon State sovereignty ever attempted. In fact, writers who reject obligatory judicial settlement on the ground of the absence of agencies of change, at the same time regard the establishment of such an effective legislature—as distinguished from the procedure of conciliation and advice by international organs—as undesirable and as tantamount to the setting up of what is called a super-State.

The problem of stability and change is one of the principal problems of the philosophy of international law and will be treated from this point of view in the chapters which follow. But it is also, as has been shown, closely connected with the question of obligatory judicial settlement, and as such is preeminently of practical importance. The insistence, on this account, on the limitation of the judicial function is based on the appeal to justice and to the requirements of peace between nations—although some may regard it as a startling revelation that, forty years after the inception of the movement for obligatory arbitration, international lawyers should have discovered that the consummation of these efforts may, in the present state of international organization, prove disastrous to the peace of the world. There should be little doubt as to the gravity of the implications of this attitude. As it is impossible to determine in advance in what disputes a legal decision may prove fraught with danger or with injustice, this test of justiciability of disputes amounts in fact to a rejection of the idea of obligatory arbitration.[1] That rejection includes even so-called purely legal disputes as connoting controversies capable of determination by an existing rule of law. In fact compulsory arbitration of legal disputes so conceived is even more dangerous from the point of view of the objection put forward.

As the purely negative character of conclusions which are drawn from the absence of an effective machinery of change is frequently concealed behind the advocacy of so-called alternative means of settlement, it will be necessary to investigate what are the possibilities of these alternative methods of settlement. An even more important task is to consider what are the existing and potential remedies calculated to obviate the inconveniences and dangers resulting from the absence of agencies of change. There are open to the international lawyer more constructive avenues of approach than the rejection of the postulate of the obligatory rule of law. First, bearing in mind that, even within the State, where the authority of the national legislature is supreme, law is to a considerable extent shaped and developed by courts, he ought to examine what are the actual extent and the possibilities of judicial law-making within the international society. Secondly, it is within his province to inquire into the scope of a deliberate extension, by the will of the parties, of the process of judicial legislation by international tribunals. Thirdly, it is his duty to consider the possibilities of political action falling short of a legislative procedure, but intended to prevent or to modify the operation of legal rules deemed to be contrary both to justice and to the peace of the world.

---

[1] See writers cited above, p. 247. See also Fischer Williams in *A.J.* xxvi (1932), p. 35, where that attitude is expressed in the submission that States (i.e., in fact, one of the disputants) must retain the liberty of determining whether a dispute is, or is not, suitable for a legal decision. This being so, it is not clear what is the advantage of a definition of a legal dispute, as suggested by the learned writer.

CHAPTER XII

INTERNATIONAL CONCILIATION AS AN INSTRUMENT OF CHANGE

§ 6. Conciliation as an Alternative Means of Settlement. The difficulties, real and imaginary, arising out of the absence of effective provisions for international change have in recent years become responsible for the prominence given to so-called alternative means of settlement, in particular to international conciliation. The view has been frequently expressed that conciliation—and not a judicial decision—is the instrument of settlement appropriate to the special needs of the international community. There has been a tendency to deprecate the insistence on judicial settlement as yet another instance of an uncritical transference of conceptions and institutions from the domain of municipal law into the field of international relations.[1] The way in which the procedure of conciliation has been raised from the position of a preliminary and ancillary means of settlement to an independent institution, rivalling, and opposed to, the normal method of judicial settlement is one of the significant phenomena in the development of legal conceptions in the international sphere.

The procedure of conciliation is to-day firmly embedded in international conventional law relating to pacific settlement. In addition to Articles 11 and 15 of the Covenant of the League, which provide for conciliation by the Council, it has been incorporated in important multilateral conventions like the General Act for the Pacific Settlement of International Disputes[2] and the General Convention of Inter-American Conciliation of 5 January 1928.[3] To these instruments there must be added a great and still growing number of bilateral treaties like the Locarno agreements,[4] the uniform conciliation treaties concluded in and after 1928 by the United States with a considerable number of non-American States,[5] and a multitude of conciliation treaties between

---

[1] See the writers referred to below, pp. 416 et seqq., 424. And see Wright, *Mandates under the League of Nations* (1930), pp. 270, 271; Potter, *The World of Nations* (1929), pp. 174, 175; Shotwell, *War as an Instrument of National Policy* (1929), pp. 246–52.

[2] See above, p. 70.

[3] Printed in *A.J.* xxiii (1929), Suppl., p. 76.

[4] See above, p. 39.

[5] See, for instance, the Conciliation Treaty between the United States and Austria of 16 August 1928, in *A.J.* xxiii (1929), Suppl., p. 197, and other identical treaties printed in the same Supplement.

various European States.[1] As a rule conciliation is adopted as
obligatory for disputes described as non-legal, or non-justiciable,
or for disputes other than those which can be settled by the
application of rules of law, or for disputes as to matters other
than respective rights. In some treaties it is prescribed as the
obligatory preliminary instrument of settlement in regard to all
disputes, whereas in others, although obligatory in regard to the
so-called non-legal disputes, it is optional in regard to controversies described as legal.[2] In general the procedure of conciliation,
as adopted in these treaties, may be described as a means of
pacific settlement in which the parties entrust a number of persons with the task of investigating the facts of a controversy, of
attempting to effect a direct settlement, or of recommending a
settlement without, however, binding themselves to accept as
conclusive either the report as to the facts or the recommendation
as to the solution of the controversy.[3] The possible advantages of
conciliation have been widely discussed by international lawyers
and others. In theory it serves a large variety of useful purposes. It
brings the parties together; through the moratorium it prevents
sudden breaches of the peace; through the elimination of the
recourse to rigid law it spreads the allaying oil of sweet reasonableness over the waves of the controversy; it is marked by
simplicity and the absence of cumbrous and costly procedure; it
may have the advantages of the services of experts; and, as its
findings are not binding in any case, it makes possible the conclusion of treaties of pacific settlement without the indefinite and
therefore destructive reservations.[4]

---

[1] For an enumeration of 110 of these treaties, up to February 1930, see Efremoff in $Z.V.$ xv (1930), pp. 383–6. See also Habicht, quoted below.

[2] See, for a useful synopsis, *Arbitration and Security*, pp. 51–3.

[3] The above definition is somewhat general and does not take into account the
various modifications of emphasis or priority in regard to the three main functions of conciliation. For an account of the machinery of conciliation see McNair
in Oppenheim (4th ed.), ii. 14–32, and the literature there quoted. See also Hyde,
'The Place of Commissions of Enquiry and Conciliation Treaties in the Peaceful
Settlement of International Disputes', in *B.Y.*, 1929, pp. 96–110; Efremoff in
Recueil des Cours, 1927 (iii), pp. 1–140; Gorgé in *R.I.*, 3rd ser., vii (1926), pp. 632–
76, and viii (1927), pp. 58–106; Revel in *R.G.* xxxviii (1931), pp. 564–607; Habicht,
Post-War Treaties for the Pacific Settlement of International Disputes (1931), pp. 1001–34.

[4] See *Arbitration and Security*, pp. 54–6, for an analysis of the reservations
accompanying conciliation treaties. It will be noted that although they do not
contain such general reservations as vital interests, independence, honour, and
interests of third States, many of them include reservations referring to previous
disputes, territorial integrity, or questions affecting domestic jurisdiction (ibid.,
pp. 55, 56).

§ 7. The Development and the Present Function of the Procedure of Conciliation.

Historically, conciliation goes back to the time when any undertakings, not only of compulsory judicial settlement, but also of obligatory procedure not involving a binding settlement, were regarded by States as unacceptable. At that stage of international organization, conciliation, as embodied in the provisions of The Hague Conventions relating to mediation and commissions of inquiry, served the function of at least bringing the parties together. It did not originally involve the duty of refraining from recourse to hostilities before the issuing of the report of the conciliation commission; and, as Governments were reluctant to permit a finding on the merits of the controversy as a whole, it was confined to an elucidation of, and finding on, the facts. In the course of subsequent development these limitations were abandoned. In the so-called Bryan treaties, the moratorium became one of the obligations of the procedure of conciliation. In subsequent conciliation treaties the conciliators were authorized to submit a recommendation as to the solution of the controversy in all its aspects. These original objects of the conciliation procedure have to a large extent been rendered obsolete by subsequent developments in the domain of obligatory judicial settlement and international organization in general. The question of the existence of facts giving rise to an international obligation has become recognized as coming within the normal function of judicial tribunals. Most treaties of judicial settlement confer upon international tribunals jurisdiction as to 'the existence of any fact which, if established, would constitute a breach of an international obligation'.[1] The principle of moratorium has become one of the main procedural rules of the machinery of pacific settlement under the Covenant. The conciliation procedure was conceived and developed at a stage of international law when there was practically no legal restraint upon States intending to engage in wars, whether stimulated by a sudden outbreak of national passion or in pursuance of a premeditated plan of aggression. That stage has been overcome now that the liberty to go to war has been substantially curtailed, and the new institutions of international organization have provided means and opportunities for consultation and negotiation.

---

[1] But see Sir John Fischer Williams in *B.Y.*, 1930, pp. 68, 69, who gives a somewhat restricted interpretation of this provision. And see below, p. 281.

The obsolescence of the original purpose of the procedure of conciliation explains why, although in the ten years following the World War there has been concluded a vast number of bilateral and multilateral conciliation treaties and although conciliation commissions have been set up and organized in advance, there has not been a single instance of recourse having been had to these bodies,[1] and why there is no likelihood of such recourse taking place.[2] It is difficult to visualize occasions on which States might feel inclined to have recourse to them. The opinion, frequently voiced, that the great majority of armed conflicts which have occurred during the last hundred years could never have been settled by the judicial procedure, is probably well founded, but it is irrelevant to the question of the usefulness of the procedure of conciliation. It is unlikely that these armed conflicts could have been prevented by such a procedure. There is no reason to assume that wars, like those waged between Austria and Sardinia, or between Turkey and the Balkan States, or between Turkey and Italy in 1911, or between the United States and Spain in 1898, or between Russia and Japan in 1904, could have been prevented by the efforts of a conciliation commission constituted in advance.[3] These armed

---

[1] The commission of investigation and conciliation set up by the protocol of 3 January 1929, between Bolivia and Paraguay, was not established under a pre-existing conciliation treaty. The function of the Commission was to determine the responsibility for the frontier incidents, which had taken place between the two countries, and to recommend measures calculated to prevent a repetition of the hostilities. It was precluded by its terms of reference from investigating or deciding on the merits of the territorial dispute. The work of the Commission did not result in a finding on the responsibility for the frontier incidents. It culminated in the Conciliation Agreement of 12 September 1929, providing for the mutual forgiveness of the offences and injuries, for the re-establishment of the *status quo* which existed before the incidents occurred, and for the renewal of diplomatic relations. The protocol of 3 January 1929 is printed in *A.J.* xxiii (1929), Suppl., p. 98. For an account of the dispute and of the work of the Commission see ibid., pp. 110–12, and xxiv (1930), pp. 122–7, 573–7.

[2] Ruegger, in a learned article in *R.I.*, 3rd ser., x (1929), pp. 91–106, surveys the reasons for the failure of conciliation commissions as a practical institution and suggests procedural remedies.

[3] In his collection of addresses entitled *International Relations* (1922), Lord Bryce enumerates, on pp. 224–30, the wars which occurred since the Treaty of Vienna in 1815, and points out that, with the possible exception of the wars between Germany and Denmark in 1864 and between Great Britain and the two South African Republics, none of these wars could have been prevented by recourse to arbitration. However, his view that most of these conflicts, like the Balkan wars or the war between the United States and Spain in 1898, could have been prevented by conciliation cannot be accepted. Lord Bryce himself mentions on p. 228 the Franco-German war of 1870 in connexion with the possible advantages of conciliation, but on p. 229 he refers to that war as to one the causes of which were deep-seated and where the differences seemed

conflicts had their roots in the desire to change the *status quo* by the invasion of the legal rights of another State—a desire stimulated by the existing international law which tolerated and permitted recourse to force, as a legal means of giving effect to claims, and provided no means for peaceful and superimposed territorial change. These wars were not due to sudden outbreaks of uncontrolled national feeling which could have been prevented if there had existed an appropriate procedure.

Neither is there good reason to believe that in the future States will be willing to entrust for effective settlement to a conciliation committee issues involving a change in the existing law. Such issues, if there is a disposition on the part of the State from which concessions are claimed to treat claims of this nature in a spirit of generosity and accommodation, can be more properly discussed in the course of laborious and confidential negotiations between the interested parties. It is to err on the side of optimism to assume that a dispute in which a State is asked to abandon its freedom of action in regard to the regulation of matters of migration, or to agree to a cession of its territory, can with advantage be treated by a conciliation commission.[1] At the same time it is unlikely that in matters of minor importance recourse will be had to the machinery of conciliation. If prolonged negotiation has in such cases failed to produce an agreement, then the probability is that the parties will prefer to have the controversy settled by the normal machinery of arbitral settlement. The procedure of permanent international tribunals may, contrary to the current assumption, be less cumbrous and expensive than that occasioned by recourse to special bodies with no experience or continuity.[2]

---

irreconcilable. See also the article by Godefroy in *R.G.* xiii (1906), pp. 559–82, devoted to the easy task of proving that the wars under review were not concerned with questions of right and could not therefore have been settled by judicial methods.

[1] This is also the reason why in disputes of this nature the part of international conferences as an instrument of pacific settlement is strictly limited. The advantages of international congresses as instruments of consultation and co-operation are obvious and numerous, but it is rightly being pointed out, by authors who have devoted special study to the functioning of international conferences, that they are not well adapted to the settlement of international disputes, and that the only justification for their function in this capacity is the present limitations of the jurisdiction of judicial tribunals. See in particular Hill, *The Public International Conference* (1929), pp. 206–18, 222.

[2] See, for instance, Article 29 of the Statute and Articles 67 and 70 of the Rules of the Permanent Court concerning the Chamber for Summary Procedure, and Judgements Nos. 3 and 4 rendered under these articles.

In view of this process of gradual obsolescence of the original function of conciliation what, it may be asked, is the reason for the continued attachment shown to it by lawyers and statesmen? The reason, it is submitted, is that to the initial purposes of conciliation there has been subsequently added another object emanating directly from the current doctrines of the inherent limitations of the international judicial function. Conciliation has been accepted as a means of an attempt at settlement of disputes which lawyers and statesmen have declared to be incapable of judicial settlement. It is easy and convenient to point to a supposed inherent distinction between justiciable and non-justiciable disputes by adducing as evidence a vast number of multilateral and bilateral treaties in which this distinction is expressly recognized by the provision of conciliation for so-called non-justiciable, and of judicial settlement for so-called justiciable, disputes. The process is not without interest for the student of the development of legal and political ideas. Conciliation has, at an early stage of its development, been called into life because there existed disputes which States were unwilling to submit for final adjudication. Subsequently, the very existence of conciliation bodies has provided an easy argument for the perpetuation of the doctrine of disputes inherently incapable of obligatory judicial settlement. Conciliation has preserved its place in international law largely in consequence of the belief that there exists a legally relevant distinction between justiciable and non-justiciable disputes. That distinction is, in turn, maintained by the existing conventional international law reserving a prominent place to the procedure of conciliation.

§ 8. The Effectiveness of the Procedure of Conciliation as an Instrument of Pacific Settlement.

Some machinery of consultation and negotiation is undoubtedly necessary and advisable before recourse is had to an international tribunal. Such machinery does in fact exist in the normal diplomatic channels. It is sanctioned by the almost universal practice of treaties of judicial settlement, which provide for negotiations as the preliminary condition of invoking a judicial decision. As between individuals, so also in relations between States, the appeal to a court ought, if necessary, to constitute the last, and not the first, stage of the controversy. States apparently attach importance to this condition, and there

have been several occasions on which Governments pleaded
to the jurisdiction of the Permanent Court on the ground that
the requirements of previous negotiations had not been
complied with.[1] In so far, therefore, as the procedure of conciliation is intended to stress the factor of negotiation and
consultation prior to recourse to judicial settlement, it may
serve a useful function, in particular in view of the fact that
international law, as interpreted by the Permanent Court,
does not in the absence of an express provision to this effect
regard previous recourse to negotiations as a condition for
invoking the obligatory jurisdiction of judicial tribunals.[2]
In so far as it is in effect used as a pretext for concealing
the determination of the States to remain free from the duty
of obligatory judicial settlement it is harmful. It is easy, by
signing a multitude of conciliation obligations, to create the
impression that an imposing edifice of pacific settlement has
been erected. The complacency with which some inter-

---

[1] See, for instance, the British plea to the jurisdiction of the Permanent Court
in the *Mavrommatis Palestine Concessions* case, Judgement No. 2, Series A, No. 2, pp.
13–15. And see the Argument of Sir Cecil Hurst, Series C, No. 5 (1), pp. 33 and 71,
and the Reply of Professor Politis, p. 50. See also the Polish plea to jurisdiction in
Judgement No. 6, Series A, No. 6, pp. 13 and 14, and Judgement No. 11, Series A,
No. 13, pp. 10 and 11. On the question of negotiations in the *Mavrommatis* case see
Feinberg, *La Juridiction de la Cour dans le système des mandats* (1930), pp. 114–21.

[2] See Judgement No. 2, where the Court said that, as the convention in question
contained no provision concerning negotiations, it was sufficient if a divergence of
opinion had manifested itself. However, the Court expressed the view that 'it would no
doubt be desirable that a State should not proceed to take as serious a step as
summoning another State to appear before the Court without having previously, within
reasonable limits, endeavoured to make it quite clear that a difference of views is in
question which has not been capable of being otherwise overcome'. It appears, therefore, that the Court has so far been unwilling to recognize that the almost uniform usage
of inserting in treaties the condition of previous negotiations has hardened into a custom.
But, even if there is no procedural rule of international law enjoining negotiations, it is
respectfully suggested that the Court might give expression to its views on the propriety
of the action of a State indiscriminately invoking its jurisdiction by availing itself of the
provision of Article 64 of the Statute, which lays down that the parties bear their own
costs apart from the cases where the Court may direct otherwise. The Court has not so
far made use of its discretionary powers in this matter. But could it not, following the
broad analogy of most legal systems, make use of this Article in order to discourage
frivolous and unnecessary appeals to its jurisdiction, in which no attempt at arriving at a
settlement through negotiations has been made? There is no substance in the view that
there is an element of punishment in the imposition of costs, as there is no substance in
the view that States, being sovereign, cannot be penalized in any form. In the *Ottoman
Debt Arbitration* of 1925 (*Annual Digest*, 1925–6, Case No. 360), the arbitrator went to the
length of asserting that the imposition of costs upon the defeated party would be
contrary to the principle of equality of States. There are sound reasons for providing
safeguards against indiscriminate use of the machinery of the Court.

national lawyers rejoice at the existence of the large number of conciliation treaties is disquieting. It lends ample support to the view that conciliation, although non-existent in practice, has become an obstacle to progress by reducing the fundamental postulate of the obligatory rule of law to one of many means of settlement of equal value. While at the period of the First and Second Hague Conferences the inimical attitude of States towards obligatory arbitration found expression in comprehensive reservations, the same attitude tended after the World War to find expression in an indiscriminate multiplication of instruments of pacific settlement devoid of the element of effective legal obligation. There is no occasion for self-congratulation because States have agreed to meet before a body of conciliators authorized to propose recommendations which Governments are not bound to accept. The practical result of conciliation and of other 'alternative means' is not to substitute one mode of peaceful settlement for another of equal force and value. The effect is to substitute a series of *attempts at* settlement for a settlement proper. Whatever the advantages of conciliation may be, it is clear that, unlike compulsory judicial settlement, it does not aim at securing the peace within international society by ascertaining in a final and binding manner the disputed rights. This is, obviously, not the only task of judicial settlement, but it is its primary task—a function which is essential to the existence of a community under the reign of law.

§ 9. Conciliation and Judicial Procedure. What has been said above must not be taken as suggesting that there is absolute certainty attaching to the peace-preserving function of judicial settlement. Like any other provision of positive law, so also a binding judicial pronouncement may be disregarded. Thus viewed, the difference between the two processes of settlement is only a relative one, and any doubt whether judicial settlement is an absolute guarantee of peace is directed against a view which no one holds and which, on the face of it, it is impossible to maintain.[1] But the difference exists nevertheless, and is of fundamental importance. In law the binding decision of an international court constitutes a final settlement in the meaning that it precludes recourse to such forms of self-help as may be otherwise

---

[1] See below, pp. 397, 398.

permitted in an undeveloped system of law. Politically, resort to self-help is still possible, just as disregard of the law and revolution are possible within the State, but legally they amount to a defiance and a breach of the rule of law, with all the political consequences of such an attitude. The moral and political effect of the judgement of a judicial tribunal is so tremendous that its legal finality has a tendency to approach actual finality. A State may disregard the finding of a concilia-tor without exposing itself to the charge of bad faith, but a Government refusing to comply with the award of a judicial tribunal is in a different position, for it then appears as a law breaker, and the most embarrassing burden of proving excess of jurisdiction, or corruption on the part of the Court, is thrown upon it if it wishes to escape the odium of having violated the law. No such restriction of the freedom of action attaches to the procedure of conciliation.

At the risk of some repetition it must be pointed out that it is not intended to deny altogether the possible usefulness—as an instrument of change—of the procedure of conciliation, operating either through a commission or, within definite lim-its, through the Council of the League of Nations.[1] The two methods are not opposed one to the other so that the choice of one necessitates the rejection of the other.[2] Even if it is conceded that some of the inconvenience of judicial settlement resulting from the absence of an international legislature may be obviated by a previous recourse to the procedure of concili-ation, can it not be urged that the proper course is to make the recourse to judicial determination dependent upon the previ-ous utilization of the machinery of conciliation in the same way in which at present, in almost all arbitration treaties, recourse to an international tribunal is made dependent upon previous diplomatic negotiation? There is little justification for the view that the eventual right to demand a judicial decision may render illusory the advantages of conciliation, inasmuch as a State, which believes itself to have the law on its side and is determined to

---

[1] See below, p. 340.

[2] There is, perhaps, some exaggeration in the view put forward by Professor Ch. de Visscher (*R.I.*, 3rd ser., ix (1928), p. 34) and others that the advocates of obligatory judicial settlement must necessarily tend to minimize the function of conciliation. This may be clearly seen, for instance, from the Report of Borel and Politis, *Annuaire*, xxxiii (2) (1927), pp. 766 et seq., which, although attributing to conciliation an important function in filling the gap arising out of the absence of an international legislature, is strongly in favour of obligatory judicial settlement.

insist rigidly on its formal right, will be disinclined to show that spirit of accommodation and broad-minded appreciation of the equitable aspect of the controversy which is an essential condition for the success of the procedure of conciliation. This pessimistic estimate lies within the domain of speculation, and it may therefore be difficult to disprove it. The same problem has arisen in connexion with the compulsory arbitration of industrial disputes, in particular in Australia, where arguments have been put forward in support of the view that the ultimate faculty to invoke the judgement of the arbitration court may frustrate the purpose of the procedure of conciliation. However, equally weighty reasons have been adduced by those who point out that, unless there is in the background a court endowed with compulsory jurisdiction, little respect is paid to the conciliator.[1]

[1] Foenander, 'The New Arbitration Act in Australia', in *International Labour Review*, xix (2), 1929, p. 164. It cannot, for instance, be said that, in the protracted Roumanian-Hungarian Optants dispute, the absence, consistently stressed by Roumania, of the duty of submitting the dispute to a final judicial adjudication had the result of making more conciliatory the State claiming freedom of action.

CHAPTER XIII

THE JUDICIAL APPLICATION OF THE DOCTRINE 'REBUS SIC STANTIBUS'

§ 10. The Doctrine 'rebus sic stantibus' as the Negation of International Law. In any discussion on the place of the doctrine *rebus sic stantibus* as a principle of change capable of judicial application it is essential to keep in mind the distinction between two fundamentally different aspects of the doctrine. It is in the first instance a pseudo-legal assertion of the absence of any binding force in international law. It is the expression of the view that the rule *pacta sunt servanda* does not apply to States with the same cogency as it applies to individuals, for the simple reason that they are States, and that their interests cannot be subjected to an obligation existing independent of their own will. As Hegel said, 'The relation of States is one of independent units which make stipulations, but at the same time stand above their stipulations'.[1] From Spinoza[2] to modern deniers of international law the doctrine *rebus sic stantibus* has been appealed to not only as a consequence, but also as the very proof of the States' independence of the law. It has been one of the manifestations of the state of nature of which the relations of States were said to afford the only historical instance.[3]

The practice of States shows few examples of actual recourse to the doctrine *rebus sic stantibus*, and probably no examples of its recognition by States against whose treaty rights it has been invoked.[4] It owes its fame and notoriety principally to writers who take it over from text-book to textbook by dint of vague but persistent references to the State's right of existence and self-preservation. Actually, even on those rare occasions on which treaties were broken under colour of the doctrine *rebus sic stantibus* it was obvious that no question of self-preservation arose unless, indeed, every change in the constellation of power enabling the State to

---

[1] *Grundlinien der Philosophie des Rechts*, § 330.

[2] *Tractatus Theologico-politicus*, xvi; *Tractatus Politicus*, iii. 14.

[3] See below, p. 401. In modern phraseology this state of nature has been referred to as the relation of co-ordination—as distinguished from subordination to law—of sovereign States. See below, pp. 405 et seqq.

[4] See Lauterpacht, *Analogies*, p. 170, n. 1. And see for a review of the more important cases Fischer Williams, *Chapters*, pp. 95–100.

disregard with impunity an onerous obligation be regarded as a material change of conditions implied in the treaty. The true function of the doctrine is to give expression to yet another aspect of the divorce of some orthodox notions of international law from general principles of law of undeniable universality—a divorce expressed, for instance, in the refusal to recognize the vitiating force of duress in the conclusion of treaties.

In fact, there is a close and not artificial connexion between the disregard of the vitiating effect of duress and the doctrine *rebus sic stantibus*. The connexion clearly exists in the domain of morals, inasmuch as it may not be absolutely repugnant to justice to maintain that a treaty imposed by force cannot claim the same sanctity as an obligation voluntarily undertaken. (The future student of international ethics will regard it as a redeeming feature of modern international law that a system of law postulating the validity of treaties concluded under the threat of physical compulsion evolved a doctrine absolving the State of its obligation as soon as it felt sufficiently strong to shake off the burdens of an imposed treaty.) But the association between the doctrine *rebus sic stantibus* and the admissibility of duress is of interest not merely from the ethical point of view. For, as a matter of historical experience, the main (although not the only) reason for invoking the doctrine *rebus sic stantibus* is in treaties imposed by force—treaties which, as a rule, do not contain any limitation of their operation in point of time,[1] whose provisions are not invariably the product of far-seeing statesmanship, which are as a rule dictated by the victor after a trial of physical strength, and which, in consequence of the nature of the conditions imposed by them, perpetuate the consciousness of their merely factual origin. There is reason to believe that this aspect of the doctrine, although it looms large in textbooks and contemporaneous politics, is not likely to retain its

---

[1] International lawyers are in the habit of advising—as a remedy calculated to obviate the necessity of recourse to the doctrine *rebus sic stantibus*—the conclusion of treaties limited in time by means of suitable denunciation clauses. But it is seldom realized that—apart from treaties imposed by force and apart from cessions or exchanges of territory—international treaties are almost universally concluded for a limited period. A glance at treaties of commerce, of extradition, of pacific settlement, or of technical unions, will show how universal is this practice. Even the charter of the organized society of States, the Covenant of the League of Nations—is subject to two years' denunciation. See, however, the Treaties of Locarno and the Pact for Renunciation of War, which are not limited in point of time.

present position in international law. It will gradually lose its *raison d'être* in an international society in which the right of recourse to war for the purpose of giving effect to claims is renounced, and whose members have undertaken to respect and to guarantee mutually their political independence and territorial integrity as against external aggression. This is believed to be the tendency, although it is not always easy (in a world in which the legal position, created under what may be called old international law, still displays its full efficacy) to realize the fundamental changes brought about by general conventions like the Covenant of the League of Nations and, to some extent, the Treaty of Renunciation of War.

These developments do not, it is clear, contain a solution of the difficulties created by existing obligations arising out of treaties imposed by force in so far as they are, or may become, unjust and obsolete. But, subject to the exceptions to be discussed presently, the remedy does not lie here with a juridical doctrine capable of application by international tribunals. It lies in the nature of things that the interpretation of a treaty, by reference to the express or implied intention of the parties, one of whom claims the change of circumstances as a reason for the dissolution of the treaty, is hardly applicable to treaties in which the intention of one of the contracting parties was of little consequence, i.e. to treaties imposed by force. The remedy lies with the appropriate political agencies, and above all in an attitude of accommodation and reasonableness on the part of the States concerned—an attitude for the manifestation of which Article 19 of the Covenant may provide a convenient starting-point. It would be prejudicial to the authority of the judicial organs of the international community and its proper function to saddle it with the duty of revising political treaties imposed by force.

§ 11. The Doctrine 'rebus sic stantibus' as a General Principle of Law.

The aspect of the doctrine *rebus sic stantibus* which is, on the one hand, an unavoidable consequence of the admissibility of duress and, on the other hand, an expression of the general weakness of international law *qua* law, does not exhaust the possibilities of the application of the doctrine itself. For, after the extra-legal elements of the doctrine have been eliminated, there still remains in it a legal residuum which, although of a limited compass, is capable of application by a judicial tribunal. The rule that compacts must be kept is certainly one of the bases of the legal relations between the members of any community. But at the same time the notion that in certain cases the law will refuse to continue to give effect to originally valid contracts is common to all systems of jurisprudence. Whether it be the rule *ad impossibilia nemo tenetur* in Roman law;[1] or the various manifestations of the doctrine of frustration or supervening impossibility of performance in English law;[2] or the express reference to changed conditions in the Austrian Civil Code;[3] or Article 323 of the German Civil Code—according to which, if the performance due from one party under a contract becomes impossible in consequence of a circumstance for which neither he nor the other is

---

[1] See, for some examples of *interitus rei* as a ground for release from the obligation, D. 7, 1, 37 ; D. 32, 1, 79, 2; D. 46, 3, 98, 8; D. 45, 1, 91, 1. And see Rabel, 'Origine de la règle impossibilium nulla obligatio' in *Mélanges Gérardin* (1907), pp. 473 et seq.

[2] See McNair, 'War-Time Impossibility of Performance of Contract' in *Essays and Lectures upon some Legal Effects of War* (1920), pp. 78–98, for a lucid discussion of the leading cases and of the tendencies in the last sixty years. See also Fischer Williams, 'Treaties and the Doctrine *rebus sic stantibus*', *Chapters*, pp. 90 ff., and Brierly in *Grotius Society*, ix (1926), pp. 11–20, for a discussion of some more recent cases illustrating the development of the doctrine. Whereas in the leading case of *Taylor* v. *Caldwell* ((1863), 3 B. and S. 826) the supervening impossibility is the physical frustration of the immediate subject-matter of the contract, in the well-known case of *Krell* v. *Henry* ([1903] 2 K.B. 740)—one of the group of the so-called *Coronation Seat* cases—the frustration was held to relate to the object of the transaction as a whole. It was 'the frustration of the adventure', as distinguished from the physical destruction of the subject-matter, which was held to be decisive in this case and in the long series of war-time cases. On the whole there was in Great Britain, as compared with continental countries, less disposition to judicial interference with contracts on account of a change of conditions resulting from the World War. The reason for this is not only the 'sweet reasonableness' of the majority of English business men, who did not insist on their strict contractual rights, but also the fact that the main reason for the difficulties on the Continent, namely, those resulting from depreciation of currency and the revolutionary changes in prices, did not occur in this country. In France a large amount of possible judicial interference was rendered unnecessary in consequence of appropriate legislative enactments (see below, p. 279), but in Germany judicial recognition in this connexion of the doctrine *rebus sic stantibus* was wide and comprehensive (see below, p. 274). As to the United States, see Dodd, 'Impossibility of Performance of Contracts due to War-Time Regulations' in *Harvard Law Review*, xxxii (1918–19), pp. 789–805. And see Holmes, J., in *The Kronprinzessin Cecilie* (244 U.S. 12), in which it was held that the failure of a German ship to deliver a cargo in England was to be excused on the ground that since war was imminent, there was grave danger of the ship being detained.

[3] See, for instance, Article 936 in regard to *pacta de contrahendo*, which lays down that an agreement to conclude a contract in the future is only binding if the circumstances have not in the meantime changed so as to frustrate the express or implied object of the agreement.

responsible, he loses the claim to counter-performance—an article to be read in conjunction with the various provisions of German law permitting the termination of the contract before its fulfilment,[1] and with the practice of German courts of abrogating or remodelling contracts vitally affected by a change of conditions;[2] or, in France, the doctrine of *imprévision* as applied by the French *Conseil d'État*,[3] or specific legislative enactments, like the *loi Failliot* embodying the substance of the doctrine,[4] or the various provisions of the *Code Civil* mitigating the rigour of the contract in case of

---

[1] See, for instance, Article 605 to the effect that the lender may give notice to terminate the loan, if, in consequence of an unforeseen circumstance, he has need of the thing lent; or Article 775 to the effect that the surety can in certain cases ask to be released if the financial condition of the debtor has become substantially worse, or in consequence of some other change in the circumstances of the principal debtor; or Article 542 relating to the termination of a contract of lease. And see, as to the termination of contracts of services, below, p. 276. As to the various aspects of the doctrine *rebus sic stantibus* in Italian law in general, see Vellani, *La revisione dei trattati e i principî generali del diritto* (1930), pp. 143 et seq.

[2] The starting-point of this aspect of the activity of courts has been the apparently rigid Article 305 of the Code which lays down, *inter alia,* that for any alteration of the substance of an obligation a contract between the parties is necessary unless the law provides otherwise. An enormous literature on this Article in relation to the clause *rebus sic stantibus* has appeared in Germany since the World War. Copious references to it, and to the relevant judicial decisions, will be found in Staudinger's *Gesammtnachtrag zur 7/8. Auflage des Kommentars zum Bürgerlichen Gesetzbuch* (1922), pp. 89–94. Of the leading decisions there must be mentioned those of the *Reichsgericht* of 7 June 1921, in which the Court, in affirming its right to modify the terms of the contract, referred to 'the elastic adaptation of the law to economic conditions' as a means of fulfilling its true function of meeting the requirements of the time (*Entscheidungen in Zivilsachen*, cii. 94. See also ibid., cvii. 78, decision of 28 November 1923).

[3] See the well-known *Bordeaux Gas* case decided on 30 March 1916, *Sirey* (1916), iii. 17, and the decision of 27 June 1919, *Sirey* (1920), iii. 25. See also Hauriou, *Précis de droit administratif et de droit public,* 11th ed. (1927), pp. 813–17; Fyot, *Essai d'une justification nouvelle de la théorie de l'imprévision* (1921); Voirin, *L'Imprévision dans les rapports de droit privé* (1922); Bruzin, *Essai sur la notion d'imprévision et sur son rôle en matière contractuelle* (1922) (with reference, *inter alia,* to the doctrine *rebus sic stantibus* in international law). And see Radoïkovitch, *La Révision de traités et le Pacte de la Société des Nations* (1930), an able monograph conspicuous for its reliance on the notion of *imprévision*. But it will be noted that, notwithstanding the insistent advocacy by writers, courts, to a large extent relieved of this task by the legislature, refuse to recognize the doctrine. See the decision of the Court of Cassation of 10 March 1919, *Sirey* (1920), i. 104, and of 6 June 1921, *Sirey* (1921), i. 193, and *Dalloz* (1921), i. 73. See also, to the same effect, Gyuot in vol. ii of the 13th edition of the treatise of Baudry-Lacantinerie (1925), § 141, who discusses the matter in detail, and Planiol, *Traité élémentaire de droit civil* (10th ed. by Ripert, 1926), ii, § 1168 *bis*. But see Page in *La Belgique Judiciaire,* 1924, columns 367–83, for a learned and lucid advocacy of the doctrine. However, the Belgian courts also have refused to recognize the doctrine, on the ground that it was for the legislature to redress the inconvenience occasioned by depreciation of currency.

[4] See below, p. 279.

non-fulfilment of the obligation for reasons independent of the debtor[1]—all these rules and doctrines show clearly that, although the protection of the right to rely upon the contract is fundamental, there is nevertheless a relatively small segment of cases in which the law will recognize that the contract has, as the result of an unforeseen change of circumstances, failed to realize the true will of the parties and that it cannot be maintained wholly or in part. The *sedes materiae* of the effect of a change of conditions on legal obligations is not limited to the formula of physical or moral impossibility of performance. Elements of it will be found in the *exceptio non adimpleti contractus* in Roman law or the various *condictiones*, in particular of the *exceptio causa data causa non secuta*; in the rules as to unjust enrichment, clearly expressed in the Roman law *condictiones*,[2] in specific provisions of some continental codes,[3] in the practice of French courts,[4] and even—in a somewhat rudimentary form—in English law;[5] in the doctrine

---

[1] See, for instance, Article 1148 of the *Code Civil*, according to which damages or interest are not payable if *vis major* or inevitable accident have prevented the debtor from complying with his obligation; or Article 1150, which lays down that the debtor is liable only for such damage as was foreseen, or might have been foreseen, provided that the obligation had not been broken by his own fault. The rigidity of Article 1134, which says that agreements cannot be revoked except by mutual consent or for reasons permitted by law, is tempered by the rule that agreements must be carried out in good faith, and by the provision of Article 1135 to the effect that the agreement binds the parties not only to what is directly stated therein, but also to all the consequences of the obligation implied by equity, custom, and law. See on this point Naquet in *Sirey* (1920), i. 105; Page, op. cit.; and Ripert, *La Règle morale dans les obligations civiles* (1905), Nos. 75 et seq.

[2] Probably the general maxim 'Jure naturae aequum est neminem cum alterius detrimento et injuria fieri locupletiorem (D. 50, 17, 206)' might be regarded as the broadest basis for this and similar doctrines.

[3] See, e.g., Article 832 of the German Code; Article 62 of the Swiss Code; Article 1119 of the Italian Code; Article 1261 of the Spanish Code.

[4] See Baudry-Lacantinerie, op. cit., ii, Nos. 689 et seq.; Planiol, op. cit., ii, Nos. 932 et seq. Although the *Code Civil* contains a number of provisions applying the doctrine in specific cases (see Articles 548, 554, 555, 1241, 1846, 1926), it was left to the practice of courts and to writers to develop it as a general doctrine. See Planiol's Note in *Dalloz*, 1891, and Ripert, ibid. (1912), i. 217. See also Renard in *Revue trimestrielle* (1920), p. 243, and Gérota, *Enrichisse-ment sans cause* (1925).

[5] It would be of interest to establish the relation between the remedy of *assumpsit*, in particular in regard to money paid for a consideration which has totally failed, and the doctrine, which has no distinct place in English law, of unjust enrichment. In 1760 Lord Mansfield in *Moses* v. *Macfarlane* (2 Burr. 1005) formulated clearly the remedy of *indebitatus assumpsit* which 'lies for money paid by mistake, or upon a consideration which happens to fail; or for money got through imposition, or extortion, or oppression, or an undue advantage taken of the plaintiff's situation'. References to *Moses* v. *Macfarlane* have now disappeared from most of the text-books. But see Friedmann, *Die Bereicherungshaftung im anglo-amerikanischen Rechtskreis in Vergleichung mit dem deutschen*

of *laesio enormis* of Roman law and the similar rules of other systems;[1] in the branches of law regulating the contract of services,[2] and the relation of partnership;[3] in the rules limiting the freedom of persons to dispose of their future property;[4] and even in the provisions as to revocability of gifts.[5] Some of these rules are found in some systems of law while they are absent in others. But their cumulative effect is to give expression to the fact that the law, in some form or other, takes cognizance of the change of conditions subsequent to the creation of the obligation.

§ 12. The Scope and Limitations of the Judicial Application of the Doctrine 'rebus sic stantibus'.

The rule *pacta sunt servanda* is a general principle of law. But so, as we have seen, is the refusal to enforce contracts whose purpose has become impossible of fulfilment, not only physically but in general, having regard to the object of the transaction. In some systems of law the emphasis is upon the frustrated common

---

bürgerlichen Recht (1930), for a scholarly and interesting attempt to demonstrate that the notion of unjust enrichment is not foreign to the law of England and that it is a notion common to most systems of jurisprudence. The common law does not countenance the retaining of advantages 'against equity and good conscience'. Mistake and failure of consideration are the basic elements of this aspect of quasi-contracts. Possibly, the relation between them and the doctrine of frustration is not unduly remote. Dr. McNair has suggested, in the fourth edition of Oppenheim (i. 753, n. 3), that 'the basis of the doctrine of frustration is probably mistake'.

[1] It will be noted that a number of international lawyers regard the notion of *laesio enormis* as the basis of the doctrine *rebus sic stantibus*. See G. F. de Martens, *Précis du droit des gens de l'Europe*, 2nd ed. (1864), ii. 166, and others referred to by Radoïkovitch, op. cit., pp. 117–32.

[2] See, for instance, Article 626 of the German Civil Code to the effect that, if a grave reason exists, the notice to terminate the service relation may be given by either party without observance of any terms of notice; or Article 624 to the effect that if the service is entered into for the lifetime of a person, or for a term longer than five years, notice of its termination may be given by the servant after the lapse of five years. And see *Boast* v. *Firth*, L.R., 4 C.P. 1, on the termination of the contract as the result of the permanent illness of the servant, and *Robinson* v. *Davison*, L.R. 6 Ex. 269. See, generally, Fry on *Specific Performance*, 6th ed. (1921), pp. 428–34, on the effect of events subsequent to the contract. And see a recent case, *Graves* v. *Cohen* (1930), 46 T.L.R., in which it was held that a contract by a jockey to ride the horses of an owner is dissolved by the death of the owner.

[3] See for the English law as to dissolution of partnership on the ground of permanent incapacity, conduct injurious to the business, and destruction of mutual confidence, the cases referred to in Lindley on *Partnership* (9th ed. 1924), pp. 688–94. And see Article 723 of the German Code to the effect that, if a grave reason exists, a partnership entered into for a fixed period may be dissolved before the expiration of that period.

[4] Ibid., Article 310, rendering void a contract whereby one party binds himself to convey his future property.

[5] Ibid., Article 530.

will of the parties, in others upon the impossibility, physical or other, of performance. Legal theory oscillates between the two tests. As a rule, inasmuch as it is based upon the failure of an implied condition, it is a combination of the two. The impossibility of performance so construed must necessarily remain a rare occurrence, because the inconvenience to the debtor, and the disappointment of his expectations as the result of a change of circumstances, constitute only one element in the process of interpretation. The other is supplied by the insistence of the law on giving effect to the legitimate expectations of the other contracting party. However, the very fact that, when a relevant change of circumstances arises, the law does not ignore it entirely, tends to increase the sanctity of the contract and to relieve the tension between the conflicting claims of change and stability.[1]

It appears thus that the effect of the doctrine *rebus sic stantibus* as usually propounded in text-books has been doubly pernicious. Not only has it introduced an element of disintegration into conventional international law, but also, as the result of its sweeping comprehensiveness, it has rendered inoperative that residuum of the doctrine which constitutes a general principle of law to be found in most legal systems. This residuum is small but, as shown, it is not without importance. Whenever it occurs it is pre-eminently suitable for judicial adjudication. Moreover, however small, it cannot properly be given effect except through the instrumentality of an impartial judicial agency eliminating the element of arbitrariness, which is necessarily involved in the faculty of a unilateral declaration of the interested party that a decisive change of circumstances has taken place. In international law the fact that the ascertainment of the change of circumstances and of the voidance of the contract have been, in the absence of a compulsory jurisdiction of international tribunals, left to the appreciation of the interested party, has not only prevented the doctrine from acquiring the authority of a generally recognized rule of positive law, but has gained for it a notoriety illustrating one of the weakest links in international law.

A recent decision given on 29 June 1925 by a quasi-international tribunal, the German *Staatsgerichtshof*, in the case

---

[1] 'Security may demand that he who does not get his due under a bilateral contract may put himself on the defensive and himself not perform'—Demogue, op. cit., p. 450.

of *Bremen* v. *Prussia*, illustrates well the possibilities and the limitations of the doctrine *rebus sic stantibus* in international law. In a treaty concluded in 1904 the two States exchanged certain portions of territory. One of the objects of the transaction was to enable Bremen to acquire land for the purpose of constructing ports and other navigation works. It was laid down in the treaty that in the territory ceded to Bremen no works connected with the fishing industry should be permitted. As a result of the World War the aspirations of Bremen in regard to shipping were frustrated for a number of reasons, and she asked, therefore, while appealing to the doctrine *rebus sic stantibus*, for a rescission of the onerous condition imposing limitations upon her in regard to fisheries. The Court, while professing to administer rules of international law and while recognizing in principle the admissibility of the doctrine, declined to apply it in the case before it. It declined to do so on the ground that the restrictive clauses of the treaty formed, in the contemplation of Prussia, an essential and determining element of the transaction, and that they could not therefore be abrogated without her consent. At the same time the Court pointed out that, although there was no room for the application of the doctrine in regard to the major issue, the Court was prepared to consider it in respect of possible modifications of the provisions of the treaty relating to the payment of certain sums or to the observance of time limits fixed therein.[1] It is seldom that one case illustrates so clearly the essential elements and the limitations of the application of a juridical doctrine. The case between Bremen and Prussia shows the recognition in principle of the doctrine *rebus sic stantibus*; it shows that its recognition in principle does not mean that

---

[1] *Entscheidungen des Reichsgerichts in Zivilsachen*, cxxii, Appendix, p. 21, and *Annual Digest*, 1925–6, Case No. 266. In fact, in those few instances in which the doctrine has been invoked before international tribunals, there has been no disposition to reject it outright. But one of the parties denied that it applied in the individual case. See, for instance, the recent decision of the Swiss Federal Court in *Thurgau* v. *St. Gallen*, of 10 February 1928 (*Entscheidungen des Bundesgerichts*, liv. i. 188, and *Annual Digest*, 1927–8, Case No. 289) in which the Court refused to apply the doctrine on the ground, *inter alia*, that the circumstances invoked as new were trifling. Similarly in the *Russian Indemnity* case, decided on 11 November 1912 by the Permanent Court of Arbitration (Scott, *Hague Court Reports*, pp. 317, 318), when Turkey pleaded that a change of conditions in the form of *force majeure* justified a delay in the payment of an agreed indemnity, the Tribunal was prepared to admit that the exception of *force majeure* may be pleaded in public international law, 'as international law must adapt itself to political necessities'. But it denied that the circumstances were such as seriously to prevent Turkey from fulfilling her obligation.

every change of conditions, or every disappointment of the hopes of one of the parties, constitute a good reason for avoiding the treaty; but it shows at the same time that the inability of a court to apply it in regard to the contract as a whole does not preclude the possibility of its application in respect of the various aspects of the execution of the contract.

Possibly it could be argued that international tribunals may be permitted, and ought to avail themselves of, a larger measure of latitude than municipal courts in taking into consideration changes of circumstances resulting in the frustration or the substantial alteration of the object of the contractual obligation. For in municipal law there is the legislature at hand which may interfere with existing contracts in a manner in which courts may feel reluctant to act. It is this very possibility of legislative interference which frequently inspires courts with an amount of caution which would dangerously approach injustice but for the fact that the legislature may be ultimately counted upon to redress the balance. This may be well seen from the way in which Belgian and French courts refused to apply the doctrine of *imprévision*—a variation of the doctrine of frustration—to contracts affected by changes of circumstances as the result of war. Thus it was left in France to a legislative enactment, the well-known *loi Failliot* of 21 January 1918, to lay down that commercial contracts concluded during the War, or three months after the armistice, may be dissolved at the request of one of the parties if it is established that, by reason of the state of war, the fulfilment of the obligation by one of the contracting parties will impose burdens, or cause damage, materially in excess of the reasonable estimate at the time of the conclusion of the contract.[1] A multitude of special enactments incorporated the principle of the doctrine in other fields of economic relations.[2] But there is no legislature in the international society, and international tribunals may there feel constrained, in order to give effect to the intention of the parties and to requirements of justice, to exercise more discretion in taking into consideration relevant changes in conditions. As has been shown in the case of *Bremen* v. *Prussia*, this discretion need not necessarily take the form of rescinding the obligation as a whole; it may consist in the

---

[1] *S. et P.*, Lois annotées (1919), p. 892.
[2] See Planiol, op.cit., ii, No. 170 *bis*.

modification of the manner of its fulfilment and in its adaptation to new conditions. Thus, for instance, in regard to pecuniary debts, the Court, while maintaining the principal obligation, might decree modifications in the mode of payment[1] by fixing the instalments, interest, and periods of payment. In regard to so-called 'state servitudes' the Court might, while leaving the servitude as such intact, take into consideration material changes in circumstances with a view to modifying the details of its execution. The function of English courts in regard to charitable trusts offers a suggestive analogy.[2]

§ 13. The Justiciability of Disputes Involving the Application of the Doctrine 'rebus sic stantibus'.

The application of the doctrine *rebus sic stantibus* in its juridical aspect is essentially a legal matter. The circumstance that it involves the consideration of facts does not, of course, deprive it of this character. The bulk of judicial activity within the State is to determine the legal relevance of facts. From this point

---

[1] On the meaning of 'mode of payment' see Fischer Williams, *Chapters*, p. 322.

[2] See, on the power of the Court to alter a scheme settled by it for the administration of a charity 'if the lapse of time and change of circumstances' make such an alteration necessary in the interest of the charity, Halsbury, *The Laws of England*, iv. 187 et seq. And see ibid., pp. 190 et seq., on the *cy-près* doctrine and its application. See also Section 84 of the English Law of Property Act, 1925, which confers power upon Official Arbitrators appointed for the purposes of the Acquisition of Land Act of 1919 (see s.-s. 11) described as 'the Authority' 'on the application of any person interested in any freehold land affected by any restriction arising under covenant or otherwise as to the user thereof or the building thereon, by order wholly or partially to discharge or modify any such restriction . . . on being satisfied: (*a*) That by reason of change in the character of the property or the neighbourhood or other circumstance of the case which the authority may deem material, the restrictive right be deemed obsolete, or that the continued existence thereof would impede the reasonable user of the land for public or private purposes without securing practical benefits to other persons, or would unless modified so impede such user.'

For the jurisdiction of the Court of Chancery apart from this provision see *Bedford (Duke of)* v. *British Museum* (1822), 2 Myl. and K. 552; *German* v. *Chapman* (1877), 7 Ch. D. 271; *Knight* v. *Simmonds*, [1896] 2 Ch. 294; *Sobey* v. *Sainsbury*, [1913] 2 Ch. 513, where the earlier cases were reviewed by Sargant, J., who held that even if there had been no implied release of the right to take proceedings to enforce the covenant, the Court was entitled 'also to take into account the general change in the character of the neighbourhood irrespective of the particular acts and omissions of the plaintiff and his predecessor in title'. He then proceeded to point out that but for this, the effect would have been 'to stereotype and perpetuate, far beyond the real intentions of the contracting parties, and to the prejudice of successive generations, restrictions which had in the course of time become obsolete and meaningless' (at pp. 529, 530). See also James, L.J., in *German* v. *Chapman*, 7 Ch. D. 271 at 279; and especially Lindley, L.J., in *Knight* v. *Simmonds*, [1896] 2 Ch. 294 at 297.

of view the Permanent Court of International Justice would be entitled to deal with any matter involving the application of the doctrine *rebus sic stantibus* under that provision of Article 36 of its Statute which entrusts it with deciding 'any question of international law'. Under that clause the Court is competent to ascertain and to decide on the relevancy of any fact or set of facts which are claimed to be creative of international rights and duties. For the phrase that the Court has to decide 'any question of international law' cannot mean that it has no jurisdiction (except in regard to international delinquencies) whenever a question of fact is raised. In the consideration of facts claimed to call for an application of the doctrine *rebus sic stantibus*, it will not as a rule be the facts which will be disputed; what will be disputed is the question whether they justify the application of the doctrine *rebus sic stantibus*. There is no good reason for interpreting the expression 'any question of international law' as meaning *ex cathedra* decisions on theoretical questions usually discussed by international lawyers, for instance, on the question whether the doctrine *rebus sic stantibus* forms part of international law.

It is true that Article 36 of the Statute refers specifically to 'the existence of any fact which, if established, would constitute a breach of any international obligation', but that does not mean that the consideration of other facts is excluded from the purview of the Court.[1] Article 36 of the Statute abounds in such repetitions *ex abundanti cautela*. It confers upon the Court jurisdiction in disputes both 'as to the interpretation of a treaty' and 'as to any question of international law', although it is clear that the first category is comprehensively covered by the second. Most probably the three remaining categories of disputes are covered by the one relating to 'any question of international law' which, in turn, covers all possible disputes which States are content to submit to an international judicial tribunal. However that may be, some of the judgements of the Permanent Court of International Justice show that there is no disposition on the part of the Court to give a one-sided restrictive interpretation of the various categories enumerated in Article 36 of the Statute

---

[1] See, however, Fischer Williams, *Chapters*, pp. 40, 41, and 100, 101, who gives a somewhat limited interpretation to the two clauses of Article 36 discussed above, and who maintains that the Permanent Court would not, under this Article, have jurisdiction to decide whether there has taken place such a material change of circumstances as to render a treaty obsolete.

and Article 13 of the Covenant. In Judgement No. 14, in which
the Court was asked in the Special Agreement to decide, *inter
alia*, whether the Government of the Kingdom of the Serbs,
Croats, and Slovenes was entitled to effect the service of certain
loans in paper francs or whether it was under an obligation to
pay the amounts due in gold or in foreign currencies, the
question was raised whether the Court had jurisdiction to decide
a dispute said to involve no question of international law, but
only one of interpreting private law contracts under municipal
law.[1] The Court held that the clause conferring upon it jurisdiction in disputes concerning 'the existence of any fact which, if
established, would constitute a breach of an international obligation' was sufficient to cover the case in hand, 'for the States
concerned may agree that the fact to be established would
constitute a breach of an international obligation', and because
'the facts the existence of which the Court has to establish may
be of any kind'.[2] This interpretation by the Court of the phrase
'the existence of any fact which, if established, would constitute
a breach of an international obligation' goes a good way towards
dispelling the doubts to which this passage has given rise. It
shows that the question whether a dispute can be brought within
the clause discussed here is mainly one of terminology. Thus the
disputed question, whether there has taken place a change of
circumstances sufficient to justify the termination of a treaty, can
well be put within the frame of the question whether the fact that a
State claims the termination of a treaty on this ground, constitutes
(having regard to the circumstances of the case) a breach of
an international obligation. Other cases in which the Permanent
Court had to interpret provisions analogous to those contained
in Article 36 of the Statute show that a too literal construction may not be altogether sound or likely to secure the approval
of the Court.[3] That aspect of the doctrine *rebus sic stantibus*

---

[1] For a statement of the objections to the jurisdiction of the Court in this
case see the Dissenting Opinion of Judge Pessôa, *P.C.I.J.*, Series A, No. 14,
pp. 62–5.

[2] Ibid., p. 19.

[3] In Judgements Nos. 6 and 7 concerning certain German interests in
Polish Upper Silesia the Court held that a convention conferring upon it
jurisdiction in regard to 'differences of opinion, resulting from the interpretation
and application' of some of its provisions, made it competent to decide whether a
breach of these provisions had taken place. In Judgement No. 8 it held that that
clause also conferred upon it jurisdiction to decide differences in regard to compensation claimed for the violation of these provisions. It referred to its Judgements Nos. 6 and 7 and, arguing *a majore ad minus*, it pointed out that 'the
decision whether there has been a breach of an engagement involves no doubt

which represents a general principle of law ought to, and can, have a place in judicial settlement of international disputes. Within its necessarily limited scope it may prove a useful instrument for adjusting contractual obligations to changed conditions.

§ 14. So-called Inter-temporal Law. Changes in the Law and Continuance of Rights.

In certain cases rights may cease to be effective as the result of the development of new rules of law attaching conditions of the continued validity of these rights. The possibilities of this mode of adapting existing rights to new conditions have been given expression in the award given by Professor Huber in April 1928 in the *Island of Palmas* arbitration between the United States and Holland. The United States claimed sovereignty over the island on the ground, *inter alia*, of its discovery by Spain in the first half of the sixteenth century. There seemed to be agreement between the parties to the dispute that the effects of the discovery by Spain must be judged in the light of contemporary law, i.e. the law in the matter of acquisition of title by discovery as it obtained in the sixteenth century. However,

---

a more important jurisdiction than a decision as to the nature or extent of reparation due for a breach of an international engagement the existence of which is already established' (Series A, No. 9, p. 23). The Court refused to attach decisive importance to the fact that Article 13 of the Covenant and Article 36 of its Statute differentiate between the various categories of these disputes (ibid.).

In the Chinese-Belgian dispute, concerning Belgian exterritoriality rights in China, Belgium maintained that the Court was competent to decide under Article 36 of the Statute the question as to the applicability of the doctrine *rebus sic stantibus*. *Belgian Mémoire* of 3 January 1927, *P.C.I.J.*, Series C, No. 16 (1), p. 22: 'C'est à la Cour permanente de Justice internationale que doit être soumise, en dernier ressort, une contestation qui surgirait relativement à l'application du principe *rebus sic stantibus* entre deux États signataires tous deux de la clause facultative de compétence. Ne s'agit-il pas, en effet, suivant la théorie la plus généralement admise, d'une clause tacite contenue dans les conventions internationales conclues sans limitation de durée, et dont l'interprétation est dès lors éminemment de la compétence de la Cour? Il est donc loisible au Gouvernement chinois de tenter devant la Cour permanente de Justice internationale la démonstration que les circonstances qui ont inspiré les clauses du Traité de 1865 relatives à l'exterritorialité ont subi une transformation tellement radicale qu'une abrogation complète s'impose.' In the French-Swiss Free Zones dispute (which, however, did not come before the Court by virtue of the Optional Clause) Switzerland did not in principle deny the right of the Court to apply the doctrine *rebus sic stantibus*. She only maintained that the *clausula* does not apply to international servitudes. See the speech of Professor Logoz, *P.C.I.J.*, Series C, No. 19 (1), pp. 196–9. The Chinese Government denied the jurisdiction of the Court, not on the ground that the consideration of the doctrine *rebus sic stantibus* did not come within the purview of the Optional Clause, but because the dispute involved highly political and important matters of State sovereignty and equality. See above, p. 200.

while prepared to assume that, as contended by the United States, mere symbolical discovery conferred at that time territorial sovereignty, he refused to agree that the title thus acquired continued irrespective of the changes which international law underwent on this subject in the following two and a half centuries. He said:

> 'As regards the question which of different legal systems prevailing at successive periods is to be applied in a particular case (the so-called inter-temporal law), a distinction must be made between the creation of rights and the existence of rights. The same principle which subjects the act creative of a right to the law in force at the time the right arises, demands that the existence of the right, in other words its continued manifestation, shall follow the conditions required by the evolution of law.'

He pointed out that under the present rules of international law requiring effectiveness of occupation as an essential condition of acquisition of sovereignty, it was impossible to recognize the Spanish title as subsisting in the eighteenth and nineteenth centuries, even if it could be assumed that mere discovery was sufficient to confer the original title.[1]

The award, which established a distinction between the creation and the continuance of rights, constitutes a clear departure from the views expressed on this subject by a number of international lawyers.[2] The conception of intertemporal law as applied by the arbitrator reveals yet another aspect of the relation between the factors of change and stability. Whereas the questions discussed in other parts of this chapter illustrated the effect of changed conditions on treaties, the award in the *Island of Palmas* arbitration shows the possible effects of a change in the customary rules of international law on existing legal rights in general. International tribunals have not so far had frequent opportunity to apply the doctrine of inter-temporal law. But it has been suggested by Lammasch, in another connexion, that if, for instance, a tribunal had to decide upon a claim for damages arising out of interference with slave traffic at a time when it was not generally condemned by international law, it would be entitled to base its decision on the law as existing at the time

---

[1] See pp. 26 and 27 of the original award, and *Annual Digest*, 1927–8, Case No. 1.

[2] See Heimburger, *Der Erwerb der Gebietshoheit* (1888), i. 139; Westlake, *International Law* (2nd ed., 1910), i. 114; and Strupp, *Der schwedisch-norwegische Grenzstreit*, in Schücking, *Das Werk von Haag*, Part II (1917), pp. 114 et seq.

of the award.[1] On two specific occasions the arbitration agreement provided that the award shall be given according to the rules of international law existing at the time of the events complained of,[2] but it appears that these provisions had reference to subsequent changes in conventional international law.[3]

---

[1] *Schiedsgerichtsbarkeit*, p. 179. But see Lapradelle and Politis, i. 683.

[2] Arbitration Agreement between the United States and Haiti in the case of *Pelletier* and *Lazare*, Moore, ii. 1750; and see Arbitration Agreement of 8 September 1900, between the United States and Russia in the cases of the *Cape Horn Pigeon, J. H. Lewis and others*, Lafontaine, p. 618.

[3] See Westlake, op. cit., p. 114, note, *in fine*.

CHAPTER XIV
THE DOCTRINE OF ABUSE OF RIGHTS AS AN INSTRUMENT OF CHANGE

§ 15. History of the Doctrine. Although as yet unknown in text-books of international law, the doctrine of abuse of rights has recently attracted the attention of international lawyers.[1] The essence of the doctrine is that, as legal rights are conferred by the community, the latter cannot countenance their anti-social use by individuals; that the exercise of a hitherto legal right becomes unlawful when it degenerates into an abuse of rights; and that there is such an abuse of rights each time the general interest of the community is injuriously affected as the result of the sacrifice of an important social or individual interest to a less important, though hitherto legally recognized, individual right. For the determination of such abuse of rights the question of subjective fault and intention may, but need not always, be material. It is easy to see why the doctrine thus conceived can be regarded as one of great potentialities in the process of judicial legislation adjusting the law to new conditions and preventing unfair or anti-social use of rights. In many cases the use of a right degenerates into a socially reprehensible abuse of right, not because of the sinister intention of the person exercising the right, but owing to the fact that, as the

---

[1] In particular, Professor Politis has treated it systematically in a series of lectures given in July 1925 at The Hague Academy of International Law under the title 'Le problème des limitations de la souveraineté et la théorie de l'abus des droits dans les rapports internationaux'. *Recueil des Cours*, 1925 (i), pp. 1–109. In these lectures, after drawing attention to certain limitations upon State sovereignty in modern international law and to the tendencies restricting the field of the so-called exclusive jurisdiction (*domaine réservé*), he attempted to show that the doctrine of *abus des droits* as applied by French courts and developed in detail by French writers constitutes a general principle of law which as such has a place in international law and is capable of application by international tribunals. See, e.g., Borel and Politis in *Annuaire*, xxxiii (2) (1927), pp. 750–5; Le Fur, ibid., pp. 786–8; Spiropoulos, *Die allgemeinen Rechtsgrundsätze im Völkerrecht* (1928), pp. 35–8; Boeck in *Recueil des Cours*, 1927 (iii), pp. 627–40; Leibholz, 'Das Verbot der Willkür und des Ermessensmissbrauches im völkerrechtlichen Verkehr,' in *Z.f.a.ö.R. und V.*, i (1) (1929), pp. 76–125; Stowell, *International Law* (1930), pp. 122, 137, 143, 171, 376, 380; Scerni, *L'abuso del diritto nei rapporti internazionali* (1930). And see for frequent references to *abus des droits* in international law Josserand, *De l'esprit des lois et de leur relativité; Théorie de l'abus de droit* (1927), especially pp. 250–62. But see Cavaglieri, *Nuovi studi sull'intervento* (1928), pp. 42–52, who rejects the application of the doctrine in international law on the ground that it is a purely natural law conception and that it is ill-suited to the individualistic character of international law.

result of social changes unaccompanied by corresponding developments in the law, an assertion of a right grounded in the existing law becomes mischievous and intolerable. The time is then ripe for judicial 'manufacturing of a new tort'[1]—a process, that is to say, which destroys the hitherto recognized freedom of action and creates a new right to legal protection from injurious interference. It is easy to see why in international society, in which there is no authoritative legislative machinery adapting the law to changed conditions, there may be both frequent occasion and imperative necessity for the judicial creation of new torts through the express or implied recognition of a principle postulating the prohibition of abuse of rights.

In fact, the view that the prerogatives of State sovereignty do not imply an unrestricted and indiscriminate use of formal rights has been expressed by many international lawyers of distinction. In 1896 Heilborn, in his *System des Völkerrechts*,[2] discussed the application to international relations of the conception of abuse of rights. Although, under the influence of the current attitude of scepticism towards analogies of private law, he admitted some hesitation in introducing it *eo nomine* into international law, he adopted it in substance. We find Westlake saying that 'no principle is more firmly established in the science of law than that which says to an owner *sic utere tuo ut alienum non laedas*'.[3] Professor Hyde has urged that 'the society of nations may at any time conclude that acts which an individual State was previously deemed to possess the right to commit without external interference, are so injurious to the world at large as to justify the imposition of fresh restrictions'.[4] A large part of the law of intervention is built upon the principle that obvious abuse of rights of internal sovereignty, in disregard of the obligations to foreign States and fundamental duties of humanity in relation to the State's own population, constitutes a good legal ground for dictatorial interference.[5] We find Ullmann pointing out that intervention is necessary, seeing that national law does not provide a remedy against abuse of rights,[6] or, again, Heilborn saying that the purpose

---

[1] See Winfield in *Columbia Law Review*, xxvii (1927), p. II.

[2] (1896), pp. 358–61.

[3] *International Law*, 1st ed. (1907), ii. 322. The statement refers to the right of the belligerent to use floating mines.

[4] Op. cit., i (1922), p. 85.   [5] See Hyde, op. cit., i. 118.

[6] *Völkerrecht* (revised ed., 1908), p. 461.

of intervention is to prevent *summum jus* from becoming *summa injuria*.[1]

§ 16. The Practice of International Tribunals.

Recently the doctrine of *abus des droits* seems to have secured some measure of recognition on the part of the Permanent Court of International Justice which has twice had occasion to refer to it in its judgements. In Judgement No. 7, in the case concerning certain German interests in Polish Upper Silesia, the Court was, *inter alia*, called upon to answer the question whether Article 256 of the Treaty of Versailles, which provided that the Powers to which German territory is ceded shall acquire all property and possessions situated therein belonging to the German Empire or to the German States, precluded Germany from disposing of her property from the day of the coming into force of the Treaty until the transfer of sovereignty over Upper Silesia in accordance with Article 88 of the Treaty. The Court held that Germany retained the right to dispose of her property until the actual transfer of sovereignty. Yet it qualified this permissive rule by saying that 'only a misuse of this right [*abus de ce droit*] could endow an act of alienation with the character of a breach of the Treaty'.[2] The Court added that 'such misuse cannot be presumed' and that 'it rests with the party who states that there has been such misuse to prove this statement'. The same terms were used in the Court's Order of 6 December 1930 in the case between Switzerland and France concerning the free zones of Upper Savoy and the district of Gex.[3] In this case the Court, while agreeing that, by virtue of certain international obligations entered into in 1815, France was prevented from levying at the political frontier duties on the importation and exportation of goods coming to and from France, rejected the Swiss contention that the duty to withdraw the customs-frontier behind the political frontier also implied the obligation not to levy duties and taxes other than those on the importation or exportation of goods. The Court held that, subject to specific obligations, France was entitled to apply her fiscal legislation in the territory of the free zones in the same manner as in any other part of French territory. But it added the *caveat* that 'a reservation must be made as regards the cases of abuses of a right [*pour le cas d'abus de*

---

[1] Loc. cit. For a number of other references see Cavaglieri, op. cit., p. 44.
[2] Series A, No. 7, p. 30.   [3] Series A, No. 24.

droit]'.[1] As in Judgement No. 7, the Court added that such an abuse of rights could not be presumed.

However, long before the doctrine of abuse of rights had been introduced, international tribunals applied it in substance in a number of cases. Their attitude towards the alleged right of expelling aliens at the absolute discretion of the receiving State may be mentioned as an instructive example. That there exists such an absolute right has been maintained by many a writer. Thus, for instance, Oppenheim maintains that a State can expel every alien according to discretion,[2] and that the expulsion of an alien without just cause cannot constitute a legal wrong.[3] It would be difficult to find a confirmation of this view in the practice of international tribunals which have been frequently called upon to adjudicate claims for wrongful and indiscriminate expulsion. In the great majority of cases, while admitting the general right of the State to expel aliens, international tribunals stressed at the same time the limitations of this right either in regard to the expulsion itself or to the procedure accompanying it. 'The country exercising the power of expulsion must, when occasion demands, state the reason of such expulsion before an international tribunal, and an inefficient reason or none being advanced, accept the consequences', said the arbitrator in a learned award in the *Boffolo* case.[4] The same principle has been expressed in a number of other awards,[5] either directly or indirectly, in the form of a refusal to grant compensation when there had been a clear reason for expulsion, for instance when the alien had taken part in subversive activities.[6] The conspicuous feature of these awards is the view that the undoubted right of expulsion degenerates into an abuse of rights whenever an alien who has been allowed to take up residence in the country, to establish his business and set up a home, is expelled without just reason, and that such an abuse of rights constitutes a wrong involving the duty of reparation. The same attitude has been adopted by some international tribunals in regard to the duties of States in connexion with

---

[1] Ibid., p. 12. See also, to the same effect, the final judgement in this case given on 7 June 1932, *P.C.I.J.*, Series A/B, No. 46, p. 167.   [2] i. p. 279.

[3] pp. 561, 562.   [4] Ralston, *Venezuelan Arbitrations of 1903*, pp. 696, 705.

[5] The *Oliva* case, ibid., p. 771; *Paquet case*, ibid., p. 265; *Ferman* case, Moore, p. 3348, and see ibid., pp. 3334–59 for a number of other cases. See for a survey of these cases, Ralston, Nos. 515–24; Politis, op. cit., pp. 101–8; Boeck, loc. cit.

[6] The *San Pedro* case, Moore, p. 3354. See also the *Maal* case, Ralston, *Venezuelan Arbitrations*, p. 914.

the closure of their ports to foreign commerce. While the right to decree such closure has never been questioned, it was held that the closing of ports without due notice to those regularly admitted to them constitutes a wrong which entails the duty of reparation. This was the award rendered on 30 November 1843 by the King of Prussia in the dispute between Great Britain and France concerning the blockade and the closure of the ports on the coast of Portendic in the French colony of Senegal.[1]

Disapproval of the anti-social use of rights has been voiced even in cases in which regard for the rights of State sovereignty appears to have been the decisive consideration. This may well be seen from the *Faber* case concerning the closing of the ports of the Catatumbo and Zulia rivers by Venezuela. Duffield, Umpire, who otherwise spoke a very Austinian language on the nature of international law,[2] and refused to question the right of the State to prohibit navigation on rivers which flow to the sea, nevertheless qualified his attitude by adding the phrases 'temporarily' and 'if necessary to the peace, safety, and convenience of her own citizens'.[3] He hastened to add that the State must be the sole judge whether the closure is so necessary, and that its decision must be final and not admitting of review. But he thought it necessary to point out 'that a case for the exercise of this discretion did exist is obvious', and his final pronouncement referred to the lawfulness of the closure 'under the circumstances which existed at the time'.[4]

§ 17. The Practice of Quasi-international Tribunals. The

---

[1] See for the award Lapradelle and Politis, i. 525, and generally on the whole case, ibid., pp. 512–44. However, see above, p. 96, on the award of the President of Chile in the dispute concerning the closure of Buenos Ayres. Cavaglieri, op. cit., p. 51, expresses the opinion that the award in the *Portendic* case can hardly be regarded as an affirmation of the doctrine of abuse of rights. In his view, the wrong consisted in the failure to comply with the duty of proper notification, a duty the existence of which a large number of international lawyers had previously assumed by analogy with the duty of notification of a war-blockade. Professor Cavaglieri's objection does not seem to the writer to be convincing. It does in effect amount to saying that the prohibition of the abuse of an otherwise uncontested right was established, not by the arbitrator in question, but by the previous consensus of international opinion.

[2] Ralston, *Venezuelan Arbitrations*, p. 555.   [3] Ibid., p. 626.

[4] Ibid. See also Nys in *R.I.*, 2nd ser., v (1930), p. 517. See also the *David J. Adams* case decided on 9 December 1921 by the British-American Claims Commission (Nielsen's *Report*, p. 526), in which the Tribunal considered and attached importance to the question whether this was a case 'of a sudden and unexpected change of a government's conduct towards a foreigner suddenly surprised by that change'.

most numerous and instructive instances of the prohibition of abuse of rights are derived from the practice of quasi-international tribunals, i.e. tribunals administering law—municipal and international—between state-members of Federal States. In particular, the Supreme Court of the United States has had occasion to check the abuse of rights in matters frequently regarded as falling within the absolute discretion of the State. The question of interference with, or diversion of, waters of rivers flowing from one State to another has frequently been the subject of the jurisdiction of the Supreme Court restraining States from exercising their rights in an unsocial manner to the detriment of other States. The jurisdiction of the Supreme Court was exercised in a similar spirit in other complaints against the abuse of rights, such as the disposing of sewage by one State so as to affect injuriously the health of citizens of another State,[1] or legislation interfering with the supply of certain commodities to the other State.[2] The Swiss Federal Court has been confronted with similar problems. In the dispute between Aargau and Zürich in 1878 it affirmed the principle that, in the case of public waters which extend over several cantons, 'none of them may, to the prejudice of the others, take such measures upon its territory as . . . may make the exercise of the rights of sovereignty over the water impossible for the other cantons, or which exclude the joint use thereof or amount to a violation of territory'.[3] And it emphasized the duty of 'rational

---

[1] *Missouri* v. *Illinois* (1901), 180 U.S. 208. In the case of *Louisiana* v. *Texas* (1900), 176 U.S. 1, in which the plaintiffs asked for a ruling enjoining the defendants from enforcing quarantine regulations injuriously affecting the citizens of Louisiana, the Court dismissed the action on the ground that the controversy was one in vindication of a grievance not of Louisiana as a whole, but only of a particular individual, and also because the Bill failed to show that Texas had authorized or confirmed the alleged action of her health officer.

[2] *Pennsylvania* v. *West Virginia* (1922), 262 U.S. 553. See *Kansas* v. *Colorado* (1901), 185 U.S. 125, in which the Court affirmed its jurisdiction in an action in which it was contended that the defendant State attempted to deprive the State of Kansas of the benefit of water from the Arkansas river which rises in Colorado and flows into and through Kansas; and, for the decision on the merits (1906), 206 U.S. 46. And see *Wyoming* v. *Colorado* (1922), 259 U.S. 419; *North Dakota* v. *Minnesota* (1923), 263 U.S. 365—an action in which the Supreme Court assumed jurisdiction in a suit against the maintenance by Minnesota of an artificial drainage system within its borders with the result that the natural capacity of the interstate stream was greatly increased and the water flooded the farms of the other State; *Wisconsin* v. *Illinois* (1929), 278 U.S. 367; (1929), 281 U.S. 179—a suit for enjoining the State of Illinois and the Sanitary District of Chicago from continuing to withdraw 8,500 cubic feet of water per second from Lake Michigan at Chicago. See below, p. 323.

[3] *Recueil des Arrêts*, iv. 46, 47, cited after Schindler in *A.J.* xv (1921), p. 170.

utilisation' of public waters 'so as not to injure the interests of the neighbours'. In the dispute between Solothurn and Aargau in 1900, a case arising out of the alleged endangering of the territory of Solothurn on account of target practice in Aargau, the Court, in answer to the plea that the latter may make use of its territory as it pleases, said that 'in international law, especially in relations within Federal States, the principle of law of vicinage holds good to the effect that the exercise of one's own rights should not prejudice the rights of one's neighbours', and that if these rights are of equal value 'a rational compromise must take place according to the natural conditions'.[1] The German *Staatsgerichtshof*, in the important case decided on 18 June 1927 between Württemberg and Prussia on the one hand and Baden on the other, not only affirmed the duty to refrain from undue interference with the flow of the river to the detriment of the lower riparian State, but also laid down that it is the duty of the riparian State to perform acts of a positive nature—like the strengthening of the banks and regulating the flow of the river— as a matter of normal policy in the interests of navigation of all riparian States.[2]

§ 18. The Prohibition of Abuse of Rights as a General Principle of Law.

Is the principle of the prohibition of abuse of rights a general principle of law entitled, by virtue of its generality, to application by international tribunals? To the English lawyer the conception of abuse of rights appears at first sight foreign to his own law. He will point to *damnum sine injuria*; he will refer to the case of *Mayor of Bradford* v. *Pickles*,[3] in which it was held that if the owner sinks a well, not in order to get water for himself, but solely in order to drain his neighbour's spring, his act is not unlawful, because 'no use of property which would be legal if due to a proper motive can become illegal because it is prompted by a motive which is improper or even malicious';[4] he will point to cases like *Allen* v. *Flood*,[5] in which it was held that whatever his motives may be a person does not act unlawfully if he persuades or induces a man, without having recourse to

---

[1] *Recueil des Arrêts*, xxvi (1), pp. 450, 451, quoted after Schindler, op. cit., p. 173.
[2] *Entscheidungen des Reichsgerichts in Zivilsachen*, cxvi, Appendix, pp. 18–45; *Annual Digest*, 1927–8, Case No. 86.
[3] [1895] A.C. 587.
[4] Lord Watson, ibid., p. 598.   [5] [1898] A.C. 1.

unlawful means, to do something which is not prohibited by law, although such act may injure another person.[1]

How far the element of malice is entirely excluded from the domain of the English law of torts is not a matter which can be here examined in detail. It is possible to find cases, decided in a period when the individualistic doctrines of economic *laisser-faire* were less predominant, in which the question of malice plays a large part.[2] And it would be idle to try to exclude it altogether from the law on the abuse of legal process (including malicious prosecution), libel, and nuisance.[3] Apart from the relevance of malice the answer to the question under discussion will depend largely on the approach to the basic problem of the law of torts, that is to say, on the question whether the law of torts is a body of rules exhaustively establishing specific injuries, so that it lies in each case upon the plaintiff to show that the act complained of falls within some established rule of liability,[4] or whether it is a branch of law governed by the comprehensive and

---

[1] Probably the English lawyer will insist that whatever may be the fate of *Allen* v. *Flood* as the result of the decision in *Quinn* v. *Leathem*, [1901] A.C. 495, the remarks there made on the point of malice still hold good.

[2] See Lord Holt in *Keeble* v. *Hickeringill*, 11 East 574, n., 11 Mod. 74: 'Suppose the defendant had shot in his own ground, if he had occasion to shoot, it would have been one thing; but to shoot on purpose to damage the plaintiff is another thing and a wrong.' And see Wigmore, 'Responsibility for Tortious Acts: Its History' in *Selected Essays on the Law of Torts* (1924), p. 76, who says that 'the principle *sic utere tuo ut alienum non laedas* was early familiar to judges, and can clearly be traced even when it is given an English garb', and quotes Holt, C.J., in *Tenant* v. *Goldwin*, 2 Ld. Raym. 1089 (1705), and Gibbs, C.J., in *Sutton* v. *Clarke*, 6 Taunt. 29 (1815). And it will be observed that even in *Mayor of Bradford* v. *Pickles* it was admitted that *animus vicino nocendi* might make a difference. Thus Lord Watson, while referring to the fact that in *Acton* v. *Blundell*, 13 L.J. Ex. 289, 67 R.R. 361 (1843), the Court relied on a passage from the *Digest* (D. 39, 3, *de aqua*, 1, § 12), in which *animus vicino nocendi* is regarded as material, explained that that passage referred to cases where the owner of the land can as well do the thing he wants to do without nuisance to his neighbour and yet wantonly does it at a place where it causes annoyance. The passage in question is: 'Marcellus scribit cum eo, qui in suo fodiens vicini fontem avertit, nihil posse agi, nec de dolo actionem: et sane non debet habere, si non animo vicino nocendi, sed suum agrum meliorem faciendi id fecit.' This Roman prototype of *Mayor of Bradford* v. *Pickles* is of some interest, as there has been a tendency recently to attach decisive importance to the Roman law maxims *feci sed jure feci* and *nullus videtur dolo facere, qui jure suo utitur* (D. 50, 17, 55) as expressive of the individualistic character of Roman law. See also D. 38, 6, 1: *neque malitiis indulgendum est*, and I. 1, 8, 2: *expedit rei publicae, ne quis sua re male utatur*.

[3] See Pollock, *The Law of Torts* (11th ed. 1920), p. 412, referring to *Christie* v. *Davey*, [1893] 1 Ch. 316, 326, and observing that although where nuisance is once proved the defendant's intention is not material, 'a proved intention to annoy the plaintiff may be relevant to show that the defendant is not using his property in an ordinary way such as good neighbours mutually tolerate, and it will naturally set the Court against him in all matters of discretion'.

[4] Salmond, *Law of Torts* (4th ed. 1916), p. 9.

pervading rule that 'it is a wrong to do wilful harm to one's neighbour without lawful justification or excuse',[1] so that prima facie the intentional infliction of damage is a cause of action requiring justification if the defendant is to escape. Which line of approach is the more in keeping with the actual content of the common law is a matter upon which the writer hesitates to pronounce an opinion. But if the latter view—advocated by authorities of the calibre of Lord Bowen,[2] Mr. Justice Holmes,[3] and Sir Frederick Pollock[4]—be correct, then it is submitted that the cleavage between English law and the modern Continental systems of law is not as deep as may be supposed.[5] For the problem of abuse of rights is only to a limited extent identical with the question of malicious

---

[1] Pollock, op. cit., p. 20.

[2] 'At Common Law there was a cause of action whenever one person did damage to another wilfully and intentionally, and without just cause or excuse.'—*Skinner & Co.* v. *Shew & Co.*, [1893] 1 Ch. 413 at p. 422. And, to the same effect, *Mogul Steamship Company* v. *McGregor*, [1889] 23 Q.B. Div. at p. 613.

[3] In *Aikens* v. *Wisconsin*, 195 U.S. 194 at p. 204; 'Justifications . . . may depend upon the end for which the act is done. . . . It is no sufficient answer to this line of thought that motives are not actionable, and that the standards of the law are external. That is true in determining what a man is bound to foresee, but not necessarily in determining the extent to which he can justify harm which he has foreseen.'

[4] Loc. cit. See also to the same effect Winfield in *Columbia Law Review*, xxvii (1927), pp. 1–11.

[5] Article 226 of the German Civil Code lays down that 'the exercise of a right is not permitted when its only object can be to cause damage to another'. For a wealth of literature and judicial authority which has grown round this subject see Staudinger's *Kommentar*, 9th ed., i. (1925). This article obviously refers to malicious abuse of rights, and ought to be distinguished from Article 826, according to which any one who deliberately inflicts damage upon another person is bound to compensate the damage.

Article 2 of the Swiss Civil Code provides: 'Every person is bound to exercise his rights and fulfil his obligations according to the principles of good faith. The law does not sanction the evident abuse of a person's rights.' See on this article pp. 10 and 11 of Reichel's *Commentary on the Swiss Code* (1911).

In France the doctrine of abuse of rights because of malicious motive—*nuire à autrui sans profit pour soi-même*—although without direct foundation in the Code and possibly not warranted by Article 544 of the Code, has been recognized and developed by the consistent practice of courts. See for an account of the French practice in the matter, Walton, 'Motive as an Element in Torts in the Common and in the Civil Law', in *Harvard Law Review*, xxii (1908–9), pp. 501–19. However, the learned author somewhat confuses *abus des droits* for malicious motives with *abus des droits* in general. Cases practically identical with *Mayor of Bradford* v. *Pickles* have arisen in France, and in each case it was held that the owners were liable in tort: see, for instance, *Badoit* v. *André*, *Cour de Lyon*, 18 April 1865, *Dalloz*, lvi (2), p. 199, and *Forissier* v. *Chaverot*, *Cour de Cassation*, 10 June 1902, *Sirey* (1903), i. 11. See also for a comparative study, Ames, 'How far an Act be a Tort because of the Wrongful Motive of the Actor', in *Harvard Law Review*, xviii (1905), pp. 411 et seq. (who shows that a large majority of American decisions follow the French and German practice), and 'Law and Morals', ibid., xxii (1908), pp. 97 et seq. And see Stoner, *The Influences of Social and Economic Ideals on the Law of Malicious Torts*, in 8 *Michigan Law Review*, p. 468.

exercise of rights. *Nuire à autrui sans profit pour soi-même* constitutes only one aspect of the problem. For it is possible to do damage to others *avec profit pour soi-même*, and it is then that the question arises whether the exercise of rights is lawful or whether it degenerates into an abuse of rights and becomes, accordingly, unlawful. It is believed that there is in this respect no difference of substance between English law and other legal systems. The major part of the law of torts is nothing else than the affirmation of the prohibition of abuse of rights. It is largely the result of a compromise, by reference to requirements of justice and of social needs, between the conflicting principles *sic utere tuo ut alterum non laedas* and *qui utitur jure suo alterum non laedit*. This, it is believed, is the proper theoretical basis of the law of torts. The usefulness, therefore, of statements like the one 'an act is lawful if done in the exercise of a common right' is limited. For the very question to be determined in each particular case is whether there has been an exercise of a common right, or whether, as the result of the manner and circumstances of its exercise, a right has ceased to be a legally protected common right.

§ 19. The Prohibition of Abuse of Rights as the Basis of the Law of Torts.

The law does not identify the common right with an abstract right regardless of the manner of its use and of the interests of others. What is a common right is a matter for the law to say. And the law says that the use of any common right is subject to the duty of abstention from injuring others, of respect of their property, and of proper care to avoid causing harm. Only such exercise of common rights is lawful as does not interfere with the interests of others in a manner which is socially reprehensible.[1] This does not imply that the law makes it its business to protect every person from any kind of injury. An injury done as the result of the exercise of a right may be painful and even ruinous; but the law will refrain from protecting the person so affected if the social advantage resulting from the upholding of the legal freedom of action is more important than the prevention of the injury resulting from the exercise of a legal right. At a certain point the law, in the form of a legislative enactment or a judicial pronouncement, declares that the

---

[1] Professor Winfield enumerates 'exercise of common right' among the absolute limitations on the right of courts to manufacture new torts (op. cit., p. 10). It is respectfully submitted that the 'common right' is no more immutable than other rights affected by the creation of new torts.

exercise of a right has become abusive—not because of the malevolent intention of the doer, but because the interests injuriously affected by the exercise of the hitherto perfectly legal right are socially and morally more important. It is clear therefore that the phrase *damnum absque injuria* means very little as a statement of legal principle. For the question is in every case whether there has been *injuria* or not. In a number of cases the law tells us definitely that the specific exercise of a right is not permitted because the interest injuriously affected is more important than the right exercised. But this enumeration of specific causes of an *injuria* is not exhaustive and is not meant to be exhaustive. Policy, as exercised by courts in their law-making capacity or by the legislature, continuously adds new causes of wrongs, that is to say, it renders certain acts unlawful which have been hitherto exercised as a common right, and it converts into legal rights interests which have hitherto enjoyed no such protection. The process is essentially one of balancing of interests. The fact that one of these interests has hitherto enjoyed the protection of the law is certainly material, but it is not decisive. It ceases to be decisive as soon as policy decides that it is socially more advantageous to restrict a right in favour of an interest which henceforth becomes a legal right. The whole branch of the law of nuisance is an illustration of this process. Liability is excluded if an act is done in the exercise of a common right; but this common right is, in regard to the use of one's property, subject to the duty of using it so as not to interfere materially with the ordinary comfort and convenience of one's neighbours. When a person uses his legal right so as to interfere with the legally recognized right of his neighbour to comfort and convenience, he abuses his right, and the law will restrain him from using it in this way, regardless of his motive.[1]

The way in which the law draws the line between interests which are entitled to such protection in the face of existing rights hitherto regarded as absolute, and those which are not

---

[1] It might, of course, be said that the conception of abuse of rights is a misnomer, inasmuch as there is *ab initio* no legal right to use one's rights in a manner prohibited by the law. Thus Planiol argues with some impatience that the idea of an abusive use of a right is impossible in juridical logic, for the simple reason that the same act cannot at the same time be in accordance with the law and contrary to it. *Traité élémentaire*, 4th ed., vol. v, No. 871. See also for a clear statement of the argument and a criticism of it, Walton, op. cit., pp. 504–5.

is not always easy to follow. Thus it may be difficult to understand why a person should be protected against noise[1] or smoke if they interfere unduly with his comfort or convenience, while protection is refused to his interest in having the use of the waters of his well (if that well is fed from a spring proceeding in an undefined channel) when that water is intercepted for purposes which cannot be held to be ordinary,[2] or may even be malicious.[3] The difficulty is not solved by saying that a person has a legal right to be protected from undue interference with his health and comfort, whereas he has no right to the waters of an undefined channel. For the answer obviously begs the question. It reveals the inadequacy of the law of torts as based on abstract propositions like the one that the exercise of a common right can never constitute a wrong. The law of torts as crystallized in various systems of law in judicial decisions or legislative enactment is to a large extent a list of wrongs arising out of what society considers to be an abuse of rights. That list is in a state of constant flux and—in view of the growing complexity of social relations and the diminishing rigidity of the law—of constant expansion. Under the influence of these factors new causes of action in tort may be and are constantly created.[4] Novelty of action is no bar to the recognition of a claim. For in addition to the recognized specific wrongs there is inherent in every system of law the general principle of prohibition of abuse of rights.[5]

---

[1] See, for instance, *Soltau* v. *De Held* (1851), 2 Sim. N.S. 133, 39, R.R. 245, concerning the persistent ringing of a bell belonging to a Roman Catholic church which, it was pointed out in the judgement, cannot claim the same privileges as a parish church in the matter of bell-ringing.

[2] *Chasemore* v. *Richards*, H. L. Cas. 349.

[3] *Mayor of Bradford* v. *Pickles*, [1895] A.C. 587.

[4] See Ames, 'Law and Morals,' in *Selected Essays on the Law of Torts* (1924), p. 9, who points to the Statute of Edward I (St. Westminster 2, 13 Ed. I, c. 24) as 'a perennial fountain of justice to be drawn upon so long as, in a given jurisdiction, instances may be pointed out in which the common law courts have failed to give a remedy for damage inflicted upon one person by the reprehensible act of another, and the continued absence of a remedy would shock the moral sense of the community'. The Statute provides as follows: 'Whensoever from thenceforth a writ shall be found in the Chancery, and in a like case falling under the same right and requiring a like remedy, no precedent of a writ can be produced, the clerks in Chancery shall agree in forming a new one; lest it happen for the future that the court of our lord the king be deficient in doing justice to the suitors.'

[5] See Lord Truro in *Egerton* v. *Brownlow*, 4 H.L. Cas. 1 at p. 195: 'Every man is restricted against using his property to the prejudice of others...the principle embodied in the maxim *sic utere tuo ut alterum non laedas* applies to the public in at least as full force as to individuals.' During the discussion of the passage of the present Article 38 of the Statute of the Court referring to general

§ 20. The Function of the Doctrine of 'Abus des Droits' in International Law.

The doctrine of abuse of rights plays a relatively small part in municipal law, not because the law ignores it, but because it has crystallized its typical manifestations in concrete rules and prohibitions. In international law, where the process of express or judicial law-making is still in a rudimentary stage, the law of torts is confined to very general principles, and the part which the doctrine of abuse of rights is called upon to play is therefore particularly important. It is one of the basic elements of the international law of torts. Only by dint of the affirmation that international law is a rudimentary system of law concerned primarily, if not exclusively, with the prevention and suppression of recourse to force can the principle of the prohibition of anti-social use of rights be regarded as inoperative. In the last resort rights are conferred by the community, and the community must see to it that the rights are not exercised in an anti-social manner. To deny this in regard to international law is to maintain that in the international sphere rights are faculties whose source lies not in the objective law created by the community, but in the will and the power of the State.

The purpose of the excursion, undertaken in the previous section, into the theory of private law of torts was to show that, notwithstanding terminological differences, the prohibition of abuse of rights is a general principle of law. In view of its general recognition by almost all systems of law the objection that is a purely natural law doctrine[1] is hardly convincing. With paragraph 3 of Article 38 of the Statute of the Court in existence, and in the face of the undoubted reaction in the science of international law against a too rigidly positivistic interpretation of its sources, there is no longer room for a sweeping condemnation of beneficent

principles of law recognized by civilized States, one member of the Committee of Jurists charged with the drafting of the Statute invoked the principle which forbids the abuse of rights as an instance of general principles of law (*Procès-Verbaux*, p. 315). And see the reference to a 'manifest and continuous abuse of sovereignty' in the report of the Committee of Jurists which examined in 1920 the question of the Aåland Islands: *Official Journal of the League of Nations, Special Supplement*, No. 3 (1920), p. 5.

[1] See Cavaglieri, op. cit., p. 46. One of the objections raised by Professor Cavaglieri against the doctrine of abuse of rights was that, in his opinion, it is adopted only by the law of a limited number of States. However, it is submitted in the present section that the doctrine represents a general principle of law inherent in the law of torts as such. The differences between various systems of law consist mainly in a different treatment of the factor of malice.

principles forming part of the common stock of legal science on the ground that they are 'pure natural law' and have not secured explicit acceptance by States.

Equally, undue importance need not be attached to the argument that the maxim *sic utere tuo ut alterum non laedas* is ill suited to the requirements of an individualistic system of law like international law. An individualistic system of law is apparently one in which the law refuses to interfere with the legally recognized self-assertion and freedom of action of the individual members of the community, even if such conduct is contrary to principles of justice and social solidarity. There is no doubt that law, in its primitive stage, is in this sense individualistic. For in its primitive stage the prevention of violence and the maintenance of security are the paramount and exclusive considerations. They cease to be so with the growth of civilization and of the social integration of the community.[1] To say that international law must remain an individualistic system of law because it was so at a certain period of its existence, is to maintain, in fact, that it cannot hope to progress from a rudimentary to a more advanced stage. It is not by accident that the notion of abuse of right lies at the bottom of most attempts to give a juristic foundation to the doctrine of individual (as distinguished from collective) intervention as one of the typical manifestations of admissibility of self-help in international relations. But self-help as a normal method of redress is as typical of a primitive stage of legal development as it is the necessary consequence of a system which provides no adequate remedy, administered by impartial agencies, against abuses of legal rights.[2]

It would be unfortunate if mere general phrases were to deprive international law of the operation of a necessary principle of change like that inherent in the prohibition of abuse of rights. It is a principle which enables courts to take cognizance, without recourse to legislation, of changes in conditions and of social developments.[3] For in a large number of cases it is on account of such developments that

---

[1] See Anzilotti, *Cours de droit international* (trans. by Gidel, 1929), p. 14.

[2] See below, p. 392, and Stowell, op. cit., pp. 122, 137, 143, 376. Phillimore's chapter on Intervention (*Commentaries*, i. § 390) begins with a statement, supported by references to Roman law and general jurisprudence, on the limitations upon the exercise of legal rights.

[3] It is of interest to note that some French writers base the theory of *imprévision*—a variation of the doctrine *rebus sic stantibus*—on the theory of *abus des droits*. See Naquet in *Sirey* (1920), i. 105.

what has hitherto been a legally recognized right ceases to be so and becomes abusive, and as such contrary to law. Hence the doctrine of abuse of rights bears closely on the theory of the non-justiciability of disputes as based on the absence of an international legislature. It enables judicial organs to develop, without the necessity for legislative interference, the international law of torts in accordance with the requirements of the international community and with the growing interdependence of States.[1]

§ 21. Further Instances of the Application of the Doctrine of Abuse of Rights in International Law.

The possibilities of the application of the doctrine of abuse of rights in relations among States are manifold. In addition to the instances, given above, of the utilization of the flow of a river, of the closure of ports, and of the expulsion of aliens, three further examples may be mentioned. One refers to the denationalization of the State's own subjects and to questions of nationality in general; the second to some questions of the sovereignty over the air; the third to the State's use of its own territory.

(a) Nationality. Matters of nationality are, subject to the international obligations of the State, left to its municipal law. A State may not only lay down rules concerning the acquisition of nationality. It may also deprive its subjects of their nationality in a variety of ways. Its law may lay down that women marrying a foreign subject lose their nationality; it may deprive its naturalized subjects of their newly acquired nationality as the result of prolonged residence abroad, or in consequences of certain offences against the law, or for other reasons; or it may decree the denationalization of its subjects for political or other offences committed abroad against the mother country. It is in particular this last category of case which, as the result of recent legislation in Russia and Italy, has raised some difficult questions of 'statelessness'. Such legislation may adversely affect legitimate rights of foreign States within whose territory the denationalized person resides. It saddles them with stateless persons whom they may find difficult to deport, but who were admitted under

---

[1] See Tourtoulon, *Philosophy in the Development of Law* (Eng. trans. 1922), p. 563, for an interesting juxtaposition of the doctrine of *abus des droits* with the 'free-law' movement in Germany, both of which are conceived of as the theoretical expressions of creative judicial activity effecting a compromise between the factors of stability and change.

the implied undertaking of their parent State that they would be received if deported from the foreign country.[1] There is no clear rule of international law at present which limits the freedom of action of States in this respect, but it is submitted that the indiscriminate exercise by a State of the right of denationalizing its subjects, when coupled with the refusal to receive them when deported from a foreign country, constitutes an abuse of rights which could hardly be countenanced by an international tribunal. The deliberations of The Hague Codification Conference of 1930 on the question of nationality have also shown that the notion of abuse of rights may not be altogether alien to the consideration of the question of the use made by the State of its right to regulate matters of nationality.[2]

(b) Air Law. While the solution of the problems arising out of abuse of rights in the matter of denationalization may still come within the purview of the violation of a legal, although not very clearly defined, right of other States, there are cases in which the abusive exercise of a right does not violate any legally recognized interest of the State injuriously affected. The exercise by a State of its rights over the air above its territory may be mentioned as an instance which is specially appropriate as illustrating the influence of a change in conditions upon the application of the doctrine of abuse of rights. At the time when Accursius, in the thirteenth century, lent his authority to the maxim *cujus est solum ejus est usque ad coelum*—a maxim adopted as the foundation of the modern principle of the State's absolute sovereignty over the air over its territory—the column of air above the land was not, for practical purposes, more than a few hundred feet high. Recent developments in aviation and wireless communication have effected an obvious change, and the law of various countries has not been slow in giving effect to this change.

---

[1] See on this subject Fischer Williams, *Chapters*, pp. 137–45.

[2] See Acts of the Conference, Meetings of the Committees, vol. ii, Minutes of the First Committee, Nationality, for a discussion of the first Article of the Convention on Certain Questions Relating to the Conflict of Nationality Laws. That article lays down that 'it is for each State to determine under its own law who are its nationals', and that 'this law shall be recognized by other States in so far as it is consistent with international conventions, international custom, and the principles of law generally recognized with regard to nationality'. See p. 20 (the observations of M. Kosters to the effect that it is 'a principle of customary law that rights may not be abused') and p. 197 for the proposal of M. Standaert and M. Rundstein to incorporate the notion of abuse of rights in the Convention *eo nomine*. See also Rundstein in *Z.V.* xvi (1931), pp. 41–5.

In Great Britain Article 9 of the Air Navigation Act of 1920[1] excluded liability in respect of trespass or nuisance 'by reason only of the flight of air-craft over any property at a height above the ground, which, having regard to wind, weather and all the circumstances of the case, is reasonable'. Article 905 of the German Civil Code, while upholding the doctrine *usque ad coelum*, provided that the owner may not oppose such acts in the air above which he has no interest in opposing. Article 667 of the new Swiss Civil Code of 1907 limits the property of the owner to such height as may be useful for the exercise of his rights.[2]

States were not slow in taking over the *usque ad coelum* doctrine for the purpose of asserting absolute sovereignty over the air above their territory. In the Air Navigation Convention of 1919 the principle of the State's complete and exclusive sovereignty over the air is expressed in unequivocal terms, and there is evidence to show that this principle has acquired an authority beyond that of a mere conventional stipulation.[3] But there has been no parallel attempt to bestow the same authority on the principle that the sovereignty over the air must not be made use of in an anti-social manner. Oppenheim asserts emphatically the existence of a rule of international law forbidding a State to alter the flow of a river so as to injure the lower riparian State,[4] but he has no doubt that, according to customary international law, a State may prevent the passage over its territory of waves emanating from foreign wireless telegraphy stations.[5] He would have had even less doubt in recognizing the right of the State to prevent, at its discretion, the passage of foreign aircraft over its territory. It cannot be denied that according to the existing law a State has such a right. But is it an absolute right against the indiscriminate and anti-social use of which

---

[1] 10 & 11 Geo. V, c. 80. See, generally, McNair, *The Law of the Air* (1932).

[2] In France the doctrine of *usque ad coelum* is adopted by Article 552 of the Civil Code. Article 544 of the Code provides that 'ownership is the right of enjoying and disposing of a thing in an unlimited manner, provided that the thing is not made use of in a manner forbidden by law or regulations'. That Article has been virtually abrogated by the activity of courts, both in relation to aviation and in other matters. See Henry-Couännier, *Éléments créateurs du droit aérien* (1929), pp. 105 ff. See also Julliot, 'De l'abus du droit dans ses applications à la locomotion aérienne' (*Revue des Idées*, 1910).

[3] See, for instance, the Report of the Committee on Territorial Waters of The Hague Codification Conference of 1930, Annex on the Legal Status of the Territorial Sea, Article 2, which lays down that 'the territory of a coastal State includes also the air space above the territorial sea'.

[4] Vol. i, p. 381.   [5] Ibid., p. 369.

the law provides no remedy? What would be the position if a State, whose territory lies in the middle of an important air-route, denounced conventions limiting its freedom of action and prohibited the passage of foreign aircraft solely to satisfy a feeling of vindictiveness or a desire to exercise pressure? What would be the position if a State arbitrarily and wantonly placed obstacles in the way of a normal and orderly development of wireless communication? To say that the injurious interference with the flow of a river is illegal because it infringes a legal right of the lower riparian State, whereas no legally recognized right is infringed as the result of a State's exercise of its sovereignty over the air, is to state the existing legal position in a somewhat narrow fashion. In fact, in 1927 the Institute of International Law adopted a resolution to the effect that a State does not possess the right to prevent the simple passage of wavelengths over its territory.[1] There is no more evidence, grounded in the practice of States, for the proposition that the lower riparian State has a legal right to the undisturbed flow of the river than there is for the proposition that a State has the right to the use of the possibilities offered by the various forms of communication in the air. The first has been generally accepted as existing law, the other has not, as yet. But there is nothing static in the existing legal position. It is conceivable that, given a specific set of circumstances—for instance, the disregard of the obvious and important interests of one State as the result of unnecessary and wanton acts on the part of another—the principle of the prohibition of an anti-social use of rights may become instrumental in transforming what has hitherto been a mere interest into a legally recognized right.

(c) *Injurious Use of Territory.* It is in particular the use of a State's territory in a manner prejudicial to the interests of other States which may give rise to the application of the prohibition of abuse of rights. Some of these prohibitions have clearly become part of international law, for instance those which lay down that a State must not permit its territory to be used as a base for organizing hostile expeditions against other States.[2] Others are far from being generally recognized, although compliance with them may gradually cease to be a matter of mere courtesy. Thus a

---

[1] *Annuaire*, xxxiii (3) (1927), p. 343.
[2] See on this subject Lauterpacht in *A.J.* xxii (1928), pp. 105–30.

State might in certain circumstances be held to have failed in its duty if it were to permit its territory to be used as a basis for constant violation of the importation and revenue laws of its neighbour.[1] Equally, a State might be regarded as abusing its powers of sovereignty by not taking the necessary quarantine, and other, measures in case of an epidemic disease threatening not only its own population, but also that of another State.[2]

§ 22. The Extent and the Limitations of the Application of the Doctrine of Abuse of Rights in International Law.

The instances, referred to above, of the possible applications of the doctrine of abuse of rights reveal at the same time its disturbing elasticity and comprehensiveness. For, in theory, there is no matter normally falling within the domain of the exclusive jurisdiction of the State which could not be brought within the purview of the operation of the prohibition of abuse of rights. The way in which some writers have attempted to prove that intercourse is an obligation of international law shows to what length the doctrine may theoretically be pursued.[3] The commercial and tariff policies of a State are regarded as the most cherished objects of exclusive jurisdiction of the State, but the history of international relations abounds in examples of official protests and remonstrances of Governments against measures of economic protection and discrimination, in a manner deemed to be unfairly injurious to the interests of the citizens of the complaining States. Such protests have frequently come from countries whose governments have traditionally attached

---

[1] See the case *Foster* v. *Driscoll*, [1929] 1 K.B. 470, and *Annual Digest*, 1927-8, Case No. 10, in which the English Court of Appeal refused to enforce as illegal a contract whose object was the illegal importation of liquor into the United States, on the ground that 'its recognition by our Courts would furnish just cause of complaint by the United States Government against our Government (of which the partners are subject), and would be contrary to our obligation of international comity as now understood and recognized...'.

[2] This class of case is mentioned by Heilborn, loc. cit., as an instance of abuse of rights.

[3] See, for instance, Stowell, op. cit., p. 138, who goes to the length of maintaining that 'the general refusal of commercial intercourse would put the State outside international law'—a doctrine pregnant with weighty possibilities at a time when a policy of high tariffs may to a large extent have the effect of limiting commercial intercourse. See also Politis, op. cit., p. 34, on the *interdiction d'isolement commercial*. For a recent affirmation of this view see Delos, *La Société Internationale et les principes du droit public* (1929), pp. 221, 229–30, and in *Archives de Philosophie du droit et de Sociologie Juridique* (1931), Nos. 1–2, pp. 109 et seq. See also Catry in *R.G.* xxxix (1932), pp. 192–218.

considerable importance to the exclusiveness of national sovereignty in these matters.[1] However, these representations have
not as a rule been made as a matter of international right; they
have been normally couched in terms of warnings against
'unfriendly acts' calculated to endanger friendly relations between
the States concerned. Accordingly, although there is little doubt
that even the most absolute and exclusive rights may be exercised
so that, having regard to the manner and effects of their exercise, a
situation may be created amounting to the commission of an
international wrong, the practice of States will itself frequently
offer a helpful guide for the determination of the question of
abuse of rights.

Apart from the practice of States such determination must be
a compromise between various factors. The fact that an act
complained of is done in the exercise of a right whose exclusiveness is regarded as forming a clear rule of international law will
undoubtedly carry weight in the decision. In certain cases freedom of action is socially more important than the prevention of
an individual injury. This is frequently the position in municipal
law.[2] It is particularly so in international relations where for
various reasons—legal, historical, and political—the State's
independence of legal regulation is more in the nature of a
rule than of an exception. The interest of the international
community—in particular its interest in encouraging the willingness of States to submit their dispute to impartial and final
adjudication, and to abide by the decisions of international
tribunals—may require that legal freedom of action should
not be hastily curtailed, and that the distinction should be
preserved between matters of international obligation and matters of international concern. But, on the other hand, the same
international interest tells us that there is nothing absolute

---

[1] See, for instance, the protest of the United States in 1885 against the proposed
increase of the duty on petroleum imported into the Dutch West Indies, *U.S. For. Rel.*
(1886), p. 737, and other examples cited by Kuhn in *A.J.* xxiii (1929), p. 816. See also
Stowell, op. cit., p. 143, on the representations made in 1929 by the United States to
the French and some other European Governments on account of regulations
limiting the importation of motion picture films from the United States. And see
the same in *A.J.* xxiv (1930), pp. 110–18, on the protest made by the United States
against the French Presidential Decree of 30 August 1927, establishing a discriminatory régime against exports from the United States. It appears that the United States,
while admitting that tariff policy is a matter of exclusive domestic jurisdiction,
maintained that no discrimination against a particular State is admissible.

[2] 'Free competition is worth more to society than it costs.'—Holmes, J., in
Vegelahn v. *Guntner*, 167 Mass. 92, 106.

even in so-called exclusive rights of domestic jurisdiction, and
that they are subject not only, as may appear from the Fourth
Advisory Opinion of the Court,[1] to the conventional obligations
of the State, but also to the changing contents of the general
body of international law in accordance with the requirements
of international peace, justice, and the growing integration of
the international community. It is for international tribunals to
achieve a reconciliation of the conflicting factors in individual
cases. Their task in this respect is admittedly a very difficult and
responsible one. But it is a task which must be performed if the
courts are to fulfil a function which lies properly within the
domain of the judiciary in every legal community, and which
is particularly urgent in a community with a rudimentary law-
creating machinery, a task, that is to say, which to a large extent
coincides with the higher synthesis of the conflicting claims of
change and stability in society. This function is one of resort to a
comprehensive legal principle of social justice and solidarity
calculated to render inoperative unscrupulous appeals to legal
rights endangering the peace of the community. But only the
existence of tribunals endowed with compulsory jurisdiction
may be able to frustrate attempts at petty appeal to formal
rights. Failing such compulsory jurisdiction selfish claims of
State sovereignty have a tendency to assert themselves in a
short-sighted and petulant manner in disregard of the purpose
of the law and of the interests of peace.[2]

---

[1] *P.C.I.J.*, Series B, No. 4, p. 24.

[2] See the Opinion of the Law Officers of the United States in the matter of the
dispute with Mexico concerning the diversion of waters from the Rio Grande river:
Opinions of Attorney-General, xxi (1893–7), p. 274. But see H. A. Smith, *The Economic
Uses of International Rivers* (1931), who suggests that differences as to the existence or
non-existence of a vital interest said to be involved in a proposed employment of an
international waterway should be regarded as a justiciable dispute suitable for
judicial determination (p. 151).

CHAPTER XV

EXTENSION OF JUDICIAL LEGISLATION BY THE WILL OF THE PARTIES

§ 23. In General. In the preceding chapters we have discussed the ways in which international tribunals, while remaining within the orbits of their strictly judicial function, are free to act in the direction of adapting the law to changed conditions. A wide scope is left to judicial discretion by means of the application, on the one hand, of general principles of law, and of doctrines like *rebus sic stantibus* and the prohibition of abuse of rights, and, on the other hand, by judicial law-making in general. Yet, beneficial as this aspect of their function may be, the possibility is not altogether excluded of judges being compelled by their judicial duty to render decisions which, although legally unimpeachable, may morally and politically be objectionable and far from fulfilling the ultimate object of the law, which is the securing of peace through justice. For much of the harshness involved in the operation of law is unavoidable and inherent in the function of the law conceived as an agency of stability and security. The judicial function cannot and must not become identical with that of a legislature. But this inescapable limitation of the powers of international tribunals does not mean that there is no remedy against the disadvantages of compulsory arbitration which result from the absence of an international legislature, nor that those disadvantages cannot be reduced by a far-seeing attitude of reasonableness, and a realization of the State's moral obligations towards the international community, whose peace cannot always be safeguarded by adherence to formal justice.[1] Some of these remedies will be discussed in the present chapter. They

---

[1] For an eloquent expression, in the course of the Swiss-French Free Zones dispute (see below, pp. 316, 332), of the sentiments underlying such attitude of accommodation, see the following passage from the speech of M. Motta on 29 March 1922 in the Swiss Federal Assembly: 'Il faut être équitable.... Les petites zones ... constituent incontestablement une servitude active pour la Confédération suisse et une servitude passive pour la France. Il n'est que très naturel qu'un pays qui est grevé d'une servitude tende à s'en libérer.... Pour la France, le régime des petites zones est une gêne; pour nous, ces petites zones ne sont pas d'un intérêt vital... Si elles constituent une gêne pour notre voisin, il est légitime, il est naturel et équitable de chercher une solution tenant mieux compte des intérêts des uns et des autres.' Quoted in the French *Contre-Mémoire* before the Court, Series C, No. 17–1, vol. iii, p. 1478, n. 2.

consist either in the voluntary extension of judicial legislation by the will of the parties, or in making, by appropriate international machinery, the judicial decision a starting-point for political modifications of the law.

§ **24. Conferment of the Power to lay down Regulations.** The parties may, when submitting a dispute for judicial settlement, either by virtue of an agreement *ad hoc* or in pursuance of a previous arbitration treaty, agree that, in case the judgement should have the effect of stabilizing conditions which have become unworkable, or of creating a deadlock which leaves without protection common interests in need of regulation, it shall be within the province of the Court either to lay down rules, or to propose recommendations calculated to establish a new legal position. There are instances of Governments entrusting the Tribunal with this form of judicial legislation. Thus Article 7 of the Arbitration Treaty of 29 February 1892 concluded between Great Britain and the United States, for the settlement of the *Behring Sea* controversy, laid down that, if the answer of the Tribunal to the questions put to it in regard to the jurisdiction in the Behring Sea 'shall leave the subject in such position that the concurrence of Great Britain is necessary to the establishment of Regulations for the proper protection and preservation of the fur-seals in, or habitually resorting to, the Behring Sea, the arbitrators shall then determine what concurrent Regulations outside the jurisdictional limits of the respective Governments are necessary and over what waters such Regulations should extend'.[1] A survey of the prolonged and occasionally acrimonious correspondence[2] preceding this arbitration agreement shows that Governments may not always be insistent on pressing their formal legal rights to their extreme consequences.[3] Great Britain resisted the attempt of the United States to exercise jurisdiction on the high seas over British vessels and subjects. But it was clear that though her attitude, based as it was on the principle of the freedom of the seas, was legally almost unassailable, the actual object of her protest was morally

---

[1] Hertslet, *Treaties*, xix. 890; Moore, i. 801.

[2] See for some of the correspondence *British and Foreign State Papers*, lxxxii (1889–90), pp. 202–91, and lxxxiii (1890–1), pp. 306–55. See also Moore, i. 776–800.

[3] See above, pp. 99, 180, on the frequent appeals by the United States to the right of self-defence.

and economically not above doubt. The United States maintained that it was protecting the seal industry from a wasteful
and senseless practice threatening to exterminate the seals in
the Behring Sea. Its claim to jurisdiction, based on prescriptive
rights said to have been acquired from Russia, proved to be
unfounded; and its claim to the property in seals, based on
somewhat far-fetched analogies to bees and other domestic
animals, was unlikely to be accepted by a judicial body. But at
the same time it was clear that, if the principle of the freedom
of the seas meant that the United States was bound to be a
passive witness of the destruction of a valuable industry closely
connected with its territory and of importance to the world at
large, then its application in that particular case was unjust,
creative of friction, and ultimately fraught with danger to the
principle of the freedom of the sea itself.

The British Government was not unmindful of this aspect of
the controversy and, while maintaining its position in regard to
the past, in effect agreed in the *compromis* to abandon its attitude
for the future. For the arbitration agreement provided that
should the award be in conformity with the British contention,
the Tribunal shall frame rules depriving British subjects of the
unrestricted freedom of action which Great Britain was legally
entitled to claim as the result of the operative part of the award.
And, as has been suggested in another part of this book,[1] it is
probably owing to this legislative authority conferred upon the
Tribunal that it was in a position to adhere, so far as the past was
concerned, to the strict letter of the law.[2] It is significant that the
United States experienced no undue difficulty in inducing Great
Britain to accept the part of the *compromis* conferring legislative
powers upon the Tribunal. As in many other cases so also in this
dispute it was not only the actual subject-matter of the controversy which was responsible for the friction produced, but
also the claim of one State to assume unilaterally the function
of the legislator in a matter of common concern.[3] Once that

---

[1] See above, p. 99, n. 4.

[2] The regulations of the Tribunal, prescribing in detail the periods and methods
of seal-fishing, were incorporated verbatim in the Schedule to the Behring Sea
Award Act, 1894 (57 Vic., c. 2; Hertslet, *Treaties*, xix. 925). On the subsequent
regulation of the Fur Seal Fisheries in the North Pacific Ocean see the Convention
between Great Britain, the United States, Japan, and Russia of 7 July 1911,
Hertslet, *Treaties*, xxvi, 348. As to the criticism of the recommendations, see
below, p. 321, n. 1.

[3] *British and Foreign State Papers*, lxxxii. 275, Note of Sir J. Pauncefote: 'Her

claim was given up, there was no insuperable difficulty in inducing Great Britain to agree to a change in the law *pro futuro* after the United States had refused to agree to an arbitration confined to the ascertainment of the legality of their action and eventual compensation.[1]

§ 25. Conferment of the Power to propose Recommendations. The conferment of legislative powers may be effected by a request or authorization, addressed to the Tribunal, to make recommendations for the future regulation of the legal relations between the parties. Such a request or authorization may be accompanied by clauses intended to render the recommendation effective in the case of the parties failing to act upon it. Thus in Article 4 of the arbitration agreement of 27 January 1909 between Great Britain and the United States for the settlement of the dispute concerning the North Atlantic Fisheries, it was laid down that the Tribunal should recommend, for the consideration of the parties, rules and methods of procedure under which all questions which might arise in the future regarding the exercise of the disputed rights of fishing might be determined in accordance with the principles laid down in the award.[2] The same Article provided that, in case the parties shall not adopt the rules and methods of procedure so recommended, then any dispute between them concerning the interpretation of the treaty of 1818, which conferred certain fishing rights upon the subjects of the United States, or concerning the application or effect of the award, shall be referred to the Permanent Court of Arbitration for decision by summary procedure. Happily, the recommendations of the Tribunal, made in pursuance

Britannic Majesty's Government are anxious to co-operate to the fullest extent of their power with the Government of the United States in such measures as may be found expedient for the protection of the seal fisheries.... But they cannot admit the right of the United States of their own sole motion to restrict for this purpose the freedom of the Behring Sea....'

[1] See ibid. lxxxiii. 307. See also ibid., p. 339, Note of Secretary Blaine, in which the United States disclaimed any intention to dispute the rule that a State cannot extend its jurisdiction more than one marine league from the shore: 'No one disputes that, as a rule; but the question is whether there may not be exceptions whose enforcement does not interfere with those highways of commerce which the necessities and usage of the world marked out.... It will mean something tangible... if Great Britain will consent to arbitrate the real questions which have been under discussion....' The British answer to the American terms of reference to the Arbitral Tribunal is contained in Lord Salisbury's dispatch of 21 February 1891 (ibid., pp. 342–8).

[2] For the terms of the agreement see the award of the Tribunal in Scott, *Hague Court Reports*, pp. 147ff.; Hertslet, *Treaties*, xxvi. 1088.

of that article, were accepted by the parties and embodied in a formal treaty.[1] It has been said, not without justice, that, although the Tribunal rejected the contention of the United States that the treaty of 1818 amounted to the creation of an international servitude, its recommendations went a long way towards conferring upon the United States rights which they claimed by virtue of a servitude.[2] Moreover, the Tribunal did not limit the application of Article 4 to recommendations of rules and methods of procedure *stricto sensu* referring to the exercise of the right of fishing. In deciding the fifth question specified in the arbitration agreement, namely, from what point must be measured the three marine miles of the coasts, bays, creeks, and harbours referred to in the treaty of 1818, the Tribunal found that its answer, 'although correct in principle and the only one possible in view of the want of a sufficient basis for a more concrete answer', was not entirely satisfactory from the practical point of view and that it left room for doubts and differences. It therefore availed itself of the permissive rule of Article 4 and proposed 'rules and methods of procedure for determining the limits' of the bays in question.[3,4]

§ 26. Recommendations by the Tribunal 'proprio motu'.

It is open to international tribunals, while rejecting the claim of the plaintiff, to state, without adding a binding recommendation, that the compliance, totally or in part, as an act of grace, with the demand of the plaintiff would be in

---

[1] Treaty of 20 July 1912, Scott, *Hague Court Reports*, p. 221; also in Hertslet's *Treaties*, xxvii. 1095.

[2] Scott in Schücking, *Das Werk von Haag* (1915), vol. i, part ii, p. 103.

[3] See the award, op. cit., pp. 188–90.

[4] Two minor instances of delegation of legislative functions to an arbitrator may be mentioned in this connexion. The first is the case of Article 9 of the Preliminary Treaty of Peace of 6 September 1897 between Turkey and Greece, which laid down that questions about which the two States shall be unable to arrive at an agreement in the course of the peace negotiations, shall be settled by a binding decision of an arbitral body composed of the representatives of the Great Powers at Constantinople (*British and Foreign State Papers*, xc (1897–8), p. 549). The substance of that article was incorporated in the final treaty of peace, and the arbitrators acting in that capacity laid down the terms of the consular convention between Turkey and Greece. The term 'arbitration' seems here to have been confused with mediation, or even intervention. See on this case Politis in *R.G.* ix (1902), pp. 202–62, 406 ff., and x (1903), pp. 69–105. For a second instance, of somewhat doubtful value as an international precedent, see the award of 6 July 1864 given by Napoleon III in the dispute between the Viceroy of Egypt and the Suez Canal Company concerning the bases of a new contract between Egypt and the Company. The case is reported and analysed in detail in Lapradelle and Politis, ii. 344–86.

accordance with justice and equity. Some of the awards given by the British-American Claims Arbitral Tribunal under the Convention of 18 August 1910 offer instructive examples of such recommendations. Thus in the case of *The Home Missionary Society*, the Tribunal, while dismissing the claim on the ground that it had no foundation in law, expressed the opinion that, in view of the services rendered by the Society in its task of peaceful development and civilization of the native inhabitants, if the British Government could avail itself of any fund from which to repair the losses sustained by the Society 'it would be an act of grace which this Tribunal cannot refrain from recommending warmly to the generosity of that Government'.[1] When in the *William Hardman* case the Tribunal rejected the claim for compensation for destruction of private property in pursuance of necessary measures of warfare, it recommended the individual affected by these measures to the favourable consideration of the United States Government 'as a basis for any friendly measure which the special conditions of the sufferer may justify'. The Tribunal pointed out that although there is no legal obligation to compensate, 'there may be a moral duty which cannot be covered by law, because it is grounded only on an inmost sense of human assistance, and because its fulfilment depends on the economical and political condition of the nation, each nation being its own judge in this respect'.[2] Similar recommendations were made in the *Cadenhead* case[3] and in the case of the *David J. Adams*.[4]

There is nothing in the existing international arbitral law to prevent the Tribunal, even without a special authorization on the part of the disputants, from expressing an opinion on these lines. But an explicit power of this nature, granted to the Tribunal in the special *compromis* concluded under a

---

[1] Nielsen's *Report*, p. 426.   [2] Ibid., p. 497.
[3] Ibid., p. 508. In this case the Tribunal expressed the desire that the British and Canadian Governments 'will consider favourably the allowance as an act of grace' of adequate compensation, but 'with the above recommendation' disallowed the claim.
[4] See also the award in the case of *Eastern Extension, Australasia and China Telegraph Company, Ltd.*: 'If the strict application of a treaty, or of a specific rule of international law, conduct to a decision which, however justified from a strictly legal point of view, will result in hardship, unjustified having regard to the special circumstances of the case, then it is the duty of the Tribunal to do their best to avoid such a result, so far as it may be possible, by recommending, for instance, some course of action by way of grace on the part of the respondent Government' (ibid., p. 79). In this case the Tribunal, having regard to the circumstances of the case, refrained from making such a recommendation.

general arbitration treaty, would both emphazise the intention of the parties not to insist on the strict provision of the law and would indicate an informal undertaking to comply with the recommendation. The history of international arbitration offers many examples of awards in which the *rigor legis* could, without impairing the juridical value of the award, have been properly mitigated by a recommendation to the generosity of the Government concerned. This course is particularly appropriate in cases in which the decision is more the result of the duty to give an award than of the conviction that it is the only possible, and legally unassailable, solution. The cause of international justice would not have suffered if in the *Savarkar* case the Permanent Court of Arbitration had added a recommendation or expression of hope in regard to the future treatment of the prisoner irregularly handed over to the British authorities.[1,2]

§ 27. Conferment of the Power to decide 'ex aequo et bono'.

The authorization to decide *ex aequo et bono* constitutes another important instance of extension of judicial legislation by the will of the parties. Agreements of this nature undoubtedly constitute an act of goodwill and accommodation on the part of the State favoured by the law in force, but the history of international arbitration testifies that such agreements are possible and practicable. A considerable number of recent arbitration conventions show that States may be prepared to entrust a tribunal with the power to decide *ex aequo et bono*, a power in effect tantamount to endowing it with a legislative function, not only in regard to a particular dispute, but also, within the purview of a general arbitration treaty, in regard to future disputes. Whatever may be thought of the desirability of this latter development,[3] it shows to what length States may be prepared to go. The authorization to decide *ex aequo*

---

[1] See above, p. 88.

[2] From an authorization as suggested in the text there must be distinguished agreements in which the Tribunal is expressly instructed to disregard rules of international law. See, for instance, Article 2 of the Convention of 19 November 1926 between Great Britain and Mexico for the settlement of British pecuniary claims in Mexico arising from loss or damage from revolutionary acts between 1910 and 1920. That article provides for examination of the claims 'in accordance with the principles of justice and equity . . . since it is the desire of Mexico *ex gratia* fully to compensate the injured parties, and not that her responsibility should be established in conformity with the general principles of International Law' (Treaty Series, No. 11 (1928)). Probably this passage does not mean that in the opinion of the parties international law is not compatible with justice and equity. See below, p. 314, n. 5, on the application of a similar provision in the French-Mexican Claims Convention.   [3] See below, pp. 328, 373 et seqq.

et bono—clearly to be distinguished from the clause instructing the Tribunal to decide on the basis of equity[1]—differs somewhat from the cases, discussed above, in which the Tribunal, after having considered the legal merits of the dispute, is instructed to supplement or to modify the existing law. In these latter cases the existing law is still the starting-point and cannot be entirely disregarded. But where a tribunal is instructed to act *ex aequo et bono*, its discretion seems to be more unfettered. This would be the proper interpretation of conventions like the one concluded on 13 January 1869 between Great Britain and Portugal, which instructed the arbitrator to decide either wholly in favour of the claim of either party 'or in the nature of an equitable solution of the difficulty';[2] or the Convention of 10 April 1897 between France and Brazil authorizing the arbitrator to choose a frontier line 's'il le juge bon';[3] or the agreement between Chile and the United States of 10 November 1858 naming the King of Belgium as arbiter 'to decide with full powers and proceedings *ex aequo et bono*'.[4] But the inference would not be wholly justified that the enlarged discretion of judges is in such cases identical with a rule of arbitrariness or with a mere power of mediation.[5] However wide may be the

---

[1] This reference to equity, in particular in arbitration agreements to which common law countries are parties, is not intended as a departure from the rules of law. This may be particularly seen from the awards of the British-American Claims Arbitral Tribunal under the Convention of 18 August 1910 which, although instructed to decide in accordance with 'treaty rights and with the principles of international law and equity', consistently refused to depart from existing rules of international law. See on this point Lauterpacht, *Analogies*, pp. 65–7.

[2] Lafontaine, p. 81 (the case of the *Bulama Island*). See also ibid., p. 171, for the Convention, concluded in similar terms, between Great Britain and Portugal, of 25 September 1872, concerning the Delagoa Bay.

[3] Ibid., p. 563.

[4] Ibid., p. 35. See also above, p. 130, on the Convention of 1889 between France and Holland.

[5] See on this point the suggestive remarks of Morgenthau, op. cit., p. 40, and of Hostie in *R.I.*, 3rd ser., ix (1928), pp. 582–5. See also below, p. 319, n. 2. And see the award in the *Georges Pinson* case decided by the French-Mexican Claims Commission (Verzijl, President) on 19 October 1928 in pursuance of the French-Mexican Claims Convention of 25 September 1924, Article 2 of which provided that the Commission shall adjudicate upon claims for losses suffered by French subjects in the course of the revolutions and disturbed conditions in Mexico between 1910 and 1920 'in accordance with the principles of equity, since Mexico wished to repair "gracieusement" the damages, and not to have her responsibility fixed according to general principles of international law'. In this award the Commission refused to apply principles of equity, as distinguished from general principles of international law, except in regard to the question of State responsibility: 'In all other respects positive international law remains paramount in the application and interpretation of the Convention. Therefore international law alone, and not the indefinite

powers conferred upon the arbitrator, he will be disinclined to avail himself of them otherwise than on the basis of rules capable of general application and having regard to the entirety of the existing law. The existing legal position is seldom so unjust or unworkable as to induce the judge to disregard it altogether in laying down new rules. The scope of legislative discretion open to the arbitrator set up on the basis of the *ex aequo et bono* clause is admittedly great. But, although such discretion implies freedom to disregard existing legal rights, it is quite compatible with an attitude which regards the existing legal position as a convenient starting-point for effecting any changes that may be necessary. This may well be seen from the dispute, to be discussed later, between Yugoslavia and France in which the ascertainment of the legal position was considered to be the necessary prerequisite for an equitable solution of the difficulty.[1] The dispute between Switzerland and France concerning the régime of the Free Zones raised the same question, but the Court was of opinion that the special agreement did not confer upon it the right to settle the dispute *ex aequo et bono* after it had decided the legal points involved.[2] At the same time this case has brought sharply into the forefront of discussion the question how far deliberate judicial legislation by way of regulation of interests is compatible with the judicial function of international tribunals, and in particular of the Permanent Court of International Justice.

principles of equity, must govern the solution of all other doubtful points of law that should arise in the course of the proceedings, such as admissibility of claims, admissibility of evidence, questions of nationality....For the same reason, the principles of equity defined in Articles 2 and 3 of the Convention are themselves constantly to be interpreted in accordance with the principles of international law.' At the same time the Commission stated that this interpretation of the *compromis* did not prevent it from applying principles of equity in the question of damages and evidence, or generally as a subsidiary source of law in those cases in which the strict application of the law would lead to 'unacceptable consequences' (*Annual Digest*, 1927–8, Case No. 318).

[1] See below, p. 331.
[2] See Order of 6 December 1930, Series A, No. 24, and the final judgement of 7 June 1932, Series A/B, No. 46. Ample information on the history of this dispute will be found in the records of the oral and written proceedings before the Court, *P.C.I.J.*, Series C, Nos. 17 and 19. See also, in addition to the literature referred to in Oppenheim, i. 435, n. 2, Chevallier in *R.I.* (Paris), ii (1928), pp. 251–74; Burckhardt in *R.I.* 3rd ser., xi (1930), pp. 90–122; Tremaud in *R.G.* xxxvii (1930), pp. 476–510. See in particular French *Contre-Mémoire* of 23 January 1929, *P.C.I.J.*, Series C, No. 17 (I), pp. 1436ff., and the Swiss *Contre-Mémoire* of 22 December, 1928, ibid., pp. 1569ff. See also the speeches of M. Paul-Boncour, Series C, No. 19 (I), pp. 49ff., and Professor Logoz, ibid., pp. 146ff.

§ 28. Regulation of Interests and the Judicial Character of International Tribunals.

The Permanent Court itself has indirectly, in the second Order given in the *Swiss-French Free Zones* case, expressed doubts whether it was authorized by its Statute to exercise a function of this nature. In rejecting the view propounded by France it observed that 'even assuming that it were not incompatible with the Court's Statute for the Parties to give the Court power to prescribe a settlement disregarding rights recognized by it, and taking into account considerations of pure expediency only, such power, which would be of an absolutely exceptional character, could only be derived from a clear and explicit provision to that effect'.[1] It is not clear whether the same doubts would prevail if the Court were asked to change undisputed rights not ascertained by a previous judgement. But, while the six judges of the majority professed some doubts on the major question, and while the six judges of the minority entertained no doubt that the Court had the right to act in conformity with a *compromis* of this nature, Judge Kellogg, in a statement of *Observations* appended to the Order and devoted exclusively to the question of the jurisdiction of the Court, expressed emphatically the view that the Court had no power under its Statute to create new rights and obligations for the parties even if such power were expressly given to it by the disputants. He pointed out that the creation of new contractual rights—as distinguished from the laying down of rules regulating in detail existing rights—was not within the competence of a judicial tribunal; that the precedents afforded by the *Behring Sea* and *North Atlantic Fisheries* arbitrations were not relevant to the issue, seeing that these adjudications were 'arbitrations pure and simple'; that the assumption by the Court of jurisdiction in such matters would amount to assumption of jurisdiction in purely political disputes, destructive of the judicial character of the Court and of its authority as a Court of Justice; that, even under the Swiss submission, the Court was asked in effect to 'pass upon questions essentially economic and political in their nature, the decision of which is not to be found in an interpretation and application of treaties between the two countries nor in the application of rules and principles of law';[2] and that the authority of the last paragraph of Article 38 of the Statute was for that purpose more apparent than real.

---

[1] Series A, No. 24, p. 10.   [2] Ibid., p. 32.

Although the objections of Judge Kellogg referred only to the competence of the Permanent Court, it is clear that they have relevance to the jurisdiction of any other international judicial tribunal. And as the majority of the Court felt compelled[1] to express doubts on the matter, it is necessary to consider here the question of justiciability of disputes submitted to judicial bodies for a decision *ex aequo et bono*. It is submitted, with the greatest respect, that the wording of Article 38 of the Statute, and general legal considerations, militate so strongly in favour of the view that there is nothing to prevent the Court from deciding *ex aequo et bono*, if the parties so desire, that the doubts expressed by the majority of the Court on this matter are hardly likely to secure general acceptance. So long as the Court does not arrogate for itself the right of deciding *ex aequo et bono*, but acts in this capacity at the express wish of the parties, that function is not fundamentally different from that envisaged in the opening paragraph of Article 38 of the Statute in which the Court is authorized to apply 'international conventions, whether general or particular, establishing rules expressly recognized by the contesting States'. Given such an agreement, the decision rendered will, it is submitted without diffidence, be a strictly legal one. It will be a decision given in accordance with rules agreed upon by the parties. These rules are in the nature of a general mandate; they are a blank cheque to be filled in by the judges. It is of no juridical importance that they contain an authorization to depart from the law as it existed before the *ex aequo et bono* agreement was made. The will of the parties is law. *Modus et conventio vincunt legem.* The 'international conventions, whether general

---

[1] Possibly, if this may be said without irreverence, the very slender size of the majority made it necessary to frame the judgement so as to satisfy a possible dissentient. Judge Huber, one of the majority judges, when referring in his presidential address, delivered in 1925, to treaties conferring upon the Court jurisdiction *ex aequo et bono*, expressed no doubts as to the right of the Court to act in that capacity; on the contrary, he was of the opinion that a clause of this nature is a welcome manifestation both of confidence in the Court and of the increasing range of the reign of law. Judge Loder, another of the majority judges, saw in 1922 no reason why the Court should not have the power to decide *ex aequo et bono* (*Annuaire*, xxix (1922), p. 233). Judge Anzilotti has stated in his treatise (*Corso di diritto internazionale*, French trans., 3rd ed. (1929), pp. 119, 120) that the *ex aequo et bono* clause has given rise to controversy, but he has refrained from associating himself with the criticism of this clause or with the denial of the rights of the Court to act in that capacity. He says: '... Tenant compte de certains besoins des rapports internationaux et dans l'intention louable de favoriser le recours à la Cour, ce texte permet aux parties d'obtenir une sentence fondée sur l'équité, plutôt que sur le droit strict. ...'

or particular, establishing rules expressly recognized by the contesting States', are rules of law, and will be applied by the Court,
even if they are in derogation of the customary rules of international law. States may have agreed in a special convention that, in
their mutual relations, the maritime belt should extend ten miles
from the low-water mark, or that their diplomatic envoys should
not enjoy immunity from taxation, or that their treaties should be
binding from the time of signature. An international court will give
effect to such provisions unless they are of an immoral character,
or run counter to universally recognized principles of international
law of an absolutely binding character. Probably it could be said
without inaccuracy that even if Article 38 did not contain its
present last paragraph, the Court would still be at liberty to
render, at the will of the parties, decisions *ex aequo et bono* by virtue
of the above quoted first paragraph of that article.[1] Like the bulk of
the rules of private law, the rules of international law are primarily
of a permissive character. It cannot be doubted that in deciding
according to these rules of conduct specifically agreed to by
the parties, the judges would be performing a strictly judicial
function.[2] This is essentially the case when judges, expressly
authorized by the parties, decide *ex aequo et bono*.

§ 29. The Right of the Permanent Court of International Justice to decide 'ex aequo et bono'.

Upon
analysis, it is not accurate to say that, in cases of a decision
ex aequo et bono rendered in pursuance of the wish of the parties,
the Court creates new contractual rights and duties as distinguished from a regulation of already existing rights and duties.
These rights and duties are already contained *in nuce* in the very
agreement conferring upon the Court jurisdiction *ex aequo et
bono*. The Court gives flesh and bones to this agreement.

---

[1] See Note by Baron Descamps on the question of Compulsory Jurisdiction in
the *Procès-Verbaux* of the Committee of Jurists of 1920, p. 255: 'The following should
be submitted to judicial procedure exclusively:... 2. Disputes which, although
unable to be stated or settled legally, are comparable, from the point of view of
jurisdiction, to disputes of a legal character by virtue of a general or special
agreement arrived at by the parties concerned.' And see the Russian Memorandum of 1899, *Hague Reports*, p. 97, on the *compromis* creating a principle of law *ad hoc*.
[2] It was therefore unnecessary—and perhaps fatal—to the French cause in the
Swiss-French Free Zones dispute to insist that the task of the Court in giving effect
to the second part of the Special Agreement was 'pas... une mission de droit, mais
plutôt une mission politique' (French *Observations* of July 1930, *P.C.I.J.*, Series C,
No. 19 (1), p. 474).

The law which it lays down is not of its own creation, although it is of its own formulation. It is the creation of the parties. It would be disconcerting to know that the Court acts judicially if it gives effect to a concrete rule, however incompatible with justice, laid down by the parties, but that its function ceases to be judicial if it acts upon a rule of a general character agreed upon by the parties. Only a conception of *ex aequo et bono* as identical with diplomatic bargaining and compromise in their questionable meaning[1] could prompt us to accept a conclusion of this nature. But, as already stated, a decision *ex aequo et bono* is not a discretionary and arbitrary ruling.[2]

Undoubtedly an authorization to decide *ex aequo et bono* imposes upon the Court a heavier and more responsible task than that involved in the interpretation or application of a single rule of conventional or customary international law. It obliges the Court to have regard to a variety of factors which it would not have to consider otherwise. However, this aspect of the matter ought not to be exaggerated. Even in interpreting and applying concrete legal rules the Court does not act as an automatic slot-machine, totally divorced from the social and political realities of the international community. It exercises in each case a creative activity, having as its background the entirety of international law and the necessities of the international community.[3] The distinction between the making of the law by judges and by the legislature is upon analysis one of degree. It has as much

[1] See on this point, Hostie, op. cit., pp. 582–4.

[2] See the Report of the League of Nations Commission (Doc. C. 400, M. 147, 1925) on the principles to govern the decision of the Council in laying down the frontier between Turkey and Iraq in accordance with Article 3, paragraph 2, of the Treaty of Lausanne. The Report is an illuminating instance of an attempt to find general principles as the basis for what was essentially a legislative decision. That a legislative decision may, its law-creating function notwithstanding, still be governed by the existing law may be seen from the Swiss-German Treaty of Arbitration and Conciliation of 3 December 1921 (*Arbitration and Security*, p. 201), which provides in Article 5 as follows: 'If, in a particular case, the legal bases mentioned above are inadequate, the Tribunal shall give an award in accordance with the principles which, in its opinion, should govern international law. For this purpose it shall be guided by decisions sanctioned by legal authorities and by jurisprudence.' See on this Article Hammarskjöld in *R.I.*, 3rd ser., ix (1928), pp. 96–8. However, the last paragraph of that Article provides that 'if the Parties agree, the Tribunal may, instead of basing its decision on legal principles, give an award in accordance with considerations of equity'.

[3] See above, p. 123. And see, in particular, the reasoning of the Court in the Twelfth Advisory Opinion in the passage affirming the rule of unanimity in the decisions of the Council of the League (Series B, No. 12, p. 29).

substance, but not more, than the traditional doctrine of separation of powers. The settling of interests is normally within the province of the legislature, but that does not mean that courts have nothing to do with composing conflicting interests. As the judicial activity is nothing else than legislation *in concreto* is it possible to assert dogmatically that the settling of conflicts of interests is outside the province of judicial tribunals?

The right of the Permanent Court of International Justice to give decisions *ex aequo et bono* if the parties wish it follows so clearly from the wording of the Statute that the doubts expressed by the majority of the Court on the matter must be read in the light of the terms of the Special Agreement under which it was requested to act. Thus it will be noted that the Court did not express doubts as to its general power to give a decision *ex aequo et bono*. Its doubts had reference rather to its power 'to prescribe a settlement *disregarding rights recognized by it*'. Apparently the majority regarded it as incompatible with the dignity of the Court to lay down, in the first part of its judgement, the existing rights of Switzerland, and then to proceed, in the second part, to decree a settlement disregarding the rights thus recognized. Would the Court have been equally doubtful if it had been asked to give a decision *ex aequo et bono* on a matter in regard to which it had not previously given a judgement; or if it had been asked to embody the award *ex aequo et bono* in a decision given separately from the judgement on the existing law? It is not easy to assume that this could have made a difference, but it is only by dint of such an assumption that the Court's doubts on the matter can be squared with the plain wording of the Statute.[1]

---

[1] It is difficult to accept the view propounded by Judge Kellogg in his *Observations* (Series A, No. 24, pp. 40, 41) to the Court's Order of 6 December 1930 that the last paragraph of Article 38 does not mean what on the face of it it must be understood to mean. 'Neither in the records of the proceedings of this Committee [of the First Assembly of the League],' says Judge Kellogg, 'nor in its report to the League, is there a suggestion that this provision of the Statute was intended to give the Court jurisdiction on political and economic questions which the Court might settle without regard to treaty rights or principles of law and equity.' The words 'political' and 'equity', as used here, are not conducive to clarity. In any case, the writer has not found Judge Kellogg's statement substantiated by the history of the clause in committee.

If, as suggested by Judge Kellogg, the term *ex aequo et bono* means legal justice not inconsistent with the existing law, then, in fact, it is difficult to see why an express authorization of the parties should be necessary in order to enable the Court to do what is plainly its duty. The power of the Court to render at the wish of the parties decisions *ex aequo et bono* has been criticized by many (see,

§ 30. The Adequacy of International Tribunals to regulate Interests 'ex aequo et bono'.

Apart from the question of the right of the Permanent Court and other judicial tribunals to regulate interests on the ground of an authorization *ex aequo et bono* the question arises whether they possess the necessary technical and expert knowledge which may be required for the determination of new rights and obligations between the parties.[1] The first answer to this question is that the expert and technical knowledge required for the creation of new rights and obligations is not necessarily greater than that necessary for the application and determination of existing rights.[2] The expert knowledge required for laying down the provisions of a new commercial treaty—a task which the Court was for a time believed to have to fulfil in connexion with the Swiss-French Free Zones dispute—is not essentially different from that required for the interpretation and application of an already existing treaty. In its Fourteenth

e.g., Scott in *A.S. Proceedings*, (1924), p. 140), but, so far as the writer is aware, there have been only a very few attempts to argue that under its present Statute the Court is prevented from acting in that capacity. See the remarks of M. Hammarskjöld, the Registrar of the Court, in *Bulletin de l'Institut Intermédiaire International*, xvii (1927–8), p. 278. See also the report submitted in 1927 to the Institute of International Law by M. de la Barra and M. Mercier, *Annuaire*, xxxiii (2), pp. 577 et seq.

[1] See, for instance, the criticism of the *Behring Sea* award by Headlam-Morley, *Studies in Diplomatic History* (1930), p. 27, who points out that the regulations laid down by the arbitrators proved in practice unsatisfactory and were eventually superseded by an international agreement (see above, p. 309, n. 2). From this he deduces a general limitation of the arbitral function, because 'a court which is very suitable for determining a point of law is not equally capable of devising a scheme for future administration, for such a scheme will probably require technical knowledge and administrative experience which a judicial authority does not possess'. As this criticism, and the inferences drawn therefrom, are frequently repeated, it ought to be stated that the arbitrators in the *Behring Sea* dispute did possess the assistance of experts. Article IX of the arbitration agreement provided for the appointment of Commissioners for an investigation and report on the questions covered by Article VII (in which the arbitrators were instructed to lay down regulations), such report to be submitted to the arbitrators. However, the Commissioners were unable to reach an agreement, except on formal and general matters, and it was left to the Tribunal to avail itself of their divergent reports in framing the regulations. The fact that the regulations (which actually worked for over ten years) proved unworkable is hardly relevant. Legislative enactments within the State, drafted with the assistance of experts, do not invariably prove workable. On the report of the joint commission of experts see Moore, p. 808.

[2] See, for an interesting example of judicial determination of interests by way of interpreting a general provision of a treaty, the award of 8 January 1921 by Hines, Arbitrator, in the dispute between Germany and France in the matter of the cessions under Article 357 of the Treaty of Versailles. The arbitrator had to decide the amount and specification of these cessions, having regard to the 'legitimate needs of the parties concerned'. For the award see *A.J.* xvii (1923), pp. 786–805, and *Annual Digest*, 1919–22.

Advisory Opinion the Permanent Court was asked to say whether, under the law in force, the powers of the European Commission of the Danube extended 'over one or more zones, territorially defined and corresponding to all or part of the navigable channel, to the exclusion of other zones territorially defined', and if so, 'according to what criteria shall the line of demarcation be fixed as between territorial zones placed under the competence of the European Commission and zones placed under the competence of the Roumanian authorities'. The technical knowledge required for the determination of these questions was not less than if the Court had been asked—as for all practical purposes it was asked—to lay down new rules of law on the matter.[1]

The second answer is that in both cases the Court may, when necessary, be assisted by experts. This is the procedure

---

[1] It is of interest to note that M. Rey, Secretary of the European Danube Commission, in his observations submitted to the Institute of International Law, expresses the opinion that, in view of past experience, the settlement of disputes in connexion with the utilization of the flow of rivers and navigation should be submitted directly to the Permanent Court of International Justice without the preliminary stage of conciliation by experts like the League of Nations Advisory and Technical Committee on Communication and Transit. *Annuaire*, xxxv (1) (1929), p. 438.

It will be noted that the Court has not been in the habit of refusing to accept certain functions of an extra-judicial nature either conferred upon the Court itself or vested in its President in the field of pacific settlement or for similar purposes. By a declaration signed on 24 July 1923 Turkey undertook to engage a number of European lawyers to be chosen from a list drawn up by the Permanent Court of International Justice from amongst subjects of States which did not participate in the World War (Series D, No. 6, p. 635). On 12 November 1923 the Court decided to accept this function, 'although this task fell, strictly speaking, outside the duties of the Court' (Series E, No. 1, p. 152). The Court then dealt with the matter in a number of sessions (ibid., pp. 152, 153, and Series E, No. 2, p. 93). The Court as such was also entrusted, in a declaration signed on 22 December 1927 (*L.N.T.S.*, xci. 283), with the function of choosing the arbitrators, in case of disagreement between the parties, in connexion with Article 273 of the Treaty of St. Germain (regulation of the position of insurance companies in the former Austro-Hungarian territory). In the Agreement (No. 11) of 28 April 1930 for the settlement of questions relating to the agrarian reforms and mixed arbitral tribunals between Czechoslovakia, Hungary, Roumania, and Yugoslavia, the parties agreed that each of the mixed arbitral tribunals set up between them shall be completed by the addition of two members chosen by the Permanent Court of International Justice from the nationals of countries which were neutral during the World War (Series E, No. 6, p. 569). On 9 May 1931 the Court decided to undertake the mission entrusted to it, and on 15 May made the required appointments (Series E, No. 7, p. 188). For other examples of documents conferring similar functions upon the Court as a whole, see Series E, No. 3, p. 105, No. 4, p. 136, and No. 6, p. 180. In addition a great number of treaties confer upon the President of the Court the function of making appointments of presidents of arbitration tribunals in the scheme of treaties of pacific settlement, of presidents of conciliation commissions, and of umpires of arbitration tribunals provided for in treaties of commerce. (See, for examples and further references, Series E, No. 7, p. 189.)

normally adopted by municipal courts, and the practice of international tribunals follows the same course. When in the case of *Wisconsin* v. *Illinois* Mr. Justice Holmes had to determine by what degrees the restoration of the rights of Wisconsin, after the diversion from Lake Michigan of 8,500 or more cubic feet of water per second had been held illegal, should take place, he had, in regard to the technical aspects of the matter, to rely on the recommendations of the master of the Court who in turn had to have recourse to the expert evidence submitted by the parties. It was only with the assistance of such expert advice and recommendations that the Court was able to issue a decree laying down that on and after 1 July 1930 the defendants are enjoined from diverting waters in excess of an annual average of 6,500 cubic feet per second, and that that amount shall be reduced on 31 December 1935 to 5,000 cubic feet and on 31 December 1938 to 1,500 cubic feet.[1] However, frequently the function of the Court consists in laying down the major principle in relation to the case in dispute while leaving it to the parties to apply the principle in detail. The way in which the German *Staatsgerichtshof* dealt with the complicated dispute between Baden, Württemberg, and Prussia is an instructive illustration of this procedure.[2]

The history of the work of the Permanent Court of International Justice shows that when necessary it may and will call in the assistance of experts. In giving its opinion on the question of the competence of the European Danube Commission, the Court relied to a large extent on the investigations of the League of Nations Advisory and Technical Committee for Communications and Transit and of a Special Committee of Inquiry. When the Court, in its Thirteenth Judgement, laid down the principles governing the award

---

[1] 281 U.S. 200.

[2] See p. 292. The Court, after having given its decision, said: '... It is doubtful whether a decision of the *Staatsgerichtshof*, even if based on detailed evidence, would in fact definitely settle the controversy. For even this subsequent decision would necessarily be limited to laying down some guiding principles. The questions brought about by the *Donauversinkung* are so complicated, their scientific and technical aspects so inter-dependent, that only a settlement by agreement will be able to produce a final settlement of the controversy. The ascertainment in the present judgment of important preliminary questions, in particular in the legal sphere, should provide the necessary basis for such an agreement. This is in fact the object of the interlocutory judgment of the *Staatsgerichtshof*. The *Staatsgerichtshof* expects that the parties will now enter into new negotiations and try to arrive at an agreement giving effect to the principles laid down in the interlocutory judgment' (*Annual Digest*, 1927–8, Case No. 86).

of damages to Poland, it made an Order setting up an expert inquiry with a view to enabling the Court to fix 'with a full knowledge of the facts' the amount of the indemnity to be paid by Poland to Germany. The Order provided for the appointment by the President of the Court of three experts, assisted by assessors nominated by the parties. The Order laid down in detail the procedure to be followed by the experts and assessors who were to make a solemn declaration and to undertake to fulfil their task 'honourably and faithfully, impartially and conscientiously'. It provides an instructive example of the way in which the Court may in the future avail itself of the assistance of experts in intricate matters. In addition, Articles 26 and 27 of the Statute provide for technical assessors to assist the special chambers of the Court in labour and communication and transit cases. The Mixed Arbitral Tribunals established by the Peace Treaties have frequently adopted the procedure of appointing experts to determine the commercial value of the object of the dispute.[1] Before the World War the arbitration agreements in the *Behring Sea*[2] and *North Atlantic Fisheries* cases afforded a clear instance of a provision for the assistance of experts in cases in which the Tribunals were asked to act in a legislative capacity.[3]

§ 31. The Need for Legislative Decisions 'ex aequo et bono' on the part of International Judicial Tribunals.
The questions must now be considered whether—assuming that the Permanent Court of International Justice is by its Statute enabled to give decisions *ex aequo et bono*—it is desirable that it should, *de lege ferenda*, possess such powers, and whether States should avail themselves of the provision of the Statute in question. These questions have been answered by many

---

[1] See, for instance, *Greek Government* v. *Vulkan Werke, Annual Digest*, 1925–6, Case No. 314, and *Antippa* v. *Germany, Recueil*, vii (1927), p. 23.

[2] See above, p. 321, n. 1.

[3] Article 3 of the arbitration agreement provided as follows: 'If any question arises in the arbitration regarding the reasonableness of any regulation or otherwise which requires an examination of the practical effect of any provisions in relation to the conditions surrounding the exercise of the liberty of fishery enjoyed by the inhabitants of the United States, or which requires expert information about the fisheries themselves, the tribunal may, in that case, refer such question to a commission of three expert specialists in such matters; one to be designated by each of the parties hereto, and the third, who shall not be a national of either party, to be designated by the tribunal. This commission shall examine into and report its conclusions on any question or questions so referred to it by the tribunal and such report shall be considered by the tribunal and shall, if incorporated by them in the award, be accepted as part thereof.'

in the negative. It has been maintained—Judge Kellogg's *Observations* in the *Free Zones* case are a representative instance of this opinion—that the exercise of such a power would compromise the judicial character of the Court, and that it would therefore be preferable that this task should, whenever necessary, be entrusted to arbitral bodies less wedded by their purpose and constitution to strictly judicial methods (such, for instance, as the Permanent Court of Arbitration), and that any advantage accruing from the exercise by the Permanent Court of exceptional powers of this nature is unlikely to compensate for the injury which may well be inflicted upon the Court as the result of the exercise of powers reminiscent of political compromise and bargaining.

It is not believed that any of these arguments will bear closer examination. The judicial authority of the Permanent Court of International Justice has now become firmly established, and there is no reason to apprehend that its prestige would suffer as the result of the exercise of a function which it may by virtue of its Statute be called upon to perform. On the contrary, it might be said, in regard to this particular function, that the fact of the Court being entrusted with it on specific occasions might well be regarded as an expression of unusual confidence in its impartiality and objectivity.[1] An international tribunal asked to act as a legislator is in effect asked to apply, not rules of arbitrary discretion, but the higher law of international justice and solidarity. For the application of that law the highest qualities of the judicial mind are required. The argument that the Court might become entangled in matters of a highly political character is hardly convincing. It has been shown elsewhere in this book that the great majority of cases brought before the Court have been cases of a pre-eminently political character closely connected with some of the most delicate and important contemporaneous problems.[2] The fact that the Supreme Court of the United States, as the result of its function of reviewing legislation from the point of view of its conformity with the constitution, in effect adjudicates upon conflicts of interests of decisive political importance does not deprive it of its judicial character.

It is not necessary to discuss here in detail the suggestion that other tribunals, like the Permanent Court of Arbitration,

---

[1] See the observation of President Huber quoted above, p. 317, n. 1.
[2] See above, p. 156.

which are said to be of a less judicial character, are the more appropriate bodies for effecting settlements of this nature. This suggestion ought to be received with caution, inasmuch as it starts from the proposition (which has been rejected as inaccurate)[1] that the rendering of decisions *ex aequo et bono* is not in accordance with a strictly judicial function, and that it lies therefore more properly within the province of international arbitral tribunals which are believed to be hybrid bodies confusing, and expected to confuse, law with bargaining and compromise. This proposition is, as will be shown later on, inaccurate and antiquated.[2] A tribunal cannot at the same time be half judicial and half non-judicial. The two functions are mutually exclusive. A tribunal must either base its decision on law or disregard the law. *Tertium non datur.* While, therefore, there is no reason why States should not submit adjudications *ex aequo et bono* to international tribunals other than the Permanent Court of International Justice, it is inaccurate to maintain that these tribunals ought to be invoked in such cases because they are strictly speaking non-judicial. The very fact that they are empowered to give a binding and final decision, as distinguished from a recommendation, constitutes an important factor in rendering their activity judicial.[3]

On the other hand, although States have, and ought to possess, freedom of action in regard to the choice of the tribunal which they may wish to entrust with the task of determining their future rights, it would not be desirable to exclude, and there is no reason to exclude, the Permanent Court of International Justice from fulfilling that function. Issues of such magnitude may arise that the parties, although willing to abide by a modification of the existing law, may feel the need that the very highest and most authoritative tribunal should determine their future rights. In the course of the Belgian-Chinese dispute concerning the termination of the treaty of 1865, the Chinese Government, while rejecting the submission of the question of the interpretation of that treaty to the Permanent Court by virtue of the Optional Clause,[4] declared its willingness, 'mindful of its obligations

---

[1] See above, p. 319.   [2] See below, p. 380.

[3] Accordingly, if the *compromis* is framed in such a way as to reserve to the parties the right to reject the judgement, the judicial character of the decision is seriously impaired. In the *Free Zones* case the Court refused to give a decision which might be disregarded by either party. Series A, No. 24, p. 14.

[4] See above, p. 200.

under Article 36 of the Statute of the said Court . . . to discuss the possibility of invoking jointly with the Belgian Government the services of this highest international tribunal, if the Belgian Government had indicated a willingness to seek a solution on the broad basis of the universally recognized principle of equality in international intercourse and that of *ex aequo et bono*'.[1] The machinery for changing the law in the international society is slight and rudimentary, and there is no reason to abandon, for the sake of unfounded fears, any one of its instruments. The Permanent Court is essentially an instrument of peace, and it is desirable that it should not be prevented from fulfilling its task as such whenever consistent with its judicial function. The history of the work of the Court provides several examples of its disregard of the defects of form in the submission to its jurisdiction because, as the Court itself said, 'judicial settlement of international disputes, with a view to which the Court has been established, is simply an alternative to the direct and friendly settlement of such disputes between the Parties', and that 'consequently it is for the Court to facilitate, so far as compatible with its Statute, such direct and friendly settlement'.[2] There is no reason why the Court should not develop, by virtue of *ad hoc* agreements of the parties, a kind of equity jurisdiction by granting relief from strict rules of law.[3] If, as the result of a deficient system of international legislation, there is a possibility and a necessity for developing by international organs a jurisdiction of this kind, modifying the existing law, then there is every reason why this should be done by a permanent body, of high authority, learning, and impartiality, which can be relied upon to shape international equity, not in a haphazard way, but in accordance with principles capable of general application.

---

[1] Memorandum of the Chinese Government of 16 November 1926, *P.C.I.J.*, Series C, No. 16 (1), p. 78.

[2] Series A, No. 22, p. 13. See Judgement No. 6, Series A, No. 6, pp. 13, 14; Judgement No. 11, Series A, No. 13, p. 16; Judgement No. 12, Series A, No. 15. See also Judgement No. 5, Series A, No. 5, p. 27, and Series A, No. 24, p. 14, where the Court declared itself competent to give a 'judgment by consent' on the ground that such a judgement, 'though not expressly provided for by the Statute, is in accordance with the spirit of that instrument'. And see also the Court's affirmation of its right to give declaratory judgements, this being 'one of the most important functions which it can fulfil' (Judgement No. 7, Series A, No. 7, pp. 18, 19).

[3] Awards given in this capacity can be easily distinguished, in form and otherwise, from decisions rendered on the basis of existing international law. They could, for instance, be printed in a separate series of the publications of the Court.

§ 32. The Practical Limits of Legislative Decisions 'ex aequo et bono'.

There is, however, one limitation of a practical nature dictated by reasons of expediency and of general respect for international law. While it may be necessary and beneficial to peace to entrust a tribunal with the legislative function by virtue of an *ad hoc* agreement, there are weighty and decisive objections against such powers being conferred in advance within the frame of obligatory arbitration. It might be said that theoretically there is no substantial difference between entrusting the tribunal with legislative powers in a special agreement and conferring upon it the same function by virtue of a treaty of obligatory arbitration; and that in both cases the legislative powers of the tribunal are grounded in the will of the parties. However, the difference between the two kinds of submission, although only one of degree, is nevertheless a substantial one. In one case a State, in the full knowledge of the circumstances, agrees to a decision disregarding the existing law because it is of the opinion that it ought not to insist on the strict application of the law. In the other case the State leaves it to the international tribunal to determine whether the existing law ought to have effect given to it. The difference although one of degree is fundamental. The mere possibility of such a power being exercised must reduce the authority and usefulness of the existing rules of international law; it would confer upon the international court unchecked and unlimited powers of legislation. No such objection attaches to the granting of such an authority in a particular case, as an act of friendliness on the part of the State which may hope to benefit from the application of strict law, or which is entitled to a judicial verdict by virtue of a general arbitration treaty.[1]

§ 33. Legislation 'ad hoc' by the Parties to the Dispute.

In appropriate cases the disputants may, while submitting the matter to the Court, themselves assume part of the legislative function either by creating new rules, or by modifying or defining more clearly in the arbitration agreement the existing law. When there is a danger that the application of certain legal rules or principles may yield results which are either unjust, or disturb so radically the established *status quo* as to be impracticable, the parties may lay down, in the arbitration agreement, specific rules calculated to guide the

---

[1] See below, pp. 331 et seqq., 372 et seqq.

Tribunal and to prevent any such result. Thus in the arbitration convention concluded on 2 February 1897 between Great Britain and Venezuela concerning British Guiana, the two countries agreed to adopt for the guidance of the Tribunal—in addition to large discretionary powers conferred upon it—a rule defining both the period and requirements of prescription as a title of acquisition of territory.[1] This course was adopted after it had become clear that although Great Britain might eventually be induced to abandon her unwillingness to arbitrate, she would do so only if a provision were inserted for making impossible a judgement rendered in accordance with formal and antiquated rules as to acquisition of title by discovery.[2] The treaty of 8 May 1871 between the United States and Great Britain which provided for the arbitration of the *Alabama* claims and laid down the well-known 'three rules of Washington', offers an example of the parties defining a disputed[3] legal rule for the purpose of the arbitration and leaving to the Tribunal the substantial task of deciding how far the claims put forward came within the rules thus defined.[4] Equally, the arbitration agreement of 13 February 1909 between the United States and Venezuela in the *Orinoco Steamship Company* case,[5] defined, in its first Article, the reasons of nullity of arbitral awards, thus supplying the arbitrators with a legal rule hitherto confined to the writings of international lawyers.[6,7]

---

[1] *British and Foreign State Papers*, lxxxix (1896–7), p. 57. See also rule (*c*) of Article 4 laying down that 'in determining the boundary line, if territory of one Party be found by the Tribunal to have been at the date of this Treaty in occupation of the subjects or citizens of the other Party, such effect shall be given to such occupation as reason, justice, the principles of international law and the equities of the case shall, in the opinion of the Tribunal, require'.

[2] See the correspondence with the United States: *British and Foreign State Papers*, lxxxvii (1894–5), pp. 1061–1107. In particular see the passages in Mr. Olney's Note of 20 July 1895 (ibid., p. 1087), and in Lord Salisbury's Note of 26 September, 1895 (ibid., p. 1107).

[3] The question whether the 'three rules' laid down new law, or whether they merely defined existing rules of law, has since been the subject of controversy among international lawyers. The predominant view seems to be that the 'three rules' did not effect any substantial change in the existing law. In the British view, expressly stated in the arbitration convention, they did have that effect. See on this subject Lapradelle and Politis, ii. 935–65, and Westlake, ii (1907), p. 198.

[4] See above, p. 151.

[5] See the *compromis* in Scott, *Hague Court Reports*, p. 235.

[6] See on this case Lammasch, *Rechtskraft*, pp. 40, 41, and Scelle in *R.G.* xviii (1911), p. 186.

[7] For another instance of the arbitration agreement laying down specific rules to govern the tribunal see Articles II and III of the Terms of Submission appended to the Special Agreement between the United States and Great Britain of 18 August 1910 (Nielsen's *Report*, p. 9).

CHAPTER XVI

JUDICIAL DECISION AS THE STARTING POINT FOR THE MODIFICATION OF LAW

I

By the Will of the Parties

§ 34. The Place of Judicial Decision in the Scheme of Change. The conferment, in various forms, of legislative powers upon an international tribunal is not the only procedure by which judicial settlement may be rendered compatible with a change of the existing law or made an instrument of it. Judicial settlement may, given the will of the parties, prove the starting-point for a required change of the law. But before such change is attempted it may be necessary to determine what the law is. For frequently a dispute is of a double nature; it consists both in a disagreement as to the existing law and in a desire to have the law changed should its rule be regarded as harsh and unreasonable. In such cases the situation tends to be doubly difficult. The latent desire for change obscures the legal issue with the State interested in the alteration of the existing legal *status quo*; on the other hand, the denial on the part of the opponent of what are believed to be obvious legal rights tends to develop, in the State favoured by the existing law, a disinclination to show such attitude of reasonableness and accommodation as it might otherwise be inclined to show. But if it is true to say that petty insistence on acquired rights produces irritation and friction, then it is equally true to say that a denial of what is believed to be a valid legal right creates the feeling that a moral wrong has been inflicted upon the State. It is not so much the denial of the object of the dispute as the denial of an impartial decision on an asserted legal right which creates the sentiment of an injury received. In cases like this the legal decision creates a convenient and welcome starting-point for an attitude of accommodation. It clears the air. Before the law can be changed it is essential to know what the existing law is; if a future relation is to be established on the basis of equity, then the existing legal position, which only in exceptional cases is entirely devoid of an element of equity and justice, must furnish one of the bases of the future settlement. It is the bridge between the statics and the dynamics of the law. It removes the element of dispute; it throws open the field of understanding. It is incompatible with the dignity of the law that it should be disobeyed, but it is not incompatible with its dignity that it should be changed, once it has been ascertained, by the agreement of the parties. Such a change may be the result of a voluntary agreement between the parties. But it may also be thought of as part of an international machinery calculated to remedy the drawbacks of the absence of an international legislature and to facilitate the transition from a static to a dynamic international law.[1]

§ 35. Judicial Decision as Preliminary to an Award 'ex aequo et bono'. The parties may agree that the legal pronouncement of an international tribunal shall be of a provisional nature, in the sense that it shall form the basis of subsequent negotiations between them, with a view to arriving at an equitable application of the judgement, and that, in case they should be unable to arrive at such an agreement, the task of reconciling the strictly judicial pronouncement of the tribunal with considerations of equity shall be left to another tribunal. There is a recent instance of two States which envisaged the entrusting of a tribunal with the settlement of a controversy after it had been decided by the Permanent Court of International Justice, on the basis of considerations not wholly identical with existing law as found by the Court. This was the case in the Special Agreement signed on 19 April 1928 between France and Yugoslavia, submitting for decision to the Permanent Court of International Justice certain questions concerning the payment of various Serbian loans floated in France.[2] Article II of that Agreement provided that, within one month from the delivery of the decision by the Court, the two Governments and the representatives of the bondholders should meet for the purpose of conducting negotiations with a view to concluding an arrangement which: (a) in the event of the Court deciding in accordance with the submission of Yugoslavia, should determine whether considerations of equity do not require the Government of that country to make

---

[1] See on this point the observations of M. Hammarskjöld in *Journal of Royal Institute of International Affairs*, ix (1930), pp. 472, 474.

[2] The Agreement is printed in *P.C.I.J.*, Series C, No. 16 (III), p. 292.

concessions over and above those which it would be obliged to make in strict law; (*b*) in the event of the Court finding in favour of the bondholders, will grant certain concessions to the Government of Yugoslavia, having regard to its financial and economic position.[1] The same Article provided that, failing such an agreement, the question of concessions referred to above shall be settled by a final decision of a special arbitral tribunal to which the matter may be referred by either of the parties.

§ 36. Judicial Decision as Preliminary to Further Negotiations. The parties may agree to avail themselves of a judicial pronouncement, as the basis of subsequent negotiations calculated to establish a new legal situation between them. An agreement of this type means that the parties reserve for themselves the legislative function instead of entrusting it to the Court. The special agreement, already referred to, of 30 October 1924 between France and Switzerland concerning the interpretation of the provision of Article 435, paragraph 2, of the Treaty of Versailles relating to the Free Zones of Upper Savoy and the District of Gex offers an example of this procedure.[2] In that convention the parties agreed to submit their dispute to the Court, with the request that the latter should consider the question in regular proceedings, but that, before giving formal judgement, it should 'unofficially' communicate to the parties its views as to the legal aspect of the matter, fixing at the same time a reasonable period within which the parties, apparently on the basis of the legal opinion of the Court, should settle between themselves the régime to be applied to the districts mentioned.[3] The same agreement provided that should the parties fail to conclude and to ratify, within that period, a treaty embodying the settlement, the Court shall by means of a final judgement pronounce both on the merits of the dispute and on the manner of its execution. This agreement, which amounted in fact to a request for an Advisory Opinion prior to the rendering of a formal judgement, asked the Court to exercise a function not envisaged by the Statute of the Court. Very wisely, if we may say so with respect, the Court considered that it could assume jurisdiction in view both of its duty to facilitate direct and friendly settlement between

---

[1] See Judgement No. 14, Series A, No. 20, p. 15.   [2] See above, p. 316.
[3] *P.C.I.J.*, Series A, No. 22, p. 7.

the parties, and of the fact that its legal opinion could conveniently be expressed in the form of the reasons underlying an Order (not having binding force), fixing the time limit within which the parties were instructed to arrive at an agreement. It is true that the Court, while complying with the request of the parties, expressed the view that it is important that 'special agreements whereby international disputes are submitted to the Court should henceforth be formulated with due regard to the forms in which the Court is to express its opinion according to the precise terms of the constitutional provisions governing its activity'; but this view is in no way expressive of the value and possible usefulness of the course adopted in the special agreement. It only states that the form of the special agreement was not in conformity with the requirements of the Statute. But one may still inquire into the desirability or appropriateness of amending the Statute so as to bring formally within its purview arbitration agreements like that concluded by France and Switzerland. It is not unreasonable to expect that the constitutions of the international agencies should conform to the needs of the international society, and the question ought in the future to be considered on its merits, namely, whether, without renouncing the benefits of a binding judicial pronouncement, it may not be useful to offer to the disputants an opportunity of arriving at a settlement of which the legal opinion of the Court should form one, but not necessarily the only, element.

§ 37. The Function of Advisory Opinions as an Instrument of Adjustment.

Arbitration agreements like those between France and Yugoslavia, and Switzerland and France, raise the question whether provision ought not to be made for enabling the parties to have direct recourse to the advisory jurisdiction of the Court. The Advisory Opinion neither has, nor is intended to have, the binding effect contemplated by the judgement. While possessing the full authority of ascertaining beyond doubt the legal position, it leaves room for its adaptation in accordance with the requirements of political expediency. In fact, a number of Advisory Opinions given by the Court at the request of the Council have proved a convenient basis for further negotiations and for the final adjustment of the controversy.[1] At present, States are in a

---

[1] See *P.C.I.J.*, Series E, No. 1, p. 208, on the negotiations and final settlement subsequent to the Sixth Advisory Opinion concerning German Settlers in

position to approach the Court with a request for an Advisory Opinion only through the Council or the Assembly of the League. Thus when in 1927 a dispute arose between Greece and Turkey concerning the interpretation of a clause in the Agreement of 1 December 1926 concerning the jurisdiction of the Mixed Commission for the Exchange of Greek and Turkish Populations, the parties asked the Council of the League to request the Court to give an Advisory Opinion on the disputed question. The Council complied with the request, and the Court gave its Opinion on 28 August 1928.[1] A similar procedure was adopted in regard to the Advisory Opinions concerning the jurisdiction of the European Commission of the Danube[2] and the Graeco-Bulgarian Communities.[3] In these cases, the request for an Advisory Opinion, far from constituting one stage in the procedure before the Council, was in the nature of a purely ministerial act, transmitting to the Court the request of the Governments concerned without an examination of the merits of the dispute. Although in these cases no undue difficulty was experienced in inducing the Council to transmit the request, it may be useful to consider whether it would not be in the

Poland. In that Opinion the Court expressed the view that the attitude adopted by Poland, in disregarding certain rights acquired by German colonists from the German Government, particularly in the period between the armistice and the ratification of the Treaty of Versailles, and in evicting these colonists, was not in conformity with the international obligations of Poland. Subsequently to that Opinion the Council declared that the case must be dealt with on the basis of the Court's Opinion. In accordance with that resolution a settlement was arrived at which provided, not for reinstatement, but for substantial compensation to be granted to the evicted settlers. See also ibid., p. 214, on the negotiations and arbitral award in settlement of the dispute dealt with in the Seventh Advisory Opinion concerning the Acquisition of Polish Nationality. See, further, op. cit., No. 4, p. 212, and No. 5, pp. 223–6, on the action taken upon Advisory Opinion No. 14 concerning the jurisdiction of the European Commission of the Danube. In that Opinion the Court, contrary to the Roumanian contention, answered in the affirmative the question whether the European Commission of the Danube has the same powers on the maritime sector of the Danube from Galatz to Braila as on the sector below Galatz. The subsequent negotiations resulted in a compromise. See *Official Journal*, April 1931, p. 735, for a Declaration, signed at Geneva on 5 December 1930 by the Governments of the Powers which are parties to the Convention instituting the Definitive Statute of the Danube. The Declaration is accompanied by a Draft Convention which, while reserving for the European Commission of the Danube the power to draw up and promulgate river police regulations for the maritime Danube (Article 1), reserves to the Roumanian Government the right to set up a Navigation Tribunal and a Navigation Court for the enforcement of these regulations (Articles 2–5). Article 12 lays down that these tribunals shall be bound by the law laid down in the Advisory Opinion.

[1] Series B, No. 16.   [2] Series B, No. 14.
[3] Series B, No. 17.

interests of peace and of international justice if the parties could directly ask the Court for an Advisory Opinion with a view to obtaining the benefits of a judicial pronouncement coupled with the provisional suspension of its effect. In certain respects an Advisory Opinion does not differ from a declaratory judgement—a task which the Court has declared to be one of its most important functions.[1] It may be of advantage not to risk the possible complications and delays incidental to the procedure before the Council, and not to impose upon it the responsibility for giving effect to the Advisory Opinion—a responsibility which it might find difficult to ignore in cases in which the request for an Advisory Opinion formally originates from the Council. Cases may occur—and have in fact occurred[2]—in which a Government, although unwilling to have the merits of a dispute ascertained by a formal judgement of the Court, may be prepared to submit it for an Advisory Opinion. The argument that, by extending thus the scope of Advisory Opinions, the Court might become involved in political controversies is as little convincing as the same argument when put forward in regard to the judgements[3] of the Court and its Opinions at the request of the Council or the Assembly.[4] The extension

---

[1] See above, p. 327, n. 2.

[2] See, for instance, the dispute concerning the jurisdiction of the European Danube Commission, in which Roumania rejected the proposal for having the case decided by a judgement of the Court, but agreed to the matter being submitted for an Advisory Opinion, on condition that it should have no binding effect and that 'the Court's Advisory Opinion having been given and the [subsequent] negotiations having led to no result, the latter should be regarded as to all intents and purposes terminated, and the four Governments should re-assume entire liberty of action': *P. C.I.J.*, Series B, No. 14, p. 21. As to the settlement of the controversy, see above, p. 334, n. 1. It will be noted that the four Governments reserved to themselves the right to bring the matter for a judgement of the Court, if necessary. See the interesting remarks of Michel de la Grotte in *R.I.*, 3rd ser., x (1929), p. 400, on the question whether the Court would be at liberty to render a judgement in a matter previously decided by an Advisory Opinion. While there seems to be no objection to the Court's confirming by a judgement a previous Advisory Opinion, it may be doubted whether the former could in substance differ from the latter. If, in point of the judicial character of the procedure, the difference between Advisory Opinions and Judgements is purely nominal, then it is difficult to see how the two procedures can result in materially different decisions, unless the Advisory Opinion proves subsequently to be based on a material error of fact or law—a contingency which, having regard to the authority of the Court, it is not necessary to contemplate.

[3] See p. 156.

[4] See, for instance, the Memorandum submitted by Judge Moore in 1922 on the occasion of the drafting of the Rules of the Court (*P.C.I.J.*, Series D, No. 2, p. 383), in which the giving of Advisory Opinions is described as not in conformity with the judicial character of the Court. See also the remarks of Mr. Elihu Root at the Committee of Jurists in 1920, *Procès-Verbaux*, p. 584. See,

of the scope of Advisory Opinions in this direction could be qualified by reserving to the Court the power to refuse, when necessary, to comply with the request. But the general and direct availability of Advisory Opinions might prove yet another instrument for the initiation of the process of peaceful change on the basis of judicial pronouncements which have in strict law no binding force, but which constitute at the same time an authoritative expression of the existing law.[1,2]

II

As Part of International Constitutional Machinery

§ 38. Judgements of Courts and the Part of Political Organs. The problem of preventing judgements of international tribunals, giving effect to obsolete or unworkable law, from becoming a source of friction and an instrument of injustice is of too great importance, even if reduced to its proper proportions, to be left entirely to the initiative of States. Alongside, therefore, of the consideration of the means, the recourse to which must be left to the initiative and the free will of the disputants, there ought to be considered methods the use of which need not be dependent upon the decision of the States which stand to benefit from the strict application and enforcement of the existing law. Means must be examined calculated to secure the assistance of the

however, Hudson, *The Advisory Opinions of the Permanent Court of International Justice* (*International Conciliation Pamphlet*, No. 214, 1925), especially pp. 370–4, and the Report of Lapradelle and Negulesco, *Annuaire*, xxxiv (1928), pp. 409–57.

[1] It will be noted that the practice of the Court and the amendments of the relevant provisions of its rules (see, for instance, Article 71) have resulted in a thoroughgoing assimilation of the advisory and contentious procedures.

[2] At the First Assembly the Argentine delegation proposed that States should be granted the right to approach the Court directly with a request for an Advisory Opinion; the International Labour Organization proposed an amendment enabling it to have recourse to the Court for an Advisory Opinion: see Lapradelle and Negulesco, op. cit., p. 434. These amendments were not adopted, probably in view of the fact that they necessitated an alteration of Article 14 of the Covenant. As to the attitude of the Permanent Court itself on the matter see, for instance, the Advisory Opinion of 8 March 1932 concerning the interpretation of the Graeco-Bulgarian Agreement of 9 December 1927: Series A/B, No. 45, p. 87. The Court refused to give an Advisory Opinion on a subject on which, in its view, the Council of the League had not asked for an Advisory Opinion, but as to which the two parties expressed the wish that the Court should pronounce an opinion. It appears, however, that the Court might perhaps have been willing to consider whether an understanding to this effect between the parties reached in the course of the proceedings would be regarded as a kind of 'special agreement', initiating a contentious proceeding before the Court.

political organs of the community of nations in overriding the consequences of obsolete law as ascertained by judgements of international tribunals. It is believed that the judicial organs of the international community could, without derogating from their judicial function and their position of impartiality, play a useful—and, it is believed, at present an essential—part in this process.

Thus, it might be considered how far, possibly by an appropriate change in the Statute, the Court should be empowered to state that the judgement, whilst given in accordance with the existing legal position, might with advantage be considered, with a view to a possible modification of its terms in the wider interest of international peace, either by the parties themselves or by the Council of the League.[1] Such an opinion on the part of the Court, if expressed either with unanimity or with a substantial majority approaching unanimity, could, as a further step, be given the effect of suspending the execution of the judgement pending the consideration of the matter by the Council. Although not accompanied by an express recommendation as to the solution of the difficulty, it would undoubtedly carry weight in any subsequent deliberations of the Council. As the law now stands there is nothing to prevent the Council from considering, under Article 11 of the Covenant, a judgement of an international tribunal, either *proprio motu* or at the initiative of any Member of the League, as was done in the Hungarian-Roumanian Optants dispute.[2] But the procedure here suggested, being grounded on the will of the Court, and the provision of the Statute of the Court, could be resorted to without producing the otherwise unavoidable result of impairing the authority of the judgement of the Court, and of international justice generally. A further

[1] The final judgement of the Permanent Court in the Swiss-French *Free Zones* case given on 7 June 1932 constitutes an important example of a pronouncement of this nature. The Court, while giving judgement in favour of Switzerland, said: 'The Court does not hesitate to express its opinion that if, by the maintenance in force of the old treaties, Switzerland obtains the economic advantages derived from the free zones, she ought in return to grant compensatory economic advantages to the people of the zones' (*P.C.I.J.*, Series A/B, No. 46, p. 169).

[2] That matter was referred by Roumania to the Council under Article 11 of the Covenant following upon the judgement of the Roumano-Hungarian Mixed Arbitral Tribunal affirming its jurisdiction in the matter of claims of Hungarian Optants in connexion with the Roumanian agrarian reform. The unsatisfactory feature of that phase of the dispute was that the Council was asked to act, not in order to remedy the disadvantages of a legal decision—no such decision on the merits had been given—but in order to prevent a possibly unfavourable legal decision.

development of this process would consist in suspending indefinitely, by the vote of an appropriate majority of the members of the Council, the execution of a judgement based on legal rules or rights which, to paraphrase Article 19 of the Covenant, have become inapplicable or whose continuance might endanger the peace of the world.

In fact the time has come to consider whether the present deadlock of Article 19 cannot, in a restricted sphere, be successfully overcome by making a judicial pronouncement having no binding effect the starting-point for putting into operation the political machinery for revising or at least for rendering provisionally inoperative existing law. Weighty objections can, no doubt, be put forward to any such scheme. Yet the problem here discussed is one calling for the examination of all possible avenues likely to assist in overcoming the difficulties resulting from the absence of an effective international legislature.[1] In especial, undue importance need not be attached to the apprehension, to which international lawyers appear to be particularly susceptible, that the exercise of a function of this nature may put into jeopardy the judicial character of the Court. Undoubtedly the use by the Court of powers of the nature here suggested might result in its becoming involved in the political controversies of the day. But the danger ought not to be exaggerated. The great majority of cases brought before the Permanent Court of International Justice have been of a highly political character. Whatever may be the nature of the Court's

---

[1] See on this matter Decencière-Ferrandière in *R.G.* xxxvi (1929), pp. 416–51, who proposes the establishment of an International Equity Court entitled to review, on the basis of equity as distinguished from law, judgements of international tribunals, including the Permanent Court. The proposal if put into practice would amount to endowing non-legal tribunals with compulsory legislative powers and is therefore open to objections indicated above, p. 328, and below, p. 373. In addition, Professor Decencière-Ferrandière's article disregards the law amending and adjusting factors already operating within the scope of existing obligatory judicial settlement. See for a criticism of his suggestions Strupp, *Das Recht des internationalen Richters, nach Billigkeit zu entscheiden* (1930), p. 118. However, proposals of this nature put forward constructive suggestions and ought to be carefully examined. They constitute an advance upon the method of approach which is satisfied with the somewhat simple solution of rejecting obligatory judicial settlement. This is, for instance, the somewhat disappointing result of the monograph of Morgenthau, *Die internationale Rechtspflege, ihr Wesen und Grenzen* (1929). M. Hostie's admirable articles on this subject—in *R.I.*, 3rd ser., ix (1928), pp. 262–81 and 562–87—are open to the same objection. M. Hostie suggests that in cases in which the Court might be compelled to give judgements which are materially unjust, and contrary to equity, it should declare the dispute to be non-justiciable and refuse to give judgement.

pronouncements, they cannot be altogether detached from the background of political controversy. It is not incompatible with the duty of the judge to criticize the law in accordance with which judgement is given and to make suggestions for its improvement. The judicial character of judgements of municipal courts is not impaired by the fact that the judges, while feeling bound to administer the existing law, frequently express strong views as to the reasonableness or justice of the legal provisions in question.

§ 39. The Function of the Council of the League of Nations in the Settlement of International Disputes. While a judicial decision may appropriately become the starting-point for any future change in the law, the task of amending the law and adapting it to changed conditions must, in so far as this function cannot be fulfilled by the normal judicial activity or by agreement of the parties, necessarily fall upon the political organs of the international community. The scope of that task is at present strictly limited by existing law.[1]

---

[1] So far as Article 19 of the Covenant is concerned, the possibilities of its effective application have not been substantially increased as the result of the resolution of the Assembly of 1929 which, at the instance of the Chinese delegation, considered the matter afresh. In that Resolution the Assembly 'Declares that a Member of the League may on its own responsibility, subject to the Rules of Procedure of the Assembly, place on the agenda of the Assembly the question whether the Assembly should give advice as contemplated by Article 19 regarding the reconsideration of any treaty or treaties which such Member considers to have become inapplicable or the consideration of international conditions the continuance of which might, in its opinion, endanger the peace of the world;

'Declares that for an application of this kind to be entertained by the Assembly it must be drawn up in appropriate terms, that is to say, in terms which are in conformity with Article 19;

'Declares that, in the event of an application in such terms being placed upon the agenda of the Assembly, the Assembly shall, in accordance with its ordinary procedure, discuss this application and, if it thinks proper, give the advice requested' (*Resolutions of the Tenth Assembly, Off. Journal, Sp. Suppl.*, October 1929, p. 18). As to the previous history of Article 19 see Oppenheim, i. 343, 344. The alternative approach towards international legislation is to endow with binding force the unanimous recommendation of the Council when acting under Article 15 of the Covenant. At present there is no obligation upon States to comply with the unanimous recommendation of the Council. In 1930 a Committee, appointed by the Council to consider some proposed amendments to the Covenant, produced a report containing a proposal which, if adopted, would have made the unanimous recommendation of the Council binding upon the States in dispute (Doc. A. 8, 1930, V). As the Council is not bound to apply existing rules of international law for the solution of disputes submitted to it, the proposed amendment amounted to conferring upon it legislative powers. However, the proposal did not secure acceptance on the part of the Eleventh Assembly of 1930, whose Legal Committee thought it desirable to return 'to

But the necessities of international life must in time lead to the abandonment of these limitations at least to the extent of allowing—as the first stage of the development—the Council and the Assembly of the League of Nations a larger measure of initiative in the process of bringing about such changes. While the legislative measures proper will, by the very nature of things, have to remain within the province of the Assembly, the initiative, either by positive measures or through temporary suspension of the operation of existing law, will more appropriately fall within the sphere of activities of the Council. It is in this field, and not in the settlement of any dispute which the parties may care to submit to its decision, that lies the proper province of the Council in the sphere of pacific settlement of international disputes. Such a conception of its function would leave it more free than hitherto to devote itself, unencumbered by the role of a judge in petty but protracted disputes, to the major task of international government in general and of initiation of international legislation in particular.

This aspect of the possible functions of the Council has been obscured in the years following upon the World War by the circumstance that the bulk of its energies has been devoted to the task of settling disputes. This one-sided preoccupation of the Council with composing controversies was in turn due not only to the conditions of the world after the political upheaval caused by the war of 1914–18, but also to the fact that the Peace Treaties entrusted it with the function of an arbiter in a large number of questions, and with partial responsibility for the execution of many of their provisions. However, this source of its activity, useful and unavoidable as it was in the initial stages of the League, cannot be regarded as being of a permanent nature. Care must be taken not to regard this aspect of the Council's activity as being its central and most important function.

It is a retrogressive attitude which regards as the normal function of the most important organ of the international community that of settling disputes between its members.

the original principles established by the Covenant'. The Committee suggested the following wording of Article 15, paragraph 6: 'If the report of the Council is unanimously agreed to by the members thereof, other than the representatives of one or more parties to the dispute, the Council shall invite the parties to comply with the recommendations of the report.' For the Report of the First Committee see *Records of the Eleventh Assembly, Plenary Meetings*, Annex 32, p. 598.

It is retrogressive because there is inherent in it the tendency to perpetuate a state of affairs proper to rudimentary communities at the lowest stage of legal development, that is to say, to communities in which the prevention of violence is the exclusive purpose of the rule of law. Only in a very rudimentary society, which has not entirely outgrown the stage of *bellum omnium contra omnes*, does every individual dispute tend to become a matter affecting the whole community, endangering its very peace and necessitating the intervention of the highest organs of organized society. This habit of contemplating disputes as the central phenomenon of social interest may itself be one of the contributory causes of insecurity. Unavoidably it results in perpetuating that rudimentary type of legal organization in a community of States with a highly developed law within their borders and with a growing interdependence and complexity of relations in their mutual intercourse.[1] The normal tendency in organized society, in which the reign of force has been replaced by the reign of law, is to remove disputes from the political sphere and to allocate them their proper place in the domain of judicial settlement. This tendency may also be observed among the Members of the League. The Covenant itself does not recognize the duty of obligatory arbitration, and even such disputes as in Article 13 are described as generally suitable for judicial settlement may, at the option of the parties, be submitted to the Council. But the position in this respect has since been substantially changed as the result of the extension of the sphere of obligatory judicial settlement in consequence of the very general acceptance of the Optional Clause of Article 36 of the Statute. Thus, for instance, a dispute like the one between Great Britain and France in 1923 concerning the Nationality Decrees in Tunis and Morocco which, in the absence of an effective treaty of obligatory arbitration,[2] had to be submitted to the Council, would under the law as it exists to-day necessarily fall within the jurisdiction of the Court— always provided that it would not come within one of the numerous reservations to the Optional Clause.[3]

---

[1] See below, p. 434.

[2] See above, p. 197.

[3] For instance—in addition to the one mentioned in the text below—the reservation limiting the scope of the signature to 'disputes arising after the ratification of the present declaration with regard to situations or facts subsequent to the said ratification', or the reservation excluding 'disputes with regard to questions which by international law fall exclusively within the

§ 40. The Council of the League and Judicial Settlement.

One of these reservations bears directly upon the question under discussion. It is the reservation which enables the parties to remove from the jurisdiction of thex Court to that of the Council, for one year in the first instance, any dispute covered by the terms of the Optional Clause.[1] This reservation is one of the manifestations of the persistent tendency of States to lapse into rudimentary methods of procedure. One of the reasons which seem to have inspired this clause was the apprehension that disputes may arise, in which the Court may be compelled to render decisions based on unsatisfactory, inequitable, and obsolete law. The reservation is to be deprecated. It is open to all the objections which have here been put forward against a procedure which makes of the Council the regular agency for settling disputes. Even in the society of States in which the rule of law is not firmly established, the natural procedure, which is likely to leave the least sense of grievance, is the submission of the dispute for a decision by law in the first instance. The second stage, namely, the search for remedies in case the law proves unsatisfactory, ought to follow and not to precede the process of ascertaining the existing law. To adopt the reverse course is to create the feeling of the benefit of the law being withheld, and to complicate comparatively simple legal issues by making them the object of the intricate and dilatory working of the political machinery of the Council. As a matter of experience, however effective may have proved the part of the Council as an instrument for preventing sudden disturbance of the peace[2] or in dealing with the enforcement of certain

---

jurisdiction of the United Kingdom.' On the meaning of these reservations see Lauterpacht, 'The British Reservations to the Optional Clause,' in *Economica* (1930), pp. 138–72, and Fischer Williams in *B.Y.* (1930), pp. 74–80.

[1] The Optional Clause was signed by Great Britain subject to the condition that 'His Majesty's Government reserve the right to require that proceedings in the Court shall be suspended in respect of any dispute which has been submitted to and is under consideration by the Council of the League of Nations, provided that notice to suspend is given after the dispute has been submitted to the Council, and is given within ten days of the notification of the initiation of the proceedings in the Court, and provided also that such suspension shall be limited to a period of twelve months or such longer period as may be agreed by the Parties to the dispute or determined by a decision of all the Members of the Council other than the Parties to the dispute'. France, Italy, and Czechoslovakia appended a similar reservation without limiting, however, the period within which the Council ought to deal with the matter. For the text of the reservations see *P.C.I.J.*, Series E, No. 6, pp. 478 et seqq.

[2] The importance of this aspect of the work of the Council may be readily acknowledged without there being any necessity for generalizing the achieve-

provisions of the Peace Treaties, its part in settling disputes has as a rule consisted in delegating the essential decision to judicial agencies. In a number of protracted cases in which it failed to adopt that course, its intervention has resulted in a serious loss to its prestige and to the authority of international justice, while the delegation of the decision to a judicial body has as a rule proved not only the most honourable, but also the most opportune solution of the difficulty.

What, then, is the proper function of the League of Nations, and in particular of its Council, in settling international disputes? That function is of the highest importance. But just because it is of the highest importance it is undesirable that it should be obscured by the performance, as a matter of course, of the task of settling all controversies which States may care to submit to it. The normal part of the Council in settling international disputes ought, it is submitted, to consist in the fulfilment of the following four functions: First, the Council must intervene whenever there is danger of a sudden and violent disturbance of the peace. Secondly, it ought to be the duty of the Council, whenever seised under Articles 11 or 15 of the Covenant, to direct the dispute to the channels of the law so that the existing rights may be impartially and authoritatively established. Its third function is, as already provided in the Covenant, to assist in giving effect to the legal position thus ascertained. The fourth is to take the initiative in causing such changes, or suspension of the operation, of existing law as may be necessary in the interests of international peace and co-operation. Some of the possibilities of the Council's action in this field were discussed in the preceding section. It is in order to be able to act thus as an *ultimum refugium pacis*, through the initiation of such changes in the law as peace and justice make necessary, that the Council must not in the future be allowed to assume, as a normal feature of its activity, the function of settling disputes between States.

ments of the Council in the direction of making it a conciliation commission for all disputes of importance. Such undue generalization mars the otherwise very useful and informative book of Mr. Conwell-Evans entitled *The League Council in Action. A Study of the Methods Employed by the Council of the League of Nations to prevent War and to settle International Disputes* (1929). See also on this aspect of the work of the Council Massart, *Le controversie internationali dinanzi al consiglio della Società delle Nazioni* (1929); Dotremont, *L'arbitrage internationale et le Conseil de la Société des Nations* (1929); Philipse, *Le rôle du Conseil de la Société des Nations dans le règlement pacifique des différends internationaux* (1929); Fischer Williams, *International Change and International Peace* (1932), pp. 59 et seqq.

§ 41. Conclusions. The Problem of Change and the Rule of Law.

This book would entirely fail in one of its main objects if it were understood to question the seriousness of the problem created for obligatory arbitration by the absence of an international legislature. At the same time, however, we believe that the difficulty arising from this defect of international organization cannot be solved by the rejection of obligatory arbitration altogether (that is by aggravating one evil by the perpetuation of another of even graver and more anarchical consequences), but by a proper assessment of the factor of change in international relations and by the exploration of all means either actually operating or likely to act towards the removal of the dangers which result from the absence of an agency to amend existing law. Thus it has been pointed out that much of this amending process is actually and necessarily performed by international judges in the ordinary exercise of their judicial function. Attention has been drawn to specific doctrines, such as the doctrine of *rebus sic stantibus* or of abuse of rights, likely to assist judges in this process. As a further possibility of effecting change, instances drawn from the practice of States have been adduced and discussed in which the parties have either agreed to extend or to modify judicial legislation as to make it conform with requirements of justice and progress, or in which they have themselves performed part of this function. It is in these voluntary agreements, dictated by a farseeing spirit of accommodation and of the realization of the ultimate solidarity of interests, and concluded, as occasion arises, within the all-embracing obligation to submit to final judicial settlement that a large part of the remedy lies. Finally, there have been considered certain institutional safeguards of international society which, although falling short of an international legislature, may prove instrumental in providing the necessary starting-point for a change in the law.

It is a clear duty of international lawyers to explore these avenues in detail and to examine their possibilities. It is not permissible to reject an institution indispensable to the life of a community under the reign of law merely because its application may, in view of the deficient organization of the international society, be fraught with danger. The obvious duty of the lawyer is, first, to weigh the consequences of the repudiation of obligatory submission to international tribunals against the contingencies of a remoter nature arising out of the absence of an international legislature; his next duty is to provide for these contingencies by propounding and examining critically both the existing legal remedies and any constructive proposals calculated to reduce to a minimum the dangers and inconveniences resulting from the absence of an effective international legislature. This Part of the present book constitutes an attempt to fulfil that task. Undoubtedly none of the existing or proposed remedies constitutes a complete solution. Remedial judicial legislation is limited by the existing legal materials, and by the necessary limitation of the judicial function. The application of the doctrine *rebus sic stantibus* cannot go beyond the scope of the application of analogous principles in private law. The prohibition of abuse of rights may have to be interpreted restrictively in a community in which freedom of action must necessarily be interpreted extensively. Extension of judicial legislation by the will of the parties and the making of the judicial pronouncement the starting-point for the law-amending process is contingent upon the parties being induced by their sense of justice, reasonableness and responsibility for international peace, to adopt that procedure. The institution, by the political organs of the League of Nations, of changes in the law on the basis of judicial decision, although not implying a radical departure, is still within the domain of proposals. But it is submitted that, however small each of these remedies may be, their cumulative effect is to supply a working alternative to a purely negative attitude.

The argument that, in view of the absence of an effective machinery of change, obligatory arbitration may result in perpetuating some crying injustices of customary and conventional international law is undoubtedly persuasive and cannot be ignored. But the rejection on this account of obligatory arbitration amounts in the last resort to a sanction of the reign of force,[1] and the question arises whether force

---

[1] See for an instructive illustration of the consequences of that attitude the essay on Arbitration in *Studies in Diplomatic History* (1930) by Headlam-Morley. The essay is full of learned observations on the merits of arbitration, but the final conclusion is the rejection of obligatory arbitration in matters of vital interest in view of the unavoidable necessity of providing for the change of the political *status quo* through war (p. 47). See the comment in *B.Y.* (1931), p. 220. The student will note with interest almost identical passages in Jellinek's *Allgemeine Staatslehre* over thirty years ago, when he insisted that 'if there existed an effective inter-state, and especially a super-state, system deciding disputes in accordance with established legal principles, it would result in conserving in the

is more likely to prove an instrument of just change. Thus viewed, the problem reduces itself to one of choice between peace and war, or law and force, as instruments for securing justice. There is no escape from the necessity of making that choice, for there is an obvious incompatibility between the current acceptance of the idea of arbitration and the accompanying limitation of that acceptance of the rule of law by the qualification that the reign of law can be accepted only in so far as the law operates justly. Such a qualification amounts to saying that a State acknowledges the supremacy of law so long as it operates in its favour, but that it rejects it when it ceases to be of advantage and imposes burdens. Even if the view be accepted—and it may be readily accepted—that the social ideal is not law, but justice, there still remains the fact that ultimately law is the more effective guarantee of securing that end.

In order to endow law with the maximum of effectiveness it is necessary to provide means for the change of law. Such means, falling short of an international legislature, but grounded in the practice of States and in existing international law, have been discussed in this Part of the book. It has been shown here that in a large number of cases it is through law that the change of law will be most conveniently effected. Recent conventional law, by forbidding changes by force, has created the necessary basis for developing these means of peaceful change. The existing tendencies in the direction of the political integration of the community of States will in the future bring about the consummation of the machinery of change through the working of an effective international legislature. This will relieve obligatory judicial settlement of the strain—some real and some imaginary—imposed upon it as a result of the present imperfections of the legislative process. For this and other reasons it is a consummation devoutly to be wished. But it is improvident to reject a working minimum because the maximum cannot as yet be obtained, especially if the desired maximum cannot by the very nature of things constitute a final solution of all diffi-

---

modern world for an indefinite time the infirm, the old and mere remnants of the past, thus rendering impossible all voluntary progress' (p. 340). And he pointed out that had that law prevailed 'Germany and Italy would still be geographical conceptions; the States of the Balkan peninsula (with the exception of Greece) would still be Turkish provinces; the maladministration of Cuba and of the Philippines would still be in force' (ibid.). But see as to Jellinek's attitude to international law p. 410 below.

culties. The conflict between stability and change and between security and justice can never be finally obliterated. It is inherent in the life of a developing society. It can be removed only at the cost of eliminating either security or social change.[1]

---

[1] It is, of course, not only in the field of law that the conflict between stability and change calls for consideration and solution. It is, on a different plane, a persistent problem of philosophy as expressed in the competing claims of philosophical theory and practical belief. See Perry, *Present Philosophical Tendencies* (1912), Chapter I, entitled 'Philosophical Theory and Established Belief'.

PART V

DISPUTES AS TO RIGHTS AND
CONFLICTS OF INTERESTS

CHAPTER XVII

'DISPUTES AS TO RIGHTS' AS A LEGAL CONCEPTION

§ 1. Claims for a Change in the Existing Law. With the limitation of the judicial function in international law on the ground that, as the result of the absence of an international legislature, international tribunals might have to apply unjust or obsolete rules of law, there is closely connected the current distinction between disputes as to rights and so-called conflicts of interests. According to that distinction a dispute is political (and therefore non-justiciable) for the reason that the claim, or the defence, which is being put forward is admittedly advanced on other than legal considerations, i.e. on political, economic, or moral grounds. In such disputes the claim (or the defence) is said to be based not on an existing legal right, but on a demand for the creation of a new right. If a State claims a portion of territory under the sovereignty of its neighbour, not because it alleges the existence of a legal right thereto based on prescription, or discovery, or conquest, but because it deems such territory to be necessary for its development; if it claims the right to prevent the union of two States, not because such a claim is grounded in a treaty or some other right under international law, but because it regards such union as dangerous to its interest; or if, without a corresponding treaty provision, it claims the right to dictate to its neighbour the form of its internal constitution, or its dynastic policy,[1] or the manner and order of the succession to the throne—in all these cases the conflict is said to be clearly non-justiciable, for the simple reason that the claimant State has itself pronounced legal judgement on its claim, and that, by having declared itself to be legally in the wrong, it has eliminated the dispute from the domain of law, and thus ousted the jurisdiction of an international judicial tribunal. It is to this class of conflicts that the fourth, and last, definition of non-justiciable disputes applies: they are those in which the claimant party does not profess to base its claim, or the defendant party its defence,

---

[1] On the dispute between Germany and France in 1870 concerning the succession to the Spanish throne—an example recently referred to by writers with melancholy frequency—see below, p. 376, n. 2.

on a rule of law; non-justiciable controversies are those in which one party or both ask for a change in the existing law; they are conflicts of interests as distinguished from conflicts of rights.

A considerable number of writers have recently been stressing the merits of this new formula of the distinction between legal and political, or justiciable and non-justiciable disputes.[1] They have pointed out that, as international organization is deficient in its legislative and judicial organs, conflicts which within the State are normally resolved by these organs assume, in international society, the form of conflicts of interests; that therefore the antinomy of disputes as to rights and conflicts of interests is the truly scientific embodiment of the traditional distinction between legal and political disputes; and that the retention of the distinction under this new form is beneficial, inasmuch as it brings to mind the necessity of providing a suitable machinery of peaceful settlement for an important class of disputes. It would thus seem that the reasons which have led to the adoption of this distinction are to a large extent the same as those advanced in support of the limitation of the judicial function on the ground of the absence of an international legislature; this has been discussed in the preceding chapters.[2]

This new formula for the orthodox distinction between

---

[1] See Castberg in *R.I.*, 3rd ser., vi (1925), pp. 155–66; Verzijl, ibid., p. 739; Rolin, quoted below; Schindler, in *Recueil des Cours*, 1928 (v), pp. 264–73, and in 'Werdende Rechte' in *Festgabe für Fritz Fleiner* (1927), p. 411; Fischer Williams, *Chapters*, pp. 43–9, and quoted below at p. 355; Clad, *Schiedsgerichtsbarkeit* (1928), p. 116. Strisower in *Der Krieg und die Völkerrechtsordnung* (1919), p. 63, and in *Annuaire* (1922), p. 51, put this distinction very clearly. See also Wehberg, ibid. And see Renault's Preface to Lapradelle and Politis, i (1904), p. xv, in which he draws attention to the difference between *droits contestés* and *une contrariété d'intérêts*. With the above formula may be compared the one proposed in 1907 by Descamps (as quoted by Lammasch, *Schieds-gerichtsbarkeit*, p. 63): 'Les différends dans lesquels les prétentions contradictoires des parties ne peuvent être formulées juridiquement, échappent en quelque sorte par leur nature à la compétence d'une juridiction appelée à dire le droit.'

[2] Possibly the approach is different in the two cases. In the class of case discussed previously, the approach is an objective one, proceeding from the supposed requirements of justice and of the international community. The distinction between disputes as to rights and conflicts of interests refers prima facie to the possibility of disputes in which the refusal to base the claim, or the defence, on legal grounds is not necessarily due to the conviction that a strictly legal verdict would not meet the cause of justice. It may frequently be a mere assertion of power. The two categories could be assimilated only by dint of the argument that an assertion of effective power is an assertion of a moral right identical with justice, or with the objective interests of the international community, and that the State asking for a change is asserting the function of the legislator in the higher international interest.

legal and political disputes has been increasingly gaining ground in conventions of pacific settlement. It was first used in the explanatory Note concerning Article 5 of the Russian Memorandum presented to The Hague Conference in 1899 where it was said: 'Arbitration being of a legal nature, its application is essentially and even exclusively restricted to cases where there is a conflict of international rights, while mediation, although of a political character, is equally applicable to conflicts of interests.'[1] The phrase was subsequently used in 1911 in the unratified arbitration treaties between the United States and Great Britain and France.[2] It reappeared in the Swiss-German treaty of 3 December 1921,[3] whose terminology was adopted in the group of the Locarno arbitration treaties.[4] A few years later it was incorporated in the Pan-American arbitration treaty, and in the General Act recommended by the Ninth Assembly of the League of Nations in 1928.[5] When in 1929 the British Government announced, in the King's speech, its intention to sign the Optional Clause, it referred to the duties of judicial settlement in regard to disputes 'as to respective rights'. Finally, the term 'as to respective rights' has been adopted in the majority of bilateral treaties of pacific settlement concluded in recent years.

§ 2. The Meaning of the Term 'Disputes as to Respective Rights'.

The formula of 'disputes as to respective rights' has been described as removing the difficulties and ambiguities created by the accepted distinction between legal and political (i.e. justiciable and non-justiciable) disputes.[6] It may be doubted whether this is so. What is a dispute 'as to respective rights'? What is a 'conflict of interests'? If the answer is that, in a dispute as to respective rights, *both* parties profess to place themselves on the ground of law, and that in a conflict of interests one or both parties admit that their claim or defence is contrary to the existing law—then the answer is clear enough. But it is an elusive and illusory clarity. A distinction in these terms between two categories

---

[1] *Hague Reports*, p. 95.
[2] See p. 37, above.   [3] See p. 40, above.
[4] See p. 39, above.
[5] See p. 38, above. For further references to these treaties see *Annuaire*, xxxiii (2) (1927), p. 705.
[6] See, for instance, Fischer Williams, loc. cit.; Rolin in *R.I.*, 3rd ser., viii (1927), p. 599.

of disputes may be of interest for the historian or the sociologist, as enabling them to make the statement that in certain cases States are willing to abide by the existing law, and that in others they put forward claims against the existing law. But it is difficult to see of what significance that distinction is for the jurist dealing with the determination of the scope of obligatory judicial settlement. Assuming that it is possible to determine, in a treaty of pacific settlement, what categories of disputes must, and what categories need not, be submitted to obligatory judicial settlement (and it is only by reference to that function that any classification of disputes has a juridical significance, a significance, that is to say, of a concept embodying definite legal rights and duties), what is the legitimate juridical function of a distinction of which each contracting party can avail itself in order to disregard any obligation assumed to have been imposed by the treaty? A treaty of pacific settlement limiting the duty of judicial settlement to disputes 'as to respective rights', in the meaning described above, merely provides that a party shall be under a duty to submit to obligatory judicial settlement any dispute which it wishes so to submit, i.e. any dispute in which it may be content to rely on law; but that it shall be under no such duty in regard to any dispute in which, by advancing or rejecting a claim in disregard of the existing law, it may wish, while remaining within the orbit of the treaty and adopting an attitude envisaged and regulated by the treaty, to oust the obligatory jurisdiction of an international tribunal.[1] Seldom have jurists put in the hands of the legislator or the statesman a conception more destructive of the legal obligation which treaties are supposed to contain. The distinction, in a legal document, between disputes as to rights and conflicts of interests, with a view to confining obligatory judicial settlement to the former category, can be preserved only by dint of the open—although obviously inconsistent—admission that the purpose of these treaties is not, and ought not to be, the imposition of rigid legal obligations. But this

---

[1] It has been claimed for this form of the distinction between legal and political disputes that it has the merit of leaving to States to determine the manner in which they wish to have their dispute settled (Fischer Williams, *A.J.* xxvi (1932), p. 35). There is some doubt whether this is really so. For the formula leaves the interested party free, by clothing its demand in the form of a legal claim, to confer jurisdiction upon a legal tribunal in a claim which may in fact be tantamount to a claim for a change in the law. The opponent would have no means of frustrating the move except by proclaiming that it wishes to base its defence on non-legal grounds.

is an admission which very nearly[1] amounts to a rejection of the institution of obligatory judicial settlement. This, for instance, is in effect the admission, it is submitted, of Sir John Fischer Williams, an international lawyer who has recently pleaded in some detail the usefulness of the definition of legal disputes as based on the distinction between disputes as to rights and those on conflicts of interests.[2]

---

[1] The residuum of legal obligation in such treaties is contained in two factors: In the first place, in cases in which both disputants admit that the controversy is as to rights—provided that there is agreement as to what 'rights' mean, and provided that they agree that it is their attitude and not the merits of the contentions which make a dispute one 'as to rights'—in such cases the duty of judicial settlement is obviously incumbent upon the parties. It is permissible to assume, however, that in cases in which there is both such admission and agreement as to the incidents of its application, the parties are obviously willing to have the matter settled judicially, and the *obligation* to have the matter thus settled is therefore of limited practical importance. Secondly, there is an undoubted legal obligation to submit disputes other than those 'as to respective rights' to the procedure of conciliation or of other so-called alternative means of settlement. However, as there is no obligation to accept the findings of the agency of settlement, the original obligation is of a strictly limited scope.

[2] *Chapters*, pp. 43–9; *A.J.* xxvi (1932), pp. 31–6; *International Change and International Peace* (1932). Sir John (op. cit., p. 14) points out that, in view of the very wide reservations usually accompanying arbitration treaties, the acceptance of the new formula would not mean any retrogression in practice. But the mere absence of retrogression is in this case tantamount to the perpetuation of the drawbacks of the original position of merely figurative and illusory obligations. There is no advantage in compelling a State 'to declare at an early stage whether it was merely seeking its legal rights or asking for a change in the law' (ibid., p. 14). It is the business of a court to find what is the nature of the plaintiff's claim. To confer that function upon the interested State is to cloak with the garb of a legal situation, envisaged and permitted by a treaty, both the claim put forward in disregard of the existing law and the resulting right to insist on a merely persuasive and legally inconclusive procedure of settlement through conciliation. If history shows very few examples of claims raised in disregard of the law (see below, p. 364), the new formula is likely to encourage rather than to discourage claims to alter rights. It sanctions the right to put forward such claims; it brings them within the orbit of treaties; it provides for a machinery for their settlement. What, it must be repeated, has hitherto been a serious step, will now be a step contemplated and authorized by a treaty. Neither will recourse to such steps be discouraged by making claims for alteration of the law appear as action in the 'higher general interest of the whole international community' (Fischer Williams in *A.J.* xxvi (1932), p. 31). What is meant by saying, that when a State, regardless of its international rights, asks for the modification of the tariff or immigration laws of another State, it does so 'in the higher international interest' (ibid., p. 33)? This phraseology is reminiscent of that used by Westlake, to the effect that a State refusing arbitration and proceeding unilaterally to a change in the law acts in lieu of an international legislature (see above, p. 15). It is, no doubt, possible that a claim for an alteration of the law *may* be justified from the wider international point of view, but it is dangerous to use terms suggesting that such a connexion is normal or natural. Whenever a State proceeds to act as a legislator, regardless of the legal rights of its neighbour, the probability is that the decisive factor of its action is to promote its own interests, and not those of the international community. These interests may at times coincide, but the very fact that they are realized by the might of the State directly concerned will ultimately determine the character

In view of the consequences of the distinction, so conceived, between disputes as to respective rights and conflicts of interests, there has recently been growing a consensus of opinion that a test, according to which the formulation of the dispute by the parties is decisive for the character of the dispute, is untenable, and that it is inadmissible that it should remain within the unfettered discretion of either party to change the character of the dispute and thus to remove it from the purview of binding judicial settlement.[1] Accordingly international lawyers, unable to resist the lure of the traditional attempt to classify international disputes, have proceeded to give to the distinction between disputes as to rights and those as to conflicts of interests another meaning which, while essentially different from the original meaning of the distinction, nevertheless preserves its terminology. Those writers interpret this distinction as meaning that the mere assertion of the disputant that the claim is one as to respective rights does not confer upon the dispute the character of a legal dispute, or upon the Court jurisdiction on the merits; that the asserted rights must be grounded in objective rights ascertained by an international tribunal;[2] and that while

of the action taken and the nature of the solution. The 'international legislation' by the United States in the matter of the Panama Canal may be adduced as a fitting instance (see above, p. 162). The phrase of States acting individually as international legislators should be used sparingly, and in full view of the fact that it is a procedure open only to powerful States acting against their weaker neighbours. It is not surprising that Westlake's insistence on the function of international legislation by individual States acting in their own interest was merely one aspect of his negative attitude towards obligatory judicial settlement (see above, p. 15). The present writer has dealt elsewhere with Westlake's great contribution to international law (Lauterpacht, 'Westlake and Present-day International Law', in *Economica*, November, 1925), but he believes that Westlake's attitude in the matter of international judicial settlement, although accurately expressing the practice of States in his time, is now antiquated.

[1] Sir John Fischer Williams has pointed out (*A.J.* xxvi (1932), p. 34) that the innovation is less objectionable than may appear at first sight, seeing that, even under a treaty not based on the distinction between disputes as to respective rights and demands for a change in the law, a State may give to a dispute a 'political' character by proclaiming that it asks for a change in existing rights. Undoubtedly it may. But such a step would bear the obvious impress of illegality. Under the treaties with the new formula it would almost be permitted; it would be regularized by means of a specific procedure of settlement; and there would be a temptation to represent it as done in the higher international interest.

[2] See, for instance, De Visscher in *R.I.*, 3rd ser., ix (1928), p. 43. See also Verzijl, ibid. vi (1925), pp. 739 and 743, who gives the following definition: 'Les différends entre États où les parties sont divisées sur un point de droit international, c'est-à-dire ou les parties, de part et d'autre, s'appuient sur des arguments qui donnent lieu à des doutes, *prima facie* raisonnables, sur le point de savoir si le droit international objectif reconnaît ou non l'existence des droits subjectifs invoqués par une partie et contestés par l'autre ou les autres.' And see Hostie, ibid., 3rd ser., x

the formulation by the parties is provisionally decisive for the character of the dispute, the final determination of its character must be grounded in a more objective test applied by an international judicial agency. In fact, almost all arbitration treaties embodying the conception of disputes as to rights contain provisions according to which, in case of disagreement as to the nature of the dispute, an international court decides upon this preliminary matter. This shows conclusively that in the contemplation of the existing treaties the formulation of the nature of the dispute by the parties is not decisive at all.[1] But, it must be repeated, if this is so, then the distinction laid down in the treaties in question fails to serve the purpose which it professes to serve, namely, the clear determination of disputes in which the parties undertake the obligations of judicial settlement.

This meaning—superimposed on the original one—of the distinction between 'disputes as to respective rights' and 'conflicts of interests' shows the confusing development of the concept. From a determination of the character of the dispute by the *ipse dixit* of the States concerned it has been transformed into an impartial adjudication, based on the probable legal merits of the dispute—a development which, in turn, is full of possibilities of further complications. For, according to this interpretation, the emphasis, in the conception of 'disputes as to respective rights', is upon the term 'rights'. In a legal document the term 'disputes as to rights' undoubtedly means disputes as to legal rights. But legal rights are such as can be determined by the application of existing rules of law, and there is therefore no question of a dispute as to 'respective rights' when it is claimed that there is a so-called 'gap' in international law. Thus the distinction between legal and political disputes reappears under one of its many traditional forms. By the same token the term 'as to respective rights' may be interpreted as referring to legal disputes, as distinguished from political controversies in the sense of controversies involving important issues.

§ 3. Disputes as to Rights and the Provisional Ascertainment of the Justiciability of a Dispute. As in legal literature

---

(1929), pp. 579–81, on the difference between the formulation of 'respective rights' in the American type of treaties and in the Locarno conventions.

[1] For, obviously, if the will of the parties, and not the nature of the claim put forward, were decisive for the determination of the character of the dispute, then there would be no room for a judicial pronouncement on the matter.

the original meaning of 'disputes as to respective rights' has been replaced by one which makes the justiciability of the dispute provisionally dependent on the legal merits of the claim advanced, the question must be asked, What is the meaning of the provision, regularly appearing in the treaties in question, that, in case of a controversy whether a dispute is one as to existing legal rights, or whether it implies a change in the existing law, the preliminary question of jurisdiction shall be decided by an international tribunal? It is submitted that the result of this interpretation of the provision in question is, in effect, that the tribunal has to decide whether the claim is in principle grounded on an existing rule of law or not. That means that the tribunal has, and is competent, to decide on the merits of the dispute from the point of view of law as distinguished from the facts; that, accordingly, it has the power to deal with a dispute each time one of the parties desires it to do so; and, finally, that the formula intended to limit the jurisdiction of the Court to a definitely prescribed category of disputes fails in its main object. In order to avoid this somewhat startling result, it has been suggested that the decision of the tribunal should, in the first instance, decide 'provisionally' whether a claim is within the frame of an existing rule of international law (in which case it is a dispute as to respective rights) or whether there is no rule of international law in its support (in which case it is a conflict of interests). How such a 'provisional' decision would, in a substantial aspect of the claim, differ from a final decision on the merits it is difficult to see. If a State puts forward a territorial claim alleged to be based on prescription, in what will the 'provisional' ascertainment whether the dispute is one as to respective rights consist? It is said that it will consist in an answer to the question whether prescription is recognized by international law. That means to a large extent a decision on the merits. If a State puts forward a claim for compensation on behalf of its subjects deprived of property rights in foreign territory as the result of general confiscatory legislation, in what will the function of ascertaining whether the dispute is one as to respective *rights* consist? Will not the 'provisional' answer have to decide on the soundness of the plea of non-discrimination, and if so, will it not largely settle the ultimate issue? It cannot avoid an examination of law and facts as thorough as that which will be necessary for the future final decision. A provisional decision stating that the alleged rule of law, adduced in support of the claim, does not exist, and that the dispute is therefore one as to a change of the existing law, is tantamount to the rejection of the claim, and nothing short of an ordinary contentious procedure would justify such a pronouncement. The remedy of a 'provisional' decision proves upon analysis to be largely meaningless.

§ 4. The Provisional Ascertainment of 'Arbitrability' in the Moroccan Claims Case.

The practice of international tribunals does not afford many instances of the plea of non-justiciability being raised *in concreto* in this form in regard to a general arbitration convention,[1] but two cases provide instructive illustration of what has been said above. In the arbitration agreement of 29 May 1923 between Great Britain and Spain, the two Governments submitted to arbitration[2] claims of British subjects or British-protected persons for damage to life and property suffered during the warlike operations in the Spanish zone of Morocco. Article 2 of that Agreement provided that, in regard to claims connected with military operations, it shall be open to the Spanish Government 'to argue that such claims are not of their nature arbitrable, and to require a decision on this point before each actual claim is examined and any award delivered with respect to the indemnity, if any, to be paid on account of such claim'.[3] Subsequently it was contended on behalf of Spain that these claims were not 'arbitrable' on the ground, *inter alia*, that they were not of an international character, seeing that there was no rule of international law in existence establishing, in regard to such claims, the responsibility of a State except in cases of denial of justice as the result of the failure to apply the provisions of the criminal law of the State in question.[4] The arbitrator[5] rejected this contention. He pointed out that, as the responsibility of one State towards another could not be determined by its own

---

[1] A plea which must be distinguished from the so-called plea to jurisdiction in regard to particular provisions conferring jurisdiction upon an international tribunal.

[2] The submission was technically for examination and report, but the agreement provided that the Report should be accepted as an arbitral award by both parties. See above, p. 200.

[3] The agreement is printed on p. 8 of the award (*Rapports*) published in 1925 at The Hague.   [4] *Rapports*, pp. 43–6.

[5] Professor Huber, at that time Judge of the Permanent Court of International Justice.

municipal law, it was necessarily a question of international law; that, apart from denial of justice, the diplomatic protection by the State of its nationals in foreign countries was one of the most important institutions of international law, and formed in the last century the principal subject-matter of the work of international tribunals; that although there may in individual cases exist rules of international law limiting or excluding the responsibility of a State, such exclusion of responsibility cannot be admitted in advance without examining the merits of each particular case; and that therefore all claims referred to in the arbitration agreement were 'arbitrable'.[1]

However, the case of the *Moroccan Claims* is instructive, not only because it shows that, in practice, an 'arbitrability' clause can be applied only by dint of being ignored altogether, but also because it brings to mind the confusion occasioned by the use of the term. For it appears from the award that the arbitrator, instead of drawing the attention of the parties, for the future guidance of States, to the lack of any actual juridical content in such an 'arbitrability' clause, proceeded to affirm its procedural value and to elaborate a distinction between different conceptions of 'arbitrability'. Basing his ruling on the history of the arbitration agreement, he found that the reference to 'arbitrability' meant that, in regard to each particular claim, the arbitrator had to examine whether or not it was supported by a rule of international law. An affirmative answer to that question, he said, would mean that the question *was* 'arbitrable', and that the arbitrator could proceed to the award of compensation. It is submitted with respect that there is little practical help which the international lawyer may hope to derive from the distinction between 'la notion formelle et abstracte' and 'la notion matérielle et concrète' of arbitrability. It serves no useful purpose to split up the consideration of a case into various stages labelled with nice distinctive terms. The question whether a claim is one covered by international law in general, whether it is supported by a specific rule or principle of international law, and whether there are actual facts bringing it within the purview of such rule or principle are in fact different aspects of one and the same action. For,

---

[1] *Rapports*, pp. 44–8. On the merits of the case the award constitutes an important contribution to a number of questions of international law such as the responsibility of States, the status of protectorates, the measure of damages, and the award of interest. See *Annual Digest*, 1923–4.

upon analysis, a claim brought before the arbitrator is in fact covered by international law only if there is a rule or principle of international law to support it; and the same claim is only then supported by a rule or principle of international law if the material facts bring it within the scope of that rule or principle.

§ 5. Provisional Ascertainment of Justiciability in the Fourth Advisory Opinion.

The theory of the possibility of a 'provisional' ascertainment of the justiciability of a dispute appears to have received some support in the Fourth Advisory Opinion of the Permanent Court of International Justice. In that case the Court was asked to give an opinion for the purpose of interpreting paragraph 8 of Article 15 of the Covenant, on the question whether a dispute between France and Great Britain as to certain nationality decrees issued in Tunis and Morocco and their application to British subjects, was or was not by international law solely a matter of domestic jurisdiction. The Court held that the matter was not solely of domestic jurisdiction, as it was clear from the submissions of the parties that the dispute involved such questions of international law as the degree of authority of the protecting State in a protectorate, the effect of the treaties between the protecting and protected States upon third States, the application of the doctrine *rebus sic stantibus*, the effect of a most-favoured-nation treaty, and so on. In giving its opinion the Court observed that 'to hold that a State has not exclusive jurisdiction does not in any way prejudice the final decision as to whether that State has a right to adopt such measures'.[1] The Court then remarked that the mere fact that a State has brought a dispute before the Council of the League, or that one of the parties appeals to an engagement of an international character, does not necessarily exclude the matter from the field of domestic jurisdiction, but

'... when once it appears that the legal grounds (*titres*) relied on are such as to justify the provisional conclusion that they are of juridical importance for the dispute submitted to the Council, and that the question whether it is competent for one State to take certain measures is subordinated to the formation of an opinion with regard to the validity and construction of these legal grounds (*titres*), the provisions contained in

---

[1] Series B, No. 4, p. 24.

paragraph 8 of Article 15 cease to apply and the matter, ceasing to be one solely within the domestic jurisdiction of the State, enters the domain governed by international law.'[1]

It has been submitted by the writer elsewhere[2] that, in so far as the Fourth Advisory Opinion lays down that, according to a preliminary judgement, a question may prima facie be one regulated by international law, but that a judgement on the merits may reveal that the question is one of exclusive domestic jurisdiction, it is of more theoretical than practical value. The argument that the Court may declare itself competent in a matter claimed by the defendant State to be within its exclusive jurisdiction, but that this need not necessarily result in a final judgement in favour of the plaintiff State, is to a large extent fallacious. In general there is no matter normally belonging to the sphere of exclusive domestic jurisdiction which cannot become the object of an international obligation. Thus even the right to determine the form of government or to select the head of the State may be regulated by a treaty. As, therefore, there is nothing of which it could be predicated in advance that it belongs to the sphere of exclusive jurisdiction, the only task of the Court is to decide whether, in the particular case, there exists a concrete rule of international law limiting the State's freedom of action. If, for instance, an immigration law of a State is made the subject of judicial proceedings, on the ground that that law is in violation of a treaty obligation, and if the defendant State raises the plea of domestic jurisdiction, it cannot be correctly maintained that the Court may find provisionally that the treaty is relevant to the immigration law (which is therefore not within the domestic jurisdiction of their State), but that a judgement on the merits may arrive at the conclusion that, although the treaty is in principle relevant to the immigration law in question, it does not in fact prohibit it. For that would

---

[1] Series B, No. 4, p. 26. And see Judgement No. 2, Series A, No. 2, p. 16, in which the Court found it necessary to embark upon a more detailed examination of questions bearing in fact upon the merits of the dispute, and to explain its attitude in the Fourth Advisory Opinion on the ground that the plea under paragraph 8 of Article 15 of the Covenant which the Court had to interpret in that case was directed against the very comprehensive jurisdiction given by that Article to the Council, and that therefore the Court was at liberty to affirm provisionally the jurisdiction of the Council in deference to the legal grounds of an international character advanced by the parties.

[2] Lauterpacht, 'The British Reservations to the Optional Clause', *Economica* (1930), p. 153.

mean that the matter *is* within the domestic jurisdiction of the defendant State, and that the relevancy, as provisionally assumed, did not in fact exist. It would mean that the provisional judgement was based on a general impression not substantiated by the investigation resulting in the judgement on the merits.[1]

It is important in considering the possibility of rendering 'provisional' decisions on the question whether a claim is or is not one as to legal rights, to distinguish such 'provisional' judgements from cases in which courts, while dealing with a plea to the jurisdiction, have provisionally to consider questions which may subsequently have to be decided at the stage when the tribunal deals with the merits of the dispute. Undoubtedly, even in this case, difficulties may arise,[2] inasmuch as decisions on the question of jurisdiction may involve matters which from the substantive point of view also have a bearing on the decision on the merits, but the practice of the Permanent Court of International Justice has shown that these difficulties are not insurmountable.[3]

§ 6. The Conception of 'Disputes as to Respective Rights' and the Practice of States.

One of the principal objections to the distinction between disputes as to respective rights and conflicts of interests is that, when embodied in arbitration treaties, it envisages situations which do not normally occur in international life. It is only in exceptional cases that States put forward demands which are admittedly against the law. It is bad policy to put oneself legally in the wrong at the outset. If an alteration of the legal *status quo* is claimed, the demand will be put forward by reference to a rule of law, even

---

[1] Ibid.

[2] See on this matter the article by Salvioli, 'Les rapports entre le jugement sur la compétence et celui sur le fond dans la jurisprudence internationale', in *R.G.* xxxvi (1929), pp. 108–15.

[3] In addition to the Fourth Advisory Opinion and to the Second Judgement referred to above there is a number of other cases decided by the Permanent Court which illustrates the relation of the judgement on jurisdiction to the judgement on the merits. See, for instance, Judgement No. 6, Series A, No. 6, pp. 15 and 16, where the Court pointed out that it is at liberty, when considering objections to the jurisdiction, to consider points touching upon the merits of the dispute. But the Court added that nothing which it 'says in the present judgment can be regarded as restricting its entire freedom of action to estimate the value of any arguments advanced by either side on the same subjects during the proceedings on the merits'. See also Judgement No. 8, Series A, No. 9, pp. 32, 33. And see Judgement No. 11, Series A, No. 13, for an instance of the Court's combining a judgement on the merits with a decision on the question of jurisdiction.

if this rule be one of disputed application and questionable reputation as is enjoyed by the doctrine *rebus sic stantibus*. A claim directed against another State's right of exclusive regulation of tariffs or of immigration will be put forward on the ground of a right to free intercourse. Occasions on which States have at the outset been content to divest themselves of the appeal to legal right have been extremely rare.[1] This may well be seen from the fact that even in those wars which are generally regarded as having their origin, not in disputes as to legal rights, but in a political clash of interests, the declarations of war and the accompanying proclamations and pronouncements show that there has been a reluctance to depart altogether from the existing law, and to base the State's action on a mere assertion of power in defiance of international law.[2] There is a danger that a not wholly

---

[1] See here Nippold, pp. 137–9. See also Fischer Williams, *Chapters*, pp. 47, 48.

[2] See, for instance, the declaration of war by Russia against Turkey in 1877. See the Russian Note of 23 April 1877 announcing the breaking off of diplomatic relations, in which reference is made to the refusal of Turkey 'à offrir les garanties réclamées par l'Europe au nom de la paix générale' (*British and Foreign State Papers*, lxviii (1876, 1877), p. 84); the Manifesto of the Emperor of Russia of 24 April 1877 pointing to the refusal of Turkey to proceed with reforms the introduction of which 'découlait, d'une façon absolue, des engagements antérieurs, solennellement contractés par le Porte vis-à-vis de toute Europe' (ibid., p. 845); and see the Turkish Manifesto of 26 April 1877 describing the Russian attitude as one of aggression and insisting on the conformity of the Turkish attitude with the obligations of 'les engagements internationaux' and 'les règles éternelles du droit des gens' (ibid., p. 857). See also the Proclamation of the Prince of Servia of 13 December 1877 on the Recommencement of the War with Turkey, basing the Servian action on alleged breaches of treaty obligations by Turkey (ibid., p. 881).

From the correspondence preceding the Russo-Japanese War of 1904 (see Martens, *N.R.G.*, 2nd ser., xxxi. 613–41) it appears that although the issue was one of a clash of political interests the final communication of Japan, announcing the rupture of diplomatic relations, referred not only to the Japanese desire 'to consolidate and defend their menaced position', but also 'to protect their established rights and legitimate interest'. In particular it was pointed out that the Russian refusal to enter into engagements to respect China's territorial integrity in Manchuria was contrary to Russian treaty engagements, and imposed upon Japan the duty to take measures of self-defence (ibid., p. 639). And see also the account in *R.G.* xii (1905), pp. 215–319.

In the correspondence preceding the Franco-German War of 1870 stress was repeatedly laid by France on the fact that her demand for the renunciation of any future attempts at placing a member of the Prussian ruling dynasty on the Spanish throne was dictated not only by her 'territorial security', but also by the threat to 'l'équilibre général des forces en Europe' (French Declaration of War of 19 July 1870, *British and Foreign State Papers*, lx (1868–70), p. 907. See ibid., pp. 784–950, for the correspondence). And see Oppenheim, i, §136, on the admissibility of intervention in the interest of the balance of power. It will also be noted that one of the reasons of the French declaration of war was the refusal of the King of Prussia to receive the French Ambassador—a step which France regarded as a refusal to continue negotiations at a time when she was admittedly prepared to put forward alternative demands. Thus, to the alleged right of

desirable change in this attitude may be brought about if legal doctrine insists on raising disregard of the law to the authority of a legislative function in the higher interest of the international community, and so-called conflicts of interests to a normal phenomenon of international life.

In this emphasis on claims for a change in the existing law we can discover a view which still regards the international community as developing in terms of conflicts of interest. This view is, in turn, based on the belief that as conditions of power within the international society are in a state of continuous flux and development, and as there is no agency to adjust the law to the changed conditions of power, conflicts of interests in disregard of the existing law are a typical phenomenon in international society. There is as yet no realization that development results not only in conflicts of interests, but also in their interdependence and integration.[1]

---

intervention in the interest of the balance of power there was added a supposed insult to national honour by the refusal of the right to negotiate.

As to the Spanish-American War of 1898, the Message of the President of the United States to Congress of 11 April 1898 (*British and Foreign State Papers*, xc (1897–8), pp. 799–812) constitutes a conspicuous attempt at a legal formulation of the dispute by reference to the rules of international law governing the recognition of States and to the various grounds of intervention.

As to the Turkish-Italian War of 1911 see the Italian ultimatum of 28 September 1911 (*A.J.*, Suppl., vi (1912), p. 11), containing, *inter alia*, charges against Turkish military and civil authorities in Tripoli and Cyrenaica of fomenting dangerous agitation against Italian subjects. In its declaration of war of 29 September 1911 the Italian Government referred to the need for safeguarding its 'rights and interests' (*Jahrbuch des Völkerrechts*, i (1913), p. 88). It will also be noted that the formal declaration of war by Germany against France in 1914 was based on alleged acts of aggression like the violation of Belgian neutrality by French aircraft, throwing bombs on German towns, &c. (*A.J.* ix (1915), Suppl., p. 298). Similar reasons underlay the French declaration of war against Turkey of 5 November 1914 (*R.G.* xxii (1915), Doc., p. 6).

In the Italian declaration of war against Austria-Hungary on 23 May 1915 (ibid., p. 213) Italy 'confiante dans son bon droit' referred not only to the protection of Italian interests, but also of Italian rights.

See for a discussion of some of these cases and for references to analogous instances, Strisower, *Der Krieg und die Völkerrechtsordnung* (1919), pp. 222–4 (note). But see Heilborn, *Das System des Völkerrechts* (1896), p. 330.

[1] See above, pp. 173 et seqq. When it is said that the practice of States shows remarkably few instances of demands being put forward in disregard of the existing law, the statement is meant to refer to demands presented in a peremptory fashion and pressed with vigour. It does not refer to claims in which the claimant State, recognizing that the demand is not grounded in law, appeals for a settlement on the basis of equity, and, when the suggestion is rejected, refrains from pressing its claim. For an instance of a claim of this character see the correspondence between Great Britain and France concerning the claims of British bondholders in regard to the repayment of the French war-debt, Cmd. 3779 (1931). The French Government refused 'a request for arbitration, which aims at increasing, on grounds of equity, the amount which a country is bound to pay in law' (French Note of 17 January 1931).

§ 7. Conflicts of Interests and the Reign of Law in International Society. It is not within the domain of legal science to discover remedies calculated to remove friction among nations, but it may not be altogether beyond the province of the lawyer to attempt to assess the place of so-called conflicts of interests in the scheme of pacific settlement of international disputes. It is submitted that, while it is dangerous to under-estimate the true causes of international conflicts, it is undesirable to exaggerate them. A conscientious survey of the causes of the chronic uncertainty in international relations, and of the possible causes of international friction would show how little substance there is in the insistence that changed conditions of internal and external power, unaccompanied by corresponding legislative changes in the international sphere, unavoidably result in conflicts of interests dangerous to the peace of the world.

In the first instance, there lies in this view the antiquated and historically false conviction that territorial changes are the only outlet for and the only expression of national development. This view has been particularly predominant in the last decade. There may have been some indefensible and irritating territorial provisions in the peace treaties concluded after the World War, and it is to be hoped that far-seeing statesmanship, aided by an improved international legislative machinery, will remove some of them. But they ought not to have the effect of making lawyers and statesmen think of international political and judicial organization in terms of the imperfections of the present territorial *status quo*. There exist territorial problems— *nomina sunt odiosa*—which cannot be satisfactorily solved by mere territorial changes, but by economic, cultural, and political adjustments conceived in a spirit of neighbourly co-operation. The exaggeration of the purely territorial aspect diminishes the chances of such adjustments being effected. Alongside the study of the possibilities of territorial changes in accordance with the requirements of national self-determination, there must always go an examination of the principal motives of the struggle for territory in the course of history. Such an examination would, it is believed, substantiate also in regard to territorial claims the view that the absence of the effective rule of law causes States to desire objects apparently of an economic nature, not because they are indispensable to the economic well-being of the State, but because they constitute an element of power either in actual war or in the diplomatic contest based on the eventuality of war.[1] The same applies to that aspect of territorial conflicts and ambitions which is connected with the problem of raw materials—a question which, but for the contingencies of war, would largely remain within the orbit of the normal economic laws of supply and demand.

Secondly, care must be taken not to distort the importance of the so-called economic causes of friction. In an international society living under the reign of law the clash of economic interests need not in itself constitute a danger to the cause of peace. High tariffs, economic discrimination, restrictions upon exports and imports, and various other ways of governmental interference with the natural flow of commerce, competitive struggle for the capture of markets—these may all affect international relations and may be productive of friction. But that does not mean that these phenomena must be treated as constituting a direct menace to international peace. Competition in the international sphere may be injurious or even ruinous to one State or another, but this may also be the result of competition in the relations between individuals. In both spheres it may prove a source of ill feeling and resentment. And yet there is within the State generally no disposition to regard economic competition as a danger to the peace of society. Under the prevailing economic system it is looked upon as a healthy and necessary factor in the life of the community. But in relations between States the various manifestations of economic competition and of governmental regulation of international trade have come to be regarded as the primary source of danger to international peace. High tariffs have been in this respect assimilated to excessive armaments. A vast literature has grown up on the economic causes of war.[2]

---

[1] See on this question Hennig, *Geopolitik* (1928), pp. 192 ff., 283 ff., who stresses the insignificant value of territorial expansion as an outlet for population. See ibid., p. 270, as to the inconsiderable part played by Italian colonies in promoting Italian emigration. See also Donaldson, *International Economic Relations* (1928), p. 597, who remarks that 'there is usually a degree of hollowness in the phrase, "outlet for congested population", even under conditions of "territorial propinquity"'. And see especially Stratton, *Social Psychology of International Conduct* (1929), pp. 141–53. See also Siegfried in *Problems of Peace*, 5th ser. (1931), pp. 101–11. For an expression of a different view see Schultze, 'Die weltwirtschaftliche Angleichung der Siedlungsschichten als Problem des Völkerrechts', in *Archiv für Rechtsphilosophie*, xix. 414.

[2] See on this subject Woolf, *Economic Imperialism* (1920); Donaldson, *International Economic Relations* (1925); D. Hunter Miller, *The Geneva Protocol* (1925), pp. 39 et seq.; Moon, *Imperialism and World Politics* (1926); Culbertson, *International*

It is submitted that in the very interest of peace it may be necessary to modify the current emphasis on economic nationalism as signifying a danger to the peace of the world. In the future, increased international co-operation and the advance on the road of co-ordinating international government will undoubtedly diminish wasteful competition and unreasonable restrictions and interference. Obvious self-interest and the large measure of economic interdependence already existing will ultimately cause Governments to refrain from such measures of economic interference as are in the long run disadvantageous to themselves.[1] In the meantime the proper approach to the problem is not to aggravate the evil by the insistence that various forms of undesirable international economic competition and restrictions are factors directly menacing the peace of the world. The fundamental analogy with the relations of private persons governs the relations of States in this as in other respects. This means that, although the clash of material interests is one of the principal factors of strife, and, generally, of human endeavour, such clash and strife do in civilized society take place within the orbit of the law and are regulated by it. It is only the precarious structure of a primitive legal system in the international society which acts as an inducement towards expressing the conflict of economic interests in terms of war or at least of danger to international peace. From this point of view it is true to say that the imperfections of the judicial and political organization of the international community—and the absence of the general duty of judicial settlement is one of those imperfections clad in the garb of juridical doctrines—are in themselves one of the causes of war. If the rule of law were supreme in international society it would be impossible

---

Economic Policies (1929); Buell, *International Relations* (2nd ed., 1929), chap. v; Salter, 'The First Results of the World Economic Conference', in *Problems of Peace*, 3rd ser. (1929), pp. 75–93 ('... if we, comfortably believing that there is a machinery for stopping war, are content to allow the economic forces of the world to move along lines which lead and guide to war, even the machinery of the League will not, at the last moment, save us from the consequences', ibid., p. 94); Burns, 'Economic Causes of War', ibid., 4th ser. (1930), pp. 86–110; Siegfried, ibid., 5th ser. (1931), pp. 91–111; Hawtrey, *Economic Aspects of Sovereignty* (1930), chap. v, pp. 105–29 (on the economic causes of war); Richardson, *Economic Disarmament* (1931).

[1] It is somewhat disturbing to see economists and statesmen who, in the domain of economic activity within the State, adopt the view that natural adjustments acting in conformity with the iron laws of economics do with inescapable necessity punish unsound and merely spiteful economic action, demonstrate alarm at unreasonable and eventually self-injurious economic interference on the part of Governments.

to speak with the same emphasis as at present of economic friction as a cause of war. Economic conflicts would receive a solution in accordance with economic laws, either on the basis of co-operation and co-ordination, or on the basis of determined competition giving victory to the more capable and more industrious nation. In an international society where the rule of law is precarious the tension occasioned by economic conflict follows the line of least resistance, i.e. of the attempt at circumventing economic laws and peaceful evolution by the short cut of force.[1] One of the causes of wars is the belief that the necessary manifestation of the co-existence of States, including the normal phenomena of economic rivalry and competition, are conflicts of interests not amenable to the reign of law. At the beginning of the present century almost the entire field of international political relations was regarded as falling within the category of mere conflicts of interests not subjected to law. This attitude was only another expression of the legal position sanctioning the right to use force in international relations—an attitude which will become obsolete when the use of force recedes into the background both as a matter of legal regulation and in deference to public opinion.

§ 8. Conflicts of Interests and the Classification of International Disputes.

As a matter of political theory, there would be no objection to dividing conflicts between States into those in which they are in disagreement as to the meaning of existing international law, and those in which they disagree because of a formal demand for a change of the existing law. What is here denied is that this distinction is relevant to the problem of the scope of the judicial function in international society, or that it has any legitimate place in a scheme of treaties providing for judicial settlement. It states a fact in the domain of international politics. It is not the nature of an individual dispute which makes it unfit for judicial settlement, but the unwillingness of a State to have it settled by the application of law. In so far as the distinction between disputes as to respective rights and other disputes is adopted

---

[1] It might be objected that the view put forward above is dogmatic, as at present the rule of law is *not* supreme in international society, and that therefore economic causes *do* at present constitute a menace to the peace of the world. The answer is that the solution can be found, not in proceeding on the basis of the existing transient absence of the rule of law, but in the endeavour to develop the judicial and political organization of mankind.

in order to secure a machinery for binding settlement in disputes in which a State seeks to challenge the legal rights of its opponent, it is—as will be submitted in the next chapter—unsound and impracticable. In so far as it is included merely in order to differentiate between disputes for which binding judicial settlement is stipulated and those to be dealt with by the purely persuasive methods of conference and conciliation, it is unnecessary and, in view of the complications to which it gives rise, mischievous. It is not necessary to provide expressly that a judicial agency shall settle only disputes as to respective rights. In the absence of an express authorization to the contrary, a judicial agency cannot, by the very nature of the function which it exercises, decide disputes other than those which are concerned with existing legal rights and duties. By designating the Permanent Court of International Justice, or any other judicial tribunal, as the adjudicating agency, the contracting parties *eo ipso* provide that the only disputes which the Court may decide are disputes as to contested legal rights and duties.

It will be asked, then, whether treaties of pacific settlement must be restricted to judicial settlement proper. We certainly do not advocate this sweeping remedy. It is possible to provide for different instruments of pacific settlement without indicating, with the help of a classification of international disputes, which category of dispute is covered by a specific machinery of settlement. It is suggested that such a solution is feasible and that it ought to be adopted in the interest of the efficacy and the clarity of treaties of pacific settlement. A treaty which, *without adopting any classification of disputes*, provides for judicial settlement of all disputes, and which, at the same time, provides for an optional procedure of conciliation to be resorted to at the request of one or both parties prior to the initiation of judicial proceedings, could achieve all the advantages claimed to be inherent in the procedure of conciliation. There are already in existence a number of conventions in which this principle has been acted upon. In these conventions there is no reference in any form whatsoever to the traditional distinction between two classes of disputes. All disputes are submitted to the procedure of conciliation as a preliminary to arbitration or to judicial settlement; all disputes are, in case of failure of the conciliation proceedings, submitted to the Permanent Court of International Justice or to an arbitral tribunal for a final decision.[1] There exists also an even larger group of treaties which, although still maintaining the traditional distinction for the purpose of authorizing the Court to decide *ex aequo et bono* in regard to so-called non-legal disputes, disregard the distinction altogether in the matter of the duty to submit all disputes to a binding settlement by a judicial tribunal.[2]

---

[1] See, for instance, the arbitration treaties of 5 July 1926 between France and Denmark, *L.N.T.S.* lxxxi. 455; of 30 November 1926 between Denmark and Czechoslovakia, ibid. lxvii. 105; of 11 December 1926 between Denmark and Lithuania, ibid. lxvii. 333; of 6 February 1930 between Italy and Austria, ibid. cv. 97; of 28 February 1930 between Denmark and Latvia, ibid. cxiii. 27. There exists also a number of arbitration treaties which, while not containing any provision for conciliation, disregard the distinction between two classes of disputes. See, for instance, the treaties of judicial settlement of 23 June 1924 between Brazil and Switzerland, ibid. xxxiii. 415; of 15 July 1925 between Brazil and Liberia, *P.C.I.J.*, Series D, No. 6, p. 120; of 28 February 1923 between Uruguay and Venezuela, *L.N.T.S.* xxxvi. 451; of 10 April 1923 between Austria and Hungary, ibid. xviii. 93.

[2] For an enumeration of some of these conventions see above, p. 42.

CHAPTER XVIII
OBLIGATORY SETTLEMENT OF SO-CALLED CONFLICTS OF INTERESTS

§ 9. Settlement of Conflicts of Interests under the Reign of Law. There are a number of recent treaties for pacific settlement which seem (at least according to one possible interpretation) to provide for the obligatory settlement *ex aequo et bono* of disputes other than those as to respective rights and which have proved incapable of solution through the procedure of conciliation. These treaties, some of which are enumerated elsewhere,[1] lay down that if a dispute—other than one as to respective rights—has not been settled by the procedure of conciliation, it shall be settled *ex aequo et bono* by a decision of an arbitral tribunal. We have said 'at least according to one possible interpretation', because even these treaties do not necessarily imply a power on the part of the judge to change the existing law. When the Swiss-Italian Treaty (and other similar treaties[2]) provides in Article 15 that, upon the failure of the procedure of conciliation, 'either party may request that the dispute be submitted to the Permanent Court of International Justice' and that 'if, in the opinion of the Court, the case is not of a juridical nature, the Parties shall agree to its being settled *ex aequo et bono*'—all depends upon what is meant by the term 'of a juridical nature'. The term may, of course, refer to a dispute which is not of a juridical nature because the party bases its claim on non-legal grounds or because the Court may think that the existing law is unjust. But it may also refer to any one of the other meanings of the conception of justiciable disputes.

However, the very possibility that the first interpretation may be correct calls for an examination of the question of obligatory settlement of so-called conflicts of interests. It is submitted that there is a fundamental fallacy in any attempt to provide, by means of a classification of controversial value, for a system of binding pacific settlement in cases in which a State formally and openly places itself outside the existing law. Should such situations be ignored? They must logically and legally be ignored in any treaty of binding pacific settlement. It is impossible, in a scheme of things devised

---

[1] See above, pp. 41, 42. [2] See above, p. 42.

to secure the reign of law, to provide machinery calculated
to enable a State to disregard the law in a manner binding
upon the party which is willing to abide by the law.[1] It is
inadmissible and impracticable to enable a State to choose,
in a manner binding upon its opponent, between judicial
settlement (if it is of the opinion that the law is on its side)
and (if it thinks that the law is against it) between another
agency of pacific settlement which may compulsorily deprive
its opponent of its legal rights. Disputes in which one party
openly professes to place itself outside the existing law,
although they may be amenable to the procedure of negotiation, conciliation, and consultation, must remain outside
the sphere of obligatory arbitration. Pacific settlement must
not be unscientifically and artificially comprehensive. The
ambition to try to remove, by way of a binding settlement
imposed by a body of arbitrators, adjudicating according
to discretion, all causes of international friction is a vain ambition. It is, in any case, peculiarly premature at a time when the
principle of obligatory arbitration in the matter of contested
legal rights has not become part of positive international law,
and when the voluntary nature of such undertakings of obligatory arbitration as exist is clearly brought to mind by denunciation and reciprocity clauses, by elastic reservations, and by the
incorporation of vague conceptions embodying all the ambiguities of the traditional distinction between legal and political
disputes. It is typical of the unreality, and of the lack of a sense
of proportion, which characterizes much international thinking, that, at a time when the very fundamentals of a legal
community, namely, preservation of peace on the basis of
legal justice, are not as yet generally accepted in the international society, legal formulas and institutions are being suggested, calculated to act as an absolute guarantee of the
preservation of peace. The only peace that the international
society can, and at present ought to attempt to, achieve is peace
within the orbit and on the basis of respect for law. In a
community under the rule of law conflicts can be settled—in
a binding manner and as a matter of obligation undertaken in
advance—only in one way: on the basis of the existing law.
That law may be changed by the appropriate means of particular or collective legislation, which partly exist already and which

---

[1] The nearest analogy to such an attempt would be a provision in a constitution
making a revolution legally admissible.

will certainly be improved as international organization develops. But this is not a task for arbitration tribunals exercising compulsory jurisdiction agreed upon in advance.[1]

§ 10. The Rejection of Obligatory Settlement of Conflicts of Interests by the General Act and Similar Conventions.

The inappropriateness of treaties of pacific settlement enabling a State to deprive an opponent of its legal rights by a binding decision of an arbitral tribunal is clearly expressed by the manner in which the General Act for the Pacific Settlement of International Disputes, drafted by the Ninth Assembly of the League of Nations, has in effect abandoned the original intention of entrusting compulsorily arbitral tribunals with legislative powers. In the General Act the parties undertake to submit to the Permanent Court of International Justice (or, if they agree, to an arbitral tribunal) all disputes with regard to which they are in conflict as to their respective rights (Article 17). They also undertake to submit to the procedure of conciliation disputes other than those in which they are in conflict as to their respective rights (Articles 1 and 20).[2] In order to provide for the final and binding settlement of this latter class of disputes, the parties undertake, in case such controversies have not been settled by the procedure of conciliation, to submit them for binding settlement by an arbitral tribunal (Article 21). But this tribunal is not at liberty to act as a legislator. It has been explicitly denied such powers. Article 28 lays down that, failing an express agreement to the contrary, the tribunal shall apply existing rules of law, namely, rules 'enumerated in Article 38 of the Statute of the Permanent Court of International Justice'. The framers of the General Act thought it necessary to reiterate in a variety of ways that the arbitrators must respect existing conventional and customary international law.[3]

---

[1] Although conflicts of interests cannot well come within general arbitration treaties in such a way as to confer in advance obligatory jurisdiction at the request of the party demanding a change in the law, there is nothing against an arbitral tribunal being entrusted with the solution of the conflict by a binding decision, if both parties in a special agreement agree thereto. In that special agreement the parties fulfil the legislative function themselves. The act of legislation consists in the agreement to have the existing law changed by the arbitral tribunal either *ex aequo et bono* or on the basis of special rules formulated by the parties. See above, p. 319.

[2] Disputes as to respective rights are subject to the procedure of conciliation only if both parties agree thereto (Article 20).

[3] See, for instance, the Resolution of the Ninth Assembly on the submission and recommendation of the General Act and a number of other conventions:

Thus disputes in which the parties are not in conflict as to their legal rights are made subject to decisions on the basis of legal rules whose only function can, in obvious logic, be to decide disputes as to contested legal rights. Disputes in which one party has put forward a demand which on its own showing is contrary to existing law (and which has therefore originally been taken out of the domain of judicial settlement) are to be decided by a legal decision confirming an admission made by the claimant at the very beginning.

This contradiction, of which no satisfactory explanation has yet been attempted, has been, and will no doubt be made in the future the object of legitimate criticism.[1] The cause of pacific settlement is not helped by self-contradictory international instruments. But it is only by dint of this unusual disregard of the obvious meaning of words[2] that the

---

'... (3) Noting that respect for rights established by Treaty or resulting from international law is obligatory upon international tribunals: (4) Recognizing that the rights of the several States cannot be modified except with their consent' (Ninth Assembly, *Plenary Meetings*, p. 488). In the Report by M. Politis of the *liaison* Sub-Committee of the First Committee of the Ninth Assembly it is stated that there was no intention to confer upon the arbitrator the power to decide as a friendly mediator: 'It had been unanimously recognized in the Sub-Committee that that would be to authorise the removal of the very basis of international relations. No treaty, not even a treaty of commerce, could continue to exist if one country, complaining of the application of a treaty of commerce by the other contracting party, went before a tribunal, and, if that tribunal, after noting that the party to whose action exception had been taken had merely been applying the treaty of commerce, could have the power to alter the Treaty...' (Ninth Assembly, *Meetings of the First Committee*, p. 62). For a similar interpretation of Article 28, as precluding the disregard of existing rights, see Muûls in *R.I.*, 3rd ser., xi (1930), pp. 689–95; Gallus, ibid., pp. 469–72; Professor Logoz before the Permanent Court, Series C, No. 19 (1), p. 383; Strupp, *Das Recht des internationalen Schiedsrichters, nach Billigkeit zu entscheiden* (1930), pp. 65–7; Borel in *Annuaire*, xxxv (1) (1929), p. 482; Fischer Williams in *Journal of the Royal Institute of International Affairs* (1928), pp. 411, 412, who says that the General Act 'as a whole will commend itself mainly, if not solely, to those States who do not expect at any time to be asking for a legislative change in the existing state of things and who are now, and expect indefinitely to be contented with the *status quo*'.

[1] See, for instance, Schücking as quoted by Borel in *Annuaire*, xxxv (1) (1929), p. 480, and Brierly in *B.Y.* (1930), pp. 125–31. In general, however, although Article 28 of the General Act has been commented upon by several writers, there has been a remarkable absence of adverse criticism. In an otherwise penetrating analysis of the General Act, Gallus simplifies the difficulty by assuming that 'les différends d'ordre non-juridique qui seront soumis au tribunal arbitral pourront avoir un aspect juridique' (*R.I.*, 3rd ser., xi (1930), p. 470), and that therefore the inconsistency is more apparent than real. Borel, op. cit., p. 483, equally finds the solution in the submission that 'tout différend—même non juridique—peut être apprécié au point de vue, sous l'angle, dans la mentalité et "sur la base" du respect du droit'. The juridical value of such an interpretation is open to serious doubt.

[2] Unless, of course, it should be argued by a dialectically minded protagonist of the General Act (the writer has not so far come across any such defence)

General Act has escaped the greater evil of conferring upon a State the right to deprive its opponent of its legal rights by a body of arbitrators acting as legislators. A considerable number of conventions of the 'General Act type' have equally refrained from conferring legislative powers upon arbitral tribunals called upon to decide disputes other than those as to respective rights subsequent to the failure of the procedure of conciliation, although in this case the contradiction has been rendered less conspicuous by the absence of a clear reference to the rules of law to be applied by the tribunal. The reference is an indirect one, namely, to the procedure laid down in The Hague Convention of 1907 for the Pacific Settlement of International Disputes.[1]

In view of the solution as finally adopted by the General Act it may pertinently be asked what useful function the distinction between disputes as to respective rights and other disputes fulfils in the General Act. It is submitted that it fulfils none.[2] According to the General Act, ultimately *all*

---

that there is a difference between conflicts of interests referred to in Article 1 and the same disputes referred to in Articles 21 and 28, namely, that the latter have been rendered 'legal' disputes on account of the obligation to submit them for a binding decision, and that therefore the application to them of legal rules is appropriate. They have become 'disputes as to respective rights' by the test adopted by Mr. Justice Baldwin in *Rhode Island* v. *Massachusetts* (*infra*, p. 442).

[1] See above, p. 41. Possibly importance has been attached to the fact that that Convention provides for the settlement of disputes 'on the basis of respect of law'— a phrase which, it has been suggested by some, does not impose the duty of a strict application of legal rules.

[2] Gallus, op. cit., whose estimate of the General Act is otherwise very favourable, admits that the distinction between legal and political disputes is open to objection as being antiquated, out of accordance with the present development of international law, and practically dangerous (pp. 225–7). But he justifies its adoption on the ground of 'des habitudes, des préjugés, des craintes, même mal fondées, dont il faut tenir compte si on veut obtenir des résultats positifs et ne pas provoquer l'abstention des États dont le concours est désiré' (p. 229). It is difficult to see how the fears and prejudices are effectively dispelled if ultimately all disputes are submitted to a decision on the basis of rules of law. The embarrassment of the writers commenting favourably upon the inclusion in the General Act, and in kindred conventions, of the distinction between legal and political disputes or of the provision concerning disputes for the solution of which international law provides no answer is clearly manifested in the reference, with pathetic uniformity, to the single example of a dispute such as the one which is presented as the direct cause of the Franco-German War of 1870. See Rolin in *R.I.*, 3rd ser., viii (1927), p. 605; Schindler in *Recueil des Cours*, 1928 (v), p. 273; Wehberg in *Friedenswarte*, October 1929; Muuls in *R.I.*, 3rd ser., xi (1930), p. 695. It is an eloquent testimony to the lack of vitality of this doctrine that writers are reduced to copying a little instructive example as the single instance of the possible application of a vital clause productive of uncertainty and confusion. What does it mean—that international law possesses no rules governing situations in which a State claims the right to prevent the dynasty of another State from acquiring the throne of a third State? Either a demand of this nature is patently put forward in an aggressive manner, in defiance of the

claims, whether referring to disputes as to respective rights or not, are to be submitted to a strictly judicial decision; according to the General Act, originally *all* disputes may be submitted to the procedure of conciliation.[1] A single clause providing for conciliation, at the option of one party, of all disputes, and for judicial settlements in case of the continuation of the dispute subsequently to the failure of the procedure of conciliation, would have had all the effect that may legitimately be expected from treaties of obligatory pacific settlement. If instead of concealing the urgency of the actual problem behind the thick veil of a traditional terminology a line of real advance had been sought, the proper solution would have been to provide for some procedure of negotiation and consultation with the object of reviewing the judicial decision in the light of political, moral, or economic considerations.[1]

§ 11. The 'ex aequo et bono' Clause of the General Act.

There is, however, one clause at the end of Article 28 of the General Act which, without substantially altering its principal feature, namely, the denial to the arbitrator of legislative powers, adds to the element of confusion, involved in the main provision, a further element of uncertainty. This clause provides as follows: 'In so far as there exists no such rule applicable to the dispute, the tribunal shall decide *ex aequo et bono*'.[2] Apparently the clause refers to that aspect of the orthodox doctrine of the limitation of the judicial function which envisages the possibility of disputes for the solution of which international law, owing to its material insufficiency,

---

existing law with the intention of provoking a conflict—in which case there is no room for obligatory pacific settlement; or such a demand is put forward on the basis of an alleged rule of law (be it even a rule of law of questionable validity like the one based on the right to intervention or on the balance of power)—in which case the matter is clearly governed by international law. The fact that international law does not contain a rule entitling a State to put forward a demand of this nature does not mean that it possesses no rule on the subject. It means that the demand finds no support in the law and must be rejected. See, on the correspondence preceding the Franco-German War, above, p. 364, n. 2.

[1] The only possible practical effect of the distinction might be that in a dispute which, in the opinion of both parties, is one concerning legal rights, a State would be at liberty to refuse to agree to a preliminary procedure of conciliation (Article 20). However, it may be doubted whether even this possibility necessarily follows from the provisions of the General Act. For, if—at least according to one possible interpretation—the character of the dispute is the function of the attitude of the parties, then the party anxious to secure the procedure of conciliation will be at liberty to remove the dispute from the legal sphere by formulating its defence accordingly.

[2] See above, p. 41.

provides no answer. The possibility of such situations has been discussed and rejected in another Part of this book and requires therefore no further elaboration.[1] That rejection must be particularly emphatic in view of the comprehensiveness of the rules of law enumerated in Article 28 of the General Act by reference to Article 38 of the Statute of the Court.[2]

However, the above interpretation of the phrase 'if there is no rule of law applicable to the dispute', although most closely in keeping with the revealed intention of the parties, is not the only possible one. For may not arbitrators be of opinion that there is no rule of law applicable to the dispute because the controversy is a 'political' one, that is to say, involving matters of the very highest importance, for instance, the right of self-defence? They may, by availing themselves of another test of justiciability, be of the opinion that there is no rule applicable to the settlement of the dispute, because the application of existing rules of law would result in an unjust decision leaving the actual controversy unsettled. They may, finally, consider that there is no rule of law applicable, because the claimant or defendant State may have put the dispute outside the pale of law by advancing contentions and defences of an admittedly non-legal character. In all these cases the arbitrators might feel that they are at liberty to proceed on the basis of *ex aequo et bono*. In view of the intention of the Assembly of the League of Nations in drafting and recommending the General Act, it is not believed that the arbitrators would be justified in adopting such an interpretation, but it may be useful not to ignore altogether the possible confusion inherent in the use of the traditional terminology.

§ 12. Arbitration and Compulsory Settlement of 'Conflicts of Interests'.

The confusing use of terms which characterizes legal thinking in the matter of pacific settlement of international disputes is clearly shown by the way in which some

---

[1] See Part II. See also for an admirable criticism of Article 28 from this point of view Brierly in *B.Y.* (1930), pp. 125–31. See also for an interpretation of that article the writers quoted above, p. 374, n. 1. It will be noted that in strict logic the very conception of disputes 'other than those as to respective rights' excludes the possibility of applying this aspect of the conception of non-justiciability. For in a 'conflict of interest' the claimant party has expressly admitted that the claim is contrary to an existing rule of law, which means that in the opinion of the claimant himself there *is* a rule of law—a negative one—applying to his claim.

[2] See above, p. 66.

recent treaties of pacific settlement prescribe recourse to arbitration. The General Act and other conventions of the same type recognize that it is undesirable and impracticable to compel States to abide by decisions of adjudicating bodies having the power to alter the existing law. Accordingly, they provide that disputes involving a demand for a change in the law shall ultimately be settled on the basis of the existing law. The General Act refers for that purpose to the rules of law laid down in Article 38 of the Statute of the Permanent Court of International Justice. Other conventions refer to The Hague Convention for the Pacific Settlement of International Disputes which instructs the arbitral tribunal to decide on the basis of respect of law. But, at the same time, there is apparent in these conventions the tendency to provide for recourse to arbitral tribunals on the vague but persistent assumption that arbitral tribunals, although bound to apply law, need not somehow apply strict law; that their function lies midway between the application of law and adjudication *ex aequo et bono*; and that, therefore, the reference to these of disputes other than those concerning respective rights introduces the possibility of the law being changed in accordance with justice and political requirements.

The view that international arbitration is not a strictly judicial procedure is not of recent date.[1] Prior to the establishment of the Permanent Court of International Justice it was propounded by well-meaning international lawyers

---

[1] Colour has been lent to this distinction between judicial settlement and arbitration by the amendments to the various Articles of the Covenant (e.g. Article 12; Article 13, pars. 1 and 4; Article 15, par. 1) adopted in 1921 by the Second Assembly. They came into force in September 1924. In these amendments the words 'or judicial settlement' were added in those passages in which originally only the term 'arbitration' appeared. However, a study of the origin of these amendments shows that they were not due to any doubts as to the judicial character of arbitration. See Second Assembly, *Records, Plenary Meeting*, pp. 698, 827, where it is stated that 'the establishment of the Permanent Court of International Justice seems to make it desirable to mention explicitly the method of judicial settlement by the Court'. And see on this matter *Annuaire*, xxxiii (2) (1927), p. 679. The same distinction was subsequently adopted in the abortive Geneva Protocol for the Pacific Settlement of International Disputes of 1924. But it appears that in the Protocol 'arbitration' was intended to serve a political function. Thus while in Article 3 the contracting parties agreed to submit to the Permanent Court of International Justice the disputes enumerated in Article 36 of its Statute, in Article 4 they agreed to submit, in the last resort, to compulsory arbitration disputes which the Council has failed to solve. Nothing is said about the character of the arbitral function. But see Wehberg in *Recueil des Cours*, 1925 (ii), pp. 55–78, who regards the arbitration provisions of the Geneva Protocol as bringing clearly to light the non-judicial character of international arbitration.

anxious to promote the cause of a permanent international judicial tribunal. One of the obvious arguments in support of such a tribunal was the plea that the existing arbitral agencies were not invariably judicial.[1] After the Permanent Court of International Justice had been established that view was not—contrary to the natural expectation—abandoned. It persists in order to fulfil the hybrid function of satisfying a supposed need for an agency able to solve 'conflicts of interests' by decisions partly legal and partly in disregard of the existing law.[2]

The practical and theoretical objections to entrusting bodies of persons with the power of settling dispute, with a binding effect, by decisions disregarding the existing law have been discussed elsewhere. But there exists in any case the very strongest objection to a view that decisions of an adjudicating body can be partly legal and partly non-legal. A body wielding such powers is not a legal body at all. A body which applies legal rules only when it deems it fit to do so and disregards them on other occasions, applies law only as it were by accident; it applies law because legal rules happen to coincide with what the arbitrator believes the law ought to be.

---

[1] See in particular Wehberg, *The Problem of an International Court of Justice* (Eng. trans. 1918), pp. 12–29; and Scott, quoted below.

[2] For a recent discussion and partial affirmation of the non-judicial character of arbitral tribunals see the Report of Borel and Politis in *Annuaire*, xxxiii (2) (1927), pp. 680–93. However, see the conclusions on p. 693, where it is stated that 'L'arbitrage proprement dit peut assurer au même titre que la Cour Permanente de Justice Internationale le "règlement judiciaire" des conflits'. It is respectfully submitted that jurists ought to speak only of arbitration 'proprement dit'. See also Scott, *Sovereign States and Suits* (1925), p. 242; *The Status of the International Court of Justice* (1916), p. 24; and *Actes et Documents*, ii. 313–21; Lapradelle in *Procès-Verbaux* (of the Committee of Jurists of 1920), pp. 694, 696; Wehberg, *Recueil des Cours*, 1925 (ii), pp. 60–78, and particularly p. 77, in which he maintains that arbitration 'maintenant comme autrefois, remplit surtout la fonction de *l'amicabilis composito*'. In emphasizing the judicial character of international arbitration, I feel somewhat perturbed by the fact that writers like Scott, Lapradelle, and Politis, whose acquaintance, if I may say so with respect, with the history of international arbitration is well known, have expressed a different opinion, but in view of the evidence available *errare malo cum* Moore (as cited below, p. 382, n. 1, and in Hyde, II. § 559). See also the literature quoted below, p. 374, n. 3, on Article 28 of the General Act. And see the opinion of Judge Kellogg in his *Observations* in the *Swiss-French Zones* case (Second Phase), *P.C.I.J.*, Series A, No. 24, pp. 33–8, and his reference, on p. 33, to the *Behring Sea* arbitration and *North Atlantic Fisheries* arbitration as being 'arbitrations pure and simple'. See also *P.C.I.J.*, Series B, No. 16, p. 22, in which the Court deprecated a somewhat loose use of the term 'arbitration'; and see Series B, No. 12, pp. 26 and 30. However, see Series B, No. 8, p. 29, where the Court speaks of a decision of the Principal and Allied Powers as 'having much in common with arbitration'. See also Series B, No. 9, pp. 14, 15.

The second objection is directed not so much against the description of such a function as arbitral—that would be a matter of mere terminology—but against the view, which it implies, that international arbitration, as distinguished from the work of the Permanent Court of International Justice, has not, from its very inception to the present day, been a strictly judicial function. Such a view fails to take into account the provisions of treaties creating arbitral tribunals and prescribing the sources of law applicable by them. Neither does it find support in the activities of international arbitral tribunals prior, and subsequent, to the establishment of the Permanent Court of International Justice. The judicial character of international arbitration is a matter of historical fact and of positive international law.[1] It is independent of the question, variously answered in various systems of jurisprudence, whether arbitrators within the State are under a duty to decide according to law or according to discretion,[2] as well as of the question

---

[1] To one who surveys, for instance, the work of post-war arbitral tribunals like the Mixed Arbitral Tribunals, the British-American Mixed Claims Tribunal under the Convention of 1910, the Mexican-American Mixed Claims Commission, or individual arbitrations like the one between Colombia and Venezuela decided in 1922 by the Swiss Federal Council, or the Ottoman Debt Arbitration of 1925, the view that international arbitration is not judicial appears to be without substance. Probably, the arbitrators in these cases would regard such a view as a grave reflection on the fulfilment of their duty. The consciousness of the judicial character of arbitration is as old as international arbitration itself. We find Greek tribunals distinguishing clearly between arbitration and mere mediation, and attempting, before pronouncing a judicial verdict, to induce the parties concerned to agree to an equitable adjustment of the difficulty. See Tod, *International Arbitration amongst the Greeks* (1913), p. 123. When in 1319 an arbitrator gave an award in the dispute between the Duke of Brabant and the Count of Holland he stressed the fact that he was bound to give his decision on legal grounds, although he would have preferred a settlement on the basis of equitable considerations. See Novakovitch, *Les compromis et les arbitrages internationaux du XIIe au XVe siècle* (1905), p. 77.

[2] It appears that in the great majority of countries arbitrators are expected to decide on the basis of rules of law. Article 1019 of the French Code of Civil Procedure provides that arbitrators shall decide according to rules of law unless the *compromis* authorizes them to act as *amiables compositeurs*. If they disregard this provision they not only run the risk of having their award set aside, but also render themselves liable according to § 1382 of the Civil Code (responsibility for damage done by fault) and to § 1992 (responsibility of the mandatory). See also, to the same effect, Article 20 of the Italian Code of Civil Procedure; Article 636 of the Netherland Code; Article 595 of the Austrian Code of Civil Procedure. And see Moore, *International Adjudications*, i, Preface, pp. xxvii–xxxvi, for a survey of the law in England and in the United States. Even if arbitration within the State were wholly non-judicial this fact would be irrelevant for the determination of the true nature of international arbitration. For the function of arbitration is different in international and municipal law. In the latter it supplements—in a manner which is not essential to the life of the community —the rule of law by yet another legal institution; in international relations it

whether judicial settlement through the Permanent Court of International Justice does not offer better guarantees of legal continuity and of authoritative development of international law. Obligatory settlement of disputes in which a State asks for a change of law cannot, and ought not to, be achieved through the questionable expedient of distorting the true character of international arbitration, past and present.[1]

lies at the very basis of the rule of law. Although voluntary in its origin, it fulfils the same function as normal judicial settlement within the State.

[1] The judicial character of international arbitration has recently been vindicated by Moore in the Preface (entitled 'Notes on the Historical and Legal Phases of the Adjudication of International Disputes') to the first volume of *International Adjudications* (1929), and by Strupp, *Das Recht des internationales Richters, nach Billigkeit zu statuieren* (1930). See Lauterpacht, *Analogies*, § 28, and the authorities there cited, and Hedges in *B.Y.* (1926), pp. 110–20. See also Pollock, *League of Nations*, 2nd ed., pp. 20–2; Hostie, op. cit., p. 582, n. 59; and see the judicious observations of Nippold, pp. 158–60. Probably the proper line of approach towards eradicating the false view of the non-judicial character of international arbitration would be to analyse in detail cases of alleged departure by arbitrators from the path of a strict application of the law. The writer has attempted this task elsewhere in regard to some cases (*Analogies*, loc. cit.). In particular, caution ought to be exercised in order not to confuse the disapproval of the legal solution adopted by the arbitrators with a charge that the tribunal has not been entirely judicial. The distinction between arbitration and judicial settlement refers therefore purely to a difference in the adjudicating institutions. As Dr. McNair puts it in Oppenheim, ii (4th ed.), p. 64: 'Arbitration' means any kind of arbitration upon which the parties to the dispute may agree, whether under the Hague Convention or not; and judicial settlement means a decision by the Permanent Court of International Justice.' Even the element of permanency cannot be regarded as a distinguishing criterion. For there exist international tribunals, such as the Mixed Arbitral Tribunals, of what has been called 'relative permanency' (Hobza in *Annuaire*, xxxiii (2) (1927), p. 830, who gives references to treaties which provide for a permanent arbitral tribunal to decide disputes arising out of the application or the interpretation of a treaty). That the practice of States does not always attach material importance to the distinction between the two agencies of judicial settlement may be seen, for instance, from the Treaty of Commerce and Navigation between Great Britain and Yugoslavia of 12 May 1927—*Treaty Series*, No. 6 (1928), Article 29 of which provides for arbitration in disputes arising out of the interpretation and application of the provisions of the treaty. The last paragraph of that Article runs as follows: 'The court of arbitration to which disputes shall be referred shall be the Permanent Court of International Justice at The Hague, unless in any particular case the two contracting parties agree otherwise.' On the other hand, when in July and December 1930 the British Government asked the French Government to consider the repayment in gold instead of paper francs of certain French *Rentes* issued in Great Britain and held by British subjects, it acknowledged that its demands were based on considerations of equity rather than on those of strict law, and proposed *arbitration* for the settlement of the dispute. The French Government refused to assent to this proposal. See Cmd. 3779 (1931).

PART VI

THE LIMITS OF THE RULE OF LAW

CHAPTER XIX

LIMITATIONS OF THE RULE OF LAW WITHIN THE STATE

§ 1. In General. The object of this book has so far been to examine the various aspects of the doctrine of the limitation of the judicial function in international society from the point of view of their relation to the practice of States and to accepted rules of international law. In addition to these aspects, expressed in the current distinction between legal and political disputes, this doctrine appears in international law as a general legal proposition, namely, as a doctrine based either on a supposed limitation of the place of law in any political community (including that of the State) or on the specific nature of international law. It is proposed to examine in this chapter the view that as the limitation of the place of law is a recognized factor *within* the State it is unreasonable and pedantic to expect law to be of all-embracing efficacy in the international sphere.

The view which bases the doctrine of the inherent limitation of the rule of law in the mutual relations of States on legal considerations drawn from the field of municipal law seems to find some support in the fact that the terms 'justiciable' and 'non-justiciable', 'judicial' and 'non-judicial', or 'legal' and 'political' are not altogether unknown in municipal law. Many a problem arising within the State offers prima facie support for the theory of the limitation of the place of law in international society. There are, indeed, within the State spheres of human activity in which the normal operation of the rule of law appears to be limited. In the first place, we are frequently confronted with administrative adjudication upon personal and property rights, commonly called administrative law, which, as the result of the modification, or exclusion, of the normal judicial process, has created the impression of a limitation of the rule of law. With the problem of administrative law there is partly connected the determination of private rights by the political action of the executive department of the Government in its relations with foreign States—a class of cases generally (although not always accurately) referred to as 'acts of State'. There is, thirdly, the wide area of the apparent limitation of the rule of law due to its very nature as an external rule of conduct, namely, its limitation to certain determined spheres of social control and regulation. There are, fourthly, the limitations of legal regulation connected with the historically determined content of the law at a given time and place. Fifthly and lastly, there is the exceptional modification of the normal process of the law as the result of the admissibility of self-help. How far do these exceptions to typical working of law and legal justice correspond to the exclusion of the obligatory rule of law in international society?

§ 2. Administrative Law. Limitations of the Law and Limitations of Judicial Process.

The vast and increasing sphere of administrative adjudication upon private rights, not only as between the individual and the public authorities, but also as between private persons, has been to a large extent responsible for fostering the view that the field of law is limited also within the State.

However, the view that administrative justice constitutes a limitation upon the rule of law cannot be admitted as a sound legal proposition. Administrative justice and legal justice are not opposed one to another. It is only judicial justice which is opposed to administrative justice. But judicial justice is not the only manifestation of the rule of law. Administrative agencies, so long as they do not act illegally, administer the law. The difference between them and ordinary courts of law is mainly a procedural one. It consists in the absence of certain safeguards traditionally connected with the conception of the judicial process. The substance of the law administered by both is necessarily different, but not the nature of law conceived as the imperative rule of conduct emanating from, or identical with, the State. It is a mistake to assume that ordinary courts administer rules of law, whereas administrative agencies act according to discretion. Both apply the law to individual cases, and both, accordingly, must exercise discretion. Undoubtedly, the reasoning underlying the decisions of judicial tribunals is more rigid, abstract, impersonal, and artificial than that applied in administrative adjudication, but this again is a difference of method explained by the special function of administration.[1] The judicial safeguards may ensure a

---

[1] The idea that all lawful authority within the State is legal authority is lucidly expressed by Krabbe, *The Modern Idea of State* (Eng. trans., 1922), pp. 118–26; see also Laski, *The Grammar of Politics* (1926), p. 387.

proper functioning of the law, but they are neither identical with the law itself nor essential to its formal function. This explains why all attempts to establish a rigid line of demarcation between judicial and administrative justice have proved unsuccessful, and why matters held, in a long series of decisions, to be judicial are no longer so treated when entrusted for decision to administrative agencies. The futility of these efforts is here even more obvious than in the parallel attempt to find a clear line of demarcation between the legislative and judicial function. The difference between judicial and administrative adjudications, far from being of a fundamental character, is to a large extent grounded in the historical experience of absolutistic and bureaucratic States, wherein the rule of executive departments was tantamount to the reign of arbitrariness.[1] Remove the judicial safeguards from ordinary courts and they will become administrative bodies. Add these safeguards to the latter and they will become courts of law in all but in name. Both administer the law of the land. Although the identification of administrative justice with the absence of law may be explained historically and psychologically as a reaction against the shortcomings and dangers of purely administrative decisions, there is no warrant for the view that the latter stands outside the realm of law or that it constitutes a limitation upon its rule.

§ 3. Act of State. Political Questions. Conclusiveness of the Statements of the Executive. Another large group of
questions which has given rise to the assertion that the sphere of law within the State is limited is the one somewhat loosely referred to under the general designation of 'act of State'.[2] It is in this connexion that the terms 'legal' and 'judicial' as distinguished from 'political' matters are frequently used in municipal law.

There are four types of cases which require consideration under this heading. There are, firstly, matters covered in

---

[1] For a clear refutation of the legal dualism of judicial and administrative decision, see Kelsen, *Allgemeine Staatslehre* (1925), pp. 80–91.

[2] See Halsbury, *The Laws of England*, xxiii. 306 ff., where there are included under this heading such questions as the general immunity of the State from suit, the conclusiveness of statements of the Crown in matters affecting foreign relations, recognition of acts of foreign Governments, &c. And see Harrison Moore, *Act of State in English Law* (1906), *passim*, where the term is similarly used in a manner calculated to cover a large variety of subjects; and Kingsbury, 'The "Act of State" Doctrine' in *A.J.* iv (1910), pp. 359 et seqq.

English law by the conception of 'act of State' in its more restricted meaning, namely, matters related to acts done in the exercise of prerogative in regard either to aliens abroad or to enemy aliens resident within British territory. This group to some extent overlaps with the second category, namely, that of questions arising out of the relations of States to one another and, in general, questions arising out of the acts of their organs done in the sphere of foreign relations.[1] This limitation upon the freedom of judicial determination may assume a variety of forms. It may amount to a legal duty of courts to refrain from determining the existence of certain legally relevant facts incidental to the main issue, and to rely for their determination on the statement of the competent executive department. This is the group of cases governed by the rule as to the conclusiveness of the statements of the political department. It includes such questions as whether a foreign community is an independent State or not; whether a portion of territory or a part of the sea is included within national territory; whether a territory is or is not included within the region of war; whether a foreign State or government has or has not been recognized; what is the status of a foreign vessel; whether there exists a state of peace or war with a foreign country; whether a person is entitled to diplomatic immunities; or whether there exist circumstances justifying reprisals. In another group of cases, courts refuse to give effect to claims arising out of events connected with the State's activities in the field of foreign relations. This applies to claims put forward against the State as successor in the liabilities of an annexed State; or to cases involving the interpretation of a treaty if such interpretation may have political consequences. Finally, the limitation of the competence of courts in this connexion means that it is not within their province to express an opinion as to the propriety or otherwise of the course taken by the Government in such matters as whether a foreign State or Government is entitled to recognition, or whether the annexation of foreign territory after war is or is not in conformity with the law.[2]

[1] For an admirable enumeration of matters political in nature in regard to foreign relations see Dickinson, *A Selection of Cases and Other Readings on the Law of Nations* (1929), pp. 73, 74. See also Oppenheim, vol. i, 4th ed. by McNair, p. 641, n. 2; Willoughby, *The Constitutional Law of the United States* (2nd ed., 1919), iii. 1326–38.

[2] See, for instance, *Oetjen* v. *Central Leather Co.*, 246 U.S. 297: 'The conduct of the foreign relations of the government of the United States is committed by the Constitution to the executive and legislative departments of the government, and

The limitation of the jurisdiction of courts in matters of this description is not confined to England and the United States. In France, in some respects, particularly with regard to the interpretation of treaties, the limitation is even more strict. The French *Conseil d'État* will as a rule refuse relief in respect of the acts of the Government in matters affecting the diplomatic relations or the external security and sovereignty of the French State.[1] On the other hand, in Germany[2] and in Italy[3] the rule does not obtain that courts are in these matters bound by the statement of the governmental department.

Can the limitation of the competence of the courts in these matters be construed as a limitation of the rule of law within the State? It is submitted that it cannot. Here as elsewhere care must be taken not to confuse the limitation upon the unrestricted freedom of judicial decision with a limitation of the rule of law. In the cases here discussed the limitations upon the freedom of judicial decision, far from amounting to a suspension of the rule of law, are the expression of a differentiation of functions, which for reasons of obvious expediency is unavoidable in the modern State. The traditional doctrine of separation of powers is, to say the least, no longer a principle obtaining with axiomatic validity. Courts perform administrative functions, and by judicial law-making encroach upon the domain of the legislative power. Administrative organs are being entrusted with judicial functions; they have, through the working of the system of devolution, assumed in practice legislative powers.

the propriety of what may be done in the exercise of this political power is not subject to judicial inquiry or decision.' So also in *Neely* v. *Henkel*, 180 U.S. 109, the Court refused to express an opinion as to the length of time Cuba should be occupied by the military forces of the United States.

[1] In particular, see on *actes de gouvernement*, Alibert, *Contrôle juridictionnel de l'administration* (1926), p. 70; Hauriou, *Précis de droit administratif et de droit public* (10th ed., 1921), pp. 431–6; Duguit, *Traité de droit constitutionnel* (2nd ed., 1923), iii. pp. 685 et seqq.; Jèze in *Revue du droit public et de la science politique* (1911), pp. 663 ff.; ibid. (1918), pp. 212 ff.; ibid. (1924), pp. 572 ff.; Bosc, ibid. (1926), pp. 186 ff.; Trotabas in *Revue critique de législation et de jurisprudence* (1926), pp. 342–451. And see Sack, 'La succession aux dettes publiques d'état,' *Recueil des Cours*, 1928 (iii), pp. 317–19; (1929), pp. 175–7, for a number of French cases relating particularly to State succession.

[2] See, for instance, *Diplomatic Immunities (German Foreign Office)* case, decided on 20 December 1926 by the Oberlandesgericht of Darmstadt and reported in *Annual Digest*, 1925–6, Case No. 244. And see Strupp in *Z̧.V.* Suppl. xiii (1926), pp. 25, 26; Anschütz, *Verfassung des deutschen Reichs* (4th ed., 1926), p. 279; Fleiner, *Institutionen des deutschen Verwaltungsrechts* (8th ed., 1929), pp. 20 ff.; Jellinek, *Verwaltungsrecht* (1928), p. 50.

[3] Granito, 'Questioni pregiudizionali', in *Rivista di diritto pubblico* (1924), i. 532.

Legislative justice, although less frequent, is not unknown. The theoretical explanation of this change has not yet struck firm roots in the minds of lawyers and students of government, but the notion is slowly gaining ground that, as a matter of juridical principle, the difference between the acts of the legislature, the executive, and the judiciary is not one of legal substance. In regard to the administration, the legal system entrusts organs, other than courts, with administering or giving effect to law on certain matters. In the domain of foreign affairs it entrusts the competent departments of the Government with the right of exclusive decision not subject to judicial review. At the same time, although the doctrine of separation of powers is being in practice reduced to its proper proportions, the elastic principle of the division of functions necessarily remains. This division of functions is particularly necessary in view of the necessity of uniformity in acts and measures affecting foreign States. Both the Government and the courts are the organs of the State, and reasons of stability and convenience in international intercourse require that a State should not address its neighbours in two voices.[1]

§ 4. Limitations of the Sphere of Law Inherent in the Nature of the Legal Function. Another source of support for the doctrine of the limitation of the place of law in relations of States has come from the fact of that undeniable limitation of the place of law in society which is conditioned by the very nature of the function of law. Law, like the State, does not embrace the totality of human relations. It cannot do it, seeing that such social ends as it is capable of achieving can be achieved only through the regulation of the external conduct of men. Law can regulate such conduct only as is suitable for universal and uniform regulation, and as is enforceable by external sanction. As in the relation of the individual to the State there is a limit to the scope of things which ought to be rendered to Caesar, so there is a limit to the scope of matters embraced by legal regulation.[2] Yet the limitation of the scope of positive legal regulation is not identical with the limitation of the rule of law. Relations

---

[1] See McNair in *B.Y.* (1921–2), p. 65. And see Weston, op. cit., below.
[2] This is very well put by McIver, *The Modern State* (1926), pp. 17–22, 149–63. See also Pound, 'The Limits of Effective Legal Action', in *International Journal of Ethics*, xxvii (1917), p. 150; Morris R. Cohen, *Reason and Nature* (1931), pp. 420–6, and the same in *Columbia Law Review*, xxvii (1927), pp. 237–50.

which are outside the scope of legal regulation are indirectly under the rule of law, inasmuch as the latter will protect them from interference by, and encroachments of unauthorized force. There is in this respect no limitation upon the rule of law in civilized society. This is the only analogy with international law which matters for the purpose of the present inquiry. The administration of law within the State—whatever the competent agency may be—is always under a duty to determine authoritatively whether a claim is or is not protected by the law, and whether, therefore, force may or may not legally be applied for the purpose of giving effect to it. It is a mistake—not less grave because commonly made—to maintain that courts have no jurisdiction over claims which the law refuses to recognize. It is, for instance, incorrect to maintain that courts do not assume jurisdiction when damages are remote, indefinite, or intangible.[1] They certainly assume jurisdiction in such claims. They dismiss them.[2] In the very fact that a tribunal has no power to give effect to a claim there lies implied the recognition, in favour of the defendant, of the continued enjoyment as 'a legal right' of the object of the claim. The field of legal regulation is not coextensive with the legal order, and while the former is necessarily limited, the latter embraces the totality of relations amenable to external regulation between those subject to the sway of law within the State.

§ 5. **Limitations of Time and Place.** Similar considerations apply to those limitations of the sphere of law which are due, not to the inherent limitations of legal regulation, but to the actual stage of cultural and political development of the society in a given place and time. The material function of the law is not permanent and fixed for all time. Its scope increases with the growth of the political coherence, the degree of civilization, and the social and economic complexity of the community in question. From its original function, i.e. the preservation of peace and prevention of violence, through the intermediary stage, i.e. the protection and maintenance of acquired rights, it proceeds to embrace wider aims such as satisfying, so far as social regulation permits, the obtainable maximum of needs, or the securing of individual freedom, or the promoting of cultural development. On the

---

[1] Thayer, 'International Arbitration of Justiciable Disputes', in *Harvard Law Review*, xxvi (1912–13), p. 417.   [2] See Appendix, pp. 445 et seqq.

whole, the circle of interests directly regulated by law expands with the growth of civilization. When the Permanent Court of International Justice, in the *Tunis and Morocco Nationality Decrees* case, expressed the opinion that the distinction between matters of domestic jurisdiction and questions regulated by international law was 'an essentially relative question',[1] it referred to a phenomenon common to all society. Social legislation in the field of industry, legislation relating to public health and education, regulation of traffic, protection of individual freedom when menaced by the consequences of unrestricted freedom of contract, legislation on public utilities, compulsory regulation, in some countries, of wages and other conditions of work, and even the protection of the aesthetic interests of the community (through legislation discouraging disfigurement of streets and unsightliness)—all these are examples of the growing scope of legal regulation.[2] It is a mistake to assume that inasmuch as certain spheres of human activity are not yet, or, perhaps, never will be, affected by explicit legal regulation, the rule of law is limited as far as they are concerned. Here again explicit legal regulation is not coextensive with the actual extent of the reign of law.

The comprehensiveness of the legal system cannot be judged by the possible scope of objects capable of regulation, but only by the scope of objects deemed at a given time to be capable of legal regulation. The absence of direct legal regulation of a particular matter is the result of the determination, or at any rate the acquiescence, of the community in the view that, in the particular case, the needs of society and the cause of justice are best served by freedom from interference. To that extent it may correctly be said that the absence of explicit legal regulation is tantamount to an implied recognition of legally protected freedom of action.[3] From this point of view the law, in the fulfilment of its basic function, namely, to ascertain through its organs whether any particular claim is entitled to legal protection or not, is unlimited and faultlessly perfect. In the field of industrial disputes, for example, modern society has not, on the whole, found it necessary or possible to evolve rules and legal standards fixing the remuneration of wage-earners. But the rule of law is nevertheless unlimited in this respect also,

---

[1] Series B, No. 4, p. 24.
[2] See here the interesting chapter on 'The Tasks and Hazards of Legislation' in Freund, *Standards of American Legislation* (1917), pp. 72–143.
[3] See above, p. 85.

inasmuch as it will protect the employer and the employee from any contract of service being determined by mere physical force. For there is no claim the legal value of which cannot be definitely adjudged by a legal rule, at least to the extent of ascertaining that it is not protected by the law. This may be called the formal justiciability of claims within the State. It represents the primary purpose of law, namely, the securing of peace. Thus conceived it has no limits in any society which has risen above anarchy. It is not to the point to adduce, by way of a superficial analogy, the fact that within the State some matters are outside positive legal regulation—although not, as pointed out, outside the law and its all-embracing protective function—as an argument in vindication of a fundamental shortcoming of present-day international law.

§ 6. Self-help. Finally, reference must be made to the supposed limitation of the place of law and of courts implied in the admissibility, even in advanced law in modern society, of various forms of self-help like the right of self-defence, retaking of goods wrongfully taken away, expelling the trespasser, the different forms of extrajudicial lien, distress for rent, abatement of a nuisance, right of appropriating or retaining debts, distress damage feasant, and so on. In assessing the importance of the institution of self-help in connexion with the question of the scope of the international judicial function, two considerations have to be kept in mind. The first is that, within the State, self-help is admitted only in well-defined cases and by way of exception. Even if the admissibility of self-help constituted a limitation of the rule of law there would be no justification for the attempt to explain the exclusion of compulsory ascertainment of legal rights in the international community by the exceptional exclusion of such adjudication within the State. The second consideration is that the recognition of the institution of self-help, far from constituting a final limitation upon the authority of the law, is only in the nature of a provisional authorization[1] to act on behalf of the law whenever there is a possibility of its ends being defeated, or of the enforcement of just claims frustrated, or of a wrong being perpetrated in a manner prejudicial to justice and order. Self-defence and other forms of extrajudicial self-help are never in law a

---

[1] See above p. 178.

definite remedy; the taking of the law into the private person's own hands is only provisional. It must ultimately justify itself before the bar of the law, and any excess or abuse of force will be visited with punishment.[1]

The fact that at a certain stage of legal development self-help plays a prominent part in the life of the community simply means that at that stage law is only partially in operation. It does not make of self-help a legal institution. Society very early becomes conscious of the incompatibility of self-help with the idea of law. It is of interest to note the rigidity with which communities with a rudimentary organization of justice discourage the resort to self-help. So pronounced is the condemnation of private force that even self-defence does not always supply an automatically effective and complete justification. The Statute of Gloucester of 1278 laid down that the slayer in self-defence shall receive a pardon by the King's favour *if he* (the King) *pleased*. And in any case the slayer forfeited his goods.[2] It has been rightly said that in our own day law allows an amount of self-help which would have shocked Bracton.[3] In Roman law, even before the *legis actiones per manus injectionem* and *per pignoris capionem* were superseded by *legis actiones per judicis postulationem* and *per condictionem* (although the former were practically nothing else than self-help sanctioned by law), it was the judge who was ultimately called upon to impose peace and to award possession. It was a rule of Roman law that a man who threw a stone in self-defence was liable if the stone happened to strike a person other than the assailant.[4] This abhorrence of *vis privata* is not difficult to understand. For the original function of any law, which has risen above its most primitive stage, is exactly the preservation of peace through the exclusion of self-help.[5]

[1] See Dicey's *The Law of the Constitution*, Appendix, Note 4, on the question of self-defence and on the 'legitimacy of necessary and reasonable force'. See also Tietze, *Die Notstandsrechte im deutschen bürgerlichen Gesetzbuch und ihre geschichtliche Entwicklung* (1907), and Japoce, *Lo stato di necessità nel diritto privato* (1917).

[2] See Wigmore, 'Tortious Responsibility', in *Select Essays in Anglo-American Legal History*, iii (1909), p. 500.

[3] Pollock and Maitland, *History of English Law*, ii (1895), p. 512. And see Fischer Williams, *Chapters*, p. 466, on the protection of independent actual possession in English real property law in the twelfth century.

[4] D. 9. 2, ad. L. Aquil. 45, § 4.

[5] See Huber in *A.J.* iii (1909), pp. 79, 80, on the total exclusion of self-help as between the Swiss Cantons, and the case of cantons *Solothurn* v. *Aargau*, decided on 1 November 1900, where the Court described the right of self-help as being contrary to the nature of the Federal State, and as inadmissible in accor-

The absence in international society of compulsory jurisdiction of courts is tantamount to a general recognition of the right of self-help. That this is so may be seen from the very attempt to find support, by reference to the admissibility of self-help in municipal law, for the existing rule of international law on the matter of the judicial settlement of international disputes. But, it must be repeated, there is an obvious objection against adducing the altogether insignificant amount of self-help within the State as a reason for its continued existence as a general rule in the sphere of international relations. There is an equal objection against placing on the same level provisional self-help, regulated by, and accountable to, courts of law with self-help calculated to give final effect to real or supposed rights without reference to an impartial adjudicating agency.

§ 7. Real and Apparent Analogy with Municipal Law. It may be submitted by way of conclusion that no valid argument can be derived from the realm of municipal law in support of the existing rule of international law denying the obligatory jurisdiction of courts in settling disputes between States. Within the State the sphere of law embraces ultimately every scope of human activity, either by regulating it directly or by affording it legal protection from forcible interference. The courts or other law-administering agencies are competent to deal with every possible claim, either by recognizing the legal right to enforce it, or by forbidding acts of force calculated to give effect to it. The phrase 'courts or other agencies administering law' is here used deliberately in view of the fact that the qualifications which it implies frequently serve the purpose of supporting limitations of the place of law in international relations by reference to such alleged limitations in the sphere of municipal law.

It has been shown that it is irrelevant whether in a particular case the legal result is reached by judicial or administrative application of the law; that there is no derogation from the rule of law as the result of the exemption, in certain States, of governmental agencies from legal liability, or in the fact that, in a definite category of matters,

---

dance with the historical foundations of the Confederation and the express provision in Article 14 of the Federal Constitution (*Recueil Official* of the decisions of the Court, xxvi (i), p. 450). See also on the institution of self-help in connexion with international arbitration the illuminating remarks of Nippold, pp. 89 ff.

usually connected with the foreign relations of the State, courts regard as binding the declarations of the executive departments; and that it is misleading to treat the fact that municipal law refrains from including within the scope of legal regulation certain aspects of human activity as an analogy justifying the exclusion of the compulsory jurisdiction of courts as a binding rule of international law. In municipal law the supposed non-justiciability of certain matters refers to what may be called the superstructure of functions added to the fundamental function of the law, namely, the function of securing peace. In international law it refers to its very basis. The gradual extension of municipal law to a wider field of matters is a luxury when compared with this elementary function of the law. There is no justification for adducing the fact that, within the State, the judicial process—not the rule of law—is not always applicable, or that the law refrains from active regulation of certain aspects of conduct as supporting the view that the limitation of the function of law is a general legal phenomenon, and that it is, therefore, nothing exceptional if law remains, in the international sphere, foreign to its primary and most essential purpose. If it could be shown that within the State there obtains a large measure of recognition of the right of the members of the community to take the law into their own hands, then, and only then, could the limitation of the rule of law be appealed to as a general legal phenomenon. No such proof has ever been successfully adduced.

The method of adducing real or imaginary exceptions in the domain of municipal law, to justify or explain certain fundamental shortcomings of international law, has been also followed by many jurists in regard to the question as to the part played by law as a factor in securing peace.[1] They point out—as yet another instance of the limitation of the function of law in general—that within the State the reign of law has not excluded the recourse to force in the form of civil war,[2] just as between States a clear obligation to have recourse to arbitration has not always had the effect of preventing war.[3]

---

[1] On the place of judicial settlement as an agency for preserving peace among States see below, p. 437.

[2] See Moore, *International Law and Some Current Illusions* (1922), p. 95.

[3] See Dupuis in *Annuaire*, xxxiii (2) (1927), p. 809, who points out that the provisions as to compulsory arbitration of disputes between the members of the German confederation did not prevent Prussia in 1866 from refusing arbitration and resorting to force.

Moreover, instances have been found and quoted of judicial decisions which far from making for peace have been instrumental in producing war. The well-known case of *Dred Scott* v. *Sanford*,[1] decided in 1857 by the Supreme Court of the United States, has become an easy prey for this particular argument.[2]

The fact that the rule of law may break down, either generally as the result of a revolution or by infringement of its particular provisions, can hardly be regarded as throwing doubt on its effectiveness as an instrument of preserving peace. Constitutions may be broken by revolutions, but there has been no disposition to express this possibility in terms of a limitation of the law within the State, or to maintain that constitutions are not necessary. The same applies to the law conceived as a whole or to any individual legal rule, including the legal rule expressed in the judgement of a court. Far from suggesting that, as the rule of law may be broken, it should be dispensed with altogether, legal principle postulates that the possibility of its being disregarded is an essential condition of the quality of a rule as a normative rule of law. Absolute certainty would transform it into a law of natural science. Equally,

---

[1] 19 How. 393.

[2] See Balch, op. cit., p. 132; Brierly, *The Law of Nations* (1928), p. 188; Wright, *Mandates under the League of Nations* (1930), p. 271. It is difficult to see what is the object of this illustration. Apparently what the reference is intended to express is that courts may become a danger to peace if they have to administer bad law, or if by corruption or otherwise they become disloyal to their judicial duty. It may be assumed that it is not suggested that courts within the State are to be dispensed with on this account. Probably the *Dred Scott* case is a somewhat unsatisfactory example in this connexion. In this case judges of the Supreme Court held that a negro could not be a citizen of the United States and that Congress had no power to exclude slavery from any of the States of the Union. It has been suggested that that decision was a contributory cause of the Civil War. That opinion is now almost generally rejected. See Warren, *The Supreme Court in United States History*, iii (1923), pp. 1–41. And see Corwin in *The American Historical Review*, xxvii (1912), pp. 52–69, and M. A. Forster, *Did the Decision in the Dred Scott Case lead to the Civil War?* (1918). Probably the best summing-up of the character of that decision is that it 'must be written down as a gross abuse of trust by the body which rendered it' (Corwin, op. cit., p. 68). The remedy against such incidents is not the abolition of the compulsory jurisdiction of courts. Neither is this a remedy against the danger arising from the fact that courts may be compelled to administer unsatisfactory laws. The remedy lies in the improvement of the law. Writers attaching importance to the *Dred Scott* case as showing the possible dangers to peace arising out of the action of courts will note with interest Lord Acton's essay on the American Revolution, in which, referring to the litigation following upon the validity of the so-called Writs of Assistance, he notes that 'John Adams, who heard the judgment, wrote that "in that hour the child Independence was born"'. *Lectures on Modern History* (1921 ed.), p. 308.

compulsory judicial settlement may not always achieve the object of securing peace, but this does not mean that normally it is unable to contribute to the achievement of that object by branding as unlawful any recourse to force intended to give effect to rights which the law refuses to recognize. Within the State the peace-promoting function of courts is enhanced by the fact that there stands behind that impartial ascertainment of legal right the physical power of the State. In international society the compulsion is less direct; and frequently the only guarantee of the effectiveness of the legal decision is the impersonal authority of the law. This factor reduces, but does not substantially impair, its function as an instrument of peace.

CHAPTER XX

THE 'SPECIFIC' CHARACTER OF INTERNATIONAL LAW AND THE RULE OF LAW IN INTERNATIONAL SOCIETY

I

The Nature of International Law as a Problem of General Jurisprudence

§ 8. In General. It is typical of the quality of the argument advanced in support of the existing rule of international law on the question of the judicial function that it is based on two contradictory assertions—frequently adduced by the same writers. One is that as the rule of law within the State is limited, there is nothing extraordinary in such a limitation of the place of law among States. This aspect of the question has been discussed in the preceding chapter. The other is that although compulsory judicial settlement of disputes is a general rule within the State, that rule cannot claim validity among States in view of the so-called specific character of international law. It is maintained that in this, as in other matters, the analogy with municipal law is not decisive, and that while the obligatory jurisdiction of courts may be a general principle of municipal law, it is not necessarily a principle of general jurisprudence. The compulsory competence of the organs of the law to adjudicate upon disputes between the members of a political society has become in the minds of many one of those mischievous analogies with private law—like State servitudes, or the principle of fault in determining responsibility, or the vitiating effect of duress on the validity of contracts—which threaten to obscure the correct appreciation of the specific character of international law. The obligatory jurisdiction of courts is represented as a peculiarity of municipal law, and warnings are sounded against a lack of criticism and imagination elevating that peculiarity to a general principle of law.

The reasoning of those who hold this view is as follows: The fact that a rule is a general principle of municipal law does not make it a general principle of law. The very admission that international law is law, although in certain aspects, regarded by municipal lawyers as fundamental, it differs radically from municipal law, shows that, far from being determined in its capacity as a body of legal rules by the general principles of municipal law, it may contribute to the higher synthesis of truly general principles of law, of which municipal law is the one and international law the other constituent element. This applies not only to particular rules and principles, but also to the very conception of law. Municipal law, it is said, is based on the principle of subordination, i.e. of subjection of persons to legal rules, imposed irrespective of their will, whereas international law is a 'law of co-ordination' in which rules of law owe their existence to obligations voluntarily undertaken. The obligatory jurisdiction of courts is one of the manifestations of a 'law of subordination' and therefore incompatible with the true character of international law.

We are thus confronted with one of the main problems of jurisprudence in general and of philosophy of international law in particular. We shall have to examine, first, what substance there is in the idea of the independence of international law from the conception of law as developed in municipal jurisprudence, and, secondly, how far theories of international law, based on this dualism, can be regarded as consistent with the legal nature of international law. For if they do in fact constitute a denial of international law—and it will be submitted that that is their practical effect—then their relevance to the question of the place of law and courts in international society may be regarded as disproved. It is for this reason that it is necessary to consider the various forms in which the negative attitude towards international law conceived as a body of legal rules may express itself.

§ 9. The Denial of the Existence of International Law.

The number of writers who deny, without any qualifications the existence of international law is comparatively small. In their view the relations of States are—in effect—governed by rules neither legal nor moral, but by laws regulating the mutual relations of physical forces. Thus Hobbes found in the relations of States the historical demonstration of what, even in his own view, would otherwise have been a mere hypothesis, namely, the existence among men of a pure state of nature,[1] coextensive with an entire absence of legal

---

[1] *Leviathan*, Part I, chap. xiii: 'But though there had never been any time, wherein particular men were in a condition of war one against another; yet

regulation. Spinoza followed him closely.[1] In the middle of the nineteenth century, Lasson, a prominent German writer, gave clear expression to the same negative attitude towards international law.[2] He found followers both before and after the World War.[3] For some of these writers this negative attitude towards international law has been merely a link in the chain of an argument calculated to support certain juridical or philosophical theories in relation to the political theory of the State. This was notably the case with Hobbes and Spinoza. With others it is an expression and a

in all times, kings and persons of sovereign authority, because of their independency, are in continual jealousies, and in the state and posture of gladiators; having their weapons pointing, and their eyes fixed on one another; that is their forts, garrisons, and guns upon the frontiers of their kingdoms; and continual spyes upon their neighbours; which is a posture of War.' This is the true meaning of Hobbes's identification of the law of nature with the law of nations: 'Concerning the offices of one sovereign to another, which are comprehended in that law, which is commonly called the *law of nations*, I need not say any thing in this place; because the law of nations and the law of nature, is the same things . . . And the same law, that dictateth to men that have no civil government, what they ought to do, and what to avoid in regard of one another, dictateth the same to commonwealths, that is, to the consciences of sovereign princes, and sovereign assemblies' (ibid., Part II, chap. xxx (*in fine*)). And see Part II, chap. x (*in fine*) of his *De Corpore Politico* (1640) for a clear statement to the effect that 'that which is the law of nature between man and man before the constitution of commonwealth, it is the law of nations between sovereign and sovereign, after'. And see also the well-known Dedication to *Elementa philosophica de Cive* (1642) for the juxtaposition of the principles *homo homini deus* and *homo homini lupus*, the first obtaining within the State, the second in the relations of States.

[1] See Lauterpacht in *B.Y.* (1927), pp. 89 et seq., and the literature there quoted; Verdross in *Zeitschrift für öffentliches Recht*, vii (1927), pp. 100 et seq.

[2] *Prinzip und Zukunft des Völkerrechts* (1897); *System der Rechtsphilosophie* (1882). He says, in the former work: 'Two States confront each other like two physical forces. It is true that they are persons endowed with intelligence enabling them to recognize what is advantageous to them and to act accordingly. But there is no other link between them than their common interests, and no form of moral will limits their attitude of selfishness' (p. 56). And he says in the latter work: 'International law lacks the quality of true law . . . not only provisionally and for the duration of a lower stage of civilization, but permanently' (p. 402). Seydel, a distinguished German constitutional lawyer, gave expression to the same views in almost identical terms: *Grundzüge einer allgemeinen Staatslehre* (1873), pp. 31, 32.

[3] See, for instance, Binder, *Philosophie des Rechts* (1925), pp. 550–93; Hold-Ferneck, *Lehrbuch des Völkerrechts* (1930). Professor Hold-Ferneck doubts whether there is in the modern world any measure of cultural or legal unity to serve as a basis for international law (pp. 23, 24). He is of the opinion that a true community of law between States is inconceivable (p. 86); that the relation between sovereign States is necessarily one of enmity, international law being merely the expression of a *modus vivendi* in the permanent state of latent warfare (pp. 12, 86, 88); that obligatory arbitration is inconsistent with the right of self-preservation, and any large measure of acceptance of the commitments of obligatory arbitration constitutes a departure 'from the wide and clear paths dictated by the very nature of the State' (p. 151).

justification of an attitude of extreme nationalism, and of a deliberate negation of the existence or of the practicability or of the need for an organized international community under the reign of law. With others it is a denunciation of the predominant attitude of complacent disregard of realities and of the actual reign of force in an admittedly transient stage in the development of international society.[1]

§ 10. The Denial of the Legal Nature of International Law.

A second group of writers while not denying the obligatory force of the rules governing the relations between States, have denied to them the character of legal rules. Thus Austin regarded rules of international law—conceived as an independent system of law[2]—as 'positive moral rules which are laws improperly so-called', i.e. 'laws set or imposed by general opinion',[3] and pointed to 'the greatest logical error of all ... committed by many continental jurists, who include in public law, not only the law of political conditions, of crimes, and of civil and criminal procedure, but also international law; which is not positive law at all, but a branch of positive morality'.[4] But he did not deny that these rules

---

[1] See Lunstedt, *Superstition or Rationality in Action for Peace? Arguments against Founding a World Peace on the Common Sense of Justice. A Criticism of Jurisprudence* (1925). See Nelson, *Rechtswissenschaft ohne Recht* (1917). And see also Fricker in *Zeitschrift für die gesamte Staatswissenschaft*, xxviii (1872), pp. 90 et seq., and 347 et seq.; ibid., xxxiv (1878), pp. 368 et seq.; and Van Vollenhoven, *The Three Stages in the Evolution of the Law of Nations* (1919).

[2] *Lectures on Jurisprudence or the Philosophy of Positive Law* (5th ed., 1885), i. 182.

[3] Ibid. ii. 754.

[4] The denial of the legal nature of international law conceived as an independent system of law is not incompatible, and must not be confused with the affirmation of the legal character of some of its rules, namely, of those which are administered as legal rules expressly adopted by the State and its courts. Austin distinguished clearly between these two aspects of the question. He pointed out repeatedly that 'although positive international morality (so-called international law) ... has no force within one nation ... a nation may adopt it and enforce it as positive law within itself' (ii. 635). This point of view is clearly expressed in *Mortensen* v. *Peters* in the High Court of Justiciary in Scotland (8 Session Cases 93): 'It is a trite observation that there is no such thing as a standard of international law extraneous to the domestic law of a kingdom, to which appeal may be made. International law, so far as this court is concerned, is the body of doctrine regarding the international rights and duties of States which has been adopted and made part of the law of Scotland.' It is generally accepted by writers on English law in so far as they touch on international law. See Stephen, *A History of the Criminal Law of England*, ii (1883), p. 35. See also Willoughby in *A.J.* ii (1908), pp. 357–65, who adopts the same attitude. With these writers international law as a body of legal rules seems to be coextensive with rules of municipal law bearing upon relations between States and international relations generally. They are what some German writers call 'external constitutional law' (*äusseres Staatsrecht*). This is practically the view of the

were binding and that they were enforced by moral sanctions like
fear of provoking general hostility and reprobation for the violation of maxims generally received and respected.[1] Recently, Felix
Somló, one of the ablest adherents of the Austinian method on
the continent of Europe, without denying the binding force of the
rules commonly referred to as international law, denied that they
partake of the character of law.[2] In his view it is not the element
of compulsion which is lacking in international law—an element
which he sees in the part played by the Great Powers and the
Concert of Europe in the last hundred years. He defines law as
the rules issued by a supreme power which are habitually obeyed,
comprehensive and permanent. Accordingly, the factors which
in his opinion destroy the legal nature of the rules of international
law are the scarcity of its rules (which cover the least essential of
the relations between nations), the precariousness of their
enforcement, and the insufficient degree of obedience shown to
them. 'This view, however,' says Somló, 'does not deny the
existence of international law'; and he adds: 'The statement
that a rule is only a rule of international law, does not mean
that it ought not to be obeyed.'[3] He therefore expresses the
opinion that the proper designation of rules governing the relations between States would be 'international' or 'supra-national'
rules. He insists that the difference is not one merely of terminology, for, he says, if we describe the rules of so-called international
law as rules of law we thereby obscure the conception of law as
generally used.[4]

§ 11. International Law as a necessarily 'Weak Law'.

Another group of writers, without denying the binding force
of international law, are in a position to assert its legal nature

---

doctrine of self-limitation discussed below. For a recent affirmation of international law as external municipal law see Wenzel, *Juristische Grundprobleme* (1920).
See also Akzin, *Les problèmes fondamentaux du droit international public* (1929).

[1] Ibid. i. 226.

[2] *Juristische Grundlehre* (2nd, unrevised, ed., 1927), pp. 153–73.

[3] Op. cit., p. 169.

[4] With this view should be contrasted that of Burckhardt who, without
questioning the legal nature of international law, denies to it the quality of
positively binding rules of law. They are, he says, dictated by the moral nature
of the State and by the necessities of international relations, but, in view of the
absence of an international organization with legislative and judicial organs,
there is no positive international law, i.e. law whose content is certain and
undisputably binding. See *Die Organisation der Rechtsgemeinschaft* (1927), pp. 374–
416. See also for a short statement of the same view *Die Unvollkommenheit des
Völkerrechts* (1919).

only by dint of the argument that it is a weak law analogous to that obtaining among primitive communities; that these undoubted shortcomings do not seriously imperil the legal nature of international law; that they are the necessary consequence of the existence of a community of sovereign States; and that to remedy them would in effect mean the termination of international law and its transformation into internal or federal law. The writings of Oppenheim are perhaps the best instance of this school of thought. In them an idealistic defence of the legal nature of international law—conceived as weak law—is coupled with the repeated assertions that its shortcomings are of a permanent nature, for there 'is not, and never will be, a central authority above the several States'.[1] This attitude is one most generally adopted by international lawyers. It is held by writers as wide apart as Holland,[2] Zitelmann,[3] and De Louter.[4] Some writers even

[1] Vol. i, p. 288. And see ibid., pp. 13–15, for an exposition of the legal character of international law notwithstanding its being a weak law. The view that there cannot and 'never will' be an organized *civitas maxima* exercising authority over States is a persistent feature of Oppenheim's treatise. But it may be doubted whether this 'immutable feature' of international society would not have disappeared from the treatise if untimely death had not prevented Oppenheim from effecting the change. That he has done so in substance may be seen from his instructive chapter on the 'Defects and Merits of the Constitution of the League' written in 1919 and left unrevised in the subsequent editions of his work. While referring to the articles of the Covenant providing for the possibility of a State leaving the League by voluntary withdrawal, or as the result of expulsion, or in consequence of its dissent from a duly ratified amendment, Oppenheim pointed out that these provisions constitute a real defect, since 'there ought to be no possibility for a member to leave the League, or to be expelled therefrom' and that 'a recalcitrant member should, if necessary, be coerced by force to submit to the decisions of the League, and to fulfil its duties' (p. 352). It is clear that a League so constituted would be 'a central authority above the several States'. Oppenheim also regarded as another real defect of the Covenant the absence, in Article 13, of a provision for compulsory jurisdiction of the Permanent Court. And see for a similar change of attitude by Liszt, p. 432 below.

[2] *The Elements of Jurisprudence* (6th ed., 1893), p. 339. International law, he says, 'is the vanishing point of Jurisprudence; since it lacks any arbiter of disputed questions, save public opinion, beyond and above the disputant parties themselves, and since, in proportion as it tends to become assimilated to true law by the aggregation of States into a larger society, it ceases to be itself, and is transmuted into the public law of a federal government'.

[3] *Die Unvollkommenheit des Völkerrechts* (1919). The present shortcomings of international law, he admits, could be removed by the League of Nations becoming the *civitas maxima* and exercising judicial and executive functions over the States. 'But then', he says, 'this would no longer be international law, seeing that the latter presupposes logically the existence of sovereign States' (p. 53).

[4] *Le droit international public positif* (1920, French trans. from the Dutch), i. 59: 'Le droit international n'a pas de législateur, et, qui plus est, n'en aura jamais. Un pouvoir législatif ne saurait exister que dans un État. Dès que le droit international cesse d'être un droit entre des États souverains, pour devenir

go to the length of maintaining that although most of these permanent deficiencies constitute legal shortcomings, they contribute towards making international law a superior type of law from the moral and social point of view.[1] The historian of legal thought will note with interest that at a certain stage of the development of international law its notional attractiveness was regarded by some as a sufficient compensation for its substantial shortcomings.

It is from this side that come most of the current 'defences' of international law which, it is said, is primitive law and must remain so under the penalty of its own extinction. The absence of a central legislative authority; the absence of tribunals endowed with compulsory jurisdiction to settle disputes; the absence of agencies enforcing the law; the absence of clear and detailed rules—all these features of existing international law are explained by what are believed to be the characteristics of primitive society.

§ 12. The So-called Specific Character of International Law.

The principal objection to some of these modern explanations of the weaknesses of the law of nations[2] is that they pave the way for the most modern form of denying international law, namely, for the negation of it by means of the assertion of its 'specific' character as a body of law. For there are two ways of viewing international law as a weak law. One, discussed in the preceding section, is the basis of the theory which, although viewing the weaknesses of international law as necessarily and permanently connected with the existence of the international society of States, admits that they are shortcomings from the more general legal point of view. But according to another view, the so-called shortcomings of international law are merely

---

le droit d'un pouvoir qui leur est supérieur et auquel tous sont soumis, les États perdent leur souveraineté et le droit international se métamorphose en droit public d'un État mondial.'

[1] 'The law of nations is of a distinctly different character from municipal law. It may truly be affirmed that the *lex gentium* is of a more elevated nature. Applying as it does *inter gentes*, it does not appeal to the policeman; it appeals to reason itself, to the sense of equity, to a higher moral consciousness': Philip Marshall Brown, *International Realities* (1917), p. 104. See also Sauer, *Lehrbuch der Rechts- und Sozialphilosophie* (1929), p. 290, to the effect that although international law is deficient *qua* law it is a superior cultural phenomenon: 'From the cultural point of view international law transcends municipal law as based on compulsion. It aspires, from the limited domain of strict law, to an affirmation, as a matter of moral conviction, of the cultural community of mankind.'

[2] For a criticism of it see below, p. 433.

the manifestation of its specific character. They are defects, it is said, only so long as they are viewed from the narrow perspective of municipal law, whereas in fact they are a reminder of the existence of a wider conception of law of which municipal law is only an historical category. Thus we find Westlake suggesting that the controversy, whether rules of international law are rules of law or of morality, can be solved if we decline 'to treat the law of the land as the only proper kind of jural law, for then, while keeping law distinct from morality, we shall not encourage an undue attribution to international law of the characters only appropriate to the law of the land'.[1] It is said that 'the orthodox concept of law is not sacrosanct'; that 'it is necessary to inquire whether it ought not to be adapted to the requirements of actual life' (actual life meaning for this purpose the existence of rules called international law);[2] and that the proper way to approach the philosophy of law is international law 'through which one is in the position to follow the delicate problem of the creation and the development of law'.[3]

It is thus that we arrive at the central problem in the question of the determination of the legal nature of international law. The answer to this question obviously depends upon the conception of law which we adopt as the basis of the investigation. To what conception of law must international law conform in order that it can accurately be described as law? Is it a conception of law deduced from the positive legal order within the State, i.e. a conception of general jurisprudence in modern society? Or is it a conception of law made so elastic as to embrace the body of rules regulating at present the mutual relations of modern States? Shall international law be guided, while admitting its own shortcomings, by the generally accepted notion of law which few would venture to deny but for the necessity of defending the legal nature of international law? Or shall it broaden

[1] *Collected Papers*, p. 14. However, Westlake himself saw the dangers of this method of approach, and admitted that 'if we give the name of law to anything which we so discover in a remote state of society before we have fixed in our minds what we mean by that name, we beg the question, and have no security that our language has any consistent, or therefore useful, sense' (ibid., p. xxii). The whole trend of his work justifies the observation of Oppenheim that 'he belonged to the legal school of international jurists who, in contradistinction to the members of the diplomatic school, desire International Law to develop more or less on the lines of Municipal Law' (ibid., p. x).

[2] Mayer in *Archiv des öffentlichen Rechts*, xxxviii (1918), p. 14.

[3] Sauer, *Grundlagen der Gesellschaft* (1924), p. 431.

it and impart to it some of its elasticity? Shall international law aim at improvement by trying to bring its rules within the compass of the generally accepted notion of law, or shall it disintegrate it and thus deprive itself of a concrete ideal of perfection?[1] Before answering these questions it is necessary to consider the doctrine in which the theory of the specific character of international law has found its current expression and which has served as a most powerful argument in support of the existing rule of international law on the question of judicial settlement. This is the so-called theory of international law as a law of co-ordinate entities or, shortly, as a 'law of co-ordination'.

II

International Law as a Law of Co-ordinate Entities

§ 13. Subordination and 'Co-ordination' in Law. It will be shown in the examination of the doctrine of co-ordination, which follows, that that doctrine, as represented by some of its exponents, amounts to a clear negation of international law as a body of binding rules of conduct, whilst as represented by others, it does not differ, its terminology notwithstanding, from a theory which claims that international law is objectively binding upon States independently of their will. In either case the doctrine must be dismissed as irrelevant to the question of the place of law and of the judicial function in international relations. The notion of international law as a law of co-ordination has recently been increasingly adopted by writers, but there has been no attempt to elaborate it in detail. In a recent text-book of Hatschek[2] we find a restatement of the theory of co-ordination, but the attempt is not particularly illuminating. He defines international law as a legal system based on co-ordination.[3] This, he says, means that, unlike municipal law which is based on subordination of persons to the legal rule, there is in international law no superior will which imposes the law. There is no

---

[1] It will be noted that the question thus put transcends the limits of a problem of international law. It becomes a problem of general jurisprudence, a problem, that is to say, whether the conception of law should be broadened by the inclusion of a generalized norm of conduct based on the relations of sovereign States as at present constituted.

[2] *Völkerrecht als System rechtlich bedeutsamer Staatsakte* (1923). An English translation by Manning of the abridged version of this book appeared in 1930.

[3] Ibid., p. 2.

super-State endowed with authority. He then proceeds to define the international law of co-ordination as a 'legal order based on the recognition of States as equal subjects of international law', a somewhat inconclusive explanation, seeing that municipal law (which is a law of 'subordination') is also based on the equality of individuals before the law. How are rules of international law created in such a system? They are created principally by parallel legislation or by customary municipal rules in various countries, for instance, by that relating to the inviolability of envoys and foreign heads of States. These rules are binding upon States not as precepts of the law, but as so-called social or conventional rules whose sanction consists merely in social compulsion.[1] They create, by the inescapable effect of reciprocity, which is the basis of all community of life, an actual, if not a legal, obligation. From these conventional rules there grows (as the result of their becoming part of the legal conviction of States) particular and, in the long run, general customary international law. We are not told what is the basis or the nature of the binding force of this customary international law.

This somewhat slender basis serves as the foundation for Hatschek's exposition of international law. But, perfunctory as it seems to be, this part of his text-book is one of the very few examples of a detailed exposition of the doctrine. Most of its adherents are satisfied with stating that, while within the State the relation of the law to the individual is one of command imposed regardless of the will of the person affected, in international society it is based on the voluntary acceptance of legal obligations.[2] However, the doctrine has

---

[1] Hatschek instances the conventions and customs of the constitution in Great Britain as an example of conventional rules. On the whole the term 'conventional rules' as used by Hatschek and other German writers is identical with Austin's 'positive morality'.

[2] See, for instance, Strupp, *Eléments du droit international public* (2nd ed., 1930), i. 11 ('Les États étant égaux entre eux, le droit international public en tant que droit entre les États est un droit de co-ordination et non un droit de subordination'); Liszt, *Das Völkerrecht* (12th ed. by Fleischmann, 1925), p. 8 ('International law is based on a corporate, not authoritarian, principle'); Walz, *Wesen des Völkerrechts und die Kritik der Völkerrechtsleugner* (1930), pp. 252–61, also bases his construction of international law on the theory of co-ordination, but there is no attempt at a detailed exposition of what the law of co-ordination really means. Ultimately the whole theory is reduced to a difference in the manner of the creation of rules of law. Waltz does not deny that rules of international law, once established, bind States independently of their will. But he attaches decisive importance to the difference in the 'process of positivation' (i.e. of creation) of rules of law. There is no explanation why this should be a reason

served as the starting-point of two distinct theories as to the basis of international obligation. One is the doctrine of auto-limitation; the other, the theory of the law-making agreement as a source of international law. One or other of these doctrines, proceeding as they do from the theory of a law of co-ordination, has been, in the last fifty years, the starting-point of most of the attempts at a juridical theory of the foundations of international law. It is therefore by reference to these theories that the meaning and the value of the doctrine of co-ordination can best be judged.

§ 14. The Doctrine of Co-ordination and the Theory of Self-limitation.

The first attempt to construe international law as a specific law of co-ordination was made by Jellinek with the help of the theory of self-limitation.[1] That theory was originally developed in order to demonstrate the partial subjection of the State to law. Sovereignty as embodying the State, says Jellinek, is the right of exclusive determination of its own competence, and of binding itself in accordance with the provisions of its own law. That sovereignty is unlimited only in so far that no other power can juridically

for regarding international law as 'a law of a specific stamp strongly differing from municipal law' (p. 295). See also Heller, *Die Souveränität* (1927), pp. 43, 44, who regards international law as 'a non-authoritarian legal order based on contract' (*herrschaftsfreie Vertragsordnung*). In fact this able monograph is a somewhat intolerant denial of international law as an independent system of law, and an affirmation of the absolute sovereignty of the State. It seems that the insistence on the specific law of co-ordination on the part of German writers has recently assumed the form of a particularly German conception of international law, grounded on the Teutonic as distinguished from the Romanist tradition, embodied in some peculiarities of the political structure of German society in the Middle Ages and in the feudal period. See, for instance, Sternberg, *Einführung in die Rechtswissenschaft* (2nd ed., Part I, 1927), p. 26. See also for an admirable survey with an extensive bibliography Borchard in *Yale Law Journal*, xxxvi (1926–7), pp. 1058–74. That the idea of the *societas inordinata* as the basis of political relations is necessarily bound up with the existence of a legal power above the *societas inordinata* is clearly pointed out by Binder, *Die Philosophie des Rechts* (1925), p. 572.

[1] The theory was first formulated in Jellinek's *Die rechtliche Natur der Staaten-verträge* (1880) and subsequently amplified and defended in his *Allgemeine Staat-slehre* (1st ed., 1900). Of the latter a French translation by Fardis appeared in two editions under the title 'L'État moderne et son droit' (2nd ed. in 1911 and 1913). The rudiments of the doctrine of self-limitation will be found in Ihering's *Der Zweck im Recht* (1880), i. 318, and possibly even in Rousseau's *Contrat Social* (Bk. I, chaps, iv, vii). See Sukiennicki, *Essai sur la Souveraineté des États en Droit International moderne* (1926), pp. 170–4. For examples of the adoption of the theory of self-limitation see Nippold, *Der völkerrechtliche Vertrag* (1894), pp. 19–22, and Zorn, *Grundzüge des Völkerrechts* (1903), p. 7. The doctrine has been accepted by some French writers, for instance, Mérignhac, *Traité de droit international*, i (1905), pp. 291 et seq.; Malberg, *Contribution à la théorie générale de l'État*, i (1920), pp. 237 et seq.

compel the State to change its law. But more than that it does not mean. In particular, it does not mean that the State is above the law in the sense that it can disregard it at will. It can change and modify the law, but so long as the law exists it is bound by it. As a juridical phenomenon Jellinek explains the process of self-limitation by saying that the State commands persons who are its organs to act in conformity with the law, and that as the acts of the organs constitute the will of the State, the State by binding its organs at the same time binds itself.

In this act of self-limitation Jellinek recognizes also the source of such binding force as international law possesses. He sees no difference between international and municipal law, except that whereas the latter is a relation of subordination of the members of the community to law, the former is one of co-ordinated entities. International law is grounded on the will of the State, and ultimately it is this formal basis of international law which is decisive. Where international law and the existence of the State conflict, the former must yield, for international law exists for States and not States for international law. Legally, says Jellinek, the State is entitled to disengage itself at any time from an obligation deemed to be inconsistent with the interests of the State.[1] This precarious nature of international obligations does not, in his view, deprive them of their legal nature, for, in addition to the purely normative aspect, there is a psychological foundation for law arising out of the fact that it is recognized as binding by the members of a society. Such obligations are not absolutely binding as a matter of law, but they possess a binding force grounded on the objective nature of international relations, which, from the point of view of their social necessity, are comparable to those obtaining among individuals.[2] Thus, although as a matter of formal legal theory the will of the State is the origin and the basis of the obligation, that will is not an entirely irrational factor.

It is not surprising that this juxtaposition of two conflicting methods of approach has led to some confusion as to the actual meaning of Jellinek's combination of the doctrine of self-limitation with the theory of a law of co-ordination.

---

[1] Cavaglieri in *Recueil des Cours*, 1929 (i), p. 325, refers to Jellinek as affirming the absolutely binding force of generally recognized rules of international law, but he gives no reference to Jellinek's writings.

[2] *Die rechtliche Natur der Staatenverträge*, pp. 46–9.

Whereas his treatment of international law is generally subjected to severe criticism and regarded as the very negation of law and a glorification of force, there are writers who draw attention to Jellinek's insistence on the objectively binding force of international law, and express the opinion that there is no substantial difference between his approach and the more recent doctrines from Triepel to Kelsen and Verdross.[1] It may be doubted whether this is so. As a legal theory the doctrine of self-limitation cannot be interpreted otherwise than as a denial of the binding force of international law. As a sociological and psychological doctrine it amounts to a negation of the ultimate supremacy of the legally sovereign State, and thus to an affirmation of the binding force of international law. This double method of approach Jellinek defended on the ground that the same object may form the subject-matter of various modes of cognition. Thus, he said, a symphony may be the subject-matter of physiology or aesthetics. In proceeding thus he laid himself open to the reproach that it is scientifically impossible to treat objects as subject-matter of various modes of cognition at the same time.[2] The fact that the juridical supremacy of the State is sociologically or morally limited by other considerations necessarily escapes juridical cognizance. In practice these considerations may or may not become operative. Political considerations may limit the State's freedom from the legal bond, but they need not do so when these very considerations dictate to the State the necessity of disregarding its obligations. The juridical theory of self-limitation leaves open that possibility. It treats the observance of the rules of international law not as a matter of legal obligation, but as the result of a calculation—which may or may not take the long view—of the compatibility of the observance of the obligation with the interests of the State. Jellinek himself admitted that as the result of a law of co-ordination thus conceived, 'the community of States is of a purely anarchical nature, and international law, originating from an unorganized authority and possessing accordingly no overriding authority, may properly be described as an anarchical law'.[3] It is not surprising that he regarded war not only as a necessary factor,

---

[1] See, for instance, Spiropoulos, *Théorie générale du droit international* (1930), pp. 46–50.
[2] See for a vigorous criticism of this 'two-sided' theory Kelsen, *Der soziologische und der juristische Staatsbegriff* (1922), pp. 114–20.
[3] *Allgemeine Staatslehre* (3rd ed., 1921), p. 379.

but also as an element of progress in this anarchical society.[1] This is, in fact, the attitude of most of the supporters of the doctrine of auto-limitation. Thus Bergbohm, one of the precursors of the doctrine, regarded the very idea of a permanent international court as incompatible with the modern conception of the State.[2] This was also the attitude of some of the followers of Jellinek. Where, as the result of the adoption of a somewhat promiscuous method, a writer's opinion lends itself to two diametrically different interpretations, then that interpretation ought to be preferred—as being the more accurate—which is most in accordance with the actual influence exercised by the doctrine.[3] It must be judged by its fruits. From this point of view there is little doubt as to the meaning and consequences of the theory of self-limitation as combined with the doctrine of co-ordination. It constitutes a negation—in all but words—of the binding force of international law. This can be clearly seen from Kaufmann's monograph on the 'Nature of International Law and the clause *rebus sic stantibus*'—the only work in which an attempt has been made at a thorough exposition of the law of co-ordination.[4]

§ 15. The Doctrine of Co-ordination and the Supremacy of Force. Kaufmann.

According to Kaufmann the law of subordination—i.e. the law imposed and binding upon the members of the community independently of their will—is possible only within the State. This is so because only the State is the instrument of an ideal which can justly claim the subjection of its members to an imposed command. That ideal is self-preservation and self-development in history in a world of competing physical forces represented by other States.[5] This ideal can be ultimately fulfilled only by physical

---

[1] See below, p. 345, n. 1.

[2] *Staatsverträge und Gesetze als Quellen des Völkerrechts* (1877), p. 32. See also the same, *Jurisprudenz und Rechtsphilosophie* (1892).

[3] For a criticism of the doctrine of self-limitation see Triepel, *Völkerrecht und Landesrecht* (1899), pp. 77–81; Duguit in *Harvard Law Review*, xxxi (1917–18), pp. 139–48; Kelsen, *Das Problem der Souveränität und die Theorie des Völkerrechts* (1920), pp. 168–74; Sukiennicki, op. cit., pp. 174–222; Verdross, *Verfassung der Völkerrechtsgemeinschaft* (1926), pp. 12–20, and in *Recueil des Cours*, 1927 (i), pp. 262–74; Chklaver, *Le droit international dans ses rapports avec la philosophie du droit* (1929), pp. 179–87; Brierly, 'Le fondement du caractère obligatoire du droit international', in *Recueil des Cours*, 1928 (iii), pp. 482–4; Spiropoulos, op. cit., pp. 46–50.

[4] *Das Wesen des Völkerrechts und die clausula rebus sic stantibus* (1911).

[5] Op. cit., pp. 130 et seq., 145 et seq.

and moral force on the part of the State; it can be fulfilled only by enlisting all the physical and moral powers of its members. The essence of the State is power as revealed in victorious war.[1] This is the reason why the law of subordination is possible only in a State-community. Only a system of justice intended as an instrument of self-preservation in history is entitled, and can be expected, to secure the obedience of all its members. This is also the reason why a world-State is impossible and why a community of States, if it existed, could not be based on the principle of subordination. It has no overriding ideal. Universal peace cannot be such an ideal. For peace is only a negative conception; it is an idea necessarily correlated to war. Between State and State there are, therefore, possible relations which the traditional theory of the law of nature assumed to have existed originally among individuals. In this state of nature each State performs for itself the distributive function which the State performs in regard to its members. Thus the basis of international relations is the competitive struggle of States, a struggle for the solution of which there would seem to exist not only no judge and no executor, but also no standards of decision. This absence of a distributive principle constitutes a much greater obstacle to the possibility of international law than the absence of tribunals and of enforcing agencies.

What, then, asks Kaufmann, is the basic principle of a law of co-ordination? How is law possible among co-ordinated entities? That principle can only be found in the maxim, 'Who can, may'.[2] That principle alone is a just and appropriate principle in regard to States which, being responsible for the preservation of the highest values, cannot be subordinated to any higher community, and which, at the same time, have to justify their separate existence by their physical and moral power. The victorious war is the vehicle of the law: it alone decides which State is in the right. Undoubtedly, in a scheme of things thus constituted, accidents are possible in which the morally stronger is not victorious, but there is no absolute guarantee of the infallibility of any kind of law.

The consequences of the law of co-ordination thus conceived are various. It means, in the first instance, that legal relations between States are based only on express recognition. There are no imposed obligations. There does not exist an all-embracing community of interests; there are no collective

---

[1] Op. cit., pp. 152 et seq.   [2] Op. cit., pp. 159 et seq., 179, 189 et seq.

interests unless they include the interest of the State concerned. Self-preservation and self-development are the overriding principles. In a law of co-ordination the subjective interests of individual members constitute objective rules of law. Accordingly, although international law owes its existence to a certain solidarity of international interests, it does not owe it to a single collective international interest. There is no such collective interest. There is, apart from the domain regulated by expressly accepted international obligations, no international community. As these obligations exist only in the limited sphere of the expressly recognized partial community of interests, the individual interests of each State must always remain the guiding consideration. In a system of a law of co-ordination the will of the State is essential not only for the creation but also for the continuation of the obligation. As Hegel said, the relation of States is one of independent entities which make promises, but at the same time stand above their promises.[1] Nothing done in the interest of the preservation of the State is illegal. The State may conclude treaties—including onerous treaties to escape major evils—but it may legally abrogate them when circumstances have changed so that they cannot be kept without disadvantage to the interests of the State. There is, in a law of co-ordination, nothing higher than the interest of *each* of the parties. If the other party is unwilling to give in, then only war can decide whose interest is legally stronger. This is not the denial of law, but the only legal proof possible in a legal system of co-ordination.

These incidents of a law of co-ordination, says Kaufmann, do not necessarily mean that it is useless and imaginary. Also large parts of the law of the State are based on the principle of self-limitation. Such community of interests as exists between States is not purely imaginary. It has produced, through treaties, a number of organs and institutions. So long as treaties are in force they do not differ from municipal obligations. And the wider interest which a State has in fulfilling its obligations may be, and frequently is, regarded as more important than the temporary interest accruing from the evasion of treaty obligations.

Probably an apology is due to the reader for this detailed account of a doctrine propounded over twenty years ago and which may not entirely express the present views of its

---

[1] Op. cit., p. 199.

author. But the references to the specific character of international law as a system of a law of co-ordination have been recently so frequent that it may be of advantage to see at close quarters what the 'law of co-ordination' really is. Writers will be less eager to base their theories on the 'specific character of international law' if they realize what is the meaning attached to it by its outspoken protagonists. It is true that Kaufmann has pressed the idea of a law of co-ordination to its extreme consequences, but it is doubtful whether in juridical logic he could have done anything else. There is no middle course between subjection to law and the negation of its binding force.

§ 16. The International Law of Co-ordination as based on Law-making Agreements.

While that branch of the doctrine of co-ordination which is based on the theory of self-limitation has necessarily resulted in a clear repudiation of international law, the effect of Triepel's rival doctrine, namely, that of international law as based on the law-making 'agreement' (*Vereinbarung*), and on the common will of the States parties to the 'agreement', has been a different one.[1] Like Jellinek, Triepel also accepts the view that the State can become bound by a rule of international law only by its own will. But he rejects the theory of self-limitation as being juridically impossible, and finds the basis of the obligatory force of international law in the common will of States which, by means of 'agreement' (as distinguished from contract), constitutes a 'common will' resulting from a combination of wills. In the *Vereinbarung* the individual wills merge in the common will which henceforth constitutes a binding rule of law, for the simple reason that the common will of States cannot without a violation of the law be changed by a single State. Thus, although the will of the State is essential for the creation of the common will, it is the latter, and not the will of the individual State, which is the source of international obligations. Triepel agreed that his theory did not explain why the *Vereinbarung* should be binding, but he

---

[1] Triepel's views on this subject are expressed with great clarity in his *Völkerrecht und Landesrecht* (1899), which is a powerful piece of juristic thinking. This work has been translated into French in 1920 by Bounet. Triepel's views are restated in *Recueil des Cours*, 1923, pp. 77–118. He defines international law as 'a law binding in the relations of a number of co-ordinated States', p. 20, n. 1. For an exposition and criticism of Triepel's theory see Jellinek, *Allgemeine Staatslehre*; Kaufmann, op. cit.; Verdross, op. cit., pp. 20, 21, and in *Recueil des Cours*, 1927 (i), pp. 275–96; Sukiennicki, op. cit., pp. 211–19.

pointed out, first, that this was a difficulty common to all theories on the binding force of law, and, secondly, that the 'common will' is not altogether a foreign will, seeing that the State's own will is one of its constituent elements. He admitted that the will of the State may subsequently undergo a change, but that, he says, means only that the State would not now undertake the same obligation, but not that the changed will liberates it from the obligation.

In general Triepel did not deny that his theory amounted to the creation of a *legal* power over States. He admitted that the theory of a law of co-ordination meant simply that international law owes its *origin* to an agreement, and not to an imposed law. He was not impressed by the objection that an international law 'above' States is contrary to State sovereignty.[1] Triepel's doctrine has remained a source of inspiration for future positivist writers, and it will be seen presently that little, if anything, has been added to it by recent jurists. Although it is based on the will of States as expressed in the *Vereinbarung*, it recognizes the authority of the law over the will of States. This was not the view of the school of thought wedded to the theory of self-limitation.[2]

§ 17. The Law of Co-ordination and the Rule 'pacta sunt servanda'. Cavaglieri and Anzilotti.

In recognizing the objectively binding force of the law-making agreement Triepel paved the way for a conception of international law which, upon analysis, proves tantamount to the abandonment of the theory of a law of co-ordination. The transition of international law from a purely contractual to an objective basis is slow, but the trend of development is clearly marked.

Thus Cavaglieri[3] still rejects the view which bases the binding force of international law on a *command* issued by a superior power. There remains, he says, only the possibility of conceiving international law as 'a system of promises between co-ordinated and juridically equal subjects'. He points out that recent studies in the general theory of law have shown that the legal rule need not necessarily assume

---

[1] 'If this were so,' he says (in 1899), 'then it is high time to embark upon an even more thorough revision of this notorious concept than with which it had recently met at the hand of competent persons.' Ibid., p. 76, n.

[2] This is an important difference between the two doctrines, and the view of Kelsen that Triepel's doctrine is merely a paraphrase of the theory of self-limitation cannot be accepted. See Kelsen, *Recueil des Cours*, 1926 (xiv), p. 285. See also Brierly, op. cit., p. 24.

[3] *Lezioni di Diritto Internazionale, Parte Generale* (1925), pp. 44 et seq.

the character of a command emanating from a superior authority, but that, in certain circumstances, it can have its origin in a promise. He adduces as an example the rules issued by the State to its organs, i.e. to itself, for regulating their conduct towards the individuals in the State, and maintains that these rules are promissory rules inasmuch as the State, being the highest power, cannot tolerate commands. It can only promise its subjects, who are subordinated to it, to act in a certain manner. Yet this analogy solves only part of the problem. For where, in the international sphere, lies the binding force of the promissory rule of conduct? This ultimate source of obligation Cavaglieri finds in the rule *pacta sunt servanda*. But unlike Anzilotti and the Austrian school represented by Kelsen and Verdross, he prefers to assume that the rule *pacta sunt servanda*, far from being an *a priori* hypothesis, is itself a legal rule which owes its existence to the practice of States and to the general conviction of States that it is of a binding nature. He then adduces in support of his contention the collective declaration of the Powers, assembled in London in 1871, affirming the binding force of treaties, as well as a number of utterances of statesmen protesting against attempts at the unilateral modification of treaties.[1]

Anzilotti goes a step further. He too starts from the proposition that the rules governing the relations of States are fundamentally different from those governing the relations of persons within the State.[2] Within the State, he says, there obtains a relation of supremacy and subordination, and the creation of legal rules is exclusively, or almost exclusively, left to organs exercising power over the people of the State so that the legal rule appears as a command issuing from above, whereas the legal rules among States cannot be anything else except agreements and promises between equals. This is the reason why within the State instruments have been created for the compulsory realization of the law by the judiciary and the administration, whereas in international

---

[1] Ibid., pp. 46–50. It would appear, however, from a more recent expression of his views on the subject, that he is prepared to assign a more independent function to the rule *pacta sunt servanda*, although he insists 'qu'elle a également le caractère de règle de droit positif acceptée par la pratique générale des États': *Recueil des Cours*, 1929 (i), p. 362. Strupp, another adherent of the positivist school, has recently also abandoned the theory of the 'common will', for which he substitutes 'la norme fondamentale *pacta sunt servanda*'. *Éléments du droit international public* (2nd ed., 1930), i. 8.

[2] *Corso di diritto internazionale* (French trans. by Gidel, 1929), p. 46.

law such organs are either rudimentary (i.e. expressed in self-help or in joint intervention of a number of States) or entirely absent. This, according to Anzilotti, is, and must remain, the true nature of the rules of international law; the establishment of a power over States would mean the end of international law. At the same time, however, Anzilotti rejects both the theory of self-limitation and that of a common will of States confronting the will of the individual State—the first on the ground that it does not explain why an obligation grounded in the will of the individual State should not be capable of dissolution by the will of that State; the second because the question of the *vis obligandi* of the common will of States is a problem which cannot be solved by purely empirical considerations, but requires a juristic foundation. That foundation Anzilotti, following Kelsen, finds in the rule *pacta sunt servanda* conceived as a necessary *a priori* assumption of the international legal systems which, although capable of explanation by reference to political or moral considerations, cannot itself be proved juridically, just as the legal force of the highest constitutional rule within the State cannot be proved as a juridical proposition. Within the State the rule *pacta sunt servanda* is one of the rules of law sanctioned by the legal order; in international society it constitutes the highest, irreducible, final criterion. The basis of international law is thus finally divorced from the will of States as its ultimate and formal source.

§ 18. The Rule 'pacta sunt servanda' and the Justiciability of International Disputes. What are the consequences, in regard to the question of the scope of the judicial function of international tribunals, of the theory of international law as a system of a law of co-ordination? It must be clear, from the exposition of the doctrine in the preceding sections, that that theory constitutes in one case, namely, as expressed in the various formulations of the theory of self-limitation, a clear negation of the binding force of international law. It is obvious that for this school of thought the rejection of the principle of obligatory adjudication of international disputes follows as a necessary conclusion from the major premiss. But for the other school of writers the conception of 'co-ordination' consists, not in the complete absence of a legal source overriding the will of the State, but merely in the rule that new law cannot be imposed upon a State against its will. Is it accurate to say that the specific structure of international law, as a system of law in which obligations cannot be imposed unless with the concurrence of the States affected, justifies the orthodox rule as to the absence of obligatory jurisdiction of courts in the international sphere?

The view that States are bound only by rules expressly accepted is obviously the assertion of the extreme positivist view. However, it is not necessary here to refute that opinion which has no reference to the question of subjection to *existing* law. It is not inconsistent with the assumption of the existence of a legal command, in the form of a basic legal hypothesis— even in its original form of the theory of the common will—to abide by obligations expressly or tacitly undertaken. So long as the binding force of this basic postulate is assumed, the view that international law is a 'system of promises' is only of secondary importance.[1] The rule *pacta sunt servanda* confronts States as an objective principle independent of their will. It is from this point of view of little importance whether we adopt the view, put forward by Verdross and Kelsen and accepted by Anzilotti, that the rule *pacta sunt servanda* is an original hypothesis which cannot be proved juridically, or whether, like Cavaglieri, we see in it a rule of customary international law. For in each case the rule, in its actual operation, confronts the State independently of its will. It does not matter whether the rule *pacta sunt servanda* is juridical or pre-legal; whether it is imposed as a matter of juridical construction or as a clear generalization from the actual practice and legal convictions of States. The result is the same. It is therefore— it is submitted—impossible to follow those writers who, from the fact that individual obligations of international law owe their origin to the will of States, deduce the existence of an essential difference between a law of co-ordination and a law of subordination. In both cases the basic rule constitutes a command, i.e. a rule existing independently of the will of the parties. It is of no consequence that in the international sphere the command does not issue from a political superior. Law may be a command without being the command of an

---

[1] It is a fatal mistake on the part of the modern positivist school—a mistake which renders the doctrine largely unreal—that it attaches decisive importance to the freedom of States not to accept new obligations, and that it disregards their subjection to rules undertaken either expressly or—and this applies to the bulk of international duties of the State—impliedly.

organized political authority. Only the antiquated view, that the law is a psychological will of a real group entity, will raise the question how a command is possible without there being an authority issuing the command. Once it is recognized that, for juristic perception, the State is identical with the law, and that the juxtaposition or opposition of the two is only a convenient mode of expression, then there is no difficulty in accepting the view that the law may be a command merely by virtue of its external nature. There is therefore an obvious *non sequitur* in the reasoning that as specific obligations of international law are—unlike laws within the State—grounded in agreement and not in a command, there is in international law no compulsory realization of the law through the instrumentality of international tribunals. From the rule that obligations of international law owe their origin to the will of States, it follows that new obligations cannot be imposed upon an unwilling State by any international legislature. But from the principle that a State is objectively bound by an obligation once undertaken there follows, with inescapable logic, the juridical postulate of the obligatory rule of law through the instrumentality of courts. For international tribunals do not impose new obligations. They ascertain existing law. They give effect and expression to the will of the State by ascertaining what obligations it has undertaken by way of express or implied consent.

§ 19. The 'Initial Hypothesis'[1] and the Rule of Law. What is the explanation of the fact that international lawyers have failed to draw the necessary conclusions from the assumption of the objectively binding force of international law as expressed in the adoption of the 'initial hypothesis'? It is believed that one of these reasons is the very form in which writers have clothed that fundamental premiss. That form seems to suggest an attitude which has in reality been abandoned. The fact that the basic principle of international law, as expressed in the rule *pacta sunt servanda*, refers exclusively to agreements of States, is responsible for much of the confusion that has arisen. The attitude —abandoned by the adoption of the initial hypothesis—

---

[1] It may be useful to refer the reader to Salmond's *Jurisprudence*, § 48 ('Ultimate Legal Principles') for a most lucid exposition of the necessity of what some continental jurists have called the 'initial hypothesis' (*Ursprungsnorm*).

that the will of the States is the ultimate source of international law, still continues to find partial adherence in the view, expressed in the formula *pacta sunt servanda*, that international law is not a command, but a system of promises. The two views are no doubt irreconcilable. It is hardly permissible to speak in one and the same breath of international law as a system of promises, and as a system governed by the objective rule *pacta sunt servanda* obliging States to abide by the rules of international law. The choice of this particular formula seems to be unfortunate, inasmuch as, at first sight at least, it refers to *pacta*, i.e. contractual agreements evidencing the direct will of States. It is only by dint of the legal construction of custom as tacit agreement that it can bring within its purview by far the most important part of international law. Only by an even more strained construction can the formula include all that customary international law to which the State has given an implied consent by virtue of its application for admission into the family of nations. And only by a further effort of legal reasoning can it be made to include those generally recognized principles of law to which States have only recently granted express recognition,[1] but which, even apart from the constant practice of States, necessarily form part of international law.

The initial hypothesis in municipal law is that the will of the State, as expressed in the constitution or, in absolute monarchies, in the will of the monarch, must be obeyed. By way of further explanation of this hypothesis it is said that the will of the State consists of duly enacted statutes, of custom as applied by its courts, of delegated legislation, of judicial decisions, and even of private agreements validated by the law. There is no reason why the original hypothesis in international law should not be that the will of the international community must be obeyed. It could be said, by way of further explanation, that although in many cases the will of the international community must be deduced from the mere fact of its existence, i.e. from 'the reason of the thing', the organs of the formation of the will of the international community are, in the absence of an international legislature, States themselves, their consent being given by custom or treaty, and being capable of impartial ascertainment and interpretation by international tribunals. An initial hypothesis expressed in the terms of *voluntas civitatis*

---

[1] See above, p. 66.

maximae est servanda would point, as the source of law, to the
will of the international society expressing itself in contractual
agreements between its constituent members, in their customs, and in the general principles of law which no civilized
community can afford to ignore; it would refer to the *civitas
maxima* as meaning that super-State of law which States,
through the recognition of the binding force of international
law *qua* law, have already recognized as existing over and
above the national sovereignties;[1] it would be compatible
with the fact that the authority of that legal super-State
extends, so far, not so much to the creation of new concrete
rules as to the maintenance and respect of obligations already
expressed or contracted by implication.

The hypothesis *pacta sunt servanda* has proved a beneficent
transition from a doctrine of international law based on
the will of sovereign States to a doctrine of the law of
nations based on the law's impersonal sovereignty. But at
present it contains the two incongruous elements. It pays
homage both to the will of States as the fountain of law and
to the heteronomous command of the rule of law. But the
synthesis is only one of words; it is not, and cannot be, one of
substance. A more satisfactory solution can be found in a
hypothesis which, by courageously breaking with the tradi-
tions of a past period, incorporates the rational and ethical
postulate, which is gradually becoming a fact, of an international community of interests and functions. The view that
such a community exists is not confined to the modern critics
of State sovereignty. By the end of the nineteenth century it
was lucidly expressed by Westlake, who saw in the fact of the
existence of the international community the true basis of
international law. It was stated on the very threshold of
international law by Grotius: 'haec vero ... societatis custo-
dia, humano intellectui conveniens, fons est ejus juris,
quod proprie tali nomine appellatur.'[2] It was expressed, by

---

[1] There has, so far, been no attempt, worthy of the magnitude of the
subject, to consider the meaning of the term 'super-State' as a legal conception, by reference to existing institutions of international law. Care must be
taken, in considering this subject, not to pay exaggerated attention to the lack
of analogy on many a point between the national and international State, and
to the respective merits of nationalism and internationalism. Probably the
realization of the essential identity, for the purposes of legal science, of the
law and the State will facilitate the adoption of the view that the international
State has already been created by the acceptance of the rule of international
law. The defective development of law-creating and law-enforcing agencies
would thus constitute only a difference of degree, not of kind, between the
international State so conceived and the national State.

[2] *De jure belli ac pacis*, Proleg., 8.

Christian Wolff, in the first scientific attempt to lay the legal
foundation of the *civitas maxima*, when he referred to *jus gentium
voluntarium* as being deduced not *ex factis gentium*, but 'ex fine
civitatis maximae quam perinde ac societatem inter omnes
homines instituit ipsa natura, ut in jus istud consentire de-
beant gentes . . .'.[1] If it is true that the initial hypothesis ought
to be not a maxim with a purely formal content, but an
approximation to a social value, then, indeed, the first postulated legal cause can fittingly be formulated by reference to
the international community as such, and not to the will of
individual States.[2]

The suggestion for a change in the formulation of the
initial premiss is not merely a matter of wording. The initial
premiss is to a large extent expressive of the nature of the
legal system in question, and it may influence its substantive
rules so far as it is in the power of a legal theory to do so. This
may be clearly seen from the fact that the initial premiss
embodied in the principle *pacta sunt servanda* could be held
compatible with the affirmation of the doctrine that a State
can legally claim the right to remain judge in disputes with
other States by the simple means of refusing to them the
benefit of judicial settlement.

III

The Judicial Function and the Legal Nature of International Law

§ 20. The Place of Courts in the Legal System. Writers
who vindicate the legal character of international law, and
who, at the same time, find no fault with the existing
rule which denies compulsory jurisdictional powers to
international tribunals, maintain that the existence of courts is

---

[1] *Jus gentium methodo scientifica pertractatum* (1749), *Praefatio*.
[2] On the question of the initial hypothesis in international law see Kelsen,
Das Problem der Souveränität und die Theorie des Völkerrechts (1920), *passim*; Verdross,
Die Verfassung der Rechtsgemeinschaft (1926), pp. 21–33; Cavaglieri, op. cit.,
pp. 40–50; Chklaver, *Le droit international dans ses rapports avec la philosophie du
droit* (1925); Ottolenghi in *Rivista*, xvii (1925), pp. 343–57; Kunz, *Völkerrechtswis-
senschaft und reine Rechtslehre* (1923), and in *Wörterbuch des Völkerrechts*, i. 787ff.;
Salvioli in *Rivista*, xiv (1921–2), pp. 20–80; Merkl in *Zeitschrift für öffentliches
Recht* (1926), pp. 497ff.; Henrich, ibid., pp. 308ff.; Métall, ibid., xi (1931),
pp. 416–23; Walz in *Archiv des öffentlichen Rechts*, lviii (1930), pp. 1–60. On the
initial hypothesis in general see Kelsen, *Die philosophischen Grundlagen der Nat-
urrechtslehre und des Rechtspositivismus* (1928).

not an indispensable condition of the rule of law at all, and that, as a matter of historical experience, law preceded the establishment of regular tribunals.[1] They adduce the conditions obtaining in primitive communities, which recognize self-help to a considerable extent, as an instance of that stage of legal development. They also point to a somewhat more advanced stage of legal organization in which there do exist tribunals, but in which submission to the judge is merely voluntary.[2]

This latter argument, so frequently and confidently repeated, may be somewhat difficult of refutation, not only because of the hypothetical character of the facts to which it refers, but also because it assumes the existence of law in communities in which, on its own showing, such existence may legitimately be the object of controversy. Whatever may be the nature of such rules the very fact that there are no impartial tribunals to adjudicate upon their operation seriously impairs their character as rules of law.[3] There is substance in the view that the existence of a sufficient body of clear rules of conduct is not at all essential to the existence of law, and that the decisive test is whether there exists a judge competent to decide upon disputed rights and to command peace. The questionable value of references to conditions prevailing in primitive communities is shown by the fact that writers of authority, including Sir Henry Maine, regard the existence of judges and tribunals as the decisive test for the assumption of the rule of law.[4] It is more easy

[1] See Bergbohm, *Staatsverträge und Gesetze als Quellen des Völkerrechts* (1877), pp. 24–32; Bluntschli, *Das moderne Völkerrecht der zivilisierten Staaten* (3rd ed., 1878), pp. 8, 9 (while admitting that the absence of the judge is even more serious than the absence of a legislator); Heilborn, *Grundbegriffe des Völkerrechts* (1912), pp. 17, 18; Fauchille, *Traité de droit international public*, i (1922), No. 28; De Louter, op. cit. i. 64; Strupp, *Grundzüge des positiven Völkerrechts* (3rd ed., 1926), p. 3; Walz, op. cit., pp. 170–2.

[2] See Lammasch, *Schiedsgerichtsbarkeit*, pp. 3–7. See also Ihering, *Geist des römischen Rechts* (2nd ed., 1866), i. 167. And see Wlassak in *Zeitschrift für Rechtsgeschichte* (Romanistic Section), xxxiii. 157, who shows that the civil procedure in Roman law originated in voluntary arbitration. See also Brunner, *Deutsche Rechtsgeschichte*, vol. i, part ii, p. 256. And see Pollock, *A First Book of Jurisprudence* (3rd ed., 1911), pp. 24, 25, who also points out that the jurisdiction of courts arose from the voluntary submission by parties. However, he admits that even in archaic society 'effectual motives for submission could be brought, sooner or later, to bear on unwilling subjects'. Possibly it might be said that such voluntary submission is voluntary in form only.

[3] See on this matter the judicious observations of Spiropoulos, op. cit., pp. 66, 67.

[4] Thus, when pointing out that the further we penetrate into the primitive history of thought the further we find ourselves from a conception of law possess-

to imagine the absence, in a community under the reign of law, of a sovereign authority imposing laws by express enactment than of agencies laying down authoritatively *quod est juris*.

There are other considerations which are relevant for the determination of the legal character of rules of conduct obtaining in society and which bear on the question of obligatory judicial settlement. The first is that only through final ascertainment by agencies other than the parties to the dispute can the law be rendered certain; it is not rendered so by the *ipse dixit* of an interested party. Such certainty is of the essence of law. The object of law to secure order must be defeated if a controversial rule of conduct may remain permanently a matter of dispute. It must so remain as long as no agencies exist capable of determining existing legal rights with finality and without appeal.[1] The second consideration is that it is essential for the rule of law that there should exist agencies bearing evidence, and giving effect, to the imperative nature of the law.[2] The law's external

ing all the elements of the conception of law as taught by Austin and Bentham, Maine says that 'it is certain that in the infancy of mankind, no sort of legislature, nor even a distinct author of law, is contemplated or conceived of' (*Ancient Law*, 1920 ed., p. 7). But he insists on the existence, even at that time, of the 'authoritative statement of right and wrong' in 'a judicial sentence after the facts, not one presupposing a law which has been violated, but one which is breathed for the first time by a higher power into the judge's mind at the moment of adjudication' (ibid.). See Walker, *The Science of International Law* (1893), p. 11 ('Custom precedes Law, and the Judge the Law-Giver'). See also Politis, *La justice internationale* (1924), p. 253, to the effect that tribunals have preceded codes, and not conversely.

[1] See on this point J. Dickinson, 'A Working Theory of Sovereignty', in *Political Science Quarterly*, xlii (1927), pp. 524–48. It will be noted that it is in particular in the common law countries that the absence of obligatory courts is regarded as the main reason for denying to international law the quality of law. See, for instance, the remarks of Lord Salisbury in the House of Lords on 26 July 1887. International law, he said, 'depends generally upon the prejudices of writers of text-books. It can be enforced by no tribunal, and therefore to apply to it the phrase "law" is to some extent misleading.' See also Gray, *The Nature and the Sources of the Law* (1909), §§ 286 and 287, who, while inclined to accept the Austinian view on the nature of international law, believed the establishment of a true international court to be impending, and saw in it a landmark in the development of international law towards true law. Borchard, 'Government Responsibility in Tort', in *Yale Law Journal*, xxxvi (1926–7), pp. 1084–6, who is inclined to defend the legal nature of self-imposed rules, largely qualifies his position by the question: 'If societal agencies, such as courts, are established, to which complaints of group violation of the established or agreed rules can be brought and from whom decisions against the group based on the rules can be obtained, why is it not proper to characterize such rules as law?' They would not be law but for the existence of courts.

[2] See Brierly, *The Law of Nations* (1928), p. 37, who says: 'Law by its very nature is imperative; there must exist an *obligation* to obey it, however we may

nature may express itself either in the fact that it is a precept created independently of the will of the subjects of the law, or that it is valid and continues to exist in respect of the subjects of the law independently of their will. Of these two aspects of the external character of law, the second is the more conspicuous and, accordingly, more important in practice. The fact that the source of law is in its creation external to those bound by it may both in primitive and in modern society be effectively concealed behind the phenomenon of customary law; for the latter is beyond the control of the individual members of a community more as a matter of legal analysis than of political and sociological fact. But there is no ambiguity possible about the external nature of the law as ascertained and enforced by courts. In international society there is lacking to a large extent that feature of the external character of law which consists in its being created regardless of the will of those who are subject to it. That shortcoming must probably remain so long as there is no international legislature in existence—a development practically identical with the establishment of what is usually called a super-State. The other manifestation of the legal nature of international law, namely, the objective ascertainment of rights by courts, is one which could be effected within the frame of the existing practice and doctrine of international law. To acquiesce in the permanent absence also of that aspect of international law is to strain its legal character to the breaking-point.

§ **21. The Meaning of the Rule 'omnis judex in re sua'.** The conception of the 'specific character' of international law has made legal thought insensible to the juristic heresy involved in the rule of international law which sanctions the absence of obligatory jurisdiction on the part of international tribunals to decide disputes between States. It has prevented

---

explain the origin of that sentiment.' See also Capitant, *L'impératif juridique* (1928). And see above, p. 419. See also Renard, *La théorie de l'Institution* (1930), p. 459; 'Si le droit international est en état d'inferiorité vis-a-vis du droit interne c'est parce que la justice internationale n'est pas encore parvenue à se détacher de ses origines contractuelles et arbitrales.' The view expressed above, as to the imperative nature of the law, does not refer to the controversy whether the law in its origin is a command or a formulation of existing custom. It refers to the external nature of legal rules independently of their origin. It is probably in this sense that Verdross—rightly, it is submitted—says: 'International law is "above" States in the same sense in which municipal law is "above" those subjected to its sway. Also international law is a law of subordination, not of co-ordination' (*Verfassung*, p. 49).

us from seeing in its true light the fact that the majority of the judgements given by the Permanent Court of International Justice has been concerned with so-called 'pleas to the jurisdiction',[1] i.e. with the refusal of one party, supported by a rigid and ingenious interpretation of relevant arbitration agreements, to accord to the other party the right, which Hobbes regarded as elementary even in a state of nature, of impartial adjudication. This has been done, as a rule, not for the reason that another international agency was competent to decide the issue, but on the ground that the State in question was not bound by any commitment to have recourse to judicial settlement. The conception of the 'specific character of international law' has prevented us from seeing any anomaly in the fact that even when the elementary duty of submission to adjudication is accepted, it is in practice often attended by elaborate reservations which reduce it to a mere formula devoid of any legal obligation. The time has come to inquire whether this is a rule which, notwithstanding its unimpeachable formal validity, is, in the present state of international law, sound and consistent with its principal doctrines and objects.[2] The international lawyer must not regard himself as being prevented from attempting that task on the ground that the Permanent Court of International Justice has repeatedly expressed the opinion that it is a clear rule of international law that a State cannot be compelled against its will to submit its disputes with other States for international adjudication, and that its jurisdiction is strictly limited by the will of States. The time has come to consider whether that rule ought not, as a matter of law, to be enunciated with more diffidence and less emphasis; whether the practice of the Permanent Court itself has not gone beyond its expressed adherence to the traditional rule;[3] and whether it ought not

---

[1] See above, p. 207, and below, p. 427, n. 3.

[2] The student of international law must observe, not without some surprise, that while successive generations of international lawyers have been at pains to explain why the vitiating effect of duress must be disregarded, no such attempt has been made in regard to the rule of international law concerning the limitation of the international judicial function.

[3] See, in particular, Judgement No. 8 (Series A, No. 9, pp. 20–5) concerning the Factory at Chorzów (Claim for Indemnity), in which the Court assumed jurisdiction in a claim for reparation, the action having been brought under an arbitration clause relating to the interpretation and application of the treaty in question (see above, p. 125). In Judgement No. 12 (Series A, No. 15, p. 23) concerning the Rights of Minorities in Upper Silesia the Court assumed jurisdiction, not by virtue of an agreement conferring jurisdiction upon it, but on the

therefore to be interpreted restrictively as being derogatory to general principles of law and to international law conceived as a system of law.

The fact that the State's right to refuse compulsory judicial ascertainment of legally contested claims is a principle of present-day international law does not mean that the international lawyer is relieved of the duty to analyse this rule in order to see whether it is consistent with other, no less fundamental, rules of international law and with other manifestations of the will of States. This may sound paradoxical, but the apparent paradox vanishes when we consider that international law is not a coherent and harmonious system of precepts governed by an all-pervading unity of the reign of law, but a body of rules largely built up as a generalization of conflicting practices, and attempting to bind together by law political entities each inclined to insist on being a law unto itself. Hence the frequent occurrence of rules generally adopted in text-books, believed to be

---

ground that Poland, in the preliminary pleadings, submitted arguments on the merits, and that even in the counter-case she did not plead to the jurisdiction. The Court said: '... There seems to be no doubt that the consent of the State to the submission of a dispute to the Court may not only result from an express declaration, but may also be inferred from acts conclusively establishing it. It seems hard to deny that the submission of arguments on the merits, without making reservations in regard to the question of jurisdiction, must be regarded as an unequivocal indication of the desire of a State to obtain a decision on the merits of the suit.' The solemn insistence of the Court on the will of States, as the sole source of its jurisdiction, can hardly diminish the importance of the fact that jurisdiction had been assumed over a sovereign State as the result of the failure to comply with the procedural rules of the Court. In the same Judgement the Court referred to Judgement No. 5 in which the Court assumed jurisdiction in pursuance of a declaration made by Great Britain in the course of the proceedings consenting to a decision of the Court on a point in regard to which the Court was of the opinion that it would otherwise have no jurisdiction. In its Twelfth Advisory Opinion—a judicial pronouncement of outstanding importance—the Court effected a deep inroad into the recognized principle of unanimity by acting upon the 'well-known rule that no one can be judge in his own suit' (Series B, No. 12, p. 32). But the difference between the facts underlying this pronouncement and those underlying the frequent insistence on its own jurisdiction being strictly limited by the will of States is not, it is submitted, a fundamental one. It is true that, in the case in hand, Turkey had previously agreed to submit the dispute for a decision by the Council of the League, but the Turkish position was that, in the absence of express provision to that effect, she was entitled to the benefit of the traditional rule of international law—sanctioned by the Covenant of the League—which required her consent to any decision on the disputed matter. The Court rejected this view on the ground that Turkey, having once agreed to the dispute being decided by the Council of the League, was bound by the general principle *nemo judex in re sua*. But, it may be asked, do the frequent pronouncements of the Court on its jurisdiction being invariably limited by the will of the parties really suggest that the principle *nemo judex in re sua* is of such general application in international law as to make it the basis of the interpretation of a treaty provision?

fundamental, and acted upon by States, but which, upon examination, reveal themselves as inconsistent in themselves, as contrary to other equally well recognized rules, and as at variance with the practice of States in other fields. Thus, for instance, the doctrine of equality of States, for a long time cherished as an obvious rule of positive internatioonal law, has been shown not to be a true reflection of the practice of States.[1] The same is true of the positivist doctrine which would restrict the sources of international law to express manifestations of the will of States.[2] It is true of the various aspects of the doctrine of sovereignty, including the refusal to recognize the obligatory competence of courts in disputes between members of the international society. There is indeed a glaring contradiction in the idea that, in a society of States which are *ex hypothesi* independent of one another, and in a relation of equality to each other, one State may legally claim the right to remain judge in a dispute in which the rights of another State are involved—a contradiction which is not solved but accentuated by the right of other States to disregard any decision thus reached, and in turn to set themselves up as judges on the disputed right. *Par in parem non habet imperium* is a maxim repeated by writers and tribunals as expressing the rule that the courts of one country may not assume jurisdiction over a foreign sovereign State without its consent. That rule is carried to its logical conclusion, in respect not only of the foreign State itself, but also in respect of its armed forces abroad, its public ships, and its property— even if, according to the jurisprudence of most States, the activities of that State are, in a given case, of the nature of private-law transactions. A vast literature and jurisprudence have grown up round the subject of jurisdictional immunities. But the existing rule, that the jurisdiction of international courts is in principle voluntary, is upon analysis nothing else than the assertion of the right to exercise jurisdiction over a foreign State, not in minor matters to which the maxim *par in parem non habet imperium* usually applies, but in international relations proper.

In municipal law the interests of the State are *summum jus*. The State is bound by its own will so long as that will exists, but, subject to certain constitutional requirements of form, it may change its will, and with it the general contents of its law. It has at its disposal general provisions of the utmost

---

[1] See Dickinson, *The Doctrine of Equality of States in International Law* (1920).
[2] See on this point Lauterpacht, *Analogies*, pp. 51–71.

flexibility which enable the organs of the State, while remaining within the orbit of the law, to overrule and change
existing rules of law in response to the political considerations
of the *salus rei publicae*.[1] The rule of international law sanctioning the State's freedom from the bonds of obligatory
judicial settlement means that the State assumes, as against
other equal members of the international community, the
same position as it enjoys in relation to the individuals
subject to itself. This is, indeed, a sufficient reason why the
application of this doctrine to the relations between States
must be rejected. Any doctrine which, in relations between
States, postulates the individual interest of the single State as
the ultimate standard of values and of legal obligation,
amounts to a negation of international law. It disregards
the fact that, while in its internal relations the State is a law
unto itself, and while its important interests are there
the decisive consideration, this is not so in its capacity as
subject to international law. This does not mean that international law disregards its important interests. It means only
that these highest interests are recognized, measured, and
adjusted by international law by reference to the equal interests of other States and to those of the international community as a whole. Undoubtedly the ultimate purpose of law
is to serve the interests of those subjected to its sway. But
that cannot mean that every important interest, so deemed
by the State in question, can claim superiority over rights,
recognized by international law, of other States. No doubt

---

[1] This part of the law is not inappropriately styled by some writers 'political
law'. (See Bilfinger, 'Betrachtungen über politisches Recht', in *Z.f.a.ö.R. und V.*
i. (1929), pp. 57–76. See also Smend, *Verfassung und Verfassungsrecht* (1928), pp. 21
et seq., and 97 et seq.) According to some, the constitution of a State as
embodying fundamental provisions relating to the State itself partakes of the
nature of 'political law'. This conception of the nature of the constitution is
advocated, not only by German writers like Ihering (*Der Zweck im Recht* (1880),
pp. 318 ff.), Jellinek (*Allgemeine Staatslehre* (1900), pp. 330 ff.), and Laband (*Das
Staatsrecht des deutschen Reichs* (3rd ed., 1895), i, 649), but also, from a slightly
different angle, by English constitutional lawyers. Dicey, referring to English
constitutional law, says: 'Conventions, understandings, habits or practices
which, though they may regulate the conduct of the several members of the
sovereign power, of the Ministry, or of other officials, are not in reality laws at
all since they are not enforced by the Courts' (*The Law of the Constitution* (8th
ed., 1915), p. 23). One may not agree with the definition of law underlying this
statement, but it is difficult to deny the existence within the State of rules, the
non-observance of which by the highest legislative or executive organs of the
State, far from amounting to a breech of law, will be constitutive of new law
expressive of the changed political necessities of the State. See on this point
Borchard, 'Government Responsibility in Tort', in *Yale Law Journal*, xxxvi
(1926), p. 789.

it is true to say that international law is made for States, and not States for international law, but it is true only in the sense that the State is made for human beings, and not human beings for the State. International law is made for States in their totality, and not for the transient benefit of the individual State. So far as the State's vital interests are concerned they are invariably within the sphere of legal protection by international law. But they are so protected as part of the international legal order. The sanctity and supremacy which metaphysical theories attach to the State must be rejected in any scientific conception of international law.[1]

§ 22. International Law and General Jurisprudence. If—
as it is submitted is the truth—the existing rule on the place of law and of the judicial function is incompatible with general principles of law and with the conception of law itself as generally recognized, then the international lawyer is confronted with his central problem, which is at the same time one of the principal problems of the philosophy of law in general. Shall international law, by refusing to admit its present imperfections and by elevating them to the authority of legitimate and permanent manifestations of a 'specific' law, abdicate the task of raising itself above the level of a primitive law of a primitive community? The results of the present

---

[1] In general, a treaty of unlimited obligatory arbitration is no more incompatible with the State's freedom of action than any other agreement in which a State binds itself to pursue, or to refrain from pursuing, a course of action. In an ordinary treaty a State binds itself to allow its will to be determined in the future by the will of the other contracting party acting in accordance with its own interest. In a treaty of obligatory arbitration it binds itself to have, in the future, its conduct determined by the will of an impartial agency deciding according to law. The only (and certainly important) point of difference is that, in so far as the doctrine *rebus sic stantibus* applies to other treaties, it cannot be applied to this particular one. For it is difficult to see how any change of circumstances can justify the refusal to have a dispute settled by law. It could, no doubt, be said that, in so far as the doctrine *rebus sic stantibus* may legitimately be put forward in regard to an ordinary treaty obligation, it may be invoked in respect of an arbitration treaty, seeing that a judicial settlement is merely the application of the existing law, and that therefore the doctrine *rebus sic stantibus*, calculated as it is to defeat the operation of existing obsolete law, may with equal justification be advanced against an arbitration treaty likely to result in an affirmation of a legal position believed to be obsolete. However, in the writer's opinion, the very idea of a plea of changed conditions being applied to the obligation to submit to judicial settlement is abhorrent to the idea of law. It can be explained only in terms of a determination to challenge the reign of law. So long as the reign of law is recognized, the doctrine *rebus sic stantibus* can be pleaded, with reference to a specific legal position said to be obsolete, within the frame of the duty of judicial settlement. In fact, so long as the doctrine *rebus sic stantibus* is claimed to be a legal doctrine, it is possible of application only through the agency of a judicial body. See above, pp. 276 et seqq.

inquiry into the scope of the international judicial function, as well as the writer's studies of the general relation of international law to private law,[1] seem to him to justify the submission that the future development of international law will be conditioned by its incorporation into the general principles and conception of law as developed by civilized communities without reference to the 'state of nature' existing among States.[2] The more international law approaches the standards of municipal law, the more it approximates to those standards of morals and order which are the ultimate foundation of all law. The time-honoured repudiation and disparagement of the analogy to municipal—and, in particular, to private—law is merely another aspect of the insistence on the so-called specific character of international law. That specific character of international law has revealed itself as the negation of the idea of law.

It is better that international law should be regarded as incomplete, and in a state of transition to the finite and attainable ideal of a society of States under the binding rule of law, as generally recognized and practised by civilized communities within their borders, than that, as the result of the well-meant desire to raise its formal authority *qua* law, it should be treated as the perfect and immutable species of a comprehensively diluted *genus proximum*.[3] There is an obvious disadvantage attaching to the application, in the domain of jurisprudence, of the principle of Gresham's Law in econo-

---

[1] *Private Law Sources and Analogies of International Law* (1927), *passim*.

[2] See the discussion by J. B. Moore of the 'essentials of an organisation which would place international law on substantially the same footing as municipal law': *International Law and Some Current Illusions* (1924), pp. 302–4. See also J. B. Scott in *A.S., Proceedings* (1930), p. 32. For an eloquent statement of the identity—save in the matter of the extent of their operation—of international and municipal law see also Krabbe, *The Modern Idea of State* (Eng. trans.), pp. 432 et seqq. See also, to the same effect, De Louter, op. cit. i. 17 (somewhat inconsequently, seeing that elsewhere he denies to international law the most prominent characteristics of municipal law: see above, p. 404).

[3] This latter course is generally followed by international lawyers. Only at times of international crises, which reveal the imperfections of the existing law, the tendency towards what we believe to be a more accurate approach stands out clearly. Liszt, the author of the well-known German text-book, was, in ten successive editions of his treatise, inculcating into the mind of the student the view that international law is based on agreement, that it is a law different from municipal law, and that the element of compulsion must necessarily be absent from it (10th ed., p. 10). But in the 11th ed., prepared by Liszt himself in 1918, there is a radical change of attitude (p. 8). International law is there said to be of the same nature as the law of the State, and the introduction of the factor of compulsion is described as the necessary practical goal of its development if it is to maintain itself as law. Oppenheim's similar change of attitude has been noted elsewhere (see above, p. 404).

mics, according to which 'bad money drives out good'. There is no good reason why primitive law, if law it be, should drive out developed law as the decisive factor in determining the conception of law. A departure from this path of juridical rectitude constitutes only an insignificant danger to municipal jurisprudence where what has been called 'the normative force of social reality' automatically acts as a corrective to misguided legal theory. In international law the effects of such methods are more pernicious. They sanction its imperfections. They prevent its development. They tend to deprive it of an attainable ideal. It may be admitted that the conception of law is an historical category, subject to changes of time and space; but, because it is an historical category, it is inadmissible that a conception of law founded on generalizations from conditions obtaining in the rudimentary stage of legal development should remain intact at a later stage, and consequently prove a cause of disintegration.

It is submitted that the arguments usually adduced in support of the legal nature of international law conceived as a 'weak law'[1] may be plausible and even scientifically accurate, but that their cumulative effect is such as to explain it away to the point of extinction. It is possible, by reference to the history of primitive communities, to assert the possibility of a legal order without a sovereign authority enacting laws; it is possible to think of a rudimentary legal order, possessing no courts with obligatory jurisdiction to ascertain disputed rights; it is possible to conceive a system of law having no organs for its enforcement, and relying for that purpose on self-help. But it is permissible to ignore the vitiating consequences of any single defect only if other essential elements are present to neutralize the results of the shortcomings in one particular sphere. To assert the possibility of the existence of a legal system in which *all* these elements are lacking is to reduce the conception of law to a shadow of its own self, or else to apply it in a meaning different from that usually attached to it.

The difficulty is not solved by the assertion that primitive communities offer an historical proof for the view that rudimentary systems of law do exist notwithstanding these shortcomings. For not only does the designation of the rules, obtaining within a community, as 'rules of law' beg the question of their legal nature; and not only is a cumulation of

---

[1] See above, p. 402.

these shortcomings unknown even to primitive society: the decisive factor is that modern States are *not* primitive communities and that there is a patent contradiction in any attempt to construe the relations between States of to-day as governed by the law of primitive peoples. Accordingly, lawyers who endeavour to explain by this method the perpetuation of the existing shortcomings of international law are engaged in a task which is as unscientific as it is unprogressive.[1] This reproach cannot be effectively met by the plea that there is nothing contradictory in the fact that relations of States with a developed system of law within their borders are governed, in their relations *inter se*, by a deficient and almost illusory system of law. Only the current personification of the metaphysical State, supported by the questionable doctrine of States as the sole subjects of international law, enables writers to assert and justify the possibility of human beings—for States and Governments are made up of human beings—adopting fundamentally differing standards of order and justice in different spheres of action.

The notion of law, with the help of which the international lawyer gauges and determines the nature of the rules which form the subject-matter of his science, is necessarily an *a priori* one. But this is an additional reason why it should be construed on the basis of what is best and most developed in legal experience—not on the basis of the emaciated, fragmentary, and historically questionable experience of primitive communities in past ages. It is of the essence of the dignity of legal science—including the science of international law—to resist the temptation to lower the standard of law to the low level of an avowedly rudimentary practice.

§ 23. The Task of the Science of International Law.
In this vindication of the dignity of their science international lawyers are confronted with two tasks, whose performance ought not, it is believed, to be delayed much longer. Both these tasks arise directly out of the subject discussed in this book. The first is the imperative necessity for abandoning a doctrine which—expressed in the traditional distinction between justiciable and non-justiciable or legal and political

---

[1] Professor Brierly (*Law of Nations* (1928), p. 52), referring to the weakness of international law in regard to the imperfections of its law-creating machinery, says—rightly, it is submitted—that such 'customary law can never be adequate to the needs of any but a most primitive society, and the international society of to-day is not, except in the matter of its law, at the primitive stage'.

disputes—has lost its original usefulness and has become an obstacle in the way of legal progress. The variety of contradictory meanings attached to this distinction, together with the disconcerting fact that a scientific discussion has been conducted for many years on a matter of fundamental importance bearing upon international life amidst a confusion of language which has rendered, and must render, that discussion fruitless, are not likely to enhance the authority of international law. Even if it could (although in fact it cannot) be shown that each of the four aspects of the conception of justiciable disputes is sound in itself, the very fact that they cover substantially different categories of disputes (so that a dispute which is justiciable according to one test is non-justiciable according to another) makes it unfit for the purpose of scientific exposition, or for the expression of legal obligations in an international treaty. The doctrine can mean so much that it does not mean anything. International lawyers have in recent years become increasingly conscious of this difficulty. However, their attitude on this question creates the impression of a passive acquiescence in an inherited evil. Baffled by the impasse into which the current distinction between the two classes of disputes has led them, some international lawyers believe that, although the distinction between legal and political disputes may be theoretically correct, its practical importance is insignificant. Others express the view that, although theoretically difficult to establish and to maintain, it may render useful service in practice. It has been shown here that the doctrine is untenable in theory and harmful in practice.

It is embarrassing to note the resignation with which most international lawyers, fully conscious of the juridical unsoundness and confusing effect of the traditional distinction between the two classes of disputes, justify the perpetuation of this distinction in international conventions on the sole ground that Governments attach importance to it. But Governments, it has been shown, attach importance to it, not only because it is a convenient means of substituting an apparent for an effective obligation, but also because of the encouragement which it receives from international lawyers.[1]

---

[1] It is apparently with reference to that doctrine that statesmen, who did not lack experience in the sphere of international action, expressed the opinion that lawyers were obstructing international arbitration in the same measure as naval experts were hampering international disarmament. See Lord Robert Cecil in *The Times*, 12 May 1929.

This is the reason why it is a duty incumbent upon the lawyer to adopt a critical attitude in regard to that doctrine in the interest not only of the dignity of the science of international law, but also of an effective peaceful organization of the international community which it is the legitimate business of international lawyers to promote. For, it is submitted, the rejection of the substance, and of the terminology, of the current doctrine—expressed in the traditional classification—of the necessary limitation of the international judicial function does not constitute a merely theoretical result. That doctrine has now become a factor possessing a reality transcending that of a mere legal theory.

In an ever-growing number of arbitration conventions States have pledged themselves to judicial settlement in all legal (justiciable) as distinguished from political (non-justiciable) disputes. The fact that the doctrine has thus found a place in leading treaties of pacific settlement has created a situation in which conventional international law is, on a subject of fundamental importance to international society, illusory and non-effective. There is little merit in an international convention the vital clause of which is based on a distinction which does not exist, or, to say the least, the meaning of which is so elastic and indefinite as to deprive the clause of practical value. Even the so-called Optional Clause of Article 36 of the Statute of the Permanent Court of International Justice, the most general and important arbitration convention, has, according to some, incorporated the current classification by qualifying, as the result of the use of the term 'legal', the four classes of disputes in regard to which obligatory jurisdiction is conferred upon the Permanent Court of International Justice. The supposed fundamental difference between justiciable and non-justiciable disputes has had the effect of increasing the emphasis upon so-called alternative means of settlement, notably conciliation. The decisive feature of these alternative means of settlement is that they do not imply any legal obligation to accept the finding or the recommendation of the body called upon to deal with the dispute. At the same time the acceptance of the obligation to have recourse to the alternative means of settlement creates the impression of a real commitment in the field of pacific settlement of disputes. Thus, under the cloak of a mere difference in procedure, a check is being put on the reign of law between nations.

It is possible that, in the initial stage of the development of international judicial settlement, the traditional classification played a useful part by allaying the apprehension of Governments over the possible consequences of undertaking the commitments of obligatory arbitration.[1] It is a common phenomenon in natural and social sciences that fictions which are, and are known to be, scientifically false are adopted and maintained for a time as a scaffolding, as it were, to aid the erection of the edifice of accurate knowledge.[2] But the same scientific experience shows that, once that object has been achieved, there ought to be no hesitation in pulling down the scaffolding and in refusing to permit the fiction to outgrow its original usefulness.

The second task with which international lawyers are confronted lies in the domain of method and general approach. The opposition, on the part of many international lawyers of authority, to the universal application of judicial settlement, and their insistence on the necessity for retaining in some form the traditional classification of disputes, come from the conviction that law must not be treated as a panacea able to secure peace in all circumstances. There is, as we have seen, certainly much force in this view. But it is essential that international lawyers should develop an attitude of criticism in regard to the very effective—although now somewhat trite—argument that law is not a panacea. Law can never, on the plane of mere fact, become an effective substitute for war. But that does not mean that law is not in itself a powerful constituent element of peace. Undoubtedly the effectiveness of the law depends to a large extent upon the prevalent practice and the general level of morality,[3] but the very fact of the reign of law is, and tends to become increasingly, part of common practice and morality. The reign of law, represented by the incorporation of obligatory arbitration as a rule of positive international law, is not the only means for securing and preserving peace among nations. Nevertheless it is an essential condition of peace. A given factor may not be the only condition of the consummation of a desired object. But that does not mean that it is not an indispensable condition of its achievement, or that there are not in existence other conditions equally essential. From the fact that obligatory

---

[1] See above, p. 5.
[2] See Vaihinger, *The Philosophy of 'As if'* (translated by Ogden, 1924).
[3] See Brierly in *Cornell Law Quarterly*, xiii (1928), p. 397.

arbitration is a *conditio sine qua non* of the normal machinery for the preservation of peace, it does not follow that peace is not equally dependent on other factors, including an enhanced consciousness of international solidarity, and a broad-minded preparedness not to rely rigidly on acquired legal rights when such rights happen to conflict with justice and with the peaceful and progressive development of international relations.

It is possible that, in dealing with questions relating to the place of law and of courts in the international society, international lawyers have attached importance to separating legal exposition from any pacifistic tendency. But if pacifism is identical with the insistence on the reign of law in international relations, then it may be doubted whether a jurist conscious of the true nature of his task may hope to achieve a rigid separation of this nature. For peace is not only a moral idea. In a sense (although only in one sense) the idea of peace is morally indifferent, inasmuch as it may involve the sacrifice of justice on the altar of stability and security. Peace is pre-eminently a legal postulate. Juridically it is a metaphor for the postulate of the unity of the legal system. Juridical logic inevitably leads to condemnation, as a matter of law, of anarchy and private force. It is one of the unsatisfactory features of modern international law that it has neglected to find a legal foundation for the so-called pacifism which it has relegated to the domain of morals and sociology. Just as positivism in the domain of international law has become unscientific by being driven, through its own exaggerations, to disregard the very practice of States which it professes to regard as the only source of law, so the desire of generations of international lawyers to confine their activity to a registration of the practice of States has discouraged any determined attempt at relating it to higher legal principle, or to the conception of international law as a whole. The latter function can—effectively, it is submitted—be performed by means of the legitimate methods of juridical criticism and analysis.

APPENDIX

LIMITATION OF THE JUDICIAL FUNCTION IN DISPUTES BETWEEN STATE-MEMBERS OF COMPOSITE STATES

As in other matters, so also in the question of the limitation of the judicial function, cases decided by quasi-international courts, endowed with compulsory jurisdiction over States which are members of composite States—in particular of Federal States—deserve special consideration. They are on the border-line between national and international adjudication; at the same time they are the first example of judicial settlement of disputes among States. Their history begins with arbitration between city States of Greek Leagues and confederations.[1] It was continued in the Middle Ages in the relations between the Federal units of Italian cities[2] and the States of the Swiss Confederation.[3] In the last hundred years it has found frequent application in the relations between the members of the American Union,[4] of the Swiss Cantons, of the States of the German *Reich*,[5] and of other Federal States,[6] for instance, of the Australian Commonwealth. The feature common to all these arbitration tribunals has been that, whenever applicable, they have had recourse to rules of international law.[7] These arbitration tribunals have thus furnished an instructive example demonstrating the operation of the obligatory rule of law among political units claiming the attributes of sovereignty. They have constituted an important link in the evolution

---

[1] See Raeder, *L'Arbitrage international chez les Hellènes* (1912), pp. 189–236, who has devoted particular attention to this aspect of Greek arbitration.

[2] Frey, *Das öffentlich-rechtliche Schiedsgericht in Ober-Italien im XII. und XIII. Jahrhundert* (1928).

[3] Usteri, *Das öffentlich-rechtliche Schiedsgericht in der schweizerischen Eidgenossenschaft des XII–XV. Jahrhunderts* (1925).

[4] On this subject the two volumes by J. B. Scott containing the reports and analysis of the cases reported and entitled *Judicial Settlement of Controversies between States of the American Union* (1918) are of great importance for the history of international arbitration and of international law in general. See also the same, *Sovereign States and Suits* (1925); and, for a short account of the work of the Supreme Court, H. A. Smith, *The American Supreme Court as an International Tribunal* (1920). And see Warren, *The Supreme Court and Sovereign States* (1924).

[5] See below, p. 451.

[6] See below, p. 445.

[7] See for clear pronouncements to this effect *Bremen (Free Hansa City of)* v. *Prussia*, decided by the German *Staatsgerichtshof*, *Annual Digest*, 1925–6, Case No. 266; and ibid., 1927–8, Case No. 289, *Canton of Thurgau* v. *Canton of St. Gallen*, decided by the Swiss Federal Court; and Case No. 86, *Württemberg and Prussia* v. *Baden*, decided by the German *Staatsgerichtshof*. See also *Kansas* v. *Colorado*, by Brewer, J., 206 U.S. 46, 97; and *Kansas* v. *Colorado*, by Fuller, J., 185 U.S. 125, 146; *Louisiana* v. *Mississippi*, 202 U.S. 1, 49; *Iowa* v. *Illinois*, 147 U.S. 1, 7 (application of the doctrine of the *thalweg*); *Nebraska* v. *Iowa*, 143 U.S. 359, 361 (river boundaries).

of the rule of law from the compulsory jurisdiction of courts over individuals to that over fully sovereign States. Indirectly they have supplied an impressive refutation of the view that the achievement of the ideal of an organized community of nations under the compulsory rule of law would mean the end of international law.[1] The consistent application of rules of international law to disputes between State-members of Federal States shows how little substance there is in this argument.

We are concerned here only with those cases decided by quasi-international tribunals in which the defendant States raised the plea of jurisdiction on the ground that the claims of the plaintiff States were political and not legal or judicial. These cases are of interest mainly for two reasons. Some of them show how lucidly these tribunals deal with this particular plea to the jurisdiction. Others, of more recent date, are an instructive instance of the manner in which these tribunals are influenced by the terminology coined by international lawyers in connexion with disputes between sovereign States.

The Supreme Court of the United States. Political Claims of Indian Tribes against the States of the Union. Article III of the Constitution of the United States provides that the judicial power of the United States shall extend to 'controversies between two or more States' and that the Supreme Court shall have original jurisdiction in all such cases.[2] This provision of the Constitution has become responsible for a wealth of judicial authority in a great variety of subjects relating to the settlement of disputes between States. In a number of these cases the Supreme Court had to give a decision on the plea that it had no jurisdiction, for the reason that the claim was political and not legal.

The first case in which the Supreme Court was confronted with this plea was the case of *Cherokee Nation* v. *State of Georgia*.[3] This was a motion for an injunction to prevent the putting into force of certain acts of the legislature of the State of Georgia in the territory of the Cherokee nation of Indians. No counsel appeared for Georgia, and it was left to the Court to deal with the question of jurisdiction from the point of view of the relation between the judicial and political power. The Court dismissed the motion. Although it was of the opinion that the actual relation of the Cherokee nation to the United States resembled that of a ward to

---

[1] See above, p. 404.

[2] By the Eleventh Amendment this jurisdiction was subsequently subjected to a restrictive interpretation, by the provision that 'the judicial power of the United States shall not be construed to extend to any suit in law or equity, commenced or prosecuted against one of the United States by citizens of another state, or by citizens or subjects of any foreign state'. For the reasons and historical antecedents of this Amendment see Scott, op. cit., pp. 13–62.

[3] (1831) 5 Peters, 1; Scott, op. cit., i. 614.

his guardian, it attached decisive importance to the fact that the Cherokee Indians were formerly a foreign nation in regard to Georgia, and that their independence was in effect denied by the proposed legislation of Georgia. The Court saw in the motion on behalf of the Cherokees an attempt to restrain a State from the exercise by force of legislative power over a foreign community whose right to independence was denied. The Court refused to grant a motion which, it said, would have the effect of controlling the legislature of Georgia and restraining it from exercising physical force. It held that such an interposition would amount to an exercise of political power, and that it did not therefore fall within the province of the judicial department. As Mr. Justice Johnson said in his opinion, the Court could not act contrary to the accepted rule that, quite independent of the general principle that for their political acts States are not responsible to judicial tribunals, it could not compel another branch of government to make good the stipulations of its treaties.[1]

This case is here referred to mainly because it raised clearly for the first time the distinction between a legal and a political decision. Mr. Justice Baldwin, whose classical pronouncement in the subsequent case of *Rhode Island* v. *Massachusetts* will be discussed in the next section, was one of the judges in this case and delivered an opinion. However, by their own submission the Cherokee Indians were a 'foreign nation', and formally no question arose as to the limitation of the competence of the Court in a dispute between members of the same legal community.

Boundary Disputes involving Questions of Sovereignty and Jurisdiction. State of Rhode Island v. *State of Massachusetts*[2] constitutes an emphatic judicial affirmation of the jurisdiction of the Supreme Court in the face of the plea challenging its jurisdiction in regard to so-called political disputes. The case is one of the *loci classici* on the question of the distinctions between legal and political disputes, and the relevant portions of the argument and of the judgement may therefore be summarized in some detail. This was a Bill filed in 1832 by the State of Rhode Island against the State of Massachusetts for the settlement of the boundary between the two States. The Bill asserted the right of Rhode Island to the disputed territory over which, at the time of the filing of the Bill, the State of Massachusetts claimed and alleged to exercise sovereignty on the ground that it was included in charters from the Crown of England. The claim was mainly based on a subsequent delimitation of the frontier by commissioners acting under the authority of the two States. It was contended in the Bill that the proceedings of the commissioners were vitiated by numerous

---

[1] 5 Peters, 30; Scott, op. cit., p. 633.
[2] 12 Peters, 657; printed in Scott, op. cit., pp. 676–748.

errors, and that the line designated by them had always been resisted by Rhode Island. The Bill asked for a restoration of the right of the latter to the disputed territory.[1] Counsel for the State of Massachusetts moved to dismiss the Bill on the ground that the Court had no jurisdiction. He contended that, by virtue of the Constitution, the jurisdiction of the Court was limited to judicial matters to be decided by the application of law and equity; that it would be manifestly absurd to extend it to political disputes of the day; that, there being no law regulating the intercourse between the States of the Union, there was no rule for settling a controversy between two or more States; and that, until such law existed, the Court could entertain no jurisdiction, because the State being above or beyond the existing law was not amenable to any superior.[2] 'This Court', it was said, 'has no jurisdiction, because of the nature of the suit. It is in its character, political; in the highest degree, political; brought by a sovereign, in that avowed character, for the restitution of sovereignty.'[3]

The Court refused to admit the relevance of these objections. As Mr. Justice Baldwin pointed out, in the last analysis the dispute resolved itself into a controversy as to the locality of a point three miles south of the southernmost point of the Charles river: i.e. 'Whether the stake set up on Wrentham Plain, by Woodword and Saffrey (the Commissioners), in 1642, is the true point from which to run an east and west line, as the compact boundary between the States. In the first aspect of the case, it depends on a fact; in the second, on the law of equity, whether the agreement is void or valid; neither of which present a political controversy, but one of an ordinary judicial nature, of frequent occurrence in suits between individuals.'[4] In view of the importance of the case the following passage of Mr. Justice Baldwin's judgement may fittingly be—and frequently has been—quoted:

'The founders of our government could not but know, what has ever been, and is, familiar to every statesman and jurist, that all controversies between nations, are, in this sense, political, and not judicial, as none but the sovereign can settle them. In the declaration of independence, the states assumed their equal station among the powers of the earth, and asserted, that they could of right do what other independent states could do; but they surrendered to congress, and its appointed court, the right and power of settling their mutual controversies; thus making them judicial questions, whether they arose on "boundary, jurisdiction, or any other cause whatever". There is neither the authority of law or reason for the position, that boundary between nations or states, is, in its nature, any more a political question, than any other subject on which they may contend. None can be settled without war or treaty, which is by political power; but under the old and new confederacy they could and can be settled by a court constituted by themselves, as their own substitutes, authorised to do that for States, which

---

[1] 12 Peters, 665.   [2] Ibid., p. 673.
[3] Ibid., p. 685.   [4] Ibid., p. 736.

states alone could do before. We are thus pointed to the true boundary line between political and judicial power, and questions. A sovereign decides by his own will, which is the supreme law within his own boundary; 6 Peters, 714; 9 Peters, 748; a court or judge decides according to the law prescribed by the sovereign power, and that law is the rule for judgment. The submission by the sovereigns, or states, to a court of law or equity, of a controversy between them, without prescribing any rule of decision, gives power to decide according to the appropriate law of the case; 11 Ves., 294; which depends on the subject-matter, the source and nature of the claims of the parties, and the law which governs them. From the time of such submission, the question ceases to be a political one to be decided by the *sic volo, sic jubeo*, of political power; it comes to the court to be decided by its judgment, legal discretion, and solemn consideration of the rules of law appropriate to its nature as a judicial question, depending on the exercise of judicial power; as it is bound to act by known and settled principles of national or municipal jurisprudence, as the case requires.

'These considerations lead to the definition of political and judicial power and questions; the former is that which a sovereign or state exerts by his or its own authority, as reprisal and confiscation; 3 Ves., 429; the latter is that which is granted to a court or judicial tribunal. So of controversies between states; they are in their nature political, when the sovereign or state reserves to itself the right of deciding on it.'[1]

The view to which Mr. Justice Baldwin thus gave classical expression was subsequently reaffirmed in the case of *State of Florida* v. *State of Georgia*,[2] with the result that in the two boundary disputes which followed—*Missouri* v. *Iowa*[3] and *Alabama* v. *Georgia*[4] —the question of jurisdiction was not even raised. The objection, unsuccessfully put forward in *Rhode Island* v. *The State of Massachusetts*, was, forty-two years later, repeated in the boundary dispute between *State of Virginia* v. *The State of West Virginia*.[5] Counsel for West Virginia contended that the Court had jurisdiction in such questions only where 'some question of a judicial nature was involved'; that the question was a political one to be decided by Congress; that in such boundary cases as *Rhode Island* v. *Massachusetts*, in which the Court had assumed jurisdiction, there was some legal element involved like the question of specific performance of contract or a question of property;[6] and that the more general pronouncements of Mr. Justice Baldwin in the *Rhode Island* case were mere dicta and unnecessary to the decision. The Court made short work of these objections. Professing to follow the established doctrine of the Supreme Court, it asserted its jurisdiction in all questions of boundary between the States of the Union, and

---

[1] Ibid., p. 730.
[2] 17 Howard, 478; Scott, op. cit., p. 939.
[3] 7 Howard, 660.
[4] 23 Howard, 505.
[5] 11 Wallace, 39; Scott, op. cit., p. 1008.
[6] Thus the English case *Penn* v. *Lord Baltimore* (1750), 1 Vesey, 444, to settle the boundary between Delaware and Maryland was referred to as involving the interpretation of an agreement for settling the boundary—'a proper head for equitable jurisdiction'.

refused to admit that that jurisdiction is defeated because in deciding such controversies it becomes necessary to construe agreements between States, or because the Court's judgement may affect the territorial status or the political jurisdiction and sovereignty of the disputant States.[1]

Claims not based on a Recognized Rule of International Law. Diversion of Waters. Another aspect of the problem of justiciability was raised in the case of *State of Kansas* v. *State of Colorado.*[2] In this case it was not the political aspect of the claim, as involving high matters of sovereignty, but the alleged absence of rules of international law preventing the defendant State from following a certain line of action. The State of Kansas asked that the State of Colorado be restrained from effecting or permitting the diversion, and certain other changes affecting the course of the waters, of the Arkansas river or any of its tributaries in a manner prejudicial to the interests of Kansas. Colorado demurred to the Bill of Complaint on the ground, *inter alia*, that the relations between itself and Kansas were governed by rules which controlled the relations of foreign and independent States; that by the law of nations, based on the right of self-preservation, it had full liberty of action in regard to the waters flowing through its territory; that mere moral obligations or obligations of comity could not be made the subject of controversy between States; and that only those controversies were justiciable in the Court which, prior to the Union, would have constituted a just cause of reprisals following, according to international law, upon a positive wrong or the with-holding of a right *stricti juris*. The Court refused to assent to these propositions. It stated that Kansas based its complaint both on the fundamental principle of law that one must use his own so as not to destroy the legal rights of another, and on the rule of common law which gives the owners of lands on the banks of a river the right to the continual flow of the stream. A dispute of this nature the Court refused to recognize as purely political. In assuming jurisdiction the Court quoted, and relied upon, the case decided in the same sense a year before between *State of Missouri* and *State of Illinois and the Sanitary District of Chicago*,[3] an action in which an injunction was sought restraining the defendants from receiving or permitting any sewage to be received or discharged into an artificial drain in order to carry off and eventually to discharge into the Mississippi the sewage of Chicago, which had been previously discharged into Lake Michigan.

In this connexion it is necessary to draw attention to the case of

---

[1] 11 Wallace, 55.

[2] 185 U.S. 125; Scott, op. cit., p. 1313.

[3] 180 U.S. 208; Scott, op. cit., p. 1286.

Louisiana v. *Texas*,[1] decided in an opposite sense, and sometimes referred to as a refusal of the Court to assume jurisdiction.[2] This was a Bill of Complaint alleging that the Health Officer of Texas, in the exercise of his powers over the establishment and maintenance of quarantines over infectious diseases, acted in a way to benefit the commerce of cities in Texas to the detriment of New Orleans. The Court refused to grant an injunction restraining the Texas officials from enforcing the quarantine laws in the manner complained of. But its refusal to grant the injunction was based, not on the ground that the dispute was a political one, but on other reasons. Thus the Court attached importance to the fact that there was no direct issue between the disputant States, no direct effort at accommodation between the States themselves having previously been made. As Mr. Justice Shiras observed in the case of *Missouri* v. *Illinois*, in *Louisiana* v. *Texas* the Supreme Court, far from declining jurisdiction, exercised it in holding that the facts alleged in the complaint did not justify the Court in granting the relief prayed for.[3]

Dismissal of the Claim and the Limitation of Jurisdiction. The State of South Australia v. *The State of Victoria.* Some interesting aspects of the problem of the limitation of the judicial function were raised in the case of *The State of South Australia* v. *The State of Victoria* decided in 1911 by the High Court of Australia.[4] This was an action brought against the State of Victoria in respect of a piece of land which had been in the occupation of New South Wales, and afterwards of Victoria, since 1847. The plaintiffs claimed, *inter alia*, possession of the said land, mesne profits till delivery, and an injunction to restrain the defendants from further trespassing upon the land. It was contended, on the part of the defendants, that the jurisdiction of the Court, as defined in Article 75 of the Constitution—which conferred upon the High Court jurisdiction in 'all matters between States'—was limited to 'justiciable' matters, and that the Court was not competent to deal with political matters such as the laying down of the boundary. They maintained that one of the reasons why disputes relating to boundaries were not justiciable was that that power resided in the Imperial Parliament, and possibly also in the Sovereign.

The Court held that it had jurisdiction. It held, by Griffith, J.,

---

[1] 176 U.S. 1; Scott, op. cit., p. 1267.

[2] See Thayer in *Harvard Law Review*, xxvi (1912–13), p. 420.

[3] In so far as Mr. Justice Fuller who, delivering in this case the judgement of the Court, was of the opinion that the subject-matter of the complaint was not susceptible of judicial decision, inasmuch as it is not 'within the judicial function to enquire into the motives of a State legislature in passing a law, or of the chief magistrate of a State in enforcing it in the exercise of his discretion and judgement' (Scott, op. cit., p. 1277), his view can hardly be accepted as sound. It was overruled in *Missouri* v. *Illinois*, 180 U.S. 208, Mr. Justice Fuller dissenting.

[4] 12 Commonwealth Law Reports, 667.

that every dispute between States is justiciable which is of such a character that it could arise between individuals and that it can be determined by a rule of law.[1] Thus, the learned judge said, in the simple case of a trespass by one State upon territory in the *de facto* possession of another, the Court would have jurisdiction. The dispute related to a boundary laid down by an Imperial statute, the Letters Patent issued under it, and a subsequent demarcation as agreed upon in 1847 by the Governors of the two States. On the merits of the dispute, the Court held that the settlement of 1847 was valid, that the claim to have that boundary rectified was not a cause of action capable of judicial decision, that the plaintiff State had no right of which the Court could take cognizance, and that the claim therefore failed. But, as mentioned, the Court refused to decline jurisdiction on the ground that the dispute was of a political and not judicial nature. The learned judge said:

> 'The law of the Empire, including the Statute law, is binding as well upon the dependencies, regarded as political entities, as upon individual subjects. If, therefore, any dependency infringes the law of the Empire governing its relations with a neighbouring dependency it is guilty of a wrong towards that other dependency. Similar wrongs committed by one independent State against another are not justiciable, because there is no tribunal which has jurisdiction to take cognizance of them.... This Court has such jurisdiction.'[2]

O'Connor, J., was even more emphatic. He pointed out that whenever a question is raised as to the position of a boundary line between two States, the Court will have jurisdiction to entertain it, if the question arises in a dispute between the States which is capable of being determined in accordance with recognized legal principles. He clearly dismissed the objection based on the alleged political character of the dispute:

> 'It is no doubt true that change of allegiance in the inhabitants of the disputed territory, and other political consequences, would necessarily follow, if it were so judged that South Australia was entitled to possession. But that does not render this a suit for the determination of political rights over the land in dispute....'[3]

The case is instructive. The Court rejected the objection to the jurisdiction based on the plea that the dispute was of a political character. But it dismissed the action on the ground that the plaintiff could adduce no legal reason for a change in the frontier as validly laid down sixty years before. Thus the Court, while assuming jurisdiction to entertain the complaint regarded as a complaint of invasion of territory, refused to give effect to a claim

---

[1] 12 Commonwealth Law Reports, 674.

[2] Ibid., p. 676. The international lawyer will note, on p. 703, the application of the doctrine of effective occupation.

[3] Ibid., p. 707.

not based on a legal right; it held that it must give effect to the legal rights of the defendant State. The remedy left open to the plaintiff was a political one, i.e. that residing in the Prerogative of the sovereign.[1] However, in order to give expression to this legal position the Court felt compelled, while answering the objection of the defendant, to use terms which, but for what has been said above, might be construed as an implied recognition of the current doctrine on the limitation of the judicial function of courts. Thus Griffith, J., declared himself prepared to assent to the view that the jurisdiction of the Court, if any is judicial, and not political; and that, so far as a controversy requires for its settlement the application of political as distinguished from judicial considerations, it is not justiciable under the Constitution. Possibly the student may be confused by the statement that a claim which cannot be supported by legal considerations is non-justiciable. Surely the Court itself did not treat it as such. It dealt with it, and dismissed it on the ground that it 'must give effect to the legal right of the defendant State'. This identification of the dismissal of the claim (as unsupported by law) with a limitation of the Court's jurisdiction is quite frequent.

The third judge in the case, who equally assented to the assumption of jurisdiction,[2] was even more apprehensive lest the jurisdiction of the Court might be extended beyond claims resting upon an alleged violation of some positive law. Such extension of jurisdiction, he said, would leave the Court 'without any limits of jurisdiction between States except the fact of some dispute,

---

[1] It will be noted in this connexion that the distinction between a political and a legal decision has been adopted in Great Britain in connexion with the question how far the jurisdiction of the Privy Council, in settling boundary disputes between colonies, was an exercise of the Prerogative of the Crown and therefore political. The question was discussed, without the terms judicial and political being used, as early as 1750, by Lord Hardwicke in his opinion in *Penn* v. *Lord Baltimore*, 1 Ves. 444; and in Scott, *Judicial Settlement*, i. 588. For a number of early cases of controversies between colonies concerning boundaries and the function of the Judicial Committee see Acts of the Privy Council, Colonial Series, iii. It appears that in these cases the view of the Privy Council was that a controversy between colonies, concerning their boundaries as laid down in their respective charters, is a judicial question to be determined by the King in Council. For other cases see *The State of South Australia* v. *The State of Victoria* (1911), 12 C.L.R. 702, *per* Griffith, J. C. The same terminology seems also to have been applied in the case of *Moses* v. *Parker* [1896] A.C. 245, in which an application was made to the Judicial Committee for leave to appeal from a decision of the Supreme Court of Tasmania, given under the statute of that colony which referred, for examination and report by the Supreme Court, certain claims to Crown lands. The Judicial Committee held that a decision given under the statute was not a judicial decision admitting of appeal, seeing that the Supreme Court was expressly exonerated from applying the rules of law and equity. See also *Sheikh Sultan Sani* v. *Sheikh Ajmondin*, 20 L.R. Ind. App. 50. See also *The State of South Australia* v. *The State of Victoria*, *supra*, for numerous references to jurisdiction of the Privy Council in boundary disputes in the eighteenth century (pp. 702–4).

[2] Isaacs, J., p. 715.

irrespective of cause or subject-matter, and therefore, possibly a controversy without any standard of right, but involving judicial interference with political and administrative action and discretion, a position unheard of, and altogether outside the pale of sober thought'. It is suggested, with great respect, that these alarming possibilities were of the learned judge's own making, and that there was no need to visualize contingencies 'altogether outside the pale of sober thought'. Apart from the interpretation of Articles 71 and 75 of the Australian Constitution, it is clear that the jurisdiction of the High Court, as indeed of every court of law, is a judicial one, i.e. one to be exercised by the application of rules of law and equity. Any other exercise of jurisdiction—unless by an agreement of the parties (in which case the content of their agreement constitutes substantive law), or by a most explicit authorization of the legislature—must necessarily constitute a dereliction of judicial duty. But it is only by an imperfect use of juridical logic that the question of the *jurisdiction* of the Court in regard to legal questions is introduced. What the Court has to decide is whether the claim is supported by law. If it rejects the claim it does so not because the claim is a 'political' one, but because there are no legal grounds to support it. By rejecting it it does not decline jurisdiction; it exercises it in a decisive manner.

The Same. Dominion of Canada v. *The Province of Ontario.* The same aspect of the problem is illustrated by the case of *Dominion of Canada* v. *The Province of Ontario*[1] decided in 1910, on appeal, by the Judicial Committee of the Privy Council. This was an action brought by the Dominion of Canada for reimbursement of certain moneys said to have been spent for the benefit of the Province of Ontario. In a treaty concluded in 1873 by the Dominion Government with a tribe of Indians the former acquired, in return for certain payments and other rights, definite title over a large tract of land about 50,000 square miles in extent, the greater part of which was subsequently found to lie within the boundaries of the Province of Ontario. As, in the view of the Dominion, the sums thus spent inured to the benefit of the Province, the Dominion sued the Exchequer Court of Canada for a declaration that it was entitled to recover from the Province of Ontario a proper proportion of the moneys paid and payable under the treaty. The Dominion Government claimed that, by the acceptance of the land in question, the Province accepted also the liabilities created in respect thereof. It contended that the Dominion acted as an agent of the Province, and that the liability incurred to obtain the surrender of the land by the Indians was, in effect, a commutation of the burden of that title upon the lands,

[1] [1910] A.C. 637.

and as such remained a charge upon the lands. The contention was put forward that, even if there were no formal grounds of municipal law supporting the claim, the case should be governed by those principles of equity and fairness which regulate the mutual relations of independent States, namely, that a State accepting the benefits of a treaty is bound also to accept the accompanying disadvantages. The Judicial Committee of the Privy Council, before which the case came, on appeal from a judgement of the Supreme Court of Canada dismissing the claim, dismissed the appeal. Their Lordships held that in order to succeed the appellants must bring their claim within some recognized legal principle, and that the contention of the Dominion could not be sustained on any applicable principle of law.

This case has also been given as an instance of the limitation of the jurisdiction of courts.[1] It is doubtful whether the example is an accurate one. The Judicial Committee did not decline jurisdiction; it dismissed the claim. There is no good reason for confusing the dismissal of a claim with a refusal to adjudicate. Dismissals of claims, on the ground of the absence of a rule of law supporting them, are normal occurrences. But no one regards them as a limitation of the place of law in society; on the contrary, they are a manifestation of the rule of law protecting the challenged right of the defendant. The situation is the same in disputes between States, although writers and judges are tempted to describe such claims, if unsupported by law, as political.

The Proposed Arbitral Tribunal in the British Commonwealth of Nations. In connexion with the cases dealt with in the two preceding sections, reference ought to be made to the report of the Conference on the Operation of Dominion Legislation and Merchant Shipping Legislation in 1929, in which the establishment of an inter-imperial tribunal for the settlement of disputes between members of the British Commonwealth was suggested.[2] This proposal, subsequently recommended by the Imperial Conference of 1930,[3] is notable both on account of the machinery and of the nature of the jurisdiction suggested. In regard to the former, it was thought desirable not to establish a permanent judicial tribunal, but to set up a panel of judges from which the disputant parties could select the members of the tribunal for each case as it arose. The Imperial Conference went further in the direction of moderation, and preferred to dispense with a panel of judges and to recommend the setting up of *ad hoc* tribunals, for the constitution of which it made certain suggestions. However, that aspect of the matter is not germane to the question here discussed. What is of interest is the passage in the Report of 1929 to the effect

[1] Thayer in *Harvard Law Review*, xxvi (1912–13), p. 423.
[2] (1930), Cmd. 3479.   [3] (1930), Cmd. 3717.

that 'there was general agreement that the jurisdiction [of the tribunal] should be limited to justiciable issues arising between governments'. The same qualification was adopted by the Imperial Conference. No attempt was made to ascertain what 'justiciable' issues are.

There is one point in the recommendations of the Imperial Conference which calls for special comment, as showing the somewhat disquieting lack of criticism in regard to the use of the term 'justiciable'. The Imperial Conference abstained from adopting obligatory judicial settlement between the members of the Commonwealth, and recommended the adoption 'of a voluntary system' instead. It is not necessary to inquire in this place what were the reasons which prevented the members of the British Commonwealth of Nations from accepting as between themselves a measure of subjection to the rule of law accepted *inter se* by most Members of the League of Nations.[1] But, it may pertinently be asked, what is the purpose of qualifying a nonexistent obligation of judicial settlement by an express provision that the arbitral tribunal has jurisdiction only in 'justiciable' disputes? The term 'justiciable' is as a rule used with the view to determining the jurisdiction of a tribunal within the frame of obligatory arbitration. In any other context it has hardly any meaning. In treaties of obligatory arbitration it serves the function, or has the effect, of obscuring or limiting the obligation of judicial settlement. In documents like that under discussion—which do not purport to impose any obligation of judicial settlement—it does not fulfil even that purely negative function.[2]

---

[1] Professor Keith, in *The Journal of Comparative Legislation and International Law*, 3rd ser., xii (1931), p. 33, strongly criticizes this attitude, and suggests that the negative result was due to the attitude of the Irish Free State, which 'declined to accept the doctrine that inter-imperial disputes are not proper subjects for the Permanent Court, and by rendering the inter-imperial system facultative sought to discredit it'. It is difficult to see how the attitude of one member of the Commonwealth could have prevented other members from accepting *inter se* the duties of obligatory arbitration. Professor Keith further suggests that, as the British Government has hitherto pursued a policy of acceding to the demands of the Irish Free State for changes in the treaty of 1921, the Irish Free State naturally felt disinclined 'to risk the necessity of honouring an arbitral award'. There seems to be no justification for this charge, seeing that the Irish Free State by signing without reservations the Optional Clause undertook that 'risk' in respect of any member of the League willing to undertake a similar obligation.

[2] On the settlement of disputes between British colonies in the eighteenth century see some of the references given above, p. 447, n. 1. See also Snow, 'The Development of the American Doctrine of Jurisdiction of Courts over States', in *Proceedings of the American Society for the Judicial Settlement of International Disputes* (1910), pp. 100–38 (reprinted in Snow, *The American Philosophy of Government* (1921), pp. 69–112); Riddell, 'Another Supreme Court', ibid. (1916), pp. 104–23; for more recent developments see Caldwell in *A.J.* xiv (1920), pp. 44–8. Under section 4 of the Judicial Committee Act of 1833 the Crown may refer to the Privy Council 'any such other matter whatsoever as his Majesty

Justiciability of Disputes between German States and Swiss Cantons. Germany and Switzerland are conspicuous for the subjection to the obligatory jurisdiction of their tribunals of matters commonly regarded as 'political' and therefore non-justiciable. According to Article 19 of the Federal German Constitution of 1919, the *Staatsgerichtshof* is competent to decide controversies of a public nature between the States, whereas controversies not of a public-law character fall within the competence of regular courts.[1] Article 76 (1) of the Federal Constitution of 1871 provided that the Federal Council shall have jurisdiction in disputes between State-members except in disputes of a private-law nature. It was generally agreed that this article conferred upon the Federal Council the widest possible jurisdiction in such matters as frontier disputes, State servitudes, interpretation of treaties between States, and so on.[2] At the same time there was general agreement that Article 76 (1) envisaged a judicial activity pure and simple.[3] The consensus of opinion on this matter is particularly significant in view of the political character of the Federal Council.

In Switzerland the Federal Court has jurisdiction not only in inter-cantonal disputes in matters of civil-law nature,[4] but also

shall think fit', i.e. matters other than appeals. It is by reference to this provision that recourse has been had to the jurisdiction of the Judicial Committee in a number of cases. See, for instance, the opening remarks of Sir John Simon (Oral Proceedings) in the case between Canada and Newfoundland concerning the Labrador boundary, decided on 1 March 1927, 43 Times Law Reports. See also White, *Boundary Disputes and Treaties* (1914; reprint from *Canada and its Provinces*), pp. 878–907, for a detailed account of the decision (following upon voluntary submission) of the Privy Council in 1884 in the Ontario-Manitoba Boundary Dispute. And see the controversy between the Government of Northern Ireland and the British Government in 1924 concerning the appointment of a representative of the former on the Boundary Commission set up by virtue of the Treaty of 1921. See *Report of the Judicial Committee*, (1924), Cmd. 2214. A number of disputes between the provinces of Canada, or between Canada and the provinces, were settled by the Judicial Committee by way of appeal from judgements of Canadian courts. Some of these raised questions of international law. See, for instance, *Attorney-General of British Columbia* v. *The Attorney-General of Canada*, [1924] A.C. 203, a case which raised the matter of the application of the most-favoured-nation treaty of 1911 between Great Britain and Japan. And see Caldwell in *A.J.* xiv (1920), pp. 45–8, for a discussion of earlier cases.

[1] See Mattern, *The Constitutional Jurisprudence of the German National Republic* (1928), pp. 291–5. For some recent cases decided by the *Staatsgerichtshof* see *Annual Digest*, 1925–6, and 1927–8.

[2] Triepel, *Die Reichsaufsicht* (1917), p. 457. And ibid., pp. 456–70, for a lucid discussion of the whole question.

[3] Triepel, op. cit., p. 142, n. 1. For an admirable historical survey of the settlement of disputes among German States from the Middle Ages down to 1866, see Laband in Lapradelle and Politis, i. 423–38. See also *British and Foreign State Papers*, xxiii (1834–5), p. 119, for the decree of the Diet, made at Frankfort, 30 October 1834, providing for the establishment of an arbitral tribunal for the purpose of deciding disputes as to the interpretation of the constitution of the Confederation and other matters.

[4] Article 110 of the Federal Constitution of 1874.

in matters pertaining to the exercise of political rights of sovereignty such as boundary disputes and application of intercantonal treaties.[1] The jurisdiction of the Federal Council is restricted to questions of a purely administrative and technical character, in particular to matters entirely regulated by Federal legislation and not affecting the sovereignty of the cantons.

---

[1] Article 110 of the Federal Constitution of 1874. See also Articles 113 and 177 of the Federal Law of 22 March 1893 on the administration of Federal Laws. See Huber in *A.J.* iii (1909), pp. 87–91, and in particular Schindler, ibid. xv (1921), pp. 151–4.

INDEX